"This lady is organized . . . well-researched guide."
San Francisco Chronicle Book Review

". . . almost overwhelmingly full of detailed information. Excellent."
San Diego Union-Tribune

"We had a great time on our California vacation. 'Weekend Adventures' was essential both during planning and execution. Thank you for a wonderful guide!"
Joleen Chambers, parent, Annapolis, MD

"Ms. Meyers has left no stone unturned in researching the recreation opportunities available in the northern half of the state."
Travelin' magazine

"Carole Terwilliger Meyers writes intelligently about family fun. She finds places kids like that adults can stomach. And vice versa."
Alice Kahn, author

"The guide is very well organized . . . Highly recommended."
Pacific Sun

". . . a gold mine of travel tips."
The Montclarion

"Carole is the doyenne-empress-goddess of family travel in the Bay Area. She invented it."
Peter Beren, co-author of The Writer's Legal Companion

"Whenever we need a break from the city routine, I reach for my copy of 'Weekend Adventures'. It's the greatest guidebook around for families who want to explore Northern California."
Dixie Jordan, Editor, Parents' Press

"Enjoyable to read . . . and loaded with photos."
Small Press magazine

". . . easy-to-follow format."
Booklist

Also by Carole Terwilliger Meyers:

The Family Travel Guide:
An Inspiring Collection of Family-Friendly Vacations (Editor)

Miles of Smiles: 101 Great Car Games & Activities

San Francisco Family Fun

How to Organize a Babysitting Cooperative and
Get Some Free *Time Away From the Kids*

Eating Out With the Kids in San Francisco and the Bay Area

Getting in the Spirit: Annual Bay Area Christmas Events

Eating Out with the Kids in the East Bay

7th Edition

Weekend Adventures in Northern California

Includes San Francisco

by Carole Terwilliger Meyers

CAROUSEL PRESS

Berkeley, California

Published by: **CAROUSEL PRESS**
P.O. Box 6038
Berkeley, CA 94706-0038
(510) 527-5849
info@carousel-press.com
www.carousel-press.com

Distributed to the book trade by Publishers Group West

This book was previously published under the titles *Weekend Adventures for City-Weary People: Overnight Trips in Northern California* (1984, 1989, and 1993 editions), and *Weekend Adventures for City-Weary Families: A Guide to Overnight Trips in Northern California* (1977 and 1980 editions).

Library of Congress Cataloging-in-Publication Data:
Meyers, Carole Terwilliger.
Weekend adventures in northern California / by Carole Terwilliger Meyers.-- 7th ed.
p. cm.
Includes indexes.
ISBN 0-917120-17-5
1. California, Northern--Guidebooks. 2. Family recreation--California, Northern--Guidebooks. I. Title.

F867.5 .M48 2001
917.9404'54--dc21

00-062176

The information in this book was correct at press time. However, the author and publisher hereby disclaim any liability due to changes, errors, or omissions, and cannot be held responsible for the experiences of readers while traveling. Specific prices are gathered in the year before publication and are mentioned only to give an approximate idea of what to expect; phone numbers are included so that readers can call to determine current rates. All establishments listed in this book are mentioned to alert the reader to their existence; they are endorsed by neither the author nor publisher. No business has paid to be included.

Reader Feedback: Text errors and typos, listing changes, exciting new discoveries, praise, even complaints—we want to hear it all.

Special Sales: Bulk purchases of Carousel Press titles are available to corporations at special discounts. Custom editions can be produced to use as premiums and promotional items. For more information, call (510) 527-5849.

Manufactured in the United States of America

10 9 8 7 6 5 4 3 2 1

for Gene

Contents

Introduction

We residents of the Bay Area are fortunate to live within easy driving distance of a wealth of exciting vacation possibilities—mountains, ocean, rivers, snow. Our biggest recreational problem is deciding, from among the many possibilities, where we should go and what we should do.

The destinations in this book radiate out from San Francisco. Most make good weekend trips, and all can be adapted easily to longer stays.

Because it is frustrating to discover after you're home that an area where you've just vacationed had an interesting attraction you didn't know about, and because it also isn't much fun finding out too late that there was a better or cheaper (depending on what you're after) lodging you could have booked into or a restaurant you would have enjoyed trying, this book is designed so that you can determine quickly what is of special interest in the area you are planning to visit. Listings are selected based on the fact that they are in some way special—bargain rates, welcoming of families, aesthetically pleasing, historically interesting, etc. Phone numbers, toll-free 800 numbers, and websites are provided for obtaining further information.

Parents especially need to have this information in advance. I know because one of the worst trips I ever experienced was the first trip my husband and I took with our first baby. I hadn't planned ahead. We took off for the Gold Rush Country and went where the winds blew us—just like before we were parents. That was a mistake. We wound up in a hotel that had no compassion for a colicky baby or his parents, and we ate a series of memorably bad meals. Now my husband and I can laugh about that trip, but at the time it wasn't funny. That fateful trip turned me into a travel writer. After that I never went anywhere without exhaustively researching it beforehand. And truthfully I've never had a bad trip since that I can blame on lack of knowledge.

With all of this in mind, I've written this book to help make your trip-planning easier, allowing you to get the most out of your weekends away.

Credits

Book design: Betsy Joyce
Cover photo: Julie Dean
Postcards appear courtesy of Lake County Discovery Museum/Curt Teich Postcard Archives
Maps: Mark T. Williams, Eureka Cartography
Computer wizardry: Gene Meyers
Printing: McNaughton & Gunn, Inc.
Images:
Inside pages: *p.7:* Carl Wilmington, San Francisco Convention & Visitors Bureau; *p.8:* San Francisco Convention & Visitors Bureau; *p.9:* George Olson, Dudell & Associates; *p.11:* Alameda Naval Air Station Public Affairs Office; *p.12:* Arne Folkedal, San Francisco Ballet; *p.14:* Robert Stinnel, Red & White Fleet; *p.19:* Herb Bettin, San Francisco Convention & Visitors Bureau; *p.20:* San Francisco Convention & Visitors Bureau; *p.21:* Haas-Lilienthal House; *p.24:* Richard Barnes, SFMOMA; *pp.25 & 26:* San Francisco Maritime National Historical Park; *p.27:* Dong Lin, California Academy of Sciences; *p.28:* Nancy Rodger, Exploratorium; *p.29:* Wax Museum at Fisherman's Wharf; *p.31:* San Francisco Convention & Visitors Bureau; *p.32:* San Francisco Recreation and Park Department; *p.34:* Michael Shay, San Francisco Zoological Society; *p.36:* Ron Scherl, Steve Silver Productions; *p.39:* Hanford Associates; *p.52:* Park Hyatt San Francisco; *p.56:* Fortune Public Relations; *p. 60:* Buca di Beppo; *p.79:* Katy Greene; *p.88:* Terry Pimsleur & Co.; *p.90:* California State Department of Parks and Recreation; *p.91:* Hostelling International; *p.93:* Santa Cruz Beach & Boardwalk; *p.99:* Janet Anderson; *p.102:* Tom's Sportfishing; *p.105:* California Artichoke Advisory Board; *p.107:* Monterey Bay Aquarium; *p.112:* Pete Amos, California Department of Parks and Recreation; *pp.117 & 118:* California Department of Parks and Recreation; p.123: Tuck Box English Tea Room; *pp.126 & 128:* California Department of Parks and Recreation; *p.131:* Theodore Osmundson, California Department of Parks and Recreation; *p.132:* John Kaestner, California Department of Parks and Recreation; *pp.137 & 138:* California Department of Parks and Recreation; *p.140:* Clerin Zumwalt, Audubon Canyon Ranch; *p.141:* Redwood Empire Association; *p.144, left:* Osmosis; *p.144, right:* Sharon Taussig, Sonoma County Convention & Visitors Bureau; *p.149:* Ansel Adams, Redwood Empire Association; *pp.150 & 156:* Redwood Empire Association; *p.169:* Paramount Parks; *p.174:* Rosicrucian Egyptian Museum; *p.175:* Winchester Mystery House; *p.181:* Valley Guild, Steinbeck Library; *p.184:* Carole Terwilliger Meyers; *p.190:* Jane Oka, Marine Mammal Center California; *p.190:* Michael Morgan, Sea Trek Ocean Kayaking Center; *p.203:* Petaluma Visitors Program; *p.211 & 223:* Carole Terwilliger Meyers; *p.226:* Redwood Empire Association; *p.229:* Vichy Springs Resort; *p.231:* California State Department of Parks and Recreation; *p.235:* Pat Cudahy, Gingerbread Mansion Inn; *p.236:* California State Department of Parks and Recreation; *p.237:* Eureka/Humboldt County C.V.B.; *p.238:* California State Department of Parks and Recreation; *p.240:* Eureka Inn; *p.244:* Ansel Adams, Redwood Empire Association; *p.250:* East Bay Regional Parks District; *p.251:* Jon Winet, Pacific Film Archive; *p.252:* California Alumni Association; *p.253:* Peg Skorpinski, Lawrence Hall of Science; *p.254:* Claremont Resort & Spa; *p.267:* Marine World Africa USA; *p.268:* Harre W. Demoro; *pp.270 & 271:* California Department of Parks and Recreation; *p.277:* Carole Terwilliger Meyers; *p.278:* unknown; *p.282:* Dunsmuir Historic Estate; *p.283:* Sonoma Valley Visitors Bureau; *p.284:* USS Potomac; *p.294:* B.F. Loomis, Poimiroo & Partners; *pp.295, 298, & 302:* John F. Reginato, Shasta-Cascade Wonderland Association; *p.296:* Carol Piechocinski, Spanish Springs Ranch; *p.305:* Gold Prospecting Expeditions; *p.308:* City Hotel; *p.310:* Moaning Cavern; *p.311:* 39th District Agricultural Association; *p.318:* Larry Paynter, California Department of Parks and Recreation; *p.320:* California Department of Parks and Recreation; *p.327:* Yosemite Concession Services; *p.328:* John Michael Flint, Oakwood Lake Resort; *p.329:* John Poimiroo, Yosemite Concession Services; *p.330:* Yosemite Research Library; *p.332:* Mono Lake Committee; *p.333:* Yosemite Concession Services; *p.336:* Sanger District Chamber of Commerce; *p.343:* Roaring Camp & Big Trees Narrow-Gauge Railroad; *pp.345 & 348:* Hal Schell; *p.355:* Gundlach-Bundschu Winery; *p.357:* Carole Terwilliger Meyers; *p.359: Sonoma Index-Tribune*, Sonoma Valley Visitors Bureau; *p.360:* Smothers Winery; *p.367:* Balloon Aviation of Napa Valley, Redwood Empire Association; *p.377:* Penn, Dr. Wilkinson's Hot Springs; *p.379:* Redwood Empire Association; *p.385, 386, & 387:* Lake Tahoe Visitors Authority; *p.391:* Greater Reno Chamber of Commerce; *p.392:* Carole Terwilliger Meyers; *p.394:* Northstar-at-Tahoe; *p.395:* David Martinez, Resort at Squaw Creek; *p.399:* Royal Gorge Nordic Ski Resort; *p.401:* Lake Tahoe Historical Society; *p.402:* California Department of Parks and Recreation; *p.403:* Bob Everson, Alpine Meadows; *pp.407 & 409:* Yosemite Concession Services; *p.411:* John M. Giosso, S.F. Recreation & Park Dept.; *p.413, left:* Shasta-Cascade Wonderland Association; *p.413, right:* California Department of Parks and Recreation; *p.414:* Rapid Shooters, Mariah Wilderness Expeditions; *p.415:* Redwood Empire Association.
Back cover: author photo by Gene Meyers.
Acknowledgments: Special thanks to the various visitors bureaus that helped in updating information pertaining to their areas.

Guidelines for Interpreting Listings

This book is organized by geographical area. Each chapter has the following subsections:

A LITTLE BACKGROUND: Historical and general background information about the area; what kinds of activities to expect.

VISITOR INFORMATION: Address and phone number of visitors bureau or chamber of commerce.

GETTING THERE: The quickest, easiest driving route from San Francisco; scenic driving routes, other transportation options.

STOPS ALONG THE WAY: Noteworthy places for meals or sightseeing.

ANNUAL EVENTS: The area's best events. When no phone number is listed, contact the visitors bureau or chamber of commerce for information.

WHERE TO STAY: Select lodging facilities, listed alphabetically and including the following information when available: Street address, toll-free 800 reservations number, phone number, fax number, website (where e-mail address can usually be obtained). Number of stories if over 3; number of rooms; if it is 100% non-smoking; price range per night for two people (see price code below); if there is a minimum stay of more than 1 night. Months closed. Policies regarding children (if children stay free in parents' room on existing beds); if facility is unsuitable for children under a specified age). If no TVs are provided; if VCRs are in rooms; if kitchens, gas or wood-burning fireplaces, or wood-burning stoves are provided; if any baths are shared. What recreational facilities are available: pool, hot tub, sauna, health spa, fitness center, par-course, tennis courts, golf course. If there is a complimentary afternoon or evening snack; if there is a complimentary breakfast; if there is a restaurant, room service. If pets are welcome. If there is a parking fee.

¢=under $50 $=$50-$99 $$=$100-$149
$$$=$150-$200 $$$+=over $200

WHERE TO EAT: Worthwhile restaurants, listed alphabetically and including the following information when available: Address, phone number, fax number, website. Meals served (B, L, D, SunBr), days open; price range (see price code below). Availability of highchairs, boosters, booths, child portions/menu. If reservations are advised, accepted (but not usually needed), or not accepted. If credit cards are *not* accepted. When parking is difficult, whether a validated parking lot or valet parking are available.

$ = inexpensive. Dinner for one adult might cost up to $15.
$$ = moderate. Dinner for one adult might cost from $15 to $30.
$$$= expensive. Dinner for one adult might cost over $30.

Projected costs are based on average entree prices and are exclusive of drinks, dessert, tax, and tip.

WHAT TO DO: Activities and sights in the area that are of special interest, listed alphabetically and including the following information when available: Address, phone number, fax number, website. Days and hours open. Admission fee.

Note that some restaurants and attractions are closed on major holidays. Always call to verify hours.

SAN FRANCISCO OVERVIEW
0
1
2
Miles
N
Golden Gate Bridge
101
Fort Point
Crissy Field
Palace of Fine Arts & Exploratorium
Blvd
PRESIDIO
Baker Beach
1
Lincoln
China Beach
Lands End
PRESIDIO HEIGHTS
Lincoln Park
Palace of the Legion of Honor
Park Presidio Blvd
Geary
Blvd
Cliff House
Masonic
RICHMOND
USF
Fulton St
de Young Museum
Panhandle
Ave
Golden Gate Park
California Academy of Sciences
Lincoln Way
HAIGHT
Pacific
UCSF
Judah St
7th Ave
SUNSET
1
Great Hwy
Noriega St
19th Ave
Sunset Res
Twin Peaks
Sunset Blvd
DIAMOND HEIGHTS
Dr
Taraval St
Portola
Mt Davidson Park
Stern Grove
Ocean
35
Sloat Blvd
Zoo
City College
280
Lake
Harding Park
SF State Univ
Geneva
Ave
Fort Funston
35
Merced
1
ba
MAP 1

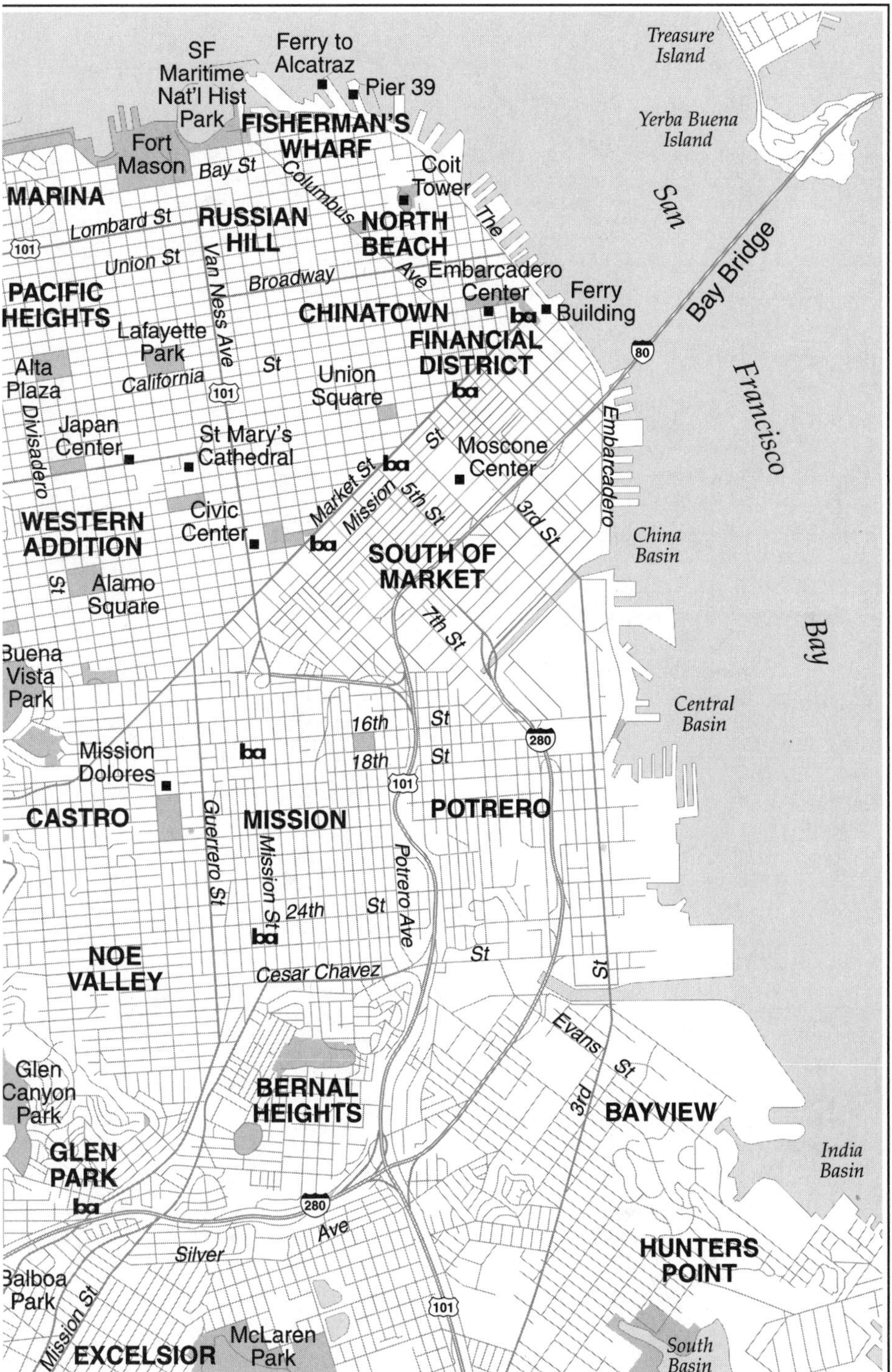
Treasure Island
Yerba Buena Island
SF Maritime Nat'l Hist Park
Ferry to Alcatraz
Pier 39
FISHERMAN'S WHARF
Fort Mason
Bay St
Columbus Ave
Coit Tower
MARINA
Lombard St
RUSSIAN HILL
NORTH BEACH
The Embarcadero
San Francisco Bay
Bay Bridge
101
Union St
Van Ness Ave
Broadway
Embarcadero Center
Ferry Building
PACIFIC HEIGHTS
CHINATOWN
Lafayette Park
FINANCIAL DISTRICT
80
Alta Plaza
California St
Union Square
101
Divisadero St
Japan Center
St Mary's Cathedral
Moscone Center
Market St
Mission St
5th St
3rd St
Embarcadero
WESTERN ADDITION
Civic Center
China Basin
SOUTH OF MARKET
Alamo Square
7th St
Buena Vista Park
16th St
18th St
Central Basin
280
Mission Dolores
101
POTRERO
CASTRO
MISSION
Guerrero St
Mission St
Potrero Ave
24th St
NOE VALLEY
Cesar Chavez St
3rd St
Evans St
Glen Canyon Park
BERNAL HEIGHTS
BAYVIEW
India Basin
GLEN PARK
280
Silver Ave
HUNTERS POINT
Balboa Park
101
Mission St
EXCELSIOR
McLaren Park
South Basin

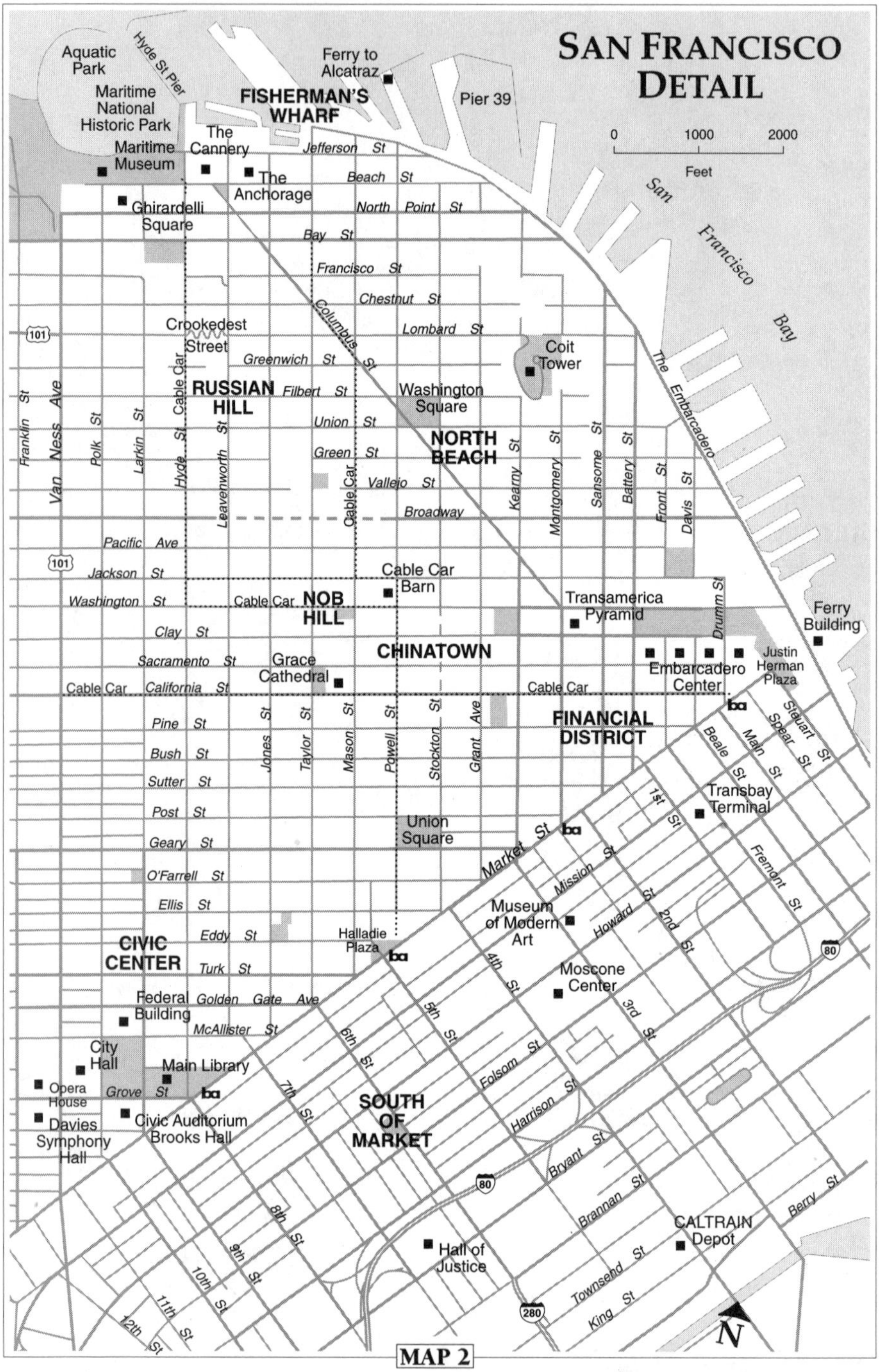
SAN FRANCISCO
DETAIL
0
1000
2000
Feet
San Francisco Bay
Aquatic Park
Hyde St Pier
Maritime National Historic Park
Maritime Museum
The Cannery
Ferry to Alcatraz
FISHERMAN'S WHARF
Pier 39
The Anchorage
Ghirardelli Square
Jefferson St
Beach St
North Point St
Bay St
Francisco St
Chestnut St
Lombard St
Greenwich St
Filbert St
Union St
Green St
Vallejo St
Broadway
Crookedest Street
Columbus St
Coit Tower
Washington Square
NORTH BEACH
RUSSIAN HILL
The Embarcadero
Franklin St
Van Ness Ave
Polk St
Larkin St
Hyde St
Cable Car
Leavenworth St
Kearny St
Montgomery St
Sansome St
Battery St
Front St
Davis St
101
Pacific Ave
Jackson St
Washington St
Clay St
Sacramento St
California St
Cable Car Barn
NOB HILL
Grace Cathedral
CHINATOWN
Transamerica Pyramid
Drumm St
Ferry Building
Embarcadero Center
Justin Herman Plaza
FINANCIAL DISTRICT
Pine St
Bush St
Sutter St
Post St
Geary St
O'Farrell St
Ellis St
Eddy St
Turk St
Golden Gate Ave
McAllister St
Jones St
Taylor St
Mason St
Powell St
Stockton St
Grant Ave
Union Square
Market St
Stuart St
Spear St
Main St
Beale St
Transbay Terminal
1st St
Fremont St
Mission St
Howard St
2nd St
Museum of Modern Art
Halladie Plaza
CIVIC CENTER
Federal Building
City Hall
Main Library
Opera House
Grove St
Davies Symphony Hall
Civic Auditorium Brooks Hall
4th St
Moscone Center
5th St
6th St
7th St
3rd St
80
Folsom St
Harrison St
Bryant St
Brannan St
Townsend St
King St
Berry St
SOUTH OF MARKET
8th St
9th St
10th St
11th St
12th St
Hall of Justice
CALTRAIN Depot
280
N

MAP 2

A LITTLE BACKGROUND

You wouldn't think such a place as San Francisco could exist. The wonderful sunlight there, the hills, the great bridges, the Pacific at your shoes. Beautiful Chinatown. Every race in the world. The sardine fleets sailing out. The little cable-cars whizzing down the city hills. The lobsters, clams, & crabs . . . Every kind of seafood there is. And all the people are open and friendly.

— Dylan Thomas

San Francisco has only one drawback. 'Tis hard to leave.

— Rudyard Kipling

One day if I do go to heaven, I'm going to do what every San Franciscan does who goes to heaven. I'll look around and say, 'It ain't bad, but it ain't San Francisco.'

— Herb Caen, June 14, 1996

You tell people you live in California and surf, and they have a picture of a "Gidget" movie. In San Francisco, however, it's more like some kind of German Expressionist film—all foggy, cold and dark, and nobody around. Just me and the sharks.

— Chris Isaak, 1999

Though the quotes above are not heard often, the saying attributed to Mark Twain, "The coldest winter I ever spent was a summer in San Francisco," is familiar to most people.

Scholars dispute that the words were Twain's, but no one who has spent a summer in San Francisco will dispute the comment.

This city is known for its morning and evening fog in summer. Locals coming in from the suburbs have learned to always bring along wraps. In summer it is easy to spot tourists. They are the ones wearing shorts . . . or white shoes, another no-no among locals. Perhaps these visitors are confusing San Francisco with the image of Southern California's warm beaches. That is a mistake.

In general the climate is temperate, ranging between 40 and 70 degrees, with the best weather usually occurring in September and October.

VISITOR INFORMATION

San Francisco Convention and Visitors Bureau *P.O. Box 429097, San Francisco 94142-9097, (415) 391-2000, fax (415) 227-2602; www.sfvisitor.org.*

Send $3 for a copy of *The San Francisco Book*. It is filled with sightseeing, shopping, and dining information. *The Lodging Guide* will be included. Or contact San Francisco FastFax at (800) 220-5747 for promptly faxed-back visitor information. Lodging reservations can be made through the bureau by calling (888) 782-9673.

Upon arrival, stop in at the **Visitor Information Center** *(Halladie Plaza, Market St./Powell St., (415) 391-2000. M-F 9-5:30, Sat 9-3, Sun 10-2.)* to get oriented.

For a recorded listing of the day's events, call (415) 391-2001. For the same information in French, call (415) 391-2003; German (415) 391-2004; Spanish (415) 391-2122; Japanese (415) 391-2101.

ANNUAL EVENTS

— January —

Chinese New Year Celebration & Golden Dragon Parade *Or in February or March, depending on the lunar calendar. (415) 391-9680; www.chineseparade.com. Free.*

First held in 1851 and held again every year since, this popular event is composed of a beauty pageant, an outdoor carnival in Chinatown, and the famous parade featuring a spectacular block-long golden dragon. (This parade is one of the few illuminated night parades in the U.S.)

— February —

Pacific Orchid Exposition *Or in March. Fort Mason Center; (415) 546-9608; www.orchidsanfrancisco.com. $10.*

Thousands of gorgeous blooming orchid plants are on display at this stunning show of amateur and professional collections. It is the largest of its kind on the West Coast. Many plants are entered for judging and show only, but hundreds more are available for purchase. Lectures by international orchid experts are scheduled. Sponsored by the San Francisco Orchid Society.

— March —

St. Patrick's Day Parade *(415) 467-8218 or (415) 467-6426. Free.*

This traditional parade has been held annually for over 80 years and is the city's largest.

— April —

Cherry Blossom Festival *(415) 563-2313, fax (415) 563-2307. Free.*

Japanese cultural events at this elaborate celebration of spring include traditional dancing, martial arts demonstrations, taiko drum and koto performances, and tea ceremonies. A Japanese food bazaar operates continuously, and demonstrations of the Japanese arts of doll-making, calligraphy, and flower arranging are usually scheduled. The festival culminates with a colorful 2-hour, Japanese-style parade.

San Francisco Decorator Showcase *(415) 447-3100. $20; seniors $18.*

Strict quality control gives this show house a reputation for being the best in the West—perhaps even the best in the entire country. Proceeds benefit San Francisco University High School.

San Francisco International Film Festival *(415) 931-FILM; www.sfiff.org. $4.50-$20.*

Known for honoring the finest in cinematic achievement, North America's oldest film festival presents recent productions from around the world. Some children's films are usually included.

— May —

Carnaval *(415) 826-1401. Free.*

This spectacular Mardi Gras-like revel is a multicultural celebration of life. It includes a parade and a two-day outdoor festival.

Cinco de Mayo Festival *(415) 826-1401. Adults $5, under 12 free.*

Commemorating the Battle of Puebla, Mexico on May 5, 1862, which marked the defeat of the powerful French Napoleonic Army by a small, poorly equipped Mexican force, this is the largest such festival in the U.S. It attracts visitors and performers from throughout Latin America and includes a free parade and a two-day festival.

San Francisco Examiner Bay to Breakers Footrace *(415), (510), or (408) 808-5000 ext. 2222; www.sfgate.com/breakers. Entry fee $20, children $15.*

The world's largest, and perhaps zaniest, footrace is usually routed through the Financial District, up the Hayes Street hill, and on through Golden Gate Park to the Great Highway. Outrageous outfits are de rigueur and in the past have included everything from a set of crayons to Humphrey the Whale. All participants receive a commemorative t-shirt and a follow-up postcard with their finishing time and ranking. Sponsored by the *San Francisco Examiner*. Proceeds benefit Bay Area charities.

— June —

Cable Car Bell Ringing Championships *Union Square; (415) 923-6160. Free.*

Competition is held in both pro and amateur divisions. The previous year's champion defends his title, and amateurs (who include some well-known Bay Area personalities) ring on behalf of non-profit organizations. The winner is then referred to as "Ding Dong Daddy." Judges are selected from among the area's musical and theatrical elite.

North Beach Festival *(415) 989-2220. Free.*

This granddaddy of street fairs, said to be the very first in the country, features Italian foods, sidewalk cafes, traditional Italian sword fighting demonstrations, bocce ball games, and a variety of entertainment.

San Francisco Lesbian/Gay/Bisexual/ Transgender Pride Parade and Celebration *(415) 864-FREE. Free.*

Though other cities now also hold annual gay pride celebrations, San Francisco's is considered the biggest and wildest. The parade is a don't-miss. A popular highlight is the Women's Motorcycle Contingent, or "Dykes on Bikes."

Stern Grove Festival *Through mid-August. 19th Ave./Sloat Blvd.; (415) 252-6252; www.sterngrove.org. Free.*

Featuring the finest of Bay Area performing arts, this program has been held in the Grove's natural outdoor amphitheater each summer since 1938. It is the country's oldest free summer performing arts festival. It is traditional to bring a picnic lunch and the Sunday paper and spend the pre-performance wait indulging in food, drink, and relaxation. Bring a blanket to sit on and a jacket in case the weather turns chilly.

The city's **croquet lawns** are available here year-round for play; for more information, call (415) 776-4104.

— July —

Fourth of July Waterfront Festival *(415) 777-7120. Free.*

Beginning in the early afternoon, a variety of music and entertainment is presented continuously. A highlight is the Sixth Army's traditional 50-cannon salute to the nation. The celebration culminates with a fireworks spectacular after sunset. Sponsored by the *San Francisco Chronicle.*

— August —

ACC Craft Show *Fort Mason Center; (415) 896-5060. Adults $8, under 12 free.*

Produced by the American Craft Council, this is the largest juried craft fair on the West Coast. It features the latest work of over 350 of the nation's premier craft artists.

San Francisco Blues Festival *Great Meadow at Fort Mason; (415) 979-5588; www.sfblues.com. $17-$20.*

Known for its all-star lineup, this upbeat affair has been called "one of the best blues events in the world." It also features a breathtaking background view of the Golden Gate Bridge.

— October —

Columbus Day Celebration *(415) 989-2220. Free.*

San Francisco's is the only Columbus Day celebration in the country that includes a re-enactment of Columbus's landing in San Salvadore. When landing at Aquatic Park, the person acting as Columbus wears a handmade Italian replica of the great navigator's clothing. The **Blessing of the Fishing Fleet** takes place the next day at Fisherman's Wharf, and the **Italian Heritage Day Parade** usually takes place the next weekend.

Fleet Week *(510) 263-1803 or (415) 981-8030; www.fleetweek.com. Free.*

To celebrate the anniversary of the Navy's birthday and to honor the men and women of the U.S. Navy and Marines, the City of San Francisco throws a gigantic birthday party each year and the public is invited. In the past there have been demonstrations of high-speed boat maneuvering, parachute drops, and a fly-by of World War II vintage aircraft. **The Blue Angels**, the Navy's premier precision flying team, also perform in a breathtaking culmination. Viewing is best from Crissy Field, the Marina Green, Aquatic Park, Pier 39, and the Marin Headlands. As part of the celebration, all Navy ships moored at the piers are usually opened for public visits. Fleet Week originated in 1908 when President Teddy Roosevelt's "Great White Fleet" of battleships sailed under the Golden Gate. Mayor Dianne Feinstein established it as an annual event in 1981.

Grand National Rodeo, Horse, & Stock Show *Cow Palace; (415) 469-6058. $7.50-$20.*

This is the largest such show held west of the Mississippi. The rodeo and horse show are scheduled each evening in the arena. Ticket holders are invited to come early to enjoy a variety of related activities: dairy animal auctions; judging contests; displays of unusual breeds of livestock, including tons of premium steers, woolly sheep, and prime swine. A special White Line Tour leads kids in to see the baby animals.

San Francisco Jazz Festival *(415) 788-SFJF, outside CA (800) 850-SFJF, fax (415) 398-5569; www.sfjazzfest.org. Free-$55.*

The Chicago Tribune calls this "the biggest and most acclaimed jazz festival in the United States."

— December —

A Christmas Carol *415 Geary St., Geary Theater; (415) 749-2ACT. $14-$47.50.*

Dickens' popular seasonal ghost tale, which celebrates the rebirth of the human spirit and the death of indifference, is sure to rekindle any lagging Christmas enthusiasm in grumpy holiday Scrooges. American Conservatory Theater's lively, colorful production enhances the story with a musical score of carols, songs, and dance. It is interesting to note that Dickens' story is credited with actually reviving the celebration of Christmas, which at the time his book was published in 1843 had slipped to the status of a quaint, almost obsolete custom. It is also considered responsible for some English social reform. Fortunately for all of us, his story still manages to wake up the spirit of human kindness. Performances run almost two hours with no intermission.

Golden Gate Park Christmas Tree Lighting *Golden Gate Park; (415) 831-2700. Free.*

San Francisco's official Christmas tree, a 100-foot Monterey cypress located at the east entrance to Golden Gate Park, is decorated each Christmas season with over 3,000 lights. The mayor is usually present to flip the switch. Santa also makes an appearance, and the audience is led in singing carols.

Guardsmen Christmas Tree Sale *Fort Mason Center; (415) 771-7463, tree lot (415) 771-7747. Trees $10-$200.*

Claiming to have the largest enclosed Christmas tree lot in Northern California, the Guardsmen sell approximately 5,000 trees each year. This sale is famous for having the best selection of noble firs but also stocks a variety of other trees, including Douglas fir, Frazer fir, and Scotch pine. Just visiting the lot is a thrill—it resembles a small forest—and imagine how nice it is on a rainy day. Trees range from table-top size to 14 feet. Garlands, wreaths, holly, mistletoe, and ornaments are also on sale. All purchases are tax-deductible, and proceeds fund camperships and educational programs for underprivileged Bay Area children.

The Nutcracker *War Memorial Opera House; (415) 865-2000; www.sfballet.org. $7-$110.*

The San Francisco Ballet has been presenting its delightful and festive version of *The Nutcracker* since 1942, when it blazed the path for all subsequent U.S. Nutcrackers by dancing the first full-length production. It has always been an extravagant interpretation, with hundreds of thousands of dollars worth of scenery and handmade costumes. Each performance features a cast of over 177 dancers that includes the company's principal dancers plus children from the Ballet School. A spectacular growing Christmas tree and a cannon that uses real gunpowder and makes a loud, smoke-producing boom are also featured. (The cannon once not only boomed but self-destructed!)

Sugar Plum Parties follow some matinee performances. They are held in the downstairs cafeteria, where guests are served sugary goodies (cookies, candy, soda) and the costumed cast members are available for autographs. Proceeds benefit the Ballet School. Purchase party tickets at the same time as purchasing Nutcracker tickets.

Union Square Window Displays.

Each year the biggest department stores—Macy's, Saks Fifth Avenue, Neiman-Marcus—treat the public to elaborate window decorations, some with moving mechanical displays. A visit to Macy's commercial, but gorgeous, seventh floor Christmas wonderland, known as Bayberry Row, is a treat; Santa is also found here. The lobby of the Westin St. Francis Hotel is also usually worth a walk-through. Street entertainers, vendors, and carolers provide further diversion.

WHAT TO DO

Guided Tours

— By Boat —

Blue and Gold Fleet Bay Tours *Depart from Pier 39, Fisherman's Wharf, (415) 773-1188; reservations (415) 705-5555, fax (415) 705-5429; www.blueandgoldfleet.com. Daily from 10am; from 11 in Jan & Feb. Adults $17, 62+ & 12-18 $13, 5-11 $9.*

This one-hour narrated cruise of the bay goes out under the world's most beautiful bridge—the Golden Gate—and also passes close to Alcatraz Island. Other boat tours include Alcatraz, Alcatraz After Hours, Angel Island, Six Flags Marine World, the Wine Country, Sausalito, and Tiburon.

Ruby Sailing Yacht *At foot of Mariposa St./near 3rd St., (415) 861-2165. Daily at 12:30 & 6, May-Nov & at other times by appt. Adults $33, under 10 $20. Reservations required.*

Captain Joshua Pryor built the 64-foot steel sloop *Ruby* himself in 1979. He also sails her himself. On the 2 1/2-hour lunch cruise, which circles Alcatraz, guests can dine on deli sandwiches either on the deck or below deck in the salon. The evening trip includes hors d'oeuvres and sails to Sausalito. Beer and wine are available at additional charge.

Whale-Watching Tours *Depart from Fort Mason Center, (800) 326-7491, (415) 474-3385, fax (415) 474-3395; www.oceanic-society.org. Sat, Sun, & some F; Jan-mid-May only. $48-$50. Children must be at least 10. Reservations required.*

Sponsored by the non-profit Oceanic Society Expeditions, these all-day trips have a professional naturalist on board to explain all about the whales and interpret their behavior. Half-day trips depart from Princeton-by-the-Sea (see page 87).

Farallon Islands Nature Cruises *(Sat, Sun, & some F; June-Nov only. $65. Children must be at least 10. Reservations required.)* take participants 25 miles across the Pacific Ocean from the Golden Gate Bridge to this National Wildlife Refuge. These islands support the largest seabird rookery in the eastern Pacific south of Alaska and are the habitat of 200,000 nesting sea birds—including tufted puffins, loons, and auklets—plus sea lions and seals.

— By Bus —

Gray Line Tours *(800) 826-0202, (415) 558-7373, fax (415) 554-0349; www.graylinesanfrancisco.com. Fares vary; children under 5 free when sitting on parent's lap. Reservations required 1 day in advance.*

Day tours are available of San Francisco, Muir Woods/Sausalito, Yosemite, Monterey/Carmel, and the Wine Country. Dinner tours of San Francisco and other Bay Area locations are also scheduled. The deluxe San Francisco tour is enjoyed aboard a red double-decker, London-style bus.

3 Babes and a Bus *Depart from Union Square, (415) 552-CLUB. F & Sat 9:30pm-1:30am. $30. Must be 21 or older. Reservations advised.*

These babes and their bus pick up guests and take them out to party in the city's hottest dance clubs. The price includes cover charges and VIP entry. There is no need to worry about parking, taxi fares, or drinking and driving, and a variety of venues are experienced.

— By Car —

49-Mile Drive.

This planned driving route through San Francisco hits most of the high points. For a free map of the route, contact the San Francisco Convention and Visitors Bureau.

— By Fire Engine —

San Francisco Fire Engine Tours & Adventures *Depart from The Cannery, Fisherman's Wharf. (415) 333-7077, fax (415) 333-7725; www.fireenginetours.com. W-M. Adults $22, under 13 $11. Reservations advised.*

This happy, exhilarating 75-minute excursion takes sightseers over the Golden Gate Bridge in a bright-red 1955 Mack fire engine. As it can get chilly in the open-air truck, authentic insulated fire-fighter jackets are available for passengers to bundle up in. Children get a lesson in fire safety through original sing-along songs. After, the tour guides go back to their home in a vintage fire house.

— On Foot —

San Francisco is a walker's paradise. The city's naturally intriguing streets become even more interesting when walked with a knowledgeable guide. Even natives have been known to learn something new on such as tour.

City Guides *(415) 557-4266; www.walkingtours.com/cityguides. Free.*

Sponsored by the San Francisco Public Library, these informative tours last approximately 1 1/2 hours and cover most of the city: Alamo Square, City Hall, Coit Tower, Haight-Ashbury, Historic Market Street, Jackson Square/Portsmouth Square, Japantown, Levi Strauss Factory, Mission Murals, Montgomery Street, Nob Hill, North Beach, Pacific Heights

Victorians, Presidio Museum, San Francisco Fire Department Museum, Union Square . . . and more! For a free schedule, send a stamped, self-addressed business-size envelope to: City Guides, San Francisco Public Library, 100 Larkin St., San Francisco 94102.

Dashiell Hammett Tour *(510) 287-9540; www.donherron.com. Sat at noon, May & June; by appt. rest of year. Adults $10, under 15 free.*

While dashing off trivia and anecdotes, guide Don Herron leads walkers to landmarks from *The Maltese Falcon* and to all Hammett's known San Francisco residences. Herron, who is always appropriately attired in trench coat and fedora, has operated this tour since 1977. Said to be the longest ongoing literary tour in the country, it lasts 4 hours and covers approximately 3 miles.

Golden Gate Park Walking Tours.

See page 34.

Mission Mural Walk *Depart from 2981 24th St./Harrison St., (415) 285-2287. Sat & Sun at 11 & 1:30. Adults $4-$10, under 18 $2.*

The Precita Eyes Mural Arts Center provides two versions of this walk. The less expensive morning walk views some of the 200-plus murals found in the Mission District. The afternoon walk includes a slide show and talk by a professional muralist.

Pacific Heights Walking Tour.

See page 22.

Wok Wiz Chinatown Tours *(415) 981-8989; fax (415) 981-2928; www.wokwiz.com. Daily at 10am. $39 with lunch, $27 without lunch; discounts for 62+ & under 12. Reservations required.*

Led by cookbook author Shirley Fong-Torres and her staff, these easy tours (no hills) take participants behind the scenes and into the heartbeat of this colorful and historic neighborhood. A dim sum lunch is optional.

For more Chinatown walks, see page 15.

— Factory Tours —

Anchor Steam Brewery *1705 Mariposa St./ DeHaro St., Potrero Hill, (415) 863-8350. M-F at 2; reservations required. Free.*

The locally popular ale that is produced here at San Francisco's only remaining brewery is distributed to almost every state. The compact brewery was built in the 1860s and has produced its well-known Anchor Steam beer ever since. After the hour-long tour, participants are treating to a generous tasting. Children are welcome but get only water at the end.

Basic Brown Bear Factory.

See page 37.

Historic Sites

Alcatraz Island *(415) 773-1188; reservations (415) 705-5555, fax (415) 705-5429; www.blueandgoldfleet.com. Daily departures; call for schedule. Adults $12.25, 62+ $10.50, 5-11 $7; includes audio tour; less expensive no-audio option available. Reservations advised.*

Before Alcatraz was opened to the public in 1973, it served as a fort in the 19th century and as a federal penitentiary from 1934 to 1963. It was occupied by Native Americans from 1969 to 1971. During the time it was a maximum security prison, it was home to some of the country's most hardened criminals: Al Capone, George "Machine Gun" Kelly, Robert "The Birdman" Stroud. Now it is run by the National Park Service as part of the Golden Gate National Recreation Area—the largest urban park in the world. And it is as good as it's cracked up to be—the boat ride, the tour, and the 360-degree bay view. After a short,

scenic ride to this infamous island, visitors follow a self-guided tour. Several ranger-led tours on special topics are also scheduled each day. A top-notch audio tour of the cell block, narrated by former inmates and guards, is optional but highly recommended. It is interesting to note that the still-operating 214-foot-tall lighthouse here was built in 1854, when it was the first on the West Coast. No picnicking is permitted. Wear comfortable shoes, dress warmly, and expect cool, windy weather—even in summer.

Cable Cars *(415) 673-6864. Daily 6am-1am. Tickets $2, under 5 free.*

These beloved objects have operated since 1873 and were designated the country's first moving National Historic Landmark in 1964. Before they were developed by Andrew Hallidie, horses had to pull carts up the city's steep hills. Many died in the process. Now 26 "single-enders" operate on the two Powell Street routes and 11 "double-enders" operate on the California Street run. Catch the Powell-Hyde line at the turnaround located at the base of Powell Street (at Market Street) and ride it up and over the hills all the way to Aquatic Park. This line goes down the steepest hills and affords the most breathtaking views. The Powell-Mason line ends at Bay Street, about 3 blocks from Fisherman's Wharf. The less used California Street line begins at Market Street and runs along California Street, passing Chinatown and then climbing over Nob Hill, ending at Van Ness Avenue. Ticket machines are provided at turnarounds, but riders can also board at designated stops along the routes and pay the conductor.

Chinatown *Bounded by Broadway, Bush St., Kearny St., & Powell St.*

With a population of approximately 80,000 residents and covering 24 square blocks, San Francisco's Chinatown is the largest Chinese community outside of Asia. The most memorable way to enter Chinatown is on foot through the ornate dragon-crested archway located at Grant Avenue and Bush Street. Designed to the Taoist principles of Feng Shui, the gate features Foo dogs to scare away evil spirits, dragons for fertility and power, and fish for prosperity. A walk along pedestrian-crowded Grant Avenue, the city's oldest street, is quite an experience. For good souvenir hunting, stop in one of the many shops. Favorite items with children include golden dragon-decorated velvet slippers, rice candy in edible wrappers, and silk coin purses.

Old St. Mary's Cathedral, which was built of brick in 1853, is the West Coast's first Roman Catholic cathedral. Half-hour **chamber music concerts** *(660 California St., (415) 288-3861. Tu & Thur at 12:30pm. $3 donation.)* follow noon Mass.

• **Chinese Culture Center** *750 Kearny St./Washington St., 3rd fl. in Holiday Inn, (415) 986-1822, fax (415) 986-2825; www.c-c-c.org. Tu-Sun 10-4; closed last 2 weeks in Dec. Free.*

This two-room gallery has rotating exhibits of historical and contemporary Chinese art by both native Chinese and Chinese-Americans.

Cultural and culinary tours of Chinatown sponsored by the Chinese Culture Foundation are scheduled year-round; all require reservations. The **Culinary Walk** *(Sat at 10:30am. Adults $30, under 12 $15.)* introduces Chinese cuisine with stops in markets, at a fortune cookie factory, at an herb shop, and at a tea shop. It concludes with a dim sum lunch. The **Heritage Walk** *(Sat at 2pm. Adults $15, under 18 $5.)* stresses the history and cultural achievements of the area. Stops might include a Chinese temple and historical society. **Chinese New Year Walks** *(Adults $15, under 18 $6. Reserve several weeks in advance.)* are given only during that time of year. A history of the holiday is presented, and all participants sample special Chinese sweets from a "Tray of Togetherness."

• **Dim Sum.**

Translated variously as meaning "touch of heart," "touch your heart," "heart's desire," and "heart's delight," dim sum items were originally served for breakfast during China's Tang Dynasty (618 to 907 A.D.) A meal of these appetizers makes an interesting change of pace for breakfast or lunch, and there is no better place to try the cuisine than here as there are said to be more dim sum parlors in San Francisco than in any other city in the U.S.

The varieties of dim sum are seemingly endless and include steamed buns, fried dumplings, and turnovers, as well as delicacies such as steamed duck beaks and feet. It is great fun to pick and choose from items brought around to tables Hong Kong-style on carts or trays that circulate non-stop. Just flag down the servers as they pass. Be aware that in crowded restaurants it can be difficult to get a server to describe what a particular item is composed of, and sometimes they don't speak or understand English very well.

Tea is brought automatically. The three most common kinds are mild green, semi-fermented oolong, and strong fermented black. Chrysanthemum combines black tea with dried flowers; jasmine combines oolong with dried flowers. To get a tea refill, do as the Chinese do and signal the waiter by turning over the lid on the tea pot. Some, but not all, establishments offer other drinks.

Note that although crossed chop sticks are usually considered an omen of bad luck, in dim sum houses they signal the server that the diner is finished.

Though this quaint custom is rapidly dying, the bill in some restaurants is determined by how many serving plates are on the table at meal's end. (This concept is reminiscent of the little hill town of San Gimignano in Italy, which was once filled with 70 bell towers. A family's wealth there was measured by the height of its bell tower.) To keep a running tab, just make a stack of the serving plates and steamers as they are emptied. Most teahouses charge about $2 to $4.50 per plate, and tips are usually divided by the entire staff.

• **Gold Mountain** *644 Broadway/Stockton St., (415) 296-7733. Daily 8-3; $. Highchairs, boosters. Reservations advised.*

Dim sum is served on floors two and three of this gigantic, bustling restaurant, which is so big that the waiters use walkie-talkies to communicate. Though floor two alone seats 280 people, there still is usually a wait. Once seated, if carts don't arrive fast enough, flag down someone who looks in charge and order directly from the kitchen. Crisp taro balls and roast duck are particularly good here.

• **Lichee Garden.** See page 17.

• **Meriwa Restaurant** *728 Pacific Ave./Grant Ave., (415) 989-8818 or (415) 989-8868. Dim sum daily 7-2:30, D daily; $.*

Able to seat 1,000 people, this popular spot roars during dim sum, and the little dishes here are among the very best and most varied currently available.

• **New Asia** *772 Pacific Ave./Stockton St., (415) 391-6666, fax (415) 391-6158. Daily 8:30-3; $. Highchairs, boosters. No reservations.*

Even with a reputed 1,000 seats, this busy spot usually requires a wait for seating in its popular ground level dining room. However, immediate seating is often available upstairs. Head servers here use walkie-talkies to communicate across the huge, noisy interior. Hesitation when offered a choice of eight teas usually is translated by the server into "green," because that tea is the most popular. Delicate shrimp dumplings, deep-fried taro balls filled with sweet poi, and cloud-like pork bows are all especially good. A dim sum-to-go counter operates by the waiting area.

• **Pearl City** *641 Jackson St./Grant Ave., (415) 398-8383. Daily 8-3, D daily; $. Highchairs, boosters. No reservations.*

The front room here is chilly and quiet, the back room warmer and noisier. Items are brought around on platters rather than carts. Excellent choices include many delicate shrimp items and very good steamed custard buns.

• **Fortune Cookie Factories.**

Always fun after a Chinatown meal is a walk through the narrow streets and alleys to find a fortune cookie factory. Though workers aren't often pleased to see tourists, it is usually possible to get at least a glimpse of the action by peeking in through a door or window. Nowadays, the traditional way of making the cookies by hand-folding is giving way to intricate machines. Proprietors are usually glad to sell cookies, and bags of broken "misfortune" cookies can be picked up at bargain prices.

• **Golden Gate Fortune Cookies** *56 Ross Alley/Washington St., (415) 781-3956. Daily 9-9.*

Tucked away in a picturesque alley in the heart of Chinatown, this factory also sells delicious mini-almond cookies.

• **Mee Mee Bakery** *1328 Stockton St./Broadway, (415) 362-3204. Daily 8-6.*

Located at the border of Chinatown and North Beach, this factory has been baking fortune cookies since 1948—longer than anyone else in town. They also sell X-rated cookies, mini-almond cookies, and both chocolate and strawberry fortune cookies.

• Herb Shop.

• Superior Trading Co. *837 Washington St./ Grant Ave., (415) 982-8722, fax (415) 982-7786. Daily 9:30-6:15.*

This interesting and somewhat mysterious shop measures out aromatic herbs on scales. Unless actually planning to purchase something, it is best just to peek in the window.

• Restaurants.

Though locals often claim good Chinese restaurants aren't found in Chinatown, in reality some are.

• Far East Cafe *631 Grant Ave./ Sacramento St., (415) 982-3245. L&D daily; $$. Highchairs, boosters. Reservations advised.*

Looking much as it did when it opened in 1920, this intriguing restaurant has 30 private wooden booths with curtains for a door. These wonderful, cozy enclosures provide the ultimate in privacy. The extensive a la carte menu includes sizzling rice soup, fried won tons, cashew chicken, deep-fried squab, and a variety of chow mein and chop suey, and the family-style Cantonese dinner is always a good choice. Exotic shark's fin, bird's nest, and seaweed soups are also available.

• Kowloon Vegetarian Restaurant *909 Grant Ave./Washington St., (415) 362-9888. L&D daily; $. Boosters. Reservations advised.*

This atmosphere-free cafe serves up some tasty gluten puffs and tofu-based dishes, as well as a large selection of dim sum. For an appetizer, don't miss the charming "bird nest" made with taro and filled with minced tofu, mushrooms, and vegetables. The house brown rice goes great with fake meat dishes such as sweet and sour "pork" and roasted "goose." For dessert, step up to the counter and pick from not-too-sweets such as giant almond cookies, and exotics such as custard balls mimicking the look of a hard-boiled egg.

• Lichee Garden *1416 Powell St./Vallejo St., (415) 397-2290. Dim sum daily 7-3; D daily; $. Highchairs, boosters. Reservations advised; accepted for dim sum 1 day in advance.*

Located on the North Beach side of Broadway, this family-style restaurant is known for its exceptional soups, Hong Kong-style crispy noodles, and crispy Peking-style spareribs. It's a good idea to come here with a large group as seating is at large round tables, portions are generous, and sodas are served in their original large plastic containers.

• Lucky Creation *854 Washington St./ Grant Ave., (415) 989-0818. L&D Thur-Tu; $. Boosters. No cards.*

In the sparest of atmospheres, this all vegetarian restaurant dishes up some of the most fabulous veggie dishes in town. Among the many choices are won tons, deep-fried taro shaped like goldfish, and a stunningly presented sautéed black mushrooms with baby bok choy. Clay pot dishes, noodle dishes (including wonderful chow fun items), and rice plates are available, as are imitation meat dishes made with gluten.

• The Pot Sticker *150 Waverly Pl./ Washington St., (415) 397-9985. L&D daily; $. Highchairs, boosters. Reservations taken.*

Situated in a picturesque alley famous for its historic buildings sporting ornate painted balconies, this spot is known for its lightly spiced Mandarin-style cuisine and handmade noodles and dumplings. Dishes tend to be lightly sauced with lots of vegetables. Good choices include hot and sour soup, Mongolian beef, and princess chicken. Dramatic Hunan crispy whole fish is served with hot sauce.

• Sam Wo *813 Washington St./Grant Ave., (415) 982-0596. L&D M-Sat; $. No reservations. No cards.*

People once came here for the experience of being insulted by, and to watch the reaction of others being insulted by, Edsel Ford Fong—the infamous waiter who reigned over the second floor. Unfortunately for those of us who actually became fond of him, Fong passed away in 1984. It is doubtful a replacement could ever be found. So now the main reason to come here is for the fresh housemade noodles and the unusual layout of the tiny dining rooms. Entering this "jook joint" through the cramped and busy kitchen and climbing the narrow stairs to the second and third floors is not unlike entering a submarine, only going up instead of down. Diners sit on stools at tables unexpectedly topped with real marble. Waiters shout orders down an ancient dumbwaiter by which finished dishes are later delivered. The house specialty, noodle soup, is available in 12 varieties. Won ton soups and chow fun dishes are also on the menu. The cold roasted pork rice noodle roll is especially good. No soft drinks, milk, or coffee are on the menu, and no fortune cookies arrive with the amazingly inexpensive check. It is worth knowing this place stays open until 3 a.m.

• **Taiwan** *289 Columbus Ave./Broadway, (415) 989-6789. L&D daily.*

For description, see page 264.

• **Tea Shop.**

• **Imperial Tea Court** *1411 Powell St./Broadway, (415) 788-6080, fax (415) 788-6079; www.imperialtea.com. Daily 11-6:30; $3-$5/person. Reservations not necessary.*

This exotic shop, decorated with a collection of bamboo birdcages, serves some of the world's most acclaimed, and expensive, teas. Sit down at one of the beautiful rosewood tables and relax while the selected tea is prepared. Like it? It's available for purchase, as are an assortment of tea accouterments.

• **Temple.**

Though there are many temples in Chinatown, only one seems to welcome visitors.

• **Tin How (or Tien Hau) Taoist Temple** *125-129 Waverly Pl./Washington St., (415) 391-4841. Daily 10-5 & 7-9pm.*

Named after the Queen of Heaven and Protector of Travelers, this temple is located in the heart of Chinatown on a lane known for its ornate, colorfully-painted balconies. It is easy to find. Just follow the scent of incense up the narrow wooden stairs to the fourth floor. Built in 1852, it is the oldest Taoist temple in the U.S. Though there is no charge to visit, donations are appreciated and an appropriate reverent behavior is expected. Bear in mind that the temple is still used for worship.

City Lights Booksellers and Publishers *261 Columbus Ave./Broadway, North Beach, (415) 362-8193, fax (415) 362-4921; www.citylights.com. Daily 10am-midnight.*

Founded in 1953 by beatnik poet Lawrence Ferlinghetti, who still looks after the business, this multi-level bookstore is said to be the first in the country to specialize in paperbacks. Many obscure titles are in its eclectic collection, providing great browsing. Don't miss stepping into the small press poetry alcove or traipsing down the creaky wooden stairs into the cellar room. Not content to just sell books, the proprietors published Allen Ginsburg's *Howl* and continue to publish unusual books.

Cliff House National Park Service Visitor Information Center *Point Lobos Ave./48th Ave., (415) 556-8642. Daily 10-4. Free.*

Learn about the history of the Cliff House area from the 1890s to the present. Adjacent **Sutro Baths**, once the world's largest indoor swimming pool complex, was filled with ocean water via an ingenious system developed by Adolph Sutro. The pools could hold 10,000 swimmers and 7,500 observers! Free ranger-led tours of the ruins are scheduled each month, but visitors can wander on their own at other times. See also page 62.

• **Musée Mécanique** *(415) 386-1170. Daily 11-7; in summer 10-8. Free admission.*

Located across from the visitors center, this "mechanical museum" is filled with old arcade games—some date from the 17th century—and provides thrills small and large. It is said to be the world's largest collection of antique coin-operated machines and is definitely one of the world's cheeriest places. For just a quarter it is possible to operate a miniature steam shovel and collect 90 seconds worth of gumballs, or to see naughty Marietta sunbathing in 3-D realism. Highlights include several player pianos, a mechanical horse ride, and jolly Laughing Sal with her original soundtrack (she was rescued from the Fun House at the now torn down Playland-at-the-Beach). But then the roller coaster made out of toothpicks and the machine that makes pressed penny souvenirs are also quite special. Beeping modern video games are in the back, where they belong.

• **Giant Camera Obscura** *(415) 750-0415. Daily 11-sunset, weather permitting. Adults $1, 2-12 50¢.*

Also nearby is this reproduction of Leonardo daVinci's 16th-century invention, which was a popular tourist attraction in the

1700s and 1800s. Built here in 1946 and once part of Playland-at-the-Beach, it uses a 10-inch mirror and two opposing plano-convex lenses to focus a live image of the shoreline outside onto a 6-foot parabolic screen inside. It rotates slowly, presenting magnified views of Ocean Beach, Seal Rocks, and the crashing waves. The personalized tour is both entertaining and educational.

• **Seal Rocks.**

Barking sea lions and brown pelicans share space on these historic rocks. They can be seen with just the naked eye or viewed through an antique telescope.

Coit Tower *At top of Lombard St., North Beach, (415) 362-0808. Daily 9-4, in summer 10-5. Adults $4, 63+ $2, under 12 $1.50.*

Located atop fashionable Telegraph Hill, this 210-foot-tall tower (approximately 18 stories) offers magnificent 360-degree views. Colorful painted murals on the ground floor walls date from 1934. Depicting area activities during the Depression, they were controversial at the time because of left-wing political content. The fee includes an attendant-operated elevator ride to the top. Parking is extremely limited. Visitors who walk or take the 39 Coit bus up, can then walk down the **Filbert Street Steps**, past the **Grace Marchant Garden**, to Levi Plaza, located near Battery Street.

Crookedest Street in the World *Lombard St. between Hyde St. & Leavenworth St., Russian Hill.*

This famous curvy street is one way downhill. Drivers must maneuver over a bumpy brick-paved road with eight tight turns while trying not to be distracted by the magnificent view. Get here by driving up the steep incline on the west side of Lombard Street, or, for an easier time of it, drive up from the south side of Hyde Street.

The **other crookedest street** is Vermont Street, between 22nd and 23rd streets on Potrero Hill. Though it has only six turns, they are said to be tighter than Lombard's.

The city's **steepest streets** are Filbert Street between Hyde and Leavenworth streets (with a 31.5 percent grade), 22nd Street between Church and Vicksburg streets (also with a 31.5 percent grade), and Jones Street between Union and Filbert streets (with a 29 percent grade).

Fort Mason *Laguna St./Marina Blvd., (415) 441-3400.*

In addition to housing the park headquarters for the Golden Gate National Recreation Area, this complex of buildings houses theaters, art galleries, museums, and myriad other facilities. Highlights include:

• **African-American Historical and Cultural Society.** See page 28.

• **Book Bay Bookstore** *Bldg. C, (415) 771-1076. Daily 11-5.*

Thousands of bargain books, as well as records and tapes, await. The West's largest **Used Book Sale** is held each September. Proceeds benefit the San Francisco Public Library.

• **Greens** restaurant. See page 68.

• **The Mexican Museum.** See page 23.

• **Museo ItaloAmericano.** See page 24.

• **Museum of Craft & Folk Art.** See page 24.

• **Young Performers Theatre.** See page 37.

Fort Point National Historic Site *Located directly under the south anchorage of the Golden Gate Bridge, at end of Marine Dr., the Presidio; take Lincoln Blvd. to Long Ave., turn left, at bottom follow road along water to fort;*

(415) 556-1693; www.nps.gov/fopo. Daily 10-5. Free; audio tour: adults $2.50, children $1.

Built in 1861, this is the only Civil War-era fort on the West Coast. Its four tiers were once home to 126 cannon. It is perhaps even more famous as the site in Hitchcock's *Vertigo* where Kim Novak's character jumped into the bay. Each winter **Candlelight Fort Tours** *(Nov-Feb; 6:30-8pm. Participants must be 15 or older. Reservations required.)* are scheduled. Participants see the fort from the viewpoint of a Civil War soldier. What was it like in the 1860s to live in drafty quarters heated by fireplaces and lighted by candles? What kind of food was eaten, and how was it prepared? These questions and more are answered on the tour and following walk through the 1870 gun emplacements located south of the fort.

Golden Gate Bridge.

Once called "the bridge that couldn't be built," this magnificent example of man's ingenuity and perseverance is one of San Francisco's most famous sights. Measuring 6,450 feet, or approximately 1.7 miles, it is the longest suspension bridge in the world, and its 746-foot-high towers are the tallest ever built. Many people are disappointed to discover that the bridge is not a golden color. In fact, it is painted with a protective dull red-orange coating. The color, known officially as International Orange, was chosen by the bridge's architect, Irving Morrow, to make it visible in dense fog. Crossing it is a must—by car, foot, or bicycle. The round-trip is about 2 miles, and views are breathtaking. It is interesting to note that bungee-jumping is said to have originated here in 1979.

Grace Cathedral *1100 California St./Taylor St., (415) 749-6300, fax (415) 749-6301. Daily 8-6; tours available. Free.*

Located atop Nob Hill, this majestic French Gothic cathedral stands 265 feet tall and is the largest in the western U.S. It is graced with more than 60 opulent stained-glass windows, and its gilded bronze entrance doors are exact replicas of Lorenzo Ghiberti's "Doors of Paradise" at the Baptistry in Florence, Italy. Concerts using the cathedral's renowned 7,400-pipe organ are often scheduled, sometimes

accompanied by the 44-bell carillon. The cathedral's reverberant acoustics and architecturally magnificent interior make these memorable experiences. Walking **labyrinths**, a unique tool for meditation and said to be a metaphor for entering one's center, where healing occurs, are available both inside the cathedral and outside on a new plaza. Patterned after one at Chartres cathedral, they are said to be the first permanent labyrinths laid in the Western hemisphere in 600 years.

Annual **Cathedral Choir Christmas Concerts** feature the Grace Cathedral Choir of Men and Boys singing both traditional and new carols. They are wondrous, inspirational events. A Festival of Lessons and a Midnight Mass are traditional on Christmas Eve, and a celebratory New Year's Eve event is also scheduled each year. And every few years the cathedral is the unusual, yet appropriate, setting for a screening of the original 1923 silent film classic *The Hunchback of Notre Dame* with live accompaniment by the organ.

Haight-Ashbury *Haight St. between Stanyan St. & Masonic St.*

It's almost possible to step back in time here to the Summer of Love. A few locals still don bell-bottoms, tie-dyed shirts, and love beads, and these items are still for sale in some shops. Not gentrified, the area is a little rough around the edges, and Haight Street is now lined with an assortment of colorful boutiques and inexpensive restaurants and coffeehouses. Wavy Gravy describes his neighborhood as "a coexistence between the punks and the hippies, a little cutting-edge U.N. in action."

Visiting here also permits the chance to see some of the area's magnificent Victorian houses, including the one at 710 Ashbury, where the Grateful Dead once lived, and the mansion at 2400 Fulton, where the Jefferson Airplane lived. Janis Joplin once lived with Country Joe McDonald in apartment 3 at 112 Page Street, Big Brother & the Holding Company formed at 1090 Page Street, and the first free medical clinic in the U.S. still operates at 558 Clayton Street. On a more somber note, the notorious Manson "family" once lived at 636 Cole Street.

Historic Houses.

San Francisco is known for its abundance of beautiful turn-of-the-century Victorian houses. At last count there were over 14,000. One of the pleasures of living here is visiting people who actually live in them. Visitors to the city interested in capturing a taste of that delight will enjoy stopping in at the two historic homes open to the public.

To see some of the city's "painted ladies," as the many colorfully painted Victorian homes are sometimes called, visit the area around **Alamo Square** at Hayes and Steiner streets. The 700 block of Steiner is packed with Queen Anne Victorians. Nicknamed "postcard row," it is often photographed commercially from the top of the park, with the skyline in the distance. Another good area is along the **Golden Gate Park Panhandle**, particularly on the Fell Street side, where well-maintained mansions are plentiful. (It is interesting to note that the Panhandle was originally the carriage entrance to the park and that it is home to some of the park's oldest trees—approximately 50 species.)

And, of course, everyone wants to see the house used in exterior scenes for *Mrs. Doubtfire*. Check it out in Pacific Heights at 2640 Steiner

Street. Seeing the house from the outside will do. Interior scenes were filmed in a studio so there is no need to peek in windows.

• **Haas-Lilienthal House** *2007 Franklin St./Jackson St., Pacific Heights, (415) 441-3004; www.sfheritage.org. House tour: W 12-3, Sun 11-4. Adults $5, seniors & under 12 $3. Strollers not permitted. Walking tour: Sun at 12:30. Adults $5, seniors & under 12 $3.*

In 1886 architect Peter R. Schmidt built this 24-room, 7½-bath Queen Anne Victorian home of fir and redwood for Bertha and William Haas, a mercantile grocer. It cost $18,500. (Average homes then cost about $2,000.) The house survived the infamous 1906 earthquake relatively unscathed, with a small bulge in the plaster the only visible damage. It also escaped the fire that followed, though Mr. Haas's downtown offices were destroyed. Family members occupied the house until 1973, when it was donated to the San Francisco Architectural Heritage. Most of the furnishings, which include a lovely and extensive set of matching art nouveau pieces in the main bedroom, are original to the house. Children often find the doll house in the second-floor nursery especially interesting.

On Sundays, a Heritage-sponsored **walking tour** of the surrounding Pacific Heights neighborhood focuses on the exteriors of some of San Francisco's finest Victorian and Edwardian homes.

• **Octagon House** *2645 Gough St./Union St., Pacific Heights, (415) 441-7512. Open 2nd & 4th Thur & 2nd Sun of month, 12-3; closed Jan. By donation.*

Built in 1861, when this architectural style was a fad throughout the country, this eight-sided house is now one of only two left in San Francisco. The National Society of The Colonial Dames of America in California has restored and furnished it and turned it into the only museum of Colonial and Federal decorative arts on the West Coast. Items on display date from 1700 to 1830 and are labeled with background information. Of special interest is a display featuring the signatures of 54 of the original 56 signers of the Declaration of Independence. The house's well-groomed garden and adjacent **Allyne Park** are both perfect for a stroll.

Mission San Francisco de Assisi *3321 16th St./Dolores St., the Mission, (415) 621-8203. Daily 9-4. Adults $2, 5-12 $1.*

Popularly known as **Mission Dolores**, this relatively small mission is sixth in California's chain of 21. The chapel, completed in 1791, is the oldest intact building in the city. Its cool adobe and redwood interior offers pleasant respite from the occasional hot San Francisco day. Of special interest is the chapel ceiling, painted in Ohlone tribal patterns and colors originally produced by vegetable dyes. A picturesque enclosed cemetery garden is landscaped to period correctness, and all the plants now found here were once used in some way by resident Native Americans. A tiny museum completes the complex.

Presidio of San Francisco *Visitor Center: on Montgomery St., Bldg. 102, (415) 561-4323. Daily 9-5. Free.*

Used as a military garrison by Spain, Mexico, and the U.S., the Presidio was established by Spain in 1776, taken over by Mexico in 1822, and then taken over by the U.S. as an Army post in 1846. It played a critical role in providing refuge for the 1906 earthquake victims. The Presidio is undergoing continuous major changes as it transforms from being an Army post into being a recreational area. Currently it has 11 miles of hiking trails and 14 miles of biking routes. Contact the Visitor Center for information on guided walks and bicycle tours.

• **Presidio Museum** *At the Visitor Center.*

This museum documents the story of the Spanish, Mexican, and American armies. Outside, the front lawn is punctuated with obsolete cannons and artillery. Inside, a warren of rooms hold displays of artifacts and an extensive collection of historic photos covering the Spanish period through Vietnam. Children particularly enjoy the large collection of uniforms and the huge dioramas showing the Spanish Presidio as it appeared at various times—in the 1790s, in the 1906 earthquake and fire, and during the 1915 Panama Pacific International Exposition. Two restored shacks used for temporary housing after the '06 quake are on view behind the museum. (Approximately 17,000 such shacks were erected all over the city after the earthquake.)

• **Burger King** *211 Lincoln Ave., (415) 673-1856. M-F 7-6, Sat & Sun 8-5; $. Highchairs, boosters, booths.*

Stop for refueling here, but forget the drive-thru. With a large-windowed room overlooking the Golden Gate Bridge, this might qualify as the most scenically situated fast-food restaurant in America.

Museums

— Art Museums —

Ansel Adams Center for Photography
655 Mission St., South of Market, (415) 495-7000, fax (415) 495-8517; www.friendsofphotography.org. Daily 10-5, to 8 on 1st Thur of month. Adults $6, seniors & 13-17 $2.

Recently relocated, this museum is dedicated to presenting photography as the model of today's visual culture. One gallery is dedicated completely to the work of Ansel Adams.

California Palace of the Legion of Honor
34th Ave./Clement St., in Lincoln Park, the Richmond, (415) 863-3330; www.thinker.org. Tu-Sun 9:30-5. Adults $8, 65+ $6, 12-17 $5; free 2nd W of month.

Situated on a scenic knoll overlooking the Golden Gate Bridge, this is the only museum in the country exhibiting primarily French art. Rodin's earliest casting of his sculpture, "The Thinker," greets visitors as they approach the entrance to this impressive neoclassical marble structure—a replica of the Hotel de Salm in Paris, where Napoleon established his new Order of the Legion of Honor in the 18th century. This museum also holds the city's collection of European and ancient art and presents free organ concerts on weekends at 4 p.m. The museum was given to the city of San Francisco on Armistice Day in 1924 and is dedicated to the memory of California men who died in World War I.

For three days every March the museum galleries are stunningly decorated with fresh flowers. For **Bouquets to Art**, members of Bay Area flower clubs and professional florists design arrangements inspired by museum paintings. Some mimic the paintings, other pick up the colors or feeling. Overall they enliven the galleries.

The entrance to the **Holocaust Memorial** is on the north side of the parking circle. A semicircular stairway leads down to an area where the cast bronze, white-painted pieces created by sculptor George Segal are displayed.

For a scenic drive, leave via Lincoln Avenue on the north side of the museum. Follow it to its conclusion at Lombard Street. This route has several vista points of the Golden Gate Bridge and passes by Baker Beach, goes through the elegant Sea Cliff residential area, and continues into the Presidio.

Cartoon Art Museum *814 Mission St./4th St., South of Market, (415) CAR-TOON; www.cartoonart.org. W-F 11-5, Sat 10-5, Sun 1-5. Adults $5, 62+ & students $3, 6-12 $2; free 1st W of month.*

Presenting both a permanent collection and changing special exhibits, this museum showcases important developments in cartoon history from the early 18th century to the present. One of only two such museums in the country, its aim is "to preserve this unique art form and to enrich the public's knowledge of its cultural and aesthetic value." Free cartooning workshops on Saturday afternoons are included with admission.

Mexican Museum *Fort Mason Center, Bldg. D, Laguna St./Marina Blvd., (415) 441-0404. W-Sun 11-5. Adults $4, seniors & 13-16 $3; free 1st W of month.*

Founded in 1975, this is the first museum in the U.S. devoted to Mexican and Mexican-American art. Exhibits change regularly. When space permits, items from the permanent pre-Columbian collection are displayed.

M. H. de Young Memorial Museum *In Golden Gate Park, (415) 863-3330; www.thinker.org. Tu-Sun 9:30-5, 1st W to 8:45. Adults $7, 65+ $5, 12-17 $4; free 1st W of month.*

A significant collection of American paintings is displayed here on colorful walls. It includes sculpture and decorative arts from colonial times into the mid-20th century as well as the country's best collection of American trompe l'oeil paintings from the turn of the century. The permanent collection of art from Africa, Oceania, Mesoamerica, and Central and South America features outstanding works from ancient to modern times; many are not seen elsewhere. Due to earthquake damage, this building is scheduled for demolition.

The cafeteria-style **Cafe de Young** *((415) 752-0116. L W-Sun; $. No reservations. No cards.)* serves simple foods prepared eloquently. The kitchen makes most items from scratch using fresh ingredients, and the menu offers a selection of salads and sandwiches along with a daily soup and pasta salad special. Diners can sit inside, where tables are decorated with fresh flowers, or outside at umbrella-shaded tables surrounding a garden fountain.

Adjoining the de Young, the **Asian Art Museum** *((415) 379-8801; www.asianart.org.)* displays the best Asian collection in the U.S. It is the largest museum in the western world devoted exclusively to Asian art, and it also holds the largest collection of Indian sculpture outside India. It has more than 12,000 objects from 40 Asian countries spanning a period of more than 6,000 years. However, due to space restraints, only about 10 percent of the collection can be displayed at any one time. This museum is scheduled to move to a Civic Center location.

Museo ItaloAmericano *Fort Mason Center, Bldg. C, Laguna St./Marina Blvd., (415) 673-2200, fax (415) 673-2292; www.well.com/museo. W-Sun 12-5. Adults $2, seniors & 12-18 $1; free 1st W of month.*

Dedicated to displaying the works of Italian and Italian-American artists, this museum's small exhibit space is stark and quiet.

Museum of Craft & Folk Art *Fort Mason Center, Bldg. A, Laguna St./Marina Blvd., (415) 775-0991, fax (415) 775-1861; www.sfcraftandfolk.org. Tu-Sun 11-5, Sat to 7. Adults $3, 62+ & 12-17 $1; free 1st W 11-7.*

Serving as a showcase for high quality contemporary crafts and folk art, this museum changes exhibits every two months.

San Francisco Museum of Modern Art *151 3rd St./Howard St., South of Market, (415) 357-4000, fax (415) 357-4037; www.sfmoma.org. Thur-Tu 11-6, Thur to 9. Adults $9, 62+ $6, students 13+ with ID $5; half-price admission Thur 6-9; free 1st Tu of month. Audio tour $3.*

Re-situated now in a striking new building, this museum was the first in the West devoted entirely to 20th-century art. Its collection includes abstract art, photography, and the work of acclaimed contemporary artists. The most efficient way to see everything is to take the elevator to the 5th floor and work down. An informative audio tour is available to the permanent collection. The museum gift shop has an array of exceptional merchandise and a particularly noteworthy section for children, and casual **Caffe Museo** *((415) 357-4500, fax (415) 357-4506.)* offers a menu of scrumptious meals and light snacks.

Yerba Buena Center for the Arts *701 Mission St./3rd St., South of Market, (415) 978-ARTS; www.YerbaBuenaArts.org. Gallery: Tu-Sun 11-6, Thur & F to 8. Adults $5, 65+ $3, under 17 free; free 1st Thur of month.*

Art shows and live entertainment emphasizing the diverse artists and communities of the region are presented here. The center is located in **Yerba Buena Gardens**, a new development that holds an outdoor stage, two cafes, a butterfly garden, a redwood grove, public sculptures, a waterfall, and a multi-language memorial to Dr. Martin Luther King, Jr.

— Floating Museums —

The collection of historic ships berthed along the San Francisco waterfront is the largest (by weight) in the world.

San Francisco Maritime Park *www.nps.gov/safr.*

• **Maritime Museum** *On Beach St./foot of Polk St., across from Ghirardelli Square, (415) 556-3002. Daily 10-5. Free.*

The architecturally interesting art deco-streamline moderne building housing this museum was built by the Work Project Administration (WPA) in 1939. Appropriately, it resembles a ship, though it was originally meant to be used as a nightclub and aquatic activities center. The main floor displays parts of old ships, elaborately carved and painted figureheads, and exquisitely detailed ship models. The second floor is home to more models as well as to artifacts, paintings, fascinating historic photos, and maps.

• **Hyde Street Pier** *2905 Hyde St./Jefferson St., (415) 556-3002. Daily 9:30-5. Adults $5, seniors & 12-17 $2, family $7.*

The vessels moored on this scenic pier represent the time period from the turn of the century through World War II—a period of rapid growth for San Francisco begun by the 1849 Gold Rush. During this time the city was an important shipping center. An annual **Festival of the Sea** in September features sea music, demonstrations of sailor arts, lectures, films, and sea poetry readings.

• ***Balclutha.*** A Cape Horn sailing ship built in Scotland in 1886, this 301-foot steel-hulled merchant ship carried whiskey, wool, and rice, but mainly coal, to San Francisco. On her return sailing to Europe she carried grain from California. Typical of Victorian British merchant ships, she is described colorfully by the men who sailed her as a "blue water, square-rigged, lime juice windbag." She is the last of the Cape Horn fleet and ended her sailing career as an Alaskan salmon ship. Renovated by donated labor and goods, she was opened to the public in 1955.

• ***Eureka.*** Originally named the *Ukiah*, this double-ended, wooden-hulled ferry was built in Tiburon in 1890 to carry railroad cars and passengers across the bay. In 1922 she was

Balclutha

rebuilt to carry automobiles and passengers and renamed the *Eureka.* Later she served as a commuter ferry (the largest in the world) between San Francisco and Sausalito, and yet later as a ferry for train passengers arriving in San Francisco from Oakland. She held 2,300 people plus 120 automobiles. Her 4-story "walking beam" steam engine is the only such engine still afloat in the U.S. A model demonstrates its operation, and a ranger-guided tour through the engine room is sometimes available. Two decks are open to the public. The lower deck houses a display of antique cars, and the main deck features original benches and a historical photo display.

• ***C.A. Thayer.*** A fleet of 900 ships once carried lumber from the north coast forests to California ports. Only two of these ships still exist. One is the *C.A. Thayer*—a three-mast lumber schooner built in Fairhaven (near Eureka) in 1895. She made her last voyage in 1950 as a fishing ship. She was the very last commercial sailing ship in use on the West Coast. Visitors can descend into her dank wooden hold to see the crew's bunk room and then ascend to the captain's lushly furnished, oak-paneled cabin—complete with a gilded canary cage. A 25-minute film of her last voyage is shown several times each day, and guided tours are available. A fascinating way to experi-

ence this ship is at one of the **chantey sings** *((415) 556-6435. Adult program on 1st Sat of month, 8pm-12; children's program on 3rd Sat, 3-3:45. Reservations required. Free.)* held in her cozy hold. Participants should dress warmly and bring something to sit on as well as a chantey or two to share. A little something to wet the whistle wouldn't hurt either.

More ships moored at the pier are not open for boarding. The ***Alma***, a scow schooner built in 1891 at Hunters Point, is a specialized cargo carrier and the last of her kind still afloat. The ***Eppleton Hall***, built in England in 1914 and used in the canals there to tow coal ships, is the only vessel in the collection not directly associated with West Coast maritime history. The ***Hercules*** is an ocean-going tugboat built in 1907. And the ***Wapama***, the last surviving example of a steam schooner, is currently being restored in Sausalito.

Non-floating displays at the pier include a turn-of-the-century ark (or houseboat), a restored donkey engine that is sometimes operated for visitors, and the reconstructed sales office of the Tubbs Cordage Company.

S.S. Jeremiah O'Brien *Pier 45, foot of Taylor St., Fisherman's Wharf, (415) 441-3101. Daily 9-4. Adults $5, seniors $4, 6-17 $3.*

This massive 441-foot-long vessel is the last unaltered Liberty Ship from World War II still in operating condition. Between 1941 and 1945, in an all-out effort to replace the cargo ships being sunk in huge numbers by enemy submarines, 2,751 Liberty Ships were built to transport troops and supplies. At that time shipyards operated around the clock. Each ship was assembled from pre-fabricated sections and took only between six and eight weeks to build. Shockingly large, the *O'Brien* was built in South Portland, Maine in 1943. She was in operation for 33 years and sailed from England to Normandy during the D-Day invasion. In 1978 she was declared a national monument. Since then dedicated volunteers, many of whom served on similar ships, have been working to restore her to her original glory. Visitors have access to almost every part of the ship, including sleeping quarters, captain's quarters, wheel house, and guns as well as the catwalks in the eerie 3-story engine room. The triple expansion steam engine is operated nine weekends each year. The public can purchase tickets for the annual **Seamen's Memorial Cruise** each May, and the **Bay Cruise** each October during Fleet Week.

USS Pampanito *Pier 45, foot of Taylor St., Fisherman's Wharf, (415) 775-1943, fax (415) 441-0365; www.maritime.org. Sun-Thur 9-6, F & Sat 9-8, in summer daily 9-8. Adults $6, 62+ & 6-12 $4.*

This 312-foot-long World War II submarine was built in Portsmouth, New Hampshire in 1943. She is credited with sinking six Japanese ships and damaging four others. She also rescued a group of British and Australian POWs from the South China Sea. The self-guided tour through the cramped belly of the sub and its meticulously restored compartments is enhanced with a recorded audio tour providing narrative by former crew members, helping listeners imagine what it must have been like for men to be cooped up in this small space for months at a time.

— Science Museums —

California Academy of Sciences *In Golden Gate Park, (415) 750-7145, fax (415) 750-7346; www.calacademy.org. Daily 10-5; in summer 9-6. Adults $8.50, 65+ & 12-17 $5.50, 6-11 $2; free 1st W of month. Planetarium: Adults $2.50, under 18 $1.25.*

Founded in 1853 following the Gold Rush, this is the oldest scientific institution in the West and one of the ten largest natural history museums in the world. And this impressive museum complex grows better all the time. Visitors can experience a simulated 4.0 and 5.7 earthquake, watch time march on via a Foucault pendulum, and view a 1,350-pound quartz cluster in the impressive Gem & Mineral Hall. The permanent Far Side of Science Gallery exhibits original *Far Side* cartoons by Gary Larson. More exhibits include bird and animal dioramas, most notably the Wild California hall featuring life-size elephant seal models and a 14,000-gallon aquarium, the African Water Hole featuring authentic animal sounds synchronized to a dawn-to-dusk lighting cycle, and Life Through Time, which focuses on evolution and takes visitors on a dinosaur-studded 3.5 billion-year journey through life on Earth.

The classic European-style **Steinhart Aquarium** exhibits hundreds of fish tanks as well as a popular Blackfooted Penguin Environment, a tropical shark habitat, and The Swamp—featuring a waterfall and home to alligators, turtles, and snakes. Said to have the most diverse collection of species in the world, the aquarium also displays the largest living tropical coral reef in the country. The California Tidepool permits handling live sea animals such as sea stars and urchins, and the donut-shaped 100,000-gallon Fish Roundabout tank puts the viewers on the inside and the fish on the outside.

The largest planetarium in Northern California, **Morrison Planetarium** has a popular Star Talk program that provides information about what can be viewed in the current night sky. **The Christmas Star** has been presented annually in December since the planetarium opened in 1952. Viewers are taken back in time to view the night sky as it is believed to have appeared to the Wise Men in Nazareth almost 2,000 years ago.

Exploratorium *3601 Lyon St., the Marina, (415) 561-0363, fax (415) 561-0307; www.exploratorium.edu. Tu-Sun 10-5, W to 9; in summer daily 10-6, W to 9. Adults $9, 65+ $7, 6-17 $5, 3-5 $2.50; free 1st W of month.*

Located inside the **Palace of Fine Arts**, which was designed by architect Bernard Maybeck in 1915 as part of the Panama-Pacific Exposition (an early World's Fair celebrating the opening of the Panama Canal) and is said to be the world's largest artificial ruin, this

cavernous museum makes scientific and natural phenomena understandable through a collection of over 650 hands-on exhibits. It has been described by a former editor of *Scientific American* as the best science museum in the world. Visitors can experience a dizzying ride on a Momentum Machine, step through a miniature tornado, and encase themselves in bubbles. To the shrieking delight of youngsters, a walk-in Shadow Box allows reverse images to remain on a wall. Teenage "Explainers" wearing easy-to-see orange vests wander the premises ready to help. Reservations should be made several weeks in advance to experience the **Tactile Dome** *((415) 561-0362. Tickets $12, includes museum admission.)*, a geodesic dome with 13 chambers through which visitors can walk, crawl, slide, climb, and tumble in complete darkness with only their sense of touch to guide them. This experience is not recommended for children under age 7. It is pleasant to picnic outside by the picturesque reflecting pond populated with ducks and even a few swans.

The **Wave Organ**, a project sponsored by the Exploratorium, is located across Marina Boulevard at the eastern tip of the breakwater forming the Marina Yacht Harbor. This unusual musical instrument was designed by artist Peter Richards in collaboration with stonemason George Gonzales. Consisting of more than 20 pipes extending down through the breakwater into the bay, the organ provides a constant symphony of natural music. Listeners can relax in a small granite and marble amphitheater and enjoy views of the San Francisco skyline. The organ plays most effectively at high tide.

— Miscellaneous Museums —

African-American Historical and Cultural Society *Fort Mason Center, Bldg. C, Laguna St./Marina Blvd., (415) 441-0640. W-Sun 12-5. Adults $2, 62+ $1, under 12 free.*

This small museum exhibits photographs of the Civil War, artifacts from World War II, and photographs collected by a black "Buffalo Soldier" Army veteran.

Cable Car Barn and Museum *1201 Mason St./Washington St., (415) 474-1887. Daily 10-5; in summer to 6. Free.*

Located 2 blocks from the heart of Chinatown, this interesting museum is inside the lovely brick cable car barn and powerhouse dating from the 1880s. Here visitors can view the huge, noisy flywheels controlling the underground cables that move the cable cars along at 9 1/2-miles per hour. Three retired cable cars—including one from the original 1873 fleet—and assorted artifacts are on display, and an informative film with vintage photographs explains how the cable cars actually work. To complete the experience, catch a cable car across the street and take a ride downtown or to Fisherman's Wharf.

California Historical Society Museum *678 Mission St./3rd St., South of Market, (415) 357-1848, fax (415) 357-1850; www.calhist.org. Tu-Sat 11-5. Adults $2, 65+ & students $1, under 6 free.*

Founded in 1871, the society has a collection of artifacts documenting California's history from the 16th century through the present. That adds up to over 500,000 photographs and 150,000 manuscripts, as well as thousands of books, maps, paintings, and emphera (the official word for "odds and ends"). Among the gems are Emperor Norton's cane and a stereoscope—the precursor to today's 3-D films. This small museum is housed within the former Hundley Hardware Building.

Musée Mécanique. See page 18.

North Beach Museum *1435 Stockton St./Columbus, on 2nd fl. of EurekaBank, (415) 391-6210. M-Thur 9-5, F 9-6. Free.*

Nostalgic photographs depicting this

area's past are displayed along with an assortment of interesting artifacts.

Presido Museum. See page 22.

Randall Museum *199 Museum Way/ Roosevelt Way, near 14th St., Corona Heights, (415) 554-9600, fax (415) 554-9609; www.randallmuseum.org. Tu-Sat 10-5. Free.*

Located below Buena Vista Park, between Upper Castro and Haight-Ashbury, this small museum has an indoor Animal Room inhabited by uncaged but tethered hawks and owls and other small, accessible animals. Most are recovering from injuries inflicted in the wild. A highlight is the Touching Pen, where children can handle domesticated animals such as rabbits, chickens, and ducks. Exhibits are few but include a replica of a 1906 earthquake refugee shack and an operating seismograph. Nature walks and children's science and arts-and-crafts classes are scheduled regularly.

On the second and fourth Saturday afternoon of each month, the Golden Gate Model Railroaders show off their **model railroad** *(12:30-5. Free.).*

Ripley's Believe It or Not! Museum
175 Jefferson St./Taylor St., Fisherman's Wharf, (415) 771-6188, fax (415) 771-1246; www.ripleysf.com. Sun-Thur 10-10, F & Sat to 12. Age 13+ $8.95, 60+ $7, 5-12 $5.95.

Among the 250-plus exhibits from Ripley's personal collection of oddities are a cable car made from 270,000 match sticks and an authentic shrunken torso from Ecuador that was once owned by Ernest Hemingway. All this, and 2,000 more curiosities. It's unbelievable!

San Francisco Fire Department Museum
655 Presidio Ave./Bush St., Presidio Heights, (415) 563-4630. Thur-Sun 1-4. Free.

The fascinating collection of antique fire apparatus found in this small museum includes engines from the hand-drawn, horse-drawn, and motorized eras of fire-fighting. Of special interest is an ornate hand-pulled engine dating from 1849, which is said to be San Francisco's, and California's, first fire engine. In addition, old photographs, memorabilia, and artifacts combine to tell the story of fire-fighting in San Francisco, beginning in 1849 with the volunteer department and emphasizing the 1906 earthquake and fire. Visitors are welcome to stop in next door at fire station #10 to see what the modern rigs are looking like.

Tattoo Art Museum *841 Columbus Ave./ Lombard St., North Beach, (415) 775-4991. M-Sat 12-9, Sun 12-8. Free.*

Located next to the studio of renowned tattooist Lyle Tuttle, this is the world's first tattoo museum. Photos and paintings trace the history of tattooing, and artifacts on display include everything from ancient bone tattooing needles to modern electric versions. To leave with a permanent souvenir, call ahead for an appointment.

Wax Museum at Fisherman's Wharf
145 Jefferson St./Taylor St., (800) 439-4305, (415) 885-4834, fax (415) 771-9248; www.waxmuseum.com. Daily 9-10; in summer to midnight. Adults $11.95, 60+ $8.95, 6-17 $5.95.

Recently completely rebuilt and expanded, this attraction displays several hundred wax celebrities situated among an assortment of backgrounds. The Chamber of Horrors intrigues older children.

Wells Fargo History Museum *420 Montgomery St./California St., Financial District, (415) 396-2619. M-F 9-5. Free.*

In homage to the Old West, this 2-story museum displays an authentic stagecoach complete with strongbox, samples of various kinds of gold found in the state, a telegraph exhibit, and, of course, a re-creation of an old banking office. All this plus gold-panning equipment and historical photos, too. The oldest bank in the West—Wells Fargo—is the sponsor, and the museum rests on the site of the bank's first office.

Parks/Spectator Sports

Angel Island State Park *San Francisco departures from Pier 41 at Fisherman's Wharf; adults $11, 5-11 $6.50. East Bay departures from Jack London Square; weekends only; call for fares; both (415) 705-8210. Tiburon departures from Main St.; adults $7, under 12 $5, bikes $1; (415) 435-2131, call for departure times. State Park information: (415) 435-1915; www.angelisland.org. Visitors Center: Sat & Sun 11-3:30; free. Tram: Daily in summer, Sat & Sun Mar & Nov, W-Sun in Apr; adults $11.50, 62+ $10.50, 6-12 $7.50.*

Half the fun of a trip to Angel Island is the scenic ferry ride over. Visitors disembark at Ayala Cove. Picnic tables and barbecue facilities are nearby, as is a pleasant little beach for sunbathing. Packing along a picnic to enjoy in some remote spot is highly recommended, but the island does have its own **Cove Cafe**. Approximately 12 miles of well-marked trails and paved roads allow hikers to completely circle the 740-acre island—the largest island in the bay. Some lead to old military ruins that are reminders of the island's past as a detention center for immigrants from 1910 to 1940 (the island was once called the "Ellis Island of the West"), as a prisoner-of-war processing facility, and as a Nike missile defense base from 1955 to 1962. A 3.2-mile loop trail leads from the cove to the top of 781-foot-high Mount Livermore, where a picnic area and a 360-degree view await. A park map is available at the Visitors Center, and a variety of guided tours are available. Except for Park Service vehicles, cars are not permitted on the island. Tram tours circle the island via the 5-mile perimeter road in summer, and bikes can be brought over on the ferry or rented on the island. Kayak tours can be reserved through **Sea Trek Ocean Kayaking Center** *((415) 488-1000; www.seatrekkayak.com; must be 6 or older.)*. Camping in primitive environmental campsites can be arranged.

Beaches.

San Francisco is *not* the place to come to go to the beach. Los Angeles is where *that* California is. Still, the city does have a few good spots to soak up some rays, weather willing. The water, however, is usually either too cold or too dangerous for swimming.

- **Aquatic Park** *Foot of Polk St., Fisherman's Wharf, (415) 556-2904. Always open. Free.*

Located in the people-congested area across the street from Ghirardelli Square, this is a good spot for children to wade and there are great views of the bay.

- **Baker Beach** *Off Lincoln Blvd./25th Ave., the Presidio, (415) 556-0560. Daily sunrise-sunset. Free.*

The surf here is unsafe and the temperature is often chilly. Still, there are usually plenty of people sunning and strolling, and the views of the Golden Gate Bridge are spectacular. **Battery Chamberlin** is located adjacent. Demonstrations of the world's last remaining 50-ton "disappearing gun" are conducted by rangers on weekends, and environmental programs are sometimes offered.

- **China Beach** *End of Seacliff Ave./28th Ave., the Richmond, (415) 239-2366. Daily dawn-dusk. Free.*

Located in an exclusive residential area, this secluded cove is surprising to come upon. Visitors park on a bluff, then walk down steep stairs to the sheltered, sandy beach. The surf is gentle, so swimming and wading are possible, and changing rooms and restrooms are available in summer.

Fort Funston *South end of Great Highway/ Skyline Blvd., (415) 239-2366; www.nps.gov/fopo. Sunrise-sunset. Visitor Center: Daily 12-4. Free.*

Acquired by the U.S. Army in 1900, these bluffs were once a link in the coastal artillery batteries lining the coast. Nike anti-aircraft missiles guarded the area from the 1950s until the fort's closure in 1963. Now part of the Golden Gate National Recreation Area, this fort's former barracks houses the Ranger Station and Environmental Science Center. Nike missile magazines can still be seen below the main parking area. A short, paved loop trail offers stunning coastal views, and an observation platform on a bluff above the ocean provides a great vantage point for whale-watching in winter, as well as a bird's-eye view of the many hang-gliders who practice their sport here.

Golden Gate National Recreation Area (GGNRA) *(415) 556-0560; www.nps.gov/goga.*

Dedicated to deceased Congressman Phillip Burton, who contributed greatly to establishing this park, the GGNRA is the world's largest urban national park and is one of the most heavily visited national parks in the U.S. Located in three California counties—San Francisco, Marin, and San Mateo—its total area is over 114 square miles, or 2½ times the size of San Francisco. These Bay Area sites are part of the GGNRA: Aquatic Park, Alcatraz, Baker Beach, China Beach, the Cliff House, Crissy Field, East Fort Baker, Fort Funston, Fort Mason, Fort Point, Gerbode Valley, Lands End, Marin Headlands, Muir Woods, Ocean Beach, Olema Valley, The Presidio, Stinson Beach, Sutro Heights Park, Sweeney Ridge, Tennessee Valley, and Tomales Bay. Also within the boundaries but not administered by the GGNRA: Angel Island State Park, Audubon Canyon Ranch, Mount Tamalpais State Park, Samuel P. Taylor State Park, and various ranches in the Tomales Bay-Lagunitas Creek area.

Golden Gate Park *Bounded by Fulton St., Stanyan St., Lincoln Way, and the Great Highway; between the Sunset and Richmond districts, (415) 831-2700, fax (415) 221-8034.*

One of the world's great metropolitan parks, Golden Gate Park encompasses 1,017 acres. It is nearly 200 acres larger than Manhattan's Central Park, after which it was originally patterned. Once just sand dunes, it is now the largest man-made park in the world.

• **Annual Events.**

Bring a blanket, a picnic, and a smile to **Comedy Day** *((415) 938-0151. Free.)* in August. Laughs are provided by local professional comedians, who in the past have ranged from upstarts—who just naturally seem to try harder—to such established luminaries as Robin Williams, Bob Goldthwait, and Father Guido Sarducci. Content is promised to be appropriate for the entire family. On Labor Day weekend in September, **A La Carte, A La Park** *((415) 458-1988. $7-$9.)* brings food from local restaurants, wine samplings, and an eclectic line-up of live music to Sharon Meadow (known as Hippie Hill in the '60s). It is a benefit for **Free Shakespeare in the Park** *((415) 666-2222. Free.)*, also held in the park in September, as well as in other Bay Area locations. Later in the month, **Opera in the Park** *((415) 777-7770. Free.)*, designed to make opera accessible to everyone, is held in Sharon Meadow. It's a great way for reluctant listeners to give this art form a try.

• **Beach Chalet.** See page 58.

• **Biking/Skating.**

On Sundays, John F. Kennedy Drive is closed to automobiles. Car traffic is replaced with heavy bike, skate, and pedestrian traffic. Skate and bike rentals are available at shops along Stanyan Street. Skates are also usually available from trucks parked along Fulton Street.

• **Buffalo Paddock** *At west end of Kennedy Dr., west of 36th Ave. across from Anglers Lodge.*

Foreign visitors seem particularly impressed with viewing this small herd of authentic buffalo.

• **California Academy of Sciences.**

See page 27.

• **Children's Playground** *On Bowling Green Dr., between King Dr. & Kennedy Dr., east of California Academy of Sciences. Daily dawn-dusk.*

Constructed in 1887, this was the very first public playground in a U.S. park. Today it is filled with creative modern play structures.

Located adjacent, an antique **Carrousel** *(W-Sun 10-4:30; to 6 in summer. Adults $1,*

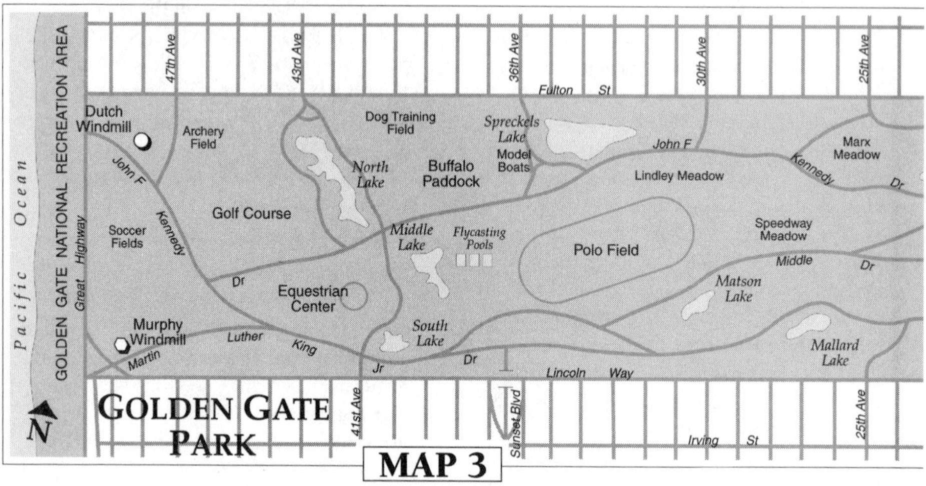

children 25¢.) makes its rounds within a protective hippodrome enclosure. Built in 1914 by Herschel-Spillman, it has 62 beautifully painted hand-carved animals and its original Gebruder band organ.

• **Conservatory of Flowers** *Closed indefinitely due to severe storm damage suffered in 1995.*

Built in Ireland in 1878 and modeled after the Palm House in London's Kew Gardens, this impressive example of Victorian architecture was shipped around Cape Horn in pieces in 1879. This tropical greenhouse is the oldest remaining building in the park and is thought to be the oldest conservatory in the U.S. as well as the only wooden conservatory in the U.S. and probably the world. It consists of a central dome flanked by two wings. Outside, 17- by 30-foot flower beds form floral messages. They are tilted at a 45-degree angle so that they can be seen from the street. This old European gardening technique, known as "carpet bedding," is costly and time-consuming and now almost extinct.

• **Golden Gate Park Stables** *John F. Kennedy Dr./36th Ave., at west end of park, (415) 668-7360, fax (415) 255-1789. Daily 8-6. $20-$25/person; riders must be 8 or older. Reservations required.*

Guided one-hour trail rides through the park are available, and on weekends trail rides to the beach are an option. Classes and private lessons are offered, and short pony rides are available for children age 1 and older.

• **Japanese Tea Garden and Teahouse** *Next to deYoung Museum, (415) 666-7200. Daily 9-6:30, Mar-Sept; 8:30-6:30 or dusk, Oct-Feb. Garden: Adults $2.50, 65+ & 6-12 $1. Tea: $2.50/person. No reservations. No cards.*

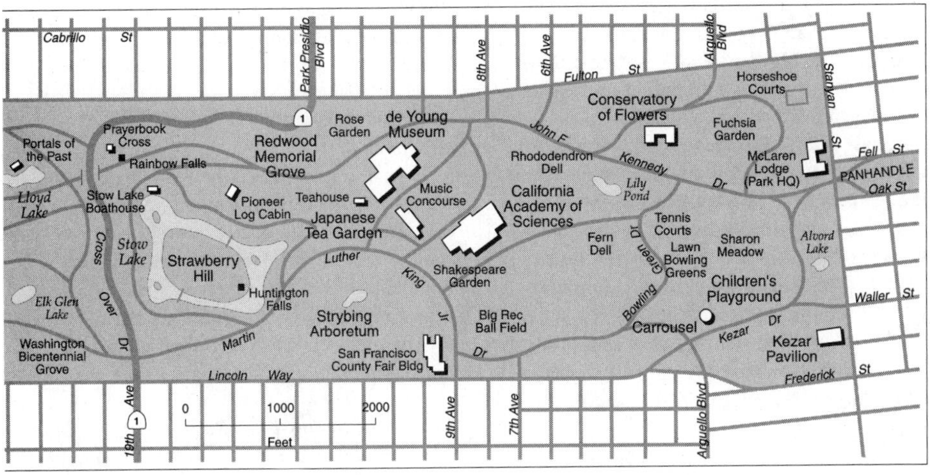

This garden is enjoyable to stroll through at any time of day, any time of year, and in almost any kind of weather. Visitors can climb up the steep arch of the "wishing bridge" (actually a drum bridge), make a wish, and drop a coin in the pond below. Steep steps lead to a miniature red pagoda, and an undulating dragon hedge is nearby. A spectacular display occurs annually during the last week of March, when the **cherry blossoms** are in bloom.

Everyone seems to enjoy stopping for refreshment at the inviting open-air teahouse, where tea and Asian cookies are served by waitresses clad in traditional Japanese kimonos. It is quite pleasant and relaxing to observe nature while leisurely sipping jasmine or green tea and munching on exotic cookies. An interesting note: Makoto Hagiwara, who designed the garden in 1893 for the Mid-Winter Exposition, is credited with introducing the fortune cookie to America here in 1914.

• **M.H. deYoung Memorial Museum.**

See page 23.

• **Shakespeare Garden** *Behind California Academy of Sciences.*

This formal, manicured garden is planted with the 150 flowers mentioned in William's plays. An attractive wrought-iron archway marks the entrance, where a brick pathway bordered by crabapple trees leads into the garden. Benches and grassy expanses invite lingering.

• **Stow Lake Boathouse** *(415) 752-0347. Daily 9-4; in summer to 5. Paddle boats, row boats, & electric boats $9.50-$14.50/hr. No cards.*

A boat on Stow Lake, the largest of the park's 11 lakes, is both an unusual and memorable picnic spot. After pushing off in a row boat, it's pleasant to find a cove where there isn't much water movement and then get down to the business of eating a picnic meal. Be warned: When bread is tossed to the ducks and seagulls, they can fairly sink a boat with enthusiasm. Though the water is shallow and it isn't possible to get very far from shore, cushions in the boats double as life preservers. Life vests are also available upon request at no additional charge. Because boats are often wet inside, consider bringing along a blanket to sit on.

• **Strybing Arboretum & Botanical Gardens** *Entrance adjoins San Francisco County Fair Bldg., (415) 661-1316; www.strybing.com. M-F 8-4:30, Sat & Sun 10-5; tours daily at 1:30, on Sat & Sun also at 10:30. Free.*

Known for its magnolia and rhododendron collections, this lovely garden displays more than 7,500 different plant species over its 70 acres. Many are unique to this climate, and most are labeled. Of special note are the Japanese-style Moon-viewing Garden, the Arthur Menzies Garden of California Native Plants, the redwood forest, the small fragrance garden, the Biblical Garden, the New World Cloud Forest, and the Primitive Plant Garden.

A variety of annual events takes place in the adjacent **San Francisco County Fair Building**. The **Mother's Day Rose Show** allows the opportunity to see a splendid variety of climbing, miniature, and old garden roses. Cuttings perfect for presenting to Mom are for sale, with proceeds benefiting the San Francisco Rose Society. It is the largest such show in Northern California. Sponsored by the San Francisco Mycological Society, the December **Fungus Fair** allows the opportunity for backyard mushrooms to be identified by experts. Wild fungi, including a number of poisonous varieties, are also displayed.

• **Walking Tours** *(415) 263-0991; www.frp.org. Call for schedule. Free.*

All of these walks are led by volunteers and require no reservations. Except for the Japanese Tea Garden tour, which lasts 45 minutes, all tours run from 1½ to 2 hours.

• The **Japanese Garden Tour** covers the history and design of the garden.

• The **Lloyd Lake Tour** explores Portals of the Past, Rainbow Falls, Prayerbook Cross, and other park secrets.

• On **McLaren's Walk**, participants see some little-known spots such as the horseshoe courts and Fuchsia Garden. They stroll through the Rhododendron and Fern Dells and visit Children's Playground.

• Participants on the **Strawberry Hill Tour** enjoy a spectacular view of the Golden Gate Bridge and San Francisco from atop the hill. They see Huntington Falls, explore the Pioneer Log Cabin, and visit the Redwood Memorial Grove and the Rose Garden.

• **Stroller Walks**, designed especially for parents of young children, cover various areas of the park.

• The **Windmill Tour** takes in Spreckels Lake, the restored windmill, and the Buffalo Paddock.

Mountain Lake Park *Entrance at Lake St./ Funston Ave, the Richmond.*

Well-hidden from the street, this park is an unexpected delight to come upon. Facilities include a lakeside path, a basketball court, tennis courts, a parcourse that begins at 9th Avenue, and a large, well-equipped playground off 12th Avenue. There are even ducks to feed. It is interesting to note that spring-fed Mountain Lake supplied all of the city's water between 1852 and 1870.

North Beach Playground *Columbus Ave./ Greenwich St.*

This simple spot is where the late baseball legend Joe DiMaggio played in his youth. It is currently embroiled in controversy, as locals want to rename it in DiMaggio's honor while representatives of the ball player's estate deem it beneath his stature. If it does get renamed, the city plans to do a $3.5 million upgrade. Either way, kids love it here.

San Francisco Zoo *1 Zoo Rd./45th Ave., (415) 753-7080; www.sfzoo.org. Daily 10-5. Adults $9, 65+ & 12-17 $6, 3-11 $3; free 1st W of month.*

A ride on the **Safari Tram** *(Adults $2.50, 65+ & under 16 $1.50.)* gives a quick 20-minute introduction to the layout of this scenic zoo. Of special note are the half-acre Gorilla World, which is one of the world's largest gorilla habitats, and the Primate Discovery Center, with its 15 species of primates and unusual nocturnal exhibit. The zoo's collection of extremely endangered snow leopards is one of the most successful breeding groups in the world. The lions and tigers are particularly interesting to visit when they are fed each afternoon from

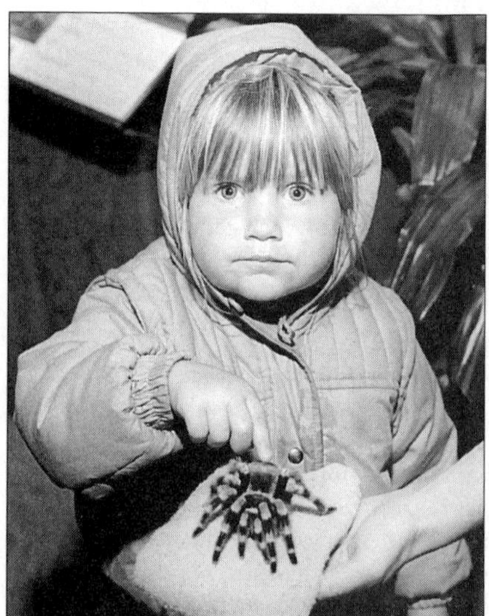

2 to 3—except on Monday, when they fast.

A separate **Children's Zoo** *(Daily 11-4.)* has a petting area with sheep and goats. An **Insect Zoo** has a functioning honeybee hive and is populated with the likes of 6- to 8-inch-long walking sticks and giant Madagascar hissing cockroaches. An adjacent butterfly garden is filled with native plants labeled with the type of butterfly they attract. Just outside the Children's Zoo is a large playground and an antique **carousel** *($2)* built in 1921 by the William Dentzel Carving Company. The perfect souvenir is a plastic Storybox Key *($2)*, which children can insert in boxes throughout the zoo to hear interesting information about the animals in four languages: English (narrated by actor and local resident Danny Glover), Cantonese, Spanish, and Tagalog.

A popular **Valentine's Day Sex Tour** is scheduled in February. Each year in July, members of the Zoological Society *($65/year/family)* are invited to **Night Tour**. Entertainment, demonstrations, behind-the-scenes tours, and admission are all free, and a picnic dinner is available for a small charge. Support the zoo and find out just what happens there after dark.

Spectator Sports.

• **Baseball.**

• **San Francisco Giants** *Pac Bell Park, King St./3rd St., near China Basin, (800) SF-GIANT, (415) 972-2000; www.sfgiants.com. April-Sept.*

Located on the city's scenic waterfront, this new ballpark features unobstructed views from every seat and plenty of restrooms. It was designed to be a state-of-the-art old-fashioned ballpark. A unique public promenade parallels the waterfront from right field to center field, and fans can watch the game through the fence here at no charge. A Family Pavilion is available where tickets are cheap, seats are reserved, and no smoking or drinking is permitted. Known for having the cheapest ticket in all of baseball, the Giants admit children 14 and younger accompanied by an adult to general seating for $1, adults $2.50, except Sundays and holidays; these tickets must be purchased at the gate.

• **Football.**

• **San Francisco 49ers** *3Com Park, 8 mi. south of downtown. (415) 656-4900. Aug-Dec.*

Sutro Heights Park *On 48th Ave., between Geary Blvd. & Anza St., outer Richmond (415) 556-8642.*

Formerly the estate of Adolph Sutro, this magnificent park has expansive views of the southern coastline. It is perfect for a picnic, but hold on to little kids, as drop-offs can be sudden and dangerous.

Performing Arts

Moving pictures got their start in 1878 when Leland Stanford placed a $20,000 bet. He hired photographer Eadweard Muybridge to prove that the four hooves of a running horse are all off the ground at the same time. The still photos were mounted on a carousel and spun so that the horse appeared to be moving. In 1880, Stanford won $20,000, and the first moving picture debuted at the exhibition hall of the San Francisco Art Association.

In preparation for a visit to San Francisco, or in remembrance of a trip past, the following movies are fun to watch. All were shot on location in San Francisco: *Birdman of Alcatraz* (1962; Burt Lancaster; NR), *The Birds* (1963; Rod Taylor, Jessica Tandy, Suzanne Pleshett; PG13), *Bullitt* (1968; Steve McQueen; NR), *The Conversation* (1974; Gene Hackman; PG), *Dark Passage* (1947; Humphrey Bogart, Lauren Bacall; NR), *Dirty Harry* (1971; Clint Eastwood; R), *D.O.A.* (1950; Edmond O'Brien; NR), *Foul Play* (1978; Goldie Hawn, Chevy Chase; PG), *48 Hours* (1982; Nick Nolte, Eddie Murphy; R), *The Graduate* (1967; Anne Bancroft, Dustin Hoffman, Katharine Ross; PG), *Greed* (1925; Erich Von Stroheim; NR), *Guess Who's Coming to Dinner?* (1967; Spencer Tracy, Sidney Poitier, Katherine Hepburn; NR), *Invasion of the Body Snatchers* (1978; Donald Sutherland, Leonard Nimoy; PG), *Jagged Edge* (1986; Glenn Close, Jeff Bridges; R), *The Maltese Falcon* (1941; Humphrey Bogart, Mary Astor; NR), *Mrs. Doubtfire* (1993; Robin Williams, Sally Field; PG13), *Pacific Heights* (1990; Melanie Griffith, Matthew Modine, Michael Keaton; R), *Pal Joey* (1957; Rita Hayworth, Frank Sinatra; NR), *Play It Again, Sam* (1972; Woody Allen; PG), *The Presidio* (1988; Sean Connery, Mark Harmon; R),

San Francisco (1936; Clark Gable, Jeanette MacDonald; NR), *Sister Act* (1993; Whoopi Goldberg; PG), *Star Trek IV—The Voyage Home* (1986; Leonard Nimoy, William Shatner; PG), *The Towering Inferno* (1974; Steve McQueen, Faye Dunaway, William Holden; PG), *True Believer* (1989; James Woods, Robert Downey Jr.; R), *Vertigo* (1958; James Stewart, Kim Novak; PG), *A View to a Kill* (1985; Roger Moore, Grace Jones; PG), *What's Up, Doc?* (1972; Barbra Streisand, Ryan O'Neal; G), *Woman in Red* (1984; Gene Wilder; PG-13).

Beach Blanket Babylon *678 Green St./Powell St., in Club Fugazi, North Beach, (415) 421-4222, fax (415) 421-4817. W & Thur at 8, F & Sat at 7 & 10, Sun at 3 & 7. Tickets $20-$55.*

Begun back in 1974 as an underground production, this fast-moving and humorous musical revue is known for its colorful, creative costumes and huge headdresses. It is the longest running musical revue in the nation. The show changes periodically but always brings pleasure. Sunday matinees are aimed at families and are the only performances open to minors (under age 21). No alcohol is served then. Parents should keep in mind that there is no profanity or violence, but sexual puns are abundant. For the past 15 years all performances have sold out, so reserve tickets early and arrive when the doors open to choose a table.

Pocket Opera *At various Bay Area venues, (415) 575-1102, fax (415) 575-1104; www.pocketopera.org. Tickets $13-$27.*

Bright and witty, this talented troupe skillfully performs sometimes dramatic, sometimes hilarious, but always enjoyable opera that is easy to understand. One of these performances makes a fabulous introduction to opera for anyone. Though most performances are appropriate for children, shows are sometimes produced especially for children.

San Francisco Mime Troupe *At neighborhood parks throughout Bay Area, (415) 285-1717; www.sfmt.org. July 4-Aug. Free.*

Since 1964, this Tony Award-winning troupe has presented sometimes caustic, always entertaining commentary on current events, political leaders, and the state of our world. The Troupe's original productions combine music, satire, and comedy. In spite of the description, children and families attend in large numbers and generally enjoy the spectacle.

Theatre on the Square. See page 45.

TIX Bay Area/Half-Price Tickets *251 Stockton St., on Union Square, (415) 433-7827; www.theatrebayarea.org. Tu-Thur 11-6, F & Sat 11-7.*

Day-of-performance half-price tickets are available for many music, dance, and theater events. They must be paid for with cash or traveler's checks, and no information is available by phone. Sunday and Monday events are available on Saturday. Full-price tickets for performances are also available and can be purchased using MasterCard or Visa. TIX by Mail permits purchasing half-price tickets through a quarterly catalog. For a copy, visit the website or write to: TIX by Mail, 870 Market Street #375, San Francisco, CA 94102.

Young Performers Theatre *Fort Mason, Bldg. C, Laguna St./Marina Blvd., (415) 346-5550, fax (415) 346-4991. Sat at 1, Sun at 1 & 3:30. Adults $8, 1-12 $5.*

A combination of professional adult performers and young actors in training, this company uses imaginative stage settings and costumes. The fast-moving productions are usually short as well, making them a good introduction to theater for children ages 4 through 10. Past productions have included *Charlie and the Chocolate Factory, Wind in the Willows,* and *The Secret Garden.*

Entertainment Complexes

Metreon *101 4th St./Mission St., South of Market, (415) 369-6000; www.metreon.com. Ticket for all attractions $17.*

Built by Sony for $85 million, this 4-story urban entertainment complex is unique. No one has ever done anything like it before. It houses a massive play area for young children on the fourth floor based on Maurice Sendak's popular children's book *Where the Wild Things Are,* a 15-screen movie theater, an IMAX theater that also shows 3-D specials, and a gaming arcade with virtual bowling. Among the nine unusual stores are **Microsoft**'s first ever, **Sony Style** showcasing the latest in electronics, and **PlayStation,** where every game in this line is available for play before purchase. Everything is related to entertainment and fun. A **Starbucks** and eight restaurants keep visitors from tarving. Similar centers are scheduled to open in Berlin and Tokyo, with Chicago and Washington, D.C. not far behind.

Rooftop at Yerba Buena Gardens *Mission St./ 4th St, South of Market, (415) 522-9860.*

Situated atop the Moscone Convention Center, this new entertainment complex holds a variety of attractions—all designed for the education and recreation of young people. Expansive lawns, fountains, a maze and play circle, and robotic sculpture invite open-air relaxation.

Zeum *(221 4th St., (415) 777-2800; www.zeum.org. W-F 12-6, Sat & Sun 11-5. Adults $7, 5-18 $5.)* is an urban park and high tech arts center designed for children ages 8 through 18. In an interactive setting they can create videos, view filmed performances in a state-of-the-art theater, and learn about animation as art.

Rounding out the rooftop offerings, an **Ice Skating Center** *(750 Folsom St., (415) 777-3727. Call for session times.)* is open year-round, as is a 12-lane **bowling center.** A historic 1906 Looff **carousel** *($1),* formerly situated at the defunct Playland-at-the-Beach, boasts 62 heavily jeweled, hand-carved animals (4 camels, 4 rams, 4 giraffes, and 44 horses, including a rare gray horse whose mouth is carved with lips shut). Beautifully restored, it twirls inside a glass enclosure.

Shopping

The Cannery *Bounded by Beach St./ Leavenworth St./Hyde St./Jefferson St., Fisherman's Wharf, (415) 771-3112, fax (415) 771-2424; www.thecannery.com. Shops open M-Sat 10-6, Sun 11-6; in summer to 8:30 Thur-Sat.*

This charming red brick shopping complex, constructed in 1907, was once the world's largest fruit and vegetable cannery. It now holds more than 45 unique shops (no chains here!), 9 restaurants and cafes, a comedy club, and other diversions. Free entertainment by street performers is scheduled daily under century-old olive trees in the inviting Courtyard.

Shops include the **Basic Brown Bear Factory** *(2nd floor, (800) 554-1910, (415) 626-0781, fax (415) 861-2660; www.basicbrownbear.com.),* which purveys handmade bears of all kinds—everything from a basic brown to a quite elaborate cream-colored Beary Godmother with pink satin wings and a magic wand. Prices are close to wholesale, and customers can stuff their own bear using a replica of a World War II-era machine that once pumped up life jackets. This is one of the few stuffed animal factories still manufacturing within the U.S., and the bears are not sold in any other stores. Free **tours** are available at the main factory *(444 DeHaro St./Mariposa St., Potrero Hill. Daily at 1; Sat also at 11am.).*

• Restaurant.

• Jacks Cannery Bar *1st floor, (415) 931-6400. L&D daily; $. No reservations.*

Fresh seafood appetizers, salads, and sandwiches are on the menu here, and 110 beers are on tap. The bar is also noteworthy for its oak-paneled Long Hall, hand-carved fireplace, ornate ceiling, and Jacobean staircase—all of which were originally part of several English manor homes built in the 1600s and 1700s and brought to America by William Randolph Hearst.

Chestnut Street *Between Fillmore St. & Scott St., the Marina.*

This is a popular neighborhood shopping area.

Clement Street *Between Anza St. & 24th St., the Richmond.*

This popular neighborhood area is heavily populated with Asian restaurants, produce markets, and bakeries.

Cost Plus Imports *2552 Taylor St./North Point St., Fisherman's Wharf, (415) 928-6200, (800) COST-PLUS; www.costplusworldmarket.com. Daily 9-9.*

The original store in a chain that now numbers 53, this gigantic importer has long been a favorite shopping stop for visitors. Back in the '60s, it was where everyone stocked up on "hippie" supplies: batik bedspreads, incense, candles. Current imports from around the world include inexpensive jewelry, kitchenware, furniture, baskets, and toys.

Embarcadero Center *Bounded by Battery St./Sacramento St./Drumm St./Clay St., (800) 733-6318, (415) 772-0700, fax (415) 982-1780. Shops open M-F 10-7, Sat 10-6, Sun 12-5; restaurants open later. Validated parking; 4 hrs. free with validation M-F after 5pm, Sat & Sun after 10am.*

This enormous 7-block complex of high-rise buildings holds 140 shops and restaurants on its lower floors, countless offices on the upper floors, and the huge Hyatt Regency hotel. A movie theater complex keeps things busy late into the night. **Justin Herman Plaza** is home to the **Vaillancourt Fountain**, nicknamed "#10 on the Richter" and described by an art critic as "something deposited by a dog with square intestines." A brochure mapping out a self-guided Sculpture Tour to the center's treasure-trove of art is available.

Factory Outlets.

• Esprit Outlet *499 Illinois St./16th St., China Basin, (415) 957-2550, fax (415) 957-2556. M-F 10-8, Sat 10-7, Sun 11-6.*

Esprit's popular line of clothing for mainly female kids and teens originates in San Francisco. Their airy outlet is constructed on three sides with floor-to-ceiling windows and is a great spot to pick up a stylish souvenir t-shirt or sweatshirt. Shoppers put items in full-size grocery carts while listening to the hippest of music, and during sales, bargain hunters have been known to wait over an hour just to get in.

• Factory Outlet Heaven *Around 3rd & Brannan sts, China Basin. Roughly M-Sat 10-4.*

Just follow the herds into the various outlet stores offering all manner of bargains.

Ghirardelli Square *900 North Point St./Larkin St., (415) 775-5500, fax (415) 775-0912; www.GhirardelliSq.com. Daily 10-6; to 9 in summer.*

Built in 1900 as a chocolate factory and converted into a festival marketplace in 1964, this beautiful brick complex is said to have been the nation's first quaint, upscale shopping center. Now it is a National Historic Landmark and home to 48 shops and 10 restaurants. Street performers are scheduled on the courtyard stage each weekend (daily in summer). A **Chocolate Festival** is held each September.

• Restaurants.

• Gaylord India *(415) 771-8822. L&D daily, SunBr; $$$. Reservations advised.*

With its posh decor of oriental carpets, potted palms, and Chippendale-style chairs, plus its killer bay view, this restaurant wouldn't really need to have good food, too. But fortunately it does. Tandoori meats, freshly baked breads, excellent curries, and many vegetarian items are on the menu.

• **Ghirardelli Chocolate Manufactory.**
See page 68.

Haight Street *Between Stanyan St. & Fillmore St.*

With unusual stores, galleries, restaurants, and nightclubs, not to mention people, this happening place is like groovy, man. Well-known for its hippy-dippy days, its shops now sell used fashions from those times. It is *the* place to get pierced and buy tie-dye.

Japan Center *Three square blocks bounded by Post St., Geary St., Laguna St., & Fillmore St., (415) 922-6776. Open daily; most shops open daily 10-5, restaurants to 9. Some businesses validate for center's garages.*

This 5-acre cultural center houses shops, restaurants, art galleries, traditional Japanese baths, a Japanese-style market, a movie theater complex, and a hotel. Designed like an indoor mall, shoppers can walk from one building to another without going outside and crossing streets. A five-tiered, 100-foot-tall Peace Pagoda that was a gift from Japan is illuminated at night, and an eternal flame, brought from the Sumiyoshi Shrine in Osaka, burns above a reflecting pool.

A **Cherry Blossom Festival** *((415) 563-2313. Free.)* is scheduled each April. This elaborate Japanese-style celebration of spring usually includes traditional dancing and martial arts demonstrations, taiko drum and koto performances, a bonsai exhibit, and tea ceremonies. A Japanese food bazaar operates continuously, and the festival culminates with a colorful Japanese-style parade. The **Nihonmachi Street Fair** is held on the first weekend in August. In addition to a food bazaar it features contemporary ethnic bands and performing arts. Admission is free.

• **Restaurants** are scattered throughout the complex. Each opens exotic avenues of food exploration.

• **Benihana** *(415) 563-4844, fax (415) 563-8022; www.benihana.com; in Kintetsu Mall. L&D daily; $$. Highchairs. Reservations advised.*

Diners here are seated at a community table with a large grill imbedded in the middle. Once the table is filled with diners, the chef dramatically begins to prepare each order as everyone watches. Though there are none, karate yells from the chefs wouldn't seem out of place. The chefs are adept performers with their knives, and the show is spectacular.

• **Isobune Sushi** *(415) 563-1030, fax (415) 563-3337, in Kintetsu Mall. L&D daily; $. Boosters. No reservations.*

At this small sushi bar, items are carried around the counter on little floating boats. Customers remove what looks interesting.

• **Mifune** *(415) 922-0337, fax (415) 567-4211, in Kintetsu Mall. L&D daily; $. Boosters, booths, child portions. No reservations.*

Specializing in serving two types of easily digested and low-calorie fresh noodles (udon—fat, white flour noodles, and soba—thin, brown buckwheat noodles), this is a branch of a well-established chain of similar restaurants in Japan. Before walking through the noren (slit curtain), take a look at the plastic food displays in the exterior windows. Topping choices for either noodle type include chicken, beef, and shrimp tempura as well as more exotic raw egg, sweet herring, and seaweed. Sesame spice salt is on each table for pepping up the basically bland dishes. The child's Bullet Train plate is served in a ceramic replica of the famous Japanese train and consists of cold noodles with shrimp and vegetable tempura.

• **Sanppo Restaurant** *1702 Post St./ Buchanan St., (415) 346-3486; fax (415) 346-0927. L&D daily; $$. Highchairs, boosters. No reservations.*

Located across the street from the center, this cozy restaurant always has a line at the door—a sure tip-off that something is worth waiting for. Among the interesting appetizers are gomaae spinach (uncooked and sprinkled with sesame seeds), harusame salad (sweet potato noodles mixed with lettuce, onion, and a creamy dressing), and housemade gyoza, which are similar to Chinese pot stickers. Entrees include a light tempura, fresh deep-fried oysters, and nasu hasamiyaki (grilled slices of ginger-marinated beef and eggplant). A large selection of noodle dishes is also available.

Pier 39 *Beach St., The Embarcadero, (415) 705-5500. Most shops open 10:30-8:30; in summer from 8:30am. Parking lot adjoins; $5/hr., less with validation.*

Following just behind Disney World and Disneyland in bringing in the most visitors annually, this popular spot offers myriad diversions in addition to more than 110 stores and 11 restaurants. Among the shops is one that specializes in puppets, another in chocolate, and another in kites. Others specialize in hats and cat-related items.

Street performers entertain daily. Bumper cars and a vast video game arcade are inside an entertainment center at the pier entrance, as is **The Great San Francisco Adventure** *((415) 956-FILM, fax (415) 956-3585. Adults $7.50, 65+ $6, under 12 $4.50.)*—an enjoyable 30-minute motion picture by Academy Award-winning Keith Merrill that shows off some of the city's best locations. At the far end of the pier is a contemporary two-tiered Venetian **carousel** *($2)* and **Turbo Ride** *((415) 392-TURBO. Adults $9, 55+ & 5-12 $5.)*—a simulated thrill ride that synchronizes hydraulically powered seats to the action on a giant movie screen. **Sea lions** have taken up permanent residence on the west side of the pier and can be seen there basking, barking, and belching on their floating docks. The newest attraction here is **UnderWater World** *((415) 623-5300, tickets (888) SEA-DIVE. Adults $12.95, 65+ $9.95, 3-11 $6.50.)*, which uses moving sidewalks to transport visitors through transparent acrylic tunnels for a diver's-eye view of the fishes, sharks, and other sea life residing there.

Each year in March, the **Tulipmania Festival** displays approximately 39,000 tulips throughout the pier. Free tours are scheduled.

• **Restaurants.**

Most of the full-service restaurants have seafood menus, but Italian, Chinese, and Mediterranean cuisines are also represented. Restaurant menu boards are found in various spots around the pier, giving visitors a chance to analyze offerings and prices. Fast-food is represented with fish & chips, hamburgers, pizza, hot pretzels, and more.

• **Bubba Gump Shrimp Co.** *(888) 561-GUMP, (415) 781-GUMP, fax (415) 781-4864. L&D daily; $$. Child menu. No reservations. Validated parking in Pier 39 garage.*

The second link in this chain operated by the Rusty Pelican and licensed by Paramount Pictures, this theme restaurant is based on the shrimping scenes in the movie *Forrest Gump.* (The first is in Monterey.) Located on the second-story level at the end of the pier, it resembles a seafood shack. Not surprisingly, the menu has many shrimp selections, most of them deep-fried, as well as fresh fish entrees and baby back ribs. The bar serves up fun drinks, including several kinds of margaritas (the Delta Sunset is particularly tasty) and some non-alcoholic, good-for-you drinks—a peanutty-chocolate Alabama Sweet Smoothie and a frothy pink Run Forrest Run. Dessert should, of course, be a box of chocolates, and that *is* an option. As a bonus, magnificent views of the bay are enjoyed from most tables. An adjacent shop sells everything Gump. (Winston Groom lived in San Francisco when he wrote *Forrest Gump*—the book. In fact, he named the main character after this city's famous department store.)

• **Eagle Cafe** *(415) 433-3689. B,L,&D daily; $. Boosters. No reservations. No cards.*

Situated at the entrance to the pier, this casual spot dates from 1920, when it was located across the street. The menu offers hearty breakfasts and a standout meatloaf sandwich at lunch, and strong drinks are always available at the antique bar.

• **Neptune's Palace** *(415) 434-2260. L&D daily; $$$. Highchairs, boosters. Reservations advised.*

Situated at the end of the pier, this airy spot stands out with its magnificent bay view of Alcatraz and tasty a la carte seafood menu. Its companion facility, the adjacent, more casual **Bay View Cafe**, offers a simple menu of soups, salads, and sandwiches as well as fresh seafood, plus it has a great view of the sea lions.

• **Yet Wah** *(415) 434-4430.* See page 82.

Union Square and Surrounds.

World-class shopping is found on the streets surrounding this large grassy square, which was originally a sand dune.

• **Britex Fabrics** *146 Geary St./Stockton St., (415) 392-2910. M-Sat 9:30-6, Thur to 8.*

Even people who can't thread a needle enjoy browsing the four floors of magnificent fabrics and notions in this unique San Francisco store. It is the largest fabric store in the West.

• **Crocker Galleria** *50 Post St./Kearny St., (415) 393-1505, fax (415) 392-5429. M-F 10-6, Sat 10-5.*

This "covered street" links Post and Sutter streets. Sixty stores and two restaurants on three floors are situated under its spectacular arched skylight. The design was influenced by Milan's famous Galleria Vittorio Emmanuelle.

Faz *(161 Sutter St., (415) 362-0404, fax (415) 362-5865. L M-F, D M-Sat; $-$$. Highchairs. Reservations advised.)* offers relaxing dining in a quietly elegant room. Among the tempting items on the Middle Eastern menu are house specialties such as dolmas (stuffed grape leaves), hummus, and tabouleh. Soups, salads, sandwiches, pizzas, and more substantial entrees, such as kabobs and seafood items, are also on the menu. Desserts include baklavah, a fig tart, a saffron brownie, and pistachio custard.

• **Department stores** include **Macy's** *(233 Geary St., (415) 397-3333; www.macys.com)*, **Neiman Marcus** *(150 Stockton St., (415) 362-3900)*, and **Saks Fifth Avenue** *(384 Post St., (415) 986-4300)*. All have restaurants.

• **FAO Schwarz** *48 Stockton St./O'Farrell St., (415) 394-8700, fax (415) 394-0439; www.fao.com. M-Sat 10-7, Sun 11-6.*

The city's largest toy store, this 3-story wonderland is filled with elaborate toy displays and exclusive, unusual, and trend-setting merchandise. Shoppers are greeted at the door by a live toy solider, and just steps from the entrance a whimsical 2-story mechanical clock tower emits charming music. A good selection of San Francisco-themed books and games is available.

• **Gump's** *135 Post St./Kearny St., (415) 982-1616. M-Sat 10-6, Thur to 7.*

Opened in 1861, this is the oldest store in San Francisco. Known for its fine oriental imports, its legendary Jade Room holds one of the finest jade collections in the world. It carries the city's largest selection of fine china and crystal and also has an eye-popping collection of American crafts.

• **Levi Strauss Store** *300 Post St./Stockton St., (415) 501-0100. M-Sat 10-8, Sun 11-6.*

Everything Levis is sold in this slick, futuristic, metallic store—a destination in itself. But the real action is up on the third floor at the shrink tub. After purchasing vintage or shrink-to-fit jeans, clients don the item and then soak in the water-filled tub along with yellow rubber duckies. They then dry off in stand-up dryers, take a private shower, and re-dress while their new, *tight* jeans are completely dried in a commercial dryer. This unusual service is free with purchase.

• **Maiden Lane** *Off Stockton St., between Post St. & Geary St.*

This charming street is closed off to cars during business hours and holds a variety of interesting shops. One not to miss is the **V.C. Morris Shop** at #140. This small, circular space was designed by Frank Lloyd Wright in 1948 to display fine china and silver. It was radical in that it had no display window. A ramp spirals up to the mezzanine along curving walls, similar to the design of New York's Guggenheim Museum. It now houses several galleries. Also worth a visit is the **Sur La Table** kitchen supply store at #77.

• **San Francisco Shopping Centre** *865 Market St., (415) 495-5656. M-Sat 9:30-8, Sun 11-6.*

Opened in 1988, this swanky 9-story indoor shopping complex is one of the few vertical malls in the U.S. A must-see 4-story spiral escalator—the only one in the U.S.—wends its way up through a sun-lit atrium into the word's largest **Nordstrom** *((415) 243-8500).*

Union Street *Pacific Heights.*

This trendy area is filled with upscale shops and restaurants (see "Where to Eat" section), many inside old Victorian and Edwardian buildings. Flower stands add a seasonal burst of color on the four blocks running between Fillmore and Octavia streets, which has the heaviest concentration of shops, but boutiques continue on in both directions and down side streets. This area is referred to as Cow Hollow, in reference to the fact that it was once the city's dairy community.

For the annual **Union Street Fair** *(June. (415) 346-4446. Free.)*, the street is usually closed off from Gough to Steiner. It begins with a Saturday morning Waiter Race in which competing servers must open a bottle of wine, pour two glasses, and carry them on their tray intact to the top Green Street and back again. Music, food, and craftspeople round out the fun.

Upper Fillmore Street *Between Jackson St. & Ellis St., Pacific Heights.*

This popular neighborhood shopping street is lined with boutiques, restaurants, and bars.

WHERE TO STAY

According to a 2000 survey, the average hotel room in San Francisco costs $155 a night.

The San Francisco Convention & Visitors Bureau has a reservations service in partnership with over 220 participating hotels. For assistance, call (888) STAY-N-SF or (415) 974-4499, or visit their website at www.sfvisitor.org.

Union Square

This is a choice area to stay in, especially if traveling *without* a car. (Hotels listed here charge between $17 and $30 per day for parking.) All of these hotels are within a few blocks of downtown, the theater district, and the cable car line. Many are quaint establishments that provide an European-style, small hotel experience.

Canterbury Hotel *750 Sutter St./Taylor St., 3 blocks from Union Square, (800) 227-4788, (415) 474-6464, fax (415) 474-0831; www.canterbury-hotel.com. 10 stories; 254 rooms; $$$-$$$+. Children under 18 free. Fitness room. Restaurant, room service. Valet parking $24.*

Built in 1928, this recently refurbished, well-priced hotel features comfortable, cozy guest rooms decorated in shades of persimmon, butter yellow, and sage green. A 20-foot mural by Jo Mora decorates the front desk, and a rooftop sun deck is among the guest amenities.

Set up in a former garden greenhouse, the wonderful glass-enclosed dining room of **Murray's Glasshouse** *((415) 474-6478, fax (415) 474-0831. B,L,&D daily; $$$. Reservations advised. Valet parking $9.)*, with its tall palms and 25-foot-high ceiling, has metamorphized into a contemporary Asian-Pacific steak and seafood house. After one of the rich and satisfying desserts, diners can retire to San Francisco's only hotel **Cigar and Cognac Lounge**, located just off the restaurant, and choose from a large selection of cigars and after-dinner drinks.

Cartwright Hotel *524 Sutter St./Powell St., 1 block from Union Square, (800) 227-3844, (415) 421-2865, fax (415) 983-6244; www.kimptongroup.com. 8 stories; 114 rooms; $$-$$$+. Children free. Afternoon tea, continental breakfast. Parking $18.*

Built in 1914 for the Panama-Pacific Exposition, this hotel is conveniently located on a fashionable shopping street. Its pleasant rooms are furnished distinctively with antiques, and fresh flowers and floral wallpaper add to the cozy, European ambiance. A complimentary tea is served each afternoon in the pleasant lobby, and guests have free use of a fitness facility located 1/2 block from the hotel.

The Clift *495 Geary St./Taylor St., 2 blocks from Union Square, (800) 65-CLIFT, (415) 775-4700, fax (415) 776-9238. 17 stories; 329 rooms; $$$+. Some VCRs. Fitness center. 2 restaurants, room service. Pets welcome ($40/day). Valet parking $28.*

This luxury historic hotel dating from 1915 has beautifully decorated rooms with high ceilings. Hefty rates put it on the list of the world's rich and famous: Mick Jagger, Madonna, and former President Jimmy Carter have all stayed here. Service is high priority for the staff, and everyone gets the royal treatment—celebrity or not. Even kids. A family plan includes two connecting rooms, and the desk loans toys for toddlers, magazines for teens, and children's books, board games, Nintendo games, and movies. The concierge has loaner strollers and can help plan family sightseeing trips. At bedtime, snacks such as cookies and milk or popcorn and soda are available from room service. Pets can be placed on the VIP (Very Important Pet) list, and upon arrival receive a basket of treats and appropriate sleeping pillows and eating bowls.

The Redwood Room *(L daily.)*, a classic art deco cocktail lounge, features its original 1933 redwood panels (it was built from a single 2,000-year-old giant redwood tree) and immense Gustav Klimt prints.

Donatello Hotel *501 Post St./Mason St., 1 block from Union Square, (800) 227-3184, (415) 441-7100, fax (415) 885-8891; www.travelweb.com. 15 stories; 94 rooms; $$$-$$$+. Children under 18 free. Hot tub, 2 saunas, spa services, fitness center. Restaurant, room service. Valet parking $25.*

Named after the Italian Renaissance sculptor, this European-style luxury hotel is said to have the largest standard guest rooms in town. The 15th-floor Penthouse Club Room and Spa has a wood-burning fireplace and a wraparound terrace with sweeping city views; it is stocked with snacks and reading material and is available at no charge to guests. More than 300 pieces of original art decorate the hotel. The lobby features 18th- and 19th-century antiques, imported Venetian chandeliers, and Italian marble quarried from the same site where Michelangelo selected the marble for his statue of David.

Grand Hyatt San Francisco *345 Stockton St./Post St., on Union Square, (800) 233-1234, (415) 398-1234, fax (415) 392-2536; www.hyatt.com. 36 stories; 685 rooms; $$$-$$$+. Children under 18 free. Some VCRs. Fitness center. Restaurants, room service. Parking $29.*

In a prime location, this hotel is well known locally for its Ruth Asawa-designed bronze fountain depicting scenes of San Francisco. Room amenities include two phones and a TV in the bathroom. **Grandviews** restaurant is on the 36th floor, and the flagship **Levi Strauss Store** operates on the ground level (see page 41).

Handlery Union Square *351 Geary St./Powell St., 1/2 block from Union Square, (800) 843-4343, (415) 781-7800, fax (415) 781-0269. 8 stories; 377 rooms; $$$-$$$+. Children under 15 free. Heated pool, sauna. Restaurant, room service. Parking $24.*

This comfortable hotel dates from 1908.

Hilton San Francisco *333 O'Farrell St./Mason St., 2 blocks from Union Square, (800) HILTONS, (415) 771-1400, fax (415) 923-5036. 46 stories; 1,900 rooms; $$$-$$$+. Children under 17 free. Heated pool, sauna, fitness center. 5 restaurants, room service. Parking $28.*

Occupying a full block and incorporating three buildings, this is the largest hotel on the West Coast. It features a dramatic sunken marble lobby.

Hotel Diva *440 Geary St./Mason St., (800) 553-1900, (415) 885-0200, fax (415) 346-6613; www.hoteldiva.com. 7 stories; 111 rooms; $$$-$$$+. Children under 12 free. All VCRs. Fitness room. Continental breakfast; restaurant, room service. Valet parking $22.*

Built in 1913, this hotel features cutting-edge contemporary design. Updated to resemble a 1920s ocean liner, each room is furnished with beds featuring sculptured steel headboards and sumptuous linens, buffed steel and maple wood furniture, cobalt blue carpeting, and black granite bathrooms. The two-room suites each have a wall bed in the living area and are especially comfortable and well-priced for families. The trip begins with the exterior window in the lobby, designed to resemble a frozen layer of glass. Movies and music videos are screened continuously on four screens above the reception desk, and the elevator is padded in cobalt blue leather to match the carpeting. This is definitely not the usual.

The airy, pleasant **California Pizza Kitchen** *((415) 563-8911. L&D daily; $. Highchairs, boosters, booths.)* operates off the lobby serving a large selection of pizzas and pastas with unusual toppings.

Hotel Monaco *501 Geary St./Taylor St., 2 blocks from Union Square, (800) 214-4220, (415) 292-0100, fax (415) 292-0111. 7 stories; 201 rooms; $$-$$$+. Children under 18 free. Some VCRs. Hot tub, sauna, steam room, fitness room. Evening snack; restaurant, room service. Valet parking $20. Pets welcome.*

Built in 1910, this landmark American beaux arts building has been completely renovated. The inviting lobby has high, high ceilings with hand-painted domes, as well as an impressive 2-story French inglenook fireplace and a grand staircase with the original bronze filigree railing and marble steps—both remains from the hotel's prior incarnation as the Bellevue Hotel. Each sumptuously decorated room features a canopy bed. Guests who miss their pets can borrow a goldfish.

The magnificent 1920s-style **Grand Cafe** *((415) 292-0101, fax (415) 292-0150. B,L,&D daily; $$-$$$. Highchairs, boosters, booths. Reservations advised.)* operates within the hotel's restored turn-of-the-century ballroom. It features an immense, high-ceilinged dining room, with ornate columns and majestic art deco-style ceiling lamps, original murals, and fanciful decorative art. Seating is in intimate booths, arranged in asymmetrical formations that give all diners a good view. The menu offers European-inspired classics and comfort foods, including items such as cassoulet, duck confit, and saffron paella. Desserts can be grand, especially a warm Valrhona chocolate cake and a poached Bartlett pear tart. The **Petite Cafe** bar area in front offers a delightful setting for a quick sandwich or pizza.

Hotel Nikko San Francisco *222 Mason St./O'Farrell St., 2 blocks from Union Square, (800) NIKKO-US, (415) 394-1111, fax (415) 421-0455; www.nikkohotels.com/amer/sanfran.html. 25 stories; 532 rooms; $$$-$$$+. Children under 18 free. Indoor heated pool, hot tub, sauna, fitness center. Restaurant, room service. Parking $27.*

Featuring clean architectural lines and a slick, marble-rich decor, this luxury hotel has San Francisco's only atrium-style, glass-enclosed, roof-top lap pool. The fitness center is equipped with a traditional kamaburo dry sauna and deep Japanese soaking tub. Rooms are elegantly contemporary.

Since the hotel caters to a large Japanese business clientelle, breakfast in elegant **Anzu** *(2nd fl., (415) 394-1100; L&D daily, SunB; $$-$$$. Reservations advised. Valet parking validated.)* features both American and Japanese fare. Among the wonders the chef whips up for the lunch and dinner menu are a large variety of sushi and sashimi, a perfect petite prime filet with Maui onion-Cabernet jus, a to-die-for side dish of wild mushroom bread pudding, a whimsical yet lucious banana-tempura split with almond brittle and honey caramel sauce—all served on exquisite Japanese-style stoneware. The popular Smooth Jazz Sunday Brunch is broadcast live by KKSF (103.7 fm) and includes assorted dim sum, sushi, and made-to-order omelettes as well as unusual entrees (sesame chicken, scallops ceviche with wasabi tobiko), and decadent desserts. An overnight hotel package is available.

Hotel Rex *562 Sutter St./Powell St., 2 blocks from Union Square, (800) 433-4434, (415) 433-4434, fax (415) 433-3695; www.sftrips.com. 7 stories; 94 rooms; $$-$$$+. Evening wine; room service. Self-parking $19.*

Aspiring to become the Algonquin Hotel of the West Coast and designed as a focal point for the arts, this theme hotel has a clubby, writer-friendly ambiance. Sketches of Martha Graham in the '30s hang in a lobby furnished with period pieces, and literary events are regularly scheduled in the wood-paneled **Lobby Bar**, where appetizers and drinks are served each evening.

The Bookstall *(570 Sutter St., (415) 362-6353, fax (415) 362-1503. M-Sat 11-6.)*, an antiquarian bookstore specializing in books for the collector, has a particularly good section on California and the West. It is located just across from the lobby.

Hotel Triton *342 Grant Ave./Bush St., 3 blocks from Union Square, (800) 433-6611, (415) 394-0500, fax (415) 394-0555. 7 stories; 140 rooms; $$-$$$+. Children free. 7 VCRs. Fitness center. Evening wine; restaurant, limited room service. Valet parking $20. Pets welcome.*

Situated across the street from the dragon-gate entrance to Chinatown in the heart of the "French Quarter," this playfully decorated hotel is sophisticated, casual, amusing, and chic all at the same time. Original art adorns public areas and guest room walls, much of it painted by local artist Chris Kidd, and bathrooms are positively slick. The Carlos Santana Suite sports hand-painted angels on the ceiling and concert posters and photos of the musician on the walls, and is stocked with meditation candles, incense, and a prayer pillow. Suites honoring Jerry Garcia and artist Wyland are also available, and another very special suite has an in-room hot tub. For guests who miss their pets, it is possible to borrow a goldfish. A must-have souvenir rubber ducky inscribed with the hotel logo is for sale in the room honor bar.

Casual **Cafe de la Presse** *(352 Grant Ave., (415) 398-2680. B,L,&D daily; $. Highchairs, boosters.)* is located adjacent to the hotel. With large windows offering views of the sidewalk, it is the place to be for breakfast. The menu offers croissants and lattes as well as waffles, pancakes, and hot oatmeal. French is often heard spoken by patrons, as this area is filled with French cafes and has become popular with French visitors, and international newspapers and magazines are for sale.

Hotel Union Square *114 Powell St./Ellis St., 1 block from Union Square, (800) 553-1900, (415) 397-3000, fax (415) 399-1874; www.hotelunionsquare.com. 6 stories; 131 rooms; $$$-$$$+. Children under 12 free. Continental breakfast. Valet parking $19.*

Built in 1913 for the Pan American Exposition, this comfortable hotel is decorated in a tailored contemporary style and situated just steps from the cable car turnaround. It is where Dashiell Hammett wrote *The Maltese Falcon*. Special features include a massive Egyptian mosaic mural in the lobby and a hand-carved wooden mermaid that once graced the bow of a ship and is now found on the sixth floor landing.

The Inn at Union Square *440 Post St./Powell St., 1/2 block from Union Square, (800) AT-THE-INN, (415) 397- 3510, fax (415) 989-0529; www.unionsquare.com. 7 stories; 30 rooms; 100% non-smoking; $$-$$$+. Afternoon tea, evening snack, continental breakfast; room service. Parking $20.*

This small, narrow, European-style hotel pampers guests with terry cloth robes, down pillows, evening turndown, complimentary overnight shoe shines, and a morning newspaper at the door. It is the first hotel in San Francisco to introduce a no tipping policy. One suite is available with a private hot tub, another with a private sauna.

Kensington Park Hotel *450 Post St./Powell St., 2 blocks from Union Square, (800) 553-1900, (415) 788-6400, (415) 399-9484; www.kensingtonparkhotel.com. 12 stories; 89 rooms; $$$-$$$+. Children under 12 free. Afternoon tea, continental breakfast; restaurant. Fitness center. Valet parking $22.*

Built in a Gothic style of architecture, this tastefully decorated circa 1924 hotel features Queen Anne-style antique mahogany furnishings and period art and accent pieces in its sophisticated rooms.

Theatre on the Square *((415) 433-9500)* presents noteworthy live performances on the hotel's second floor.

The King George Hotel *334 Mason St./Geary St., 1 block from Union Square, (800) 288-6005, (415) 781-5050, fax (415) 835-5991; www.kinggeorge.com. 9 stories; 143 rooms; $-$$$. Children under 12 free. 2 kitchens. Room service. Self-parking $16.50.*

Thomas Edison was an original investor in this pleasant hotel, built in 1914, and it was he who convinced management to switch from gaslight to electricity. With thick walls, it is very quiet, and a large bowl of complimentary apples is always available at the desk.

A moderately-priced continental breakfast and afternoon tea are served in **The Bread & Honey Tea Room** *(B daily, tea W-Sun 3-6; $. No reservations.)* and open to non-guests. Simple tea spreads consist of a choice of ten kinds of tea and either a crumpet, a giant housemade muffin, a raisin scone, fruit and custard tarts, or traditional finger sandwiches. Additionally, a rich chocolate layer cake is available, as are sherry and port.

Room service is provided by **Lori's Diner** *(336 Mason St., (415) 392-8646. B,L,&D daily; $. Other nearby locations: 500 Sutter St./Powell St., (415) 981-1950; 149 Powell St./O'Farrell St., (415) 677-9999.)*, located next door. Featuring a '50s decor and dispensing the likes of burgers, fries and onion rings, and shakes, Lori's never closes.

Pan Pacific Hotel *500 Post St./Mason St., 1 block from Union Square, (800) 327-8585, (415) 771-8600, fax (415) 398-0267; www.panpac.com. 21 stories; 330 rooms; $$$+. Children under 18 free. Restaurant, room service. Valet parking $27.*

The luxurious rooms in this tranquil hotel feature marble bathrooms with TVs and terry bathrobes, and an on-site fluffing machine creates pillows to specification in about 1/2 hour. Glitzy window-walled interior elevators traverse the 21 stories, and complimentary transportation via a fleet of luxury cars is provided within the city.

The acclaimed hotel restaurant, **Pacific** *((415) 929-2087. B&L M-F, D daily, Sat & SunBr; $$-$$$. Reservations advised.)*, is situated off the sedate marble lobby. Elegant marble columns grace the attractive space, and fresh flowers decorate each table. Brunch, when the menu features eggs Benedict topped with the freshest of crabmeat, is a particularly fine time to dine here.

Petite Auberge *863 Bush St./Mason St., 4 blocks from Union Square, (800) 365-3004, (415) 928-6000, fax (415) 775-5717. 5 stories; 26 rooms; 100% non-smoking; $$-$$$+. Some fireplaces. Afternoon tea, continental breakfast. Valet parking $20.*

Located on the lower slopes of Nob Hill, this small, ornate, baroque-style building now operates as a B&B. Rooms are furnished with French country antiques, and breakfast is served in a cheery room sporting a view of a tiny garden and decorated with a wrap-around painted mural depicting a French market scene. Special features include a beveled-glass door leading to the entry, curved bay windows, and an unusual vintage elevator. A sister property, The White Swan Inn, is just a few doors away.

Savoy Hotel *580 Geary St./Jones St., 3 blocks from Union Square, (800) 227-4223, (415) 441-2700, fax (415) 441-0124. 7 stories; 83 rooms; $$-$$$+. Afternoon tea, restaurant. Valet parking $18.*

Built in 1913, this well-priced hotel offers attractively decorated rooms with fluffy feather beds and goose down pillows, plus a complimentary overnight shoeshine service.

With dark wooden walls, comfortable benches, and a horseshoe-shaped zinc-topped bar, cozy **Brasserie Savoy** *((415) 441-2700, fax (415) 441-7172. B&D daily; $$-$$$. Reservations taken. Valet parking $7.)* perfectly captures the essence of a Parisian brasserie. Menus change weekly, and the food matches the best found in France but geared to American tastes. For breakfast try the traditional oeuf (egg) dishes and pastries, for lunch a croque-monsieur sandwich or beef cheek hash. Dinner possibilities include tender, tasty beef cheeks in burgundy sauce with horseradish mashed potatoes and a classic roasted chicken, followed by dessert choices of crème brulee and chocolate Charlotte with raspberry sauce. Wines are exclusively French.

Sir Francis Drake Hotel *450 Powell St./Sutter St., 1 block from Union Square, (800) 227-5480, (415) 392-7755, fax (415) 677-9341; www.sirfrancisdrake.com. 21 stories; 417 rooms; $$$-$$$+. Restaurant, room service. Valet parking $27.*

When built in 1928, this Gothic-Renaissance building was the tallest in town and the last word in hotels. Innovations at the time included an indoor golf course, ice water on tap, and radios in every guest room. Height is no longer its claim to fame, though it is still famous for its glamorous art deco **Harry**

Denton's Starlight Room *((415) 395-8595.)* rooftop bar, which offers fancy cocktails, light supper, and dancing to a full orchestra as well as panoramic views of the city. The grand two-level lobby retains its magnificent original marble walls, recessed mirrors, and murals depicting the life of explorer Sir Francis Drake. Rooms are tastefully decorated in contemporary style, and guests have access to a full-service health club located nearby. Afternoon tea and drinks are available in the mezzanine lobby lounge. The most famous of the hotel's doormen, who all wear a colorful bright red Beefeater uniform, is Tom Sweeney—known for having a terrific memory for faces. Cable cars stop at the front door.

Villa Florence *225 Powell St./Geary St., 1 block from Union Square, (800) 553-4411, (415) 397-7700, fax (415) 397-1006. 7 stories; 180 rooms; $-$$$. Children under 12 free. Evening wine; restaurant, limited room service. Parking $17.*

Built in 1908, this conveniently located hotel has a colonnaded entrance with a Giotto-style wishing fountain, and its lobby is decorated with a rare 17th-century velvet tapestry and a trompe l'oeil mural depicting 16th-century Florence. A Medici-style wood-burning fireplace warms guests in the lobby, where a piano player entertains nightly.

A popular restaurant, **Kuleto's** *(221 Powell St./Geary St., (415) 397-7720, fax (415) 986-7050. B,L,&D daily, Sat & SunBr. Highchairs, boosters, booths. Reservations advised.)*, operates off the lobby serving superb northern Italian cuisine in elegant surroundings. For a snack or light meal, a Crostini Bar serves housemade toasts with a variety of toppings. Should tables be filled, a seat at the counter can often be had at the last minute, providing the additional treat of watching the skilled kitchen staff in action. Grilled items are particularly good, including appetizers of red potatoes and eggplant with an aioli sauce, and desserts are exceptional. A good souvenir is the 100-percent cold-pressed extra virgin California olive oil used in the restaurant and attractively bottled to take home.

The Westin St. Francis *335 Powell St./Geary St., on Union Square, (800) WESTIN 1, (415) 397-7000, fax (415) 774-0124; www.westin.com. 32 stories; 1,192 rooms; $$$+. Children under 18 free. Fitness center. 3 restaurants, room service. Small dogs welcome; other pets upon approval. Valet parking $30.*

Built in 1904, this classy landmark hotel has a superb location opening right onto Union Square. It consists of both an older 12-story section and a newer 32-story tower with an outside glass elevator that goes non-stop from the lobby to the 32nd floor in less than 30 seconds. The posh lobby holds a famous Magneta clock that was made in Austria in 1856 and installed here at the post-earthquake reopening in 1907. This is the only hotel in the world that launders its money—literally and legally—a custom that began in 1938 to keep women's white gloves from being soiled by dirty coins. Upon check-in, children 12 and under get a free Westin Kids Club packet filled with an assortment of age-appropriate amenities, and strollers, cribs, highchairs, bottle warmers, potty seats, and step stools can be placed in the room at no additional charge.

Dewey's sports bar *((415) 774-0169. B,L,&D daily; $. Highchairs, boosters. No reservations.)* offers a casual, clubby, pub-like atmosphere and an all-you-can-eat, make-your-own-sandwich buffet lunch. The cable cars are visible from most tables. A revitalizing tea can be enjoyed seated among the staid, plush, Old World splendor of the elegant room housing **The Compass Rose** *((415) 774-0167. Tea daily 3-5; $24-$27. Highchairs, boosters. Reservations advised.)*. Diners choose from a variety of caffeinated and herbal teas. The complete tea service includes a scone, several delicate tea sandwiches sans crust, fresh berries topped with Grand Marnier cream, and several petit fours. Items can also be ordered a la carte. And all the while a violin-bass-grand piano trio provide relaxing musical background. Lunch, evening snacks, and elegant cocktails are also served here daily. The more trendy **St. Francis Cafe** *((415) 774-0264. B&D daily; $$. Highchairs, boosters, booths, child items. Reservations accepted.)* features comfortable booths and artsy tableware, and offers a menu that includes an appetizer salad of flavorfully dressed baby lettuce topped with perfect barbecued shrimp plus entrees such as a fresh grilled red snapper with a full-flavored dried tomato-fennel-spinach sauce, and a homey, tender oven-braised veal shank. Among the house-made desserts are a strawberry-rhubarb pie with lemon mascarpone cream and a trio of profiteroles stuffed with Ben & Jerry's ice cream.

White Swan Inn *845 Bush St./Mason St., 4 blocks from Union Square, (800) 999-9570, (415) 775-1755, fax (415) 775-5717. 4 stories; 26 rooms; 100% non-smoking; $$-$$$+. Children under 5 free. All fireplaces. Fitness room. Afternoon tea, full breakfast. Valet parking $20.*

Built after the 1906 earthquake in 1915, this charming hotel resembles an English manor house, with curved bay windows, warm dark woods, and handsome antique furnishings. The cheery reception area, cozy living room, and book-lined library all have fireplaces and are inviting places to relax. The large guest rooms are individually decorated with English floral wallpapers. Each has a separate sitting area and is furnished with a mahogany bed fitted with a warm European wool mattress cover. Amenities include terry robes, evening turndown service, and a morning newspaper. Breakfast is served in a dining room just off a tiny English garden. A sister inn, Petite Auberge, is just a few doors away.

South of Market

Referred to by old-timers as "South of the Slot," signifying its location south of the street car tracks on Market Street, this colorful area was city center in the mid-1800s. Rapidly being refurbished, it is now home to many art museums and to the Moscone Convention Center.

Argent *50 Third St./Market St., (877) 222-6699, (415) 974-6400, fax (415) 543-8268; www.argenthotel.com. 36 stories; 667 rooms; $$$+. Children under 18 free. 2 saunas, fitness center. Restaurant, room service. Valet parking $26.*

Each room in this sleek contemporary hotel is equipped with three phones. The entire 23rd floor is devoted to "Green Suites" using recycled paper goods, all natural amenities, and state-of-the-art air and water filtration systems. All guests have complimentary access to the San Francisco Tennis and Health Club.

Harbor Court Hotel *165 Steuart St./Mission St., (800) 346-0555, (415) 882-1300, fax (415) 882-1313; www.harborcourt.com. 8 stories; 131 rooms; $$$-$$$+. Indoor heated pool, hot tub, sauna, fitness center, health spa. Evening wine. Parking $24.*

Featuring an Old World flavor, this historic 1907 landmark building has an attractive vintage brick façade and offers some rooms with spectacular views of the bay and Treasure Island.

Hotel Griffon *155 Steuart St./Mission St., (800) 321-2201, (415) 495-2100, fax (415) 495-3522; www.hotelgriffon.com. 5 stories; 62 rooms; $$$+. Continental breakfast; restaurant; room service. Parking $18.*

Among the guest rooms in this stylish boutique hotel are eight with expansive bay views plus three penthouse suites. All feature white-washed brick walls, tall ceilings, and window seats. Guests have complimentary access to a nearby fitness center with an indoor pool and hot tub.

Focusing on delicious, unusual seafood dishes, **Red Herring** *((415) 495-6500; L M-F, D daily; $$-$$$. Child menu. Reservations advised. Valet parking D M-Sat.)* operates off the hotel lobby. Boldly-flavored, winning dishes on the regularly changing menu include the whimsical, such as an appetizer of savory crêpe cones filled with lobster-mango-avocado salad. Items such as a hearty Moroccan salmon tagine, prepared with large Israeli couscous and served sizzling in the dish, and a whole, very red tandoori snapper are among the innovative main courses. For dessert, a trio of chocolate delights—each made with a different premium chocolate—and a trio of citrus delights are primo, but warm chocolate chip cookies are pretty good, too. An interesting mixed-drink menu is worth considering along with the wine list, and children are nicely accommodated with a special "guppies" menu offering such items as fusilli pasta and mini-burgers. Comfortable booths are among the seating options in the restive interior, with bay views in the back and attractive street views in the front bar area.

Hotel Palomar *12 Fourth St./Market St., (877) 294-9711, (415) 348-1111, fax (415) 348-0302; www.hotelpalomar.com. 198 rooms; $$$-$$$+. Fitness center. Restaurant, room service. Valet parking $29.*

Featuring an urbane, sophisticated interior design, with details like faux leopard-skin carpeting, this well-located hotel operates on the fifth through ninth floors of a completely refurbished 1907 landmark building.

The **Fifth Floor** *((415) 348-1555. D M-Sat; $$$.)* restaurant features tailored furnishings, dramatic lighting, and more faux carpet (this time zebra), and is reputed to be on "the culinary wild side."

Palace Hotel *2 New Montgomery St./Market St., (800) 325-3535, (415) 512-1111, fax (415) 543-0671; www.sheraton.com. 8 stories; 550 rooms; $$$+. Children under 18 free. Indoor pool, hot tub, sauna, health spa. 3 restaurants. Valet parking $20.*

When this grande dame hotel opened in 1875, it was the largest and most luxurious in the world. Though that original hotel burned to the ground after the 1906 earthquake, it was rebuilt in 1909 as the present structure. A dubious claim to fame from its past is the fact that this was where President Harding, who was staying in the Presidential Suite, died in 1923. Nowadays anyone with $2,600 can stay in the Presidential Suite, and the list of those who have includes Sophia Loren and Whoopi Goldberg. **Tours** are given of the public rooms by City Guides; make reservations through the hotel at (415) 557-4266.

One of the most elegant public rooms is the **Garden Court**. Filled with tall marble columns and enormous potted palms, its most glorious feature is a 25,000-pane stained-glass dome said to be worth over $7 million, and it is the only *room* on the National Register of Historic Places. **Afternoon tea** *((415) 546-5089. W-Sat 2-4:30, Sun 2-3:30; $18+.)* here is an elegant affair, with fussy sandwiches, rose petal jam, and a classical harpist providing background ambiance. A special **Princess Tea** *($15/child.)* welcomes children with a crown or scepter and includes kid-friendly hot chocolate and peanut butter & jelly finger sandwiches. The **Pied Piper Bar** and adjoining restaurant hold three noteworthy murals: Maxfield Parrish's "Pied Piper" and two Antonio Sotomayers depicting famous San Franciscans—one of Mark Twain and the other of madam Sally Stanford.

San Francisco Marriott *55 Fourth St./Mission St., (800) 228-9290, (415) 896-1600, fax (415) 896-6177. 39 stories; 1,500 rooms; $$$. Indoor pool & hot tub, 2 saunas, fitness center. 3 restaurants, room service. Valet parking $25.*

Referred to by locals as the "Jukebox Marriott" in recognition of its distinctive architectural design, this well-positioned mega-hotel is the second-largest in San Francisco. It opened at 9 a.m. on October 17, 1989 and closed at 5:04 p.m. the same day, just after the strongest earthquake since 1906 hit this city. Fortunately, it sustained only cosmetic damage. Its spacious public areas are enhanced by the soothing sounds of a variety of water fountains. Most rooms have sweeping views of the city, and panoramic views are available from the 39th-floor **View Lounge**. Occasionally one of the hotel's restaurants will offer the Golden Gate Spectacular—an impressive, award-winning dessert designed by the hotel's pastry chef that reconstructs the famous span in chocolate and cream.

W *181 Third St./Howard St., (877) W-HOTELS, (415) 777-5300; www.whotels.com. 31 stories; 423 rooms. VCRs, CD players. Indoor lap pool & hot tub; fitness center. 2 restaurants; room service.*

Situated next door to the Museum of Modern Art, this brand-new slick and stylish hotel greets guests with a 3-story-high octagonal lobby. Rooms are decorated in attractive taupe, moss green, or rich brown fabrics, with furniture accents in blue. Each is equipped with two phones, a big 27-inch TV screen, and high-speed internet and e-mail access. Aveda amenities, stunning city views, and inviting down duvets complete the pretty picture. Turndown brings sassy fortune cookies: "Sleep naked," "Dance more than you should."

Nob Hill

After its steep slopes were conquered by Andrew Hallidie's development of the cable car in 1873, Nob Hill became one of the city's most exclusive residential areas. It was known as the "Hill of Palaces" because it held so many opulent mansions. Unfortunately, all of them burned down in the fire that followed the 1906 earthquake, save the brownstone shell of what is now the private Pacific Union Club. Because of its spectacular views and steep streets, Nob Hill has been the setting for many films. Most memorable, perhaps, is *Bullitt* with Steve McQueen.

Fairmont Hotel *950 Mason St./California St., (800) 527-4727, (415) 772-5000, fax (415) 772-5013. 24 stories; 596 rooms; $$$+. Children under 17 free. Fitness center. 4 restaurants, room service. Valet parking $30.*

Situated at the top of one of San Francisco's highest hills, this elegant landmark hotel welcomes guests with a gargantuan lobby filled with marble columns and a valuable art collection. The hotel has hosted many international heads of state, including President Clinton, and numerous celebrities, and it has starred in movies—*Vertigo, Shoot the Moon, Sudden Impact.* Its lobby and grand staircase were the setting for the *Hotel* TV series. Guest rooms are spacious, with goose-down pillows, terry cloth robes, and twice-daily maid service, and the cable cars, which stop in front of the hotel, can be heard from some. The hotel's crown is the historic eight-room Penthouse Suite—the most opulent and expensive in the U.S. It rents for $8,000 per night and features a 2-story circular library, a game room with a stained-glass skylight, and 24-karat-gold-plated bathroom fixtures.

The **Lobby Lounge** is the perfect place to relax over afternoon tea *(M-Sat 3-6, Sun 1-6.)* accompanied by live classical string music. In the **Tonga Room Restaurant & Hurricane Bar** *(Ext.5278; www.tongaroom.com. D daily; $$. Reservations advised.)*, simulated tropical rainstorms occur every 40 minutes in a Tiki-hut atmosphere. It is *the* place to stop in the evening for an exotic drink, and a bargain during the happy hour buffet *(M-F 5-7; $6/person, under 5 free.)*. A live dance band floating aboard a boat in the room's indoor lagoon (a converted swimming pool dating from 1929) entertains beginning at 8 p.m. *($3 cover charge)*. And the famous glass elevators are always ready to whisk diners up to the breathtaking views in the lavish **Crown Room** *(Ext.5131. Cocktails daily from 11am. D buffet daily, SunBr; $$.)* situated atop the hotel.

Mark Hopkins Inter-Continental *One Nob Hill, California St./Mason St., (800) 662-4455, (415) 392-3434, fax (415) 421-3302; www.markhopkins.net. 18 stories; 392 rooms; $$$+. Children under 14 free. Some VCRs. Fitness center. 2 restaurants, room service. Parking $27.*

Built on the spot where once stood the mansion of Mark Hopkins, who founded the Central Pacific Railroad, this hotel opened in 1926. Combining an architectural style that is part French château, part Spanish Renaissance, it has a central tower and two wings affording spectacular city views.

The tower is crowned by the legendary **Top of the Mark** *((415) 616-6916, fax (415) 392-0822. Cocktails daily from 3. Tea M-F 3-5. SunBr 10-2. Reservations advised.)*, which has a 360-degree view of the city and features live jazz. It is said that proposing marriage by presenting a diamond engagement ring in the bottom of a drink glass is played out more frequently here than anywhere else in the world. A plaque on the wall by the bar commemorates this as being a favorite spot for World War II Marines to have a last drink before sailing off to battle in the Pacific.

Nob Hill Lambourne *725 Pine St./Stockton St., 3 blocks from Union Square, (800) BRITINN, (415) 433-2287, fax (415) 433-0975; www.sftrips.com. 20 rooms; 100% non-smoking; $$$-$$$+. All VCRs & kitchens. Evening wine, continental breakfast. Valet parking $24.*

Sitting pretty in a residential area midway up Nob Hill, this intimate, contemporary hotel offers guests a quiet, posh retreat with easy access to downtown sights. Designed primarily for the business traveler, each room has personalized voice mail and a fax, and laptop computers with Internet access can be borrowed. In the interest of having guests feel healthier when they leave the hotel than when they arrived, each of the six suites here is outfitted with an instrument of torture, otherwise known as an exercise machine, and turndown brings an antioxidant supplement and inspirational quote. The honor bar is stocked with organic goodies, and music is piped from a radio in the bedroom into the bathroom. A room for spa treatments is on the main floor (packages are available), and just outside are the **Joice steps** up to California Street, which could easily qualify as Satan's StairMaster north (the more famous southern version is in Santa Monica). Carrying the theme yet further, wellness videos can be borrowed from the front desk, as can a great selection of movies filmed in San Francisco.

Renaissance Stanford Court Hotel
905 California St./Powell St., (800) HOTELS-1, (415) 989-3500, fax (415) 391-0513. 8 stories; 393 rooms; $$$+. Children under 18 free. Fitness center. Restaurant, room service. Valet parking $29.

Built on the site where Leland Stanford's mansion once stood—it was described as "a mansion that dominated the city like the castle of a medieval hill town"—this grand old hotel is blessed with striking turn-of-the-century detail, a beaux-arts fountain in the carport, and a lobby dome of Tiffany-style stained glass. Its elegant lobby is furnished with fine antiques, including Baccarat chandeliers and an 1806 grandfather clock once owned by Napoleon Bonaparte. Guest room pampering includes marble bathrooms with heated towel racks, plus complimentary amenities: coffee and newspaper delivered to the room in the morning, overnight shoeshine, and downtown limousine service.

Among the lobby shops is **John Small Ltd.** A small shop indeed, specializing in traditional British regimental items, it was the hotel's first shop. Among the many treasures dispensed here is an authentic Metropolitan brand bobby whistle imported from England.

The celebrated **Fournou's Ovens** *((415) 989-1910. B,L,&D daily, Sat&SunBr; $$-$$$. Highchairs, boosters, child menu. Reservations advised.)* is known for its massive, beautifully tiled European-style roasting ovens and intimate, finely appointed dining rooms. Specialties are roasted meats and seafood. The wine cellar holds more than 8,000 bottles and has one of the country's largest selections of California wines. In the **Lobby Lounge**, live piano music accompanies afternoon tea and evening cocktails.

The Ritz-Carlton *600 Stockton St./California St., (800) 241-3333, (415) 296-7465, fax (415) 986-1268; www.ritzcarlton.com. 9 stories; 336 rooms; $$$+. VCRs in suites. Indoor heated pool, hot tub, sauna, steam room, fitness center. 2 restaurants, room service. Valet parking $30.*

Occupying a full square block about halfway up Nob Hill, just off the California Street cable car line, this branch of the classy chain is set within a restored 1909 neoclassical landmark building. The completely new interior features Italian marble, silk wall-coverings, Bohemian crystal chandeliers, Persian carpets, and antique furnishings. A museum-quality collection of 18th- and 19th-century European and American art and antiques is displayed throughout. Room amenities include a morning newspaper, terry robes, and twice-daily maid service.

The Terrace offers the only outdoor hotel dining in San Francisco. In fair weather, its dressy al fresco Sunday jazz brunch *(Adults $50, 5-12 $25.)* is sublime. Diners sit outside on a red brick courtyard that is surrounded by a colorful flower garden and protected on three sides by the building's "U" shape. Inside, a battery of buffet tables offer delicacies that include a variety of caviars, smoked salmon, imported cheeses, fresh fruits, tasty cold salads, and hot entrees such as eggs Benedict, blintzes, and fish and meat courses. There is also a heavily laden pastry table, and a killer dessert table. Coffee and freshly squeezed orange juice are included. Everything is carefully prepared and elegantly presented by a well-trained kitchen staff.
The Dining Room *(D daily; $$$. Highchairs, boosters, booths. Reservations advised.)* is considered one of the city's top restaurants, and **The Lobby Lounge** serves a relaxing afternoon tea *(Daily 2:30-4:30; $26-$38. Reservations advised.)*. Two special teas for children are held annually: The **Easter Bunny Tea**, with service

by the Easter Bunny, and **Teddy Bear Teas** during the weeks leading up to Christmas.

Financial District

Hyatt Regency San Francisco *5 Embarcadero Center/Market St., (800) 233-1234, (415) 788-1234, fax (415) 398-2567. 17 stories; 805 rooms; $$$+. Children under 18 free. 2 restaurants, room service. Parking $30.*

Built in 1973, this elegant hotel resembles a pyramid, and every room has a view of either the city or the bay. Nifty glass elevators run the height of the hotel's magnificent 17-story atrium interior, and one end of the California Street cable car line is just outside the front door. **Equinox**, Northern California's only revolving rooftop restaurant, offers a 360-degree view of the city.

Mandarin Oriental, San Francisco *222 Sansome St./Pine St., (800) 622-0404, (415) 276-9888, fax (415) 433-0289; www.mandarinoriental.com. 48 stories; 158 rooms; $$$+. Children under 12 free. 2 VCRs. Fitness center. Restaurant, room service. Valet parking $30.*

Located in the heart of the Financial District, this luxury hotel occupies the first two floors of a skyscraper with its lobby, lounge, and two restaurants. Then it shoots up into the air and places guest rooms in twin towers on the top 11 floors of the 48-story building. This translates into quiet rooms with stupendous views. Furnishings are tasteful, contemporary, and a bit oriental, and a pot of hot jasmine tea is delivered to the room upon check-in. All bathrooms are stocked with fine English soaps and lotions, and some bathtubs feature a city view, permitting bathers to literally soak up the sights.

Appointed sumptuously, with silk-themed art created especially for the restaurant, **Silks** *((415) 986-2020. B&D daily, L M-F; $$-$$$. Highchairs, child menu. Reservations advised. Valet parking.)* offers an excitingly sophisticated menu of California cuisine with an Asian accent. Sample starters include an unusual chicken and shitake spring roll with Vietnamese salad, and a mild celeriac and roasted garlic soup with grilled bay scallops. Entrees are items such as seared lobster and scallops with spinach risotto cake and lemon-herb essence, and teriyaki salmon with carrot and daikon sprout salad and a smoked salmon-avocado roll. Desserts include the familiar—a banana split—and the wild—a gooey chocolate cake served with a raspberry-truffle swirl ice cream sandwich.

Park Hyatt San Francisco *333 Battery St./Clay St., (800) 233-1234, (415) 392-1234, fax (415) 421-2433. 24 stories; 360 rooms; $$$+. Children under 12 free. Restaurant, room service. Parking $30.*

Built in 1989, this hotel is conveniently located across the street via an overstreet walkway from the upscale Embarcadero Center shopping complex. Luxurious in every way, its public areas are decorated with fine art (an "Art in the Park" brochure provides a self-guided tour). Each room has a bay or city view, and amenities include fresh flowers and terry cloth bathrobes. Guests also get complimentary shoeshines and have a Mercedes Benz available to shuttle them around. **Teddy Bear Teas** are held for children in December and include seasonal edibles as well as a teddy bear memento.

Fisherman's Wharf

The major chains are well represented in this very popular area.

Best Western Tuscan Inn at Fisherman's Wharf *425 North Point St./Mason St., (800) 648-4626, (415) 561-1100, fax (415) 561-1199; www.tuscaninn.com. 4 stories; 221 rooms; $$$-$$$+. Children under 18 free. Some VCRs; 1 wood-*

burning fireplace. Evening wine; restaurant, room service. Pets welcome. Valet parking $20.

This comfortable, pleasantly appointed small hotel is reputed to be popular with filmmakers.

The appealing **Cafe Pescatore** *(2455 Mason St./North Point St., (415) 561-1111. B,L,&D daily, Sat&SunBr; $-$$. Highchairs, boosters, booths, child menu. Reservations advised.)* has windows that open to the sidewalk in warm weather and features a menu of fresh fish, pastas, and pizza baked in a wood-burning oven.

Dockside Boat & Bed *At Pier 39, (800) 436-2574, (415) 392-5526, fax (510) 444-0420; www.boatandbed.com. 13 yachts; $$-$$$+. All VCRs & galleys. Continental breakfast. Self-parking $8.*

Spend the night on a yacht anchored near Fisherman's Wharf. All vessels have separate state rooms; most have two or three. Catered candlelight dinners can be arranged, and the Snooze and Cruise package brings a captain on board to take her out for a cruise.

Hilton San Francisco Fisherman's Wharf *2620 Jones St./Bay St., (800) HILTONS, (415) 885-4700, fax (415) 771-8945. 234 rooms; $$$-$$$+. Children under 18 free. Fitness center, parcourse. Restaurant, room service. Self-parking $12.*

This motel claims to have the largest guest rooms at Fisherman's Wharf. A secluded sun deck and jogging track are among its amenities.

Holiday Inn Fisherman's Wharf *1300 Columbus Ave./North Point St., (800) HOLIDAY, (415) 771-9000, fax (415) 771-7006. 4 stories; 580 rooms; $$-$$$. Children under 19 free. Heated pool. 2 restaurants. Self-parking $15.*

This well-located hotel is situated in two buildings across the street from each other. A coin-operated laundry is available.

Hyatt at Fisherman's Wharf *555 North Point St./Jones St., (800) 233-1234, (415) 563-1234, fax (415) 749-6122; www.hyatt.com. 5 stories; 317 rooms; $$-$$$+. Heated pool, hot tub, sauna, fitness center. Restaurant, room service. Valet parking $24.*

Built on the site of an historic marble works building and incorporating that façade into its new architecture, this attractive hotel has been constructed using some of the original bricks recycled into a modern interpretation of the building's inceptive design. Rooms were renovated recently, and washers and dryers are located on each floor.

Radisson Fisherman's Wharf *250 Beach St./Powell St., (877) 497-1212, (415) 392-6700, (415) 986-7853. 4 stories; 355 rooms; $$-$$$. Children under 18 free. Heated pool. Restaurant. Free parking.*

Covering an entire block, this lodging has many rooms with bay and city views. Family rooms are large, with two double beds and a double sofa bed. An outdoor pool is located within an enclosed, landscaped courtyard.

San Francisco Marriott Fisherman's Wharf *1250 Columbus Ave./Bay St., (800) 228-9290, (415) 775-7555, fax (415) 474-2099; www.marriott.com/sfofw. 5 stories; 285 rooms; $$$-$$$+. Children under 18 free. Health spa. Restaurant, room service. Valet parking $24.*

Plenty of comfortable public spaces enhance the comfort of this posh hotel.

Sheraton at Fisherman's Wharf *2500 Mason St./Beach St., (800) 325-3535, (415) 362-5500; www.sheratonwharf.com. 4 stories; 524 rooms; $$-$$$+. Children under 17 free. Heated pool, fitness room. Restaurant, room service. Valet parking $24.*

This huge, contemporary-style hotel takes up an entire city block. It features spacious rooms and that rarest of San Francisco amenities—a heated swimming pool.

Suites at Fisherman's Wharf *2655 Hyde St./North Point St., (800) 227-3608, (415) 771-0200, fax (415) 346-8058. 24 suites; $$$+. Children under 12 free. All kitchens. Evening wine, continental breakfast. Self-parking $15.*

Staying in this small building, it is possible to feel like a local rather than a visitor. In addition to offering most of the comforts of home, the lodging is located across the street from Ghirardelli Square, is right on the Hyde Street cable car line, and is very close to the best aspects of the Fisherman's Wharf area. It also has a rooftop sun deck with a spectacular view of the Golden Gate Bridge, and a newspaper is delivered to the door each morning.

Chinatown and North Beach

Royal Pacific Motor Inn *661 Broadway/ Columbus Ave., (800) 545-5574, (415) 781-6661, fax (415) 781-6688. 5 stories; 74 rooms; $. Sauna. Free parking.*

Situated on the Chinatown-North Beach border, this bargain motel is right in the thick of it.

San Remo Hotel *2237 Mason St./Chestnut St., (800) 352-REMO, (415) 776-8688, fax (415) 776-2811; www.sanremohotel.com. 62 rooms; $. All shared baths. Restaurant. Parking nearby $10-$12.*

Tucked away in a quiet residential neighborhood between Fisherman's Wharf and North Beach, this family-owned and -operated Italianate Victorian hotel was built by the founder of Bank of America just after the big earthquake in 1906. Reception and the charming, comfortable, European-style rooms are upstairs, reached via a steep and narrow staircase. With their lace-covered windows and mish-mash of antique furnishings, rooms are situated off a warren of narrow hallways made cheery by well-placed skylights. Many have views of famous city landmarks. With the exception of a rooftop penthouse featuring a great bay view, all rooms share baths; half have sinks in the room. Downstairs, the main restaurant dining room features white-painted embossed tin ceilings.

The Washington Square Inn *1660 Stockton St./Filbert St., (800) 388-0220, (415) 981-4220, fax (415) 397-7242; www.wsisf.com. 15 rooms; 100% non-smoking; $$-$$$+. Afternoon tea, continental breakfast. Valet parking $20.*

This charming North Beach gem features a super location that permits late-evening coffeehouse hopping, and it is just a few blocks from an uncrowded cable car stop. Each room is individually decorated and furnished with English and French antiques. Several choice rooms in the front have bay windows overlooking Washington Square Park and the beautiful St. Peter & Paul church, the bells from which can be heard tolling the hour. Amenities include terry cloth robes, down pillows and comforters, and a morning newspaper delivered to the room. Tea is served in the cozy lobby, and breakfast is delivered to the room.

Japantown

Surprisingly, this quiet part of town is just 10 blocks from bustling Union Square. Both of these hotels have an exotic Asian flavor.

Best Western Miyako Inn *1800 Sutter St./ Buchanan St., (800) 528-1234, (415) 921-4000, fax (415) 923-1064. 8 stories; 125 rooms; $-$$$+. Children under 18 free. Restaurant. Self-parking $10.*

Many of these large rooms have dramatic views of the southwestern portion of the city. Some are equipped with steam baths.

Radisson Miyako Hotel *1625 Post St./Laguna St., (800) 333-3333, (415) 922-3200, fax (415) 921-0417; www.miyakohotel.com. 13 stories; 220 rooms; $$$+. Children under 18 free. Fitness center. Restaurant, room service. Valet parking $20.*

This exotic hotel has two traditional Japanese-style suites with futon feather beds on tatami mats, as well as western-style rooms with Japanese touches. Most of the serene rooms here have deep furo bathing tubs, and some suites have a private redwood sauna. The tasteful lobby overlooks a Japanese garden where guests can stroll.

Pacific Heights/Presidio Heights

El Drisco Hotel *2901 Pacific Ave./Broderick St., (800) 634-7277, (415) 346-2880, fax (415) 567-5537; www.eldriscohotel.com. 4 stories; 43 rooms; 100% non-smoking; $$$+. Evening wine, continental breakfast. No parking.*

Built in 1903, before the '06 quake, this Edwardian-style building is in a quiet residential neighborhood. It maintains its original dark-wood interior trim and is elegantly decorated and furnished. Turn-of-the-century millionaires are said to have kept their mistresses lodged here. Later in the century, President Eisenhower bunked here due to its close proximity to the Presidio. Rooms are spacious and comfortable, and the suites have good views.

The Laurel Inn *444 Presidio Ave./California St., (800) 552-8735, (415) 567-8467, fax (415) 928-1866; www.thelaurelinn.com. 4 stories; 49 rooms; $$. Children under 12 free. All VCRs; some kitchens. Continental breakfast. Pets welcome. Free parking.*

Located far from the usual tourist haunts in a nice residential area, near Sacramento Street shopping, this motel has spacious rooms and a stylish 1950s modern decor. East-facing rooms have good city views, and it's hard to beat the price.

Haight-Ashbury/Golden Gate Park

Stanyan Park Hotel *750 Stanyan St./Waller St., (415) 751-1000, fax (415) 668-5454; www.stan yan park.com. 36 rooms; $$-$$$+. Some kitchens. Afternoon snack, continental breakfast. No parking.*

Located at the park's edge, this 1904 Victorian mansion survived the great quake of '06. It has been renovated and turned into a pleasant hotel with attractively decorated rooms.

By the Sea

Ocean Park Motel *2690 46th Ave./Wawona St., the Sunset, (415) 566-7020, fax (415) 665-8959. 24 rooms; $. Some kitchens. Hot tub. Dogs welcome. Free parking.*

Located near the ocean and just a block from the zoo, this art deco-style motel dates from the '30s, when it was San Francisco's first motel. Maintaining its original nautical decor, some windows are shaped like portholes. Rooms are attractive and homey, and several spacious family suites are available. Amenities include a playground, barbecue area, and several gardens.

Miscellaneous

The American Property Exchange *(800) 747-7784, (415) 447-2000, fax (415) 440-1008; www.We-Rent-SanFran.com. 1-30 stories; 400 units; $70-$250. All VCRs & kitchens; some wood-burning & gas fireplaces. Some pools, hot tubs, saunas, fitness centers, & tennis courts. Some free parking.*

Live like a native. This service offers lodging in interesting residential areas. Among the possibilities are a cottage with a garden and view of the Golden Gate Bridge, and a penthouse with city views. According to this office, "We have it all. Just call."

The Archbishop's Mansion *1000 Fulton St./Steiner St., on Alamo Square, (800) 543-5820, (415) 563-7872, fax (415) 885-3193; www.sftrips.com. 15 rooms; $$$-$$$+; 2-night min. on weekends. Some fireplaces. Afternoon snack, continental breakfast; limited room service. Free parking.*

Located in a area rife with Victorian architecture, this fabulous French-style château dates back to the Victorian era and was once the residence of the town's second Archbishop. Each romantic room is named after an opera and decorated uniquely, and, though all are desirable, some are more so than others. Rooms circle a 3-story, curved mahogany grand staircase surmounted by a leaded-glass skylight, which is truly worthy of the title "grand." A tiny elevator is also available. All guest rooms are cozy and furnished with antiques, and many feature partial canopied beds. The magnificent Don Giovanni Suite features two fireplaces and an extraordinary four-poster bed with a full wooden canopy (the perfect place to be in the event of an earthquake). The bed, which originally graced a French castle, has a crocheted lace and silk trim and is decorated with carved feet, cherub faces, wolves, and more. The suite poses guests with the delightful dilemma of choosing between a soothing shower that surrounds them with seven spraying heads, or a long soak in a bubbly tub. When the shower wins, bathers are enveloped in a warmth as complete as that of a deep, deep tub. Public rooms feature painted frescoes and beautiful woodwork, and the lobby holds a 1904

Bechstein grand piano once owned by Noel Coward. Delightfully, breakfast is delivered to the room along with the morning paper.

Bed & Breakfast California.

See page 416. Most of the San Francisco host homes listed with this reservations service cannot accommodate more than two people in a room, but at least a dozen are appropriate for families. One room is in a "painted lady" and another in a former candy store.

Hostels.

• **Union Square:** *312 Mason St./Geary St., (415) 788-5604, fax (415) 788-3023. 260 beds; private rooms.*

• **Fisherman's Wharf:** *At Fort Mason, Bldg. 240, Bay St./Franklin St., (415) 771-7277, fax (415) 771-1468. 150 beds; private rooms.*

The hostel near Union Square is well-located and in a good area. The one at Fort Mason is in a former Civil War barracks situated on a peaceful knoll with a magnificent view of the bay. It is the largest and busiest hostel in the country. See also page 417.

Motel Row.

A plethora of lodgings lines the 20-block corridor stretching along Lombard Street from Van Ness Avenue to the Presidio.

WHERE TO EAT

There are far too many good restaurants in San Francisco to permit listing them all here. Those that are included are excellent in some way. Don't be afraid to try places discovered while wandering. If the people dining inside look animated and happy, give it a try. It is amazing how infrequently a bad meal is served in this food-fanatical town. Even hotel restaurants (described in the "Where to Stay" section), which are often best overlooked in other places, are usually good here. More restaurants are listed in the "Shopping" section. They don't call San Francisco "Food City" for no reason. In fact, there are said to be more restaurants per resident in San Francisco than in any other city in the U.S.

And do try some of the local food products. The fortune cookie, Irish coffee, and martini were all invented here. Pisco punch, an unusual drink made with Peruvian brandy, dates back to the Gold Rush. Sourdough bread is credited to Isidore Boudin, a French immigrant who in 1849 got some sourdough from a gold prospector and mixed it in with his French bread to produce the world's first sourdough French bread. (Look around town for Boudin cafes, where soups and stews are served in hollowed-out bread rounds.) Dry salame is made by several local companies, including Molinari and Cariani, which both date back to the 1890s. The original Swensen's Ice Cream shop still operates at Hyde and Union streets dishing out its Sticky Chewy Chocolate and Turkish Coffee specialties. It's It—an ice cream sandwich made with oatmeal cookies, vanilla ice cream, and a coating of chocolate—was developed in 1928 at now-gone Playland-at-the-Beach; the confections are sold now in grocery stores. Another frozen delight, the Popsicle, was created here in 1905 when 11-year-old Frank Epperson carelessly left out a mix of powdered soda and water with a stirring stick on one very cold San Francisco night. Green Goddess salad dressing was created in 1923 at the Palace Hotel by chef Philip Roemer, who named it after a play of the same name by William Archer. Double Rainbow is the ice cream of choice, Anchor Steam the beer,

Calistoga (from the Wine Country) the mineral water, Ghirardelli the chocolate, Torani the flavored syrup, and Tom's the cookie.

Note that a state law makes it illegal to smoke in any California restaurant or bar, or in any public place of business. Valet parking averages around $7.

Acquerello *1722 Sacramento St./Van Ness Ave., (415) 567-5432; www.acquerello.com. D Tu-Sat; $$$. Reservations advised.*

Formerly a church, the romantic, intimate dining room of this upscale Italian gem features a rustic, pitched, wooden Moorish ceiling. It is the kind of place where the Mayor might be seated at the next table. Menu selections include a four-course tasting menu with wines. Definitely not the usual, the delicious preparations are derived from a refined style of Italian cuisine known a cucina della nonna, or "grandmother's cooking," and feature complex reduced sauces achieved through slow, home-style cooking. Examples include an exquisite tortelloni stuffed with brandy-plumped figs and ground pork in a nut dough, and a flavorful pepper-crusted pork loin with carmelized endive and tiny chianti-poached pears topped with gorgonzola. Complimentary little treats are sent out occasionally from the kitchen, perhaps a tiny citrus appetizer cocktail or a plump, perfect scallop sitting on mashed potatoes splashed with truffle oil. Desserts are also a pleasant surprse. Service is elegant and formal, with meals served on fine china and crystal enhanced by paper doilies.

Ana Mandara *891 Beach St., in Ghirardelli Square, Fisherman's Wharf, (415) 771-6800, fax (415) 771-5275; www.anamandara.com. L M-F, D daily; $$$. Reservations advised. Valet parking.*

Located within a fabulous high-ceilinged, open dining room, this delightful restaurant, whose name translates as "beautiful refuge," is owned by TV's *Nash Bridges* stars Don Johnson and Cheech Marin. It's rumored that the elaborate decor and the theatrical ceiling lights, which mimic a star-studded evening sky, are going to do double-duty occasionally as stage sets. Full-grown potted palms and antique Vietnamese artifacts complete the effect, making this space resemble a Vietnamese village. It is a desirable place to be. And then there's the food. Though portions are small, the modern Vietnamese cuisine is delicious. Appetizers include crispy spring rolls filled with crab and shrimp, and occasionally superb seafood-stuffed zucchini blossoms. Main dishes such as marinated grilled quail and fresh fish steamed in banana leaves are excellent choices, especially with a side of spicy grilled okra. Elegant cocktails, including a spicy Tapari Poison and a refreshing mint-lemongrass Ana Mandara, and beers provide the perfect accompaniment, and an extensive wine list is also available. Vietnamese coffee and green tea, grown on the chef's family plantation in Vietnam, are available with dessert. At some point, be sure to go upstairs and check out the luxurious bar area.

Andale Taqueria *2150 Chestnut St., the Marina, (415) 749-0506.*

For description, see page 167.

Aqua *252 California St./Battery St., Financial District, (415) 956-9662, fax (415) 956-5229. L M-F, D M-Sat; $$$. Reservations essential. Valet parking.*

With a large dining room and a tall, tall ceiling, this is a physically beautiful space enhanced by gorgeous oversize flower arrangements. It is chic, bustling, and romantic all at the same time and delivers food of equal caliber. Creative, full-flavored, impeccably fresh seafood items dominate the menu, and it seems impossible to choose a wrong dish. Presentations are dazzling, with colorful flavored oils often drizzled around the perimeter of plates, and some dishes involve "table theater," with the waiter dramatically mixing and preparing items at table. Signature dishes include a savory black mussel soufflé, a theatrical and delicious lobster pot pie, and grilled tuna layered with foie gras. Non-fish entrees include duck, foie gras, and a vegetarian tasting menu. Desserts are equally good and include a daily soufflé, a variety of cheeses, and the house specialty updated root beer float enhanced with chocolate "straws." A five-course tasting menu with optional wine pairings is a good way to go for those who just can't decide.

A. Sabella's *2766 Taylor St./Jefferson St., Fisherman's Wharf, (415) 771-6775, fax (415) 771-6777. L&D daily; $$$. Highchairs, boosters, child menu. Reservations accepted. Free validated parking.*

In the family since 1920, this restaurant's chef, Michael Sabella, is the great grandson of its founder. Though the restaurant changed location once in 1939, moving here from across the street, it is well settled into its third-story perch—where through large arched windows all tables enjoy a view of the wharf and the bay beyond. It is a definite exception to the rule that "locals don't eat at the Wharf because there is no fresh fish there." Fresh Dungeness crab is a specialty (indeed, the restaurant maintains saltwater tanks filled with Dungeness crab, abalone, and Maine lobster). A delightful starter is a martini glass filled with a crab Louis cocktail prepared with avocado and housemade Louis dressing. Crab cakes with Remoulade sauce are also very good. Main courses include several crab dishes—cioppino, garlic-roasted in the shell, and whole cracked with black bean sauce—as well as mesquite-grilled salmon and swordfish, and sautéed petrale sole with a delicate lemon and caper sauce. Several meats and some vegetarian pastas are also available. Desserts include the light—a poached pear with lemon-pecan bars—and the heavy—a New York-style cheesecake made from a Sabella family recipe. Note that the menu here is available in French, German, Italian, Japanese, Russian, Portuguese, Korean, and Spanish!

Beach Chalet *1000 Great Highway/Ocean Beach, Golden Gate Park, (415) 386-VIEW, fax (415) 386-4125; www.beachchalet.com. L&D daily, SunBr; $-$$. Child menu. Reservations advised. Free parking lot adjoins.*

Designed in 1925 by San Francisco architect Willis Polk, this historic colonnaded Spanish stucco building with terra-cotta roof tiles is at the western end of Golden Gate Park, across the street from the Pacific Ocean. In the past it has served as a tea house and as an Army signal station, but now the upstairs is a wildly popular brewpub with ocean views from every table. Target a visit for lunch, when the menu is less pricey and the views can be enjoyed uninterrupted by sun-shielding shades. Don't miss the beer sampler or the full-flavored, though essentially fizzless, housemade root beer. Two standouts on the menu are a hamburger made with flavorful Niman Ranch ground chuck and an herb-crusted rotisserie roasted chicken with garlic mashed potatoes. Sausage dishes are also usually available, and the kitchen is famous for its achiote-spiced chicken wings. Desserts are costly, but the fussy Chocolate Treasure Chest—made with hard chocolate sides and filled with espresso mousse—and the pastry chef's signature Sandcastle—the ultimate vertical dessert, whimsically composed of a flourless chocolate truffle cake with bittersweet chocolate sauce and placed vertically between two chocolate castle-shaped cookies—are worth it. A nickel from each beer sold goes to charity, and live music is scheduled every night but Sunday. When the restaurant isn't too busy, informal **brewery tours** are available upon request.

Downstairs, the **Visitors Center** *((415) 666-7024; www.sfparks.org.)* displays natural history exhibits and colorful WPA wall frescoes depicting life in San Francisco during the Depression. Interesting local souvenirs, including authentic street signs and parking meters, can be purchased in the **City Store** *((415) 831-4758)* operating in an alcove.

Betelnut *2030 Union St./Buchanan St., Pacific Heights, (415) 929-8855. L&D daily; $-$$. Highchairs, boosters. Reservations advised. Validated parking.*

With a menu of native dishes from throughout Asia and a streamlined, exotic interior featuring lacquered walls and some very comfortable half-moon booths, this casual spot is always bustling. A favorite area to sit is in the bar, where large windows overlook the sidewalk traffic. Though most dishes are full-flavored and satisfying, truly exceptional items include minced chicken in lettuce cups, red-cooked pork in a spicy-sweet sauce, and tea-smoked duck. Portions are small and meant to be shared tapas-style. Modeled after the beer restaurants found in Asia, the menu accordingly offers a selection of brews. Prime is the ice-cold house rice ale, which is perfect with a plate of sun-dried anchovies, peanuts, and chilies to munch on. An assortment of unusual mixed drinks is also available. Desserts are limited, but an exotic Chinese tea can provide a satisfying conclusion.

Bill's Place *2315 Clement St./25th Ave., (415) 221-5262. L&D daily; $. Highchairs, boosters, child portions. Reservations accepted.*

A variety of hamburgers named after celebrities star on the menu here along with hot dogs and sandwiches. Choice shoulder chuck is ground in the kitchen daily for the tasty burgers. Sides include perfect French fries made from fresh potatoes and made-from-scratch soups, potato salad, and coleslaw. Milkshakes are served in old-fashioned metal cannisters. Breakfast items are on the menu until 1 p.m. Seating is at tables or at a counter with swivel stools, and a collection of Presidential china decorates the walls. In mild weather, a pleasant outdoor patio, landscaped with a Japanese garden complete with waterfall, is inviting.

Black Cat *501 Broadway/Kearny St., North Beach, (415) 981-2233, fax (415) 281-3280. L&D daily; $$-$$$. Reservations advised. Valet parking.*

With its cluster of comfortable, short, tomato-red leather booths and wide open dining room, this bustling spot resembles an upscale coffee shop. It's named after a Beatnik-era hangout of the same name, and its specialty is American and Chinese cuisine. Among the best appetizers are a crisp fritto misto (artichokes, fennel, shaved Parmesan), roasted mussels brought to the table in an iron skillet, and any of the unusual soups. For entrees, pastas are a good choice, and fresh crab and lobster are selected from tanks visible to the entire dining room (struggling chefs have been seen getting snipped by cranky crustaceans). For dessert, either rich doughnut balls filled with vanilla custard or baba rhum are the way to go. Both are especially nice with herbal tea served in a petite but heavy metal pot resembling a black mouse. An intimate subterranean live jazz club, the **Blue Bar**, has no cover charge and operates at the conclusion of a cobalt-blue stairwell leading downstairs. Seating is on overstuffed chairs covered in blue mohair, and special appetizer-size portions from the cafe menu can be ordered.

Boulevard *One Mission St./Stewart St., the Embarcadero, (415) 543-6084, fax (415) 495-2936. L M-F, D daily; $$$. Highchairs, boosters, booths. Reservations advised. Valet parking.*

Co-owned by chef Nancy Oakes and acclaimed local restaurant designer Pat Kuleto, this sumptuous restaurant offers a feast for both the palate and the eyes. Diners enter the gorgeous 1889 French-style building via a revolving door. The belle epoque-style interior features stunning mosaic tile floors as well as sensuous blown-glass light fixtures and pressed tin and ironwork accents. Some tables have three-landmark views—of the Ferry Building, Embarcadero Center, and the Bay Bridge. Large, serious forks foreshadow the exciting, full-flavored dishes to follow. One flawless meal here began with a Chinese-seasoned appetizer of two perfect prawns intertwined over a plump rock shrimp dumpling. The entree was a delicious, thick, honey-cured pork loin served with roasted potatoes and baby spinach. A pear tart with caramel sauce and vanilla bean ice cream provided the perfect finish.

Buca di Beppo *855 Howard St./Fourth St., South of Market, (415) 543-POPE. D daily; $$. Limited reservations.*

The party begins upon entering the door at this festive, happy, old-time southern Italian spot, whose name translates as "Joe's basement." Choose from a warren of small subterranean rooms, or pick one of the comfortable booths in the boisterous upstairs bar where kids can wiggle and squirm to their heart's content, then study the menu posted on the wall while being entertained by favorite tunes from the '50s. Portions are huge and meant to be shared. Lord have mercy on anyone who orders a "large" of anything here, and on the poor soul who arrives without a BIG appetite. The oblong, thin-crusted pepperoni pizza is nothing short of great and is served high on a footed tray so as not to crowd a tall bowl of spaghetti with one very large meatball and perhaps a tasty salad, too. Or skip the pizza and order the satisfying garlic bread. More pastas and some chicken and veal dishes are also on

the menu. Even those who order small portions have leftovers to take home that can feed them for a night or two more. Kids have been known to grow saucer eyes when they find out soft drink orders include *two* refills.

The Buena Vista *2765 Hyde St./Beach St., Fisherman's Wharf, (415) 474-5044. M-F 9am-2am, Sat & Sun from 8am. No reservations. No cards.*

In 1952 the owner of this legendary bar challenged local travel writer Stanton Delaplane to help him re-create the Irish coffee served at Shannon Airport in Ireland. The biggest deterrent to success was getting the cream to float. Once mastered, the result is history. It is de rigueur to stop at this cozy spot and find out what all the fuss is about. Casual meals are also served.

Cafe Bastille *22 Belden Pl./Bush St., Financial District, (415) 986-5673, fax (415) 986-1013. L&D M-Sat; $. Reservations advised for D; no reservations for L.*

Located in the middle of a quaint alley in the "French Quarter," this Very French bistro provides a quick fix for Francophiles. Seating is at a long row of tight tables with a wall bench on one side and a chair on the other, or in the Bohemian atmosphere of the crowded cellar. In warm weather, tables are set up outside in the alley. The Americanized menu includes salads, sandwiches, a pizzetta, crêpes, and more substantial entrees such as boudin noir (black sausage) and quiche. Authentic French desserts include crème caramel, chocolate mousse, and both crêpes Suzette and a fabulous crêpe topped with chocolate sauce, toasted almonds, and whipped cream. Live music is performed upstairs Tuesday through Saturday.

Cafe de Paris L'Entrecote *2032 Union St./Buchanan St., Pacific Heights, (415) 931-5006. L M-F, D daily, Sat & SunBr; $$-$$$. Highchairs, boosters. Reservations advised. Valet parking at D.*

Situated within the shell of the first mansion built west of Van Ness Avenue, which was also the home of the dairy that gave the name "cow hollow" to this district, this authentic French bistro opened on Bastille Day in 1983. In a bow to history and city dictates, an unusual sort of greenhouse cafe was built around a glass-encased palm tree planted in front of the house in 1867; it is a choice room to be in during daylight, as views of the sidewalk parade are prime then. The restaurant's signature dish is a charbroiled New York steak served with their 12-ingredient secret sauce (made downstairs, out of sight even of the chef!), a flawless butter lettuce salad, and crisp pommes frites. The menu also holds seasonal surprises such as a deep-fried soft shell crab appetizer (the French would definitely love this) and house-smoked salmon. Crêpes and omelettes, a hamburger, and several daily specials are also available. A full-flavored tarte tatin—a sort of French caramelized apple pie—is the dessert specialty of the house. Other endings include pêche Melba, profiteroles with chocolate sauce, and the classic crème brulee. Both the secret steak sauce and salad dressing are available bottled to take home. On weekend evenings, live music is scheduled in the bar until 2 a.m. A Cafe de Paris also exists in Geneva, and a L'Entrecote de Paris in Paris.

Cafe Trieste *601 Vallejo St./Grant Ave., North Beach, (415) 392-6739. Daily 6:30am-11pm; $. No reservations. No cards.*

This Very Cool coffeehouse was a favorite hangout with the Beat Generation and was once frequented by Jack Kerouac, Allen Ginsberg, and friends, and it is where Francis Ford Coppola wrote part of *The Godfather* script. In traditional Italian style, the owners perform live opera every Saturday at noon.

Caffe Sport *574 Green St./Columbus, North Beach, (415) 981-1251. L&D Tu-Sat; $$. Reservations advised. No cards.*

The bad news is that the cramped and

uncomfortable seating here of yore remains, but the good news is that the infamous slow and surly service is gone. And it is easy now to get a reservation. Celebrate by checking out the still-funky decor and still-incredible food. Waiters seem trained to nudge diners into ordering more than they think they need, but it's the exception to be disappointed with their recommendations. The scrupulously fresh prawns in garlicky white sauce and the pasta in pesto are both especially good.

California Culinary Academy *625 Polk St./Turk St., (800) BAY-CHEF, (415) 292-8241, fax (415) 775-5129; www.baychef.com. L&D M-F; SunBr on occasion; $-$$. Reservations advised.*

Founded in 1977, this training school for professional chefs operates two very different restaurants, both of which are completely student-run while overseen by chef-instructors. **Tavern** offers an intimate setting and features American and Italian specialties. The more formal **Carême** operates in a grand room with an 80-foot-high ceiling and fine architectural details. It serves an elegant global cuisine and puts on fabulous Thursday and Friday evening buffets that showcase student work. The school's retail store sells housemade salads and pastries as well as logo apparel and cooking utensils.

Calzone's Pizza Cucina *430 Columbus Ave./Green St., North Beach, (415) 397-3600, fax (415) 397-3446. B,L,&D daily; $-$$. Highchairs, boosters, booths, child menu. Reservations accepted.*

Reflecting the colors of the Italian flag, walls reaching to a high ceiling are painted dark green and decorated with colorful Italian cooking ingredients. Diners seated at small Formica tables downstairs enjoy superb views of sidewalk traffic, while some upstairs diners are entertained by overviews of the downstairs diners. Meals begin with a crusty hunk of Italian bread. A favorite appetizer is the light and crunchy deep-fried calamari served with a tangy basil pomodoro sauce. Crisp-bottomed pizzas prepared in a wood-fired brick oven are available with a large selection of delicious toppings. Contrary to what one expects given this restaurant's name, only a few delicious calzones (pizza turnovers) are available. Fresh fettuccine, linguine, and angel hair pastas are prepared with a variety of interesting toppings, and housemade lasagna and gnocchi are also on the menu. (Note that a free limo shuttle operates from downtown for lunch; call for details.)

For dessert, **Stella Pastry and Cafe** is just next door. It is famous for its trademarked sacripantina cake, described by *Gourmet* magazine as "a San Francisco concoction of cream, air, and magic . . ."

Capp's Corner *1600 Powell St./Green St., North Beach, (415) 989-2589. L M-F, D daily; $$. Highchairs, boosters, booths, child portions. Reservations advised. Validated parking.*

After entering the saloon-style swinging doors, diners are in what is reputed to be the liveliest and noisiest of the North Beach family-style restaurants. When there is a wait for a table, a seat at the Victorian-era bar can make time fly. In the cozy, friendly interior dining room, where photos of prior happy diners decorate the walls, noisy family groups rub elbows with swinging singles while enjoying the hearty Italian food. The bountiful three-course dinner includes minestrone soup, a green salad, and an entree (steak, roast duck, chicken breast picatta, ossobuco, lasagna, seafood cannelloni, etc.).

Carnelian Room *555 California St./Montgomery St., 52nd fl. in Bank of America bldg., Financial District, (415) 433-7500. D daily, Sun Br; $$$. Basement garage.*

In a luxurious setting atop San Francisco's tallest building, this elegant restaurant provides diners a feast for their eyes with walnut panelling and fine art on one side and breathtaking bay views on the other. A fine-dining menu and a wine cellar holding 40,000 bottles offer fitting fare. A three-course, fixed-price menu offers items such as sweet pea ravioli with Meyer lemon-mint broth, peppercorn-crusted ahi tuna with ginger mashed potatoes, and a banana pecan tart.

Cha-Am *701 Folsom St./3rd St., South of Market, (415) 546-9711, fax (415) 546-0354. L M-Sat, D daily.*

For description, see page 259.

Charles Nob Hill *1250 Jones St./Clay St., Nob Hill, (415) 771-5400, fax (415) 771-3542; www.nextcenturyrestaurants.com. D Tu-Sun; $$$. Reservations advised. Valet parking.*

Tucked off the lobby of an exquisite vintage apartment building, this intimate, romantic, and elegant restaurant offers the best in attentive service, impeccable food, and lush accouterments. Servers seem to really care whether everything is perfect. The menu features luxury items such as caviar, lobster, foie gras, quail, abalone, and filet mignon. And the silverware is *real* silver, the china is the best, and, though simple in design, even the wineglasses are top quality. A six- and nine-course tasting menu, available with an optional wine pairing, permits sampling the chef's talents. Current chef, Ron Siegel, was in 1999 the first American to win the Japanese Iron Chef competition. It is interesting to know that this building is said to be the highest object in San Francisco, due to a Motorola antenna atop it.

Chaya Brasserie *132 The Embarcadero/Mission St., (415) 777-8688, fax (415) 247-9952. L M-F, D daily; $$$. Reservations advised. Valet parking.*

Featuring magnificent views of the bay and Bay Bridge that are especially pretty at night, this new restaurant is a branch of a successful Los Angeles venue. With French-style parquet floors, Japanese-style bamboo ceilings, and dramatic contemporary art hanging on natural brick walls, this spot is a combination of a French brasserie and a Japanese teahouse, or "chaya." The Franco-Japanese menu offers up main dishes such as grilled salmon with fingerling potatoes and herb-Dijon mustard sauce, and grilled free-range chicken with Maine lobster tail and wild-rice risotto. A full sushi bar dining area is also on the premises. Desserts are a highlight. A warm Valrhona chocolate cake with raspberry sauce is to-die for, and the carmelized banana tart with crushed walnut pralines is pretty good, too.

Chevy's *150 4th St./Howard St., South of Market, (415) 543-8060. Highchairs, boosters, booths, child menu. L&D daily; $-$$.*

When you're hankering for some reliably tasty Tex-Mex, try this prolific spot, which seems to be everywhere. Everyone's favorites are on the menu—tacos, enchiladas, burritos, tamales—and their acclaimed fajitas are fun for the whole family to share. Waiting for the food to arrive is almost painless with a frosty margarita and plenty of the superb house salsa and thin, crisp corn chips. Crayons and coloring menus are provided for children, who also are usually interested in El Machino—the restaurant's intriguing tortilla-making machine.

Chinatown restaurants. See page 17.

The Cliff House *1090 Point Lobos Ave., Outer Richmond, (415) 386-3330, fax (415) 387-7837; www.cliffhouse.com. L M-F, D daily, Sat & SunBr; $$-$$$. Highchairs, boosters, booths. Reservations advised.*

Perched solidly on bedrock at the edge of the Pacific, this historic treasure is the only ocean-front restaurant in San Francisco. It has been around for quite some time, since 1863 to be exact, but in three different renditions, having twice burned to the ground. The most recent version was constructed in 1909. Though it has gone through many changes, the structure has always housed a restaurant and since 1977 has been part of the National Park Service's Golden Gate National Recreation Area. Diners choose between three dining rooms and two bars—all with spectacular views of the ocean and Seal Rocks. On the main level, **Phineas T. Barnacle Bar and Deli** serves a casual menu of soups, salads, and sandwiches, as well as snacks and mixed drinks, while the main dining room, the **Seafood & Beverage Company**, serves a more formal menu of steak and fresh seafood and is the choice spot for Sunday brunch. **Upstairs at the Cliff House** has a more informal, family-friendly atmosphere and a menu offering 30 different omelettes, both hot and cold sandwiches, a Louis salad, chili, and a hamburger. At dinner, the upstairs menu adds pasta and seafood entrees and becomes more pricey. On Sundays, the downstairs **Terrace Room** is opened for a buffet Champagne brunch. See also page 18.

Cordon Bleu *1574 California St./Polk St., (415) 673-5637. L Tu-Sat, D Tu-Sun; $. No cards.*

With just nine counter seats and three

tiny tables, this miniscule Vietnamese restaurant is one of the oldest in the city and has been under the same management since 1976. From the counter, diners can watch the entire cooking process while sipping a complimentary mug of hot tea. Satisfying one-plate meals consists of a large scoop of rice topped with light tomato-based meat gravy and a choice of deep-fried imperial roll, tasty barbecued beef satay (listed on the menu as shish kebab), or barbecued chicken. That's it!

The **Lumiere** movie theater *((415) 352-0810)* is right next door, and a host of interesting shops are just around the corner.

dallaTorre *1349 Montgomery St./Union St., North Beach, (415) 296-1111, fax (415) 982-2055. D W-Sun; $$-$$$. Reservations advised. Valet parking.*

Situated atop Telegraph Hill, in one of the city's most hidden and splendidly scenic locations, this restaurant's name translates as "at the tower." It features bright rooms, with stone floors and a gabled ceiling in the main dining room. Adding a Mediterranean feel, walls are painted warm Tuscan colors and windows look out upon gardens and the bay, and the charming third-floor Rooftop Room overlooks a multicolored slate roof to a spectacular bay view beyond. The perfect time to dine here seems to be as soon as it opens at 5 p.m., when the light permits seeing the panorama at its clearest, but most diners arrive much later in favor of seeing the even more romantic evening lights. While perusing the sophisticated Italian menu, delicious olives are brought for nibbling. Dessert here should be taken in three courses. First, select one from the menu—perhaps a chocolate Nutella bread pudding or a tiramisu—to savor with a leisurely coffee. Second, take a climb up the **Filbert Steps**, which pass by the restaurant's front door and terminate near Coit Tower. Third, view *Dark Passage*, the 1946 classic with Humphrey Bogart and Lauren Bacall that was filmed in the art deco building across the street.

Delancey Street Restaurant *600 The Embarcadero/ Brannan St., (415) 512-5179. L Tu-F, D Tu-Sun, Sat&SunBr; $-$$. Highchairs, boosters. Reservations advised. Valet parking at L & F-Sun D.*

The comfortable open room here lets in plenty of light and even a glimpse of the bay. Though that is enough to lure in plenty of diners, this special restaurant is also a training school of the Delancey Street Foundation—the country's largest and most acclaimed self-help residential organization for former hard-core criminals. It is completely self-supporting. All tips are considered donations, and all restaurant profits go directly to caring for the residents. Interestingly, no resident who has finished the 2-year training program has ever gone on to commit a serious crime. In this win-win atmosphere, it seems impossible to leave unsatisfied. Lunch is a particular bargain, with plenty of well-priced, well-executed sandwiches—roasted ginger pork loin and chutney on sourdough bread, blackened chicken breast on a Kaiser roll—and hot dishes—Thai red curry prawns and vegetables over rice. A hamburger, a hot dog, and an assortment of light items—including desserts such as a Chocolate Decadence that claims only 200 calories and 6 grams of fat—are also available. The menu changes daily and is composed based on the current residents' backgrounds.

Dim Sum restaurants.

For explanation and for restaurants in Chinatown, see page 15.

- **Fountain Court** *354 Clement St./5th Ave., the Richmond, (415) 668-1100. Daily 11-3; $. Highchairs, boosters. Reservations advised.*

Unusual items served at this authentic Shanghai-style restaurant include bowls of savory soy bean milk seasoned with hot chili-sesame oil and topped with floating slices of Chinese doughnut; pan-fried turnip rice cake; pan-fried pork buns wrapped in fried, then steamed, bread dough; marinated pig ears; eel noodle soup; and braised boneless pigs' feet. Though there are some more common dishes, such as pot stickers and beef chow fun, this is definitely a spot for the dim sum adventurer.

- **Harbor Village** *Four Embarcadero Center, lobby level, Financial District, (415) 781-8833. Daily 11-2:30, Sat & Sun from 10:30; $. Highchairs, boosters. Reservations accepted for M-F. Validated parking in center garage.*

It is worth the wait generally required to dine on the upscale dim sum served at this

Hong Kong-style spot. The back room, with its large windows overlooking the treetops to the Vaillancourt Fountain and Ferry Building, is choice. Special touches include doilies and pretty blue-patterned dishes that actually match. The selection of delicious items brought around on carts changes daily. They are made with impeccably fresh ingredients, and a tasty complexity characterizes many of the refined renditions.

• **Ton Kiang** *5821 Geary Blvd./22nd Ave., the Richmond, (415) 387-8273. Daily 11-3; $. Highchairs, boosters. No reservations.*

Operating on two floors, this attractive spot specializes in Hakka-style cuisine. Exemplary dim sum items are considered by many to be the very best in San Francisco and include deep-fried taro croquettes, puffy deep-fried stuffed crab claws, miniature egg-custard tarts, and crisp walnut cookies filled with lotus paste, as well as positively ethereal chive-shrimp dumplings and exquisite steamed pea shoots.

A branch is located at 3148 Geary Boulevard *(at Spruce St., (415) 752-4440).*

• **Yank Sing** *427 Battery St./Clay St., Financial District, (415) 781-1111. M-F 11-3, Sat & Sun 10-4; $. Highchairs, boosters. Reservations advised.*

In 1957, when it opened in a previous location on Broadway in Chinatown, this was the first dim sum parlor in the city to serve the cuisine as it was known in Hong Kong. Two compelling reasons to forsake tradition and visit this now upscale parlour at it location outside of Chinatown are that they take reservations and that the parking is easier. The tasteful, brightly lighted upstairs interior here is a warren of dining rooms. Downstairs, tables are separated by etched-glass partitions and a peaceful bamboo fountain sets the tone. Tablecloths, fabric napkins, and fresh flowers grace each table. Soft drinks and bottled water can be ordered, and servers are friendly and can usually answer questions. Top items include cloud-soft rice noodles stuffed with a variety of meats, succulent stuffed black mushroom caps, deep-fried crab claws, sweet deep-fried taro balls, flaky-crusted custard tarts, and especially for kids—wedges of orange peel filled with shimmering orange Jell-O.

It is a Cantonese custom to introduce a new baby to family and friends at a Red Egg and Ginger Party. Named for some of the food items included in the luncheon menu, these parties are catered here and set menus are available.

A branch is located at 49 Stevenson Street *(at 1st St., (415) 495-4510).*

Doidge's *2217 Union St./Fillmore St., Pacific Heights, (415) 921-2149. B&L daily, D W-Sat; $-$$. Boosters. Reservations advised.*

Breakfast here is a winner, and it's available all day. Eggs are cooked to order and served with toast and a side of either cottage fries or sliced tomato. Eggs Benedict, omelettes, pancakes, housemade granola, and French toast made from a choice of six different breads are among the other items available. Don't miss the Motherlode bacon, a flavorful honey-cured variety made without preservatives. And then there are the fresh-squeezed orange and grapefruit juices and hot chocolate made with milk. For lunch it's a variety of hamburgers, sandwiches, housemade soups, and a beautiful fresh fruit salad. Often there is a wait for seating in the cozy dining room. However, there is usually room at the counter, where the bonus is watching the busy, colorful cooks.

E&O Trading Company *314 Sutter St./Grant Ave., 2 blocks from Union Square, (415) 693-0303; www.eotrading.com. L&D daily; $$. Reservations advised.*

The sleek, quiet exterior here belies the warm, roaring interior designed to resemble an Indonesian trading company warehouse. Live piano music keeps things jumping in the busy bar and is also enjoyed throughout the restaurant. Well-positioned seating for meals is found both upstairs, where some diners have views of the street and others can watch the action in the bar downstairs, and adjoining the bar, where there is also a counter with tall stools overlooking the kitchen. Housemade English-style beers and tropical sodas prepared with housemade fruit syrups are the perfect accompaniment to the mild-mannered but complexly flavored Indonesian fare. Sharing a variety of items from the unusual southeast Asian menu is the way to go. A fabulous dinner can be composed of lamb naan (stuffed bread); Cambodian lettuce cups filled with an exotic mixture of pork, shrimp, peanuts, and coconut; Thai crab cakes with a tangy red curry sauce; papaya-avocado salad with spicy Asian greens; and delicious Hawaiian walu fish with black-and-tan sesame seed crust served atop a bed of rice atop green long beans. Noteworthy "small dishes," the menu's strong point, include crispy Indonesian corn fritters and satays with spicy peanut sauce. Desserts are all made in-house. For the perfect finale, select one from the bamboo tray brought to each table—perhaps a mango crème brulee or a tropical Napoleon—and order up some fragrant World Peace licorice-peppermint loose leaf tea, served in a heavy metal pot. Before leaving, check out the bamboo birdcage collection hanging just off the bar area, the restroom decor, and the basement beer-brewing vats.

Elite Cafe *2049 Fillmore St./California St., Upper Fillmore, (415) 346-8668. D daily, SunBr; $$. Highchairs, boosters, booths. No reservations.*

Parties of four get the best seats here, in enclosed wooden booths left from the restaurant's prior life as an old-time Chinese restaurant. In addition to Cajun martinis and other exotic bar drinks, plus appetizers such as Cajun popcorn, the menu offers a selection of authentic spicy Cajun-Creole dishes: gumbo, jambalaya, blackened salmon, chicken and dumplings, barbecue ribs.

El Mansour *3123 Clement St./32nd Ave., Outer Richmond, (415) 751-2312, fax (510) 669-0444. D daily; $$. Child portions. Reservations advised.*

Upon entering the double doors of this Moroccan restaurant, diners are encased in another world. Cloth is draped from the ceiling of the intimate dining room, giving occupants the illusion of being inside a sultan's tent. Adding to the sensuous feeling are floors covered with plush oriental carpets and seating on hassocks at low tables of inlaid wood. After diners select an entree from the fixed-price menu, a waiter dressed in a long caftan appears to perform the ritual hand washing. Hands are gathered over a large metal pot placed in the middle of the table, then splashed with warm water. When the first course arrives—a tasty lentil soup—diners drink it right from the bowl, since no eating utensils are provided here. A bland Moroccan bread is offered to accompany it. The next course is a salad plate of spicy marinated rounds of carrots and cucumbers and a delicious mixture of tomatoes and green peppers meant to be scooped up with the bread. Then comes a bastela—a fragrant pie containing a sweet chicken and almond mixture wrapped in filo pastry and sprinkled with powdered sugar. Among the entree choices are seafood, rabbit, couscous, and shish kabob. Both succulent roasted chicken and tender stewed lamb are also offered with a choice of toppings such as almonds, honey, or prunes. Dessert is fried bananas with honey and a repeat of the hand-bathing ritual. And finally the waiter pours mint tea, skillfully and beautifully, from up high. Belly dancers perform nightly.

Enrico's *504 Broadway/Kearny St., North Beach, (415) 982-6223, fax (415) 397-7244. L&D daily; $$. Highchairs, booths. Reservations advised; accepted for same day only. Valet parking.*

Though no longer run by Enrico Banducci—the well-known original owner, who now operates a hot dog cart in Richmond, Virginia—this landmark restaurant was the city's first coffeehouse. Coffee and snacks are still served on the informal outdoor patio, which is heated in cool weather and is one of the best spots around for people-watching. More substantial meals can also be ordered there as well as in the large interior room, where paintings by local artists adorn the walls and jazz is performed nightly from 9 p.m. The dinner menu offers a large selection of tapas plus several soups, salads, pastas, and pizzas. More substantial entrees include delicious items such as salmon coated with a fruit mustard and served with garlic mashed potatoes, and a surprisingly flavorful top sirloin served with a braised onion and perfect oven-roasted potatoes. Accomplished housemade desserts, such as malt ice cream in a chocolate cookie sandwich with toasted pecans, are hard to resist. Special events are sometimes scheduled.

Epplers Bakery *3465 California St./Laurel St., Presidio Heights, (415) 752-0825. M-Sat 6:30-7, Sun 8-5; $. 1 highchair. Free parking lot adjoins.*

This bakery is famous for its extensive assortment of baked goods, including cakes, pastries, tortes, petit fours, cookies, muffins, and tea cakes. Specialty cakes include a Grand Marnier and Black Forest. All stops are pulled out for Christmas, when specialty items include gingerbread, marzipan, fruit cakes, mincemeat and pumpkin pies, several kinds of buche de noel, and elaborate gingerbread houses. A variety of candies are also available. Though there is no table service, a sit-down area invites relaxing over a bakery selection and tea or coffee.

More Epplers are located at 750 Market Street near Union Square *((415) 392-0101)*, at Stonestown shopping center *((415) 731-5544)*, and at Embarcadero Center *((415) 982-5383)*.

Farallon *450 Post St./Powell St., off Union Square, (415) 956-6969, fax (415) 834-1234. L M-Sat, D daily; $$$. Booths. Valet parking.*

The long bar entryway leads under gorgeous lighting fixtures posing as jellyfish to the magnificent back room of this spectacular restaurant. An elaborate painted mosaic, successfully designed to look old, covers the three Gothic arches of the main dining room ceiling (it was once the celing for the Elks Club saltwater swimming pool on the floor below) along with some gargantuan belle epoque sea urchin light fixtures. No table in the tiered room is bad, and many are attached to exquisitely comfortable booths. The seasonal "coastal menu" includes innovative preparations of fish (ginger-steamed wild salmon and striped bass "pillows" with crayfish mousse and foie gras coulis), a large selection of raw items (including housemade caviar), and a whole roasted 1 1/2-pound lobster, plus some locally-raised meat items. Unusual appetizers have included a black truffled Dungeness crab and sea urchin gratin and a conch chowder, and luscious desserts have included a caramel-chocolate brulee, warm apricot dumplings with vanilla ice cream and huckleberry sauce, and a Bing cherry Napoleon.

Fior d'Italia *601 Union St./Stockton St., North Beach, (415) 986-1886, fax (415) 986-7031. L&D daily; $$-$$$. Highchairs, boosters, booths. Reservations advised. Valet parking.*

Opened in 1886, when great sailing ships were seen in the bay and goats roamed Telegraph Hill, this venerable traditional northern Italian restaurant is the oldest in the U.S. The small dining area in the bar is graced with a large composite mural depicting the Church of St. Francis of Assisi in Tuscany, while the spacious main dining area in back is decorated with historic San Francisco memorabilia and outfitted with plenty of comfortable oversize booths. Experienced servers, attired in traditional black-and-white uniforms, offer expert assistance in navigating the extensive menu. Always a good choice is the four-course, fixed-price dinner; main courses include seafood, veal, and chicken. Additionally, the regular menu offers fresh pasta, risotto, and polenta. Desserts include the classic tiramisu, fresh berries, and sometimes a delicious poached pear in caramel sauce and cream.

The Fly Trap Restaurant *606 Folsom St./2nd St., South of Market, (415) 243-0580. L M-F, D M-Sat; $$. 1 highchair, boosters. Reservations advised. Valet parking.*

Once, long ago, in a former incarnation, the restaurant in this spot solved its fly problem by putting fly paper on the tables, prompting the GIs of the 1898 Spanish-American war to refer to it as the "fly trap." The flies stuck and so did the name. When the original owner's cousin reopened the restaurant after the 1906 earthquake and fire, he irreverently named it "The Fly Trap Restaurant," and it is still called that today. A replica of Louie's Restaurant, a turn-of-the-century Market Street eatery, it has a spiffy updated interior that features high ceilings and a bank of small tables perfect for solo diners. Some unusual items are found on the menu. Among the starters are several soups, including a chilled vichyssoise, and a variety of salads, including a tasty celery Victor. House specialties include an exquisite chicken coq au vin, the hard-to-find Hangtown fry, and an Old World wiener schnitzel. Steaks, seafood, pastas, and a hamburger are also available. Each entree is accompanied by thick, crispy, ridged housemade potato chips. The rich housemade desserts range from a banana split to a chocolate torte with marscapone cream, and intriguing drinks such as the Fly Trap Coffee, prepared with Godiva and Frangelica liquors, are also available.

42 Degrees *235 16th St./Illinois St., China Basin, (415) 777-5558. D W-Sun; $$-$$$. Reservations accepted.*

For those who are sick and tired of looking for a parking place, this hidden-away restaurant is the place to head for, as spaces are plentiful and free in the huge lot it shares with the Esprit Outlet. Featuring an industrial chic atmosphere in a warehouse space, with white tablecloths mixed with aluminum chairs and a 22-foot-high ceiling, this lively spot has an open first-floor dining room and a more sedate second level with comfy 3/4-moon booths. More seating is available on an inviting, heated outdoor courtyard surrounded by trees and flowers. The kitchen serves up rustic, flavorful Mediterranean cuisine (42 degrees is the latitude of Provence) along with live jazz. For evenings when the appetite is light, pair an inspired soup and a pizza-like flatbread topped with something unusual such as wild nettles with mozzarella and red onions. Entrees have included tender veal cheeks with an herb-mustard crust and an absolutely fabulous pancetta-wrapped scallop dish with fettucine, broccoli Romanesque, and capers. A dessert chef prepares delicacies such as orange-olive oil cake and heavenly persimmon pudding with caramel ice cream.

Franciscan Restaurant *At foot of Powell St./The Embarcadero, Pier 43 1/2, Fisherman's Wharf, (415) 362-7733, fax (415) 362-0174. L&D daily; $$-$$$. Highchairs, boosters, booths, child menu. Reservations advised. Parking validated at adjacent lot.*

Though the outside of this restaurant is one of the ugliest bits of architecture imaginable, the inside is tasteful, with staggered tiers of seating, some in cozy half-moon booths, and every diner gets a fabulous bay view. A drink menu starts things off with some playful concoctions, including several non-alcoholic versions, and that famous San Francisco sourdough bread keeps hunger at bay. The favorites are all here, though updated for contemporary tastes. Starters include a delicious clam chowder with bits of bacon and thyme, as well as crabcakes, seafood cocktails, and oysters on the half shell. The crab Louis is made with Dungeness crab (according to the waiter it has "seen ice, but carefully"), mixed lettuces, and a delicious housemade dressing. The seafood combo is an attractive arrangement of grilled —not fried—fresh fish, prawns, and scallops positioned around a wild rice cake topped with ginger-cilantro sauce. A satisfying exception to the calorie-heavy desserts is a trio of full-flavored sorbets. Fish-hating kids will love the special coloring menu offering spaghetti and a hamburger as well as grilled prawns.

Fringale *570 Fourth St./Brannan St., South of Market, (415) 543-0573. L M-F, D M-Sat; $$. Reservations advised.*

Cheery yet intimate, this bright, very popular spot is owned by French-Basque chef Gerald Hirigoyen. He offers a seasonal menu of light Franco-California bistro fare that American's can recognize. Appetizers might include a soup du jour of creamy fava bean purée, house-cured salmon, foie gras medallions, and a mashed potato croquette. Dinner entrees have included delicate steamed salmon topped with threads of deep-fried onions and served on a bed of tart braised leeks, a lemon-chicken breast with a side of couscous and dates, and a marinated roast rack of lamb. Among the possible desserts are a tangy lemon tart with fresh raspberries and a wonderful clafouti made with toasted almond slices and fresh raspberries. In French "fringale" means "the urge to eat," and that urge is delightfully satisfied here.

Gabbiano's *One Ferry Plaza/The Embarcadero, (415) 391-8403, fax (415) 391-1617. L&D daily, SunBr; $$-$$$. Highchairs, boosters, child menu. Reservations accepted.*

The main reason to dine here is for the incredible view of Treasure Island and the Bay Bridge afforded from the second-floor dining room, where all seats are good seats. Fortunately, the food is tasty as well. The menu is eclectic, with an extensive selection of sandwiches and salads at lunch and, at dinner, items such as crab cakes and oysters on the half shell among the appetizers, and paella and lobster in puff pastry among the entrees. The Sunday champagne brunch extravaganza should please anyone. Note that weekend lunch is served only on the first floor.

Ghirardelli Chocolate Manufactory *900 North Point, in Ghirardelli Square, Fisherman's Wharf, (415) 771-4903. Sun-Thur 10am-11pm, F & Sat to 12; $. Highchairs. No reservations.*

A small working chocolate factory that uses original equipment from the early 1900s still operates in the back of this classic ice cream parlor. All of the chocolate sauces and syrups are made on site, as are some of the candies sold in the shop. After reading the mouth-watering menu, which can be kept as a souvenir, each ice cream-lover takes a seat and awaits the fulfillment of their ice cream fantasy. Special concoctions include The Alcatraz Rock (rocky road and vanilla ice cream covered with a shell of chocolate, chopped almonds, whipped cream, and a whole cherry) and The Earthquake Sundae, which serves four or more people (eight flavors of ice cream with eight different toppings accented with bananas, whipped cream, chopped almonds, and cherries). Hot fudge sundaes, sodas, and milkshakes are also available. Ghirardelli chocolate goodies, including a 5-pound chocolate bar, are sold in a small adjoining shop.

Gira Polli *659 Union St./Columbus, North Beach, (415) 434-4472. Daily 4:30-9:30pm; $.*

Solve the dilemma of circling North Beach, searching unsuccessfully for a parking place, by dashing in here and picking up a great take-home dinner while the driver circles yet again. In a flash, the "special" is ready to go—a fragrant rotisserie-roasted chicken prepared in a wood-fired oven and packed with sides of potatoes, fresh vegetables, and rolls. Soups and salads, pastas and risottos, and housemade desserts such as cannoli, lemon-flavored cheesecake, biscotti, and tiramisu are also on the menu. For those with a parking space, in-shop seating is available.

Golden Turtle *2211 Van Ness Ave./Vallejo St., (415) 441-4419; D Tu-Sun; $$. Highchairs, boosters. Reservations advised.*

Located within a converted Victorian with a koi pond at the entrance, this elegant, sedate Vietnamese restaurant is decorated with intricately hand-carved wooden plaques and light sconces constructed from tree branches. It serves a cuisine that is a cross between Cantonese and Szechwan Chinese. A good starter is crisp-fried imperial rolls stuffed with a pork-seafood mixture and served with thin rice noodles, lettuce, and a mild dipping sauce. More dramatic appetizers include barbecued quails flambé and sizzling rice soup. Main dishes include a tasty grilled beef kabob, aromatic lemon grass curry prawns, steamed whole sea bass in a subtle ginger sauce, and fresh catfish in a clay pot. The Seven Jewel beef dinner consists of seven special beef dishes served in a specific order; each dish can also be ordered separately. Tea comes with the meal, and a sweet fresh-squeezed lemonade is among the drink selections. For dessert, don't miss the spectacular presentation of bananas flambé.

Gordon Biersch Brewery Restaurant *2 Harrison St./The Embarcadero, (415) 864-2333; www.gordonbiersch.com. L&D daily; $.*

Brewmaster Dan Gordon is the only American in over 40 years to graduate from the rigorous 5-year brewing program at The Technical University of Munich in Weihenstephan, Germany. Call for the schedule of **brewer's lunch tours** scheduled once each month. An **Oktoberfest** is staged each October, complete with plenty of seasonal Wiesenhelles lager, platters of traditional Bavarian culinary delights, waitstaff in lederhosen, and live oom-pah bands. For more description, see page 178.

Greens *Laguna St./Marina Blvd., at Fort Mason Center, Bldg. A, (415) 771-6222. L Tu-Sat, D M-Sat, SunBr; $$. Highchairs, boosters. Reservations essential. Free parking lot adjoins.*

With high ceilings, large windows framing the Golden Gate Bridge, and colorful modern art hanging on the walls, this trendy, all-vegetarian restaurant packs 'em in. Starters on the ever-changing menu might include a fragrant and flavorful black bean chili or a delicate watercress salad with pears and walnuts. Entrees include pastas and a tasty pita sandwich. Desserts are uncomplicated but delicious—perhaps a pear-almond upside down cake or a fabulous apricot tart with pistachio nuts and toasted almond ice cream. Cafe-style dinners are served Monday through Friday; on Saturdays, a fixed-price three-course dinner is presented. The brunch menu is a la carte. Greens is run by the San Francisco Zen Center, and many of the fresh herbs and vegetables are grown at the center's West Marin farm.

Greens To Go *((415) 771-6330, fax (415) 771-3472. M-F 8am-9:30pm, Sat 8-4, Sun 9-3:30.)* dispenses many menu items as well as their delicious breads and an assortment of pastries and desserts.

Hamburger Mary's *1582 Folsom St./12th St., South of Market, (415) 626-1985. L&D daily; $. Highchairs, boosters. Reservations advised.*

With a sound system rivaling that of the Hard Rock Cafe and a decor as eclectically mixed as the clientele it serves, this funky spot dishes up its signature charbroiled hamburger until the wee hours in a *very* relaxed atmosphere. The menu also offers a variety of sandwiches and salads, and breakfast is served all day. Ten beers are on draft, and the cream pitcher is a baby bottle. In sum, it's the kind of place that would make Dorothy say to Toto, "We're not in Kansas anymore!"

Hard Rock Cafe *1699 Van Ness Ave./Sacramento St., (415) 885-1699. L&D daily; $-$$. Highchairs, boosters, booths, child portions. Reservations accepted Sept-May.*

Sitting in one of the roomy booths positioned on raised platforms around the perimeter of the cavernous dining room here (it was formerly a new car showroom) allows first-rate people-watching. Bizarre wall decorations include half a Cadillac convertible, Elvis's rhinestone-bedecked white cape, and Kurt Cobain's guitar. And, as might be expected from the name, rock & roll blasts out at ear-splitting levels. Considering the sensory overload and the fact that many people come here to look and to be seen, it is impressive that the American-style food is quite good, the service attentive, and the prices reasonable. The house salad is crisp, cold romaine lettuce, and the housemade Thousand Island dressing is tangy with fresh onion. Hamburgers are served on whole wheat sesame buns and are just plain good. The menu also offers an assortment of sandwiches, housemade chili, grilled fresh fish, and rich, old-fashioned desserts. A plethora of souvenir items can be ordered at the table and added to the tab.

Hornblower Cruises *Pier 33, Bay St./The Embarcadero, (415) 788-8866, fax (415) 394-8251; www.hornblower.com. L, call for schedule, $35; D daily, $69-$81; Sat&SunBr, $55; children 4-12 half price, under 4 free. Reservations required.*

Cruises board 1/2-hour before departure. Diners at brunch are seated as they board, and the maitre d' announces to each table when it is their turn to visit the bounteous buffet. Magnificent views of San Francisco and the bay are enjoyed as the boat goes out under the Golden Gate Bridge, past Sausalito and Angel Island, and beside Alcatraz. Live music plays in the background, and the Captain makes the rounds to greet everyone. After dining, there is time to tour the vessel. The four-course dinner is more formal, with waiters serving diners. Special events are often scheduled. Note that though highchairs and booster seats are not available, parents are welcome to bring strollers with wheel locks on board, and children are given crayons and coloring books to keep them busy.

House of Prime Rib *1906 Van Ness Ave./Washington St., (415) 885-4605. D daily; $$$. Highchairs, boosters, booths, child portions. Reservations advised. Valet parking.*

The specialty of the house in this posh spot is the finest aged prime rib—served right from the cart and carved to order table-side. (In fact, the only other entree on the menu is grilled fresh fish.) Choose a City Cut (for small appetites), an English Cut (several thin slices), or a King Henry VIII Cut (for those with king-size appetites). The complete dinner includes a chilled green salad prepared at the table and presented with *chilled* forks, bread and butter, either mashed potatoes and gravy or a baked potato, fresh horseradish sauce, creamed fresh spinach, and Yorkshire pudding. Come here hungry.

Hunan Restaurant *924 Sansome St./Broadway, outskirts of North Beach, (415) 956-7727. L&D daily; $-$$. Boosters. Reservations accepted.*

Once upon a time this was a tiny, obscure restaurant located in Chinatown. It seated 29 people. Then it was described in *The New Yorker* as "the best Chinese restaurant in the world." Lines formed, and it was no longer possible to just saunter in and sit down at one of the few tables or at the counter, where half the pleasure was in watching the cooks in action. To satisfy demand, the restaurant moved to this huge warehouse, which seats 314 and permits instant seating once again. The kitchen uses unsaturated oils, lean meats, and skinned chicken, and it uses no MSG or sugar; salt-free dishes are available. Appetizer dumplings here are like pot stickers only spicy hot; the unusual Diana's Special consists of spicy meat sauce and lettuce sandwiched between two deep-fried flour pancakes. Harvest pork (a traditional dish fed to farm workers and pallbearers to give them strength), hot and sour chicken, and bean sprout salad are all especially good, as is the cold chicken salad mixed with shredded cucumbers, shiny noodles, and peanut dressing. Specialties include excellent fresh seafood dishes and unusual house-smoked ham, chicken, and duck cured over hickory wood, tea leaves, and orange peels. The distinctive hot bean sauce—a combination of fermented black beans, powdered red peppers, garlic, oil, and vinegar—is available to go. With some of this sauce and a souvenir copy of the owner's book, *Henry Chung's Hunan Style Chinese Cookbook,* available at check-out, it is possible to try out more of these unusual dishes at home.

Branches are located at 1016 Bryant Street *(at 8th St., (415) 861-5808. L&D M-Sat.)* and 674 Sacramento Street *(at Kearny St., (415) 788-2234. L&D M-F.).*

Jackson Fillmore Trattoria *2506 Fillmore St./ Jackson St., Upper Fillmore, (415) 346-5288. D daily; $$. Highchairs, boosters. Reservations advised; accepted only for 3+.*

Those who show up here without reservations usually find themselves standing in a line that stretches out the door. Even those with reservations can wind up sitting at crowded tables or on a stool at the counter. However, the exceptional antipastos and pastas make it all worthwhile. Cloud-like gnocchi, fresh fish items, and truffle dishes are also served, and a classic zabaglione is the perfect dessert.

Japanese Restaurants. See page 39.

John's Grill *63 Ellis St./Powell St., near Union Square, (415) 986-DASH, (415) 982-2583; www.johnsgrill.com. L&D M-Sat; $-$$. Highchairs, boosters, booths.*

One of the settings in Dashiell Hammett's *The Maltese Falcon,* this restaurant's cozy interior features its original gaslight fixtures, some original period furnishings, and mahogany-paneled walls covered with photos of famous patrons and old San Francisco scenes. The lunch menu offers a variety of salads as well as a hamburger, several pastas, and that hard-to-find Hangtown fry (an early California dish prepared with oysters and eggs). Dinner brings on extensive seafood selections. One of the most popular dishes is straight-out-of-the-book Sam Spade's Chops (broiled rack of lamb with a baked potato and sliced tomatoes). This is one of only two national literary landmarks in California (the other is City Lights bookstore).

Just Desserts *248 Church St./Market St., Upper Market, (415) 626-5774, fax (415) 626-7212; www.justdesserts.com. Daily 8am-11pm; $. Booths. No reservations.*

Bakery cases here are filled with goodies such as almond croissants, black-bottom cupcakes, chocolate chip cookies, and a variety of pastries, muffins, cheesecakes, and pies. Personal favorites are the cakes, which include such wonders as carrot cake with cream cheese frosting, chocolate fudge cake with a rich fudge frosting, lemon cake topped with a choice of lemon or bittersweet chocolate glaze, and sublime weekend cake—devil's food with cream cheese frosting and a mocha filling. And on and on. And although they *are* fattening, they are made *without* preservatives, artificial colorings, or artificial flavorings.

Branches are all over town: Three Embarcadero Center *((415) 421-1609);* 836 Irving Street *(at 10th Ave., the Sunset,*

(415) 681-1277); 3735 Buchanan Street *(at Marina Blvd., near Fort Mason, (415) 922-8373).*

Katia's: A Russian Tearoom *600 5th Ave./ Balboa St., the Sunset, (415) 668-9292. L Tu-F, D Tu-Sun; $$. Reservations taken.*

Located in the heart of San Francisco's Russian neighborhood, among sidestreets filled with interesting vintage houses, this intimate restaurant offers entree into a different world. By all means start with the traditional thick beet and cabbage borscht. Prizes among the main courses are breaded chicken cutlets Pozharski, and golubtsi—cabbage leaves stuffed with ground beef. For dessert, boiled cheese dumplings topped with exquisite fresh sour cream should not be missed. A live guitarist plays some evenings.

Across the street, teeny, tiny **Globus** (*332 Balboa St., (415) 668-4723, same fax; Tu-Sat 12-5.*) specializes in selling Slavic books.

Khan Toke Thai House *5937 Geary Blvd./24th Ave., the Richmond, (415) 668-6654. D daily; $. Boosters. Reservations advised.*

Diners remove their shoes in the entryway before entering a maze of lushly decorated small dining rooms. Most diners recline on floor pillows at richly embellished tables, but some tables are also available with wells in the floor underneath, into which legs can dangle. Many of the unusual Thai herbs used in preparing dishes for the extensive, well-executed menu are grown in a courtyard behind the restaurant. An all-inclusive dinner includes an appetizer of fried fish cakes, spicy and sour shrimp soup, a green salad, a choice of two entrees, either a pudding or fried banana, and hot tea or coffee. Also, a good selection of vegetarian items is available.

La Mediterranée *2210 Fillmore St./California St., Upper Fillmore, (415) 921-2956; and 288 Noe St./Market St., the Castro, (415) 431-7210.*

For description, see page 260.

La Taqueria *2889 Mission St./25th St., the Mission, (415) 285-7117. L&D daily; $. Highchairs. No reservations. No cards.*

To experience fast food Mexican-style, step through one of the two arches here and head to the counter to place an order. Then pick a table, and kick back. Entertainment is provided by a colorful folk mural decorating one wall, by cooks in the open kitchen busily preparing orders, and by a jukebox with Mexican music. The menu is simple. Choose between tacos made with two steamed corn tortillas and burritos made with flour tortillas. Fillings are a choice of pork, beef, sausage, chicken, or vegetarian (beans and cheese). Pinto beans and fresh tomato salsa round things out; avocado and sour cream cost a bit more. Depending on the season, delicious housemade fresh fruit juices include strawberry, cantaloupe, orange, banana, and pineapple.

Walk-away desserts can be picked up next door at **Dianda's Italian-American Pastry** (*(415) 647-5469*), where everything is made from scratch and the cannoli are particularly good.

Le Colonial *20 Cosmo Pl./off Taylor & Post, near Union Square, (415) 931-3600, fax (415) 931-2933. L M-F, D daily; $$$. Reservations advised. Valet parking.*

Operating on the site that was formerly home to legendary Trader Vic's, this branch in a successful upscale chain brings accomplished Vietnamese cuisine to town. (Other branches are in New York, Philadelphia, Chicago, and Los Angeles.) With a tropical decor evoking 1920s Vietnam—vintage black-and-white photos of turn-of-the-century Saigon adorn the walls while ceiling fans quietly and gently stir the air—the outdoor verandah and elegant interior dining rooms offer sanctuary from the street bustle. Among the appetizers are several kinds of spring rolls and a tasty steamed crêpe dumpling stuffed with chicken, woodear mushrooms, and bean sprouts. Main courses include a delicate sea bass fillet steamed in a banana leaf and a flavorful tiger prawns-mango-eggplant-basil-coconut curry. Unusual dishes include abalone and scallop tempura with roasted seaweed, and wok-sautéed morning glories with minced garlic. Fresh tropical fruit and housemade sorbet and cookies are winning desserts. An inviting upstairs lounge serves an hors d'oeuvres menu and presents live jazz on Friday evenings after 7 and Sunday after 8.

Leon's Bar-B-Q *2800 Sloat Blvd./46th Ave., the Sunset, (415) 681-3071. L&D daily; $. Highchairs, boosters, booths. No reservations.*

Located across the street from the zoo, this tiny, extremely casual spot is known for delicious, messy pork ribs slathered with a tangy sweet sauce. Good beef ribs, hot links, and barbecued chicken are also available. Meals come with a corn muffin and choice of baked beans, spaghetti, potato salad, or coleslaw. The menu is rounded out with a half-pound hamburger, housemade chili, and tiny pecan and sweet potato pies. Everything can be prepared to go, and the picnic area in the zoo or the nearby beach are both good places to take it.

Little City *673 Union St./Powell St., North Beach, (415) 434-2900; www.littlecitysf.com. L M-F, D daily, Sat & Sun Br; $$. Reservations suggested.*

Though seating is tight, the ambiance here is cheery and cozy, and many tables offer views of the sidewalk parade. Heated outside seating is also available. Tables in the back room have the additional interest of walls filled with vintage black-and-white photos depicting the area's beatnik days. Speaking of which, the restaurant also continues to attract Lawrence Ferlinghetti, star beatnik poet and currently the city's poet laureate. The menu offers interesting antipasti (baked Brie and roasted garlic; grilled eggplant timbale), distinctive salads (carmelized walnuts with fresh pear and Roquefort cheese), housemade pastas and a risotto of the day, and heartier fish and meat entrees. A hamburger served with housemade chips is also available. Dessert includes the ubiquitous tiramisu but also a fabulously flavorful blackberry-ginger sorbetto.

Liverpool Lil's *2942 Lyon St./Lombard St., the Presidio, (415) 921-6664. L M-F, Sat & Sun Br, D daily; $-$$.*

This atmosphereic pub serves a limited menu—a decent hamburger and a few finger foods—in its cozy front alcoves and in a small area outside the entrance that is inviting on a warm day. The on-tap brews are refreshing, and two TVs are tuned to sports. A larger menu is available in the popular back dining room,

Lovejoy's Tea Room *1351 Church St./Clipper St., Noe Valley, (415) 648-5895. Tu-Sun 11-6; $. Reservations taken for 4+.*

Cozy as anything encountered in England, this tiny, absolutely charming spot provides a welcome retreat from the city streets. And diners can shop while they sip: Everything is for sale—from the tea cups to the furniture. The menu offers all things English—toasted crumpets, scones, tea sandwiches, sausage rolls, pasties. Tea service ranges from a simple cream tea to an expansive high tea, and a special Wee Tea is served to children. I say, old chap, what fun!

LuLu Restaurant *816 Folsom St./4th St., South of Market, (415) 495-5775, fax (415) 495-7810; www.lulu.com. B,L,&D daily; $$. Highchairs, boosters. Reservations advised. Valet parking at D.*

Outrageously popular, this casual restaurant operates in the large, open, high-ceilinged room of a converted 1910 warehouse. The house specialty is simply-prepared foods of the French and Italian Riviera served family style. Especially tasty items include almost anything from the wood-fired rotisserie or oven, but especially tasty items include an appetizer of delicate fritto misto with artichokes and an entree of crisp rosemary-scented roast chicken. Among the unusual nightly specials are suckling pig on Friday and air-dried duck on Saturday. An adjoining cafe serves the same menu but takes no reservations.

MacArthur Park *607 Front St./Jackson St., Financial District, (415) 398-5700. L M-F, D daily; $$. Reservations advised.*

For description, see page 167.

Magic Flute Garden Restaurant *3673 Sacramento St./Spruce St., Pacific Heights, (415) 922-1225, fax (415) 922-1257. L M-F, Sat&SunBr, D W-Sat; $-$$. Highchairs, boosters. Reservations advised.*

Located within a lovely vintage Edwardian on a low-key, high-quality shopping street, this pleasant spot offers comfortable indoor tables as well as outdoor seating in a garden, weather permitting. The manicured Tuscan-style garden is furnished with Italian market umbrellas and marble tables with iron chairs. It has heat lamps and is partly tented. Inside, the colorful work of local artists decorates the walls. Lunch items include smoked trout, soothing polenta spiced up with a pepper sauce, and a great Black Angus ground chuck hamburger on a housemade bun with sides of pommes frites, a Napa greens salad, and a kosher pickle. At brunch, the menu changes to cheese blintzes, Belgian waffles, and fresh seafood. The tempting desserts, which usually include an array of cakes (the double fudge chocolate cake is a house specialty), are all housemade by their own pastry chef.

Mama's on Washington Square *1701 Stockton St./Filbert St., North Beach, (415) 362-6421. B&L Tu-Sun; $$. Highchairs, boosters. No reservations. No cards.*

Located on a corner of Washington Square, this cozy, cheery, often crowded spot has cafeteria-style service. Breakfast choices include blueberry pancakes, thick French toast made from various breads, a variety of omelettes, and fresh-squeezed citrus juices. Lunch brings on salads, sandwiches, hamburgers, hot dogs, and a zucchini and cheese frittata. Delicious desserts and fresh strawberry creations—even out of season—are a house specialty.

Marrakech *419 O'Farrell St./Taylor St., near Union Square, (415) 776-6717. D daily; $$. Reservations accepted. Valet parking on Sat.*

After passing through the doors of this oasis in the urban jungle, diners enter the enveloping womb-like warmth of an exotic Middle Eastern bazaar. Resembling a posh adult playpen, the main room has comfortable padded benches and round tables circling the perimeter with low stools as supplemental seating. Diners have a choice of six complete dinners. The traditional Moroccan foods include a kaleidoscope plate of colorful vegetable salads, a flaky bastella pastry filled with a sweet chicken-toasted almond mixture, and couscous. Main course choices include a simple but divine chicken with lemon and olives as well as several rabbit, lamb, and shrimp dishes. Belly dancing is scheduled nightly. Families fit in fine here, and are usually given a corner area with more space.

Masa's *648 Bush St./Powell St., in Hotel Vintage Court, near Union Square, (800) 258-7694, (415) 989-7154, fax (415) 989-3141. D Tu-Sat; $$$. Closed most of Jan. Reservations essential. Valet parking.*

This highly acclaimed, elegant, and very expensive restaurant serves a menu of classic French cuisine at tables set luxuriously with Hutschenreuther china and Christofle silver. Guests are expected to dress accordingly, with men in coat and tie. Menu highlights include shellfish and game dishes—such as lobster salad with truffle vinaigrette, and roast breast of pheasant with morels and pears—and a dessert tasting platter. Adding intrigue, the restaurant bears the name of its founding chef, Masa Kobayashi, who was murdered off the premises long ago in a still unsolved case.

Max's Diner *311 3rd St./Folsom St., South of Market, (415) 546-MAXS; www.maxsworld.com. L&D daily; $$. Boosters, booths. Reservations accepted.*

Specializing in serving large portions of '50s food, this popular spot continues the theme with lots of chrome and Formica, miniature tabletop jukeboxes filled with '50s tunes, comfortable oversize vinyl booths that offer privacy to families, and waitresses dressed in black-and-white uniforms and bobby sox. The extensive menu offers crispy-coated chicken-fried steak, New York deli-style sandwiches, a gigantic hamburger with bacon and cheese, and a blue-plate special of well-seasoned, moist meatloaf served with tasty made-from-scratch mashed potatoes indented with a gravy-filled crater. A few appetizers and side dishes are a meal in themselves: country-style ribs, sliders (baby burgers), spicy chicken wings with blue cheese dip, giant onion rings, a salad (a wedge of iceberg lettuce topped with housemade dressing), slaw, and tasty housemade chili. Among Max's famous gargantuan desserts are a tapioca pudding layered with strawberries and topped with whipped cream, a bread pudding with vanilla sauce, a delicious seven-layer cookie topped with hot fudge and ice cream, and a large selection of ice cream concoctions. To top it all off, each diner receives a piece of Bazooka bubble gum with the check.

Across town, **Max's Opera Cafe** *(601 Van*

Ness Ave./Golden Gate Ave., Civic Center, (415) 771-7300. L&D daily; $$. Boosters, booths. No reservations.) offers similar fare but with the added bonus of talented servers who also take turns serving entertaining stints singing at the mike between 7 and 11 p.m.

McCormick & Kuleto's Seafood Restaurant *900 North Point, in Ghirardelli Square, Fisherman's Wharf, (415) 929-1730. L&D daily; $$-$$$. Highchairs, boosters, booths, child menu. Reservations advised. Validated parking in Ghirardelli Square garage.*

Spectacular views are available from most tables in this splendidly appointed seafood restaurant, though the half-circle booths on the second of three tiers are choice. High ceilings, floor-to-ceiling leaded glass windows, and fantastical light fixtures add to the overall elegant ambiance. The extensive menu, which changes daily, is designed to please every appetite. Starters include delicious crab cakes; sweet, crisp rock shrimp popcorn; and a satisfying, nicely seasoned clam chowder. Among the many seafood dishes, which are fresh whenever possible, are an excellent pan-fried petrale sole with caper-lemon butter and a delicious blackened sea bass with a side of homey mashed potatoes. Pastas, salads, sandwiches, and a variety of meats round things out. Desserts—perhaps a plate-size fresh peach tart with a flaky crust and crème fraîche topping, or a banana cream pie with fresh caramel sauce—are not an afterthought.

The restaurant's more casual **Crab Cake Lounge** offers the same incredible view with a less expensive, less extensive menu and the additional options of pizza and a hamburger.

Mel's Drive-In *2165 Lombard St./Fillmore St., the Marina, (415) 921-2867. B,L,&D daily; $. Highchairs, boosters, booths, child menu. No reservations. No cards. Free parking lot adjoins.*

When Mel's was a *real* drive-in, carhops brought trays out to clamp on windows for in-car dining. Now the eating goes on inside the restaurant. Seating is at a long counter, in booths, or at tables with chairs, and an oldie but goodie can be played for two bits on a computerized mini-jukebox. (An interesting aside: Jukeboxes were invented in San Francisco in 1888.) Dress is just-off-the-jogging-trail casual. Menu items include the Famous Melburger with all the trimmings, a variety of veggie burgers, fries with the skins still on, and, of course, big onion rings. All this, plus salads, soups, and sandwiches galore. For more substantial appetites, the menu also offers a chicken pot pie, meat loaf served with lumpy mashed potatoes and gravy, and the day's blue-plate special. Among the drinks are flavored cokes and thick, old-fashioned milkshakes made with Carnation deluxe ice cream and served in the mixer tin. Desserts include chocolate fudge cake, banana cream pie, and a banana split. Teens call this place "cool."

A branch at 3355 Geary Boulevard *(at Stanyan St., Presidio Heights, (415) 387-2244.)* is the exact location of one of the three original Mels.

Mike's Chinese Cuisine *5145 Geary Blvd./16th Ave., the Richmond, (415) 752-0120. D W-M; $$. Boosters. No reservations.*

Located far from the crush of Chinatown, this is one of the best Chinese restaurants in town. Tables are covered with white linens, and the tastefully decorated, well-insulated downstairs dining room keeps the noise level low. House specialties include crispy chicken, a cold shredded barbecued chicken salad. and Peking duck (order one day in advance). More winners include a spicy, fragrant hot and sour soup, an incredible smoky and tender Mongolian beef served on a bed of crispy rice noodles, and a large selection of colorful sweet and sour dishes and pan-fried chow mein noodle items that are popular with children.

Millennium *246 McAllister St./Larkin St., in the Abigail Hotel, Civic Center, (415) 487-9800, fax (415) 487-9921. L Tu-F, D Tu-Sun; $$. Reservations advised.*

Specializing in richly flavored vegan and vegetarian cuisine, this stylish restaurant operates in a hotel's transformed carriage house. The eclectic menu also interests non-vegetarians, especially those watching their fat intake. No animal products are used, most items are prepared with little or no oil, and organic ingredients are used whenever possible. Menu selections might include a crisp sesame-shitake phyllo spring roll or a stack composed of sautéed vegetables, smoked tofu, and barley salad flavored with Thai green curry sauce. Delicious desserts adhere to the program, too, including a Mad Good Chocolate Cake with a ganache center served with coconut sorbet and caramel-rum sauce. Beverages include a selection of premium California wines as well as interesting non-alcoholic drinks, including ginger beers and housemade herbal elixirs. Once a month, on the Sunday evening closest to the full moon, an Aphrodisiac Night package is offered that includes a four-course, fixed-price menu of aphrodisiac delights, plus a room for the night in the hotel.

Moose's *1652 Stockton St./Union St., North Beach, (415) 989-7800, fax (415) 989-7838; www.mooses.com. L Thur & F, D daily; $$$. Highchairs, boosters. Reservations advised. Valet parking.*

A large, open room at this always bustling spot makes most tables good ones, and carpeting keeps the din to a minimum. Live piano music in the evenings adds to the inviting atmosphere. Samples from the eclectic, ever-changing menu include both asparagus soup accented with prawns and fresh oven-roasted chicken breast with housemade gnocchi and roasted artichokes, and the menu always has a pasta, pizza, and Moose Burger. Save room for an unusual dessert, which might be a lemon-scented vanilla rice pudding or a warm mango and coconut cream tart. Tea lovers will appreciate the rare varieties, including jasmine pearls and monkey-picked Tikuanyin.

North Beach Pizza *1499 Grant Ave./Union St., North Beach, (415) 433-2444. L&D daily; $. Boosters, booths. No reservations.*

Lacking pretension and finesse, this restaurant serves an unfussy kind of pizza in a relaxed, easy atmosphere. The pepperoni and cheese and the spicy-hot sausage versions are both particularly tasty, with an excellent crust, and a salad tossed with the creamy house Italian dressing is the perfect accompaniment. An outstanding cannelloni is among the pasta choices, and barbecued ribs and chicken plus a submarine sandwich are also on the menu.

A branch is one block up the street at 1310 *((415) 433-2444).*

One Market Restaurant *1 Market St./Steuart St., the Embarcadero, (415) 777-5577, fax (415) 777-4411. L M-F, D daily, SunBr; $$$. Highchairs, boosters. Valet parking.*

Situated in a scenic corner of an attractive historic building dating from 1917, just across from the bay, the airy, substantial interior of this popular restaurant is a delight to be in. It is co-owned by celebrity chef Bradley Ogden. On his all-American menu, appetizers include items such as crab cakes and barbecued oysters. For entrees, the changing menu might offer tender Yankee pot roast with roasted turnips and potatoes, or succulent rosemary-roasted chicken breast with three kinds of garlic mashed potatoes and wild mushrooms. For dessert, expect new takes on old favorites—strawberry shortcake with orange ice cream, peach cobbler topped with a dab of fresh peach sorbet—plus stellar cookies and fruit sorbets. A Sunday jazz brunch offers a menu of breakfast favorites, and the kitchen makes English muffins from scratch for the eggs Benedict.

Palomino Euro Bistro *345 Spear St./Steuart St., in Hills Plaza, the Embarcadero, (415) 512-7400, fax (415) 512-0648; www.palominosf.com. L&D daily; $$-$$$. Highchairs, boosters, child menu. Reservations advised. Validated parking.*

Offering a great view of the Bay Bridge, this bustling spot has a raised seating area, unusual glass lighting fixtures, and interior palm trees that echo those lining the street outside. Kids get a color-in place mat to occupy them while parents contemplate a more sophisticated menu. All dinners start with a crusty loaf of bread and a delicious crushed tomato-Feta cheese-kalamata olive spread. Crisp hearts of Romaine deliciously tossed with a creamy herb vinaigrette, toasted pine nuts, and Gorgonzola makes a choice appetizer before an entree of either fish or a spit-roasted meat. Kids might enjoy a pasta or the pizza with cracker-thin crust prepared in an apple wood-fired oven. Sixteen beers are on tap, and a large selection of wine varietals are available by the glass.

Perry's *1944 Union St./Laguna St., Pacific Heights, (415) 922-9022. B&L M-F, Sat & SunBr, D daily; $$.*

Consistency is a strong point at this popular watering hole. Drinks are strong and tasty, and the cafe food seems always just as remembered. A good hamburger comes on a Kaiser roll with a side of thin, greaseless fried potato rounds, and a neatly chopped corned beef hash is topped with two poached eggs. Chops, steaks, and fresh fish items flesh out the menu. For dessert, try the housemade apple brown Betty or one of the array of delights brought in from Just Desserts. Unfortunately, the wait-service can be less than attentive. Atmospheres vary: sidewalk tables, the boisterous bar area, the dark but quiet back room, and a sunny, sky-lighted back porch.

A branch is at 185 Sutter Street *(at Kearny St., (415) 989-6895).*

Picnic Pick-Ups.

• **Andronico's** *1200 Irving St./Funston Ave., near Golden Gate Park, (415) 661-3220. Daily 7am-11pm.*

For description, see page 262.

• **Anna's Danish Cookie Co.** *3560 18th St./ Valencia, the Mission, (415) 863-3882, fax (415) 863-7408. Open Tu-Sat 8:30am-5pm. $6.85/ pound.*

Sold nowhere but at this store, Anna's Danish butter cookies have been made here since 1933. Buy just a few, or a box or tin filled to the brim.

• **Lucca Delicatessen** *2120 Chestnut St./Steiner St., the Marina, (415) 921-7873. M-F 9-6:30, Sat & Sun 9-6. No cards.*

Owned by the same family since 1929, this deli prices its made-to-order sandwiches by weight. Housemade salads, handmade bread sticks, and a large selection of Italian wines are also available.

• **A North Beach Picnic.**

Florence Italian Delicatessen & Ravioli Factory *(1412 Stockton St./Vallejo St., (415) 421-6170. M-Sat 7-7, Sun 9-3.)* is a traditional Italian deli that has been in business since the 1920s. Across the street, **Panelli Bros. Italian Delicatessen** *(1419 Stockton St./Vallejo St., (415) 421-2541. M-Sat 7-5:30.)* has been around almost as long. Then there's **Molinari Delicatessen** *(373 Columbus Ave./Vallejo St., (415) 421-2337; M-F 8-6, Sat 7:30-5:30.)*, which has been on its present corner since 1912 and claims to be the oldest Italian deli in town. All can provide the makings for a great picnic. Dash into one of the Chinese markets for some fresh fruit, and into **Victoria Pastry Co.** *(1362 Stockton St./ Vallejo St., (415) 781-2015. M-Sat 7-6, Sun 8-5.)* for a dessert—perhaps a cannoli or their specialty St. Honoré cake—and that's picnicking North Beach-style!

• **Say Cheese** *856 Cole St./Carl St., Haight-Ashbury, (415) 665-5020. M- Sat 10-7, Sun 10-5.*

A variety of sandwiches, salads, pâtés, crackers, cheese spreads, and fresh cookies are available, plus almost 300 kinds of cheese.

• **Shenson's Kosher Style Delicatessen** *5120 Geary Blvd./15th Ave., (415) 751-4699. Daily 8-5:45. Highchairs.*

This fragrant spot has been making picnickers happy since 1933. Among the offerings are blintzes, pastries (including a delicious cherry strudel), housemade Kosher dill pickles and pickled tomatoes, and a great corned beef with coleslaw and Russian dressing on rye.

• **Sweet Things** *3585 California St./Spruce St., in Cal-Mart in Laurel Village, the Richmond, (415) 221-8583; M-Sat 8-7, Sun 9-6.*

For description, see page 196.

• **Vivande Porta Via** *2125 Fillmore St./ California St., Upper Fillmore, (415) 346-4430. Daily 10-10. 1 highchair.*

All items here are prepared in the heavenly smelling open kitchen and are, in keeping with the literal meaning of the deli's name, "food to carry away." The Italian fare varies, but main dishes might include succulent roasted chicken, mushroom or chicken turnovers in a flaky crust, or torta Milanese (a tall pie layered with ham, spinach, and cheese). Salads include cannellini beans and caviar, caponata (eggplant with raisins and pine nuts), and several fresh pastas. Sandwiches are made to order with freshly baked breads, and tempting dolci (sweets) beckon from a display case. Comfortable seating is also available for dining on the premises.

Plouf *40 Belden Pl./Bush St., Financial District, (415) 986-6491, fax (415) 986-6492; www.plouf.com. L M-F, D M-Sat; $$. Reservations advised.*

Specializing in steamed mussels and offering eight different versions, this seafood bistro is so contemporary French that after just a few minutes diners feel they've been beamed onto the French Riviera. One waiter witnessed here, dressed in a white-and-black-striped shirt and sporting a charming, authentic French accent, could do no wrong. He brought a huge iron pot full of mussels pastis (about 50 or 60 prepared with fennel, tomato, and onion) with a side of perfect thin, crisp pommes frites, and he regularly removed bowls of discarded shells. More seafood items are on the menu, including fish & chips with aioli sauce, along with a variety of meats and several pastas. Good wine choices straight out of France include Muscadet, Sancerre, and Burgundy. For dessert, don't miss the profiteroles—little cream puff shells filled with banana ice cream and topped with warm chocolate and caramel sauces. Outside, tables fill the alley (closed to cars) just as they do in the south of France, however the weather here isn't as divine as it is there, so heat lamps attempt to take off the chill. The dining room features a high, pressed-tin ceiling and has booths as well as a bank of intimate bench-and-chair tables for two. In sync with the name, which translates as "splash," stuffed sports fish decorate the walls.

Polly Ann Ice Cream *3142 Noriega St./39th Ave., Outer Sunset, (415) 664-2472. Daily 11-10, F & Sat to 11; $. No cards.*

Claiming to be the only ice cream store in the world where both dogs and babies get a free ice cream cone, this small shop is notable for yet other reasons. Where else is there a constantly changing choice of over 425 flavors of ice cream? Where else does the owner make all of his own ice cream and smile happily as he declares, "Tonight I think I'll make watermelon"? At least 52 flavors are available every day. Some are seasonal, and some are trendy—like Batman (black-colored vanilla with lemon swirls) and Star Wars (blue-colored vanilla with rainbow marshmallows). Among the many unusual flavors are sunflower seed, vegetable, red bean, chocolate-peanut butter, and American beauty made with rose petals. Believe it or not, some very traditional flavors are also available, and vanilla is always the number one best seller. According to the owner, "Anything is possible."

Postrio *545 Post St./Mason St., in the Prescott Hotel, near Union Square, (415) 776-7825, fax (415) 776-6702. B M-F, L M-Sat, D daily, SunBr; $$-$$$. Highchairs, boosters, booths. Reservations advised. Valet parking.*

Owned by Los Angeles celebrity chef Wolfgang Puck, and referred to inelegantly by some as Puck's Place, this grand spot is entered via a dramatic staircase leading down to an attractive contemporary dining room. It is a place to see, to be seen, and to enjoy a fabulous meal. Among the California-style cuisine, with Mediterranean and Asian accents, are such specialties as fried quail with pineapple glaze and Chinese-style duck with mango sauce. Desserts are generally excellent. As would be expected in any restaurant owned by Mr. Puck, a bar menu with great pizzas is also available. And don't overlook having a power breakfast here. The menu then features fresh crab omelettes, sourdough waffles, and breakfast pizzas.

Prego *2000 Union St./Buchanan St., Pacific Heights, (415) 563-3305. L&D daily; $$-$$$. Highchairs, boosters. Reservations advised.*

Said to have originally introduced to the San Francisco restaurant scene such now-standard items as tiramisu and buffalo mozzarella, this popular spot also seems to be a magnet for celebrities. Any of the various dining rooms seem choice—the bustling bar area has some tables with a great view of the sidewalk scene, while several other rooms have comfortable booth seating. A great way to start is with several antipasti—perhaps a Parma prosciutto with fruit, or deep-fried eggplant with garlic and tomato sauce. In fact, the assorted appetizer platter can make a satisfying light meal. Contorni such as roasted Yukon Gold potatoes with rosemary and garlic, polenta, and pan-braised greens are also available. Pastas here are housemade and exceptional, with wonderful renditions such as fazzoletti al salmone (large green and white-striped raviolis filled with fresh salmon, mozzarella, and arugula and topped with a delicate tomato cream sauce) and mezzelune alle melanzane (half-moon spinach pockets filled with ricotta and topped with grilled eggplant, fresh tomato, and fresh basil). Pizzas and calzone, along with fresh fish and assorted meat dishes, round out the menu. Among the desserts is a plate of housemade cookies that are perfect with a cappuccino.

Red Crane *115 Clement St./12th Ave., the Richmond, (415) 751-7226, (415) 386-5979. L&D daily; $. Highchairs, boosters.*

Good service and delicious interpretations of Chinese vegetarian and seafood dishes makes this otherwise simple neighborhood restaurant quite popular. Menu winners include vegetarian pot stickers, hot braised string beans in a tasty sauce, and Szechwan eggplant. Gluten and bean curd substitute for meat in many dishes, and there is an extensive seafood menu.

Rubicon *558 Sacramento St./Montgomery St., Financial District, (415) 434-4100, fax (415) 421-7648; www.myriadrestaurantgroup.com. L M-F, D M-Sat; $$$. Reservations advised. Valet parking at D.*

With celebrity investors including Robin Williams, Francis Ford Coppola, and Robert DeNiro, this bustling, sophisticated spot seems to have no choice but to be a hit. The two-level dining area is tucked between attractive brick walls decorated with modern art, and beams criss-cross near windows as an earthquake safety measure. Diners can choose between two fixed-price menus as well as from an a la carte menu. Full-flavored dishes include items such as rock shrimp ravioli, pan-roasted chicken on garlic mashed potatoes, and tasty oven-roasted venison with root vegetable hash. Exceptional desserts are prepared by a special pastry chef and include delights such as coconut cake topped with mango ice cream, chocolate truffle cake, and cookies and housemade cherry ice cream. This restaurant is known for its impressive wine list and temperature-controlled cellar.

Scott's Seafood Grill & Bar *2400 Lombard St., the Marina, (415) 563-8988; and 3 Embarcadero Center, (415) 981-0622.*

For description, see page 289.

Sears *439 Powell St./Sutter St., Union Square, (415) 986-1160. B&L W-Sun; $. Boosters. No reservations. No cards.*

Known for its extensive menu, this busy downtown institution is caught in a '50s time warp. A wait in line is usually required before being seated at one of the tables covered with lacy tablecloths under protective see-through plastic. Seating is often faster at the counter, with its convenient hooks underneath for purses and where everyone seems to know the waitresses. Breakfast is available all day and includes silver dollar pancakes, crisp waffles, French toast served with homemade strawberry preserves, banana-nut bread, an imposing fresh fruit bowl (a must in summer), a huge baked apple with cream, and housemade yogurt.

Soku's Teriyaki & Sushi *2280 Chestnut St./Scott St., the Marina, (415) 563-0162. L&D M-Sat; $. 1 highchair, 1 booster.*

What's lacking in atmosphere here is more than made up for in delicious bargain fare and fast service. The extensive menu offers a surprisingly large choice of traditional Japanese items: teriyaki, tempura, sashimi, sukiyaki, nabe, sushi, donburi, udon noodles, and more. Dessert is ice cream in either green tea or tempura flavor.

South Park Cafe *108 South Park Ave./2nd St., South of Market, (415) 495-7275. B,L,&D M-F; on Sat D only. Highchairs, boosters. Reservations accepted for D.*

With large windows overlooking the small and popular park that fills the center oval of this unique street (designed originally to resemble London's Berkeley Square), this is a great place to sit down for a continental breakfast or simple lunch. Somehow reminiscent of a New York City cafe, it is actually French-owned.

Just a few doors down, **Lumbini** *(156 South Park Ave., (415) 896-2998, fax (415) 896-2995. M-F 9:30-6.)* purveys an eclectic collection of unusual accent items for the home.

Speckmann's *1550 Church St./Duncan St., Noe Valley, (415) 282-6850. L&D daily; $-$$. 1 highchair, boosters. Reservations advised.*

If someone were dropped into this restaurant blindfolded, they very well might be convinced they were in Germany when the blindfold was removed. Waitresses wear lacy tops and white aprons, tables are covered with red-and-white-checked cloths, and some of the patrons converse in German. When additionally offered a menu with a variety of German specialties, it isn't a stretch to imagine being in Germany itself. Diners can sit in either a restaurant-like winestube in front or in a more informal bierstube adjacent to a bar in back. Menu choices include Ungarisches goulasch (Hungarian goulash with spatzle), sauerbraten (marinated beef with potato pancakes), an assortment of schnitzels, and several wursts (sausages). Imported and draft beers are, of course, available. The dessert tray is heavy with strudels and rich pastries, including a traditional Black Forest cake. A take-out delicatessen also operates on the premises.

Stars *555 Golden Gate Ave./Van Ness Ave., Civic Center, (415) 861-7827, fax (415) 554-0351. L M-F, D daily; $$-$$$. Highchairs, boosters, booths. Reservations advised. Valet parking at D.*

No longer owned by celebrity chef Jeremiah Tower, this popular restaurant has changed but still offers a good meal. All seats seem to be good seats, with many comfortable booths permitting most diners good views of the surrounding action. The menu of rustic regional cuisine changes daily, with the crispy-skinned wood-roasted chicken and juicy spit-roasted meats being standouts. Desserts are all winners, especially the flavorful caramel pot de crème with Belgian nut cookies. Specialty cocktails prepared at San Francisco's longest bar add to the fun.

The Steps of Rome Trattoria *362 Columbus Ave./Grant St., North Beach, (415) 986-6480, fax (415) 984-0611. D W-M; $$. Reservations accepted.*

Reminiscent of one of the many tiny Italian restaurants found in New York City, this charming little spot has several tables in a street-level room, plus more up narrow stairs in a second-floor dining room—all with sidewalk views. The menu is a choice of delicious housemade pastas and more substantial meat entrees, but the kitchen seems willing to produce any request. Desserts are exceptional and include a cliché tiramisu as well as a memorable creamy gelatin with fruit sauce. Service is attentive and cheerful and the food quality surprisingly good considering a barker is used to bring people in. Just a few doors down, the related, though more informal, **Steps of Rome Cafe** offers less expensive dining with a similar menu.

St. Francis Fountain *2801 24th St./York St., the Mission, (415) 826-4200. L&D daily; $. Boosters, booths, child portions. No reservations. No cards.*

Run by the same family since 1918, this informal coffee shop features old-time wooden booths and a counter with swivel stools. It was last decorated in 1949 and claims to be the oldest ice cream parlor in San Francisco. Patrons can try any of the 20 flavors of housemade 14 percent-butterfat ice cream in such delights as giant double-dip sodas or triple-scoop milkshakes served in an old-time metal canister. Sundae syrup toppings are housemade, too. There is even an authentic New York egg cream and a root beer made from housemade syrup. In fact, most items are made from scratch, including the soups, salads, sandwiches, mayo, and potato salad. At a candy counter in front, made-on-the-premises sweets include peanut brittle, old-time German-style fudge, and rum truffles. Best sellers are rocky road (they make the marshmallow fresh, too, of course) and coconut clusters.

The Stinking Rose *325 Columbus Ave./ Broadway, North Beach, (415) 781-ROSE, fax (415) 403-0665. L&D daily; $$. Highchairs, boosters. Reservations advised.*

A warren of unusual rooms awaits garlic-lovers here, as does some delicious food made with as much garlic as possible. A don't-miss item is the bagna calda, consisting of tender, soft, almost sweet cloves of garlic served with bread for spreading. Among the winning dishes are a wild mushroom-roasted eggplant lasagna, a delectable thick-cut pork chop served with garlic relish and garlic mashed potatoes, and 40-clove garlic chicken. For dessert, the truly adventurous can try garlic *ice cream*! For those who still haven't had enough, a tiny shop in front sells all things garlic.

Straits Cafe *3300 Geary Blvd./Parker Ave., the Richmond, (415) 668-1783, fax (415) 668-3901. L&D daily. Highchairs, boosters.*

In a nod to the tropics, columns have been transformed into pseudo palm trees in this airy, casual cafe. The delicious Singaporean cuisine is a complex, refined, and aromatic combination of Malaysian, Indonesian, Chinese, and Indian cuisines. It seems impossible to order wrong. However, particularly tasty items include murtabak (Indian bread stuffed with spiced minced beef), spicy basil chicken, green beans sambal (long beans stir-fried with chilies), and chili crab. Meats are cooked slowly and literally fall off the bone. The mixed bar drinks are outstanding—Raffles punch, Singapore sling, Midori margarita—and some are available in frozen versions. Great smoothies, a delightful housemade ginger-vanilla soda, and a variety of luscious fruit syrup sodas are also available.

Tadich Grill *240 California St./Battery St., Financial District, (415) 391-1849, fax (415) 391-2373. L&D M-Sat; $$. Highchairs, boosters.*

Begun in another location in 1849 as a coffee stand, this Old San Francisco institution has been here since 1967. With its dark wood walls, long lunch counter, and private enclosed booths, it has an old-fashioned clubby feel and is a fabulously cozy place to be on a rainy day. The wait to get in can be long, but persevere. Then be wise and order simple, unsauced dishes. Pan-fried seafood is particularly good and is served with tasty housemade tartar sauce, and steaks and chops are also on the menu. Unusual Hangtown fry—scrambled eggs, bacon, and oysters—is also available. Though the housemade rice pudding has been on the menu for over 100 years, desserts are weak.

Taiwan *445 Clement St./6th Ave., the Richmond, (415) 387-1789. L&D daily.*

For description, see page 264.

Tavolino *401 Columbus Ave./Vallejo St., North Beach, (415) 392-1472, fax (415) 397-7244. 11:30am-1am daily; $$. Valet parking.*

With two walls of windows and tables wrapped around the narrow L-shaped interior, this casual Venetian-inspired wine bar gives everyone a good view of something. When weather permits, alfresco sidewalk dining can be enjoyed. Cicchetti—small dishes of finger food that are Italy's answer to Spain's tapas—comprise the menu: Amaretto-braised duck on polenta, steamed shellfish, tramezzini sandwiches, sea bass with pine nuts, addictive anchovy-stuffed deep-fried olives, and the house specialty—sturgeon saltimboca. Over 100 Italian and Italianesque wines, including sparkling Prosecco, are offered, as is a classic bellini and a variety of grappas. Simple, delightful desserts include tiny chocolate amaretti and buckwheat cake filled with bitter orange marmalade.

T.G.I. Friday's *685 Beach St./Hyde St., Fisherman's Wharf, (415) 775-8443.*

For description, see page 161.

ThirstyBear *661 Howard St./3rd St., South of Market, (415) 974-0905, fax (415) 974-0955; http://thirstybear.com. L&D daily; $-$$. Highchairs, boosters. Reservations accepted.*

With several seating areas in a large, open room of concrete floors and aged brick walls, this is a most unusual brew pub. Do order a 3-ounce taster of each of the seven different house brews. It will probably be impossible to pick a favorite until all are sampled, and by then most people forget which is which and have to start over—or come back again. The authentic Spanish menu is prepared by a chef from Spain. To adequately sample it, try several tapas—perhaps the tender fried fish cheeks and gambas al Pil-Pil (shrimp in garlic wine sauce)—and share a paella or one of the larger plates. But save room for a fabulous dessert. The unique, dramatic "Madonna's Bra" (formerly tagged "La Sagrada Familia" after the famous church in Barcelona) features two delicious chocolate sugar cones stuffed with smooth chocolate mousse presented sitting upright on a cloud of chantilly cream. Food and drink can also be enjoyed upstairs by pool tables.

Tommaso's *1042 Kearny St./Broadway, North Beach, (415) 398-9696, fax (415) 989-9415. D Tu-Sun; $$. Highchairs, boosters. No reservations.*

In 1935, when this spot was known as Lupo's, it was the first restaurant to bring pizza from New York City to the West Coast. (Pizza was introduced to the U.S. at the Lombardy Pizza Restaurant in New York City in 1905.) And for quite a while it was the only restaurant in the entire U.S. to prepare all of its baked foods in a genuine oak wood-burning brick oven. (In fact, world-renowned Chez Panisse in Berkeley used this oven as a model for their own, which then began producing a trend-setting gourmet mini pizza.) Truly a family operation, the owner is a waiter, his sister is hostess, his mother and another sister are cooks, his father keeps the books, and his wife does a little bit of everything. Movie director Francis Ford Coppola has been known to dash in from his nearby office—sometimes to chow down from the menu, other times to whip up his own creations in the kitchen. Seating in the dimly-lit cellar consists of both a large community dining table and smaller tables in semi-private compartments separated by wooden partitions. Wall murals dating to 1935 depict scenes of Naples and the Amalfi Coast. Any of the marinated salads—broccoli, string beans, or roasted peppers—make a good starter, and do use the crusty bread to soak up excess marinade. Almost 20 kinds of pizza are made with a superb thin, crisp-yet-chewy crust. Several calzones (a sort of pizza turnover) are also available, as are pastas, seafood, veal, and chicken entrees. For dessert there's a cannoli, spumoni ice cream, and a housemade tiramisu.

Tommy Toy's *655 Montgomery St./Washington St., in Washington and Montgomery Tower, Financial District, (415) 397-4888, fax (415) 397-0469. L M-F, D daily; $$$. Reservations advised. Valet parking at D.*

It's hard to imagine a more elegant, more romantic restaurant than this well-established hideaway, where men are required to wear a coat and tie. After passing through the dark entry, diners are greeted by the striking sight of giant goldfish in a tank and then seated in a refined room displaying authentic Asian antiques. The pampering service begins immediately and doesn't stop. Chopsticks appear only by request. To begin, diners can order delicious crisp drinks from the bar to sip while perusing the menu. Specializing in haute cuisine Chinoise, the specialty here is a blend of classic Chinese dishes with traditional French presentation. The amazing fixed-price, six-course Signature Dinner includes: minced squab Imperial; seafood bisque in a coconut shell crowned with puff pastry; an artistically presented whole fresh Maine lobster, shelled and sautéed with pine nuts and fresh mushrooms in a peppercorn sauce and served on a bed of angel hair crystal noodles; Peking duck wrapped in lotus buns; tender wok-charred medallion of beef with garlic and wine, served with four-flavors fried rice; and peach mousse in a strawberry compote beautifully swirled with hearts. The elaborate, elegant presentations are served on oversize plates, and a fresh hot finger towel is offered after each course.

Tosca *242 Columbus Ave./Broadway, North Beach, (415) 986-9651. Open daily 5pm-2am; $. No cards.*

Opened in 1919, this popular bar roars with excitement. It is a hangout for actors and writers, and the jukebox is said to have great selections—if only it were possible to *hear* them. Seating is at an uninspired collection of tables surrounded by wall-hugging, comfy red booths. The house drink is a yummy brandy-laced Ghirardelli hot chocolate.

Waterfront Restaurant & Cafe *Pier 7, The Embarcadero/Broadway, (415) 391-2696. L&D daily; $$-$$$. Reservations advised. Free valet parking.*

Located next to a public walking pier, this veteran restaurant was recently remodeled. The menu in the smaller downstairs cafe/bar is more casual and less expensive than upstairs in the more formal restaurant, but both areas offer the same mesmerizing jewel of a bay view overlooking Treasure Island and the Bay Bridge. Pelicans, sailboats, and the occasional tugboat compete with the cuisine for attention. In addition to a large variety of seafood items, the cafe menu offers salads, pastas, and steaks. And certainly, in America, if it's good enough for the President of the country to seek out, it is good enough for the populace.

World Wrapps *2257 Chestnut St./Pierce St., the Marina, (415) 563-9727, fax (415) 563-9719; www.worldwrapps.com. L&D daily; $. Child portions.*

This noteworthy fast-food chain offers tasty, wholesome meals that are made to order. Items include an international array of stuffed tortillas as well as some "unwrapped" rice bowls and soups. Signature mixtures include salmon and asparagus, portabello mushroom and goat cheese, and Thai chicken. They all go particularly well with the various smoothies. The decor is colorful, and the seating offers great people-watching. This location is especially pleasant for solitary diners, and take-out orders can be placed online.

A branch is at 2227 Polk Street *(at Vallejo St., (415) 931-9727, fax (415) 931-9729).*

Yet Wah *2140 Clement St./23rd Ave., the Richmond, (415) 387-8040. L&D daily; $$. Highchairs, boosters. Reservations advised.*

Once just a little hole-in-the-wall at a different location on this same street, this modest establishment has blossomed into something more. The long menu lists over 200 dishes, and the quality is generally good. Favorites include hot and sour soup, fried won tons stuffed with Chinese sausage, pot stickers, mu shu pork, Szechwan spiced beef, and ginger-garlic lamb. Explore the menu and enjoy the adventure of trying something new. How about dragon's eye fruit for dessert?

Branches are at 5238 Diamond Heights Boulevard *(at Clipper St., Twin Peaks, (415) 282-0788.)* and Pier 39 *(Fisherman's Wharf, (415) 434-4430.).*

Zao *2406 California St./Fillmore St., Upper Fillmore, (415) 345-8088. L&D daily; $. Child items. No reservations.*

Offering quick and inexpensive meals featuring oodles of noodles with lots of flavor, this new local chain features a high-energy, casual atmosphere. The delicious, healthy cuisine of Thailand, Vietnam, China, and Japan are featured. Menu standouts include Middle Kingdom chicken cups (a flavorful appetizer consisting of a minced mixture of chicken, shitake mushrooms, and water chestnuts wrapped in lettuce), a low-fat chicken salad, and the surf 'n turf—a big bowl of fresh handmade fat noodles topped with a sautéed mixture of chicken, prawns, and vegetables flavored with ginger, garlic, and chilies. For fussy children, a simple chicken dish is available along with a bowl of plain noodles or a cup of rice. Drinks of choice include myriad beers, premium whole leaf teas, sakes, and a tangy housemade sparkling ginger-orange cooler and lemonade. For dessert, try the popular deep-fried banana spring roll with chocolate sauce, or the unusual Japanese mochi ice cream consisting of mango, green tea, and Kona coffee ice cream balls in individual rice wrappers. For single diners and general overflow, a communal dining table runs through the center of the room.

A branch is at 2031 Chestnut Street *(at Fillmore St., the Marina, (415) 928-3088).*

Zarzuela *2000 Hyde St./Union St., Russian Hill, (415) 346-0800, fax (415) 346-0880. L&D M-Sat; $$. No reservations.*

With an open, yet cozy dining room warmed by butter-yellow Mediterranean walls, this gem serves delicious Spanish tapas. Each meal starts with bread and olive oil and a complimentary plate of exquisite olives. For a terrific tapas dinner, begin with a shared salad and small plate of salted almonds. Continue with grilled eggplant rolled around creamy goat cheese, crisp fried potatoes with garlic and sherry vinegar, and shrimps sautéed in garlic and olive oil. For a filling, well-priced meal, add a daily special such as fresh sardines. Larger plates such as traditional Catalan seafood stew, grilled lamb chops, and ox-tail stew are also available, as is, of course, paella. Wash it all down with a traditional sherry. Sponge cake stuffed with fruit and soaked in liqueur is a perfect ending. After, jump on one of the cable cars passing by outside and take a refreshing ride.

Zuni Cafe *1658 Market St./Franklin St., (415) 552-2522, fax (415) 552-9149. L&D Tu-Sun; $$. Reservations suggested. Valet parking at D.*

It seems that all seats are good in this cheery warren of oddly shaped spaces, where the Market Street parade and chefs in the kitchen are all part of the visual treat. The menu changes *twice* each day. For a delightful brunch consider an antipasto plate spread with delicious Molinari salami and baked ricotta followed by a pizza baked in the wood-burning brick oven, topped perhaps with artichoke hearts and capers. Other options might include eggs baked with tomato, fennel, and white beans and served in an oversized earthenware bowl, or the acclaimed house-ground hamburger on grilled rosemary focaccia bread. The roasted chicken and Caesar salad are also good choices. It seems impossible to order wrong. But do leave room for dessert, especially if the divine rhubarb tart is one of the choices.

Just outside the door, **Red Desert** *(1632-C Market St./Franklin St., (415) 552-2800. Open daily.)* invites walking across its sand-strewn floors to check out an impressive supply of cacti and other succulents, and interesting antique shops are found on both sides of Market Street.

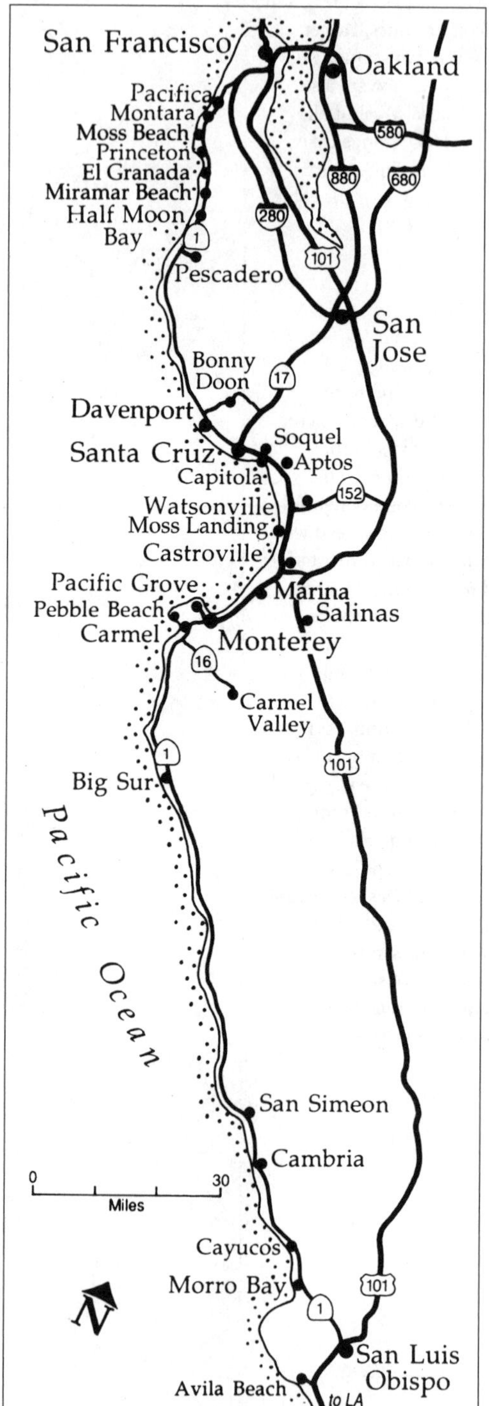
San Francisco
Oakland
Pacifica
Montara
Moss Beach
Princeton
El Granada
Miramar Beach
Half Moon Bay
Pescadero
San Jose
Bonny Doon
Davenport
Santa Cruz
Soquel
Aptos
Capitola
Watsonville
Moss Landing
Castroville
Pacific Grove
Pebble Beach
Carmel
Marina
Salinas
Monterey
Carmel Valley
Big Sur
Pacific Ocean
San Simeon
Cambria
Cayucos
Morro Bay
San Luis Obispo
Avila Beach
to LA
580
680
880
280
101
1
17
152
16
0
30
Miles
N
MAP 4

A LITTLE BACKGROUND

The trip down Highway 1 from San Francisco features a breathtaking, cliff-hugging ride along the Pacific Ocean.

After passing ridges of boxy houses in pastel tones (referred to as being made of "ticky-tacky" by folk singer Malvina Reynolds in her famous '60s song "Little Boxes") and the beach town of Pacifica, Highway 1 winds to the ocean through a eucalyptus-lined path in the coastal foothills. A stretch of this road known as Devil's Slide hugs cliffs dropping steeply into the sea. In fact, part of the road itself occasionally drops off, causing traffic congestion due to detours. Though many people make informal stops in the Devil's Slide area to take pictures, it is quite unsafe. Restraint is in order until an obvious parking area is observed. Once the road passes this hilly area, it moves inland and becomes more flat and straight.

When the Bay Area is blazing with sunshine, this area can be disappointingly socked in with fog. And vice versa. In fact, on many late summer and early fall days, when San Francisco is covered with fog, this area is at its most beautiful. The area's spectacular unspoiled beaches are a popular destination anytime, but they are especially so then, when the weather is usually warm and clear.

Be careful, though, about going in the water as tides can be dangerous. Always check with a ranger station or lifeguard before swimming.

Pacifica

WHERE TO STAY

Seabreeze Motel *100 Rockaway Beach Ave., (650) 359-3903, fax (650) 359-5624. 20 rooms; $. Continental breakfast; restaurant.*

This is the place for a quick, inexpensive escape. Rooms are simple, but the beach is only a few steps away, and a merry steak and seafood restaurant, **Nick's** *((650) 359-3900. B,L,&D daily; $$. Highchairs, boosters, booths, child portion. Reservations advised.)*, which is under the same ownership, is just next door.

WHERE TO EAT

Taco Bell *5200 Hwy. 1, (650) 355-0591. L&D daily; $. Highchairs, child portions. No reservations. No cards.*

Located inside an attractive redwood building, this fast-food restaurant's exceptional beachfront location makes it worthy of a stop-in. Free entertainment is provided by always-present surfers in the ocean just outside.

Montara

WHERE TO STAY

Point Montara Lighthouse Hostel *On 16th St., (650) 728-7177, same fax; www.norcalhostels.org. 45 beds; private rooms.*

This restored 1875 lighthouse is now the cliffside setting for a picturesque retreat. Lodging is in a modern duplex that was formerly the lightkeeper's quarters. Facilities include two kitchens, a laundry, a private beach, an outdoor hot tub (fee), and bicycle rentals. See also page 417.

Moss Beach

WHAT TO DO

James Fitzgerald Marine Reserve *At the end of California Ave., (650) 728-3584. Daily sunrise to sunset. Free.*

Excellent tidepooling is available here. Usually some pools are accessible, with the occasional sea star or hermit crab caught by the tide. And because visitors are not permitted to remove anything, the sand is rich with shells and interesting natural debris. To see a large variety of specimens, visit when the tide is out. Naturalist-led walks are usually scheduled then on weekends. Call for times. Though the parking area can be deceptively warm and calm, the area by the ocean is usually windy and cold. Take wraps. Picnic tables are provided near the parking lot.

WHERE TO STAY

Seal Cove Inn *221 Cypress Ave., (800) 995-9987, (650) 728-4114, fax (650) 728-4116; www.sealcoveinn.com. 10 rooms; 100% non-smoking; $$$-$$$+. All wood-burning fireplaces. Full breakfast.*

The owner of this coastal inn is well-known for traveling through Europe evaluating other people's inns. She is Karen Brown, author and publisher of the popular *Karen Brown's Country Inns* series of guidebooks. Set way back from the road, her inn fronts a bank of mature cypress and offers access to secluded beaches and tidepools. Antiques and original watercolors cozy up the interior of the newly constructed lodge, and comfortable public areas include a sitting room with a wood-burning fireplace and a patio with views of the distant ocean. All rooms feature a private terrace or balcony, complimentary wine and soft drinks, a towel warmer, fresh flowers, and turn-down service. Breakfast can be taken privately in-room or with other guests in the dining room.

WHERE TO EAT

Moss Beach Distillery *Beach Way/Ocean Blvd., (800) 675-MOSS, (650) 728-5595; www.mossbeachdistillery.com. L M-Sat, D daily, SunBr; $$$. Reservations advised (not accepted for lunch).*

Magnificently situated on a scenic bluff, this out-of-the-way surf & turf dinner house dates from the Prohibition era of the 1920s, when it was a notorious speakeasy, and is now reputed to be haunted (it was once featured on TV's *Unsolved Mysteries.* It is well worth searching out for a romantic repast. Plan to arrive before sundown so there is time to take in the incredible cliff-top view and snuggle under one of the blankets thoughtfully provided on the ocean-side cocktail deck. A few lucky folks manage to snag a wooden bench swing, too. Tables in the cozy interior also offer fabulous views.

Princeton-by-the-Sea

A LITTLE BACKGROUND

This scenic fishing village makes an inviting stop. Known as being a hotbed for bootlegging during Prohibition, now it is known for its surfers and seafood restaurants.

GETTING THERE

Located about 25 miles south of San Francisco.

WHAT TO DO

Surfer-watching.

The legendary surfing spot known as **Maverick's**, found just north of Pillar Point Harbor, sports killer waves, literally, in the winter. It was here on December 23, 1994 that world-famous surfer Mark Foo was killed while surfing the world-class monster waves that break in this treacherous area. He had flown in from Honolulu that day especially to surf the unusually large waves, which have been know to reach up to 30 feet. Maverick's is rated one of the world's three best surfing spots (the others are Todos Santos Island off Ensenada in

Baja California, Mexico, and Waimea Bay on the North Shore of Oahu in Hawaii).

Whale-watching.

Expeditions are scheduled January through April on Saturdays, Sundays, and some Fridays. Sponsored by non-profit **Oceanic Society Expeditions** (*(800) 326-7491, (650) 474-3385. $29-$32. Children must be at least 7. Reservations required.*), each boat trip has a professional naturalist on board to educate participants about the whales and interpret their behavior. See also page 13.

WHERE TO STAY

Pillar Point Inn *380 Capistrano Rd., (800) 400-8281, (650) 728-7377, fax (650) 728-8345; www.pillarpointinn.com. 11 rooms; 100% non-smoking; $$$-$$$+. Unsuitable for children under 12. All VCRs & gas fireplaces. Afternoon snack, full breakfast.*

Facing a picturesque small boat harbor, this contemporary inn features a Cape Cod-style of architecture. Some of the spacious rooms have private steam baths; all sport cloud-like feather beds and harbor views. A complimentary video library is also available. Several good seafood restaurants and the busy harbor itself are just across the street.

WHERE TO EAT

Barbara's Fishtrap *281 Capistrano Rd., (650) 728-7049, fax (650) 728-2519. L&D daily; $-$$. Highchairs, boosters, child portions. No reservations. No cards.*

A view of the harbor and a casual atmosphere make this tiny roadside diner a pleasant stop for a quick meal. In addition to a rustic interior room, a glassed-in deck is kept warm with heat lamps. Though there is sometimes a short wait to be seated, service is quick, encouraging a fast turnover. Lunch is served until 5 p.m. and includes New England-style clam chowder, bouillabaisse, fish & chips, and calamari as well as steak and a hamburger. The dinner menu additionally offers scallops, prawns, and steak—all served with a choice of soup or salad, French bread, French fries or baked potato, and a vegetable. The house specialty—rockfish fresh off the harbor fishing boats—is available either broiled or dipped in batter and deep-fried tempura-style.

Miramar Beach

A LITTLE BACKGROUND

A few miles north of Half Moon Bay, a turn toward the sea on Magellan Avenue leads to peaceful Miramar Beach. Off the beaten path, it provides a chance to view the area in the way some of the luckier local residents do. Brown pelicans and scurrying sandpipers can be observed from the beach, reached by climbing down a breakfront constructed with large boulders.

WHAT TO DO

Bach Dancing and Dynamite Society
307 Mirada Rd., (650) 726-4143, fax (650) 712-0506; www.bachddsoc.org. Sun at 4:30; closed Jan, Sept, & Dec. Adults $20, students under 21 half-price, under 14 free.

Live jazz and classical music are performed at this beach house. The door opens at 3 p.m., and the music begins at 4:30. Arrive early, as there are no advance reservations. A buffet, with a wine and juice bar, is available, and minors are welcome. Call for schedule.

WHERE TO STAY

Cypress Inn *407 Mirada Rd., (800) 83-BEACH, (650) 726-6002, fax (650) 726-1138; www.cypressinn.com. 12 rooms; 100% non-smoking; $$$-$$$+. Children free. Some TVs, all fireplaces. Afternoon snack, full breakfast; room service by arrangement.*

Located on a quiet frontage road across the street from the ocean, this impressive inn is decorated with bright accents of Mexican folk art. Each room in the main inn faces the ocean, so guests can always hear the soothing sound of the ocean in the background, and each also has a private balcony, ocean view, and fireplace. Many guests enjoy just sitting in their room and watching the brown pelicans dive for fish. To experience a bit of heaven, reserve the third-floor Las Nubes room. Its name meaning literally "the clouds," this penthouse room has a luxurious tiled bathroom with an over-size whirlpool tub, plus a bank of windows overlooking the ocean. Occupants want to stay forever. Four rooms are located in a newly added beach house behind the main inn. The afternoon snack includes tea and exquisite hors d'oeuvres.

WHERE TO EAT

Miramar Beach Inn *131 Mirada Rd., (650) 726-9053, fax (650) 726-5060; www.beachfront dining.com. L M-Sat, D daily, SunBr; $$-$$$. Highchairs, boosters, booths, child menu. Reservations advised.*

Situated across the street from the ocean in a somewhat isolated spot, this casual restaurant offers expansive views and is especially nice at lunch and Sunday brunch. The lunch menu has salads, hot sandwiches, hamburgers, omelettes, and housemade chowder with garlic bread. Pricier dinners include seafood, steak, and pasta and come with salad, fresh vegetables, and rice pilaf. After dining, visit the beach behind the rocky breakfront across from the restaurant to take a walk, build a sand castle, or maybe observe a flock of brown pelicans bobbing on the surf and diving for food.

Half Moon Bay

A LITTLE BACKGROUND

The oldest of the coastal towns in this area, Half Moon Bay has an interesting Main Street. Uncutesied, it looks much as it always has.

VISITOR INFORMATION

Half Moon Bay Coastside Chamber of Commerce and Visitors Bureau *520 Kelly Ave., (650) 726-8380, fax (650) 726-8389; www.half moonbaychamber.org.*

Harvest Trails *765 Main St., Half Moon Bay 94019, (650) 726-4485.*

For a free map to the area's farms, send a self-addressed, stamped, legal-size envelope.

GETTING THERE

Located approximately 25 miles south of San Francisco.

ANNUAL EVENTS

Chamarita *May or June. (650) 726-2729.*

Held here for over 100 years, this Portuguese festival takes place seven weekends after Easter and includes a barbecue, parade, and carnival.

Half Moon Bay Art and Pumpkin Festival *October. (650) 726-9652; www.miramarevents. com. Free.*

Children are invited to wear costumes and participate in the Great Pumpkin Parade. Rounding out the fun are pumpkin-carving and pie-eating contests, arts and crafts booths, a variety of pumpkin foods, and assorted on-going entertainment. Pumpkin patches, brightly colored with their seasonal loot, are open nearby for picking, and a pumpkin weigh-off, which in 1999 squashed the world record with a 991-pounder, is held mid-week,

WHAT TO DO

Obester Winery *12341 San Mateo Rd. (Hwy. 92), 2 mi. east of town, (650) 726-WINE, fax (650) 726-7074. Tasting daily 10-5.*

On Bottle Your Own days, customers bring in their own bottles to be filled directly from the barrel. Call for schedule. Usually a non-alcoholic grape juice varietal, such as Gewurztraminer or Pinot Noir, is served to kids while their parents taste the real thing.

Picnic.

Put one together by visiting old-fashioned **Cunha's Country Store** *(Main St./Kelly Ave.,*

(650) 726-4071.), which has been in the same building for over 50 years, and the **Half Moon Bay Bakery** *(514 Main St., (650) 726-4841.)*, which is still using its original brick ovens and known for its French bread and Portuguese sweet bread. The bakery also makes its own donuts, and sandwiches are available to go.

While picking up supplies, allow some time for poking around in some of the shops on Main Street. Don't miss **Half Moon Bay Feed & Fuel** *(331 Main St., (650) 726-4814.)*, an old-time farm supply store established in 1911 that sells farm, pet, and garden supplies to locals and has plenty of chicks, ducklings, bunnies, and other small farm animals to pet and purchase.

The area's spectacular beaches are popular picnic destinations summer through fall, when the weather tends to be warm and clear. **Dunes Beach**, which is part of **Half Moon Bay State Beach**, is prime.

WHERE TO STAY

Beach House Inn *4100 N. Cabrillo Hwy., (800) 315-9366, (650) 712-3300, fax (650) 712-0693; www.beach-house.com. 54 rooms; $$$-$$$+. All CD players, mini-kitchens, & wood-burning fireplaces. Heated pool, hot tub, fitness center. Evening wine, continental breakfast.*

Those who are particularly lucky arrive here at dusk on a night when the fog clings above the water on a fluffy cloud, setting off a continuous bleat from a nearby fog horn. Contemporary-style rooms have private balconies and views of the ocean beyond the harbor, permitting the occasional sighting of an egret or brown pelican. Fragrant Aveda amenities and impressive water pressure await in the bathroom. Beds, made with comfortable cotton blankets and feather duvets, face the peaceful fishing harbor. A 6-mile coastal trail runs adjacent, leading into nearby Princeton-by-the-Sea, the perfect destination for dinner. Breakfast includes fresh-squeezed orange juice, great coffee, and an assortment of scones, muffins, and croissants; all can be gathered in the lobby and taken to the room to enjoy at leisure. Plan ahead and pre-order a scrumptious box lunch to enjoy the next day on the beach.

Half Moon Bay Lodge *2400 S. Cabrillo Hwy., (800) 368-2468, (650) 726-9000, fax (650) 726-7951; www.woodsidehotels.com. 81 rooms; $$$-$$$+. Children under 12 free. Some wood-burning fireplaces. Heated pool, hot tub, fitness center.*

Located at the quiet southern end of town, this modern hacienda-style lodge motel overlooks the fourth fairway of the **Half Moon Bay Golf Links**—designed by Arnold Palmer and rated first in the Bay Area. An oversize hot tub is within a semi-enclosed room.

San Benito House *356 Main St., (650) 726-3425. 12 rooms; 100% non-smoking; $-$$. Unsuitable for children under 10. No TVs; some shared baths. Sauna. Continental breakfast; restaurant.*

Upstairs, guest rooms feature vividly colored solid walls, high ceilings, and bathrooms with old-fashioned clawfoot tubs. Rooms are decorated with European antiques, contemporary paintings, and historical photographs. Guests can stroll in the formal English garden and, perhaps, indulge in some competition on the croquet lawn. Breakfast can be served in-room or even in bed.

Downstairs, the charmingly decorated **restaurant** *(D Thur-Sun; $$-$$$. Highchairs, boosters, child menu. Reservations advised.)* invites romantic dining. Fresh local produce and seafood are used for the Mediterranean-style cuisine, and the soups and French pastries are particularly delicious. Make reservations when booking a room, as this cozy dining room is very popular with locals. (Overnight guests get a 10 percent discount in the restaurant.) A **deli** *(Daily 11-3.)* dispenses inexpensive salads and sandwiches, and a lively Western-style **saloon** *(Daily from 4pm.)* is the perfect spot for a nightcap.

WHERE TO EAT

2 Fools Cafe & Market *408 Main St., (650) 712-1222. B Sat&Sun, L daily; $. No reservations.*

This popular, informal cafe offers a good selection of tasty housemade items, including soups, salads, sandwiches, fish & chips, and both a sirloin burger and veggie burger. Fresh local salmon is used in both a salad and sandwich. The Foolish Kids Coloring Menu gives children a choice of a peanut butter & jelly or grilled cheese sandwich, a cheeseburger, and fish & chips, plus a picture to color. Seating is in either a cheery interior room or out on a tiny, quiet patio in back. If the wait is too long, consider ordering take-out.

Pescadero

A LITTLE BACKGROUND

Named for the town creek that once was filled with trout ("pescadero" means literally "fishing place"), this tiny burg was settled by Portuguese farmers. Now this peaceful place is best known for its agricultural product: straw flowers and artichokes. And Duarte's Tavern.

Do take a walk through this tiny agricultural town. Of special note are the colorful fields of straw flowers, the old-fashioned general store, and a picturesque 130-year-old church.

For a lovely ride through the backcountry, follow the quiet, winding road that begins in front of the restaurant (State Road) 7 miles north to San Gregorio, where the **San Gregorio General Store**, an old-fashioned country emporium, provides an interesting stop for picnic supplies or a snack. After stocking up, head to nearby **San Gregorio State Beach**, which often has sun when none is to be found elsewhere along this stretch of coast, for a picturesque picnic spot. Note that about a mile north of here is a popular clothing-optional beach.

GETTING THERE

Located 50 miles south of San Francisco.

WHAT TO DO

Año Nuevo State Reserve *New Year's Creek Rd., (800) 444-4445, (650) 879-0227; www.anonuevo.org. Tours Dec-Apr; reservations required & can be made up to 8 weeks in advance. $4/person + $5/vehicle.*

Huge elephant seals return to this beach each year to mate and bear their young. It is the only elephant seal rookery on the U.S. mainland. Docent-guided tours, lasting 2 1/2 hours and covering 3 miles, take visitors close enough to observe the seals basking in the sun or sleeping. Usually that is the extent of the activity

seen, but occasionally one of the weighty bulls (some weigh almost 8,000 pounds!) roars into battle with a challenging male. When picking a tour date note that the males arrive in December (when most of the battles occur), the females arrive in January, and the babies start being born in late January. Mating usually occurs in February, when the population is at its peak. Then the adult seals, and tourists, begin to leave, making March and April—when the weaned pups are still around—a somewhat quieter time to visit. An even quieter time is the rest of the year, when advance tickets aren't necessary. Call ahead for schedule. Note that no food service is available at the reserve, and no drinking water is available along the tour trail.

Depending on the season, pick-your-own olallieberries (June and July), pumpkins (October), kiwi fruit (November), or Christmas trees are waiting across the street at 476-acre, usually sunny **Coastways Ranch** *(640 Cabrillo Hwy. (Hwy. 1), (650) 879-0414; www.well.com/user/dmsml/coastways. June-July daily 9-5, Oct-Dec 10-4; closed Jan-May & Aug-Sept.).* This little piece of paradise, with twisting dirt trails, has been farmed by the Hudson family since 1917. Call ahead for current information on crops, and bring along garden gloves to protect hands. Picnic facilities and light snacks are available.

Pescadero State Beach *New Year's Creek Rd., (650) 879-2170.*

Sand dunes at the north end invite sliding, a creek invites wading, and tidepools invite exploring. The **Pescadero Marsh Natural Preserve**, a 210-acre refuge for waterfowl and wildlife teeming with migrating birds and native plants, adjoins. Marked trails are available for hiking, and docent-led nature walks are scheduled on weekends. Tidepool explorations are also scheduled when the tides are right. Call for current schedule.

WHERE TO STAY

Costanoa Coastal Lodge & Camp *2001 Rossi Rd., (877) 262-7848, (650) 879-1100, fax (650) 879-2275; www.costanoa.com. 40 rooms, 12 cabins, 135 tent cabins; $-$$$+. No TVs. Hot tub, saunas, steam rooms, health spa. Continental breakfast.*

Situated on a bluff on the up side of Highway One, this new "boutique campground" offers an upscale camping experience. Guests can stay in tents and bring their own sleeping bags, stay in tent bungalows equipped with bedding that includes heated mattress pads and down comforters, or stay in comfortable cabins with fireplaces, an expansive pastoral view, and private decks with porch swings. Any of these choices bring with them the adventure of trekking through the chilly local air to communal "comfort stations." The upscale part means that they look attractive, smell nice, and have heated floors. (Regulations governing use of this prime coastal land limit restrooms and prohibit building a full service restaurant.) Alternatively, regular hotel rooms with bathrooms en suite are also available. (Traditional campsites for tents and RVs are scheduled to open soon.) Prices reflect the various levels of pampering. Simple deli meals are available in a General Store, and the property abuts four state parks and offers easy access to their hiking trails. Amenities include mountain bike rentals and a children's mega-sandbox.

Pigeon Point Lighthouse Hostel *210 Pigeon Point Rd., (650) 879-0633, fax (650) 879-9120; www.norcalhostels.org. 52 beds; private rooms; hot tub $3/person.*

Named after the first big ship that crashed on the rocks here, the *Carrier Pigeon*, this scenic lighthouse, built in 1871, is the second tallest freestanding lighthouse in the U.S. Guests are housed in adjacent bungalows, and a

cliff-top hot tub is open in the evenings. See also page 417.

Forty-minute public **lighthouse tours** are available *((650) 879-2120. Sat & Sun 11-4, also F in July & Aug. Adults $2, children $1.)*, and excellent tidepools are located just to the north.

WHERE TO EAT

Duarte's Tavern *202 Stage Rd., (650) 879-0464. B,L,&D daily; $-$$. Highchairs, boosters, booths. Reservations advised for D.*

Diners have been coming here since 1894 to enjoy drinks in the old-time bar, and since 1936 for a home-cooked meal in the cozy, casual coffee shop. (The name is pronounced "Do-arts.") Breakfast, served until 1 p.m. on weekdays, features giant buttermilk pancakes and outstanding omelettes—especially the sautéed garlic and artichoke and the linguica (a spicy Portuguese sausage) versions—as well as more usual items. At lunch or dinner try the delicious creamy artichoke heart or green chili soups, giant boiled artichokes with garlic mayo dip, fried oysters, homemade pie, and fresh applesauce. Grilled fresh fish is available at dinner, and a popular fixed-price cioppino feed is scheduled each Friday, Saturday, and

Sunday night by reservation. (Artichoke items are made with artichokes picked fresh in nearby fields.)

Norm's Market *287 Stage Rd., (650) 879-0147. M-Sat 10-7, Sun 10-6.*

This is the best spot in the area for picnic supplies. A deli in the back makes sandwiches to go. Do try the delicious local goat cheese and artichoke salsa, and be sure to pick up extra of the super artichoke-garlic and artichoke-pesto breads to finish baking at home, and don't forget some garlic-herb croutons and olallieberry muffins.

Davenport

A LITTLE BACKGROUND

Once a well-known whaling town, this tiny village was wiped out by a fire in 1915. All that remains from those days is the town jail.

GETTING THERE

Located 70 miles south of San Francisco, and 9 miles north of Santa Cruz.

WHAT TO DO

Bonny Doon Vineyard *10 Pine Flat Rd., Bonny Doon, 1 mi. south of town, then 5 mi. up the hill, (831) 425-4518; www.bonnydoonvineyard.com. Tasting daily 11-5; tours by appt.*

The pleasant side trip taken to reach this winery follows a meandering country road to the tiny mountain town of Bonny Doon. Picnic facilities are provided in a redwood grove complete with a gurgling creek. Winery specialties include exotic French and Italian varietals and a muscat Canelli. A rich, raspberry-flavored framboise dessert wine makes delicious sipping. Do try one of the unusual, brandy-like fruit eaux de vie.

Davenport Jail Museum *2 Davenport Ave./Ocean Ave., (831) 429-1964. Call for schedule. Free.*

Due to the generally peaceful nature of the area's residents, this two-cell jail, built in 1914, was used only twice. In 1987 it was transformed into a small museum with exhibits on the history of Santa Cruz county's north coast.

Rancho del Oso Nature and History Center *3600 Hwy. 1, 7 mi. north of town, (831) 427-2288. Park: daily sunrise-sunset; guided nature walk on Sun at 1. History center: Sat & Sun 12-4. Free.*

Located on Waddell Creek and part of **Big Basin Redwoods State Park**, this bucolic spot has a marked nature trail leading through one of the few remaining native Monterey pine forests. Former president Herbert Hoover's brother Theodore settled this valley in 1914, and his family home is now the museum. After viewing vintage photos and checking out the old logging artifacts and wildlife exhibit, consider a picnic either in the sheltered courtyard or on the deck overlooking the preserve.

Just across the street, **Waddell Beach** is a popular spot for windsurfing and hang-gliding.

WHERE TO STAY

Davenport Bed & Breakfast Inn *31 Davenport Ave./Hwy. 1, (800) 870-1817, (831) 425-1818, fax (831) 423-1160. 12 rooms; 100% non-smoking; $-$$. No TVs. M-F credit toward breakfast in restaurant, Sat & Sun full breakfast; restaurant.*

Some of the eclectically decorated, colorful rooms here have skylights and ocean views. All guests are greeted with a complimentary drink in the restaurant bar.

WHERE TO EAT

Davenport Cash Store Restaurant *(800) 870-1817, (831) 426-4122, fax (831) 423-1160. B,L,&D daily. Highchairs, boosters. Reservations advised.*

Rebuilt on the site of an old-time cash store that was destroyed by fire in the 1950s, this spot's eclectic menu includes Mexican items, a hamburger, vegetarian dishes, and a variety of fresh housemade bread and pastries—all served in a comfortable, large open space. The adjoining store features yet more eclecticism, with everything from Italian soaps to African hats for sale.

Santa Cruz

A LITTLE BACKGROUND

Close enough to San Francisco to visit just for the day, Santa Cruz has long been a popular summer destination. Weather is reliably clear and sunny, and the beach features fine sand and a gentle surf. In fact, it is a Very Southern California-style beach town. The beach people add to the simile with zinc on their noses, surfboards hanging out of their cars, and the Beach Boys blaring from their tapedecks. Why, even the police officers wear shorts!

The 1989 Loma Prieta earthquake wreaked havoc here. The damage was severe along the popular Pacific Garden Mall, which has now been rebuilt and is better than ever.

VISITOR INFORMATION

Santa Cruz County Conference & Visitors Council *1211 Ocean St., (800) 833-3494, (831) 425-1234, fax (831) 425-1260; www.santacruzca.org.*

GETTING THERE

Located approximately 65 miles south of San Francisco. Take either Highway 101 or the more scenic Highway 280 to Highway 17; or take magnificently scenic Highway 1 all the way.

ANNUAL EVENTS

Cabrillo Music Festival *August. (831) 426-6966, fax (831) 426-6968. Free-$25.*

This is said to be one of the country's best small music festivals. The program includes a variety of contemporary orchestral works, including world premieres, and some events are scheduled at Mission San Juan Bautista.

WHAT TO DO

Antonelli Brothers Begonia Gardens *2545 Capitola Rd., (831) 475-5222. Daily 9-5. Free.*

Acres of indoor plants, ferns, and beautiful begonia baskets can be viewed and purchased here. Peak of bloom is August and September, but a good show can also be enjoyed April through October. Picnic tables are available in the Hanging Begonia Room.

Beach & Boardwalk *400 Beach St., (831) 423-5590; www.beachboardwalk.com. From 11am, daily June-Sept, weekends Oct-May; call for closing time. Admission to Boardwalk free; individual rides $1.50-$3, all-day ride ticket $21.95; miniature golf $4.75-$5.75.*

Fortunately, this is one beach boardwalk that has not degenerated over the years. Built in 1907, it was spiffed up a few years ago with a cheerful painting. Now the only boardwalk left on the West Coast and the oldest amusement park in California, it offers a variety of arcade games, fast-food stands (don't miss the salt water taffy and caramel apples at **Marini's**), and souvenir shops—plus 23 major rides and 11 kiddie rides. The half-mile-long concrete walkway parallels a clean, gorgeous beach. Thrill rides include the **Giant Dipper**, a rickety wooden roller coaster built in 1924 and rated by *The New York Times* as one of the ten best in the country, and Logger's Revenge, a refreshing water flume ride. An old-fashioned **merry-go-round**, built in New Jersey by Charles Looff in 1911 and the largest of the four remaining classic carousels in Northern California, features 70 hand-carved horses (all with authentic horse-hair tails) and 2 chariots as well as its rare, original 1894 342-pipe Ruth Und Sohn band organ and a ring toss—one of the few left in the world. Both the roller coaster and the carousel are now National Historic Landmarks, and the Boardwalk itself is a California Historic Landmark. All this plus free band concerts on Friday nights in summer and indoor miniature golf, too!

Lighthouse Point *On West Cliff Dr.*
• **Santa Cruz Surfing Museum** *(831) 420-6289, fax (831) 469-4371. Thur-M 12-4; closed W Dec-Mar. Free.*

This unique museum is housed within the small brick **Mark Abbott Lighthouse**. A scenic 3-mile bike and pedestrian pathway begins here.

• **Seal Rock**, home to a herd of sea lions, is visible off shore.

• **Steamer Lane.** Surfers can be viewed in action from here.

Museum of Art & History *705 Front St., (831) 429-1964. Tu-Sun 12-5, F to 7. Adults $4, under 12 free.*

The permanent collection exhibited here focuses on the social history of Santa Cruz county. Contemporary works by local artists are also displayed.

The Mystery Spot *465 Mystery Spot Rd., 3 mi. north of town (call for directions; finding it can be a bit of a mystery, too), (831) 423-8897, fax (831) 429-6653; www.mystery-spot.com. Daily 9-5; in summer to 8. Adults $4, 5-11 $2.*

Located in a grove of redwoods, this small, quiet, cool spot measures only about 150 feet in diameter. Visitors are given a guided tour during which gravitational forces appear to be defied, and everyone leaves with a souvenir bumper sticker.

Natural Bridges State Beach *2531 West Cliff Dr., at north end, (831) 423-4609. Daily 8am-sunset. $6/vehicle.*

Enjoy a picnic in the sun on the sandy beach, or in the shade at sturdy tables. All but one of the mudstone arches, after which the beach is named, have collapsed, but there are still plenty of tidepools to explore. Swimming in the ocean is recommended only when a lifeguard is on duty, but sometimes a lagoon forms where small children can wade safely. From October through February large numbers of monarch butterflies make their winter home here. A short nature trail leads to good viewing points where they can be observed hanging in clusters on mature eucalyptus trees. Guided walks are often scheduled. During monarch season, the Visitors Center *(Daily 10-4.)* displays informative exhibits.

Pacific Avenue/Downtown Santa Cruz *Pacific Ave. between Water St. & Cathcart St.*

These five landscaped blocks comprise downtown Santa Cruz. Once the park-like setting was home to a variety of boutiques, art galleries, and restaurants operating from within restored historic buildings. But the 1989 Loma Prieta earthquake turned the area into a disaster zone of destruction. Now things are hopping again, especially in the evening. Don't miss impressive **Bookshop Santa Cruz** *(1520 Pacific Ave., (831) 423-0900. Daily 9-11.)*, which had temporarily relocated inside a canvas tent but is now in a grand new building.

Santa Cruz City Museum of Natural History *1305 East Cliff Dr., (831) 420-6115, fax (831) 469-4371. Tu-Sun 10-5. Adults $2, 13-18 $1.*

Located across the street from wonderful **Seabright Beach**, this museum displays the county's natural treasures. Exhibits include Native American relics, fossils, local wildlife specimens, an operating beehive, and a "touch tank" of live sea animals, plus a life-size whale sculpture for kids to climb on.

Santa Cruz Mission State Historic Park *144 School St., (831) 425-5849, fax (831) 429-1840. Thur-Sun 10-4; call for tour times. Adults $2, 6-18 $1, family $5.*

A restored adobe building here is all that remains of the original mission complex and is now the only remaining example of mission Indian housing in California. Among the exhibits contained in its rooms is an example of living quarters for Native American families. Just off the adobe, a large Victorian garden gone wild, with several tall redwoods and a giant avocado tree that is one of the oldest in the state, invites leisurely picnicking. Living History Day, when docents in period dress oversee a variety of crafts activities, is scheduled each month.

A block away, **Mission Santa Cruz** *(126 High St., (831) 426-5686. Tu-Sat 10-4, Sun 10-2; call to verify schedule. By donation.)*, built in 1794, is 12th in the chain of missions. Completely destroyed in an earthquake in 1857, the mission was rebuilt in 1931 as this half-size replica. It now houses a small museum displaying original statues, candlesticks, and paintings, as well as ornate vestments and a baptismal font.

Santa Cruz Municipal Wharf *Near the Boardwalk, (831) 420-6025. Daily 5am-2am.*

It is possible to either walk or drive to the end of this half-mile-long pier. Fishermen angle from the side, and seafood restaurants, snack stands, and picnic tables are scattered along its length. Seals can be fed through fishing holes at the end of the pier, and deep-sea fishing trips originate at concessions located here.

Seymour Center at Long Marine Lab *West end of Delaware Ave., (831) 459-3800. Tu-Sat 10-5, Sun 12-5; tours 1-3. Adults $5, 60+ & 6-16 $3; free 1st Tu of month.*

Part of a marine research station for U.C. Santa Cruz, this new center provides impressive views of the Monterey Bay National Marine Sanctuary. It features exhibit galleries, aquariums stocked with local sea life, and a touching pool stocked with hermit crabs, sea stars, and sea anemones. It also displays the skeleton of an 86-foot-long blue whale that washed ashore up the coast on Pescadero Beach in 1979. Research is conducted here on a variety of topics, including marine mammal behavior, fish diseases, and coral genetics. Guided tours include viewing the tanks where sea lions are housed for study.

University of California, Santa Cruz Campus *1156 High St., (831) 459-0111. Free parking Sat & Sun, M-F $3.*

Located high in the hills above town, the buildings of this spectacularly beautiful campus are hidden among a forest of old-growth redwoods. Gorgeous views of the Monterey Bay are enjoyed from many locations. Pick up a map at the Public Information Office *((831) 459-2495.)* and take a self-guided walking tour. **Guided tours** *((831) 459-4008. M-F at 9:30, 12:30, & 3. Reservations required. Free.)* are also available, and free shuttle buses loop the campus daily. The **Arboretum** *((831) 427-2998. Daily 9-5.)* has an extensive collection of plants from Australia and New Zealand and of South African protea. **Whole Earth** *(In Redwood Tower bldg., (831) 426-8255. B&L daily, D M-F; $. No reservations. No cards.)* is a cafeteria-style natural foods restaurant with seating on a spacious deck under mature redwoods. **Bay Tree Bookstore** *((831) 459-4544. M-F 8:30-5:30, Sat 10-4.)* dispenses student books and supplies as well as the now-famous "U C Santa Cruz Banana Slugs" t-shirt worn by John Travolta in *Pulp Fiction.*

Wilder Ranch State Historic Park *1401 Old Coast Rd., off Hwy. 1, 2 mi. north of town, (831) 426-0505. Thur-Sun 10-4; tours Sat & Sun 11-4. $6/vehicle.*

The perfect spot to spend a lazy day in the country, this 5,000-acre turn-of-the-century ranch complex invites visitors to bring along a picnic. Formerly a dairy, it was built in an arroyo, or valley, that protects it from whipping coastal winds, and is reached via a short walk down from the parking lot. Visitors can inspect the owner's large Queen Anne Victorian home, an even older adobe, a bunk house, several barns, a chicken coop, and miscellaneous other structures. Among the domesticated animals bringing life to the old buildings are horses, cows, goats, chickens, and guinea hens. Docents add to the atmosphere by dressing in old-fashioned garb. The Old Cove Landing Trail provides a 4-mile nature walk on which, if all goes well, pond turtles, cormorants, and harbor seals might be sighted; a fern grotto is also on the itinerary. A self-guiding brochure is available at the trailhead.

WHERE TO STAY

Babbling Brook Inn *1025 Laurel St., (800) 866-1131, (831) 427-2437, fax (831) 427-2457; www.babblingbrookinn.com. 13 rooms; 100% non-smoking; $$$. Unsuitable for children under 13. Some wood-burning & gas fireplaces. After-*

noon & evening snack, full breakfast; limited room service.

Shaded by tall redwoods, this secluded hillside inn was built as a log cabin in 1909. Rooms have been added through the years. Now it is the oldest and largest B&B in the area and is on the National Register of Historic Places. Most guest rooms are named after impressionist painters and decorated in the artist's favorite themes and colors. And the inn delivers what its name promises: a babbling brook runs through the property, plus there are even a few cascading waterfalls. The acre of beautifully landscaped grounds surrounding the inn has paths, a covered footbridge, an 18th-century water wheel, and a lacy wrought-iron gazebo.

Casa Blanca Inn *101 Main St., (800) 644-1570, (831) 423-1570, fax (831) 423-0235; www.casablanca-santacruz.com. 39 rooms; $-$$$+. Some kitchens; some wood-burning & gas fireplaces. Restaurant, limited room service.*

Located across the street from the beach and Boardwalk, this converted 1918 mansion features spacious, pleasantly decorated rooms. More rooms, boasting terraces and a country-style decor, are available in a newer 1950s annex.

The **Casablanca** restaurant *((831) 426-9063; D daily, SunBr; $$-$$$. Highchairs, boosters, child portions. Reservations advised).* has the largest wine cellar in the county and features a sophisticated menu of seafood, pastas, and meats.

Chateau Victorian *118 First St., (831) 458-9458. 7 rooms; 100% non-smoking; $$. Unsuitable for children under 18. No TVs; all wood-burning fireplaces. Afternoon snack, continental breakfast.*

Built around the turn of the century, this B&B is only a block from the beach and Boardwalk. Attention to detail is displayed throughout. A favorite room is the L-shaped Lighthouse Room on the second floor. The inn's largest room, it is furnished with an armoire, a queen-size brass bed, and two very comfortable oversize, rolled-arm chairs positioned on either side of the fireplace.

Ocean Echo Inn and Cottages *401 Johans Beach Dr., (831) 462-4192, fax (831) 462-0658; www.oceanecho.com. 15 units; $-$$; 2-night min. in summer. Some kitchens.*

Located a few miles south of the Boardwalk, these attractive rooms and cottages are on a private beach within sound of the surf.

Santa Cruz Hostel *321 Main St., (831) 423-8304, fax (831) 429-8541; www.HI-Santa Cruz.org. 40 beds; private rooms.*

Located within the restored 1870s Carmelita Cottages on Beach Hill, this hostel is just 2 blocks from the Boardwalk action. See also page 417.

Sea and Sand Inn *201 West Cliff Dr., (831) 427-3400, same fax. 20 rooms; $-$$$+; 2-night min. on Sat. Children under 12 free. Afternoon snack, continental breakfast.*

Perched on a cliff high above the beach, all rooms have views of the ocean and Boardwalk. The soothing sound of the surf breaking on the shore below is continuous, and an extensive grassy area in front of the rooms is bordered with colorful plants and flowers and furnished with tables and chairs, inviting repose. Though there is no direct beach access, it is just a short walk to the beach and Boardwalk.

West Coast Santa Cruz Hotel *175 West Cliff Dr., (800) 426-0670, (831) 426-4330, fax (831) 427-2025; www.westcoasthotels.com. 10 stories; 163 rooms; $$-$$$+. Children under 12 free. All VCRs; some kitchens. Heated pool, child wading pool, hot tub, sauna. 2 restaurants, room service.*

Formerly known as the Dream Inn, this hotel is located right on the beach within easy walking distance of the Boardwalk. Each room has a private balcony or patio overlooking Cowell's Beach and Monterey Bay. The pool and hot tub are one story up from the sand and enjoy the same view.

The **Mainsail** *((831) 426-4330.)* has a fantastic beach and ocean view, and its windows are usually open to the sounds of waves breaking on the shore.

Motel Row. Many motels are located in the area surrounding the Boardwalk, including some inexpensive ones dating from the 1930s. Rooms are usually available at the last minute.

WHERE TO EAT

Crow's Nest *2218 East Cliff Dr., (831) 476-4560, fax (831) 476-6085; www.crowsnest-santacruz.com. L&D daily; $$. Highchairs, boosters, child menu. Reservations advised in summer.*

Fresh local seafood at reasonable prices is the specialty here, but steaks, salads, and an enchilada are also on the menu. Children get a color-in menu and a goodie from the treasure chest. Diners can enjoy ocean views outdoors, protected by a glass windbreaker, and watch yachts come and go from the Santa Cruz Yacht Harbor. A cocktail lounge upstairs offers live entertainment and dancing.

El Palomar *1336 Pacific Ave., (831) 425-7575, fax (831) 423-3037. B,L,&D daily, SunBr; $-$$. Highchairs, boosters, booths, child menu. No reservations.*

Housed in the cool, attractively remodeled back room of a 1930s hotel, with high ceilings and colorful wall murals, this restaurant serves well-prepared, authentic Michoacan-style Mexican food. Tortillas are made by hand each day, and there is a large selection of Mexican beers. Unusual menu items include pozole (pork and hominy stew), carne asada (barbecued beef), and occasionally menudo (tripe soup). The fresh seafood specials are also usually quite appealing. Children especially enjoy the sopes (little tortillas shaped like boats and filled with chicken, guacamole, or tasty ground beef).

Gabriella Cafe *910 Cedar St., (831) 457-1677, fax (831) 423-3919. L&D daily, Sat & SunBr. Highchairs. Reservations advised.*

In an intimate space, with fresh flowers and candles adorning the tables and angel images throughout, this romantic, European-style hideaway produces delightful northern Italian fare. For starters, a roasted garlic-rosemary spread is one of several available to enhance the complimentary house-baked focaccia. Among several salads made with local organic produce are a house salad with edible flowers and a panzanella (bread salad). Main courses include 8-inch pizzetas, several kinds of pasta and a risotto, and fish or meat dishes such as chicken Diavola—a flavorfully marinated chicken breast grilled under a brick and served with a side of soft polenta and a sautéed vegetable. Housemade desserts include a raspberry jam bread pudding and a rich tiramisu.

Hobee's *740 Front St., (831) 458-1212. B&L daily, D W-Sun. Highchairs, boosters, child menu. No reservations.*

The secret to success here is tasty, wholesome food prepared with plenty of vegetables and tofu and served in a cheerful atmosphere in comfortable surroundings. The breakfast menu, available all day, offers a selection of omelettes and scrambles as well as items such as whole-wheat pancakes, granola, cinnamon-orange swirl French toast, and their famous blueberry coffeecake. Lunch and dinner bring on a salad bar, housemade soups, and a variety of sandwiches and hamburgers.

India Joze *1001 Center St., (831) 427-3554, fax (831) 427-0230. L M-Sat, D daily, SunBr; $$. Highchairs, boosters, child menu. Reservations advised.*

A variety of Southeast Asian, Persian, and Indian cuisines, plus many vegetarian and vegan dishes, appear on this restaurant's exciting, exotic menu. The pleasant dining area is light and airy, and a large patio exudes a tropical atmosphere. The kitchen is well-known for its splendid desserts, which can also be enjoyed sans meal in an informal dining area. Each August the menu reflects the fact that the restaurant is the home of the **International Calamari Festival**. Before or after a meal here, browsing is pleasant in the adjoining **Santa Cruz Art Center** shops.

Santa Cruz Brewing Co. & Front Street Pub *516 Front St., (831) 429-8838, fax (831) 429-8915. L&D daily; $. Boosters, child menu. Reservations advised.*

Located downtown, this cheerful spot claims to be "the first brewery on California's central coast since Prohibition." It dispenses made-on-the-premises brews: an European-style Lighthouse Lager, a Lighthouse Amber, and a dark Pacific Porter. A root beer made from an old-time recipe is also available. Like the brews, the pub food is made fresh on the premises and includes steaks, oyster shots (spicy oysters in a shot glass), beer bread (made from the spent grains of beer-making), and fish & chips (battered deep-fried halibut). All this, plus an assortment of sandwiches and "munchies."

Capitola

A LITTLE BACKGROUND

Dating back to 1861, this artsy-craftsy beach town was the state's first seaside resort. The lovely mile-long beach is sheltered between two bluffs and offers both swimming in calm ocean waters and wading in the fresh water of Soquel Creek. Be cautious, however, as sometimes that creek water isn't so pristine.

Fronting the beach, the Esplanade is lined with coffeehouses and restaurants serving everything from hamburgers to lobster. Many have outdoor patios overlooking the beach.

In summer free shuttle buses are in service taking visitors from parking lots on Bay Avenue to the beach. Some shuttle bikes are also available for loan.

VISITOR INFORMATION

Capitola Chamber of Commerce *621-B Capitola Ave., (800) 474-6522, (831) 475-6522, fax (831) 475-6530; www.capitolachamber.com.*

GETTING THERE

Located approximately 5 miles south of Santa Cruz.

ANNUAL EVENTS

Begonia Festival *September. (831) 476-3566. Free.*

Begun years ago as a way to make use of the beautiful blooms discarded by local begonia growers interested only in the bulbs, this popular festival includes a sand castle contest, fishing derby, and nautical parade of flower-covered floats down Soquel Creek. Throughout the festival, the town's merchants and homeowners put on their own shows with begonia displays and decorations. (The only other begonia festival in the world is held in Ballarat, Australia.)

WHAT TO DO

Bargetto Winery *3535 N. Main St., Soquel, (800) 422-7438, (831) 475-2258, fax (831) 475-2664; www.bargetto.com. Tasting & tours M-Sat 9-5, Sun 11-5.*

This small family winery is known both for fruit wines, including olallieberry and apricot, and excellent homemade wine vinegars. It also produces an unusual and authentic Mead (honey wine). Bring a picnic to enjoy on the rustic outdoor patio overlooking gurgling Soquel Creek.

WHERE TO STAY

Capitola Inn *822 Bay Ave., (831) 462-3004, (831) 462-0835. 56 rooms; $-$$$+. Children under 6 free. Some kitchens & gas fireplaces. Heated pool. Continental breakfast. Small dogs welcome.*

Located away from the beach, this tasteful, modern lodging facility has rooms with private patios.

Capitola Venetian Hotel *1500 Wharf Rd., (800) 332-2780, (831) 476-6471; www.capitola venetian.com. 20 units; $-$$$+; 2-night min. on weekends. All kitchens; some fireplaces.*

Built in the 1920s, this mini-village of charming stucco apartments is located right on the beach. It was California's first condominium complex. Some units have balconies and ocean views, and one spectacular unit has both a panoramic ocean view and a fireplace in the bedroom.

Harbor Lights Motel *5000 Cliff Dr., (831) 476-0505. 10 rooms; $-$$$. Children under 5 free. Some kitchens; 1 fireplace.*

This ordinary motel boasts an extraordinary location just across from the beach. Some rooms have views of Monterey Bay, the village, and the beach.

WHERE TO EAT

The Country Court Tea Room *911-B Capitola Ave./Hill St., (831) 462-2498. High tea, Sun 4:30-5:30; $12.95. B&L M-Sat; $. Reservations advised. No cards.*

Operating within a vintage mansion's converted carriage house, this cozy spot is filled

Capitola Venetian Hotel

with nooks and crannies in which to enjoy a traditional high tea. Though the artistically presented items vary, round one might consist of a golden raisin and apricot scone topped with fresh fruit; round two, a tray of delicate finger sandwiches; round three, angel food cake with fresh raspberries and cream. Call ahead for the current menu, or don't and be surprised. Tea is served in tiny individual pots topped with cozies. Most of the decorative items in the rooms are for sale.

Dharma's Natural Foods Restaurant *4250 Capitola Rd./42nd Ave., (831) 462-1717, fax (831) 464-TOFU. B,L,&D daily; $. Highchairs, boosters. No cards.*

Legend has it that this vegetarian and vegan haven—the oldest completely vegetarian restaurant in the U.S.—once suffered a "Big Mac attack" by McDonald's, who sued over its former name of McDharma's. Formerly just a food stand by the beach in Santa Cruz, it has settled into a pleasant, spacious spot in a suburban shopping center. Items on the extensive menu include several vegetarian burgers, a variety of Mexican dishes, sautés, salads, pastas, and soups; at breakfast it's tofu scrambles. Ingredients are organic when available.

Gayle's Bakery & Rosticceria *504 Bay Ave./ Capitola Ave., (831) 462-1200. Daily 6:30am-8:30pm; $. No reservations.*

The talent behind it all here is Gayle, who once was a pastry chef at Berkeley's Chez Panisse, and her husband Joe, who once was a house painter and musician. Their story is of the little bakery that grew and grew, expanding from a tiny storefront operation to occupying the entire building. It is an unpretentious bakery extraordinaire, featuring cases laden with a plethora of soul-satisfying, made-from-scratch choices that sometimes make a person dissolve into an abyss of indecision. What to put on the lunch tray? The German red potato salad, in which the potatoes are actually cooked thoroughly? Yes. Christie's coleslaw made with fresh ginger, cilantro, and peanuts? But of course. The albacore sandwich prepared with house-made mayo and focaccia cheesebread? Most definitely. But leave room for a dessert—perhaps the divine, moist German chocolate cake, or maybe an eclair or Napoleon or crocodile bar or some other decadent delight. Sidle up to the coffee bar for a drink and then settle down at one of the indoor "earthquake tables" made from crockery broken in that infamous 1980s quake, or outdoors at one of the cheery tables on the heated brick patio. A take-home order can be prepared for pick-up after dining; don't forget to include a loaf or two of European-style bread, a bag of the melt-in-your mouth crostini, and maybe one of the dome-shaped lavender marzipan-frosted princess cakes, too. Oh, and then there are the soups, not to mention the pizzas and spit-roasted meats prepared in a brick roasting oven imported from Italy. . .

Margaritaville *221 Esplanade, (831) 476-2263. B,L,&D daily, SunBr.*

For description, see page 192.

Shadowbrook Restaurant *1750 Wharf Rd., (831) 475-1511 or (831) 475-7664; www.shadowbrook-capitola.com. L&D daily, SunBr; $$-$$$. Highchairs, boosters, child menu. Reservations advised.*

Located on the banks of Soquel Creek, the heart of this popular restaurant is a log cabin originally built as a summer home in the 1920s. Diners descend to the restaurant either by riding a bright red, self-operated cable car down a flower-laden hill from the street above, or by strolling down a winding step-path. Most tables offer views of the creek, often with the added entertainment of ducks and geese cavorting on the water. The menu features prime rib and fresh fish as well as a variety of specials. A house specialty is scampi prepared with succulent giant prawns. Dinners include a choice of either Caesar salad or creamy artichoke soup, a fresh vegetable, and freshly baked sourdough bread. Each evening a jukebox provides music for dancing in the bar, where live entertainment is scheduled on weekends. Though children are truly welcome, this restaurant exudes a romantic atmosphere.

Aptos

A LITTLE BACKGROUND

Located just a few miles south of the well-known coastal towns of Capitola and Santa Cruz, this tiny, less frenetic burg often gets lost in the shuffle. But that's all the more reason to head here for a restorative getaway.

Aptos was first inhabited by the Oholne Indians, and then by Rafael Castro, who received it in 1833 as a 6,000-acre land grant to raise cattle. The property started breaking up in 1872 when sugar millionaire Claus Spreckles bought 2,400 acres from Castro. He built a summer home and deer park, which he stocked with deer, elk, and other game. Most of the village was built between 1850 and 1900, when it was a busy logging town, and at one time it bustled with 13 saloons and 2 railroad stations.

Because Aptos is a very confusing town to navigate, it's smart to carry a good map (the chamber of commerce will send one free). Otherwise it is possible to just go round and round in scenic circles. The town has three basic areas: Aptos Village, Seacliff State Beach area, and Rio Del Mar. Tiny Aptos Village is sprinkled for 2 blocks along Soquel Drive just northeast of Highway 1, and is home to several restaurants, an assortment of shops, and an historic inn.

Be particularly careful in late afternoon at the poorly marked intersection of Spreckles and Soquel drives, which seems designed especially to snag out-of-towners. Making a left-hand turn here can leave even a careful driver with an unwanted souvenir ticket.

VISITOR INFORMATION

Aptos Chamber of Commerce *7605 Old Dominion Ct. #A, (800) APTOSCC, (831) 688-1467; www.aptoschamber.com.*

ANNUAL EVENTS

West Coast Antique Fly-In & Airshow *May. In Watsonville; (831) 763-5600. Free-$10.*

Always held on Memorial Day Weekend, this is one of the largest antique fly-in and air shows on the West Coast. It features an assortment of vintage and classic planes, including some from World Wars I and II and some home-built models.

Roses of Yesterday and Today *May & June. In Watsonville, 803 Browns Valley Rd. (call for directions); (831) 728-1901, fax (831) 724-1408. Daily 9-4. Free; catalog $3.*

Tucked into a redwood canyon, this demonstration garden for a mail-order nursery is an extraordinary sight when its approximately 450 varieties of old-fashioned roses bloom in unison. Picnic tables are available.

Fourth of July Parade *July. (831) 688-1467.*

This is billed as "the world's shortest parade."

WHAT TO DO

The Forest of Nisene Marks State Park *On Aptos Creek Rd., behind Aptos Village, (831) 763-7063. Sunrise-sunset.*

Back among tall, dense redwood groves, Aptos Creek Road meanders into this scenic 10,000-acre park. An easy trail leads to the epicenter of the devastating 1989 Loma Prieta earthquake, which flattened buildings as far away as 80 miles north in San Francisco.

Seacliff State Beach *201 State Park Dr., (831) 685-6500. Sunrise-sunset. $6/car.*

Following the area's winding roads aimlessly often eventually leads to this locally popular beach. After parking in a meter-free area, it is a short, scenic walk to view the *Palo Alto.* This former tanker was converted into a nightclub in 1930, and soon after cracked up in a storm. Its current incarnation is as an unusual fishing pier. Campsites are available.

WHERE TO STAY

KOA Kampground *1186 San Andreas Rd., Watsonville, (800) KOA-7701, (831) 722-0551.*

Located 1 mile from the beach, this particularly posh campground has a heated pool, several hot tubs, two kiddie pools, and a water-fun playground. See also page 415.

Mangels House *570 Aptos Creek Rd., behind Aptos Village, (831) 688-7982. 6 rooms; $$$. Unsuitable for children under 13. Some fireplaces. Afternoon snack, full breakfast.*

Located on 4 acres of lawn, orchard, and woodland set way back from any well-traveled road, and with no TVs or radios, this secluded B&B is adjacent to the state park and enjoys blissfully silent nights. Built in 1886 by the brother-in-law of Claus Spreckles, this Italianate Victorian mansion is a delight to explore. Afternoon port and cookies are served in a huge communal drawing room with an unusual rough-cut granite fireplace. Inside, shelves of books invite browsing, and outside, a well-tended English-style garden with gazebo and fountain invites lingering. A Ping-Pong table beckons from the back porch, and a porch swing begs for movement on the front of the wraparound verandah. By appointment, a therapeutic massage or footbath is available in a tiny adjacent cottage. The attractive high-ceilinged guest rooms are individually decorated and accented with lace-edged bed linens and fresh flowers from the garden. The Guest Room has a fabulous marble sink that is original to the house and an unusual Victorian door-window leading out to an upstairs porch.

Rio Sands Motel *116 Aptos Beach Dr., (800) 826-2077, (831) 688-3207, fax (831) 688-6107. 50 rooms, $-$$$; 2-night min. on summer weekends. Children under 5 free. Some kitchens. Heated pool, hot tub. Continental breakfast.*

Located just 1 block from the beach, this 1950s-era traditional motel offers the bonus of a nice garden-pool area with barbecue facilities.

Seascape Resort *One Seascape Resort Dr., Rio Del Mar, (800) 929-7727, (831) 688-6800, fax (831) 685-0615; www.seascaperesort.com. 285 rooms; $$$-$$$+. All kitchens & fireplaces. 2 pools, hot tub, sauna. Restaurant; room service.*

This cliff-top resort offers spacious contemporary condominium units with expansive ocean views. Want to have a marshmallow roast on the beach? A bellman is available to take guests down to the beach in a golf cart, build a fire, and leave them with the makings for s'mores. Guests have access to an adjacent 18-hole golf course and a sports club with 9 tennis courts and a fully equipped fitness center. Special facilities for families include a playground and, in summer, an inexpensive children's program for ages 5 through 10. A small shopping center and full-service day spa are just across the street.

WHERE TO EAT

Bittersweet Bistro *787 Rio Del Mar Blvd., in Deer Park Shopping Center, Rio Del Mar, (831) 662-9799, fax (831) 662-9779; www.bittersweetbistro.com. L&D Tu-Sun; $$-$$$. Reservations advised.*

Though situated at the edge of a shopping center, this restaurant, operating inside an historical building that once sat right smack in the middle of Highway 1, does not disappoint. Beautifully remodeled, with original art decorating the walls, it is simple yet elegant—just like the food. The chef uses high quality local ingredients whenever possible. One dinner here started with a shared pear and blood orange salad accented with Roquefort cheese and arranged on a plate splashed with a colorful balsamic glaze. Entrees were a delicious Mediterranean angel hair pasta with tomatoes, pine nuts, and Feta cheese, and a delicate grilled fresh Mahi Mahi served atop garlic mashed potatoes and sautéed fresh spinach. Portions are large, but some people manage to save room for Death by Chocolate—a giant platter showcasing some of the from-scratch chocolate desserts the restaurant is justly famous for. Enough for three or four people, it holds a variety of outrageous concoctions, including a heavenly chocolate mousse and a devilishly refined chocolate bread pudding.

Britannia Arms *8017 Soquel Dr., in Aptos Village, (831) 688-1233. B,L,&D daily; $.*

This informal spot serves authentic pub fare—including bangers and mash, with some American concessions, such as baby back ribs—in an authentic pub atmosphere. It also features 16 imported draft beers, satellite TV, darts, and pool. For those staying nearby, an authentic black English taxi is available at no charge for pick up and return.

Palapas Restaurant y Cantina *21 Seascape Village, Rio Del Mar, (831) 662-9000. L&D daily; $$. Reservations advised.*

Featuring a Mexican-style thatched roof and boasting both comfortable half-moon booths and expansive ocean views, this popular restaurant specializes in fresh seafood. Among the temptations are sand dabs grilled in white wine and served with a light tomatillo sauce, a spicy version of scampi, and crabmeat enchiladas. Vegetarian selections include a delicious enchilada filled with marinated tofu and topped with guacamole. All this and fabulously crisp complimentary tortilla chips with just-right dipping salsa, too, not to overlook handmade tortillas, fresh sauces, mango margaritas made with fresh Mexican fruit, and 26 different tequilas.

Moss Landing

A LITTLE BACKGROUND

There is actually enough to see and do in this commercial fishing port to fill a weekend itinerary. This small town is home to over 25 antique shops, most on quiet Moss Landing Road. Among the most interesting are artistically arranged **Hamlin's Antiques, Martin & Company Antiques** with its eclectic collection displayed in a warren of cozy rooms, and another shop operating out of a recycled train caboose. Hours are casual, but most are open Wednesday through Sunday from 11 a.m. to 4 p.m. Also on Moss Landing Road, the tiny post office acting as the town's unofficial museum displays historical photos of Moss Landing's past as a shipping port, whaling station and cannery, and then fishing village.

By the docks, fishing boats can often be seen unloading their catch. **Tom's Sportfishing** *((831) 633-2564. $35-$45/person. Departs daily at 6am.)* takes visitors out on the *Kahuna* for some deep-sea fishing.

This area also is prime for bird-watching. Pelicans, cormorants, gulls, terns, herons, and egrets are all drawn here to feast on the rich marine life. Rarer birds often show up during migrations.

VISITOR INFORMATION

Moss Landing Chamber of Commerce
8071 Moss Landing Rd., (831) 633-4501; www.monterey-bay.net/ml.

Marina Chamber of Commerce *211 Hillcrest, Marina, (888) 428-0627, (831) 384-9155.*

GETTING THERE

Located 8 miles north of the Monterey Peninsula and 8 miles west of Salinas. Turn off Highway 1 just before reaching the two landmark smokestacks on the eastern side of the highway, and before **Little Baja** and its Mexican pottery on the western side.

WHAT TO DO

Elkhorn Slough Safari *(831) 633-5555; www.elkhornslough.com. Adults $24, 3-14 $18, unsuitable for children under 3. Call for schedule. Reservations required.*

The best way to see great numbers of birds up close in their natural habitat is to take this tour in an open-air, flat-bottomed aluminum pontoon boat. Tours last 2 hours and travel through Elkhorn Slough. (Wondering what a "slough" (pronounced "slew") is? Simply "a wet, muddy place.") One of the state's largest wetlands, it winds inland for 7 miles and provides an important feeding and resting place for a variety of wildlife. A naturalist is aboard to point out unusual specimens, and participants are encouraged to help count various kinds of birds for an on-going research project. Lots of cute sea otters are also usually spotted, and sometimes a "raft" of them can be seen holding onto each other while floating. Don't forget binoculars and a camera.

Fort Ord *In Marina.*

A few miles south of Moss Landing, the expansive sand dune area that was formerly the Fort Ord military base is now operated by the Bureau of Land Management. It is slowly metamorphizing into recreational use. Hiking and mountain biking trails snake through its 8,000 acres. Hot air ballooning and skydiving facilities also are based here. (For those who are afraid of skydiving, here's some food for thought: At **Skydive Monterey Bay** *((888) BAY-JUMP, (831) 384-3483, fax (831) 384-7522; www.skydivemontereybay.com. Skydive $185/person; balloon ride $165/person.)* they claim that "skydivers aren't afraid of dying, they're afraid of not living."). For those who prefer to check out the skies from the ground, the new **Monterey Institute for Research in Astronomy (MIRA)** *(200 Eighth St., (831) 883-1000, fax (831) 883-1031; www.mira.org.)* schedules Star Parties regularly at its **Weaver Student Observatory**, giving participants the chance to look through a 14-inch telescope.

The largest art foundary on the West Coast, the **Monterey Sculpture Center** *(711 Neeson Rd., (831) 384-2100, (831) 384-1700, fax (831) 834-0575.)* permits seeing sculptures manufactured from beginning to end. Informal tours view clay being carved for molds, molten metal being poured into the molds, and patina colors being applied to the finished product. Discounts are available in an impressive gallery shop stocked with finished projects, and future plans call for a sculpture park set on the scenic dunes out front.

Monterey Bay Kayaks *2390 Hwy. 1, (800) 649-5357.*

For description, see page 108.

Western Hang Gliders *1 Reservation Rd., Marina, (831) 384-2622. Daily 9-sunset. Reservations recommended. 3-hr. beginners course, $89.*

Located on the dunes at secluded **Marina State Beach**, this hang-gliding school provides lessons and equipment to the daring.

The beach has a boardwalk trail over the sand dunes, where the endangered Smith's Blue Butterfly makes its home, and pods of dolphins can sometimes be spotted looping through the surf. The beach also provides a spectacular spot to watch the sun set.

WHERE TO STAY

Monterey Dunes Co. *(800) 55-DUNES, (831) 633-4883, fax (831) 633-3722; www.montereydunes.com. 120 homes; $$$+. All kitchens & wood-burning fireplaces. Pool, hot tub, saunas, 6 tennis courts.*

Fabulous beachfront vacation homes nestled on 125 acres of sand dunes can be rented. All have spectacular views, some have private hot tubs, and facilities include a sand volleyball court and basketball court.

Pajaro Dunes *2661 Beach Rd., Watsonville, (800) 675-8808, (831) 722-9201, fax (831) 728-7444; www.pajarodunes.com. 120 units; $$$+; 2-night min. on weekends. All VCRs, kitchens, & wood-burning fireplaces. 19 tennis courts.*

Situated in the shoreline dunes, this private compound consists of condominiums, townhouses, and homes. Hiking and biking trails, jogging paths, and volleyball and basketball courts round out the recreational facilities. Bike rentals are also available.

Scenic Bay Destinations *(888) 880-ROOMS, (831) 633-8000.*

This personalized reservations service specializes in matching visitors with the perfect lodging.

Travelodge *3290 Dunes Dr., Marina, (800) 550-0055, (831) 883-0300, fax (831) 384-8137. 84 rooms; $-$$$+. Hot tub.*

This inexpensive lodging is situated amid the dunes just a short walk from Marina State Beach.

WHERE TO EAT

Maloney's Harbor Inn *(831) 724-9371. L&D Tu-Sun; $$. Highchairs, boosters, child portions. Reservations advised.*

Perched on pilings over the slough, this casual spot offers an off-the-boat-fresh fish menu along with fine pelican-watching.

Phil's Fish Market and Restaurant *7640 Sandholdt Rd., (831) 633-2152, fax (831) 633-8611. Daily 8:30am-7pm, later in summer; $. Child menu.*

Begun as a fish market in 1982, when Phil was a commercial fisherman, this humble spot has evolved into a wildly popular restaurant. That's because owner Phil, a warm and kind man, takes his Italian grandmother's peasant recipes and marries them to great effect with the freshest seafood and rock-bottom prices. Diners glut on steamed Sicilian stuffed artichokes (with a bread crumb-garlic-mozzarella filling), hearty fresh Manhattan chowder, and blackened salmon with sun-dried tomato sauce or Monterey Bay spot prawns sautéed in white wine, capers, and roma tomatoes with a lemon-caper butter sauce. A seafood quesadilla, seafood salad, fish & chips, and even a burger are also on the extensive menu. Why, even the Schwarzeneggers—Arnold, Maria, and the kids—have eaten here.

The Whole Enchilada *(831) 633-3038. L&D daily; $-$$. Highchairs, boosters, Reservations advised.*

This roadside cantina, just off Highway 1, serves a slew of margaritas, including papaya and prickley pear flavors, and also lines up some unusual suspects on its menu: seafood flautas, oyster shooters, an Oaxacan tamale wrapped in banana leaves. And, of course, because Castroville, the "artichoke capital of the world," is just a few miles east of town, it also offers a big artichoke appetizer.

Monterey Peninsula

A LITTLE BACKGROUND

Popular for years because of its proximity to San Francisco, this area (Monterey, Pacific Grove, Pebble Beach, Carmel, and Carmel Valley) is well-established as a vacation destination. A vast variety of overnight accommodations and restaurants is available. Due to the area's immense popularity, there is no off-season, and reservations are essential for both lodging and the more popular restaurants.

Recently established, the **Monterey Bay National Marine Sanctuary** is the nation's eleventh and largest protected marine area. It covers more than 300 miles—from the Farallon Islands near San Francisco in the north to Cambria in the south. Protected resources include the nation's most expansive kelp forests, one of North America's largest underwater canyons, and a deep ocean environment that is the closest to shore in the continental U.S. The Monterey Bay Aquarium acts as the sanctuary's interpretive center.

GETTING THERE

Located approximately 40 miles south of Santa Cruz.

STOPS ALONG THE WAY

Giant Artichoke Restaurant *11261 Merritt St., off Hwy. 1, Castroville, (831) 633-3204. B,L,&D*

daily; $. Highchairs, boosters. No reservations.

Located in "the artichoke capital of the world," where three-quarters of the nation's artichokes are grown, this novelty restaurant makes a good rest stop. To find it, just look for the giant artichoke. Artichoke specialties include French-fried artichokes with mayonnaise dip, artichoke soup, artichoke salad, artichoke quiche, and artichoke cake. Other more standard short-order items are also on the menu.

Monterey

VISITOR INFORMATION

Monterey Peninsula Visitors & Convention Bureau *380 Alvarado St., (831) 649-5358, fax (831) 648-5373. M-F 8:30-5.*

Monterey Visitors Center *Franklin St./Camino El Estero, at Lake El Estero, (831) 649-1770, fax (831) 648-5373. Hours vary.*

ANNUAL EVENTS

Adobe Tour *April or July. (831) 372-2608. Adults $10, 6-18 $1.*

This is a very popular self-guided walking tour of historic adobe homes and buildings. Some privately-owned homes and gardens are included.

Castroville Artichoke Festival *May. In Castroville; (831) 633-CHOK; www.artichokefestival.org. Adults $6, under 12 $3.*

This is one of the state's oldest agricultural festivals. It was at this festival in 1947 that then-starlet Marilyn Monroe became the very first California Artichoke Queen.

Monterey Scottish Festival and Highland Games *May. At Monterey Fairgrounds; (831) 899-3864, fax (831) 899-7907; www.montereyscotgames.com. Adults $10, 65+ & 7-16 $8.50.*

Celebrating everything Scottish, this event is described as being much like a Celtic three-ring circus. One ring features piping (as in bagpipes) and drumming contests, with massive pipe bands competing against each other. Another ring features unusual athletic events such as the Caber Toss (in which a huge pole is tossed end-over-end for accuracy) and Putting the Stone (in which a heavy stone is tossed). And another presents the Highland Dancing Championships, which today is participated in predominantly by females. Events, including several sheepdog demonstrations, run continuously.

Monterey Historic Automobile Races *August; www.montereyhistoric.com.* **Grand Prix** *September. Both at* **Laguna Seca Racetrack** *in Salinas; (800) 327-SECA, (831) 648-5111; www.laguna-seca.com.*

Originally held in Pebble Beach, the Historic Automobile Races demonstrate the abilities of a broad range of vintage sports and racing cars. At the Grand Prix, Indy cars take the stage for three days featuring the world's best drivers.

Monterey Jazz Festival *September. At Monterey Fairgrounds; (831) 373-3366, fax (831) 373-0244; www.montereyjazzfestival.org. Tickets $150-$210, under 2 free.*

The oldest continuously presented jazz festival in the country, this well-known event offers three days of non-stop entertainment. Tickets are for the full three days and usually sell out by the end of July.

Christmas in the Adobes *December. (831) 646-5640. Tickets $10-$13, 6-17 $2.*

Each year Monterey lights up a group of historic adobes festively decorated for the holidays. Entering their cozy warmth from the chill of the night, participants tour each of the historic buildings decked with period decorations and illuminated only by candlelight. Luminarias guide participants along walkways, and docents dress in period costumes. Musical entertainment and fragrant refreshments, including Mexican hot chocolate and several wassails, are part of the mix. In addition to the adobes that are always open to the public—including the **Colton Hall Museum**, where California's first constitution was drafted, and the Stevenson House, where prior resident Robert Louis Stevenson is portrayed by an actor and Scottish music and bagpipes provide enchanting entertainment—participants are provided entry to a few adobes that are usually closed to the public, including the Casa Amesti, now a private men's club. Purchase tickets in advance as this event often sells out.

La Posada *December. (831) 646-3427. Free.*

This street parade re-enacts the hardships suffered by Mary and Joseph as they tried to find shelter in Bethlehem. A low-key, feel-good community event, it is composed almost entirely of locals. Participants meet at the Monterey Conference Center, where candles are passed out, and then, transformed into pilgrims, they form a parade following a mariachi band down the area's closed-off streets, stopping at various locations to sing carols. This event is gloriously filled with children. After, everyone returns to the conference center to relax over complimentary cider and cookies and more mariachi music while blindfolded children excitedly whack at candy-filled piñatas. In a sort of six-ring circus that for fairness divides the kids by sex and age, roars of joy explode whenever someone releases candy. (In Mexican culture, the piñata traditionally symbolizes a colorfully dressed Satan. The treasures inside symbolize temptation, the blindfold represents blind faith, and the stick is virtue. The candies that fall out reward the faithful.)

WHAT TO DO

Cannery Row.

Once booming with sardine canneries, Cannery Row became a ghost town in 1945 when the sardines mysteriously disappeared from the area's ocean. In *Cannery Row*, John Steinbeck described it as "a poem, a stink, a grating noise, a quality of light, a tone, a habit, a nostalgia, a dream." Now this mile-long road houses restaurants, art galleries, shops, a **Bargetto Winery Tasting Room** *(#700, (831) 373-4053; www.bargetto.com. Tasting daily 10-6.)*, **Steinbeck's Spirit of Monterey Wax Museum** *(#700, (831) 375-3770, fax (831) 646-5309. Open daily, hours vary. Adults $7.95, 6-12 $3.95.)*, and the **Monterey Bay Aquarium** *(see page 107)*. **A Taste of Monterey** *(#700, (831) 646-5446, fax (831) 375-0835. Tasting daily 11-6; fee $3, applies to purchase.)* provides samplings from local wineries along with a 180-degree view of the bay and a theater presenting wine-related videos.

Reading John Steinbeck's *Cannery Row* provides background for visiting this historic street. Lee Chong's Heavenly Flower Grocery, mentioned in Steinbeck's novel, is now **Wing Chong Market**—a collection of shops *(#835)*, and La Ida's Cafe is now **Kalisa's** sandwich shop *(#851)*. Doc's lab *(#800)* is currently owned by the city.

Just a block north of the aquarium, the **American Tin Cannery Premium Outlet** *(125 Ocean View Blvd., (831) 372-1442. M-W & Sat 10-6, Thur & F 10-9, Sun 11-5.)* is worth a detour. Within its attractive industrial interior are some especially noteworthy outlets: Carter's, Come Fly a Kite, Royal Doulton. Also, **First Awakenings** *(#105, (831) 372-1125. B&L daily; $. Highchairs, boosters, booths, child menu. No reservations.)*, with its pleasant outdoor patio and soothing live guitar music, is a good choice for breakfast items such as fresh fruit crêpes and a variety of omelettes, as well as for salads and sandwiches.

Edgewater Family Fun Center *640 Wave St., (831) 649-1899, fax (831) 649-2387. Daily 11-10, in summer 10-1.*

This family entertainment center has the latest video games and a candy shop stocked with cotton candy, caramel apples, and popcorn. It also is home to what might be the world's fastest **merry-go-round.** Built by Herschell-Spillman in 1905, it has 36 horses and 2 chariots.

Bay Bikes *((831) 646-9090. Daily 9-5, in summer to 7. $10+/2 hrs., $22+/day.)* rents both 21-speed mountain bikes and multi-passenger Italian surrey bikes to ride on the spectacular waterfront bike trail that hugs the bay from Fisherman's Wharf to Lover's Point. Children's bikes, child seats and trailers, and jogging strollers are also available. Safety equipment is included with rentals.

El Estero Park *Del Monte Ave./Camino El Estero/Fremont Blvd., (831) 646-3866. Daily 10-dusk. Free.*

Hiking and bike trails and a lake filled with hungry ducks await here. Paddle boats and canoes can be rented, and children may fish from boats. Located by the lake on Pearl Street, **Dennis the Menace Playground** features colorful play equipment designed by former area resident Hank Ketchum—creator of the *Dennis the Menace* comic strip. Notable are a hedge maze with a corkscrew slide in its center, a long suspension bridge, and an authentic Southern Pacific steam train engine (number 1285) to climb on. Picnic tables and a snack concession are available.

Fisherman's Wharf *(831) 373-0600, fax (831) 373-2027. Shops daily 10-10.*

Lined with restaurants and shops, the Wharf also offers inexpensive entertainment. Sometimes an organ grinder greets visitors at the entrance, his friendly monkey anxious to take coins from children's hands. Sea lions hang out around the wharf pilings and sometimes put on a free show. The **Glass Bottom Boat** *((800) 200-2203, (831) 372-7150, fax (831) 372-7152; www.sealifetours.com. Call for schedule. Adults $6, under 12 $5.)* runs 20-minute narrated harbor tours, and several businesses also offer deep-sea fishing expeditions.

Jacks Peak County Park *25020 Jacks Peak Park Dr., off Hwy. 68 to Salinas, (831) 372-8551. Daily 11-7; in winter 9-5. $2-$3/vehicle.*

This 525-acre park has 8 miles of trails and a variety of picnic areas. Follow the nature trail up to Jacks Peak for a great view of Monterey Bay, Carmel Bay, and the valley.

Maritime Museum of Monterey *5 Custom House Plaza, (831) 375-2469, fax (831) 655-3054. Daily 10-5. Adults $5, 65+ $4, 13-18 $3, 6-12 $2.*

Beginning with the history of the Spanish ships that anchored in the area four centuries ago, this new museum celebrates California's seafaring heritage. See ship models, bells, compasses, and related items, and learn about the area's naval history. Most impressive is the 2-story-tall, 10,000-pound 1889 Fresnel lens once used at the Point Sur Lighthouse.

Monterey Bay Aquarium *886 Cannery Row, (831) 648-4888; www.montereybayaquarium.org. Daily 10-6; in summer 9:30-6. Adults $15.95, 65+ & 13-17 $12.95, 3-12 $7.95. Advance reservations: (800) 756-3737; $3/order.*

Built on the site of what was once the Row's largest sardine cannery, this spectacular $112 million facility is one of the nation's largest seawater aquariums. It is run by a non-profit organization with the mission of stimulating interest in, increasing knowledge about, and promoting stewardship of Monterey Bay through innovative exhibits, public education, and scientific research. Well-arranged and architecturally interesting, the aquarium provides a close-up view of the underwater habitats and creatures of Monterey Bay—an area

known for its spectacular and varied marine life. Among the more than 100 galleries and exhibits is one that displays a 3-story-high kelp forest and another that displays the area's playful sea otters. More than 350,000 fish, mammal, bird, invertebrate, and plant specimens are on display, and almost all are native to Monterey Bay. Don't miss the special walk-through aviary of shorebirds or the bat ray petting pool. Children especially enjoy the Touch Pool, where they can handle a variety of sea stars and other tidepool life. The Outer Bay, which features the world's largest acrylic window, permits peeking into a simulated ocean, with sharks, ocean sunfish, green sea turtles, and schools of tuna swimming in a million gallons of water. This area also has a fascinating display of sea jellies, including a don't-miss psychedelic tank filled with orange sea nettles shown against a bright blue background. Both a fast-food cafeteria and a pricier restaurant are available inside; picnic tables are provided outside. Or get a hand-stamp for re-entry and dine somewhere nearby.

Monterey Bay Kayaks *693 Del Monte Ave., (800) 649-5357, (831) 373-KELP, fax (831) 373-0119; www.montereykayaks.com. Daily 9-6, in summer to 8. $50/3-hr. tour.*

Observe sea lions and otters up close near Fisherman's Wharf and along Cannery Row. Tours guided by marine biologists include a half-hour of safety instruction, and no experience is necessary. Tour kayaks hold two people. Children must be at least 4 1/2 feet tall; smaller children can be accommodated in a triple kayak with two adults.

Monterey Peninsula Museum of Art *559 Pacific St., (831) 372-7591, fax (831) 372-5680. W-Sat 11-5, Sun 1-4, 3rd Thurs to 8. Adults $3, students $1.50; free 1st Sun 1-4 & 3rd Thur 5-8.*

Located downtown, this museum has been called "the best small town museum in the United States." Indeed it provides the delight of a small collection of regional art and photography well displayed. Important artists of the Monterey Peninsula, including Ansel Adams and Edward Weston, are represented. A strong graphics collection includes works by Rembrandt, Manet, and Picasso.

An extension of the museum, the historic **La Mirada adobe** *(720 Via Mirada, (831) 372-3689, (831) 372-6043. Thur-Sat 11-5, Sun 1-4. Adults $3, students $1.50; free 1st Sun 1-4.)* is located several miles away. One of the first adobes built during the Mexican occupation of Monterey, it features a dramatic contemporary addition and displays antique furnishings, early California art, and works by contemporary regional artists. Dramatic gardens are filled with more than 75 varieties of rose and 300 varieties of rhododendron.

Monterey State Historic Park *20 Custom Plaza, (831) 649-7118, (831) 647-6236. Daily 10-4, in summer to 5; walking tour daily, call for schedule. Tickets $1-$5.*

Part of the California State Park system, this facility consists of both historical sites and preserved adobes. (Downtown Monterey holds the largest collection of historic buildings west of Williamsburg.) Guided tours are scheduled for the very special **Stevenson House** (said to be haunted by a forlorn woman dressed in black), the **Cooper-Molera Adobe** (a 2-acre complex with chickens, sheep, carriages, and a visitor center), the **Larkin House**, and the **Casa Soberanes**.

The First Theater *(Pacific St./Scott St., (831) 375-4916. Call for schedule, reservations, & ticket prices.)* was once a saloon and boarding house for sailors. The first play was presented here in 1848, and the Troupers of the Gold Coast are still going strong. Nowadays the melodramatic shows and olios change periodically, but they are still presented in the tiny theater just like they were in the old days. All productions were written before 1900.

The Path of History, a self-guided walking tour following gold-colored tiles embedded in the sidewalk, leads past 44 historic buildings and gardens.

Rent-A-Roadster *229 Cannery Row, (831) 647-1929, fax (831) 647-1928; www.rent-a-roadster.com. Daily 10-6. $29.95+/hr.*

Easy-to-drive, authentic reproductions of 1929 Model A Ford Roadsters can be rented for a drive down the coast or a tour of the 17-Mile Drive. Roadsters seat four—two in the front and two in the rumble seat—and a red 1930 deluxe Phaeton model seats five. It is worth the rental price just to honk the old-fashioned horn and watch reactions.

Ventana Vineyards *2999 Monterey-Salinas Hwy. (Hwy. 68), (800) BEST-VIN, (831) 372-7415. Tasting daily 12-5.*

The tasting room here is in the historic, atmospheric Old Stone House. Don't miss sampling the white wines, particularly the Chardonnays and Rieslings it is known for. A flower-beladen deck surrounded by tall pines is available for picnicking.

WHERE TO STAY

Casa Munras Garden Hotel *700 Munras Ave, (800) 222-2446 CA, (800) 222-2558 US, (831) 375-2411, fax (831) 375-1365; www.casamunras-hotel.com. 166 rooms; $-$$$. Children under 12 free. Some gas fireplaces. Heated pool. Restaurant.*

One of the first residences built outside the walls of the old Presidio in 1824, the original Casa was built of individual adobe bricks made by hand from native materials. Parts of the dining room and porch of the original house remain. Converted into a hotel in 1941, its grounds are spacious, attractive, and peaceful, and all rooms are furnished with brass beds.

Hotel Pacific *300 Pacific St., (800) 554-5542, (831) 373-5700, fax (831) 373-6921; www.hotelpacific.com. 105 rooms; $$$-$$$+; 2-night min. on weekends. Children under 12 free. All VCRs & gas fireplaces. 2 hot tubs. Afternoon snack, continental breakfast; limited room service.*

Situated near the Wharf, this lodging melds the amenities of a hotel with the convenience of a motel. It features adobe-style architecture and attractive gardens with fountains. All rooms are spacious suites equipped with down comforters and pillows as well as featherbeds, and nightly turndown service is provided.

Hyatt Regency Monterey *One Old Golf Course Rd., (800) 228-9000, (831) 372-1234, fax (831) 375-3960. 575 rooms; $$-$$$. Children under 18 free. 2 heated pools, 2 hot tubs, fitness center, parcourse, 6 tennis courts (fee, some night lights). Restaurant, room service.*

Located on the outskirts of town, this quiet, luxurious resort is adjacent to the scenic **Old Del Monte Golf Course**—the oldest golf course west of the Mississippi. **Knuckles Historical Sports Bar** has 14 big-screen TVs tuned to the action in a casual, peanut-shells-on-the-floor atmosphere.

Monterey Bay Inn *242 Cannery Row, (800) 424-6242, (831) 373-6242, fax (831) 373-7603; www.montereybayinn.com. 4 stories; 47 rooms; $$$-$$$+; 2-night min. on weekends. Children under 12 free. All VCRs. 2 hot tubs, sauna, fitness center. Evening snack, continental breakfast; limited room service.*

Located a short walk from the aquarium, all rooms in this waterfront lodging feature private balconies, sleeper sofas, and plush robes. Most rooms also have spectacular bay views, and all guests have access to the rooftop hot tub and its breathtaking view of the bay. Breakfast is brought to the room.

Monterey Marriott Hotel *350 Calle Principal, (800) 228-9290, (831) 649-4234, fax (831) 372-2968. 10 stories; 341 rooms; $-$$$+. Children under 18 free. Heated pool, hot tub, fitness center. 1 restaurant, room service. Valet parking $12.*

Located near the Wharf, this attractive hotel is built on the former site of the grand old Hotel San Carlos. It is the tallest building in town and offers spectacular views. Rooms are quiet and tastefully appointed, and a sports bar presents live music in the evening.

Monterey Plaza Hotel & Spa *400 Cannery Row, (800) 334-3999, (831) 646-1700, fax (831) 646-0285; www.woodsidehotels.com. 285 rooms; $$$-$$$+; 2-night min. on weekends. Children under 18 free. Health spa. Restaurant, room service. Valet parking $8.*

Built partially over the bay, with rooms on either side of the road, this well-situated luxury hotel features comfortably appointed, attractively decorated rooms with marble bathrooms. Some have private balconies and magnificent bay views. A new penthouse-level health spa is equipped with two hot tubs on a sundeck, two saunas, and a fitness center—all available free to guests who book a treatment and for an additional daily fee otherwise.

Dinner at a bayside window table in the **Duck Club** *(B,L,&D daily; $$-$$$. Highchairs. Validated valet parking.)* is a delight. For starters try the crab-laden crab cakes or delicious traditional Caesar salad. Entrees include several housemade pastas, a selection of fresh seafood, and, of course, duck: crisp-roasted with Valencia orange sauce or wood-roasted with green peppercorn mustard sauce. Dessert choices include a chocolate layer cake, a large selection of housemade ice creams, and a plate of housemade cookies.

Old Monterey Inn *500 Martin St., (800) 350-2344, (831) 375-8284, fax (831) 375-6730; www.oldmontereyinn.com. 10 rooms; $$$+; 2-night min. on weekends; 100% non-smoking. Unsuitable for children. No TVs; some fireplaces. Full breakfast.*

Built in 1929, this aesthetically magnificent half-timbered, Tudor-style inn resembles an elegant English country house. It is located in a quiet neighborhood near enough to downtown to permit walking. Though any room here should please, a few are quite special. The private Garden Cottage has a cozy fireplace and two-person whirlpool tub. The Library has book-lined walls and a large stone fireplace, and the Serengeti Room sports a bed covered by genuine jungle mosquito netting and antique travel mementos for decorations. All rooms have a unique and tasteful decor, with fluffy beds made with soft feather beds on the mattress topped by down comforters. Thoughtful touches such as small chocolates held in silver boxes, candles by the bathtub, terry-lined silk robes, a CD player equipped with a soothing classical disc, a fabulous collection of books, and stamped postcards make guests feel well cared for. Some sort of snack is always available. And then there is the acre of tended flower gardens surrounded by massive Monterey Pines. In the morning, coffee is delievered to the room, with breakfast served later at an enormous, beautifully-set table in a dining room graced by plank floors, a huge copper fireplace, and a hand-plastered ceiling. Alternatively, breakfast can be served in bed.

Spindrift Inn *652 Cannery Row, (800) 841-1879, (831) 646-8900, fax (831) 646-5342; www.spindriftinn.com. 4 stories; 42 rooms; $$$-$$$+; 2-night min. on weekends. Children under 10 free. All VCRs & wood-burning fireplaces. Afternoon snack, continental breakfast; limited room service. Valet parking $6.*

Located right in the heart of Cannery Row, just 2 blocks from the aquarium, this tasteful lodging offers comfortable rooms. Many have bay views, permitting occupants to greet a foggy morning as Steinbeck described in *The Grapes of Wrath* journal, "I remember how grey and doleful Monday morning was. I could lie and look at it from my bed . . ." Some rooms have faux canopy beds, and all are equipped with gas-started fireplaces that accept wood. Breakfast is brought to the room on a silver tray, along with a newspaper. The inn's backyard is tiny McAbee Beach, where ruins of concrete sardine holding tanks await exploration.

West Wind Lodge *1046 Munras Ave., (800) 821-0805, (831) 373-1337, fax (831) 372-2451; www.westwindlodge.com. 52 rooms; $-$$. Children under 10 free. Some VCRs, kitchens, & gas fireplaces. Indoor heated pool & hot tub, sauna. Continental breakfast.*

Though the architecture of this motel is unpresumptious, its facilities are noteworthy.

Motel Row.

Modern motel accommodations abound along Munras Avenue.

WHERE TO EAT

Abalonetti Seafood Trattoria *57 Fisherman's Wharf, (831) 373-1851, fax (831) 373-2058. L&D daily; $-$$. Highchairs, boosters, child portions. Reservations advised.*

This small, unpretentious restaurant is named for a famous dish in which squid (or calamari) is pounded until tender, breaded, and then sautéed in butter. Over half the menu is devoted to squid dishes—the house specialty. Other seafood and Italian dishes, as well as pizza, are also available, and the dining room has a good view of Monterey Bay.

Bubba Gump Shrimp Co. *720 Cannery Row, (888) 560-GUMP, (831) 373-1884, fax (831) 373-0354; www.bubbagump.com. L&D daily; $.*

Highchairs, child menu. No reservations.

Based on the movie *Forrest Gump*, which won six Oscars, this is the first in the chain of seafood restaurants revolving around memorabilia from the movie—script pages, storyboards, costumes, photos, scrawled Gumpisms on tabletops. And all the while the movie plays continuously on video monitors. By the way, the men's room is Bubba's, the women's room Jenny's. For more description, see page 40.

Fresh Cream *99 Pacific St., 100-C Heritage Harbor, (831) 375-9798, fax (831) 375-2283; www.freshcream.com. D daily; $$$. Reservations advised.*

Situated on the second story of a building across from the Wharf, this classy, serene restaurant offers a great harbor view along with excellent classical French cuisine. Appetizers include housemade lobster raviolis with a rich lobster butter sauce and a sprinkling of both black and gold caviars. Among the entrees, which include fresh local fish and veal, is a flawless rack of lamb Dijonnaise and a succulent roast duck with black currant sauce. The spectacular desserts include a Grand Marnier soufflé and an incredible edible chocolate box holding a mocha milk shake.

Ghirardelli Chocolate Shop & Soda Fountain *660 Cannery Row, (831) 373-0997.*

This is a much smaller version of the fountain in San Francisco. For description, see page 68.

Mike's Seafood Restaurant *25 Fisherman's Wharf, (831) 372-6153. L&D daily; $-$$. Highchairs, boosters, child portions. Reservations advised at D.*

Arrive before sundown to take advantage of the excellent bay views afforded from the tables in this busy and popular seafood restaurant. Steaks, hamburgers, and chicken are also on the menu.

Montrio *414 Calle Principal/Franklin St., (831) 648-8880; www.montrio.com. L&D daily. Reservations advised.*

Operating within a dramatically remodeled 1910 firehouse, with tall ceilings and odd contemporary lighting, this popular spot is always buzzing. If full, opt for a seat in the bar and order there. Innovative items include a roasted beet salad with apples and Feta cheese, and Basmati rice cakes. Favorites are crispy crab cakes, risotto, and juicy rotisserie chicken with mashed potatoes.

The Sardine Factory *701 Wave St., (831) 373-3775, fax (831) 646-8900; www.sardinefactory.com. D daily; $$$. Highchairs, boosters, child menu. Reservations advised.*

Once home to a canteen patronized by cannery workers, this building now houses an elegant, award-winning restaurant with five very different dining rooms and over 30,000 bottles of wine in its cellar. The kitchen is known for its fresh seafood and aged beef. Special items include fresh abalone, fresh Australian lobster tail, and aged beef. Appetizers include a highly acclaimed abalone cream bisque created for President Reagan's inaugural, as well as fresh clams, mussels, oysters, and dungeness crab in season. But no sardines. A knock-out dessert features a spectacular foot-high lighted ice swan bearing a scoop of sorbet.

Stokes Adobe *500 Hartnell St., (831) 373-1110, fax (831) 373-1202. L M-Sat, D daily; $$$. Reservations advised.*

Dating from 1833 and one of the oldest buildings in Monterey, this historic 2-story structure now has a comfortable, airy, modernized interior. Owner-chef Brandon Miller showcases local ingredients, and his always evolving menu usually includes an acclaimed lavender-infused grilled pork chop and sometimes a really good cassoulet. The refined soups are particularly delicious, and small tapas plates make nice starters or, for smaller appetites, a few can compose a satisfying meal.

Whaling Station Inn Restaurant *763 Wave St., (831) 373-3778, fax (831) 373-2460; D daily; $$$. Highchairs, boosters, child portions. Reservations advised.*

Situated inside a building that dates from 1929 and once housed a Chinese grocery store, this restaurant produces creative and delicious food. On one visit seafood selections included barbecued Monterey Bay prawns—the fresh, sweet, firm-fleshed kind that are so hard to find nowadays—and blackened fresh salmon.

Entrees were served with a house salad consisting of Cajun-spiced walnuts resting on a bed of Belgian endive, spinach, and baby lettuce—all tossed with a sweet dressing fragrant with sesame oil. Steamed baby carrots and asparagus on a bed of purple cabbage accompanied the entrees, and a diamond of spicy polenta completed the plate. Grilled quail, rack of lamb, and prime steaks are among the non-seafood entrees. Desserts are made fresh in the kitchen each day, and an irresistible tray of them is presented at the end of each memorable repast.

Wharfside Restaurant *60 Fisherman's Wharf, (831) 375-3956, fax (831) 375-2967. L&D daily; $$. Highchairs, boosters, child portions. Reservations advised.*

In the window downstairs it is sometimes possible to watch the various varieties of ravioli (meat and spinach, cheese, squid, salmon, shrimp, crab, lobster) being laboriously prepared. Dining takes place upstairs, where great views of the bay can be enjoyed. The menu is rounded out with other pastas and seafood.

Pacific Grove

A LITTLE BACKGROUND

Originally settled as a Chinese fishing village, Pacific Grove was established in 1875 as a Methodist Episcopal Church summer camp. Some modest summer cottages and distinctive Victorian-style homes remain today. Due to some of the ordinances put into effect in those early days, only recently, in 1969, was a liquor store opened within the town limits. In fact, Pacific Grove was the last dry city in California. Still old-fashioned, the main shopping street has free diagonal parking with an additional row in the center of the street.

VISITOR INFORMATION

Pacific Grove Chamber of Commerce
584 Central Ave., (800) 656-6650, (831) 373-3304, fax (831) 373-3317.

ANNUAL EVENTS

Victorian Home Tour *April & October. $15. Children must be 12 or older.*

Monarch Butterflies *October. Free.*

Each year hundreds of thousands of stunning orange-and-black monarch butterflies return to Pacific Grove to winter on the needles of favored local pine trees. They migrate all the way from western Canada and Alaska and stay until March, when they again fly north.

Somewhat of a mystery is how they find their way here each year since, with a lifespan of less than a year, no butterfly makes the trip twice. It is, in fact, the great-grandchildren of the prior year's butterfly visitors that return. Somehow the monarchs program a genetic message into their progeny, which then return to these same trees the following fall and repeat the cycle.

Reacting to the weather somewhat as does a golden poppy, monarchs prefer to flutter about on sunny days between the hours of 10 a.m. and 4 p.m. In fact, they can't fly when temperatures drop below 55 degrees. So on cold and foggy days, which are quite common in this area, they huddle together with closed wings and are often overlooked as dull pieces of bark or dead leaves. On cold days observers must be careful where they step: Monarchs that have dropped to the ground to sip dew off the grass might be resting there, having found it too cold to fly back to their perch.

During early March the butterflies can be observed mating. Watch for females chasing males in a spiral flight. (Males are recognized by a characteristic black dot on their wings.) When a female finds a male she likes, they drop to the ground to mate. Literally standing on his head at one point, the male, while still mating, then lifts the female back to a perch in a tree, where they continue mating for almost an entire day!

Butterfly nets should be left at home. To discourage visitors from bothering these fragile creatures, Pacific Grove has made molesting a butterfly a misdemeanor crime carrying a $1,000 fine.

To celebrate the annual return of the butterflies, the town of Pacific Grove, also known as Butterfly Town U.S.A., has hosted a **Butterfly Parade** every October since 1938. Completely non-commercial, this delightful parade provides the low-key pleasure of viewing local grade school children marching down the street dressed as butterflies. Traditional bands and majorette corps from local schools also participate. Weather always cooperates: This parade has *never* been rained on.

For more information on the monarchs, contact non-profit Friends of the Monarchs *(P.O. Box 51683, Pacific Grove 93950-6683)*. To receive a child's packet of information on the monarch (stories, a coloring page, etc.), send a request and $1 for postage and handling.

WHAT TO DO

Lover's Point *626 Ocean View Blvd.*

Located at the southern tip of Monterey Bay, this park holds a chunky granite statue honoring the monarch butterfly. It offers a pleasant beach for sunbathing and wading, and a grassy picnic area with barbecue pits.

Monarch Grove Sanctuary *1073 Lighthouse Ave., (888) PG-MONARCH, (831) 375-0982. Daily dawn-dusk. Free.*

The densest clusters of monarchs congregate in the pine and eucalyptus grove located behind the Butterfly Grove Inn. Guided tours are available from mid-October through mid-February.

Pacific Grove Museum of Natural History *165 Forest Ave./Central Ave., (831) 648- 3119, fax (831) 372-3256; www.pgmuseum.org. Tu-Sun 10-5. Free.*

Opened in 1882, this museum is dedicated to telling the natural history of Monterey County through exhibits of marine and bird life, native plants, shells, and Native American artifacts. Butterfly-related exhibits include photographs and displays, as well as an informative 10-minute videotape. The life history of the monarch is portrayed in drawings, and during the summer larvae are often on view. Milkweed—the only plant on which the female monarch will lay her eggs—attracts butterflies to a native plant garden outside the museum.

Each year during the third weekend in April this tiny museum sponsors a **Wildflower Show**. As many as 600 varieties are displayed.

Point Piños Lighthouse *On Asilomar Blvd., about 2 blocks north of end of Lighthouse Ave., (831) 648-3116, fax (831) 372-3256. Thur-Sun 1-4. Free.*

Docents dressed in period costume give informal tours of this oldest continuously operating Pacific Coast lighthouse, built in 1855 out of granite quarried nearby. The area surrounding the lighthouse is a good spot to walk, picnic, and observe sea otters; note that Doc's Great Tide Pool, from Steinbeck's *Cannery Row*, is here.

Poor Man's 17-Mile Drive.

There is no charge for taking this scenic 4.2-mile drive that passes rugged seascapes and some impressive Victorian homes. Begin at Ocean View Boulevard and 3rd Street. At Point Piños, turn left on Sunset Drive. Tidepooling is good in several spots, and from April to August beautiful lavender ice plant cascades in full bloom over the rocky beach front.

Special Shops.

- **Antique Clock Shop** *489 Lighthouse Ave., (831) 372-6435.*

This charming converted cottage holds a constantly changing inventory of clocks. Be there on the hour for a chiming treat.

- **The Cubby Hole** *580 Lighthouse Ave., (831) 648-5344, fax (831) 648-1019.*

It's easy to feel a bit like Alice while browsing the wonderland of accessories here. Don't miss the very unusual TV bed in the back, or the myriad items made from vintage chenille.

WHERE TO STAY

Andril Fireplace Cottages *569 Asilomar Blvd., (831) 375-0994, fax (831) 655-2693; www.andrilcottages.com. 16 units; $-$$; 1-week min. in summer. Children under 5 free. VCRs avail.; all kitchens & fireplaces. Hot tub. Pets welcome.*

These woodsy, pine-paneled cottages make for very comfortable lodging, especially for longer stays. Situated around a tree-shaded courtyard furnished with picnic tables, they are just a block from the ocean.

Asilomar Conference Grounds *800 Asilomar Blvd., (888) 733-9005, (831) 372-8016, fax (831) 372-7227; www.asilomarcenter.com. 314 units; 100% non-smoking; $-$$$. Children under 2 free. Some TVs, kitchens, & wood-burning fireplaces. Heated pool. Full breakfast; dining room.*

Founded as a YWCA camp in 1913 and boasting eight buildings designed by architect Julia Morgan, this 105-acre facility is now used mainly as a conference grounds. It is part of the California State Parks system. Rooms are divided among 28 lodge buildings. When underbooked, rooms are made available to the general public. Reservations cannot be made more than a month in advance; last-minute accommodations are often available. In Spanish the word "asilomar" means "retreat by the sea," and, indeed, the grounds are located in a quiet, scenic area just a short walk from the ocean. Both guests and non-guests are welcome to participate in inexpensive, family-style conference meals (breakfast from 7:30 to 9, lunch from noon to 1, dinner from 6 to 7); reservations are not necessary, and highchairs and booster seats are available.

Beachcomber Inn *1996 Sunset Dr., (800) 634-4769, (831) 373-4769. 26 rooms; 100% non-smoking; $$; 2-night min. on weekends. Heated pool, sauna. Continental breakfast; restaurant.*

Factors rendering this typical motel special include its oceanside location, a 90-degree pool, and free bikes and safety helmets for the use of guests.

The **Fishwife Restaurant** *(1996 1/2 Sunset Dr., (831) 375-7107. L&D W-M, SunBr; $-$$. Child portions.)* is located adjacent and justly popular with locals. A large variety of fresh seafood and pastas is featured, and the soups and flautas are also quite good.

Butterfly Grove Inn *1073 Lighthouse Ave., (800) 337-9244, (831) 373-4921, fax (831) 373-4921; www.bflyinn.qpg.com. 28 rooms; $-$$$; 2-night min. on weekends. Some kitchens & fireplaces. Heated pool, hot tub. Small dogs welcome.*

This attractive complex offers a choice of either suites in a vintage house or regular motel rooms. Located on a quiet side street, it is adjacent to the Monarch Grove Sanctuary.

The Centrella *612 Central Ave., (800) 233-3372, (831) 372-3372, fax (831) 372-2036; www.centrellainn.com. 26 rooms; 100% non-smoking; $$-$$$+; 2-night min. on weekends. Children under 5 free. Some TVs & wood-burning & gas fireplaces. Afternoon snack, full breakfast.*

This restored turn-of-the-century Victorian has won awards for its interior decor. Rooms are furnished with antiques and feature Laura Ashley wallpapers and fabrics, and some bathrooms have clawfoot tubs. Suites on the third floor are particularly nice. Families with children under 12 are accommodated only in the more expensive cottage suites, each of which has a fireplace and private garden.

The Gosby House Inn *643 Lighthouse Ave., (800) 527-8828, (831) 375-1287, fax (831) 655-9621; www.foursisters.com. 22 rooms; $-$$$. No TVs; some fireplaces & shared baths. Afternoon tea, continental breakfast.*

Located in the heart of the town's shopping area, this Queen Anne Victorian features a charming rounded corner tower and many bay windows. Built in 1887 by a cobbler from Nova Scotia, it is now an historic landmark. Noteworthy features include particularly attractive wallpapers, a well-tended garden, and an assortment of stuffed bears and bunnies that welcome guests throughout the inn (all available for purchase).

For a hopelessly romantic getaway, make dinner reservations at **Gernot's Victoria House Restaurant** *(649 Lighthouse Ave., (831) 646-1477. D Tu-Sat; $$-$$$. Boosters, child portions.*

Reservations advised.). Located just next door in another restored Victorian, this lovely dining room offers a continental menu with selections such as Austrian wiener schnitzel and wild boar Bourguignonne.

Seven Gables Inn *555 Ocean View Blvd., (831) 372-4341. 14 rooms; 100% non-smoking; $$$-$$$+; 2-night min. on weekends. Unsuitable for children under 12. No TVs. Afternoon tea, full breakfast.*

Located across the street from the ocean, this elegant yellow Victorian mansion was built in 1886. Rooms and cottages all have ocean views and are decorated with fine European and American antiques.

Motel Row.

Numerous motels are located at the west end of Lighthouse Avenue and along Asilomar Boulevard.

WHERE TO EAT

Bay Cafe *589 Lighthouse Ave., (831) 375-4237. B&L daily; $. Highchairs, boosters, child portions.*

The all-American menu here includes plate-size pancakes, house-baked meats, and made-from-scratch mashed potatoes and gravy.

Lighthouse Cafe *602 Lighthouse Ave., (831) 372-7006. B&L daily; $. Highchairs, boosters.*

This small, comfortable cafe specializes in fluffy omelettes, char-broiled chicken and hamburgers, and housemade soups, salads, and sandwiches.

Old Bath House *620 Ocean View Blvd./17th St., (831) 375-5195, fax (831) 375-5379. D daily; $$$. Highchairs, boosters. Reservations advised.*

Every table in this elegant Victorian has a splendid view of Monterey Bay. Entrees include imaginative preparations of meats and fish, including house specialty Beef Bindel—filet mignon in puff pastry with foie gras and wild mushrooms. Divine desserts are made in the restaurant's own pastry kitchen, and the Grand Marnier soufflé is well worth the wait for preparation.

Red House Cafe *662 Lighthouse Ave., (831) 643-1060. B&L Tu-Sun, D Thur-Sat; $. No cards.*

Lunch on tasty, attractive sandwiches and salads and sublime soups in this cute little cottage converted into a charming cafe. Drinks include made-from-scratch lemonade and unfiltered apple juice, and desserts are devastatingly delicious.

Hidden around back is **Miss Trawick's Garden Shop** *(664 Lighthouse Ave., (831) 375-4605, fax (831) 656-0960.)*, and what a find it is. Do stop in for a browse through the myriad garden-related delights tucked here and there throughout the warren of spaces.

Tinnery *631 Ocean View Blvd., (831) 646-1040. B,L,&D daily; $$. Highchairs, boosters, booths, child portions.*

Located at Lover's Point, this comfortable, casual restaurant offers outstanding views of the bay. Breakfast is particularly pleasant, with omelettes, egg dishes, and strawberry pancakes on the menu. The extensive, eclectic international dinner menu includes entrees such as tempura prawns, pasta primavera, and prime rib.

Carmel-by-the-Sea

A LITTLE BACKGROUND

They had take the direct country road across the hills from Monterey, instead of the Seventeen Mile Drive around by the coast so that Carmel Bay came upon them without any fore-glimmering of its beauty. Dropping down throgent pines, they passed woods-embowered cottages, quaint and rustic, of artists and writers, and went on across wind-blown rolling sand hills held to place by sturdy lupines and nodding with pale California poppies. Saxon screamed in sudden wonder of delight, then caught her breath and gazed at the amazing peacock-blue of a breaker, shot through with golden sunlight, over-falling in a mile-long sweep and thundering into white ruin of foam on a crescent beach of scarcely less white.

— Jack London,
Valley of the Moon, 1913

A well-established getaway destination, Carmel is best known for its abundant shops, cozy lodgings, and picturesque white sand beach.

It is also known for the things that it doesn't have. No street signs, streetlights, electric or neon signs, jukeboxes, parking meters, or buildings over 2 stories high are allowed in town. No sidewalks, curbs, or house numbers are found in the residential sections. These absent items help Carmel keep its small-town feeling.

Do be careful. Eccentric laws in the town make it illegal to wear high-heeled shoes on the sidewalks, throw a ball in the park, play a musical instrument in a bar, or dig in the sand at the beach other than when making a sandcastle.

It seems that almost every weekend some special event is scheduled in the area, making available lodging perpetually scarce. Make accommodation reservations far in advance, especially for the quainter lodgings, and consider taking advantage of the special rates often available for mid-week stays.

VISITOR INFORMATION

Carmel Visitors Center/Business Association *San Carlos/5th, (800) 550-4333, (831) 624-2522, fax (831) 624-1329; www.carmelcalifornia.org.*

ANNUAL EVENTS

AT&T Pebble Beach National Pro-Am *January & February. In Pebble Beach; (800) 541-9091. $15-$25.*

This was formerly known as the Bing Crosby Golf Tournament.

Carmel Art Festival *May. (831) 642-2503. Free.*

Among the events are special exhibits, art demonstrations in the galleries, and the kick-off to the town's annual **Art Walk**—when galleries stay open late on Friday nights and host special events.

Carmel Bach Festival *July & August. (831) 624-2046, fax (831) 624-2788; www.bachfestival.org. $10-$50.*

Held annually since 1935 (except for two years off during World War II), this baroque music festival varies its highlights from year to year. Candlelight concerts are usually presented in the town's picturesque mission, and a special children's concert is always scheduled.

Concours d'Elegance *August. In Pebble Beach; (831) 372-8026, fax (831) 659-0663.*

Car buffs don their dressiest summer attire for a stroll on the spacious lawn at the Lodge at Pebble Beach, where this elegant affair is held. Classic vintage and antique automobiles are displayed.

WHAT TO DO

Art Galleries.

- **Galerie Blue Dog** *6th/Lincoln, (831) 626-4444, fax (831) 626-4488. Daily 10-6.*

This gallery is devoted entirely to the pop art blue dog of Louisiana Cajun artist George Rodrigue.

- **New Masters Gallery** *Dolores/Ocean, (800) 336-4014, (831) 625-1511, fax (831) 625-5137; www.newmastersgallery.com. Daily 10-5.*

The work of accomplished contemporary artists is shown here.

Beaches.

- **Carmel Beach** *At the foot of Ocean Ave., (831) 626-2522.*

Known for its white powdery sand and spectacular sunsets, this world-famous beach is a choice spot for a refreshing walk, a picnic, or flying a kite. Swimming is unsafe.

The **Great Sand Castle Contest** *((800) 550-4333)* is held here each September or October, depending on the tides. Contestants are encouraged to bribe judges with food and drink.

- **Carmel River State Beach** *At the end of Scenic Rd., (831) 649-2836. Daily 9-dusk. Free.*

Very popular with families and divers, this beach has a fresh-water lagoon and an adjoining bird sanctuary. It is located behind the Carmel Mission, where the Carmel River flows into Carmel Bay, and offers beautiful views of Point Lobos. Locals refer to it as Oliver's Cove; the southern end is known as Monastery Beach. Swimming is dangerous. Picnic facilities are available.

Mission San Carlos Borromeo del Rio Carmelo *3080 Rio Rd., 1 mi. south of town off*

Hwy. 1, (831) 624-3600. M-Sat 9:30-4:30, Sun 10:30-4:30; services on Sun. By donation.

Father Junipero Serra, who established this mission in 1770 and used it as his headquarters for managing the entire chain of missions, is buried here at the foot of the altar. It is also referred to as the Carmel Mission. An intriguing star window graces the rough sandstone walls and Moorish bell tower of the façade, and a museum displays Native American artifacts, mission tools, and re-creations of both the original mission kitchen and California's first library. A quadrangle courtyard garden, featuring a restful fountain stocked with colorful koi, accents the cemetery where over 3,000 mission Indians are buried. A **fiesta** is held each year on the last Sunday in September.

Across the street, 37-acre **Mission Trail Park** *((831) 624-3543. Daily dawn-dusk. Free.)* has several hiking trails. The broad Serra Trail is an easy uphill hike. Doolittle Trail goes further on for great views of the bay and a visit to the 1929 Tudor **Flanders Mansion**, where it is possible to tour the grounds and stroll through the **Lester Rowntree Arboretum**.

Pacific Repertory Theatre *Monte Verde/8th, in Golden Bough Playhouse, (831) 622-0700, fax (831) 622-0703; www.pacrep.org. Performances Mar-Oct. Tickets $8-$20, under 5 not admitted.*

In a building reconstructed on the site of a playhouse that has burned to the ground twice in the past (each time after performances of *By Candlelight!*), this ambitious company presents varied fare in an intimate venue.

Pebble Beach Equestrian Center *Portola Rd./Alva Ln., Pebble Beach, (831) 624-2756, fax (831) 624-3999. Group rides daily at 10, 12, 2, & 3:30. $47/person. Riders must be 7 or older. Reservations required.*

Escorted rides follow the extensive bridle trails winding through scenic Del Monte Forest, around the legendary Spyglass Hill Golf Course, down to the beach, and over the sand dunes. Riders have a choice of English or Western saddles, and English riding lessons are available.

Point Lobos State Reserve *3 mi. south of town off Hwy. 1, (831) 624-4909. Daily 9-dusk; interpretive center 12-5. $7/vehicle.*

Described as "the greatest meeting of land and water in the world," Point Lobos provides the opportunity to see the rustic, undeveloped beauty of the Monterey Peninsula. The flat-topped, gnarled-limbed Monterey cypress trees are native to just the 4-mile stretch between here and Pebble Beach, and sea otters are often spotted in the 1,250-acre reserve's protected waters. Self-guiding trails are available, and guided ranger walks are scheduled daily in summer. A restored whaler's cabin, built in 1851 by a Chinese fisherman, now serves as an interpretive center. Artifacts and photographs tell about the area's history and one display highlights the location's various incarnations in movies. Dress warmly, and bring along binoculars, a camera, and maybe a picnic, too.

17-Mile Drive *At Pebble Beach exit off Hwy. 1, between Carmel & Monterey, (831) 649-8500. Daily sunrise-sunset. $7.50/vehicle.*

The scenery along this world-famous drive is a combination of showplace homes, prestigious golf courses, and raw seascapes. Sights include the Restless Sea, where several ocean crosscurrents meet; Seal and Bird Rock,

Sea otter

where herds of sea lions and flocks of shoreline birds congregate; the Pebble Beach Golf Course, one of three used during the annual AT&T National Pro-Am tournament; and the landmark Lone Cypress clinging to its jagged, barren rock base. Picnic facilities and short trails are found in several spots.

Consider splurging on lunch or dinner at one of the ocean-view restaurants (one is a reasonably-priced coffee shop) at the elegant Inn at Spanish Bay (see page 119) or Lodge at Pebble Beach (see page 120). The gate fee is reimbursed when the meal check is paid.

Shopping Complexes.

• **The Barnyard** *Hwy. 1/Carmel Valley Rd., (831) 624-8886. Daily 10-5:30, restaurants 8am-10pm.*

This unusual complex is filled with shops worthy of a browse. Don't miss **Succulent Gardens** *((831) 624-0426)* with its rare and unusual varieties of flowering cacti and succulents. **Thunderbird Bookshop & Cafe** *((831) 624-1803, fax (831) 624-0549. L daily, D Tu-Sun; $-$$. Highchairs, boosters, child portions.)*, a combination bookstore/restaurant, features dining among world-famous authors. Sandwiches and hamburgers are available at lunch, full meals at dinner, coffee-and during the off hours.

• **Carmel Plaza** *Ocean/Junipero, (831) 624-0137, fax (831) 624-5286. M-F 10-5:30, Sun 12-5.*

The upscale collection of noteworthy shops here surrounds a courtyard filled with flowers.

Special Shops.

• **The Mischievous Rabbit** *Lincoln/Ocean, (831) 624-6854. M-Sat 10-5, Sun 12-5.*

This tiny shop specializes in delightful Beatrix Potter-illustrated items.

• **The Secret Garden** *Dolores/5th, (831) 625-1131. M, Tu, & Thur 11-3, F-Sun 11-5.*

Tucked down a tiny pathway, this peaceful shop purveys a charming collection of garden accents.

Tor House *26304 Ocean View Ave., (831) 624-1813, (831) 624-1840; www.torhouse.org. Tours F & Sat on the hour 10-3. Adults $7; children must be 12 or older. Reservations required.*

Poet Robinson Jeffers built this medieval-style house and tower retreat out of huge granite rocks hauled up from the beach below. He did much of the work himself and was of the opinion that the manual labor cleared his mind and that, as he put it, his "fingers had the art to make stone love stone." All of his major works and most of his poetry were written while he lived with his wife and twin sons on this craggy knoll overlooking Carmel Bay.

WHERE TO STAY

Carmel River Inn *Hwy. 1 at bridge, (800) 882-8142, (831) 624-1575, fax (831) 624-0290. 43 units; $$-$$$+; 2-night min. on weekends. Some kitchens & wood-burning fireplaces. Heated pool.*

Located on the outskirts of town on the banks of the Carmel River, this lodging facility stretches over 10 acres. Guests have a choice of motel rooms or individual cottages, many of which have balconies or patios overlooking the river.

Cobblestone Inn *Junipero/8th, (800) 833-8836, (831) 625-5222, fax (831) 625-0478; www.foursisters.com. 24 rooms; 100% non-smoking; $$$-$$$+. Children under 2 free. All gas fireplaces. Afternoon snack, full breakfast.*

Located only 2 blocks from the main shopping street, this charming inn is filled with teddy bears awaiting guests in fanciful poses. Should one capture a heart, all are available for adoption by purchase. Spacious guest rooms are furnished with country-style pine furniture and iron-frame beds. Shutters provide privacy, and fireplaces constructed with large river rocks provide atmosphere and warmth. Refrigerators are stocked with complimentary cold drinks. In the morning all guests are greeted with a newspaper at their door, and breakfast can be enjoyed either outside on a sunny slate-and-brick-paved courtyard filled with English flowers blooming in stone containers, or inside with the bears. Two bicycles are available for guests to borrow.

Cypress Inn *Lincoln/7th, (800) 443-7443, (831) 624-3871; www.cypress-inn.com. 33 rooms; $$-$$$+; 2-night min. on weekends. Some gas fireplaces. Evening snack, continental breakfast. Pets welcome ($20/night).*

Featuring a Moorish Mediterranean style of architecture, this inn dates from 1929 and is located right in town. Owned now by actress Doris Day along with several partners, its rooms are distinctively decorated and comfortable and a few have ocean views. All guest rooms are equipped with a decanter of cream sherry, a fruit basket, bottled drinking water, and fresh flowers.

Green Lantern Inn *7th/Casanova, (888) 414-4392, (831) 624-4392, fax (831) 624-9591; www.greenlanterninn.com. 19 rooms; 100% non-smoking; $$-$$$+. Children under 5 free. Some fireplaces. Continental breakfast.*

Operating as an inn since 1926, this pleasant group of rustic multi-unit cottages is located on a quiet side street just a few blocks from the village and 2 blocks from the beach.

Highlands Inn, A Park Hyatt Hotel *On Hwy. 1, 4 mi. south of town, (800) 682-4811, (831) 620-1234, fax (831) 626-8105; www.highlands-inn.com. 142 rooms; $$$+. Children under 18 free. Some kitchens & wood-burning fireplaces. Heated pool, 3 hot tubs, fitness center. 2 restaurants, room service. Small dogs welcome.*

Located in a fragrant pine forest in the scenic Carmel Highlands, up a hill just pass the town gas station with its old-time pump and two authentic red English phone booths, this inn was built on its spectacular cliffside setting in 1916. Through the years it has been the host to many famous guests, including the Beatles and two presidents—Kennedy and Ford. Luxurious contemporary-style guest rooms are designed for privacy, making it possible to just hole up and listen to the birds tweeting and the sounds of the not-too-distant surf. All have ocean views and are equipped with robes and even binoculars. Complimentary bikes are available to guests, and upon check-in children are given a special amenities bag filled with goodies.

At breakfast it's an expansive buffet and at lunchtime hamburgers and specials in the casual, moderately priced **California Market**, where diners can enjoy an expansive view of the rugged coastline either inside or outside on a balcony. The celebrated **Pacific's Edge** *(L&D daily, SunBr; $$$. Reservations advised.)* restaurant also features a stunning view (plan to dine during daylight hours). One dinner enjoyed here included a perfectly prepared boiled artichoke appetizer served with sesame mayonnaise; ginger-carrot soup; a colorfully presented entree of grilled swordfish on grilled Maui onions topped with a chunky sauce of kalamata olives, oven-dried tomatoes, and parsley; and a classic crème brulee chosen from an array of elegant desserts.

The Inn at Spanish Bay *2700 17-Mile Drive, Pebble Beach, (800) 654-9300, (831) 647-7500, fax (831) 644-7955; www.pebblebeach.com. 270 rooms; 100% non-smoking; $$$+. All VCRs & gas fireplaces. Heated pool, hot tub, sauna, fitness center, health spa, 8 tennis courts (fee; 2 with night lights), 18-hole golf course. 3 restaurants, room service.*

Nestled ocean-front beside a protected marine sanctuary, this luxury resort was designed to complement its spectacular surroundings. The decor blends in with the misty wash of natural colors seen outside, and most rooms have a patio or balcony. Bicycle rentals, a shuttle to Carmel and Monterey destinations, and milk and cookies at bedtime can be arranged. A full time Nature Concierge is on the staff, as is a talented floral arranger, and the **Ansel Adams Gallery** *(M-F 10-6.)* operates as one of the resort's shops. The Scottish-style **Links at Spanish Bay** golf course—which Jack Nicklaus considers "possibly the best in the world" and about which Tom Watson enthuses,

"Spanish Bay is so much like Scotland, you can almost hear the bagpipes"—surrounds the resort.

Roys' at Pebble Beach *((831) 647-7423, fax (831) 644-7957. B,L,&D daily; $$.)* offers spectacular ocean views across the dunes along with the celebrated, strikingly colorful Euro-Asian cuisine of Hawaii-based chef Roy Yamaguchi. Noteworthy on the lunch menu are tasty spring rolls in a chili-plum sauce and a well-seasoned Thai chicken salad with minty dressing. Fresh local seafood and designer pizzas are also on the menu, as are gorgeous, killer desserts.

Lamp Lighter Inn *Ocean Ave./Camino Real, (831) 624-7372. 9 units; 100% non-smoking; $$-$$$+. Children under 1 free. Some kitchens; 1 wood-burning fireplace.*

Conveniently located between the village and the ocean, this enclave has both charming rooms and gingerbread-style cottages. It very well might fulfill guest's fairy tale fantasies. Several of the cozy, comfortable cottages accommodate families; the "Hansel and Gretel" has a special sleeping loft for kids. Another, the "Blue Bird Room," has a cathedral ceiling of age-patinaed redwood and a picture window looking into a large oak tree. Children especially enjoy finding all 17 elves in the Elves Garden. Accommodations in an annex, located 1 block closer to the beach, are a little less expensive and a lot less interesting; however, several have ocean views.

La Playa Hotel *Camino Real/8th, (800) 582-8900, (831) 624-6476, fax (831) 624-7966. 80 units; $$-$$$+. Children under 12 free. Some kitchens & fireplaces. Heated pool. Restaurant, room service.*

This luxury Mediterranean-style hotel is conveniently located just 2 blocks from the beach and 4 blocks from town. Taking up an entire square block, it is the largest hotel, as well as the only full-service resort hotel, in Carmel. Guest room beds have rustic carved headboards sporting the hotel's mermaid motif, and the beautifully maintained gardens are abloom with colorful flowers year-round. A group of charming, spacious cottages situated a block closer to the ocean are also available.

The casual **Terrace Grill** *(B,L,&D daily.)* features an elaborate Sunday brunch with a buffet of fresh fruits and pastries, Belgian waffles, and made-to-order omelettes. Diners can also opt to order from a menu, and a perfect spicy Bloody Mary is available from the bar. The restaurant's namesake terrace has both ocean and garden views and is covered overhead and heated, so al fresco dining can be enjoyed regardless of the weather.

Lincoln Green Inn *Carmelo/15th, (800) 262-1262, (831) 624-1880, fax (831) 626-1243; www.vagabondshouseinn.com. 4 units; $$$; 2-night min. on weekends. Some kitchens; all gas fireplaces. Pets welcome.*

Located on the outskirts of town, just a few blocks from where the Carmel River flows into the ocean, this cluster of comfortable English housekeeping cottages features living rooms with cathedral-beamed ceilings and stone fireplaces.

The Lodge at Pebble Beach *17-Mile Drive, Pebble Beach, (800) 654-9300, (831) 624-3811, fax (831) 626-3725. 161 rooms; $$$+; 2-night min. on weekends. All fireplaces. Heated pool, children's wading pool, sauna, 14 tennis courts (fee). 3 restaurants, room service.*

Complete luxury and the best of sporting facilities await guests here. Golfers can enjoy playing some of the best courses in the country, and horse rentals and equestrian trails are nearby, as are jogging and hiking trails and a parcourse.

Non-guests are welcome to stop in and enjoy the spectacular ocean view here over a drink or meal. Try the **Club XIX** *((831) 625-8519. L&D daily; $$-$$$. Reservations advised.)* at lunch, when diners can sit on a terrace overlooking both the 18th hole and the ocean while enjoying fare as casual as their dress—a Cobb salad, a club sandwich. Dinner is more elegant, with diners seated in the plushly appointed dining room and feasting on refined dishes such as cassoulet of lobster and duck confit, and boneless quail stuffed with sweetbreads and morels.

Mission Ranch *26270 Dolores St./Rio Rd., (800) 538-8221, (831) 624-6436, fax (831) 626-4163. 31 rooms; 100% non-smoking; $-$$$+; 2-night min. on weekends. Some gas fireplaces. Fitness center, 6 clay tennis courts (fee). Continental breakfast; restaurant.*

Owned by actor Clint Eastwood, who has invested a fistful of dollars in furnishings, this former dairy farm is located near the Carmel Mission. It has operated as a lodging facility since 1937. Special accommodation choices include roomy cottages that work well for families, the 1857 Victorian-style Martin Family Farmhouse with B&B-style rooms, and the 1852 Bunkhouse cottage; simpler rooms are also available. Eastwood fans take note: The 19th-century pot-belly stove that appeared in *Unforgiven* is found in the inn restaurant.

Normandy Inn *Ocean Ave./Monte Verde, (800) 343-3825, (831) 624-3825, fax (831) 624-4614; www.normandyinncarmel.com. 48 units; $-$$$; 2-night min. on weekends. Children free. Some kitchens & wood-burning fireplaces. Heated pool (unavail. Jan-Mar). Afternoon sherry, continental breakfast.*

Conveniently located on the town's main shopping street and just 4 blocks from the ocean, this inn features an attractive half-beamed Normandy style of architecture and has several large cottages. The comfortably appointed rooms are decorated in French country style, with feather mattresses, and the pool is invitingly secluded.

Pine Inn *Ocean Ave./Monte Verde, (800) 228-3851, (831) 624-3851, fax (831) 624-3030. 49 rooms; $-$$$+; 2-night min. on weekends. Children under 18 free. 1 gas fireplace. Restaurant, room service.*

Decorated in an elegant Victorian style, this inn opened in 1889 and is the oldest in town. It is conveniently located in the center of town.

San Antonio House *San Antonio/7th, (831) 624-4334. 4 rooms; 100% non-smoking; $$$-$$$+; 2-night min. on weekends. Unsuitable for children under 12. All gas fireplaces. Continental breakfast.*

This attractive guest house offers large rooms, a lovely garden, and a location in a quiet residential area just 1 block from the beach. One room has a private patio, another its own doll house, and a breakfast tray is brought to each room in the morning.

Sea View Inn *Camino Real/12th, (831) 624-8778, fax (831) 625-5901. 8 rooms; 100% non-smoking; $-$$$; 2-night min. on weekends. Unsuitable for children under 12. No TVs; some shared baths. Afternoon & evening snack, continental breakfast.*

Located 3 blocks from the beach, this converted Victorian home offers pleasantly appointed rooms. The most requested guest room features a cozy canopy bed.

The Stonehouse Inn *8th/Monte Verde, (800) 748-6618, (831) 624-4569; www.carmelstonehouse.com. 6 rooms; 100% non-smoking; $$-$$$+. Unsuitable for children under 12. Some shared baths. Afternoon snack, full breakfast.*

Built by local Indians in 1906, this rustic stone country house is close to the village. The original owner often entertained well-known artists and writers, and the antique-furnished rooms are now named in honor of some of those guests.

Sundial Lodge *Monte Verde/7th, (831) 624-8578, fax (821) 626-1018; www.sundiallodge.com. 19 rooms; 100% non-smoking; $$$-$$$+; 2 night min. on weekends. Unsuitable for children under 5. Some kitchens. Afternoon snack, continental breakfast; restaurant.*

Located just 1 block from the center of town, next to City Hall (known for a while as "Clint's Place"), this charming hotel is built around a flower-filled brick courtyard. Tea and sherry are served to guests each afternoon.

Vagabond House Inn *4th/Dolores, (800) 262-1262, (831) 624-7738, fax (831) 626-1243; www.vagabondshouseinn.com. 11 rooms; $-$$$; 2-night min. on weekends. Unsuitable for children under 12. Some kitchens & wood-burning & gas fireplaces. Continental breakfast. Pets welcome.*

This rustic English Tudor-style building features cozily furnished rooms that open off a quiet, flower-bedecked courtyard.

WHERE TO EAT

Carmel Bakery *Ocean/Lincoln, (831) 626-8885. Daily 6:30am-7pm.*

Caramel apples and both alligators and turtles made of marzipan bread are just a few of the delicacies available at this popular bakery. Also particularly good are the apricot log pastries, wild blueberry scones, and focaccia with spicy pepper topping. Pastries and drinks can be enjoyed on the premises or while walking the boutique-laden streets.

Cottage of Sweets *Ocean Ave./Lincoln, (831) 624-5170, (831) 620-0106; www.cottageofsweets.com. M-Thur 10-7, F-Sun to 8.*

Among the sweet surprises in this charming candy cottage are imported chocolates, diet candy, gourmet jelly beans, and taffy.

Em Le's *Dolores/5th, (831) 625-6780, fax (831) 625-0563. B&L daily, D F & Sat; $. Boosters.*

Football broadcaster John Madden is part-owner of this cozy, casual spot touted as a "vintage soda fountain." Among the large variety of breakfast items are buttermilk waffles, in a choice of light or dark bake, and wild blueberry pancakes. The basic all-American cuisine includes fried chicken, meatloaf, mashed potatoes, and apple pie. Pleasant views of sidewalk traffic and counter seating add to the low-key Carmel charm.

The General Store *5th/Junipero, (831) 624-2233, fax (831) 624-3522. L&D daily, SunBr; $-$$. Highchairs, child menu. Reservations advised.*

In a warren of spaces that includes a heated outdoor patio, this popular spot serves an eclectic menu of fresh seafood, pasta, pizza, salads, and sandwiches as well as Mexican and vegetarian items, and it stays open late for night owls.

Jack London's *San Carlos/5th, (831) 624-2336, fax (831) 626-0941. L&D daily, SunBr; $-$$. Highchairs, boosters.*

Even locals come here to enjoy the excellent bar drinks and cozy bistro atmosphere. Kids are welcome and can order fancy non-alcoholic drinks. Menu specialties include individual-size pizzas, a variety of hamburgers, and deep-fried calamari. Fresh fish selections change daily. Rich, velvety pasta carbonara Milano and a New York steak round out the eclectic menu. Dinner entrees come with a generous house salad topped with ranch dressing.

La Boheme Restaurant *Dolores/7th, (831) 624-7500, fax (831) 624-6539; www.laboheme.com. D daily; $$. Closed part of Dec or Jan. 1 booster, child portions. No reservations.*

Cozy and colorfully decorated, and featuring an overhanging indoor roof built by a retired French race car driver, this charming petite cafe is outrageously romantic. Just one three-course fixed-price dinner is served each evening, plus one vegetarian entree option. With no menu choices to fret over, diners are free to concentrate on each other. The French and Italian country-style dishes are served informal family-style. One dinner enjoyed here began with a large, crisp salad accented with olives and substantial slices of ham, salami, and cheese. Then came a perfectly seasoned cream of broccoli soup, followed by a main course of pork loin in a cream sauce flavored with juniper berries. Strawberries Romanoff cost additional and made a refreshing, light dessert. The soup and entree change each evening, so it is a good idea to call ahead for the night's menu.

Patisserie Boissiere *Mission/Ocean, (831) 624-5008. B Sat & Sun, L daily, D W-Sun; $$. Reservations advised at D.*

The menu at this elegant little gem offers housemade soups as well as more substantial entrees. Though it would be hard to do so, don't overlook the pastries and desserts—lemon cheesecake, chocolate whiskey cake, zabaglione, and plenty more.

Piatti *6th/Junipero, (831) 625-1766.*

For description, see page 356.

Picnic Pick-Ups.

• **Mediterranean Market** *Ocean/Mission, (831) 624-2022. Daily 9-6.*

This well-stocked delicatessen offers freshly marinated artichoke hearts, sandwich meats, cheeses, skinny French baguettes, exotic beers, wines, bottled waters, and soft drinks.

Caviar is also available, as are picnic baskets to carry it all away in.

• **Wishart's Bakery** *Ocean/Mission, (831) 624-3870. Daily 6:30am-7pm.*

This is a popular branch of the Carmel Bakery (see page 122).

Rocky Point *On Hwy. 1, 12 miles south of town, (831) 624-2933. L&D daily; $$-$$$. Highchairs, boosters, child portions. Reservations advised.*

Take a scenic drive down the coast toward Big Sur, stopping here to enjoy the spectacular view along with a multi-course charcoal-broiled steak or fresh seafood dinner. Sandwiches and hamburgers are on the lunch menu, making it a relative bargain.

Sans Souci Restaurant *Lincoln/5th, (831) 624-6220. D Thur-Tu. Highchairs, boosters. Reservations advised.*

Elegant dining and a quiet, relaxing ambiance greet diners at this oasis of civility. Each course is perfectly executed and presented with flair. One meal enjoyed here began with sautéed wild mushrooms and asparagus tips with a sherry cream sauce. Then came grilled apple sausage and duck confit with raspberries and goat cheese over Carmel Valley greens moistened with a creamy balsamic-date vinaigrette. The entree was a rich lobster fricassée in the flakiest of puff pastries. The dessert soufflé, for which the restaurant is well known, was flavored with aromatic passion fruit, however just about any flavor imaginable can be prepared. Servers are attentive and attired in tuxedos. An Early Bird menu is often available from 5 to 6:30 p.m.

Toots Lagoon *Dolores/7th, (831) 625-1915, fax (831) 625-4096; www.tootslagoon.com. L&D daily; $-$$. Highchairs, boosters, child menu. Reservations advised.*

Roaringly popular with locals, this friendly spot is known for its ribs prepared with a choice of four sauces. Brick oven-baked pizza, housemade pasta, and fresh fish are also on the eclectic menu. Desserts include mud and turtle pies as well as green Jell-O tequila shooters, eaten by loosening the edge with a toothpick and then chucking it down the hatch.

Tuck Box English Tea Room *Dolores/Ocean, (831) 624-6365, fax (831) 624-5079. B, L, & afternoon tea daily; $. Boosters. No reservations. No cards.*

Featuring fairy-tale architecture and verily reeking of quaintness, this tiny dining room can be quite difficult to get seated in. If ever it is without a long line in front, go! Additional seating is available on a tiny outdoor patio. The limited breakfast menu offers simple egg items served with delightful fresh scones and a choice of either homemade olallieberry preserves or orange marmalade. At lunch sandwiches, salads, and omelettes are available along with Welsh rarebit and a daily entree special. Afternoon tea features scones, pies, delicious English trifle, and, of course, plenty of hot English tea.

Across the street, tiny **Picadilly Park** invites relaxing contemplation with its benches, flower garden, and goldfish pond.

Village Corner *Dolores/6th, (831) 624-3588, fax (831) 622-8855. B,L,&D daily; $-$$. Highchairs, boosters, booths, child menu. Reservations advised.*

The large patio here, which is heated year-round, provides the chance to relax and watch the rest of the town stroll by. The Mediterranean bistro menu offers bruschetta and deep-fried local calamari for appetizers. Entree choices include several interesting pastas as well as a delicious Cajun-style blackened salmon and a dramatic paella for two. Local wines pair perfectly.

Carmel Valley

A LITTLE BACKGROUND

Reliably sunny and peaceful, Carmel Valley is often overlooked by visitors to the Monterey Peninsula. That's a shame, because it is a wonderful place to relax and only a few miles inland from Carmel. Lodgings, restaurants, and shops dot Highway 16/Carmel Valley Road along its 15-mile stretch east into the hub of town.

VISITOR INFORMATION

Carmel Valley Chamber of Commerce *13 W. Carmel Valley Rd., (831) 659-4000, fax (831) 659-8415.*

WHAT TO DO

Bernardus Winery *5 W. Carmel Valley Rd., 13 mi. from Hwy. 1, (831) 659-1900, fax (831) 659-1676. Tasting W-Sun 11-5.*

The father of owner Ben (Bernardus) Pon is the designer of the Volkswagen bus and was the person who first exported the Beetle to the U.S. Ben himself has been a professional race driver for Porsche and represented Holland in skeet shooting at the 1972 Olympics. With such an accomplished background it isn't surprising that he would make a success of his upstart winery, which makes wines in the old French Bordeaux and Burgundian styles and is known for its Chardonnay and Sauvignon Blanc.

Château Julien Wine Estate *8940 Carmel Valley Rd., 5 mi. from Hwy. 1, (831) 624-2600, fax (831) 624-6138. Tasting M-F 8:30-5, Sat & Sun 11-5; tours daily at 10:30 & 2:30.*

Styled after an actual château located on the French-Swiss border, this castle-like structure has no formal tasting bar. Tasters just gather informally around a large table in the middle of a high-ceilinged room. While their parents are enjoying an informal tasting of Chardonnays and Merlots—the two varietals this winery is noted for—children can partake of juice and crackers. A garden patio invites picnicking.

Garland Ranch Regional Park *Off Carmel Valley Rd., 8.6 mi. from Hwy. 1, (831) 659-4488, fax (831) 659-5902. Daily sunrise-sunset. Free.*

Running along the banks of the Carmel River, this park boasts more than 5,000 acres. The 1.4-mile Lupine Loop Trail provides an easy nature walk; more self-guided hiking trails lead up into the mountains. This park is home to the very spot in the Carmel River where the boys in Steinbeck's *Cannery Row* caught frogs. Though frog collecting is not permitted, relaxing is. A Visitors Center provides orientation and maps.

WHERE TO STAY

Carmel Valley Ranch Resort *One Old Ranch Rd., 6 mi. from Hwy. 1, (800) 4-CARMEL, (831) 625-9500, fax (831) 624-2858; www.grandbay.com. 144 rooms; $$$+; 2-night min. on weekends. Children under 17 free. All wood-burning fireplaces. 2 heated pools, hot tub, sauna, fitness center, 12 tennis courts (fee; 2 clay), 18-hole golf course. 3 restaurants, room service.*

Built in an elegant ranch-style architecture featuring local stone and oak, this luxurious all-suite resort is situated on 1,700 scenic acres surrounded by rolling hills. It is the only resort on the Monterey Peninsula with a guarded gate. Each suite features cathedral ceilings and has a large private deck, two TVs, and three two-line phones. Some suites have decks with private outdoor hot tubs. A children's playground is provided, a special children's program operates in the summer, and horseback riding is available on-site.

The Oaks restaurant *(B,L,&D daily, SunBr. Highchairs. Reservations advised.)* sports a stunning view of the valley.

John Gardiner's Tennis Ranch *114 Carmel Valley Rd., 11 mi. from Hwy. 1, (800) 453-6225, (831) 659-2207, fax (831) 659-2492; www.jgtr.com. 14 rooms; $$$+; 5-day rate ($1,725-$2,250/person) includes lodging, meals, & tennis instruction. Closed Dec-Mar. Unsuitable for children under 18. Some wood-burning fireplaces. 2 pools (1 heated), hot tub, sauna, 14 tennis courts.*

Begun by John Gardiner in 1957, this legendary tennis retreat has been visited by three presidents (Nixon, Ford, and Reagan). The 5-day clinics run Sunday through Friday and include approximately 25 hours of instruction; shorter programs are also available. And with one court per guest room, there is never any waiting. When guests aren't on the courts, they're usually either relaxing on the private patio of their luxurious cottage, admiring the extensive flower gardens, or satisfying their worked-up appetites with a sumptuous meal. Low-cal diets haven't been discovered here yet. Meals include items such as soufflés, beef Wellington, and fresh fish with popovers.

Quail Lodge Resort & Golf Club *8205 Valley Greens Dr., 3 mi. from Hwy. 1, (888) 828-8787, (831) 624-2888, fax (831) 624-3726; www.quail-lodge-resort.com. 100 units; $$$+. Children under 12 free. Some gas fireplaces. 2 pools (1 heated), hot tub, health spa, 4 tennis courts (fee), 18-hole golf course. Continental breakfast; restaurant, room service. Pets welcome.*

These lakeside cottages are situated on 850 acres of golf fairways, meadows, and lakes that were once the site of the Carmel Valley Dairy. Guests can use hiking trails and visit 11 lakes that are also wildlife sanctuaries. Attracting a classy crowd, the resort's parking lot has been witnessed holding a DeLorean and several Ferraris at the same time.

The dressy **Covey Restaurant** *(D daily. Highchairs, boosters, booths. Reservations advised.)* overlooks a lake and offers refined European cuisine with a California touch.

Tassajara Zen Mountain Center
39171 Tassajara Rd., 40 mi. from Hwy. 1. Reservations: (415) 865-1899 (M-F 9-12:30 & 1:30-4); www.sfzc.com. 29 units; 100% non-smoking; $$$+; rate includes 3 vegetarian meals; 2-night min. on weekends. Closed Sept-Apr. Number of children permitted is controlled. No TVs; some fireplaces; some shared baths. Hot springs pool, steam rooms. Day use: (831) 659-2229; adults $14-$17, children $8-$10; reservations essential.

Owned by the Zen Center of San Francisco, this traditional Zen Buddhist monastery is located deep in the Ventana Wilderness in the Los Padres National Forest and is home to 50 male and female monks. Getting there requires a 14-mile drive down a steep dirt road (a four-wheel-drive or stick-shift is strongly advised), but overnight guests have the option of arranging a ride in on a four-wheel-drive "stage." The famous hot mineral springs are semi-enclosed in a Japanese-style bathhouse. Men's and women's baths and steam rooms are separated, and swimsuits are optional. More activities include hiking, river wading, and picnicking. Guests stay in simple wood or stone cabins with no electricity. Lighting is provided by kerosene lamps, and one phone is shared by everyone. This isn't a place to sleep in—bells go off at 5:30 a.m. to announce meditation time for any guests who want to participate. Getting a reservation can be difficult. Call early. For overnight stays, reservations open on April 3. For day visits, reservations open on April 25. Day guests must bring their own towels and food.

WHERE TO EAT

Katy and Harry's Wagon Wheel *Hwy. 16/Valley Greens Dr., in Valley Hills Shopping Center, 3 mi. from Hwy. 1, (831) 624-8878. B&L daily; $. No reservations. No cards.*

Extremely popular with locals, this spot is usually packed. Tables are tiny, but portions are generous. Breakfast seems to be the busiest meal and is served until the 2 p.m. closing time. The menu includes omelettes, eggs Benedict, oatmeal, assorted styles of pancakes (don't miss the owner's favorite—raspberry), and fresh-squeezed orange juice. A late breakfast permits chowing-down more than enough grub to satisfy a tummy until dinner. The hamburgers, French fries, and homemade beans are also reputed to be very good.

Big Sur

A LITTLE BACKGROUND

Whoever settles here hopes that he will be the last invader.

— Henry Miller, *Big Sur and the Oranges of Hieronymus Bosch*

Big Sur is such a special place that many people who have been here don't feel generous about sharing it. However, facilities are so limited that it's hard to imagine the area getting overrun with tourists. Except, perhaps, in the thick of summer.

The town of Big Sur seems to have no center. It stretches along Highway 1 for 6 miles, offering a string of amenities. Then, as one continues driving south, the highway begins a 90-mile stretch of some of the most spectacular scenery in the U.S.

Note that the river's bottom here is rocky. Bring along waterproof shoes for wading.

VISITOR INFORMATION

Big Sur Chamber of Commerce *P.O. Box 87, Big Sur 93920, (831) 667-2100; www.bigsur california.org.*

Monterey Peninsula Visitors & Convention Bureau. See page 105.

GETTING THERE

Located approximately 25 miles south of the Monterey Peninsula.

WHAT TO DO

Big Sur is so non-commercial that there is little to list in this section. Visitors can look forward to relaxing, swimming in the river, picnicking on the beach, or taking a hike through the woods. Look out for poison oak, and bring along a good book.

Andrew Molera State Park *On Hwy. 1, (831) 667-2315. $4/vehicle.*

Located near the photogenic **Bixby Bridge**, this beach park has plenty of hiking trails. Several are short and easy: The 2-mile (round trip) Bluffs Trail follows the ocean to a promontory, and the 5-mile (round trip) Bobcat Trail follows the Big Sur River through dense redwoods. Walk-in campsites are available.

Molera Horseback Tours *((800) 942-5486, (831) 625-5486, fax (831) 624-4789. Daily at 9, 1:30, and 4 hours before sunset. Closed Dec-Mar. $25+/person; riders must be 7 or older. Reservations advised.)* offers rides to the beach.

Henry Miller Library *On Hwy. 1, just south of Nepenthe restaurant, (831) 667-2574, same fax; www.henrymiller.org. Thur-Sun 11-6 .*

Miller lived in Big Sur for 18 years. The former home of his good friend, Emil White, has been turned into a shrine honoring the late artist and author. It is filled with memorabilia, photos, and letters, and the bathroom features erotic tiles by Ephraim Doner. The library also serves as a community art center and book store, and picnicking on the redwood-sheltered lawn is encouraged. Special events are often scheduled on weekends.

Pfeiffer Beach.

Watch for unmarked Sycamore Canyon Road on the west side of Highway 1. This narrow road begins about 1.7 miles south of Fernwood Resort and winds for 2 lovely miles to a beach parking lot. The only easily accessible public beach in the area, it features striking rock formations and arches carved out by the rough surf. Visitors can wade in a stream that meanders through the sandy beach but should stay out of the turbulent ocean. If it all looks vaguely familiar, it might be because this is where Elizabeth Taylor and Richard Burton acted out some love scenes in *The Sandpiper.*

Pfeiffer-Big Sur State Park *On Hwy. 1, (831) 667-2315. Daily 10-10. $6/vehicle.*

Activities at this 821-acre park include hiking (among the many trails is a half-mile nature trail), river swimming, and ranger-led nature walks and campfires, and an open meadow is perfect for playing baseball or throwing a Frisbee. Facilities include picnic tables, a restaurant, and a store. Campsites are available.

Point Sur State Historic Park *Off Hwy. 1, 19 mi. south of Carmel, (831) 625-4419. Sat at 10 & 2, Sun at 10. Adults $5, 13-18 $3, 5-12 $2. No strollers.*

The **Point Sur Lightstation**, which is the center of this park, was built in 1889. It is now open for strenuous 3-hour guided tours that include a half-mile hike and a 300-foot climb. Tours are not recommended for small children. Because parking is limited, only the first 40 people to arrive can be accommodated.

WHERE TO STAY

Big Sur Lodge *Off Hwy. 1, (800) 4-BIG-SUR, (831) 667-3100, fax (831) 667-3110; www.bigsurlodge.com. 61 rooms; $-$$; 2-night min. on weekends. Children stay free. No TVs; some kitchens & fireplaces. Heated pool. Restaurant (May-Sept only).*

Situated within Pfeiffer-Big Sur State Park, this complex has many spacious two-bedroom motel units. They are distributed throughout spacious, grassy grounds where deer are often seen grazing; those close to the pleasant pool area seem most desirable. Guests also have access to the state park's facilities. A casual, moderately-priced coffee shop serves meals all day in season.

Esalen Institute *Off Hwy. 1, (831) 667-3000, fax (831) 667-2724; www.esalen.org. Heated pool, hot tubs.*

Located on a breathtaking crest above the ocean, this legendary educational facility offers lodging and dining in conjunction with its workshops. Space is open to the general public when the facility is underbooked. Then a bed space runs $90 to $150 per person per day and includes three meals. Special family rates are available. Call for reservations no earlier than 5 days before date of desired visit. Some will want to be forewarned, others informed, that nude bathing is de rigueur in the hot tubs and swimming pool. Self-exploration workshops include massage, meditation, yoga, vision improvement, etc. Call for a copy of the workshop catalogue.

New Camaldoli Hermitage *2 mi. off Hwy. 1, 20 mi. south of town, (831) 667-2456, (831) 667-2341, fax (831) 667-0209; www.contemplation.com. 9 rooms; $45 donation/person. Includes 3 simple vegetarian meals.*

Founded in 1958 by three Benedictine monks from Camaldoli, Italy, this quiet 800-acre wildlife and wilderness preserve allows guests to meditate, read, rest, and pray. Solitary, silent, non-directed retreats, in the Catholic tradition of the Benedictine order, are offered here and open to people of all faiths. Chapel services are available for those who wish to participate, and each modest room has a private garden and ocean view.

A **gift shop** *(Daily 8:30-11 & 1:15-5.)* sells pottery and religious items as well as brandy-dipped fruitcake and date-nut cake made by the resident Camaldolese monks.

Ripplewood Resort *On Hwy. 1, (831) 667-2242; www.ripplewoodresort.com. 16 cabins; 100% non-smoking; $-$$. Children under 12 free. No TVs; some kitchens & wood-burning fireplaces. Restaurant.*

Rustic, pleasantly decorated redwood cabins are located both above and below the highway. The ones below are in a dense, dark grove of redwoods just a stone's throw from the Big Sur River. A cafe serves breakfast and lunch.

Ventana Inn & Spa *On Hwy. 1, (800) 628-6500, (831) 667-2331, fax (831) 667-2419; www.ventanainn.com. 59 rooms; $$$+; 2-night min. on weekends. Unsuitable for children under 18. All VCRs; most wood-burning fireplaces. 2 heated pools, hot tub, sauna, health spa, fitness center. Afternoon snack, continental breakfast; restaurant.*

The striking, clean-lined, and award-winning architecture of this serene resort seems to fit in perfectly with its spectacular, secluded location in the hills 1,200 feet above the ocean. It is a choice spot for a restive, revitalizing, and hedonistic retreat. Rooms are distributed among 12 buildings. All have either a private balcony or patio and either an ocean or mountain view, and some have private hot tubs. Clothing is optional in the Japanese hot baths and sun decks.

Known for its accomplished California-style cuisine, **Cielo** *(L&D daily. Highchairs, boosters.)* has seating both in a cedar-paneled dining room with mountain and ocean views and out on a large terrace with a panoramic ocean view.

WHERE TO EAT

Deetjen's Big Sur Inn *On Hwy. 1, (831) 667-2378. B&D daily; $-$$$. Highchairs, boosters, child portions. Reservations advised for D.*

For aesthetic pleasure it's hard to beat lingering over a hearty breakfast in this Norwegian-style inn, especially when it's raining outside and the table is situated in front of the fireplace. The mellow, rustic, and informal setting provides a complementary background to the fresh, simple, and wholesome foods produced by its kitchen. Dinner by candlelight is more expensive and sedate, and children don't fit in as well then.

Rustic, casual **lodging** *(20 rooms; $-$$$. Some wood-burning fireplaces & stoves; some shared baths.)* is available in units built of local redwood, situated comfortably amid a forest of redwoods and firs. Rooms are usually booked up far in advance.

Nepenthe *On Hwy. 1, (831) 667-2345, (831) 667-2394. L&D daily; $$. Highchairs. No reservations.*

Located at the top of a cliff 808 feet above the ocean and offering a breathtaking view of the coastline, this famous restaurant was designed by a student of Frank Lloyd Wright. It is an elaboration of a cabin that was originally built by Orson Welles as a retreat for him and Rita Hayworth. When the weather is mild, lunchers can dine outside on a casual terrace. The menu features simple foods such as steak, fresh seafood, roasted chicken, housemade soup, and a very good hamburger. It is also possible to stop in at the bar for just a drink. Overall this restaurant seems to be living up to the promise of its name, which refers to a mythical Egyptian drug that induced forgetfulness and the surcease of sorrow.

Cafe Kevah *((831) 667-2344. Closed Jan & Feb.)*, located downstairs, serves moderately-priced brunch and lunch items on a patio featuring the same striking view. On a warm afternoon it is an especially choice spot to enjoy a refreshing cold drink and tasty pastry.

The classy **Phoenix** gift shop provides pleasant browsing before or after dining.

San Simeon and Cambria

A LITTLE BACKGROUND

Located in the small town of San Simeon on the wind-blown coast south of Big Sur, the spectacular **Hearst Castle**™ is perched atop La Cuesta Encantada ("The Enchanted Hill"™). It was designed by architect Julia Morgan and is filled with art treasures and antiques gathered from all over the world. Though unfinished, the estate contains 56 bedrooms, 102 bathrooms, 19 sitting rooms, a kitchen, a movie theater, 2 libraries, a billiard room, a dining hall, and an assembly hall! Colorful vines and plants grace the lovely gardens, and wild zebras, tahr goats, and sambar deer graze the hillsides—remnants of the private zoo that once included lions, monkeys, and a polar bear.

Before 1958 visitors could get no closer than was permitted by a coin-operated telescope located on the road below. Now maintained by the State of California Department of Parks and Recreation as an Historical Monument, the castle is open to the public. Five tours are available; all include a scenic bus ride up to the castle.

• **Tour 1** is suggested for a first visit and includes gardens, pools, a guest house, and the ground floor of the main house—Casa Grande.
• **Tour 2** covers the upper floors of the main house, including Mr. Hearst's private suite, the libraries, a guest duplex, the kitchen, and the pools.
• **Tour 3** covers the 36-room guest wing and includes the pools and a guest house.
• **Tour 4** stresses the gardens. It includes the elegant 19-room Casa del Mar guest house, the wine cellar, and the pools. This tour is given only April through October.
• The **Evening Tour** combines highlights of the daytime tours and additionally features volunteers in period dress, bringing the magnificent surroundings to life. This tour is given only in spring and fall on most Friday and Saturday evenings.

Reservations are recommended and can be made by calling (800) 444-4445. Tickets can also be purchased at the Visitor Center ticket office after 8 a.m. on the day of the tour. The charge for each of the four day tours is $14 for adults, $8 for children ages 6 through 12; the night tour is $25 for adults, $13 for children. For more information, check the website at www.hearstcastle.org.

Note: Children under 6 are free only if they sit on their parent's lap during the bus ride. Tours require walking about 1/2 mile and climbing approximately 150 to 400 steps; comfortable shoes are advised. Strollers are not permitted. Tours take approximately 2 hours. Picnic tables and a snack bar are available near the Visitor Center.

VISITOR INFORMATION

San Simeon Chamber of Commerce *250 San Simeon Dr. #3A, San Simeon, (800) 342-5613, (805) 927-3500, fax (805) 927-8358.*

Cambria Chamber of Commerce *767 Main St., Cambria, (805) 927-3624, fax (805) 927-9426; www.cambria-online.com.*

GETTING THERE

Located approximately 75 miles south of Big Sur.

For a more leisurely trip, try the train package offered by Key Holidays *((800) 783-0783, (925) 945-8938), fax (925) 256-7597.).* Via rail is the way guests used to travel to the castle in its heyday. Invitations then always included train tickets. Today travelers can still relax and enjoy the scenery while Amtrak's Coast Starlight transports them to San Luis Obispo. From there, after seeing the local sights, they are transported by bus for a tour of the coast and on to Morro Bay for overnight accommodations. The next day participants are bused to the famed castle for a guided tour, then down scenic Highway l for a stop in the village of Cambria, and then back to San Luis Obispo for the return train ride. The package does not include meals. Rates vary, and discounts are available for children.

ANNUAL EVENTS

Christmas at the Castle *December. Adults $14, 6-12 $8.*

During the entire month the castle and guest houses are lighted and decorated in splendid fashion for the Christmas holidays—just as they were when Mr. Hearst lived here.

WHAT TO DO

The Pewter Plough Playhouse *824 Main St., Cambria, (805) 927-3877, fax (805) 927-1023. Performances F & Sat at 8, some Sun matinees at 3. Tickets $12.50. Reservations advised.*

Stage plays are scheduled year-round in this intimate theater. Free dramatic readings occur on Wednesday evenings at 7, and jazz is presented in the lounge every Sunday evening from 7 to 11 p.m.

The Soldier Factory *789 Main St., Cambria, (805) 927-3804. Daily 10-5.*

An ideal souvenir stop, this shop offers everything from an inexpensive unpainted pewter animal to a dearly-priced and elaborately-painted Alice in Wonderland chess set. Assorted sizes and styles of pewter soldiers from various wars and nations are also for sale.

William Randolph Hearst Memorial State Beach *San Simeon. Daily 8am-sunset. $3/vehicle.*

In addition to providing a very nice swimming beach, this park has a 640-foot-long fishing pier. No license is required to fish from the pier, and equipment rentals are available.

WHERE TO STAY

Bluebird Motel *1880 Main St., Cambria, (800) 552-5434, (805) 927-4634, fax (805) 927-5215. 37 rooms; ¢-$$. Children under 6 free. Some VCRs & gas fireplaces.*

Situated by Santa Rosa Creek and within easy walking range of the village, this attractive motel surrounds a landmark mansion dating from 1880. Many rooms are creekside, with private balconies or patios, and one spacious two-bedroom family suite is available.

The Blue Whale Inn *6736 Moonstone Beach Dr., Cambria, (800) 753-9000, (805) 927-4647; www.bluewhaleinn. 6 rooms; 100% non-smoking; $$$-$$$+; 2-night min. on weekends. All gas fireplaces. Afternoon snack, full breakfast.*

Situated across the street from the ocean, this luxurious inn boasts ocean view mini-suites with canopy beds and private outdoor entrances. Guests have access to a communal sitting area with a panoramic ocean view, and breakfast is served in an adjacent room with a similar view.

Cambria Pines Lodge *2905 Burton Dr., Cambria, (800) 445-6868, (805) 927-4200, fax (805) 927-4016; www.cambriapineslodge.com. 125 units; $-$$$. Children under 3 free. Some wood-burning fireplaces. Indoor heated pool & hot tub, sauna. Full breakfast; restaurant. Dogs welcome.*

Located on a pine-covered hill above town, this is a spacious 25-acre facility with rustic cabins. The lodge was originally built in 1927 by an eccentric European baroness who wanted to live in opulent style near the Hearst Castle. Recently updated, the new Main Lodge now houses a moderately-priced restaurant and the woodsy, casual Fireside Lounge, where live entertainment is scheduled every night in front of its large stone fireplace. Colorful peacocks run loose on the property, and a volleyball area is available to guests. A nature trail leads down into the village.

Cavalier Oceanfront Resort *9415 Hearst Dr., San Simeon, (800) 826-8168, (805) 927-4688, fax (805) 927-6472; www.cavalierresort.com. 90 rooms; $-$$$. Children free. All VCRs; some wood-burning fireplaces. 2 heated pools, hot tub, fitness center. Restaurant, room service. Pets welcome.*

The only ocean-front resort in San Simeon, this contemporary-style resort motel has over 900 feet of ocean frontage. Many rooms have expansive ocean views, and some also have private patios. Firepits are lit on the beach each night at sunset, where guests can relax in chairs.

Fog Catcher Inn *6400 Moonstone Beach Dr., Cambria, (800) 425-4121, (805) 927-1400; fogcatcherinn.com. 60 rooms; 100% non-smoking; $$-$$$. All mini-kitchens & gas fireplaces. Heated pool, hot tub. Continental breakfast.*

Situated across the street from the ocean, this pseudo English Tudor-style inn has a big two-bedroom suite for families and another ocean-view suite for honeymooners. Many rooms have ocean views.

The J. Patrick House *2990 Burton Dr., Cambria, (800) 341-5258, (805) 927-3812, fax (805) 927-6759; www.jpatrickhouse.com. 8 rooms; 100% non-smoking; $$-$$$; 2-night min. on weekends. No TVs; all wood-burning fireplaces or stove. Afternoon & evening snack, full breakfast.*

Situated in the woods above the East Village, this authentic log cabin holds one guest room; seven more are found in an adjacent Carriage House. All beds are covered with duvets and handmade quilts. Afternoon wine and hors d'oeuvres and bedtime chocolate chip cookies and milk are included, as is an exclusively vegetarian breakfast served in the sun room.

Pickford House *2555 MacLeod Way, Cambria, (805) 927-8619. 8 rooms; 100% non-smoking; $$. Some gas fireplaces. Afternoon snack, full breakfast.*

Though this inn was built in 1983, it is far from modern in feeling. All rooms have claw-foot bathtubs and bear the names and personalities of silent film stars. Notable among them is the Valentino Room, which is furnished with dark-wood antiques and has a great view. A late afternoon snack of fruit breads and wine is served at a massive inlaid mahogany bar dating from 1860, and breakfast features the traditional Danish pancake fritters known as aebleskivers.

White Water Inn *6790 Moonstone Beach Dr., Cambria, (800) 995-1715, (805) 927-1066, fax (805) 927-0921; www.whitewaterinn.com. 17 rooms; 100% non-smoking; $-$$$; 2-night min. on weekends. All VCRs & gas fireplaces. Continental breakfast.*

Situated across the street from the ocean, this contemporary motel court has two mini-suites with a private patio and oceanview hot tub, plus six rooms with oversize whirlpool bathtubs. Breakfast is delivered to the room, and movies can be borrowed from the desk.

Motel Row.

Numerous motels are located along scenic Moonstone Beach Drive in Cambria.

WHERE TO EAT

The Brambles Dinner House *4005 Burton Dr., Cambria, (805) 927-4716, fax (805) 927-3761; www.bramblesdinnerhouse.com. D daily, SunBr; $$-$$$. Highchairs, boosters, booths, child portions. Reservations advised.*

Located inside a rambling 1874 English-style cottage with Victorian decor, this cozy dinner house has some very private booths and a special room for families. Known for its prime rib, traditional Yorkshire pudding, and fresh salmon barbecued over an oak-wood pit, the kitchen also prepares an extensive selection of steaks, chicken items, and fresh seafood. Hinting at the owner's heritage, several Greek dishes appear on the menu: a tasty salad with Feta cheese, dolmathes (stuffed grape leaves), and saganaki (fried cheese). A hamburger is also available, and a rich English trifle is among the desserts. Interesting paintings and china plates decorate the walls, and the entrance is crowded with a collection of clocks that are for sale.

Linn's Main Bin Restaurant *2277 Main St., Cambria, (805) 927-0371. B,L,&D daily; $. Highchairs, child menu.*

For description, see Linn's Downtown SLO Bin on page 186.

Robin's *4095 Burton Dr., Cambria, (805) 927-5007, fax (805) 927-2712; www.robinsrestaurant.com. L&D daily; $-$$. Highchairs, boosters, child menu. Reservations advised.*

Situated within a converted house, this pleasant spot uses homegrown herbs to prepare delicious renditions of ethnic and vegetarian dishes. The seafood bisque is a must, and curries are prepared to order. The menu includes a variety of salads, sandwiches and pastas, as well as seafood and tofu dishes. A selection of housemade desserts rounds out the offerings. Patio seating is available.

Sebastian's General Store/Patio Cafe *422 San Simeon Rd., San Simeon, (805) 927-4217; www.sebastians.com. Store: daily 8:30-5:30. Cafe: B&L daily; $; closed Nov-Mar; no reservations; no cards.*

Built in 1852 and moved to its present location in 1878, this store is now a State Historical Landmark. Inexpensive short-order items are served in the outdoor cafe. In winter watch for monarch butterflies congregating in the adjacent eucalyptus and cypress trees.

The Tea Cozy *4286 Bridge St., Cambria, (805) 927-8765, same fax; www.teacozy.com. Tea W-Sun 10-5. No reservations.*

In England it is customary to conclude a visit to one of the stately homes with a stop at a local tea room, and the English proprietors here are attempting to interest Americans in this tradition. Situated within a modest 1890s school teacher's house, this cozy tea room offers light meals and pastries along with a nice cup of tea (or coffee). The extensive Royal Tea and smaller Cream Tea are served all day. Imported English foods and an interesting collection of antique china are also available for purchase.

Morro Bay

A LITTLE BACKGROUND

Named "El Morro" in 1542 by explorer Juan Rodriguez Cabrillo, because it reminded him of a turbaned Moor, over time the name of the huge volcanic rock here, visible from just about everywhere in town, evolved into "Morro," which means "knoll" in Spanish. The area is also referred to as the "Gibraltar of the Pacific." The rock stands 576 feet high and is now a State Monument. Peregrine falcons, said to be the fastest moving animal in the world and an endangered species, nest at the top.

Because the area's wide variety of landscapes offer myriad nesting sites for some of California's most interesting birds, bird watching is particularly good here.

Commercial fishing is this small, picturesque town's main industry. Albacore and abalone are the local specialties, and they frequently show up on restaurant menus.

Lodgings often fill up on weekends, so reservations should be made well in advance.

VISITOR INFORMATION

Morro Bay Chamber of Commerce *880 Main St., (800) 231-0592, (805) 772-4467, fax (805) 772-6038; www.morrobay.org.*

GETTING THERE

Located approximately 30 miles south of San Simeon.

ANNUAL EVENTS

Morro Bay Harbor Festival *October. (800) 366-6043, (805) 772-1155, fax (805) 772-2107. Adults $5, 1-12 free.*

General merriment includes a sand sculpture spectacular, a Hawaiian shirt contest, and ship tours, plus live entertainment and plenty of seafood and wine tasting. Proceeds benefit community nonprofit organizations, which volunteer their time to the festival.

WHAT TO DO

Coleman Beach Park *Embarcadero Rd./ Coleman Dr., east of Morro Rock.*

Children are sure to enjoy this idyllic playground in the sand.

Fishing.

The pier is a prime spot for fishing. Chartered fishing boats are also available.

Giant Chess Board *Embarcadero/Front, in Centennial Park, (805) 772-6278, fax (805) 772-2693.*

At the base of a 44-step stairway is one of the two largest chess boards in the U.S. (The other is in New York City's Central Park.) The redwood chess pieces stand 2- and 3-feet high and weigh from 18 to 40 pounds—making a game here physical as well as mental exercise. From noon to 5 p.m. each Saturday the Morro Bay Chess Club sponsors games on the giant 16- by 16-foot concrete board, and the general public is welcome to challenge. The board is otherwise available weekdays from 8 to 5. Reservations must be made by filling out an application at the Recreation & Parks Department. Call for details.

Morro Bay Aquarium *595 Embarcadero, (805) 772-7647. Daily from 9:30, closing time varies. Adults $2, 5-11 $1.*

This teeny, tiny aquarium is a draw for the gift shop located in front. However, the price is right, and over 300 live marine specimens can be observed. All are said to be injured and distressed animals that can't be returned to the wild. Some preserved specimens are also displayed, and very noisy seals beg to be fed.

Morro Bay State Park *At south end of town, on State Park Rd., (805) 772-2560.*

- **Bird Sanctuary.**

Following a trail through the marsh and hills allows for the possibility of catching glimpses of over 250 species of birds. This is said to be the third largest bird sanctuary in the world.

- **Heron and Cormorant Rookery** *At Fairbank Point, off State Park Rd.*

No one is allowed inside the rookery, which is one of the last where the Great Blue Heron can be found, but the herons can be viewed from an observation area.

- **Museum of Natural History** *(805) 772-2694. Daily 10-5. Adults $3, 6-12 $1.*

Situated at White Point on a scenic perch over the bay, this small museum presents lectures, slide shows, and movies about the wildlife and Native American history of the area. Large windows provide excellent views of the estuary, and a telescope permits up-close viewing of wildlife. Guided tours are sometimes available. In winter, guided walks are scheduled to see the monarch butterflies that congregate at Pismo State Beach; it is the largest overwintering colony of monarchs in the United States.

The Shell Shop *590 Embarcadero, (805) 772-8014, fax (805) 772-4137. Daily 9:30-7, to 5 in winter.*

The perfect souvenir stop, this shop has the largest selection of sea shells on the West Coast and offers them at bargain prices.

Tiger's Folly II Harbor Cruises *1205 Embarcadero, (805) 772-2257. Daily June-Sept; Sat & Sun Oct-May; call for schedule. Adults $10, 4-12 $5.*

The 1-hour harbor cruise aboard this sternwheeler requires no reservation, but the special Sunday champagne brunch cruise does.

WHAT TO DO NEARBY

Avila Beach *20 mi. south of town off Hwy. 101.*

This tiny, old-fashioned beach community is a great place to watch surfers and to swim in a generally mild surf.

Cayucos *6 mi. north of town on Hwy. 1.*

This quiet little beach town has a string of inexpensive motels. It also boasts both a fine beach with a gentle surf and a 400-foot-long fishing pier where equipment rentals are available.

WHERE TO STAY

Blue Sail Inn *851 Market Ave., (888) 337-0707, (805) 772-7132, fax (805) 772-8406; www.bluesailinn.com. 48 rooms; $-$$. Some fireplaces. Hot tub.*

This streamlined modern motel is centrally located, allowing guests to walk to restaurants. The hot tub area has a view of Morro Rock, as do most of the rooms.

Embarcadero Inn *456 Embarcadero, (800) 292-ROCK, (805) 772-2700, same fax; www.embarcaderoinn.com. 32 rooms; $$-$$$+. Children under 12 free. All VCRs; some gas fireplaces. 2 indoor hot tubs. Continental breakfast.*

Situated in a quiet spot at the south end of the busy Embarcadero strip, this attractive modern motel is constructed of weathered wood. All rooms have bay views, and most have balconies. A library of videos is available at no charge to guests, and local calls are free.

The Inn at Morro Bay *60 State Park Rd., (800) 321-9566, (805) 772-5651, fax (805) 772-4779; www.innatmorrobay.com. 98 rooms; $$-$$$+. Children under 12 free. Some fireplaces. Heated pool, health spa. Restaurant, room service.*

Located at the southern end of town in Morro Bay State Park, this small resort is sheltered by a strand of old eucalyptus and provides a quiet, restful spot to spend the night. Choice rooms have gorgeous views of the estuary, and some have private decks and hot tubs. The spa is a full-service massage center, and complimentary use of mountain bikes is available. An 18-hole public golf course is just across the street, and a heron rookery located in an adjacent grove of eucalyptus often treats guests to the raucous rantings of its occupants.

The **Dining Room** restaurant offers diners a mesmerizing panoramic view of the estuary and sand spit, and the wildlife watching from here is very good. Depending on the time of year, viewers see herons carrying nesting materials or sea otters basking on their backs. Kayaks and sailboats come and go as well. A different theme menu is served each night. The three-course Sunday brunch is ordered from a menu that offers both a perfect eggs Benedict served with a side of scalloped potatoes topped with wispy deep-fried potatoes, and a savory paella prepared with fresh local catch. Each entree includes a glass of champagne, fresh-squeezed orange juice, coffee, and access to a dessert bar laden with items such as giant chocolate-dipped strawberries and housemade ice cream with a variety of toppings.

WHERE TO EAT

Dorn's Original Breakers Cafe *801 Market Ave., (805) 772-4415, fax (805) 772-4695. B,L,&D daily; $-$$. Highchairs, boosters. Reservations advised.*

This casual restaurant features a great bay view and is especially pleasant at breakfast. The menu then offers a choice of hearty breakfasts, plus novelty items such as chocolate chip pancakes with chocolate syrup. The extensive dinner menu features fresh local fish and an award-winning Boston clam chowder.

The Great American Fish Company *1185 Embarcadero, (805) 772-4407. L&D daily; $$. Highchairs, boosters, child portions. No reservations.*

Located a short, scenic stroll from the center of town, this restaurant provides a comfortable, casual atmosphere and good views of the rock. The extensive menu includes mesquite-grilled fresh fish and shark, as well as deep-fried fresh local prawns and Monterey squid. A steak and hamburger are also available.

Hofbrau der Albatross *571 Embarcadero, (805) 772-2411, fax (805) 772-5001. L&D daily; $. Highchairs, boosters, child portions. No reservations.*

Popular with locals and visitors alike, this casual spot features cafeteria-style service. The fish & chips are superb, and a very good French dip sandwich and hamburger are also available. Seating is a choice of inside or outside at harbor-view tables. A cafe just opposite beckons for dessert.

Pacific Cafe *1150 Embarcadero, (805) 772-2965. L Tu-F, D Tu-Sun; $-$$. 1 highchair, boosters. Reservations advised.*

Situated across from the rock and featuring several heated outdoor tables, this casual, chef-owned restaurant operates in extremely tight quarters and has a strong repeat clientele of locals. At dinner, the perfect starter is the house special of scampi fra Diavalo, which consists of perfect prawns in a tasty red sauce suitable for dunking with the soft, hot house bread.

Entrees are listed on a chalk board and sometimes include a salmon Lilliano—poached and wrapped around spinach and topped with a light red sauce—and snapper Griglia—grilled and topped with a light white wine sauce. All meals end with a complimentary liqueur, but don't miss dessert when it is marinated fresh strawberries, fresh peach cobbler, or house-made vanilla ice cream. Lunch is a less expensive selection of salads, sandwiches, and hamburgers.

Rose's Landing *725 Embarcadero, (805) 772-4441. L&D daily; $$-$$$. Highchairs, boosters, child menu. Reservations advised.*

Good views can be enjoyed here in both the downstairs bar and the upstairs restaurant. Seafood dominates the dinner menu, but steaks and a few other items are also available. Complete dinners include a relish tray, either the house-specialty seafood chowder or a salad, either a baked potato or rice pilaf, steamed vegetables, and hot garlic bread. Lunch is a less expensive selection of salads, sandwiches, fish & chips, and burgers.

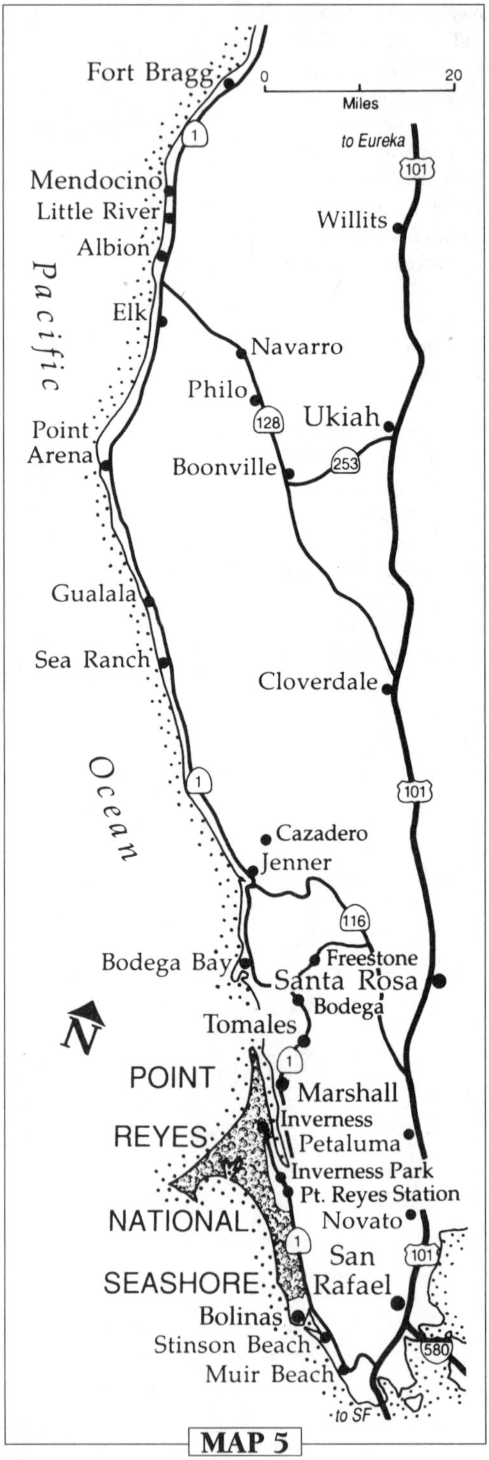
Fort Bragg
0
20
Miles
1
to Eureka
101
Mendocino
Little River
Albion
Willits
Pacific
Elk
Navarro
Philo
128
Ukiah
Point
Arena
Boonville
253
Gualala
Sea Ranch
Cloverdale
Ocean
1
101
Cazadero
Jenner
116
Bodega Bay
Freestone
Santa Rosa
Bodega
N
Tomales
1
POINT
Marshall
Inverness
REYES
Petaluma
Inverness Park
Pt. Reyes Station
NATIONAL
Novato
1
San
101
SEASHORE
Rafael
Bolinas
Stinson Beach
580
Muir Beach
to SF

MAP 5

A LITTLE BACKGROUND

Highway 1 north from San Francisco allows an escape into a quieter, less-populated area. The two-lane road leading to Stinson Beach winds through fragrant eucalyptus groves, then rustic countryside rife with wildflowers in spring. For long stretches it hugs oceanside cliffs, riding like a roller coaster and providing breathtaking views. The inland route known as Panoramic Highway is steep, with many blind curves. One of its nicknames is Kamikaze Alley, bestowed as a result of accidents occuring regularly in the fog. On sunny summer days both roads can become congested when everyone heads to the beach to soak up some of the famous California sunshine that is so elusive in the northern part of the state.

A word of warning: The rocky cliffs and beaches along the coast are scenic and beautiful. In their awe, people sometimes forget that they are also dangerous. Though it is tempting to stand at the edge, where the surf is pounding, people have been washed out to sea doing just that. Don't be one of them. Be careful. Stay on trails. Obey posted signs. And take special care not to let children run loose.

VISITOR INFORMATION

Redwood Empire Association *In San Francisco. (800) 200-8334, (415) 394-5991, fax (415) 394-5994; www.redwoodempire.com.*

Information on the coastal counties north of San Francisco can be obtained here.

West Marin Chamber of Commerce
11431 Hwy. 1, Point Reyes Station, (415) 663-9232, fax (415) 663-8818; www.pointreyes.org.

GETTING THERE

From San Francisco, take Highway 101 to Highway 1 north.

Muir Beach

A LITTLE BACKGROUND

It was in this area (the exact spot is still disputed) more than 400 years ago that Sir Francis Drake beached the *Golden Hinde*, formerly known as the *Pelican,* and claimed California for Queen Elizabeth I.

WHAT TO DO

Green Gulch Farm Zen Center *1601 Shoreline Hwy., just before town, (415) 383-3134, fax (415) 383-3128; www.sfzc.com.*

Reached via a sharp downhill turnoff, this Zen retreat offers public meditation programs daily. On Sundays, a longer program includes a dharma talk. Visitors are also welcome to take informal afternoon walks in the organic garden, which supplies the herbs and vegetables for Greens restaurant in San Francisco.

Overnight lodging is available in a peaceful Japanese-style **Lindisfarne Guest House** *(12 rooms; $-$$$. 100% non-smoking. No TVs; all shared baths. Vegetarian meals included.)*, and guests may take their meals with the permanent residents. A separate apartment is available for families with children.

Mount Tamalpais State Park *801 Panoramic Hwy., (415) 388-2070. Summit visitor center open irregular hours; guided hikes on Sat & Sun at 9:30am. $5/vehicle.*

From some locations, Mt.Tam, as the mountain is affectionately nicknamed, resembles the resting figure the local Native Americans called "The Sleeping Maiden," who was said to safeguard the area. This 6,233-acre park offers 50 miles of hiking trails, and the view from its 2,571-foot peak is spectacular. It is interesting to note that the mountain bike was first developed here for use on the park's hills, and it is said to be "the best spot on Earth to shoot a car commercial." Campsites are available.

Since 1904, the 7.1-mile **Dipsea Race** has been run on the first Sunday of each June. Hordes of runners tromp the trail then from the center of Mill Valley to Stinson Beach. The **Mountain Play** (*June. (415) 383-1100, fax (415) 383-4848; www.mountainplay.com. Adults $18-$22, 65+ & 3-7 $12-$15.*) has been presented in the natural outdoor amphitheater atop the mountain annually since 1913. Plays have run the gamut from the obscure to Shakespeare to well-known Broadway musicals. In the old days people came on burros, by stagecoach, or on the old Mount Tamalpais Scenic Railway, also known as the "Crookedest Railroad in the World" because it had 281 curves, including a five-fold switchback known as the Double Bow

Knot, along its 8 1/4-mile route. Now many audience members ride the free shuttle buses up the mountain and, after the performance, hike 4 miles down to board a shuttle bus for the rest of the journey back to the parking area.

Muir Beach.

Reached by turning onto a leafy, blackberry-lined lane located just south of the Pelican Inn, this popular beach is unsafe for swimming. However, it is excellent for sunbathing and people-watching, and picnic tables are available.

Muir Beach Overlook.

Panoramic coastline views make this is great picnic spot. In winter, it is a good perch from which to watch the whale migration.

Muir Woods National Monument *Off Hwy. 1, on Panoramic Hwy., (415) 388-2595; www.nps.gov/muwo. Daily 8-sunset. Adults $2, under 17 free.*

Located just off Highway 1 and enveloping 560 acres, this magnificent, fragrant old-growth redwood forest has 6 miles of walking trails. Among them are the easy paved Main Trail with interpretive exhibits; seven more-challenging, unpaved trails lead away from the crowds. Naturalist John Muir, for whom the forest was named, said of it, "This is the best tree lover's monument that could be found in all the forests of the world." The largest tree here measures 240 feet high by 16 feet wide. Because nearly two million people come here each year, only a visit early or late in the day (before 10 or after 4) provides the hope of some solitude; rainy days are also quiet. And no matter what time of year it is, visitors are advised to bring along warm wraps. The dense forest lets in very little sunlight, and the weather is usually damp, foggy, and cold. Discovery Packs filled with tools that assist children in exploring nature can be borrowed free from the Visitors Center. Picnicking is not permitted, but a snackbar dispenses simple foods.

Slide Ranch *2025 Shoreline Hwy., (415) 381-6155, fax (415) 381-5762; www.slideranch.org. $10-$15/person. Reservations suggested.*

Perched dramatically on the ocean side of Highway 1 near Muir Beach, this ranch offers the city-slicker a chance to get back to the land . . . a chance to learn about a self-sustaining rural lifestyle through exposure to frontier arts . . . a chance to slow the pace. During Farm Day programs, adults and children learn together about things such as cheesemaking, composting, and papermaking. Though the program varies according to the season and the ages of participants, a typical day begins with smiling staff members greeting visitors in a fragrant grove of eucalyptus. A visit to the sheep and goat pen usually follows, giving children the chance to "pet a four-legged sweater" and milk a goat. More activities include collecting eggs, feeding chickens, carding and spinning sheep wool, making bread and cheese, helping in the garden, and hiking along one of the coastal wildland trails.

WHERE TO STAY AND EAT

The Pelican Inn *10 Pacific Way, (415) 383-6000, fax (415) 383-3424; www.pelicaninn.com. 7 rooms; $$$-$$$+. No TVs. Full breakfast; restaurant.*

Sheltered by towering pines and alders, this authentic reconstruction of an actual 16th-century English Tudor inn was built in 1979. It offers snug rooms furnished with English antiques, canopied beds, and oriental carpets.

The lunch menu in the pub **restaurant** *(L&D daily; $-$$. Highchairs, boosters, child portions. Reservations accepted.)* consists of housemade traditional English pub fare such as bangers and mash, cottage pie, and the ever-popular ploughman's plate. Dinner brings on prime rib, beef Wellington, and rack of lamb. British ales and beers that complement the food are on tap, and a simple tea service is always available. Diners can be seated outside on an enclosed patio or inside in a rustic candle-lighted dining room furnished with several long communal tables and a number of more private individual ones. On cold, foggy days a fireplace warms the interior.

Stinson Beach

A LITTLE BACKGROUND

This town has no gas station. According to a local resident, "It disappeared one night and didn't come back."

WHAT TO DO

Audubon Canyon Ranch's Bolinas Lagoon Preserve *4900 Hwy. 1, 3.5 mi. north of town, (415) 868-9244. Sat, Sun, & holidays 10-4; mid-March through mid-July. By donation.*

Situated on picturesque Bolinas Lagoon just north of town, this 1,000-acre ranch is a non-profit project sponsored by the four Bay Area Audubon Societies. It is open only during the breeding season. Breeding pairs of Great Blue Herons (measuring 4 to 5 feet tall and with a wingspan of nearly 6 feet), snowy egrets, and Great Egrets nest noisily in the tall redwood trees located in the ranch's Schwarz Grove. Approximately 60 other bird species also make their home here, making this a bird watcher's paradise. Nests contain an average of two to five eggs, which incubate for about 28 days. Once hatched, baby birds, covered in fluffy down, waddle about their nests while waiting for their parents to return from gathering a meal of fish and crustaceans in nearby Bolinas Lagoon. (Baby egrets fly at 7 weeks, herons at 9 weeks.) A self-guiding nature trail, and several other scenic trails of varying length

and challenge, lead to an overlook where telescopes are available and a ranch guide is on hand to interpret and assist. Visitors can rest on benches and observe these graceful birds as they court, establish a pecking order, build their nests, and begin rearing their young.

Exhibits in the Display Hall museum, a converted milking barn left from the days when the ranch was a dairy, give visitors more detailed information about the birds as well as about the geology and natural history of the area. Nearby, a stream-side, sod-roofed Bird Hide is designed so observers can see out, but birds can't see in. Its feeders attract a variety of unsuspecting birds, including many colorful hummingbirds. A picnic area, from which the nesting site can be viewed, provides a scenic spot to relax and enjoy a leisurely lunch in peaceful surroundings.

Stinson Beach Park *(415) 868-0942. Free.*

This magnificent beach offers a little taste of the Southern California beach scene. Conditions often permit swimming here, though the water is cold and lifeguards are on duty usually only in summer. Since the weather is often different than everywhere else in the Bay Area, it is wise to call and check conditions before setting out *((415) 868-1922).*

WHERE TO STAY

Casa del Mar *37 Belvedere Ave., (800) 552-2124, (415) 868-2124, fax (415) 868-2305; www.stinsonbeach.com. 4 stories; 6 rooms; 100% non-smoking; $$-$$$+; 2-night min. on weekends. Children under 6 free. No TVs; 1 wood-burning fireplace. Afternoon snack, full breakfast.*

Perched on a hill above town, this peachy-colored, Mediterranean-style stucco structure has three rooms with great views of the ocean and three with views of Mount Tamalpais—the inn's back yard. Its terraced garden was planted in the 1930s for use as a teaching garden by the U.C. School of Landscape Architecture in the '70s. Now the owner tends to it and invites guests to pinch and prune, should the mood strike. The house itself was completely rebuilt. Wonderful breakfasts, sometimes prepared with ingredients fresh from the garden, greet guests in the morning in a sunny dining area.

Steep Ravine Cabins *On Hwy. 1, 1 mi. south of town, (800) 444-7275, (415) 388-2070. 10 cabins; $. No TVs; all wood-burning stoves.*

Perched on a rocky bluff overlooking the ocean, within Mount Tamalpais State Park, each of these primitive cabins dates from the 1930s and sleeps up to four people. Each has a small wood-burning stove, a picnic table and benches, sleeping platforms, and an outdoor barbecue. They do not have running water, electricity, or shower facilities. Primitive toilets, water faucets, and firewood are nearby. Guests must provide their own bedding, cooking equipment, and light source. Paths lead down to the beach, where six primitive campsites are also available.

WHERE TO EAT

Stinson Beach Grill *3465 Hwy. 1, (415) 868-2002. L&D daily; $-$$. Highchairs, boosters. Reservations advised.*

Overlooking Highway 1, this informal grill has an eclectic menu offering everything from hamburgers to osso bucco. In between are a Greek salad, an impeccably fresh salmon with tomato-basil sauce, and a spicy blackened snapper. A large variety of complementary beers from micro-breweries are also available.

Bolinas

A LITTLE BACKGROUND

So shy of visitors is this tiny oceanside hamlet that residents spirit away directional signs as soon as they are posted. All visitors are hereby warned that reception in town can be chilly.

WHERE TO STAY

One Fifty-Five Pine *(415) 868-0263, fax (415) 868-0201. 2 cabins; 100% non-smoking; $$; 2-night min. on weekends. Children under 1 1/2 stay free. No TVs; all kitchens & wood-burning fireplaces. Full breakfast.*

It's impossible not to relax in one of these two knotty-pine cabins situated at the end of a rural dirt road. They were built by two brothers on 3 private, quiet acres just above Duxbury Reef, an area once considered a healing spot by the native Miwok Indians, and are a short walk from beach and tidepools. One of the kitchens has multi-paned windows overlooking a huge rosemary bush that frames a grassy, brambly expanse to the ocean. This same cabin has an alcove with a cozy, narrow captain's bunk bed for kids and a bedroom with a skylight allowing the old folks to fall asleep under the stars. It is wise to bring along dinner. Breakfast items are provided so that guests can prepare what they like, when they like.

WHERE TO EAT

Bolinas Bay Bakery & Cafe *20 Wharf Rd., (415) 868-0211, fax (415) 868-9408. B&L daily; $. Highchairs, boosters, child portions. No reservations.*

Situated at the end of a gravel pathway in a big old house, this pleasant spot offers an eclectic menu. Pastas, hamburgers, and pizza made with both organic crust and organic tomato sauce are available. Bakery items are extensive and exceptional, and all are made with organic flour. The deli has plenty of salads, soups, and "other stuff" ready to go, plus six beers on tap.

Point Reyes Area

WHAT TO DO

Johnson's Drakes Bay Oyster Company
17171 Sir Francis Drake Blvd., Inverness, (415) 669-1149, fax (415) 669-1262. Tu-Sun 8-4.

A visit to this scenically situated enterprise allows viewing the various stages of the oyster-farming process. Oysters are available for purchase.

Point Reyes National Seashore *West of Olema, (415) 663-1092; www.nps.gov/pore. M-F 9-5, Sat & Sun 8-5. Free.*

Known for its beaches and hiking trails, this 71,000-acre refuge has plenty of other interesting things for visitors to do. Many activities are clustered around the Park Headquarters. A Visitor Center houses a working seismograph and a variety of nature displays. The **Morgan Horse Ranch**, where pack and trail animals for the national parks are trained, is adjacent. (The Morgan was the first American horse breed.) A short walk away a replica coast Miwok Indian village, **Kule Loklo**, has been re-created using the same types of tools and materials as the Native Americans themselves originally used.

Trails beginning near the headquarters include the .5-mile self-guided Woodpecker Nature Trail, the .6-mile-long self-guided Earthquake Trail, which follows the San Andreas fault and passes a spot where the Pacific plate moved 16 feet north in about 45 seconds during the 1906 earthquake, and the popular 4.1-mile Bear Valley Trail, which winds through meadows, fern grottos, and forests before ending at the ocean. The area has 147 miles of hiking trails, most of which are open to horses, and guided trail rides, buggy rides, hayrides, and overnight pack trips are available at nearby **Five Brooks Stables** *(1000 Hwy. 1, Olema, (415) 663-1570.)*. Also, mountain bikes are permitted on some trails, and walk-in backpacking campsites are available for a fee by reservation *((415) 663-8054)*.

Farther away from the headquarters is the 1870 **Point Reyes Lighthouse** *((415) 669-1534. Steps open Thur-M 10-4:30. Lighthouse hours irregular.)*, where winds have been recorded blowing at 133 miles per hour—the highest rate in the continental U.S. The bottom line is that it can get mighty windy, cold, and wet at this scenic spot. The lighthouse is reached by maneuvering 300 steps down the side of a steep, rocky cliff. This is a popular spot in winter for viewing migrating gray whales. **Shuttle buses** *(Daily 9-5, weather permitting; Jan-April. $3.50, under 13 free.)* depart regularly then from the Drake's Beach visitor center.

Drake's Beach offers easy beach access and has a great little short-order cafe. The **Ken Patrick Visitor Center** *((415) 669-1250. Sat & Sun 10-5; daily in summer.)* here has maritime history displays and a 250-gallon salt water aquarium. At the **Tule Elk Reserve** on Tomales Point, a herd of approximately 500 elk can often be observed grazing. Nearby, historic **Pierce Point Ranch** is open for a self-guided tour of its barn, bunkhouse, old and new dairy, and blacksmith shop.

The Point Reyes National Seashore Association offers seminars and classes in natural history, environmental education, photography, and art. To request a free catalog, call (415) 663-1200.

WHERE TO STAY

Reservations Services.

For information on the area's B&Bs call:

- **Inns of Marin** *(800) 887-2880, (415) 663-2000, fax (415) 669-7242; www.innsofmarin.com.*
- **Inns of Point Reyes** *(415) 663-1420.*
- **Point Reyes Lodging** *(800) 539-1872, (415) 663-1872, fax (415) 663-8431; www.ptreyes.com.*

Holly Tree Inn *3 Silverhills Rd., Point Reyes Station, (800) 286-HOLL, (415) 663-1554, fax (415) 663-8566; www.hollytreeinn.com. 4 rooms, 3 cottages; 100% non-smoking; $$-$$$+; 2-night min. on weekends. No TVs; some kitchens & wood-burning fireplaces & stoves. Hot tub. Afternoon snack, full breakfast.*

Tucked away in its very own valley just beneath the Inverness Ridge, this rustic B&B offers four attractively appointed rooms and a spacious cottage with a wood-burning stove, a stereo and tapes, and a clawfoot tub. A stream runs picturesquely through the property, and an informal playground with a wooden plank swing invites children to play. A rustic cottage, perched over Tomales Bay and featuring a solarium with a hot tub, is also available.

Manka's Inverness Lodge *30 Callender Way/ Argyle Ave., Inverness, (800) 58-LODGE, (415) 669-1034, fax (415) 669-1598; www.mankas.com. 14 units; 100% non-smoking; $$-$$$+; 2 night min. on Sat. Children free in cabins. Some TVs & VCRs; some kitchens & gas wood-burning fireplaces. Hot tub. Restaurant, limited room service. Dogs welcome.*

This rustic 1917 arts and crafts-style hunting lodge was the first place in town with a phone. During the 40's, it was a speakeasy. Both cozy lodge rooms and larger cabins are available. Rooms 1 and 2 boast both a large weathered deck overlooking Tomales Bay and a clawfoot tub. Several rooms have a large four-poster bed made with unpeeled whole cypress logs: Guests climb a step stool, then sink into peaceful slumber upon its featherbed under a fluffy down comforter. Six other rooms have open-air showers.

Local game grilled in the fireplace is often on the dinner menu in the inn's intimate **dining room** *(D Thur-M. Highchairs, boosters.)*.

Breakfast is optional, inexpensive, and not to be missed. Served fireside in the lobby, one such gustatory extravaganza featured eggs scrambled with local goat cheese and hand-gathered mushrooms, a side of toasted herb bread, and both homemade rhubarb purée and blood orange marmalade.

Point Reyes Hostel *1380 Limantour Rd., Point Reyes Station, (415) 663-8811, same fax. 44 beds; private rooms.*

Nestled in a secluded valley, this former ranch house offers both a kitchen and outdoor barbecue for preparing meals. Two cozy common rooms with wood-burning stoves are also available to guests. See also page 417.

WHERE TO EAT

The Station House Cafe *11180 Hwy. 1, Point Reyes Station, (415) 663-1515, fax (415) 663-9443. B,L,&D daily; $-$$. Highchairs, boosters, booths, child menu. Reservations advised on weekends.*

Menu choices in this casual, popular spot include sandwiches, light and inexpensive entrees, and pricier daily specials that always feature fresh fish and local shellfish. Hamburgers are prepared with ground chuck from organically fed cattle raised at the local Niman Ranch. Desserts include apple pie, devil's food cake, bread pudding, butterscotch pudding, and seasonal fruit pies. Truly all stages of hunger can be satisfied here at the same table. Additionally, service is fast and unpretentious.

Tomales Bay Area

A LITTLE BACKGROUND

A former railroad stop, Marshall was the site of the first wireless communications system on the West Coast. Also once a dairy center, it now is better known for its oysters, clams, and mussels.

WHAT TO DO

Tomales Bay State Park *(415) 669-1140. Daily 8-sunset. $5/vehicle.*

Access to the warm bay waters for swimming and wading is available at popular **Heart's Desire Beach.** The easy self-guided Indian Trail begins here and leads to a Miwok garden, where native plants used for food and medicine are labeled. It then climbs a slope that skirts the bay and ends at Indian Beach.

WHERE TO EAT

Tony's Seafood *18863 Hwy. 1, Marshall, (415) 663-1107. L&D F-Sun; $. Highchairs, boosters. No reservations. No credit cards.*

Many restaurants in this area offer oyster dishes made with the fresh local supply. Here, at tables with relaxing views of Tomales Bay, the specialty is oysters barbecued in the shell. Deep-fried oysters are also available, as is fresh fish and a hamburger. Beer, which seems to go especially well with oysters, is available from the bar.

Bodega Bay

A LITTLE BACKGROUND

Claimed for England in 1579 by Sir Francis Drake and later discovered by Don Juan del la Bodega of Spain, this area was settled in the early 1800s when Russian settlers arrived to trap sea otters. It is the second largest salmon port on the Pacific coast and the busiest commercial fishing port between San Francisco and Eureka. But it is probably best known as the location for the 1962 Alfred Hitchcock film *The Birds.* Now a private residence, the old Potter School featured in the movie still stands in the tiny inland town of Bodega, as does St. Theresa's church, a picturesque building dating from 1859 and Sonoma County's oldest continuously active Catholic church and a state historical landmark.

VISITOR INFORMATION

Bodega Bay Area Chamber of Commerce *575 Hwy. 1, (707) 875-3422, same fax; www.bodegabay.com.*

GETTING THERE

Located approximately 75 miles north of San Francisco via Highway 1, or via Highway 101 to Highway 116 west to Highway 12 west.

ANNUAL EVENTS

Fisherman's Festival *April. (707) 875-3422; www.bodegabay.com. Adults $3, seniors $2, under 13 free.*

Held each year at the beginning of the commercial salmon season, this festival's highlights are a traditional parade of colorfully decorated commercial fishing boats and a Blessing of the Fleet, but bathtub races, stunt kite demonstrations, and a juried art show are also part of the fun. All proceeds benefit local nonprofit organizations.

WHAT TO DO

Chanslor Guest Ranch *2660 Hwy. 1, (707) 875-3333, fax (707) 875-2785; www.chanslor.com. Daily 9-5. Horses $30+/hr., ponies $10/10 min. Riders must be 8 or older.*

Guided trail rides through a wetlands preserve and beach rides across sand dunes are offered at this 700-acre working guest ranch. Pony rides are available for kids under 8.

Lodging (*(707) 875-2721. 6 rooms; 100% non-smoking. Continental breakfast.*) is available.

Osmosis Enzyme Bath & Massage *209 Bohemian Hwy., Freestone, 5 mi. east of town, (707) 823-8231, fax (707) 874-3702; www.osmosis.com. Daily 9-9. Enzyme bath with blanket wrap $65, with massage $140. Unsuitable for children. Reservations required.*

Long popular in Japan, the enzyme bath here is something like a mud bath—only lighter, more fragrant, and dry. It is said to improve circulation, break down body toxins, and relieve stress, and this is the only place in the U.S. where it is available. The experience begins in a tranquil tea garden with a soothing cup of enzyme tea to aid digestion. Then bathers, either nude or in a swimsuit, submerge for 20 minutes in a hot mixture of Hinoki cedar fiber, rice bran, and over 600 active plant enzymes that naturally generate heat. This is followed by a blanket wrap or massage. Private massages are given in serene outdoor Japanese pagodas nestled in a wooded area near Salmon Creek.

Sonoma Coast State Beach *(707) 875-3483, fax (707) 875-3876. Daily 8-sunset. Free.*

Actually a series of beaches separated by rocky bluffs, this state beach extends for 18 miles from Bodega Head to Meyers Gulch, just south of Fort Ross State Historic Park. It is accessible from more than a dozen points along Highway 1, and campsites are available.

- **Goat Rock Beach** *Off Hwy. 1, 4 mi. south of Jenner, (707) 875-3483, (707) 865-2391.*

Located where the Russian River flows into the ocean, this beach is popular with harbor seals. March is the beginning of pupping season, when Seal Watch volunteers are on hand to interpret and answer questions for viewers. Seeing the baby seals, many people are tempted to get closer, but visitors should stay at least 50 yards away. When pups are born they depend on the mother's milk for the first 48 hours. During that critical period the mother will often go out to feed, leaving newborn pups by themselves. If a mother finds humans around her pup when she returns, she will abandon it. Seals hang around this area in large numbers through July. Then the population thins out until the following March. Driftwood collecting is encouraged because pile-ups of wood debris are a potential fire hazard to the town. Note that swimming in the ocean is hazardous due to sleeper waves and riptides.

WHERE TO STAY

Bodega Bay Lodge *103 Hwy.1, (800) 368-2468, (707) 875-3525, fax (707) 875-2827; www.woodsidehotels.com. 78 rooms; $$$+; 2 night min. Children under 12 free. Most wood-burning fireplaces. Solar-heated pool, hot tub, sauna, health spa, fitness room. Restaurant.*

Situated at the southern end of town, overlooking the scenic wetlands marsh and sand dunes of **Doran Park** and the ocean beyond, this rustically attractive modern motel features rooms with stunning ocean views. A wonderful whirlpool hot tub is sheltered from the elements by glass walls, but its ceiling is open to the possibility of a light mist or rain providing a cooling touch. Golfing can be arranged at an adjacent 18-hole course.

A convenient ocean-view **restaurant** *(D daily. Reservations required.)* serves elegant dinner fare prepared with the best local ingredients: fresh Tomales Bay oysters on the half shell, Petaluma escargot with Enfant Riant truffle butter, rack of Sonoma lamb with olive-basil Zinfandel glacé and minted Sebastopol apples. Breakfast is choice here, and the ocean view is often at its best then. Delectable box lunches—packed with such goodies as marinated local fresh vegetables, herb-stuffed Petaluma game hens, and croissant sandwiches filled with Valley Ford lamb—are also available.

WHERE TO EAT

The Tides Wharf Restaurant *835 Hwy. 1, (707) 875-3652, fax (707) 875-3285. B,L,&D daily; $$. Highchairs, boosters, child portions. Reservations advised.*

Always crowded, this recently remodeled spot offers a well-priced breakfast and serves it until noon. Lunch and dinner menus offer an extensive selection of seafood entrees. A tasty tartar sauce is freshly made, and the Dungeness crab cocktail, though made with frozen crab, is delicious. Complete dinners come with a starter of either a delicious potato-rich New England clam chowder, or equally delicious seafood chowder, or a green salad with shrimp garnish, plus a vegetable and sourdough bread. Several vegetarian items, fried chicken, and steak are offered for those who don't care for fish. In addition to fish & chips, the children's menu offers a hamburger, hot dog, and grilled cheese sandwich. (One kid was overheard here saying, "It's a really good hamburger for a *nice* restaurant.") Because most tables afford sweeping views of Bodega Bay, it is worth scheduling a meal here before sunset.

Attractive contemporary rooms with ocean views are available across the street at **The Inn at the Tides** (*800 Hwy. 1, (800) 541-7788, (707) 875-2751, fax (707) 875-2669; www.innatthetides.com. 86 rooms; $$-$$$+. Children under 12 free. VCRs to rent; some kitchens & wood-burning fireplaces. Heated indoor-outdoor pool, hot tub, sauna. Continental breakfast; 2 restaurants, room service.*). At monthly Dinners with the Winemaker, five-course meals are paired with wines from a guest winery whose representative is on hand to comment. These events are fun, and the delicious food is served in gut-busting portions.

Jenner

WHAT TO DO

Fort Ross State Historic Park *19005 Hwy. 1, 11 mi. north of town, (707) 847-3286. Daily 10-4:30. $6/vehicle.*

Built by Russian and Alaskan hunters in 1812 as a trading outpost, this historic fort has been authentically restored by the state. The compound consists of two blockhouses equipped with cannons, a small Russian Orthodox chapel, a manacor's house, and a barracks. Picnic tables are available. Outside the gates, a picturesque bluff at the edge of the ocean offers a path leading down to the beach. An architecturally striking Visitors Center is located adjacent to the parking area.

Living History Day, which allow visitors to step back in time to the 1800s, is held annually on the last Saturday in July. Then, costumed staff and volunteers perform musket drills and fire cannons, craftspersons demonstrate their skills, and a blacksmith pounds at his forge.

Kruse Rhododendron State Reserve *On Kruse Ranch Rd., 22 mi. north of town, (707) 847-3221. Daily sunrise-sunset. Free.*

Best known for its spring floral display in April and May, depending on weather, this 317-acre park has 5 miles of hiking trails that take visitors over picturesque bridges and through fern-filled canyons.

Salt Point State Park *25050 Hwy. 1, 20 mi. north of town, (707) 847-3221. Daily sunrise-sunset. $5/vehicle.*

A popular spot with skin divers, this park is also choice for a walk along the beach. Stump Cove has an easy, short trail down to its scenic beach. Campsites are available.

WHERE TO STAY

Fort Ross Lodge *20705 Hwy. 1, 12 mi. north of town, (800) 968-4537, (707) 847-3333, fax (707) 847-3330; www.fortrosslodge.com. 23 units; $-$$$+. Children under 12 free. All VCRs; most wood-burning fireplaces. Hot tub, sauna.*

This collection of comfortable rustic-modern cabins is situated on a large, open, grassy bluff on the ocean side of the highway. Some units have ocean views; all have a small refrigerator, a coffee maker, a microwave oven, and a barbecue on a private patio. A beach access trail is available to guests.

Jenner Inn *10400 Hwy. 1, (800) 732-2377, (707) 865-2377, fax (707) 865-0829; www.jennerinn.com. 13 units; 100% non-smoking; $-$$$+; 2-night min. on weekends. Children under 5 free. No TVs; some kitchens & wood-burning fireplaces & stoves. Afternoon snack, continental breakfast; restaurant.*

Tucked into a curve in the highway at the point where the Russian River runs into the Pacific Ocean, this inn offers a choice of lodge rooms, cottages, and private homes. Three rooms in the River House get unobstructed views of the estuary and share a hot tub. A communal lounge is kept cozy by an antique wood-burning stove and offers guests a library filled with books and games.

Salt Point Lodge *23255 Hwy. 1, 17 mi. north of town, (800) 956-3437, (707) 847-3234, fax (707) 847-3354; www.saltpoint.com. 16 rooms; $-$$; 2-night min. on weekends. Some wood-burning stoves. Hot tub, sauna. Restaurant.*

Located across the street from the Pacific Ocean, this motel features a large expanse of lawn dotted with a swing set and giant sculpted slide designed and built by local artist Bruce Johnson. Special family rooms have a queen bed and two twin bunk beds, and two rooms for two have an ocean view and a private deck and hot tub.

Timber Cove Inn *21780 Hwy. 1, 14 mi. north of town, (800) 987-8319, (707) 847-3231, fax (707) 847-3704; www.timbercoveinn.com. 47 rooms; $-$$$+; 2-night min. on Sat. Unsuitable for children. No TVs; some fireplaces. Restaurant.*

Perched on a rocky seaside cliff, this inn offers many rooms with magnificent ocean views and some with sunken tubs and private hot tubs. A tall Bufano sculpture, which acts as a landmark, juts above the lodge, and the lobby bar and restaurant feature a dramatic Japanese-modern style of architecture and expansive ocean views.

The Sea Ranch

WHERE TO STAY

Home Rentals. *Rams Head Realty & Rentals, 1000 Annapolis Rd., (800) 785-3455, (707) 85-2427, fax (707) 785-2429; www.ramsheadrealty.com. 120 units; $$$-$$$+; 2-night min. All kitchens; some fireplaces. Pets welcome in some homes.*

Stunningly beautiful wind-swept coastal scenery is the backdrop for the approximately 1,500 luxury vacation homes situated in this development. Each home is unique. For example, the spectacular oceanfront Monette House has three bedrooms and a very special hot tub in an enclosed room with sliding glass doors opening to the ocean. Rustic hike-in cabins are also available. Guests have access to two recreation centers and to hiking and jogging trails as well as a children's playground. A 9-hole golf course, designed in the Scottish manner by Robert Muir Graves, can be played at extra charge.

The Sea Ranch Lodge *60 Sea Walk Dr., (800) 732-7262, (707) 785-2371, fax (707) 785-2917; www.searanchlodge.com. 20 rooms; $$$-$$$+; 2-night min. on weekends July-Oct. Children under 5 free. No TVs; some wood-burning fireplaces & stoves. Restaurant, room service.*

At this rustic modern facility, each room has an ocean view. Two rooms have private courtyards with hot tubs.

Gualala

A LITTLE BACKGROUND

Named for an Indian word that is pronounced "wha-LA-la" and means "water coming down place," this town is located in a banana belt of regularly warm weather. The area's many celebrity property owners include singer Kris Kristofferson and comedian Robin Williams.

VISITOR INFORMATION

Redwood Coast Chamber of Commerce *P.O. Box 338, Gualala 95445-0338, (800) 778-LALA, fax (707) 884-9004; www.gualala.com.*

WHERE TO STAY

Gualala Hotel *On Hwy. 1, (707) 884-3441, fax (707) 884-3908. 19 rooms; ¢-$. Some shared baths. Breakfast; restaurant.*

Built by the town's founders in 1903, when guests arrived from San Francisco by stagecoach, this historic inn's rooms are decorated with period antiques. Five have private baths and ocean views.

Family-style dinners are served in the restaurant, and an atmospheric logging bar, once frequented by Jack London, is now popular with locals.

Mar Vista Cottages *35101 Hwy. 1, 5 mi. north of town, (877) 855-3522, (707) 884-3522; www.marvistamendocino.com. 12 units; $-$$. No TVs; all kitchens; some wood-burning fireplaces & stoves. Hot tub. Pets welcome.*

Most of these one- and two-bedroom cottages have ocean views; all are just a short walk from a sandy beach with a gentle surf.

The Old Milano Hotel *38300 Hwy. 1, 1 mi. north of town, (707) 884-3256; www.oldmilanohotel.com. 9 units; 100% non-smoking; $$-$$$+; 2-night min. on Sat. Unsuitable for children under 16. No TVs; some wood-burning stoves; some shared baths. Hot tub. Full breakfast; restaurant.*

Built originally in 1905 as a railroad rest stop and pub, this cliffside Victorian hotel is elegantly refurbished and listed in the National Register of Historic Places. A garden cottage and a converted caboose—complete with upstairs brakeman's seats where occupants can watch the sun set—are available in addition to the hotel rooms. An expansive ocean view is enjoyed from the cliff-top hot tub.

Serenisea *36100 Hwy. 1, 3 mi. north of town, (800) 331-3836, (707) 884-3836; www.serenisea.com. 23 units; $-$$$; 2-night min. on weekends. Children under 1 free. Some TVs & VCRs; all kitchens; some wood-burning fireplaces & stoves. Pets welcome in some units.*

Most of these housekeeping cabins and vacation homes are spread over a scenic ocean bluff. Some have private hot tubs, and one has a private sauna. A trail leads down to the beach.

St. Orres *36601 Hwy. 1, 2 mi. north of town, (707) 884-3303, fax (707) 884-1543; www.saintorres.com. 8 rooms, 11 cottages; $-$$$; 2-night min. on weekends. No TVs; some wood-burning fireplaces; some shared baths. Hot tub, sauna. Full breakfast; restaurant.*

This unusual inn is built of weathered wood in a Russian style of architecture featuring onion-domed turrets.

A fixed-price, three-course dinner is served in the striking 3-story-tall **dining room** *(D daily, SunBr; $30. Reservations advised.)* featuring large windows with ocean views Dishes often make use of locally foraged ingredients and wild game such as boar and venison.

Whale Watch Inn *35100 Hwy. 1, 5 mi. north of town, (800) WHALE-42, (707) 884-3667, fax (707) 884-4815; www.whalewatchinn.com. 18 rooms; 100% non-smoking; $$$-$$$+; 2-night min. on weekends. No TVs; some kitchens; all wood-burning fireplaces. Sauna. Full breakfast; limited room service.*

Perched on an oceanside cliff, this dramatic contemporary-style inn offers plenty of peace and quiet. Rooms are spread among five buildings; all have private decks and ocean views, and eight have two-person whirlpool bathtubs. The Bath Suite has a spiral staircase leading to a whirlpool bathtub for two that is positioned under a skylight and features an ocean view. The Crystal Sea offers a mesmerizing view of an ocean cove—from a couch, the bed, and another of those whirlpool tubs for two. In the morning, a delicious breakfast is brought to the room in a large willow basket tray. Guests can relax in the communal Whale Watch Room equipped with a cozy circular fireplace, panoramic view of the ocean, and telescope for whale-watching. Guests also have access to a half-mile stretch of private beach.

Point Arena

WHAT TO DO

Point Arena Lighthouse *At the end of Lighthouse Rd., 2 mi. off Hwy. 1, (877) 725-4448, (707) 882-2777; www.mcn.org/1/palight. Daily 11-2:30; in summer M-F 11-3:30, Sat & Sun 10-3:30. Adults $2.50, under 12 50¢. House rentals: 3 units; $$; 2-night min. All VCRs; all kitchens & wood-burning stoves.*

Originally built in 1870, this lighthouse was destroyed in the '06 quake and then rebuilt. It was finally automated in 1976. Visitors can take a self-guided tour of the museum, which is filled with historical photos and features a whale-watching room. Then it's a 145-step climb (equivalent to 6 stories) up the 115-feet-tall light for a guided tour of the tower. Those who want to stay the night can book one of the bargain three-bedroom, two-bath lightkeeper's homes located adjacent.

Manchester

GETTING THERE

Located 5 miles north of Point Arena and 30 miles south of Mendocino.

WHAT TO DO

Manchester State Beach *(707) 937-5794.*

This 650-acre park is located where the San Andreas Fault meets the sea. It is the closest spot in North America to Hawaii.

WHERE TO STAY

KOA Kampground *(800) KOA-4188, (707) 882-2375.*

Situated within a thick grove of pine and cypress, this campground has Kamping Kottages and boasts a heated pool, a hot tub, a game room, and beach access. For description, see page 415.

Elk

WHERE TO STAY

Harbor House Inn *5600 Hwy. 1, (800) 720-7474, (707) 877-3203; www.theharborhouseinn.com. 6 rooms, 4 cottages; 100% non-smoking; $$$-$$$+; 2-night min. on weekends. Unsuitable for children under 12. No TVs; some wood-burning fireplaces. Full dinner & breakfast included.*

Built entirely of redwood in 1917, this lovely inn has a path leading to a private beach where guests can sun, explore tidepools, and gather driftwood. Meals are served in a beautifully appointed dining room with a spectacular ocean view.

Mendocino

A LITTLE BACKGROUND

Mendocino provides a rejuvenating, quiet escape from the hectic pace of city life. Now an Historical District, this remote burg is built in a pastel Cape Cod-style of architecture and exudes the feeling that it belongs to a time past. In the early 1800s, it was a center for redwood mills and the main shipping port for sending lumber to San Francisco. In the late 19th century, it was known as "The Town of the Water Towers." Today, some of these picturesque towers have been converted into lodgings, and the town is better known for its charming shops and art galleries. Visitors can really slow down their systems by leaving their cars parked for the duration of a visit. It is easy to get anywhere in town via a short walk.

Visitors are advised that Mendocino has a volunteer fire department with an alarm that has been known to go off in the middle of the night. Resembling the scream of an air-raid siren, it can be quite startling, even when a person is aware of what it is. On a cheerier note, quarterly Sunday morning pancake breakfasts are held here.

The night life here is of the early-to-bed, early-to-rise variety. Consider this itinerary: dinner out, a stroll through town, a nightcap at the Mendocino Hotel, and then off to bed.

Make lodging reservations as far in advance as possible; in-town lodging is limited and popular.

VISITOR INFORMATION

Fort Bragg-Mendocino Coast Chamber of Commerce *332 N. Main St, (800) 726-2780, (707) 961-6300, fax (707) 964-2056; www.mendocinocoast.com.*

GETTING THERE

Located approximately 150 miles north of San Francisco. Take Highway 101 to Highway 1, or Highway 101 to Highway 128 to Highway 1.

ANNUAL EVENTS

Mendocino Coast Whale Festival *March. In Mendocino & Fort Bragg; (800) 726-2780.*

In Mendocino, the fun includes a wine tasting, seafood chowder tasting, and classic rock concert. In Fort Bragg, it takes the form of a microbrewery beer tasting, a seafood chowder tasting, and a classic car show, and whale-watching cruises are available.

Mendocino Music Festival *July. (707) 937-2044, fax (707) 937-1045; www.mendocinomusic.com. $14-$40; under 18 $12.*

A variety of performances—including orchestra, chamber music, opera, and jazz—are presented in a small oceanside tent in Mendocino Headlands State Park. Master classes are scheduled, and free pre-concert lectures educate the audience about the music being performed.

WHAT TO DO

Beachcombing.

Follow down to the beach the little path behind the **Mendocino Presbyterian Church** on Main Street. (Built in 1868 from local redwood, this American Gothic church is California's oldest continuously-used Presbyterian church and is a town landmark. It is considered a masterpiece.) While there, make a kelp horn by cutting the bulb off the end of a long, thin

piece of fresh bull kelp. Rinse out the tube in the ocean so that it is hollow. Then wrap it over one shoulder and blow through the small end. The longer the tube, the greater the resonance.

Catch A Canoe & Bicycles, Too *On Comptche-Ukiah Rd., (800) 320-BIKE, (707) 937-0273, fax (707) 937-0305. Daily 9:30-5:30. $10+/hr.*

Drifting down calm Big River affords the opportunity to picnic in the wilderness, swim in a secluded swimming hole, and observe a variety of wildlife. Canoe rentals include paddles and life jackets. Bicycle rentals are also available.

Ford House Museum and Visitor Center *735 Main St., (707) 937-5397. Daily 11-4. $1 donation.*

Inside this historic 1854 home, an interpretive center focuses on the cultural and natural history of the area. During whale-watching season, a related short orientation film is presented. Information on interpretive programs held at nearby **Mendocino Headlands State Park** can also be obtained here then. (From December through April, whales migrate close to shore and from the headlands can sometimes easily be seen "breaching," or jumping out of the water.) In good weather, a picnic at tables in the backyard offers a spectacular ocean view.

Kelley House Historical Museum *45007 Albion St., (707) 937-5791. F-M 1-4; daily in summer. Adults $1.*

A gigantic cypress tree grows in the front yard of this home built by William H. Kelley (Daisy MacCallum's father) in 1861. The restored first floor displays a collection of photos from the 1800s, as well as changing exhibits of local artifacts and private collections.

Mendocino Art Center *45200 Little Lake St., (800) 653-3328, (707) 936-5818. Daily 10-4. Free.*

Three rooms display art here. Cookies and coffee are sometimes available in the lobby, and an inviting courtyard garden seems the perfect place to enjoy them. Activities related to fine arts and crafts are scheduled year-round, and the **Mendocino Theatre Company** presents performances March through December.

Russian Gulch State Park *On Hwy. 1, 2 mi. north of town, (707) 937-5804, fax (707) 937-2953. Daily dawn-dusk. $5/vehicle.*

A protected beach, a 36-feet-high waterfall, and a blow-hole are among the features of this rustic park. Picnic tables overlook an ocean cove, and campsites are available.

Van Damme State Park *8125 Hwy. 1, Little River, 2 mi. south of town, (707) 937-5804. Park: daily dawn-dusk; Visitor Center: daily 10-4. $5/vehicle.*

Among the interesting features in this 2,069-acre park is a canyon wall covered with ferns and the 1/3-mile Bog Trail leading to a large area of skunk cabbage. Picnic facilities and campsites are available.

An unusual **Pygmy Forest,** where stunted trees grow in leached soil, is nearby. It has a short boardwalk trail, and a brochure describing the various types of trees is available at the trailhead. To reach the forest, follow Little River Airport Road approximately 3 miles inland.

WHERE TO STAY IN TOWN

Blair House Inn *45110 Little Lake St., (800) 699-9296, (707) 937-1800, fax (707) 937-2444. 5 rooms; 100% non-smoking; $-$$$+; 2-night min. on weekends. Unsuitable for children under 6. Some shared baths. Pets welcome.*

Famous as the exterior for Jessica Fletcher's house in the TV series *Murder, She Wrote*, this delightful 1888 Victorian was constructed of now abusurdly expensive virgin clearheart redwood. All the rooms are nicely decorated with antiques and hand-crafted quilts, but the particularly nice Angela Suite, where Angela Lansbury actually stayed while filming, has a Victorian dip sink and a clawfoot tub. The exterior of the house is surrounded by a picket fence and a cottage garden and looks much as it did when originally built.

Hill House Inn *10701 Palette Dr., (800) 422-0554, (707) 937-0554, fax (707) 937-1123; www.hillhouseinn.com. 44 rooms; $$$-$$$+; 2-night min. on Sat. Some wood-burning fireplaces. Continental breakfast; restaurant, room service.*

Located on a hill above the village, this charming lodging facility was built in 1978. It has become famous as the setting for many of the early episodes of the TV series *Murder, She Wrote*, and the Bette Davis Suite is where the namesake star lodged for 6 weeks while filming her final movie. Because of this Hollywood connection, it attracts many stars as patrons. Rooms are spacious and furnished comfortably with brass beds and lace curtains.

John Dougherty House *571 Ukiah St., (800) 486-2104, (707) 937-5266; www.innaccess.com/jdh. 6 rooms; $-$$$+. Unsuitable for children. Some wood-burning stoves. Full breakfast.*

Situated on a quiet back street, this cozy salt box-style inn, built in 1867, is one of the oldest houses in town. An adjacent water tower has been converted into a charming two-room suite with an 18 foot-high beamed ceiling and a fireplace, and two cottages are situated in an English garden. Most of the rooms have great ocean views.

Joshua Grindle Inn *44800 Little Lake Rd., (800) GRINDLE, (707) 937-4143; www.joshgrin.com. 10 rooms; 100% non-smoking; $$-$$$+; 2-night min. on weekends. Unsuitable for children. No TVs; some wood-burning fireplaces & stoves. Afternoon snack, full breakfast.*

Situated on a 2-acre knoll at the edge of town, the Victorian farmhouse that comprises this small inn was built in 1879 by the town banker. It has a New England country atmosphere, and Early American antiques furnish every room. Guest rooms are in the main house, a cottage, and a water tower.

MacCallum House Inn *45020 Albion St., (800) 609-0492, (707) 937-0289; www.maccallumhouse.com. 19 rooms; 100% non-smoking; $$-$$$; 2-night min. on weekends May-Dec. Children under 10 free. No TVs; 1 kitchen, some wood-burning fireplaces & stoves. Restaurant.*

Built in 1882 by William H. Kelley for his newlywed daughter, Daisy MacCallum, this converted Victorian home was one of the first B&Bs in the area (though it no longer serves breakfast). The attractively decorated rooms are furnished with antiques, many of which belonged to the original owner. A water tower suite is fitted with a bed on the first floor, a bathroom with ocean view on the second, and another bed with ocean view on the third. Accommodations are also available in newer structures adjacent to the house.

In the evening, **MacCallum House Restaurant** (*(707) 937-5763; www.maccallumhousedining.com. D daily. Closed Jan-mid-Feb. Boosters. Reservations advised.*), an independent operation, serves elegant seafood and game entrees in the house's magnificent dining rooms. On cold nights, guests are warmed by crackling fires in two fireplaces built of smooth river stone. Light dinners and snacks are available across the hall in the cozy **Grey Whale Bar**, also operated by the restaurant. Interesting drinks include Daisy's Hot Apple Pie (a blend of apple cider, Tuaca, cinnamon, and whipped cream) and a non-alcoholic Velvet Rabbit (a frothy mix of cream, grenadine, and strawberries served elegantly in a brandy snifter).

Mendocino Hotel & Garden Suites *45080 Main St., (800) 548-0513, (707) 937-0511, fax (707) 937-0513; www.mendocinohotel.com. 51 rooms; $-$$$+; 2-night min. on weekends. Children under 14 free. Some TVs & fireplaces; some shared baths. 2 restaurants, room service.*

Built in 1878, this authentic Victorian hotel dates back to when the town was a booming port for the logging trade. Its small rooms combine 19th-century elegance with modern convenience. Contemporary cottages, located behind the hotel amidst almost an acre of well-tended gardens, have luxurious suites featuring canopied beds and marble bathrooms. Antiques are found throughout the hotel, but one of the most interesting is the registration desk —an ornate teller's cage from a Kansas bank.

A casual **cafe** with ocean views serves both breakfast and lunch. The eggs Benedict is perfect, and the potato cake wedges are both unusual and delicious. Dinner is available in a more formal **restaurant** *($$$. Highchairs, boosters, child portions. Reservations advised.)* furnished in vintage oak. Fresh seafood and meat entrees are on the a la carte menu. Starters include a French onion soup and a very good Caesar salad, and the dessert tray always includes the house specialty—deep-dish olallieberry pie with homemade ice cream. A Victorian lady ghost is said to haunt tables six and eight. The hotel's lobby **bar,** with its stained-glass dome (believed to be a Tiffany), is a good spot to enjoy a fancy drink among beautiful specimens of stained glass and antique oriental carpets.

Mendocino Village Inn *44860 Main St., (800) 882-7029, (707) 937-0246; www.mendocinoinn.com. 10 rooms; 100% non-smoking; $-$$$; 2-night min. on weekends. Unsuitable for children under 10. No TVs; some wood-burning fireplaces & stoves; some shared baths. Afternoon snack, full breakfast.*

Built in 1882, this Queen Anne Victorian is known as "the house of the doctors" because it was originally built by a doctor, and then was bought in turn by three more doctors. All the cozy rooms are decorated with antiques and contemporary art. A suite with a private deck and ocean view is available in a converted 2-story water tower.

Sea Gull Inn *44594 Albion St., (888) 937-5204, (707) 937-5204, fax (707) 937-3550; www.mcn.org/a/seagull. 9 rooms; 100% non-smoking; $-$$$; 2-night min. on weekends. 1 TV. Continental breakfast; room service.*

Built in 1877 as a town house, this simple inn has a casual, friendly atmosphere. A mature garden, with giant fuchsias and a century-old rosemary bush, surrounds the inn. Breakfast includes hot beverages, orange juice, muffins, and raspberry scones.

Sweetwater Inn *44840 Main St., (800) 300-4140, (707) 937-4076, fax (707) 937-1549. 8 rooms; 100% non-smoking; $-$$$+; 2-night min. on weekends. No TVs; some kitchens; some wood-burning fireplaces & stoves; some shared baths. Pets welcome.*

Guests here have the choice of staying in an 1870 Victorian house, a cottage, or a converted water tower. Each room is stocked with a complimentary bottle of wine. Additional rooms are available in Little River.

Whitegate Inn *499 Howard St., (800) 531-7282, (707) 937-4892, fax (707) 937-1131; www.whitegateinn.com. 6 rooms, 1 cottage; 100% non-smoking; $$-$$$+; 2-night min. on weekends. Children under 2 free. Some wood-burning fireplaces & stoves. Evening snack, full breakfast.*

Built in 1880, this converted Victorian home has a view of the ocean and town and is surrounded by a garden with a white picket fence and gate. It is tastefully furnished with French and Victorian antiques. Live orchids grace every room, and lace-edged sheets and lofty down comforters adorn every bed. Some bathrooms feature clawfoot tubs. Homemade cookies are always available, chocolates arrive at bedtime, and a lavish breakfast is served on antique china and sterling silver.

WHERE TO STAY NEARBY

Fensalden Inn *33810 Navarro Ridge Rd., Albion, 7 mi. south of town, (800) 959-3850, (707) 937-4042; www.fensalden.com. 8 rooms; 100% non-smoking; $$-$$$; 2-night min. on weekends May-Dec. Unsuitable for children under 7. 1 TV & VCR; some kitchens & wood-burning fireplaces & stoves. Evening snack, full breakfast.*

Originally a Wells Fargo stagecoach way station in the 1860s, this restful B&B sits atop 20 tree-lined acres of headlands meadow offering quiet respite. Among the rooms in the large main house is an upstairs two-room suite with a sweeping view of a pasture lined with cypress trees. Another 2-story suite is built around an 1890s water tower, and a private bungalow with an unobstructed ocean view is situated at the head of the pasture. Antique furnishings are used throughout.

Glendeven Inn *8205 N. Hwy. 1, Little River, 1 1/2 mi. south of town, (800) 822-4536, (707) 937-0083, fax (707) 937-6108; www.glendeven.com. 10 rooms; 100% non-smoking; $$-$$$+; 2-night min. on weekends. Unsuitable for children under 8. All CD players; most fireplaces. Afternoon & evening snack, full breakfast.*

Built in 1867, this attractive New England-style farmhouse is set back from the highway on 2 1/2 quiet acres overlooking the headland meadows and bay at Little River. Rooms are in the farmhouse as well as in a restored hay barn, water tower, and well-designed addition. All are furnished tastefully and eclectically with antiques and contemporary art. Handmade quilts cover beds and walls, and peaceful views are seen from every window. Favorites include charming Eastlin, hidden behind a bookcase door in the main house, and Briar Rose, featuring a view of both the ocean *and* fireplace from its bed. Breakfast can be delivered to the room.

Near the entrance, **The Gallery at Glendeven** displays the work of a cooperative of local artists.

Heritage House *5200 N. Hwy. 1, Little River, 4 mi. south of town, (800) 235-5885, (707) 937-5885, fax (707) 937-0318; www.heritage-houseinn.com. 66 rooms; $$-$$$+. Closed Jan to mid-Feb. Children under 6 free. No TVs; many wood-burning fireplaces; some gas fireplaces. Afternoon snack; full dinner & breakfast included; restaurant.*

Located on a craggy stretch of coast with magnificent ocean views and over 37 acres of well-tended gardens, this luxurious inn offers rooms and cottages furnished either with antiques or in contemporary style. Most have ocean views and decks. If it all looks familiar, it could be because it's been seen before in the movie *Same Time Next Year*, which was filmed here. The cabin the movie was filmed in has been divided into one called "Same Time" and another called "Next Year." Note that though some family amenities exist, children are generally discouraged.

Fine dining is available in an elegant cliff-side **restaurant** *(B M-F, D daily, Sat & SunBr; $$$. Highchairs, boosters. Reservations advised for D.)*. Non-guests are welcome.

Little River Inn *7751 Hwy. 1, Little River, 2 mi. south of town, (888) INN-LOVE, (707) 937-5942, fax (707) 937-3944; www.littleriverinn.com. 65 rooms; $-$$$+; 2-night min. on weekends. Children under 16 free. All VCRs; 1 kitchen; some wood-burning fireplaces & stoves. Health spa, 2 tennis courts (night lights), 9-hole golf course. Restaurant, room service.*

Built on this spectacular location in 1853 by an ancestor of the current owner, this gingerbread Victorian house became an inn in 1939 and now offers a choice of cozy attic rooms, cottages, and standard motel units. Most have expansive ocean views. On the ocean side of Highway 1, new rooms have both an indoor whirlpool tub and a private outdoor hot tub. The beach and hiking trails of Van Damme State Park are adjacent, and a new spa offers pampering body treatments and restorative massage.

The lovely full-service, garden-view **restaurant** *(B&D daily. Highchairs, boosters.)* and oceanview **bar**, which is perfect for a light meal, are open to non-guests.

Mendocino Coast Reservations *1000 Main St., Mendocino, (800) 262-7801, (707) 937-5033, fax (707) 937-4236; www.mendocinovacations.com. 70 units; $-$$$+; 2-night min., 1-week in July & Aug. All kitchens; some fireplaces. Dogs welcome in some units.*

This vacation home rental service arranges lodging in privately-owned studio apartments, cabins, cottages, inns, and houses located on the Mendocino coast. Some units are oceanfront, some have ocean views, and some have private hot tubs.

Stanford Inn by the Sea *On Comptche-Ukiah Rd., Mendocino, (800) 331-8884, (707) 937-5615, fax (707) 937-0305; www.stanfordinn.com. 33 rooms; 100% non-smoking; $$$+; 2-night min. on Sat. Children under 4 free. All VCRs; some kitchens; all wood-burning fireplaces. Indoor heated pool & hot tub, sauna, fitness center. Afternoon tea, evening snack, full breakfast. Pets welcome.*

Located on the outskirts of town, upon a bluff above a scenic llama farm and duck pond that is home to black swans, these luxurious yet cozy pine- and redwood-panelled contemporary rooms are decorated with antiques, fresh flowers, and the work of local artists. All are furnished with either a four-poster or sleigh bed, and many have views overlooking the gardens to the ocean beyond. Operating as a self-sufficient ecosystem, this unique property has a certified organic garden, nursery, and working farm spread over 10 acres. The greenhouse-enclosed pool and hot tub are like a tropical retreat, and mountain bikes are available for guests to borrow at no charge. Dogs get VIP treatment with special bedding, bones, biscuits, water dishes—even baggies for owners to clean up their messes. Cats are welcome, too, as are, in fact, all pets.

In a large, open, very comfortable dining room, a new, exceptional, *totally* vegetarian restaurant, **The Ravens** *(D Thur-M; $$.)*, offers exciting, refined cuisine using only the freshest ingredients. In addition to serving complex dishes such as wild mushroom galette and blackened tofu Creole, this elegant, creative gourmet venue also offers pizza, polenta, and a portabella burger.

WHERE TO EAT

Cafe Beaujolais *961 Ukiah St., (707) 937-5614, fax (707) 937-3656; www.cafebeaujolais.com. D daily; $$. Closed Dec. Child portions. Reservations advised.*

Gone here are the days of great breakfasts and informal lunches. Now it is dinners only, using local meats, fish, and organic produce. Wonderful breads, including a dense Austrian sunflower bread and an unusual hazelnut, are baked on the premises in a wood-burning oven. A three course, fixed-price country menu is available Tuesday through Thursday.

Mendocino Bakery *On Lansing St., (707) 937-0836. Daily 8-7; $. 1 booster.*

The perfect spot for a light lunch, this super bakery dispenses tasty housemade soup and thick-crusted pizza warm from the oven. A hunk of fragrant, moist gingerbread makes a memorable dessert, as do chewy cinnamon twists and chocolate chip-oatmeal Cowboy Cookies. The bakery also dispenses an assortment of breads and breakfast pastries made without mixes or preservatives. Everything is exceptional.

Next door, the **Mendocino Chocolate Company** *(10483 Lansing St., (800) 722-1107, (707) 937-1107; www.mendocino-chocolate.com. Daily 10-5:30.)* purveys delicious handmade candies. Samples are always available.

Behind the bakery, tiny **Mendo Burgers** *((707) 937-1111. M-Sat 11-7, Sun to 5; $.)* dishes up the obvious in a variety of delicious renditions (beef, chicken, turkey, veggie, fish, kid-size) plus hot dogs, fresh fish & chips, housemade soups, salads, and fresh-cut fries. Seating outdoors at roomy picnic tables is prime on a sunny day.

Fort Bragg

A LITTLE BACKGROUND

The largest city on the Mendocino coast, Fort Bragg also has the largest working sea port between San Francisco and Eureka. Known as Noyo Harbor, it is home to popular seafood restaurants serving fresh fish from the daily catch.

GETTING THERE

Located 10 miles north of Mendocino.

ANNUAL EVENTS

John Druecker Memorial Rhododendron Show *May. (800) 726-2780. Free.*

One of the largest such shows in the West, this is hosted by the Noyo chapter of the American Rhododendron Society. An enormous exhibit includes everything from alpine dwarf species to huge trusses of hybrids.

World's Largest Salmon Barbecue *July. (800) 726-2780, (707) 964-6535. Adults $12, under 12 $7.*

In addition to feasting on king salmon, participants can look forward to music, dancing, a variety of educational salmon displays, and a fireworks show over the ocean. Proceeds benefit the non-profit Salmon Restoration Association and assist them in restocking Northern California salmon runs.

WHAT TO DO

Downtown Shopping.

A walk along Main and Laurel streets allows a look at some of the town's most interesting shops. On North Main Street, stop in at the **Mendocino Chocolate Company** at #542 *((800) 722-1107, (707) 964-8800. Daily 10-5:30.)* for hand-dipped chocolates and truffles. Visit **Round Man's Smoke House** at #412 *((800) 545-2935, (707) 964-5954, fax (707) 964-5438.)* for smoked meat, fish, cheese, and an assortment of jerkeys. At #401, the informal **Laurel Deli** *((707) 964-7812. M-F 7-4, Sat 8-4.)* dishes up freshly made soups and sandwiches as well as gigantic blackberry muffins and delicious housemade pies. At #362 the **Northcoast Artists Gallery** *((707) 964-8266. Daily 10-6.)* displays and sells the works of local artists, and at #330 **The Hot Pepper Jelly Company** *((800) 892-4823, (707) 961-1422, fax (707) 961-5462. Daily 10-5:30. Closed all of Jan.)* dispenses charming doily-topped jars of delicious pepper jelly and many other local food products.

The Fort Bragg Footlighters Gaslite Gaieties *248 Laurel St., (707) 964-3806. W & Sat at 8pm; summer only. Tickets $7. Reservations advised.*

Gay Nineties music and nonsense highlight a program that appeals to all ages.

Georgia-Pacific Tree Nursery *90 W. Redwood Ave., (707) 964-5651. Daily 9-4. Free.*

Visitors here get a view of four million seedling trees. A nature trail and picnic tables are available.

Glass Beach *On north side of town, across from Noyo Bowl at 900 N. Main St.*

It's best to ask for precise directions when in town. Park in the dirt lot and then walk down the path to the beach. Many years ago this was a dump, but now it is the source of great joy for kids as they scoop up bits of pottery and glass that have been smoothed into jewels. Local artists make jewelry from their finds, but anyone can easily put them in a clear glass of water at home for a fabulous, free souvenir.

Guest House Museum *343 N. Main St., (707) 961-0902. Sat & Sun 10-2. By donation.*

Get a sense of this area's history by viewing the old logging photos and artifacts on display inside this beautifully restored 1892 mansion constructed entirely of redwood.

Jughandle State Reserve *On Hwy. 1, 3 mi. south of town, (707) 937-5804. Daily dawn-dusk. Free.*

A unique self-guided nature trail takes hikers through an ecological staircase consisting of five wave-cut terraces that demonstrate how plants and soils affect one another. During the 5-mile walk (allow 3 hours), the terrain changes from grass-covered headlands, to a pine and redwood forest, to a pygmy forest filled with full-grown trees measuring only 1 to 2 feet tall. Wear sturdy shoes, and bring water and a lunch.

Mendocino Coast Botanical Gardens *18220 N. Hwy. 1, 2 mi. south of town, (707) 964-4352, fax (707) 964-3114. Daily 9-5; Nov-Feb 9-4. Adults $6, 60+ $5, 13-17 $3, 6-12 $1.*

A self-guided tour leads through 47 acres of flowering plants. Known for its rhododendrons, fuchsias, and heathers, this garden also boasts a major collection of succulents, camellias, and old heritage roses. An impressive collection of unusual perennials is sold in the gift shop, and picnic facilities are available.

Diners can sit on a sunny deck overlooking the gardens at **The Gardens Grill** *(18603 N. Hwy. 1, (707) 964-7474. L M-Sat, D Thur-Sat, SunBr, in summer; hours change for rest of year; $-$$. Highchairs, boosters, child portions. Reservations advised.).* Among the light lunch and dinner specialties are grilled items prepared over mesquite or apple wood, creative vegetarian entrees (perhaps a delicious torte of wild mushrooms and spinach), and refined housemade desserts.

Ricochet Ridge Ranch *24201 Hwy. 1, across from MacKerricher State Park, (888) TREK-RRR, (707) 964-7669, fax (707) 964-9669; www.horse-vacation.com. Daily at 10,12,2,&4. $28/hr.; riders must be 6 or older. Reservations required.*

Equestrian excursions vary from by-the-hour guided rides on the beach to week-long trips with nightly stops at inns. They include treks on Fort Bragg's Ten Mile Beach and in Mendocino's majestic redwood forests. Catered trips, camping expeditions, and private tours can also be arranged.

Skunk Train/California Western Railroad *Foot of Laurel St., (800) 77-SKUNK, (707) 964-6371, fax (707) 964-6754; www.skunktrain.com. Daily; schedule varies. Round trip: adults $26, 5-11 $12, under 5 free if they don't occupy a seat. Reservations advised.*

This train gets its name from the fact that the original logging trains emitted unpleasant odors from their gas engines. Loggers said they "could smell 'em before they could see 'em." Most of the trains today are pulled by diesel engines as they travel through dense redwood forest, through deep mountain tunnels, and over many bridges and trestles on the run between Fort Bragg and Willits, where there is a stopover for lunch. Quick stops are made along the way to deliver mail. A half-day trip is also available.

WHERE TO STAY

Colonial Inn *533 E. Fir St., (707) 964-9979. 8 rooms; 100% non-smoking; $-$$. Closed part of Oct & part of spring. Children under 5 free. Some TVs; some wood-burning fireplaces.*

Located in a quiet residential area, this massive 1912 wood-frame home was turned into a guest house in 1945. It features tastefully decorated rooms, one with an oversize fireplace. A public tennis court is just a block away.

DeHaven Valley Farm *39247 N. Hwy. 1, in Westport, 10 mi. north of town, (707) 961-1660, fax (707) 961-1677; www.dehaven-valley-farm.com. 8 rooms; 100% non-smoking; $-$$. Closed Jan. Children under 6 free. No TVs; some wood-burning fireplaces & stoves; some shared baths. Hot tub. Afternoon snack, full breakfast.*

Romance and family fun are both possible here. For romance, request the cozy Valley View room and enjoy its private bathroom, small corner fireplace, and view of the valley. The spacious Eagle's Nest, with its Franklin stove and expansive windows overlooking the valley, is another winner. With kids in tow, opt for one of the two cottages. One teenager who stayed here actually uttered, "Mom, you did right. This place is great!" A cozy communal living room in the traditional Victorian farmhouse is the gathering spot for afternoon refreshments. It holds a grand piano for self-entertainment and a TV with a large video library. Guests are welcome to play with the many resident cats and to walk the goats—although sometimes the goats seem to be walking the guests. The tidepools of Westport Union Landing Beach await just across the highway, and a hilltop hot tub offers views of the valley and ocean. Delicious, intimate four-course dinners are available to guests by reservation.

The Grey Whale Inn *615 N. Main St., (800) 382-7244, (707) 964-0640, fax (707) 964-4408; www.greywhaleinn.com. 14 rooms; 100% non-smoking; $$-$$$; 2-night min. on Sat. Some TVs & VCRs; some kitchens; some wood-burning & gas fireplaces. Full breakfast.*

Originally built as a hospital, this stately redwood building was converted into an especially spacious inn in 1976. Some of the pleasantly decorated rooms have a private deck, some have ocean views that permit viewing the whale migration, and one has a whirlpool bathtub for two. A large communal guest area is equipped with a TV, fireplace, pool table, and plenty of board games. The elaborate breakfast buffet sometimes includes a heavenly concoction of fresh bananas and blueberries mixed with a light cream cheese sauce. A relaxing stay here can be just what the doctor ordered.

Pine Beach Inn *16801 Hwy. 1, 4 mi. south of town, (707) 964-5603. 51 rooms; $$-$$$. 2 tennis courts. Restaurant.*

This motel complex is located on 12 acres of private land. Facilities include a private beach and cove.

Motel Row.

Three traditional motels on the northern end of town offer good value and an extraordinary beachfront location.

- **Beachcomber Motel** *1111 N. Main St., (800) 400-SURF, (707) 964-2402; www.thebeachcombermotel.com. $-$$$+.*
- **Hi Sea Inn** *1201 N. Main St., (800) 990-SEAS, (707) 964-5929. $-$$.*
- **Quality Inn Suites/Oceanview Lodging** *1141 N. Main St., (707) 964-1951. $$-$$$+.*

WHERE TO EAT

Cap'n Flint's *32250 N. Harbor Dr., (707) 964-9447. L&D daily; $. Highchairs, boosters, child portions. No reservations. No cards.*

Popular with locals, the menu here offers various kinds of fish & chips, clam chowder, and the house specialty—deep-fried shrimp won tons made with a tasty cream cheese filling. Hamburgers, hot dogs, sandwiches, and wine-based drinks are also available. Though the decor consists of well-worn, mismatched furniture, the view of picturesque Noyo Harbor is excellent.

Egghead's Restaurant *326 N. Main St., (707) 964-5005. B&L daily; $. Highchairs, boosters, booths, child portions. No reservations.*

Decorated with movie photos from *The Wizard of Oz* and related knickknacks, this cheerful, popular, and tiny diner serves 40-plus varieties of crêpes and *big* omelettes. Regular breakfast items and an assortment of sandwiches are also available. Families will appreciate the privacy afforded by enclosed booths.

Old Coast Hotel Bar & Grill *101 N. Franklin/Oak, (888) 468-3550, (707) 961-4488, fax (707) 961-4480. D Thur-M; $$.*

Extensively renovated and restored to its 1892 glory, this historic building features really spectacular original pressed-tin walls and is home to both a restaurant and hotel. The airy, open dining room has an attractive bar area and beautiful original wooden floors throughout. The dinner menu offers appetizers such as onion rings, popcorn shrimp, and roasted mussels. Entrees consist of seafood, pasta, pizza, and an assortment of specialties—grilled salmon, shellfish cioppino, scampi, rosemary roasted rotisserie chicken, and, on Friday and Saturday nights, prime rib.

The upstairs **hotel rooms** *(6 rooms; $-$$$. Some fireplaces. Continental breakfast.)* are simple but comfortable, and all are equipped with warm down comforters.

The Restaurant *418 N. Main St., (707) 964-9800. L Thur-F, D Thur-Tu, SunBr; $$. Highchairs, boosters, booths, child portions. Reservations advised.*

An ad for this restaurant reads, "If you like to eat, you'd probably like to eat at a place where people who like to eat, eat what they like—and like it!" It's an unusual ad—just like the restaurant, which, in completely unpretentious surroundings, serves good food at reasonable prices. The eclectic menu changes regularly, but the emphasis is on fresh local seafood and vegetarian items. A sample lunch menu offers a variety of sandwiches, plus a hamburger, Philly cheesesteak, chicken flauta, vegetable chili, and several salads and soups. Desserts are a chocolate shortcake with fresh berries and cream, a housemade ice cream, and a lemon tart. Dinner entrees the same night include Thai-style shrimp in green curry sauce, Denver lamb riblets with sweet & sour glaze, and chicken breast Amalfi topped with lemony arugula.

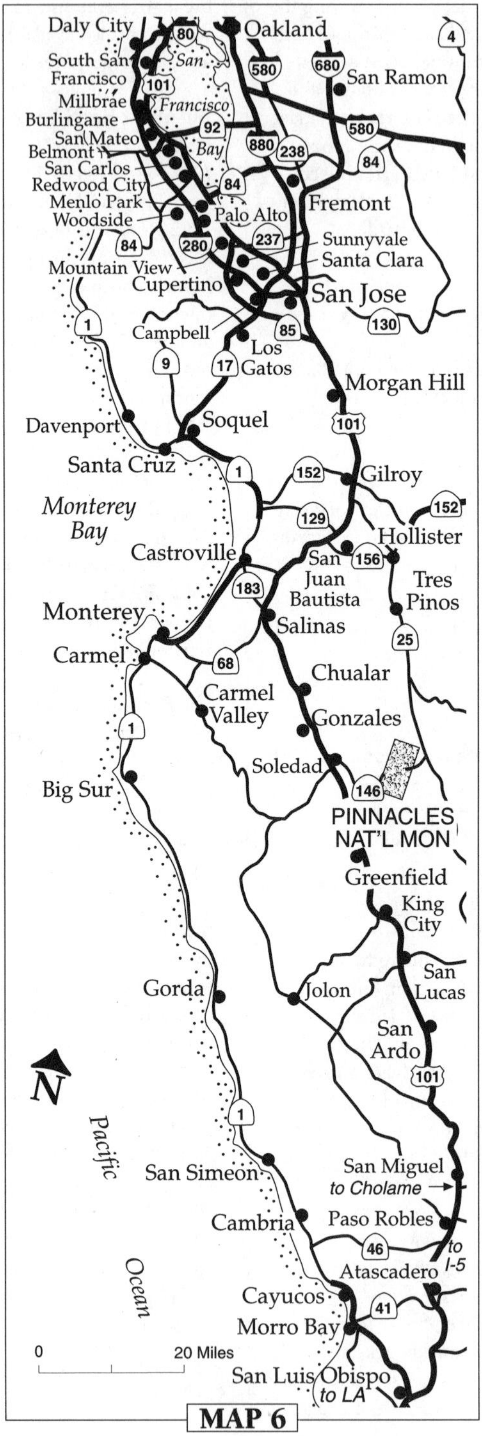
Daly City
Oakland
South San Francisco
San Francisco Bay
Millbrae
Burlingame
San Mateo
Belmont
San Carlos
Redwood City
Menlo Park
Woodside
Palo Alto
San Ramon
Fremont
Sunnyvale
Santa Clara
Mountain View
Cupertino
San Jose
Campbell
Los Gatos
Morgan Hill
Davenport
Soquel
Santa Cruz
Gilroy
Monterey Bay
Hollister
Castroville
San Juan Bautista
Tres Pinos
Monterey
Salinas
Carmel
Chualar
Carmel Valley
Gonzales
Soledad
Big Sur
PINNACLES NAT'L MON
Greenfield
King City
San Lucas
Gorda
Jolon
San Ardo
Pacific Ocean
San Simeon
San Miguel
to Cholame
Cambria
Paso Robles
to I-5
Atascadero
Cayucos
Morro Bay
San Luis Obispo
to LA
0
20 Miles
MAP 6

Millbrae

WHERE TO EAT

Fook Yuen *195 El Camino Real/Millbrae Ave., (650) 692-8600. L&D daily; $. Reservations accepted.*

On Chinese restaurant row, this popular spot—a branch of a chain found also in Hong Kong, Singapore, and Australia—stands out with its delicious, distinctive food. Dim sum is served at lunch, with a Cantonese menu at dinner. Specialties include tank-fresh seafood, pork with pickled plums, and crispy chicken.

Hong Kong Flower Lounge *51 Millbrae Ave./El Camino Real, (650) 692-6666 or (650) 878-8108. L&D daily; $$. Reservations advised.*

Authentic Hong Kong-style fresh seafood dishes, superior dim sum, and the restaurant's signature Peking duck are served in a cavernous, yet stylish room said to seat 400.

Burlingame

VISITOR INFORMATION

San Mateo County Convention & Visitors Bureau *11 Anza Blvd. #410, (800) 288-4748, (650) 348-7600, fax (650) 348-7687; www.sanmateocountycvb.com.*

WHAT TO DO

Burlingame Museum of Pez Memorabilia
214 California Dr./Howard Ave., (650) 347-2301; www.burlingamepezmuseum.com. Tu-Sat 10-6. Free.

Operating in the front of a computer store, this homespun exhibition includes some interative exhibits and displays hundreds of plastic Pez candy dispensers dating from the 1950s to the present. Snoopy, Bugs, and Fred (Flintstone) are all on display, along with Tweety Bird, who starred in a *Seinfeld* episode. A large selection of current and collectible Pez dispensers are for sale, as are the hard-to-find candy refills.

WHERE TO STAY

Embassy Suites *150 Anza Blvd., (800) EMBASSY, (650) 342-4600; www.embassy-suites.com.*

Located 2 miles south of the airport, this branch has a **Bobby McGee's** restaurant serving prime rib, steak, and fresh seafood. For description, see page 364.

WHERE TO EAT

Benihana *1496 Old Bayshore Hwy./Broadway, (650) 342-5202, fax (650) 342-6896.*

For description, see page 39.

Copenhagen Bakery & Cafe *1216 Burlingame Ave./Lorton Ave., (650) 342-1357, (650) 344-4937;*

www.copenhagenbakery.com. Bakery: M-Sat 6-6, Sun 8-4. Cafe: B&L daily, D W-Sun. $. Booths.

This combination bakery and coffee shop produces great six-grain bread and sweet French bread. For lunch try a delicious German bologna on sweet French bread with a side of potato salad, a grapefruit-quinine Danish soda, and, of course, a dessert pastry. Order at the back counter, then find a seat in the cheery open dining room with views of sidewalk.

Max's Opera Cafe *1250 Bayshore Hwy., (650) 342-MAXS.*

For description, see page 73.

Pisces *1190 California Dr./Broadway Ave., (650) 401-7500, fax (650) 401-8321; www.nextcenturyrestaurants.com. L M-F, D daily, SunBr; $$-$$$. Reservations advised.*

Operating within the town's beautifully restored and stylishly updated historic train station, this upscale yet casual spot specializes in fresh fish items. In addition to raw, seared, grilled, and smoked seafood there is the option of trying the signature rotisserie-style fish dishes. For an appetizer, crispy calamari spiced with red pepper and served with a sesame-mint aioli is delicious. A refined, thin New England clam chowder, served with a few whole clams, is also unusual and quite good. For entrees, a porcini-crusted petrale sole with roasted garlic mashed potatoes is comforting, and a sweet miso-glazed sea bass with lobster tortellini is boldly flavorful. A few meat dishes round out the menu. Desserts—including a layered milk chocolate mousse and a signature root beer float with warm chocolate chip cookies—have flair. Since the building is trackside, a whole lotta shakin' goes on as trains pass by.

World Wrapps *1318 Burlingame Ave., (650) 342-9777, fax (650) 342-9731.*

For description, see page 82.

San Mateo

GETTING THERE

Located approximately 20 miles south of San Francisco.

WHAT TO DO

Acres of Orchids *914 S. Claremont St./9th Ave., (650) 871-5655, fax (650) 373-3913; www.rodmclellan.com. M-Sat 10-6, Sun 12-5.*

One of the largest orchid nurseries in the world, this family-owned business began small in the 1890s. They were the first to bag supersoil and sell it to consumers (an irony being that anything will grow in it except orchids) and is famous for its well-draining Danish black plastic pot. Now all of the growing is done in green houses in Watsonville. However, a self-guided tour here permits seeing a variety of orchids and learning how they are propagated and cared for. Plants are available for purchase, with assistance provided in choosing the best variety for any home environment, and for a small fee sick plants can be boarded for intensive care in the "orchid spa."

Coyote Point Recreation Area *On Coyote Point Dr. Park: (650) 573-2593; www.coyoteptmuseum.org. Daily sunrise to sunset. $4/vehicle. Museum: 1651 Coyote Point Dr., 650-342-7755. Tu-Sat 10-5, Sun 12-5. Adults $3, 62+ & 13-17 $2, 4-12 $1; free 1st W of month.*

This 670-acre park is equipped with a barbecue area, several playgrounds, inviting grassy areas, an 18-hole golf course, a rifle range, and a swimming beach with bathhouse (lifeguards in summer). It is one of the best windsurfing sites in the U.S. and considered prime for beginners. As if all this isn't enough, it's also located on the descent route for the San Francisco International Airport, making it a wonderful place to just sit and watch planes landing.

Surrounded by an aromatic grove of eucalyptus trees, the architecturally impressive **Coyote Point Museum** was the first environmental museum in the U.S. It aims to educate visitors about local ecology and the environment with numerous hands-on and multimedia displays and live colonies of ants, termites, and bees. Exhibits in the impressive outdoor Wildlife Habitats area include live native animals (burrowing owls, a porcupine, a banana slug), a walk-through aviary of native Bay Area birds, and a colorful demonstration garden composed of plants that attract hummingbirds and butterflies. The new Nature's Marketplace shows how Native Americans used plants, shrubs, and trees in everyday life.

Japanese Garden *E. 5th Ave., in Central Park, (650) 377-4700; M-F 10-4, Sat & Sun 11-4; free.*

This tidy garden has a teahouse and a central pond divided by a narrow bridge. Koi are fed daily at 11 a.m. and 3 p.m. Rare and unusual plants include a weeping beech and umbrella pine.

WHERE TO EAT

Draeger's Market Place *222 E. 4th Ave./B St., (650) 685-3700. Daily 7am-10pm.*

This enormous market includes a sushi bar, wine tasting room, smoothie bar, deli, and bakery as well as a cooking school.

On the second floor, in an open space drenched with light, upscale **Viognier** restaurant *((650) 685-3727. B,L,&D daily; $$-$$$. Booths.)* serves a rustic Mediterranean menu of salads, pizzettas, grilled and rotisseried meats, and pastas. The namesake wine is featured on the wine list.

Heidi Pies *1941 S. El Camino Real/20th Ave., (650) 574-0505. B,L,&D daily; $. Highchairs, boosters, child menu. No reservations.*

The selection of freshly-baked pies is replenished constantly from this old-fashioned coffee shop's own kitchen. Pie choices include fruit (raisin and gooseberry in addition to more common varieties), meringue (black bottom, banana), and specialty (German chocolate, pecan, cream cheese). The house specialty is hot apple pie—served plain, a la mode, with hot cinnamon sauce, with whipped cream, or with either Cheddar or American cheese. A vast selection of short-order items, including a hamburger and grilled cheese sandwich, comprise the rest of the menu. Weekdays between 2 and 4 p.m. coffee is only 55 cents when ordered with pie. Whole pies are available for take-out.

La Michoacana *251 S. B St., (650) 348-9610. L&D daily; $. Highchairs, boosters.*

This tiny Mexican restaurant provides comfortable seating in its 2-story dining area. Everything is made fresh and is of exceptional taste, quality, and value, and a la carte and combination plates allow a satisfying meal whatever the stage of hunger. A small selection of Salvadorian dishes includes pupusas—handmade corn tortillas stuffed with delicious cheese and flavorful seasoned pork. Horchata, Mexican hot chocolate, and wine margaritas are among the drink choices, and flan is the single dessert.

Mei's Restaurant *71 East 3rd Ave., (650) 347-2722, fax (650) 347-8988.*

For description, see King Yen on page 260. Both restaurants are under the same ownership, and the menu and decor are similar.

North Beach Pizza *240 E. 3rd Ave., (650) 344-5000.*

For description, see page 75.

The Pot Sticker *3708 S. El Camino Real/37th Ave., (650) 349-0149. L&D daily; $$. Highchairs, boosters. Reservations advised.*

The Chinese Mandarin-style cuisine served here is lightly spiced, has very little sauce, and is heavy on the vegetables. Interesting menu items include hot and sour soup, sizzling rice soup, Mongolian beef, princess chicken, and, of course, pot stickers. More exotic items made with beef tripe and beef tendon are also available.

T.G.I. Friday's *3101 S. El Camino Real/Hillsdale Blvd., (650) 570-4684. L&D daily, SunBr; $-$$. Highchairs, boosters, child menu. No reservations.*

This comfortable fern bar produces tasty drinks from a massive bar dominating its center, and its vast menu offers everything from a French dip sandwich to a hamburger to a chimichanga to blackened filet mignon. The children's menu—which doubles as a coloring book and offers kids everything they love most prepared the way they like (for instance: a grilled cheese sandwich made with American cheese on white bread)—just might qualify as the world's most extensive. Furthering its family-friendly rep, kids are given a helium balloon as a parting gift.

San Carlos

WHAT TO DO

Hiller Aviation Museum *601 Skyway Rd., just off Hwy. 101, (650) 654-0200; www.hiller.org. Daily 10-5. Adults $7, 65+ & 12-17 $5, 8-11 $2.*

Recently reopened in its new home at San Carlos Airport, this huge 53,000-square-foot museum is heaven for aviation buffs. Approximately 50 aircraft and 100 exhibits span the 128-year history of aviation. Many displays are interactive. Some show aircraft operations in motion, and some demonstrate robotic aircraft of the future. Visitors can also see vertical take-off and landing craft, hypersonic craft, and various wing configurations. A restoration workshop is viewed through giant windows, allowing a glimpse of the museum's latest acquisitions while they are being restored. Multi-media presentations and a library enhance the experience and educate about this area's powerful influence on aviation (for example, the first "aeroplane" with three-axis control flew in this very area in 1869—three decades before Kitty Hawk).

Redwood City

WHAT TO DO

Malibu Grand Prix/Malibu Castle *Grand Prix: 340 Blomquist St./Seaport Blvd., (650) 366-6442. Malibu Castle: 320 Blomquist St., (650) 367-1905. Both daily 11am-10pm; prices vary.*

Bring your dare-devils to the Grand Prix to race Indy-style cars in a safe, fun environment. One- and two-seat Virage cars can be driven by ages 18 and older with a valid driver's license (younger passengers are permitted in the two-seaters), and junior drivers measuring 4'8" or taller can drive scaled-down F-50s. The adjacent Castle rounds out the fun with three 18-hole miniature golf courses, a video-game arcade, go-karts, and batting cages.

WHERE TO STAY

Hotel Sofitel San Francisco Bay *223 Twin Dolphin Dr., 12 mi. from airport, (800) SOFITEL, (650) 598-9000, fax (650) 598-0459; www.hotelsofitelsfbay.com. 9 stories; 421 rooms; $-$$$+. Pool, hot tub, sauna, fitness center, parcourse. 2 restaurants.*

Taste France without leaving the Bay Area. This link in the sleek French hotel chain is situated near the bay among equally sleek hi-tech companies. French touches include the charming accents of many employees, bath mitts instead of wash cloths, and a complimentary freshly-baked baguette from the hotel's bakery to take home at check-out. Pampering includes Nina Ricci bathroom amenities and evening turndown with a fresh rose and chocolate.

Elegant **Le Baccarat** serves classic French cuisine in posh surroundings.

WHERE TO EAT

Pizza & Pipes *821 Winslow St./Broadway, (650) 365-6543. L&D daily; $. Highchairs. Reservations accepted.*

When the huge Wurlitzer theater pipe organ here is being played *(W-Sun 6:30-10.)*, all conversation is drowned out by lively renditions of songs such as "The Mickey Mouse Club Theme," "Chattanooga Choo Choo," and other all-time favorites. Kids love it. Some sing along, while others jump out of their seats to view through windows the movement of the pipes. This is definitely the place to go when children are cranky and ill-behaved. If they don't actually change their mood and have a good time, at least no one will hear them. Incidentally, the pizza is quite good.

Woodside

A LITTLE BACKGROUND

Though located just a few miles from bustling El Camino Real, Woodside feels very rural. It has been called the "horsiest community in the United States," and, indeed, it has more horses per capita than any other community in the county. Hitching posts found outside some of the town's restaurants seem to back up the claim, and on weekends horses and wagons are often found "parked" by them. With the recent heavy influx of people who have made their bundle in Silicon Valley, a millionaire here is now considered average—a member of the middle class. Fortunately the restaurant prices don't reflect this reality.

GETTING THERE

Located on Highway 84, approximately 5 miles west of Highway 101.

WHAT TO DO

Filoli Estate *86 Cañada Rd., (650) 364-8300; www.filoli.org. Guided tours Tu-Thur, by reservation; self-guided tours Tu-Sat 10-2; mid-Feb-Oct. Adults $10, 2-12 $1, under 2 free.*

Under the protection of the National Trust for Historic Preservation, this 654-acre country kingdom surrounds a 43-room Georgian Revival mansion. Built in 1917 by architect Willis Polk, its ballroom is gilded with 200 pounds of gold extracted from the original owner's Empire Mine in Grass Valley. (The mansion is the setting for the 1978 film *Heaven Can Wait* and was seen as the exterior of the Carrington home shown at the beginning of TV's *Dynasty*.) Tours of the 16 landscaped acres of mature formal gardens include such delights as two herbal gardens, a garden designed to resemble a stained-glass window in Chartres cathedral in France, and a practical cutting garden. For information on the many special events held here, call (650) 366-4640.

Menlo Park

A LITTLE BACKGROUND

Developed in the 1800s by two Irishmen, this peaceful, tree-filled suburb is centered around its historic train station—the oldest passenger station in the state. Leland Stanford and Mark Hopkins, both rail tycoons in their time, once boarded the train here for the ride into San Francisco. Today the station is a shelter for CalTrain passengers.

WHAT TO DO

Sunset Magazine Garden *Willow Rd./ Middlefield Rd., (650) 321-3600. M-F 9-4:30. Free.*

Visitors here are welcome to take a self-guided walking tour through the 7 acres of landscaped gardens surrounding an impressive 1.3-acre lawn.

WHERE TO STAY

Stanford Park Hotel *100 El Camino Real, (800) 368-2468, (650) 322-1234, fax (650) 322-0975; www.woodsidehotels.com. 4 stories; 162 rooms; $$$+. Children under 12 free. Some fireplaces. Pool, hot tub, sauna, fitness center. Evening snack; restaurant, room service.*

Located just north of town, this hotel offers spacious rooms furnished with custom-made English yew wood furniture. It was one of the first hotels in the U.S. to offer the innovative computer-operated "video on command" system.

WHERE TO EAT

Allied Arts Guild Restaurant *75 Arbor Rd., (650) 324-2588. L M-Sat at 12, 12:30, 1, & 1:15; afternoon dessert & beverage M-F 2-2:30; $. Highchairs, boosters. Reservations required. No cards.*

Originally a tearoom, this restaurant was opened by the Palo Alto auxiliary of Children's Hospital at Stanford in 1932. In those days guild members prepared food in their homes and transported it to the premises for serving. Now a modern kitchen lets volunteers prepare three-course luncheons that include a soup, hot entree with vegetable or salad, freshly-baked rolls, dessert, and choice of beverage. The menu is different each day, and all the recipes are for sale. In warm weather an attractive patio is opened for dining; request it when reserving. All profits and tips are used to help support Children's Hospital. Allow time to wander through the attractive Spanish Colonial-style estate, once part of the vast Rancho de las Pulgas, a Spanish land grant dating back to the late 1700s. Shops invite browsing, and the peaceful 3.5-acre gardens—designed after the Alhambra Gardens in Granada, Spain—invite a leisurely stroll.

Draeger's *101 University Dr., (650) 688-0688. Daily 7am-10pm.*

For description, see page 161.

Gaylord India Restaurant *1706 El Camino Real/Encinal, (650) 326-8761. L&D daily.*

For description, see page 38.

Late for the Train *150 Middlefield Rd./Willow Rd., (650) 321-6124. B&L M-F, Sat&SunBr, D daily; $$. Highchairs, boosters. Reservations advised.*

This formula-free restaurant has several different dining areas, including an outdoor patio that is particularly pleasant in warm weather, and an interesting collection of old-time sugar bowls and salt-and-pepper shakers decorates the tables. Meals are made to order with organic, additive-free ingredients whenever possible, and very little red meat is used. Brunch items include delicious eggs piperade (a two-egg omelette served with a fantastic scone and sides of both delicious fried potatoes and a mixture of lightly sautéed bell peppers, onions, and tomatoes), blintzes, whole grain pancakes, and an assortment of sandwiches, salads, and hot entrees. Lunch and dinner menus feature seafood, chicken, pasta, and vegetarian entrees.

Palo Alto

A LITTLE BACKGROUND

With wide tree-lined streets and impressive mansions on its outlying boulevards, Palo Alto historically has been home to upper-class residents, many of whom are affiliated with Stanford University. More recently it has become known for being a part of that nebulous area known as Silicon Valley. The University Avenue exit off Highway 101 leads under a canopy of magnolias, then oaks, then, upon entering the Stanford campus, palms.

VISITOR INFORMATION

Palo Alto Chamber of Commerce *325 Forest Ave., (650) 324-3121, fax (650) 324-1215.*

GETTING THERE

Located approximately 13 miles south of San Mateo, and 32 miles south of San Francisco.

WHAT TO DO

Birthplace of Silicon Valley *367 Addison Ave./Waverley St.*

The product and the company that launched the high tech industry were developed in this garage by William Hewlett and David Packard. A monument beside the driveway tells the story.

Elizabeth F. Gamble Garden Center *1431 Waverley St./Embarcadero Rd., (650) 329-1356, fax (650) 329-1688. House: M-F 9-noon. Free. Garden: Daily dawn to dusk. Free.*

Once the home of Elizabeth F. Gamble, heiress to the Procter & Gamble fortune, this Georgian Revival house features enormous pieces of beautiful redwood paneling unmarred by knots. Today both the house and the beautifully manicured classic Edwardian gardens are maintained by volunteers. Gardens include small "rooms" and an assortment of soothing fountains and scattered benches for quiet reflection.

Palo Alto Children's Theatre *1305 Middlefield Rd., (650) 329-2216. Adults $2, under 18 $1.*

The seasonal productions here are performed by child actors ages 8 through 18 and appeal especially to children. Past shows have included such favorites as *The Tales of Beatrix Potter* and *Charlotte's Web.* Summer performances are usually staged outside, and picnics are encouraged. Call for current schedule.

Palo Alto Duck Pond *At east end of Embarcadero Rd. Daily sunrise-sunset. Free.*

Located in a quiet, unpopulated area away from town, this is one of the Bay Area's best spots to feed ducks and birds. Usually it attracts a hefty number of hungry ducks and seagulls, sometimes even a few swans. In winter, plenty of unusual migrating birds are mixed in. A nearby small airport provides plane-watching fun.

Nearby, the **Lucy Evans Baylands Nature Interpretive Center** *((650) 329-2506. Call for hours. Free.)* has exhibits that orient visitors to the area. Workshops, films, and slide shows are scheduled regularly. During daylight hours, visitors can walk out over the 120-acre salt marsh on an 800-foot-long raised wooden walkway.

Naturalist-led walks are scheduled on weekends.

Palo Alto Junior Museum & Zoo *1451 Middlefield Rd./Embarcadero, (650) 329-2111. Tu-Sat 10-5, Sun 1-4. Free.*

Opened in 1934, this was the first children's museum on the West Coast. Exhibits are of the hands-on variety and especially fun for young children. Special programs and workshops are scheduled regularly. An outdoor mini-zoo houses local and exotic animals, including raccoons, ravens, and crows.

Stanford Shopping Center *On El Camino Real, just north of Stanford campus, (800) 772-9332, (650) 617-8585, fax (650) 617-8248; www.stanfordshop.com. M-F 10am-9pm, Sat 10-7, Sun 11-6.*

Beautifully designed, this is the only shopping center in the world owned by a university. In addition to being an environmentally conscious mall, with recycling receptacles throughout, it is a showcase for California artists. Look for David Gilhooley's "Merfrog Fountain," Larry Binkley's "Flying People," and John Pugh's 180-foot-long mural of an 18th-century Parisian street scene. Among the 150 fashionable stores are a branch of the Wine Country's **Oakville Grocery** (see page 372), filled with esoteric foods; a branch of Berkeley's **Andronico's** (see page 262); **Gleim Jewelers**, where the world's largest emerald is sometimes on display; the world's first **Victoria's Secret**, opened here in 1977; California's first **Bloomingdales; Cornelia Park**, an exceptional housewares store that is reminiscent of the Mad Hatter's tea party; and an unusual open-air **Polo/Ralph Lauren** shop. **The Health Library**, operated by Stanford University Hospital as a community service, provides an archive of medical information and helpful volunteer reference librarians. A variety of restaurants attract diners at all hours, including a branch of **Max's Opera Cafe** (see page 73) and a branch of **Piatti Ristorante** (see page 356).

The Stanford Theater *221 University Ave., (650) 324-3700. Adults $6, 65+ $4, under 18 $3.*

This 1,175-seat movie palace has been meticulously restored to its 1925-era grandeur by former classics professor David Packard, Jr., son of the computer tycoon. Plush red mohair seats, elaborate ceiling paintings, and magnificent tile work in the lobby help take audiences back in time as they view pre-1950 Hollywood films. Some movies play here that can be seen nowhere else. Retrospectives are scheduled regularly, and silent films are often accompanied by an organist on the theater's Wurlitzer. Proceeds from the box office are used for film restoration and preservation.

Stanford University Campus *Entrance at El Camino Real/University Ave., (650) 723-2560; www.stanford.edu. Facilities sometimes closed during academic breaks; call to confirm.*

Founded by Leland Stanford in 1885 on what had been his family's horse farm, California's premier private university is dedicated to the memory of Stanford's son, who died of typhoid fever at the age of 15. It is fittingly nicknamed "The Farm" and is home to 13 Nobel Prize winners. The **Quadrangle**, which is the oldest part of the campus, features buildings of Mission-style architecture. Hour-long **campus tours** *((650) 723-2560. Daily at 11 & 3:15. Free.)* leave from the Visitor Information Booth at Memorial Auditorium. Tours of the 2-mile-long **linear accelerator** are available by appointment *((650) 926-2204. Free.)*. East of the Quad, **Hoover Tower** *((650) 723-2053. Daily 10-4:30. Adults $2, 65+ & under 13 $1.)*, Stanford's shorter version of the University of California's campanile, stands 285 feet tall—affording a panoramic view of the area from its observation platform, reached by an elevator. At the tower's base, a museum that is part of the **Hoover Institution on War, Revolution, and Peace** honors Stanford graduate and former president Herbert Hoover. Nearby, the **Thomas Welton Art Gallery** is home to revolving exhibitions of international and regional artists' works.

Built in 1892, the neoclassical **Iris & B. Gerald Cantor Center for Visual Arts** *(Museum Way/Lomita Dr., (650) 723-4177; www.stanford.edu/dept/ccva. W-Sun 11-5, Thur to 8; docent tours W at 12:15 & Sat at 2, family tour 2nd Sat at 3. Free.)* is the oldest museum west of the Mississippi and the first building constructed of structurally reinforced concrete.

Having suffered severe damage in the 1989 earthquake, it has been attractively repaired and is once again showing its eclectic collection of extraordinary jades, Asian and Egyptian treasures, Stanford family memorabilia, and California Native American exhibits (a noteworthy object in this latter collection is a canoe carved by Yurok Indians from a single redwood log). Its also displays the gold spike that marked the meeting of the two sections of the Transcontinental Railroad in 1869, and is home to an adjacent 1-acre **Rodin Sculpture Garden** *((650) 723-3469. Daily dawn-dusk; tours Sat at 11 & Sun at 3.)* holding 20 bronzes, including "The Gates of Hell." Together the museum and garden hold the world's second-largest collection of Rodin sculpture (the largest Rodin is in Paris).

The Winter Lodge *3009 Middlefield Rd./Oregon Expressway, (650) 493-4566, fax (650) 493-3294; www.winterlodge.com. Daily 3-5, call for other session times; Oct-Apr only. Admission $5, under 4 $2, skate rental $2.*

An *outdoor* ice skating rink in Palo Alto? Well, it's *not* on a frozen lake. Indeed, it's located in a nicely manicured residential section of town. But it *is* removed from traffic and surrounded by tall eucalyptus trees, and it's the *only* outdoor rink west of the Sierra. Designed for families and children, the rink measures about two-thirds the size of an average indoor rink, making it too small for competitive skating.

WHERE TO STAY

Crowne Plaza Cabana Palo Alto *4290 El Camino Real/San Antonio Rd., 4 mi. from downtown, (800) 2-CROWNE, (650) 857-0787, fax (650) 496-1939. 8 stories; 194 rooms; $$. Children under 18 free. Heated pool, hot tub, fitness center. Restaurant, room service. Pets welcome.*

This attractively renovated hotel has a curving entry hugged by 16 of its original Italian cypress trees planted in 1962. Once owned by Doris Day (and still reflecting that fact today with its pet-friendly policy) and co-owned by Jay J. Sarno (who designed and built Caesar's Palace in Las Vegas), it was popular with Rat Pack members Sammy Davis, Jr. and Frank Sinatra. It made another big splash in 1965 when the Beatles took over the eighth floor during a concert tour (a suite on that floor now honors them). All guest rooms have refrigerators with complimentary cold drinks, and complimentary car service is available within a 5-mile radius.

Mediterranean-inspired cuisine is served in **4290 Bistro & Bar**, which also offers heavenly outdoor seating during nice weather.

Garden Court Hotel *520 Cowper St./University Ave., (800) 824-9028, (650) 322-9000, fax (650) 324-3609; www.gardencourt.com. 4 stories; 62 rooms; $$$+. Children under 12 free. All VCRs; some wood-burning fireplaces. Fitness center. Restaurant, room service.*

Located just off the main street, this attractive hotel offers posh comfort. A central courtyard with fountains and flowers conveys a far-away-from-it-all feeling. Staff strives to give personal service and claims never to forget a name. The tastefully appointed guest rooms have private terraces and four-poster beds with European-style down bedding. Amenities include terry cloth robes, complimentary video tapes, shoeshine, nightly turndown, and local shuttle service.

On the ground floor directly beneath the hotel, **Il Fornaio Restaurant** *((650) 853-3888. Reservations advised.)* serves up rustic pizzas in an elegant interior space as well as out on a sunny, peaceful courtyard.

Hidden Villa Hostel *26870 Moody Rd., Los Altos Hills, (650) 949-8648, fax (650) 948-4159. 35 beds; some private rooms. Closed June-Aug.*

Located on a 1,600-acre ranch in the foothills east of town, this facility was built in 1937 as the first hostel on the Pacific Coast. Guests sleep in rustic cabins. The property includes a working farm, organic garden, and land preserve. See also page 417.

Sheraton Palo Alto *625 El Camino Real/University Ave., (800) 874-3516, (650) 328-2800, fax (650) 327-7362. 4 stories; 343 rooms; $$$-$$$+. Children under 18 free. Some kitchens. Heated pool, fitness center. Restaurant, room service. Pets welcome.*

Centrally located and offering the amenities typical of the chain, this comfortable lodging has an attractively landscaped garden area with a large koi pond.

WHERE TO EAT

Andale Mexican Restaurant *209 University Ave., (650) 323-2939. L&D daily; $.*

Surprisingly delicious regional Mexican items inlude fresh fish tacos, vegetarian flautas stuffed with mashed potatoes, and seasonal fresh-fruit drinks. Items are prepared to order, using fresh ingredients and no lard, and meats are continuously sizzling on the open grills. Many interesting vegetarian choices are also available. On weekends from 11 to 2, special Mexican brunch items join the menu. In good weather, choice seating is provided on a sidewalk-side patio, and sometimes live music provides free entertainment from a public square across the street. Costs are kept low by placing orders at a back counter.

Blue Chalk Cafe *630 Ramona St., (650) 326-1020, fax (650) 326-1022. L M-F, D M-Sat; $-$$. Highchairs, boosters. Reservations accepted.*

Operating within a historical building dating from 1927, this busy spot features an inviting open-air front patio and an interior equipped with pool tables. The kitchen dishes up delicious down-home Southern cuisine. Appetizers include roasted Blue Lake green beans, catfish chips, and hoppin' john (black eyed peas). Dinner is a choice of salads—a blackened chicken Caesar, a warm spinach with smoked chicken—and hefty dinner plates—house-smoked pork chops, old-fashioned meatloaf, barbecued short ribs. Don't miss a side of roasted garlic mashed potatoes or housemade buttermilk biscuits. If interested, servers can provide a complete description of the original Southern folk art and photography decorating the premises.

Buca di Beppo *643 Emerson St., (650) 329-0665.*

For description, see page 59.

Chef Chu's *1067 N. San Antonio Rd./El Camino Real, Los Altos, (650) 948-2696. L&D daily; $$. Highchairs, boosters, booths. Reservations advised.*

Chef Chu watches closely over his large kitchen staff and sees to it that excellence prevails in this well-appointed restaurant. Impressive dishes include crisp fried won tons, tasty Szechwan beef, and a magnificent, sesame oil-fragrant hot and sour soup. Mu shu pork is served with unusual square pancakes for wrapping, and the beautifully presented lemon chicken consists of deep-fried whole chicken breasts, each glazed with lemon sauce and topped with a thin slice of lemon and a bright red maraschino cherry. Should there be a wait for seating, a large window in the reception area provides views of the busy kitchen.

Draeger's *342 First St., (650) 948-4425.*

For description, see page 161.

Good Earth Restaurant *185 University Ave./Emerson St., (650) 321-9449. B,L,&D daily; $-$$. Highchairs, boosters, booths, child menu. No reservations.*

An impressive selection of tasty and nutritious dishes is on the menu in this comfortable spot. Breakfast items include hot cakes with molasses-honey syrup and a variety of muffins. Omelettes, served with ten-grain toast, are available all day. Salads, creative sandwiches (including a popular and delicious cashew-chicken), several veggie burgers and pizzas, and an assortment of hot entrees and pastas flesh out the menu along with enticingly named fruit shakes and smoothies made with non-fat yogurt and high protein powder.

Gordon Biersch Brewing Company *640 Emerson St., (650) 323-7723.*

For description, see page 178.

MacArthur Park *27 University Ave./near El Camino Real, (650) 321-9990. L M-F, D daily, SunBr; $$-$$$. Reservations advised. Free valet parking.*

Situated just off the beaten path, this popular restaurant operates within a designated Historical Landmark. Designed for the U.S. War Department in 1918 by Julia Morgan, the architect of Hearst Castle, the building is now divided into several dining areas, including two indoor balconies and a grand barn-like room on the main floor. The kitchen is celebrated for its dry-aged steaks, California game, and baby back ribs cooked in an oak wood smoker. Dessert selections are presented on a menu decorated with a mouth-watering color reproduction of Wayne Thiebaud's "Two Meringues."

Ming's *1700 Embarcadero Rd., (800) 355-6001, (650) 856-7700, fax (650) 855-9479; www.mings.com. L&D daily; $-$$. Highchairs, boosters, booths, child menu. Reservations advised.*

Located just off Highway 101, this sedate restaurant has existed in Palo Alto since the 1950s, when it opened on El Camino Real. Ming's beef—a somewhat sweet dish prepared with tender wok-charred beef, and a generic item on many Chinese menus—was this restaurant's invention, as was its delicately flavored chicken salad. Made with shredded, deep-fried chicken, the salad is labor-intensive to make and in such heavy demand that one chef is employed to prepare just that. Every morning another chef prepares fresh dim sum delicacies—among them steamed shark's fin dumplings, delicious fresh shrimp items, and an electric-bright mango pudding in strawberry sauce—that are available from 11 a.m. to 5 p.m. Other noteworthy dishes include dramatic drunken prawns flambé and steamed fresh garlic lobster. A full vegetarian menu is also available.

Peninsula Fountain and Grille *566 Emerson St./Hamilton Ave., (650) 323-3131. B,L,&D daily; $. Highchairs, boosters, booths. No reservations.*

Opened by the Peninsula Dairy in 1923 and featuring red leatherette booths and an authentic soda fountain, this popular spot is known for serving tasty simple food—oatmeal and buttermilk pancakes in the morning, a variety of sandwiches and hamburgers at lunch, and chicken pot pies and pork chops at dinner—at reasonable prices. Fountain items are made with ice cream from the nearby Peninsula Creamery and include their famous hand-blended milk shakes. Other favorites include sour cherry pie, housemade soups, and cherry coke.

Scott's Seafood Grill & Bar *2300 E. Bayshore Rd./Embarcadero, (650) 856-1046.*

For description, see page 289.

Spago Palo Alto *265 Lytton Ave./Ramona, (650) 321-4466. L&D daily; $$$. Reservations advised.*

Operating within a lovely Mission-style stucco building, this is a branch of the famous Los Angeles restaurant owned by celebrity chef Wolfgang Puck. The art-filled main dining room has a view of the wood-burning oven, and an outdoor courtyard features dining under a huge oak tree. In addition to the celebrated pizzas, the menu offers items such as succulent tamarind-glazed rack of lamb, Chinese-style roast duck, and truffled lobster-potato salad.

Straits Cafe *3295 El Camino Real/Lambert, (650) 494-7168. L&D M-Sat.*

For description, see page 80.

World Wrapps *201 University, (650) 327-9777, fax (650) 327-8679.*

For description, see page 82.

Zao *261 University Ave., (650) 328-1988.*

For description, see page 82.

Mountain View

WHAT TO DO

NASA/Ames Research Center *Moffett Field, off Hwy 101, (650) 604-5000, tour reservations (650) 604-6497; www.arc.nasa.gov. Tours: M-F, usually at 9:30 & 1:30; reservations required; children must be 9 or older. Visitor Center: M-F 8-4:30. Free.*

Research in aeronautics and space technology is conducted at this 430-acre facility. Tours last 90 minutes and are given by reservation only. Each tour is a little different and might include a visit to the world's largest wind tunnel, to a flight-simulation facility, or to a huge hangar to see research aircraft (these immense hangars were built in the 1930s to hold dirigibles). Be prepared to walk approximately 2 miles. The Visitor Center is open for drop-ins, and a gift shop sells unusual science-related items. An open house extravaganza is held approximately every two years, usually in September.

Santa Clara

GETTING THERE

Located off San Tomas Expressway (G4), 2 miles west of Highway 101.

VISITOR INFORMATION

Santa Clara Chamber of Commerce & Convention-Visitors Bureau *1850 Warburton Ave., (800) 272-6822, (408) 244-9660; www.santaclara.org.*

WHAT TO DO

Intel Museum *2200 Mission College Blvd., (408) 765-0503; www.intel.com/go/museum. M-F 9-6. Free.*

Located in the main lobby of the Robert Noyce Building at Intel Corporation's headquarters (Intel is the world's largest semiconductor company and the inventor of the Pentium processor), this technology museum teaches how computer chips are made and how they are used in everyday life. Visitors can learn the differences between various types of chips, how they are constructed, and trace their history. Hands-on educational exhibits appealing to both children and adults change regularly, and a live video feed from the company's chip-fabrication facility can be viewed. The Intelligent Home exhibit demonstrates how computers can enhance a home.

Mission Santa Clara de Asis *500 El Camino Real, (408) 554-4023, fax (408) 554-4373; www.scu.edu. Daily sunrise-sunset. Free.*

The original Santa Clara mission, founded in 1777 by Father Thomas de la Pena, was built on a site beside the Guadalupe River. It was destroyed by fire. Rebuilt in 1928, this replica of the eighth mission in the chain of California missions is on the picturesque grounds of Santa Clara University—California's first institution of higher learning and the state's first coeducational Catholic university. Now a State Historical Landmark, it holds some interesting relics, including three bells that were a gift from the king of Spain, and original artwork by professional artist Agustin Davila, who painted the original mission's interior, is exhibited throughout. Extensive lush gardens showcase thousands of roses—several of which are classified as antique varieties—and a wide variety of trees and plants, some of which are among the oldest cultivated plants in California: flourishing olive trees planted by Franciscan friars in 1822, a giant 123-year-old Jacaranda tree, and the oldest grapevine in Northern California. Full bloom occurs April through May.

Paramount's Great America *On Great America Parkway, off Hwys. 101 & 237, (408) 988-1776; www.pgathrills.com. Call for schedule. Closed Nov-Feb. Age 7-59 $39.99, 60+ $29.99, 3-6 or under 48" tall $19.99; parking $6.*

There's no question about it. The thrill rides at Northern California's most elaborate theme park are spectacular, and the roller coasters are great shocking fun: The Vortex is the West's first stand-up roller coaster; the Demon features two 360-degree loops and a double helix; and the Grizzly is a classic wooden coaster based on the extinct Coney Island Wildcat. The circa 1976 double-decker Carousel Columbia is the world's tallest, and

the Drop Zone Stunt Tower free-fall ride is Santa Clara's tallest structure. The new Kidzville has colorful rides and attractions especially for children 12 and under, and eight live shows round out the fun.

WHERE TO STAY

Biltmore Hotel & Suites *2151 Laurelwood Rd., (800) 255-9925, (408) 988-8411, fax (408) 986-9807, www.hotelbiltmore.com. 372 rooms. Lap pool, hot tub, fitness center. 2 restaurants.*

Offering style and elegance, this hotel is situated 3 miles from San Jose International Airport and 5 miles from downtown San Jose. A courtesy shuttle operates within a 5-mile radius.

Embassy Suites Hotel *2885 Lakeside Dr., (800) EMBASSY, (408) 496-6400, fax (408) 492-9121; www.embassy-suites.com/es.santa-clara. 10 stories; 257 rooms; $$$+. Children under 18 free. Indoor heated pool, hot tub, sauna, fitness center. Evening cocktails, full breakfast.*

All guests get a spacious two-room suite consisting of one bedroom plus a separate living room with sofabed. Each suite is equipped with two TVs and a mini-kitchen with coffeemaker. A complimentary cooked-to-order breakfast is served in the **Valley Plaza Cafe**, and complimentary cocktails are served at an evening reception. The hotel is just minutes from Paramount's Great America theme park and offers packages including admission tickets.

Madison Street Inn *1390 Madison St., (800)-491-5541, (408) 249-5541, fax (408) 249-6676. 6 rooms. Some shared baths. Pool, hot tub. Evening snack; full breakfast.*

Located just 10 minutes from the San Jose Airport and 15 minutes from downtown, this comfy B&B is surrounded by 1/3 acre of landscaped gardens. Breakfast includes fresh fruit juice, muffins, and eggs Benedict, and homemade chocolate chip cookies and sherry are provided each evening.

WHERE TO EAT

Crocodile Cafe *2855 Stevens Creek Blvd., in Valley Fair mall, (408) 260-1100. L&D daily. Highchairs, boosters, child menu.*

The menu offers a variety of salads, sandwiches, pizzas, calzones, and pastas, plus oakwood-grilled meats, and the kids' coloring menu has all their favorites.

Pizza & Pipes *3581 Homestead Rd./Lawrence Expressway, (408) 248-5680, fax (408) 248-5389. L&D daily.*

For description, see page 162. Unfortunately, this location has no Wurlitzer organ.

World Wrapps *3125 Mission College Blvd., (408) 486-9727, fax (408) 486-9774.*

For description, see page 82.

San Jose

A LITTLE BACKGROUND

Currently touting itself as the "capital of Silicon Valley" (a title that seems valid considering that 24 of the area's largest computer companies have headquarters or divisions here), San Jose—the country's eleventh-largest city and California's third-largest and oldest, having been founded as a Spanish pueblo in 1777 (it also was the state capital from 1849 to 1851)—receives relatively little attention for its attractions. But that seems to be changing as the city concentrates on revitalizing its downtown area. Now, visitors to the city center can enjoy its many cultural offerings as well as its reliably mild climate.

VISITOR INFORMATION

San Jose Convention & Visitors Bureau *333 W. San Carlos St. #1000, (800) SAN-JOSE, (408) 295-9600, fax (408) 295-3937; www.sanjose.org.*

GETTING THERE

Located approximately 50 miles south of San Francisco.

WHAT TO DO

Alum Rock Park *End of Alum Rock Ave. (east of Hwy. 101), (408) 27-PARKS. Daily 8-dusk. Free; parking $4 on weekends, daily in summer.*

Located in the foothills of the Diablo Range northeast of town, this 730-acre park,

California's first, is maintained by the city for hiking, horseback riding, bicycling, and picnicking. In some spots, mineral water bubbles up from sulphur spings—a reminder of the park's past as a nationally known health spa in the early 1900s. Facilities include picnic tables, barbecue pits, and a children's playground. The privately-operated **Youth Science Institute** *((408) 258-4322; www.ysi-ca.org. Tu-F noon-4:30; in summer, Tu-Sun. Adults 50¢, kids 25¢.)* displays live birds of prey, including hawks and owls, as well as other native animals and a large taxidermy collection. Hands-on activities are available especially for children.

Cathedral Basilica of St. Joseph *80 S. Market St., (408) 283-8100; www.stjosephcathedral.org. M-F 9-5. Free.*

Designed by architect Bryan J. Clinch and constructed in 1877, when it was known as St. Joseph Cathedral, this is one of downtown San Jose's most architecturally stunning buildings. It replaced the Pueblo de San Jose's first small adobe church built in 1803. Renovated in 1990 to the tune of $17 million, the cathedral features some extraordinary stained glass and murals as well as a completely restored multi-domed edifice. The choir loft holds a circa 1886 mechanical Odell organ that is one of only four in the entire U.S. and the only one in its original condition on the West Coast.

Children's Discovery Museum of San Jose *180 Woz Way, (408) 298-5437, fax (408) 298-6826; www.cdm.org. Tu-Sat 10-5, Sun 12-5; also M in July & Aug. Adults $6, 55+ $5, 2-18 $4. Parking $2-$4.*

Children ages 3 through 13, for whom this museum was designed, are sure to be entertained. Located in Guadalupe River Park, this striking lavender-colored building housing the largest children's museum in the West was designed by Mexico City architect Ricardo Legorreta. Fortunately he included plenty of places for adults to sit and watch while their kids have a great time doing everything from making a tortilla from scratch, to blowing gigantic bubbles, to climbing on a full-size fire engine. A snack bar serves inexpensive things that kids like to eat: hot dogs, hamburgers, peanut butter & jelly sandwiches. Steve Wozniak, of Apple Computer fame, sponsored the Jesse's Clubhouse exhibit named in honor of his son. Guess who the street the museum is located on, Woz Way, is named for?

Emma Prusch Farm and Park *647 S. King Rd., at Hwys. 680 & 280, (408) 926-5555, fax (408) 277-3820. Daily 8:30-6, during Daylight Savings Time to 8:30. Free.*

One of the things discovered when visiting this old-fashioned farm is that not all apples are computers. Deeded to the city of San Jose in 1962, this 47-acre dairy farm, surrounded now by the city, presents the opportunity to step back in time to San Jose's rural past. The restored original 19th-century white farmhouse is now the information center. The barn, which is the city's largest and the third largest in California, is home to an assortment of domesticated farm animals that includes cows, sheep, and pigs—all thriving in spite of their closeness to the freeway. Don't miss the fruit orchard where over 100 kinds of rare fruits grow, among them limequat, pawpaw, gumi, and sapote as well as exotic varieties of cherries, guavas, persimmons, grapefruit and other citruses, and—apples.

The Gaslighter Theater *400 E. Campbell Ave., Campbell, (408) 866-1408, fax (408) 866-4162; www.gaslighter.com. F & Sat at 8. Adults $15, 60+ $13, under 12 $12.*

A staff member says that this cozy theater is located "in lovely downtown Campbell—Santa Clara County's fastest-growing ghost town." And, indeed, at night this seems to be the only show in town. After being greeted in the street and at the door by the exuberant cast, the whole family has fun inside hissing the villain and cheering the hero—while munching on, and throwing, complimentary popcorn. The two-part shows are not at all subtle, making them great for school-age children. Shows include both a melodrama (such as *Ignorance Isn't Bliss* or *No Mother to Guide Her*) and a vaudeville performance featuring dancing, singing, and comedy.

Japantown *Between N. Fifth & Jackson sts., (408) 298-4303. Free.*

Dating back to the late 1800s, when bachelors from Japan migrated to the area, this historic neighborhood today features modern streets lined with cherry trees that bloom spectacularly in the spring. Historical sites of particular interest include the Buddhist Church Betsuin dating from 1937, the Wesley United Methodist Church built in 1941, and the circa 1910 Issei Memorial Building, now housing the **Japanese-American Historical Museum** and its photographic exhibits of Japanese-Americans who migrated to the Santa Clara Valley in 1890. Shops and galleries abound, as do Japanese restaurants, and on Sunday mornings a bustling **Farmers' Market** unfolds. Annual festivals celebrating the changing seasons include **Nikkei Matsuri** in May, the **Obon Festival** in July, and the **Aki Matsuri** in September. Japantown is just south of downtown and can be reached via the Light Rail line.

Kelley Park. *Parking $3.*

• **Happy Hollow Park and Zoo** *1300 Senter Rd./Keyes Rd., (408) 295-8383, fax (408) 277-4470. Daily 10-5. Admission $4.50, 65+ $4, under 2 free; rental strollers $1.50.*

Children through age 10 love this mini-amusement park—the only combination park and zoo in the U.S. Spacious and shady, it offers a satisfying combination of kiddie rides and over 150 zoo animals, including a family of endangered golden-eyed black-and-white ruffed lemurs. The zoo also has a small seal pool, a bird enclosure, and a petting area, where for small change children can hand-feed animals. Five rides, daily puppet shows, and use of a concrete maze and playground equipment are included with admission. Picnic tables are also available. Note that mothers get in free here on Mother's Day, and fathers on Father's Day.

• **Kelley Park Express Train** *Irregular schedule. Round-trip $1.50.*

Boarded just outside the zoo, this miniature choo-choo train makes stops at the following two park sites.

• **Japanese Friendship Garden** *(408) 277-4192. Daily 10-dusk. Free.*

Patterned after the Korakuen Garden in San Jose's sister city of Okayama, this 6 1/2-acre garden includes four heart-shaped ponds populated with rare koi. Walk on the Moon Bridge for good luck; cross the Zigzag Bridge to get rid of evil spirits.

• **San Jose Historical Museum** *1600 Senter Rd., (408) 287-2290. M-F 10-4:30, Sat & Sun 12-4:30. Adults $4, 65+ $3, 6-17 $2.*

This ever-growing 25-acre complex incorporates many turn-of-the-century San Jose buildings along with structures from other periods, including a Chinese temple from the mid-1800s and a gas station from the 1920s. In all, over 28 relocated or replicated historic homes and business buildings highlight the culture and history of San Jose and the Santa Clara Valley. Begin a visit at the Pacific Hotel, where docent-led tours commence; a self-guided tour brochure is also available. Stop for refreshments in **O'Brien's Ice Cream and Candy Store**—the first place west of Detroit to serve ice cream and sodas.

Lick Observatory *On Mount Hamilton Rd., 23 mi. east of downtown, (831) 274-5061; www.ucolick.org. M-F 12:30-5, Sat & Sun 10-5. Tours on half-hour, M-F 1-4:30, Sat & Sun 10:30-4:30; open some evenings in summer. Free.*

Situated at the top of 4,372-foot-high Mount Hamilton, far from city lights, this observatory, built in 1887 and now a division of U. C. Santa Cruz, is reached via the original carriage trail—a laborious 19-mile drive up a narrow, winding two-lane road with no less than 347 curves. But its view overlooking San Jose and the Santa Clara Valley makes the struggle worthwhile. Guided tours include seeing, but not looking through, the world's second-largest refractor telescope (it measures 120 inches), which has been in use for more than a century. Visitors get to look through a smaller 36-inch refractor scope, which has been here from the beginning and was the largest in the world when the observatory was built. Allow 90 minutes to reach the observatory and 2 hours to tour it. Note that no food or gas is available in the area.

Municipal Rose Garden *On Naglee Ave./Dana Ave., (408) 27-PARKS; wwwsjparks.com. Daily 8am-sunset. Free.*

Located west of downtown, 2 blocks from the Egyptian Museum, this 5 1/2-acre garden, formerly a prune orchard, dates from 1931. It boasts 3,500 rose bushes representing 189 varieties of heritage, modern, and miniature roses. Hybrid-teas comprise 75 percent of the collection. The garden is centered around a two-tiered fountain and surrounded by green lawns and tree-shaded picnic tables. Other features include a reflection pool, a sun dial, concrete benches, and a natural grass stage surrounded by redwood trees. The roses are at their showy peak in May and June but continue blooming through October.

Overfelt Gardens *2145 McKee Rd./Educational Park Dr. (between Hwys. 680 & 101), (408) 251-3323, fax (408) 251-2865. Daily 10-dusk. Free.*

Featuring expansive lawns and a sometimes gurgling stream, this peaceful 33-acre park is filled with native and exotic plants. Special features include a paved arboreal trail that meanders through the entire park, a California native plant and wildlife area, several natural wildlife sanctuaries, a fragrance garden, and three small percolation ponds that hold water for the Santa Clara Valley's water table. A 5-acre Chinese Cultural Garden is decorated with impressive statuary, including a 30-foot bronze-and-marble statue of the ancient Chinese philosopher Confucius overlooking a reflecting pond. Don't miss the ornamental Friendship Gate at the main entrance or the 15-ton piece of black marble mined in the Republic of China and presented to San Jose from Tainan City, her sister city in China.

Peralta Adobe & Fallon House Historic Site *San Pedro St./W. St. John St., (408) 993-8182; www.serve.com/sjhistory. Tours Tu-Sun 12-3:30. Adults $6, seniors $5, children $3.*

Situated in a small downtown park, both of these historic houses, surrounded now by modern high rises, offer a look into the daily life of two prominent early San Jose families. Built in 1797, the Peralta Adobe is San Jose's oldest structure remaining from when the city was El Pueblo de San Jose de Guadalupe and is a legacy to the city's Spanish influence. Named after Luis Peralta, who occupied the adobe from 1807 to 1851 and was one of the state's first millionaires, it has two rooms outfitted in period style—a bedroom furnished in 1777 style and a living room furnished to reflect the 1830s—plus an outside working horno oven. Across the street, the lavish Victorian Fallon House mansion dates from 1855. It was built by an early mayor and has 15 furnished rooms decorated in the style of the 1860s.

Raging Waters *2333 S. White Rd. (Capitol Expressway/Tully Rd.), (408) 238-9900, fax (408) 270-2022; www.rwsplash.com. Daily 10-6, June-Aug. Closed Sept-May. Admission $18.95, under 43" $14.95, after 3pm $12.95, 60+ $9.95. Parking $3.*

Located in Lake Cunningham Regional Park, this water-oriented amusement park is the Bay Area's largest and claims to have the fastest waterslides this side of the Rockies. Sliders can reach speeds up to 25 miles per hour and can be dropped 6 stories into a catchpool below. An inner tube ride, a sled ride, a rope swing, and myriad other water activities round out the fun. Importantly, an army of 40 lifeguards watch over frolickers, and facilities include free changing rooms and showers plus inexpensive lockers. Where else can a family find such good clean fun? Note that foods and beverages may not be brought into the park. Food service is available, and a public picnic area is provided just outside the main gate.

Rosicrucian Egyptian Museum *1342 Naglee Ave., (408) 947-3636, fax (408) 947-3638; www.rosicrucian.org. Daily 10-5. Adults $7, 65+ $5, 6-15 $3.50. Strollers not permitted.*

This museum houses the largest exhibit of Egyptian, Babylonian, and Assyrian artifacts in the western U.S. Highlights of the collection include mummies, fine jewelry, and a full-size reproduction of a 4,000-year-old rock tomb—the only such tomb in the United States. Among the six human mummies is one that has a 9-inch metal pin in his knee—an exciting discovery documenting the first known attempt at knee surgery. Also in the collection are the mummies of several cats, some fish, a baboon,

and the head of an ox. The surrounding 7.5-acre park is stunningly adorned with exotic trees and flowers and unusual Egyptian statuary. Picnicking is permitted. The **Rosicrucian Planetarium** located adjacent is closed indefinitely for repairs.

San Jose Flea Market *1590 Berryessa Rd. (between Hwys. 680 & 101), (408) 453-1110, fax (408) 437-9011; www.sjfm.com. W-Sun dawn-dusk. Free. Parking $1-$5.*

Said to be the largest in the world, bigger even than the famous Paris market that started the whole thing, this outdoor flea market was the first in the U.S. It features over 2,700 vendors spread out over 120 acres. Most everything can be found here, and at bargain prices. In addition, there are more than 35 restaurants and snack stands, and a 1/4-mile-long section that is California's largest outdoor produce market. A variety of free entertainment is provided, and for a fee kids can play skee-ball and ride on a pony, a merry-go-round, and go-carts. Thursdays and Fridays are least crowded; weekends and Wednesdays are usually quite busy.

San Jose Museum of Art *110 S. Market St./San Fernando St., (408) 294-2787, fax (408) 294-2977; www.sjmusart.org. Tu-Sun 10-5, Thur to 8. Adults $7, 62+ & 6-17 $4; free 1st Thur of month. Strollers avail. for loan.*

Holding a collection of primarily contemporary American art, this unusual part-1892 Romanesque sandstone/part-1991 stark modern building is said to serve as a metaphor for contemporary art's ties to tradition.

The Tech Museum of Innovation *201 S. Market St., (408) 294-TECH, fax (408) 279-7167; www.thetech.org. Tu-Sun 10-5, 3rd Thur to 8. Adults $8, 65+ & 3-12 $6.*

Originally called "The Garage," in whimsical reference to the garages in which many Silicon Valley inventions had their humble beginnings (the most famous being the personal computer developed by Steve Jobs and

Stephen Wozniak in their garage), the nickname was dropped in favor of something more befitting the major science and technology museum it has become. Focusing on current projects at local technology companies, museum exhibits allow visitors to see how silicon chips are produced, to design a bike, and to meet Vanna the spelling robot. Guided tours of each individual exhibit gallery are scheduled, and volunteers are on hand to answer questions. Operating within the museum but with a separate admission fee (a combination ticket is available, and advance tickets are advised), the **IMAX Dome Theater** is a must-see. Audiences are almost completely surrounded by a film projected onto an 82-foot-diameter screen—the only one in Northern California. When leaving this electric mango-and-purple-colored building, don't miss the whimsical, mesmerizing autokinetic sculpture by George Rhoads located just outside the exit.

Winchester Mystery House *525 S. Winchester Blvd., (408) 247-2101, fax (408) 247-2090; www.winchestermysteryhouse.com. Tours Sun-Thur 9-5, Fri & Sat 9-7. Adults $13.95, 65+ $10.95, 6-12 $7.95. Strollers not permitted.*

The story goes that Sarah Winchester, heir to the $20 million Winchester rifle fortune, believed that to make amends for a past wrongdoing she had to build additions to her circa 1884 Victorian mansion continuously, 24 hours a day. Her eccentric ideas resulted in some unusual features: asymmetrical rooms, narrow passageways, zigzag stairwells, and doors opening into empty shafts. The tour of this city landmark takes in 110 of the 160 rooms, climbs more than 200 steps, and covers almost a mile. The **Winchester Historical Firearms Museum**, which holds one of the largest collections of Winchester rifles on the West Coast, provides an interesting way to pass time while waiting for the tour to begin. Food service and picnic tables are available. A self-guided tour of 6 acres of Victorian gardens, sprinkled liberally with fountains and statues, is included with admission. Spooky flashlight **Halloween Tours** are scheduled annually in October.

Wineries.

• **J. Lohr Winery** *1000 Lenzen Ave., (408) 288-5057, fax (408) 993-2276; www.jlohr.com. Tasting 10-5 daily; tours Sat & Sun at 11 & 2.*

Operating on the site of a former beer brewery, this premium winery is tucked into a residential part of the city near Highway 880. All wine is made on the premises, but the grapes are grown on Lohr-owned vineyards scattered from Paso Robles to St. Helena.

• **Mirassou Winery** *3000 Aborn Rd. (E. Capitol Expressway exit off Hwy. 101), (408) 274-4000, fax (408) 270-5881; website: www.mirassou.com. Tasting M-Sat 12-5, Sun 12-4; tours M-Sat at 1 & 3, Sun at 2.*

This area's Wine Country can be sampled by taking a freeway ride into the suburbs, where rows of grapevines announce this winery's entrance. At this location since 1937, it is now operated by the fifth generation of the same family, making Mirassou the country's oldest wine-making family. It all began when Pierre Pellier arrived in the fertile Santa Clara Valley in 1854 and planted the varietal cuttings he had carried with him from France. Today his descendents continue the tradition of fine winemaking that he began. Special events are scheduled regularly and include cooking classes as well as Sunday brunches and sunset dinners featuring refined, elegant menus.

• **Ridge Vineyards** *17100 Monte Bello Rd., Cupertino, (408) 867-3233, fax (408) 867-2986. Tasting Sat & Sun 11-3; no tours.*

Started by three Stanford Research Institute engineers in 1959, this destination winery is positioned high on a limestone ridge way back in the Santa Cruz Mountains and is reached via a beautiful, curvy back roads route. On warm days tasting occurs outdoors, and by reservation picnics can be enjoyed at vineyard-side tables offering a magnificent view of the bay below. On cooler days, tasting occurs inside a 100-year-old barn. Ridge, know for its Cabernets and Zinfandels, has been called "the Château Latour of California," and the wines *are* good. So good, in fact, that a Zin brought to Paris as a gift to a native was personally witnessed being sniffed by that native, who expressed surprise and then swallowed with absolute delight.

WHERE TO STAY

Briar Rose Bed & Breakfast Inn *897 E. Jackson Street/N. 19th, (408) 279-5999. 6 rooms; $-$$. No TVs. Full breakfast.*

Once home to a commercial walnut orchard, this 1875 Victorian farmhouse, complete with inviting wrap-around porch, is carefully restored and converted into a comfortable lodging. Walls are papered with authentic Victorian designs by Bradbury & Bradbury, and period furniture is used throughout. One room features a Murphy wall bed, another a clawfoot tub, and two share a bath. Fond of Maxfield Parrish, the owners have a small library of books about the artist in the main floor sitting room and have covered the walls with their extensive Parrish art collection. The surrounding grounds hold a detached 2-story Victorian guest cottage, a pond, an arbor, and a gazebo, as well as a half-acre of English gardens and some mature trees planted long ago. Breakfast is served on the porch in warm weather. Located north of downtown, the inn is close to public transportation

Campbell Inn *675 E. Campbell Ave., Campbell, (800) 582-4300, (408) 374-4300, fax (408) 379-0695; www.campbell-inn.com. 95 rooms; $-$$$+. Children under 13 free. Some fireplaces & VCRs. Heated pool, hot tub, fitness center, parcourse, 1 tennis court (night lighting). Full breakfast. Pets welcome.*

In this B&B-style inn, guests choose from one and two-bedroom suites. Facilities include an adjacent 16-mile jogging/bicycle/nature trail that passes through forests and alongside a stream and two lakes, connecting to a full-series par course, and the hotel provides complimentary use of 10-speed bikes. A lavish European-style hot breakfast consisting of fruits, cheeses, meats, and eggs as well as granola, croissants, and muffins is served in the poolside Breakfast Room (a no-cholesterol breakfast is provided upon request). The inn is situated close to upscale shopping, and a complimentary airport shuttle is available.

Crowne Plaza *282 Almaden Blvd., (800) 2-CROWNE, (408) 998-0400. 9 stories; 239 rooms; $-$$$+. Children under 17 free. Pool, fitness center. Restaurant.*

Centrally located in downtown San Jose, this hotel is across the street from the San Jose McEnery Convention Center and within easy walking distance of all the downtown attractions. Rooms are spacious, and on the Concierge Level guests get complimentary evening cocktails and hors d'oevres plus a continental breakfast. The fitness center is open around the clock, and tennis courts, racquetball courts, and jogging paths are nearby

Double Tree Hotel *2050 Gateway Pl., (800) 222-TREE, (408) 453-4000, fax (408) 437-2898; www.doubletreesanjose.com. 10 stories; 505 rooms; $-$$. Children under 19 free. Heated pool, hot tub, sauna, fitness center. 3 restaurants.*

Located adjacent to the airport, 5 miles from downtown, this hotel offers convenient access to the convention center and downtown via the Light Rail. A complimentary shuttle is available to the airport. Everyone gets freshly baked cookies at check-in, and on the Executive Level guests also get a continental breakfast, terry robes, and nightly turndown.

Fairmont Hotel *170 S. Market St., (800) 527-4727, (408) 998-1900, fax (408) 287-1648. 20 stories; 541 rooms; $-$$$+. Children under 18 free. Some fireplaces. Heated pool (unavail. Nov-Apr), sauna, fitness center. 2 restaurants, room service.*

Built on the site of what was California's capitol building from 1849 to 1851, this luxury high-rise hotel is located within convenient walking distance of all downtown attractions. Guest rooms are equipped with goose-down pillows and comforters, and terry robes and turndown are included.

Hayes Conference Center *200 Edenvale Ave., (800) 420-3200, (408) 226-3200; www.hayes conferencecenter.com. 135 rooms; $$-$$$+. Pool, hot tub, fitness center, tennis courts.*

Once the largest private home in Northern California, this fabulous mansion, located about 15 minutes from downtown, is now a conference center during the week but open to the general public for weekend stays. The spacious rooms in the original house are a particular delight to stay in, but the newer rooms were built to match the mansion's architectural style and feature contemporary comforts. Guests have access to volleyball courts and a jogging/walking trail running through a scenic park across the entry drive. It is a delightful challenge to find the "hidden" subterranean billiards room bar.

Dinner in the exquisite dining room that houses **Orlo's** *(L M-F, D daily. Reservations advised.)*, furnished with antiques and featuring a beautiful antique crystal goblet collection, is not to be missed. The cuisine matches the setting. The **Silver Creek Dining Room**'s expansive weekend brunch is also exceptional.

Hensley House *456 N. Third St., (800) 498-3537, (408) 298-3537, fax (408) 298-4676. 8 rooms; $-$$. All TVs & VCRs; some kitchens & fireplaces. Afternoon hors d'oeuvres, full breakfast.*

San Jose's only downtown B&B, this beautifully restored 116-year-old Queen Anne Victorian home is just a few blocks from the convention center and Light Rail. The dark wood interiors of the house have been carefully restored, and it is decorated with crystal chandeliers and antiques. All of the lavishly decorated guest rooms have private baths, queen-size beds, and robes. The Judge's Chambers, which features a whirlpool bath and fireplace, is worth the splurge and is said to sometimes attract the ghost of Superior Court Judge Perley F. Gosbey, who once owned the house.

Hotel De Anza *233 W. Santa Clara St., (800) 843-3700, (408) 286-1000, fax (408) 286-0500; www.hotelDeAnza. 10 stories; 101 rooms; $$-$$$. All VCRs. Fitness center. Evening snack; restaurant, room service. Parking $8.*

Referred to as the "Grand Lady of San Jose," this 1931 hotel is new again. Refurbished to its art deco grandeur, it exudes a cozy feeling and features attractively appointed, spacious rooms and well-designed tile bathrooms equipped with a phone and TV. Amenities include evening turndown, complimentary shoeshine, terry cloth robes, and a Raid Our Pantry nighttime snack buffet that permits bathrobe-clad guests to perch on the kitchen counter while gobbling up goodies such as chocolate chip cookies and salami cracker sandwiches. For a small additional fee, an extensive breakfast buffet can be enjoyed in a charming room, cleverly painted bright yellow to bring a cheery atmosphere into a windowless room.

Italian dinners are served in **La Pastaia Restaurant**, and the attractive **Hedley Club** lounge presents live jazz most evenings.

Hyatt Sainte Claire *302 S. Market St., (800) 824-6835, (408) 885-1234, fax (408) 287-5700. 6 stories; 170 rooms; $$-$$$+. Fitness center. Restaurant, room service. Parking $10.*

A national historic landmark dating from 1926, this meticulously restored downtown hotel was designed in a Spanish Revival Renaissance style by the same architects who did the Mark Hopkins in San Francisco. It boasts beautiful original hand-painted ceiling panels and an elegant public sitting lounge. Amenities in the attractively, sometimes whimsically decorated rooms, include featherbeds and cotton kimonos. In good weather, breakfast can be taken in an inner garden courtyard featuring vibrantly colored, hand-painted Spanish ceramic tiles.

A branch of the celebrated Tuscan-style **Il Fornaio** serves as the hotel restaurant.

The Pruneyard Inn *1995 S. Bascom Ave., Campbell, (800) 559-4344, (408) 559-4300, fax (408) 559-9919. 116 rooms; $$$+. Children under 13 free. Some VCRs & fireplaces. Heated pool, hot tub, fitness center, parcourse. Full breakfast.*

One of only three hotels in the western U.S. that is located in a shopping center, this tastefully decorated hotel is adjacent to the attractive **Pruneyard** shopping complex. In spite of the location, it manages to provide a secluded feeling. Turndown service and a lavish European-style breakfast is included.

San Jose Hilton and Towers *300 Almaden Blvd., (408) 287-2100, fax (408) 947-4489; www.sjhilton.com. 17 floors; 355 rooms; $$-$$$+. Heated indoor lap pool, hot tub, fitness center.*

Directly adjoining the San Jose McEnery Convention Center, with indoor access, this hotel is located in the heart of downtown San Jose. It has 15 luxurious corner suites and 2 VIP tower floors.

The **City Bar & Grill** offers regional American dishes, with outdoor seating in good weather and an extensive Sunday champagne brunch.

WHERE TO EAT

Buca di Beppo *1875 S. Basom Ave, Campbell, (408) 377-7722*

For description, see page 59.

Emiles *545 S. Second St., (408) 289-1960, fax (408) 998-1245; www.emiles.com. L on F, D Tu-Sat; $$$. Reservations advised. Valet parking $3.*

Owner-chef Emile Mooser grew up in the French part of Switzerland. He was trained in the wine country of Lausanne, above Lake Geneva, and now he produces a California-moderated synthesis of all that experience. In his long-lived, elegantly appointed downtown restaurant, the menu changes with the season. Sample appetizers include a vegetable ragoût with truffle oil, baked burgundy snails, and French onion soup. Entrees include several styles of fresh fish, rack of lamb, and a seasonal game—perhaps a tender, mild moose or wild boar flavored with a classic game sauce. Prompted by the chef's own need to cut butter from his diet, lighter dishes that avoid fats—cuisine minceur—are always available. Desserts are seductive, and the signature soufflé for two, flavored perhaps with cappuccino or Grand Marnier, is definitely to-die for, excuse the expression. Adding to the overall tone of the experience, service is excellent, dishes arrive under silver warming domes, and chef Emile finds time to personally visit each table and chat amiably with diners.

Gordon Biersch Brewery Restaurant *33 E. San Fernando St./1st St., (408) 294-6785, fax (408) 294-4052; www.gordonbiersch.com. L&D daily; $-$$. Highchairs, boosters. Reservations advised.*

Located downtown, this upscale restaurant offers pleasant patio dining as well as seating in a spacious, airy dining room overlooking stainless steel brew tanks. The eclectic menu changes regularly and features salads, sandwiches, and individual pizzas as well as more serious entrees and desserts. In addition to three styles of housemade beer, the menu offers a selection of varietal wines and coffees, and the house bread is often a wonderful sourdough pumpernickel. Live jazz is sometimes scheduled outdoors on Sunday afternoons, and a variety of music is occasionally scheduled inside in the evening.

Hamburger Mary's *170 W. St. John, in San Pedro Square, (408) 947-1667. B,L,&D daily; $.*

For description, see page 69. This branch, housed in an old laundry building, turns into a gay dance club in the evening.

La Taqueria *15 S. First St., (408) 287-1542. L&D daily.*

For description, see page 71.

The Old Spaghetti Factory *51 N. San Pedro St./St. John St., (408) 288-7488, fax (408) 288-5241. L M-F, D daily; $. Highchairs, boosters, child portions.*

Oodles of noodle selections await spaghetti connoisseurs here. There is spaghetti with regular marinara sauce, with mushroom sauce, with white clam sauce, and with meat sauce. For those who can't make up their minds, there is spaghetti with a sampler of sauces. Meatballs, spinach tortellini, and baked chicken are also available. Complete dinners come with bread, soup or salad, drink (coffee, tea, or milk), and spumoni ice cream. The restaurant is housed in what was once the warehouse for the *San Jose Mercury News.* It features bordello decor and a variety of interesting spots to be seated: an antique barber's chair in the bar, within a restored streetcar, on a brass bed converted into a booth.

Scott's Seafood Grill & Bar *185 Park Ave./Market St., (408) 971-1700. L M-F, D daily.*

For description, see page 289.

San Juan Bautista

A LITTLE BACKGROUND

Once the largest city in central California, this town is now a sleepy remnant of that time. It's hard to believe that at one time seven stage lines operated out of the town and that there were numerous busy hotels and saloons. Now the town holds just a few Mexican restaurants, boutiques, and antique shops.

VISITOR INFORMATION

San Juan Bautista Chamber of Commerce
1 Polk St., (831) 623-2454, fax (831) 623-0674; www.sanjuanbautista.ca.us.

GETTING THERE

Located approximately 45 miles south of San Jose. Take Highway 101 south, then Highway 156 east.

ANNUAL EVENTS

Early Days at San Juan Bautista *June. (831) 623-4881.*

Visitors to the state historic park on these days witness re-enactments of 19th-century townspeople performing everyday tasks, such as tortilla-making and baking bread in a hornito oven, and the restored **Plaza Hotel's** famous bar is opened for business.

La Virgen del Tepeyac *December. (831) 623-2444.*

This early California folk opera is presented in the mission by El Teatro Campesino, a local acting company. Also scheduled are a candlelight tour of the mission and **La Posada**—a procession through the city streets in which Mary and Joseph are portrayed seeking shelter.

WHAT TO DO

Fremont Peak State Park *At end of San Juan Canyon Rd., 11 mi. from town, (831) 623-4255, fax (831) 623-4612; observatory (831) 623-2465. Daily 8-sunset. $3/vehicle.*

A popular destination for picnickers and hikers, this park's summit is an easy 15-minute climb from the parking area. An observatory with a 30-inch reflecting telescope is open to the public twice each month; call for schedule. Campsites are available.

San Juan Bautista State Historic Park
19 Franklin St., (831) 623-4881, fax (831) 623-4612. Daily 10-4. Adults $2, 6-12 $1.

This park's assortment of restored buildings allows visitors to see what life was like in this area in the early 1800s. The **Castro Adobe** sits on the plaza in a picturesque area perfect for picnicking.

Mission San Juan Bautista *(402 S. Second St., (831) 623-4528. Daily 9:30-5. By donation.)* was founded in 1797 and is 15th in the chain of 21 California missions. Owned by the Catholic Church, it has the largest church of all the missions, and Thomas Doak, the first American settler in California, painted its bright red and blue reredos and altar. If everything looks familiar, it could be because this park was a major location in the Hitchcock movie *Vertigo.*

WHERE TO STAY

KOA Kampground *900 Anzar Rd., (800) KOA-7572, (831) 623-4263.*

For description, see page 415.

Posada de San Juan Hotel *310 Fourth, (831) 623-4030. 34 rooms; $-$$$. All gas fireplaces.*

This attractive mission-style inn makes lavish use of tiles. It is situated just a block from town, and is connected by a breezeway to the main street.

WHERE TO EAT

Jardines de San Juan *115 Third St., (831) 623-4466; www.jardinesrestaurant.com. L&D daily; $. Highchairs, boosters, child portions. Reservations accepted.*

What a wonderful fair-weather experience it is to sit outside under a sheltering umbrella on the brick courtyard here. Among the profusely flowering gardens, with autumn-colored roosters sometimes running loose, diners peruse the menu while sipping icy-cold margaritas and dipping tortilla chips in tasty salsa. Flautas consist of shredded beef rolled in a deep-fried tortilla and topped with guacamole. Tacos, enchiladas, and a deliciously spicy tamale are available, as are plenty of a la carte items and veggie dishes. On weekends after 5 p.m., regional specialties join the menu. Red snapper Veracruz is available on Fridays, shrimp fajitas on Saturdays, and drunken chicken on Sundays. Limited amounts of these specialties are prepared, so diners must call to reserve their portion. Live music is scheduled on the outdoor stage each Saturday and Sunday from noon to 3:30.

San Juan Bakery *319 Third St., (831) 623-4570. Daily 8-6.*

This old-fashioned bakery makes a wonderful sourdough French bread, a down-soft buttermilk bread, and an assortment of delicious pastries. The sugar cookies are particularly good and make a great car snack. Picnic supplies are also available.

Salinas

A LITTLE BACKGROUND

Salinas is one of the biggest cities in the Salinas Valley. Known as "the salad bowl of the nation," this valley is where author John Steinbeck spent his formative years, and many of his novels are set here. In fact, the first working title for *East of Eden* was "Salinas Valley."

VISITOR INFORMATION

Salinas Valley Chamber of Commerce *119 E. Alisal St., (831) 424-7611, fax (831) 424-8639; www.salinaschamber.com.*

GETTING THERE

Located approximately 20 miles south of San Juan Bautista, and approximately 100 miles south of San Francisco. It is also possible to take Amtrak from Oakland or San Jose and return the same day. Call (800) 872-7245 for more information.

ANNUAL EVENTS

California Rodeo *July. (800) 771-8807, (831) 757-2951. $10-$18.*

First presented in 1911, this outdoor rodeo is ranked fourth largest in the world. It is especially noted for its trick riders, clowns, and thoroughbred racing. Prize money totals over $200,000, attracting the best of the cowboys to the competitions.

Steinbeck Festival *August. (831) 753-7401, fax (831) 753-0574; www.steinbeck.org.*

Each year one of Steinbeck's many novels is emphasized in this intellectual festival honoring the town's native son. Bus and walking tours, films, lectures, and panel discussions are all part of the festivities.

John Steinbeck and his sister Mary on Jill — the inspiration for The Red Pony

WHAT TO DO

National Steinbeck Center *One Main St., (831) 796-3833; www.steinbeck.org. Daily 10-5. Adults $7, 62+ $6, 11-17 $4.*

The tour here begins with a 10-minute introductory film detailing highlights of Steinbeck's life. Then six galleries of interactive exhibits illustrate famous scenes from his books and his life, enhanced by selected quotes and film clips. *East of Eden* is represented by a full-size boxcar filled with faux iced lettuce (visitors actually *feel* the cool air) and clips from the movie featuring James Dean. *The Red Pony,* which Steinbeck wrote while living in his boyhood home a few blocks away, features a corral exuding the aroma of fresh hay and equipped with a replica pony that kids can mount. But the premiere exhibit seems to be the original "Rocinante"—the custom-built pick-up camper that Steinbeck drove when he traveled around the country writing *Travels with Charley.* Outside the main exhibition hall a small Art of Writing Room invites visitors to write responses to various Steinbeck quotes, and to learn a little more about writing in general. Children can use word magnets for composing poems. Another gallery houses changing art exhibits.

WHERE TO STAY

Motel Row.

On the east side of the freeway, the whole of North Main Street offers inexpensive generic lodging.

WHERE TO EAT

Cottage Cafe *737 Sanborn Pl. (Monterey Peninsula exit off Hwy. 101), (831) 754-1968. B&L M-Sat; $. 1 highchair, boosters.*

This tiny, friendly roadhouse produces a particularly good, crisp green salad, which makes sense since this area is known as the nation's salad bowl. Some seating is available in comfortable booths, and counter seating permits a fast in and out. Breakfast items are available all day, and hamburgers and a variety of sandwiches, including a great French dip, are on the menu.

Fast-food heaven *1300 block of N. Main St.*

First Awakenings *171 Main St., (831) 784-1125.*

For description, see page 106.

The Steinbeck House *132 Central Ave., (831) 424-2735, fax (831) 757-5806; L M-Sat; $. Closed 2 weeks in Dec. Highchairs, boosters, child menu. Reservations advised.*

In 1902, John Steinbeck was born in the front bedroom of this beautifully renovated 1897 Victorian house. In *East of Eden* he described it as ". . . an immaculate and friendly house, grand enough but not pretentious . . . inside its white fence surrounded by its clipped lawn and roses . . ." Now a volunteer group owns the house and operates it as a gourmet luncheon restaurant. Serving seasonal produce grown in the Salinas Valley, the restaurant's menu changes daily and includes items such as crunchy, cool gazpacho soup and tasty chicken-walnut salad. Lunch includes soup or salad and entree for $7.50; dessert and beverage are extra. Though the dining rooms are elegantly decorated, with Steinbeck memorabilia covering the walls, the atmosphere is casual. Comfortable travel attire is acceptable, and children are welcome. After lunch, a well-priced cellar gift shop invites browsing and perhaps selecting a souvenir book by Steinbeck. **Guided house tours** operate in summer *(10:30, 2:30, & 3:30; $4-$5.).*

Gonzales

GETTING THERE

Located approximately 20 miles south of Salinas.

WHAT TO DO

Mystic Cliffs Wine Center *800 S. Alta St., (831) 675-8838, fax (831) 675-2611. Tasting daily 11-6; tours by appt.*

This attractive modern winery displays changing art exhibits. Picnic tables, a pond populated with ducks and geese, and lush grassy areas offer a relaxing respite from freeway traffic.

Soledad

WHAT TO DO

Mission Nuestra Señora de la Soledad *36641 Fort Romie Rd., off Paraiso Springs Rd., 3 mi. west of Hwy. 101, (831) 678-2586. W-M 10-4. By donation.*

Named for the Spanish word for solitude, this isolated mission was built in 1791 next to the Salinas River, where it sits among peaceful green pastures and rolling hills. It was the 13th in the chain of missions. In 1835, it was abandoned and then crumbled into ruin. In 1935, volunteers rebuilt the living quarters and the chapel, which retains its original tile floor.

Pinnacles National Monument *12 mi. southeast of town, (831) 389-4485, fax (831) 389-4489. Daily 9-5. $4/vehicle.*

Formed by ancient volcanic activity, this scenic area is home to craggy pinnacles and spires that are particularly surprising to come across because the area is otherwise so flat. Spring and fall are the best times to visit for hiking and camping, spring being particularly popular because of the stunning display of wildflowers. At other times, the temperature can be uncomfortable. A variety of raptors—prairie falcons, red-shouldered hawks, turkey vultures, and golden eagles—nest in the rocks and are sometimes sighted. The more developed east side of the park is reached by taking Highway 25 south, then Highway 146 west. There, a Visitor Center offers orientation, and a moderately difficult 2-mile loop trail leads to the Bear Gulch Caves.

King City

WHAT TO DO

Mission San Antonio de Padua *On Jolon Rd., 23 mi. southwest of Hwy. 101 via Jolon Rd., in Fort Hunter Liggett, (831) 385-4478. Daily 8-6. By donation.*

Founded in 1771 by Father Serra, this is one of the largest restored and rebuilt missions. Original remains at the remote but picturesque site include the well, grist mill, tannery, and parts of the aqueduct system. The imposing façade of its church is known for both the campanile located in front and its archway bells. Both the church and the quadrangle have been restored to an authentic approximation of their original luster. Known as the "Jewel of the Santa Lucias," it was the third mission. A museum exhibits Native American artifacts, and an annual **fiesta** is held the second weekend in June. It is especially beautiful in the spring, when the surrounding grasslands are ablaze with a profusion of wildflowers.

San Miguel

GETTING THERE

Located approximately 65 miles south of Soledad.

WHAT TO DO

Mission San Miguel Arcangel *775 Mission St., (805) 467-3256, fax (805) 467-2448. Daily 9:30-4:30. By donation.*

Founded in 1797, this is the 16th in the chain of California's 21 missions. The present mission building was constructed in 1816. Though the outside architecture is simple, the delicate original and unretouched neoclassical paintings inside, done by parish Indians under the direction of professional artist Esteban Munras, are especially noteworthy. The reredos feature marble pillars with intricate geometric patterns displaying a dazzling array of colors, and original sheepskin windowcoverings can also be viewed. Beehive ovens and olive presses are displayed in the gardens, and shaded picnic tables are provided. A **fiesta** is held each September on the third Sunday.

Don't miss the 1846 **Rios Caldonia Adobe** located across the street. Once part of the mission estate, this 2-story adobe has served as a hotel, stagecoach office, school, and family home. It has been restored and furnished to reflect the past.

Paso Robles

VISITOR INFORMATION

Paso Robles Visitors & Convention Bureau
1225 Park St., (800) 406-4040, (805) 238-0506, fax (805) 238-0527.

GETTING THERE

Located approximately 5 miles south of San Miguel.

WHAT TO DO

James Dean Memorial *On Hwy. 46, 25 mi. east of town, in Cholame (pronounced "show-LAMB"), (805) 238-1390.*

Depending on a person's mood, this can be an interesting or bizarre side trip. This is where legendary actor James Dean crashed his racing-model Porsche roadster and died in 1955. A concrete-and-stainless steel obelisk shrine to Dean's memory stands just 900 yards from the actual death site. Constructed and maintained by a Japanese national who comes to pay homage twice a year, it is located in the parking lot of the **Jack Ranch Cafe**.

Wine Tasting.

This area's limestone soil is similar to that found in Provence in the south of France and produces flavorful grapes. The long, hot summers turn them into fodder for ripe, robust Merlots and Zinfandels.

A scenic **back roads tour** begins at the Vineyard Drive exit off Highway 101 just north of Templeton. Take Vineyard Drive west for about 8 miles through bucolic, oak-studded farm land, passing Peachy Canyon Road (which returns to the freeway). At Adelaida Road, turn right and continue for about 2 miles to **Adelaida Cellars** (*5805 Adelaida Rd., (800) 676-1232, (805) 239-8980, fax (805) 239-4671. Tasting daily 11-5; fee.*), a scenically-situated winery specializing in producing small quantities of low-tech premium wines fermented with natural yeast. Of special interest here is an expansive walnut orchard, the bountiful fruit of which is sold in the tasting room. Continue about 10 miles east on Adelaida Road toward town, crossing 101, to **Eberle Winery** *(On Hwy.*

46 East, 3.5 mi. east of Hwy. 101, (805) 238-9607. Tasting 10-5 daily; in summer to 6.). The winery's excellent reds can be tasted in a room filled with medals and awards from competitions, and picnic tables are provided on a sheltered patio. Tours of the cool caves are given sporadically.

For a free map to this area's many wineries, contact the **Paso Robles Vintners and Growers Association** *((800) 549-WINE, (805) 239-VINE, fax (805) 237-6439).*

WHERE TO EAT

A&W Rootbeer Drive-In *2110 Spring St., (805) 238-0360. Daily 10am-11pm; $. Child portions. No cards.*

An oasis off Highway 101, this A&W stand is right out of the '50s. A waitress appears when a car's headlights are turned on, and food is served on a tray that attaches to a partially rolled-down window. Choices are simple: hamburgers, hot dogs, French fries, onion rings, and cold root beer.

Atascadero

VISITOR INFORMATION

Atascadero Chamber of Commerce *6550 El Camino Real, (805) 466-2044.*

WHAT TO DO

The Charles Paddock Zoo *9305 Pismo St., off Hwy. 41, 1 mi. west of Hwy. 101, (805) 461-5080. Daily 10-4; in summer to 6. Adults $3, 65+ $2.25, 3-15 $2.*

Though small, this 5-acre zoo takes good care of its diverse population. An adjacent park has shady picnic tables and a lake with paddleboat rentals.

San Luis Obispo

VISITOR INFORMATION

San Luis Obispo Chamber of Commerce *1039 Chorro St., (805) 781-2777, fax (805) 543-1255; www.slochamber.org & www.visitslo.com.*

San Luis Obispo County Visitors & Conference Bureau *1037 Mill St., (800) 634-1414, (805) 541-8000, fax (805) 543-9498; www.SanLuisObispoCounty.com.*

GETTING THERE

Located approximately 30 miles south of Paso Robles via Highway 101, and approximately 45 miles south of San Simeon via Highway 1. It is also possible to take Amtrak; call (800) 872-7245 for more information.

WHAT TO DO

California Polytechnic State University (Cal Poly) *On Grand Ave., (805) 756-1111. Tours: (805) 756-5734; M, W, F at 10 & 2; free.*

Tours of this attractive campus begin in the lobby of the Administration Building.

Gum Alley *Next to 733 Higuera St.*

For several decades gum-chewers have been depositing their product on these brick walls. Some have even taken the time to make designs. A vulgar, tacky eyesore to many, it is a cheap thrill for gum aficionados and most children. So don't get stuck here without a stick. Stock up on different colors of gum before arriving, and note that Double Bubble is reputed to stick best.

Hot Springs.

• **Avila Hot Springs Spa, Campground & RV Park** *250 Avila Beach Dr., (800) 332-2359, (805) 595-2359. Daily 8am-10pm. Adults $7.50, 2-12 $5.*

At this family-friendly spot, inner tubes can be rented to use in a warm pool. RV and tent campsites include a continental breakfast, and a fitness center, pool, and hot tub are among the facilities.

• **Sycamore Mineral Springs Resort** *1215 Avila Beach Dr., (800) 234-5831, (805) 595-7302, fax (805) 781-2512; www.sycamoresprings.com. 55 rooms; $$-$$$+. Some kitchens & fireplaces. Heated pool, 23 public hot tubs. Restaurant.*

Situated on a back road leading to the coast, this inn has outdoor mineral spring hot tubs that can be rented by the hour, and each guest room has a private hot tub. Massage treatments are available. The springs' history dates to 1897, when two men drilling for oil were disappointed to find sulfur-based mineral water instead. First called the "oil wells," the springs became popular in the 1920s when W. C. Fields and other celebrities who stayed at Hearst Castle stopped in.

Mission San Luis Obispo de Tolosa *782 Monterey St., (805) 543-6850. Daily 9-4; in summer to 5. By donation.*

Founded in 1772, this is the fifth mission in the California chain. It was the first mission to introduce the red clay roof tile, which successfully repelled the flaming arrows used in attacks by Native Americans. The complex has been extensively restored and includes a fragrant rose garden and a museum exhibiting rare early California photos. Its charming chapel has a simple façade with a belfry and vestibule (unique among the state's missions) and is still used for services. An adjacent plaza and park provide shady trees, large grassy areas, stream-hugging paths, and inviting open-air cafes.

The nearby **San Luis County Historical Museum** *(696 Monterey St., (805) 543-0638. W-Sun 10-4. Free.)* is appropriately filled with historical exhibits that include a hurdy-gurdy (or calliope) and a school bell.

San Luis Obispo Children's Museum *1010 Nipomo St., (805) 544-KIDS, fax (805) 545-5875; www.slonet.org/slokids. Call for schedule. Admission $4.50, under 2 free. Strollers not permitted.*

Located within a transformed transmission shop, this museum especially for kids holds numerous hands-on exhibits that entice them to explore and interact. They can become encased in a giant bubble, pilot a space shuttle to the moon, and anchor a newscast. Children under 16 must be accompanied by an adult.

SLO Trolley *Schedule varies. Free.*

This streetcar makes getting around downtown easy and fun.

WHERE TO STAY

Embassy Suites Hotel *333 Madonna Rd., (800) 864-6000, (800) EMBASSY, (805) 549-0800, fax (805) 549-9138; www.embassy-suites.com. 4 stories; 196 suites; $-$$$. Children under 18 free. Indoor heated pool & hot tub, fitness center. Full breakfast; restaurant, room service.*

This branch of the all-suites hotel chain is located adjacent to a beautifully landscaped open-air shopping mall. For description, see page 364.

Garden Street Inn *1212 Garden St./Marsh St., (800) 488-2045, (805) 545-9802, fax (805) 545-9403; www.gardenstreetinn.com. 13 rooms; 100% non-smoking; $-$$$. Unsuitable for children under 16. Some fireplaces. Hot tub. Afternoon snack, full breakfast.*

This enormous 1887 Italianate/Queen Anne-style mansion is beautifully restored and just a block from downtown. Fragrant old citrus trees greet guests at the front gate, and a communal parlor area features an interesting browsing library.

Hostel Obispo *1619 Santa Rosa St., (805) 544-4678, fax (805) 544-3142; www.hostelobispo.com. 22 beds; some private rooms.*

Located just 1 block from the Amtrak station and within walking distance of downtown, this hostel has a B&B atmosphere. Bicycles are available for rental, and complimentary pancakes are served each morning. See also page 417.

KOA Kampground *4765 Santa Margarita Lake Rd., 10 mi. from town, (800) KOA-5619, (805) 438-5618.*

For description, see page 415.

Madonna Inn *100 Madonna Rd., (800) 543-9666, (805) 543-3000, fax (805) 543-1800; www.madonnainn.com. 109 rooms; 100% non-smoking; $-$$$. Children under 18 free. Some fireplaces. 2 restaurants.*

Begun in 1958 with just 12 rooms, this sprawling pink motel now has more than 100 guest rooms. All are uniquely decorated, some more uniquely than others—like the Cave Man Room, with its stone walls, ceilings, and floors and cascading waterfall shower; and the Barrel of Fun Room, in which all the furniture is made from barrels. A photo file at the check-in desk is available to help guests decide which room to book.

For those not spending the night, a snack in the flamboyant coffee shop or dinner in the more formal **Alex Madonna's Gold Rush Steakhouse** *(D daily. Highchairs, boosters, booths, child menu. Reservations advised.)*—where the menu is surf & turf-style and all the supporting courses are included—is a must. A separate bakery dispenses goodies such as French cream puffs, cinnamon pull-aparts, and an assortment of pies. And don't miss the restrooms—especially the men's room.

Motel Inn *2223 Monterey St., (805) 543-4000.*

Opened on December 12, 1925, this is the world's very first motel. It is currently closed.

Quality Suites *1631 Monterey St., (800) 228-5151, (805) 541-5001, fax (805) 546-9475; www.qualitysuites.com. 138 suites; $-$$; 2-night min. on summer weekends. Children under 18 free. All VCRs. Heated pool, children's wading pool, hot tub. Evening snack, full breakfast.*

This chain is known for its spacious rooms and made-to-order buffet breakfasts. A complimentary evening cocktail hour is also provided, giving guests a chance to relax and mingle.

Motel Row.

A vast array of motels lines the north end of Monterey Street.

WHERE TO EAT

Benvenuti *450 Marsh St., (805) 541-5393. L M-F, D daily; $$. Reservations advised.*

Operating from within a transformed Victorian home, this romantic restaurant offers an extensive menu of refined northern Italian dishes. Its namesake dish, fettucine Benvenuti, tops the pasta with a combination of prawns, scallops, and mushrooms in a tasty tomato sauce. The petto di pollo alla Diavola consists of a breaded chicken breast sautéed with brandy and Dijon mustard. More entrees include a pheasant with vodka sauce crowned with glazed white grapes, and ossobuco alla Milanese—braised veal shank with saffron risotto. Selections from the dessert tray include a housemade light tiramisu and, in season, perfect fresh red raspberries topped with Grand Marnier.

Farmers' Market and Street Faire *600 & 700 blocks of Higuera St., (805) 541-0286, fax (805) 781-2647; www.downtownslo.com. Thur 6-8:30pm. Free.*

Shoppers here can buy dinner fully prepared or pick up the fixings. This market is known for its delicious barbecued items, and live entertainment is provided free.

Hobee's California Restaurant *1443 Calle Joaquin, (800) 462-3376, (805) 549-9186; www.hobees.com. B,L,&D daily; $. Highchairs, boosters, booths, child menu. No reservations.*

For description, see page 97.

Linn's Downtown SLO Bin *1141 Chorro St./Marsh St., (805) 546-8444; www.linnsfruitbin.com. B,L,&D daily, SunBr; $. Highchairs, boosters, child menu. No reservations.*

Known for its delicious breakfasts, expansive salad bar, and large selection of pies and desserts, this pleasant dining spot has a varied menu that includes delectable pot pies as well as stuffed potatoes, stir-frys, and sandwiches. Everything is handmade in their own kitchen. An adjoining shop purveys the restaurant's own line of gourmet food products, which are also available through a mail-order catalogue.

Pepe Delgado's *1601 Monterey St., (805) 544-6660. L&D Tu-Sun; $. Highchairs, boosters, booths, child portions. No reservations.*

Comfortable booths and large, solid tables make this popular Mexican spot an especially good choice for families. The hacienda-style building features tile floors, velvet paintings, and papier-mâché parrots on perches hanging from the ceiling. Potent fruit margaritas and daiquiris come in small, medium, and large, helping diners get festive. A large variety of traditional Mexican items is on the menu, and many are available in small portions. Fajitas are particularly fun to order because they arrive sizzling on raised platters and are kept warm on the table by candles.

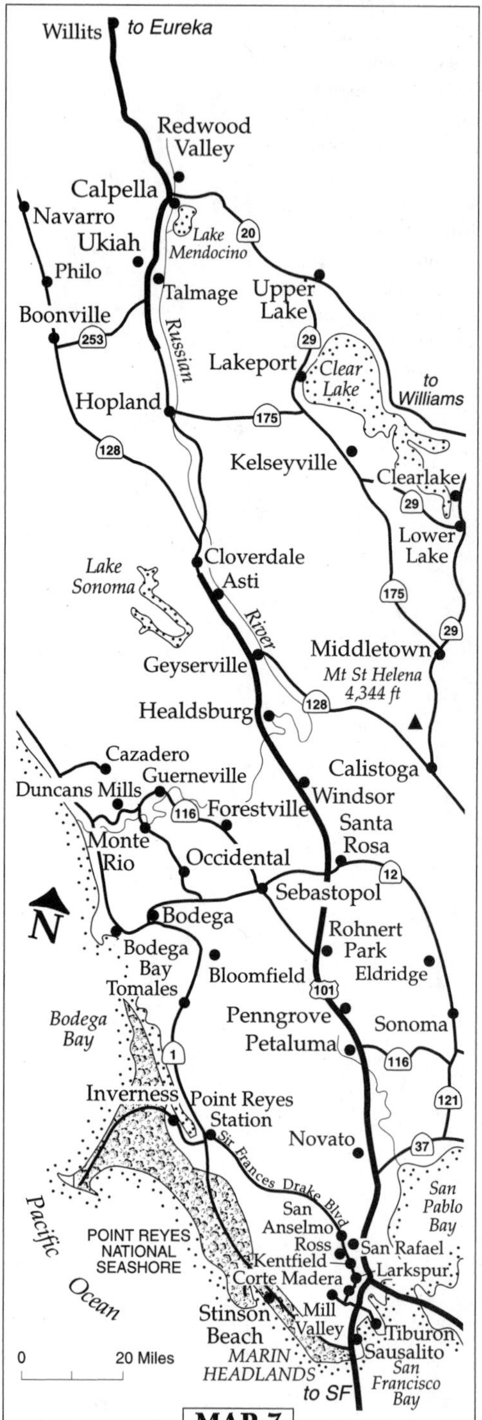
Willits
to Eureka
Redwood Valley
Calpella
Navarro
Ukiah
Lake Mendocino
20
Philo
Talmage
Upper Lake
Boonville
253
Russian
29
Lakeport
Clear Lake
to Williams
Hopland
175
128
Kelseyville
Clearlake
29
Lower Lake
Cloverdale
Lake Sonoma
Asti
175
River
29
Middletown
Geyserville
Mt St Helena 4,344 ft
Healdsburg
128
Cazadero
Guerneville
Calistoga
Duncans Mills
116
Forestville
Windsor
Santa Rosa
Monte Rio
Occidental
12
Sebastopol
N
Bodega
Rohnert Park
Bodega Bay
Bloomfield
Eldridge
Tomales
101
Bodega Bay
Penngrove
Sonoma
Petaluma
116
1
121
Inverness
Point Reyes Station
Novato
37
Sir Frances Drake Blvd
San Anselmo
San Pablo Bay
Pacific Ocean
POINT REYES NATIONAL SEASHORE
Ross
San Rafael
Kentfield
Larkspur
Corte Madera
Mill Valley
Stinson Beach
Tiburon
Sausalito
0
20 Miles
MARIN HEADLANDS
San Francisco Bay
to SF
MAP 7

A LITTLE BACKGROUND

Across the Golden Gate Bridge from San Francisco, spectacularly scenic Marin County comprises a number of prosperous bedroom communities. It is home to numerous rock stars and celebrities, including *Star Wars* filmmaker George Lucas, who built his studios in the hilly back country.

Books and films have poked fun at the generally upscale residents, creating a stereotype of people with an easygoing, laid-back approach to life, seeking nothing more than to tickle each other with peacock feathers while soaking in a hot tub, and emphasizing their New Age flakiness. The reality is, of course, somewhere in between.

Consistently fair weather makes this area a popular destination with Bay Area residents, especially when other areas are covered by fog.

VISITOR INFORMATION

Marin County Convention and Visitors Bureau *1013 Larkspur Landing, (415) 499-5000; www.visitmarin.org.*

Marin Headlands

A LITTLE BACKGROUND

Get oriented to this 12,000-acre park at the **Visitor Center** *(Alexander Ave. exit off Hwy. 101, (415) 331-1540. Daily 9:30-4:30. Free.)* located inside Fort Barry's old chapel. Then take a soul-soothing walk along Rodeo Beach. When leaving, follow McCullough Road east to Conzelman Road, which leads past some of the old bunkers and gun batteries that attest to the area's military past. **Hawk Hill**, at Battery 129, is considered the best site on the West Coast to view birds of prey; over 25,000 hawks and other raptors migrate over this area each year. Farther on, several twists in the road offer magnificent views of the Golden Gate Bridge, and behind it, San Francisco. A picture taken here makes the subject look as if they are standing on the edge of the earth.

WHAT TO DO

Bay Area Discovery Museum *557 McReynolds Rd./East Fort Baker, (415) 487-4398, fax (415) 332-9671; www.badm.org. Tu-Thur 9-4, F-Sun 10-5; in summer Tu-Sun 10-5. Adults $7, 1-18 $6.*

This activity-oriented, hands-on museum is especially nice as a rainy day outing. Themes include the bay environment, art, multimedia, and architecture. Among the related activities spread among seven buildings: constructing a model suspension bridge; crawling through a simulated ocean; building a personal enclosure in the Space Maze. The excitement is catching, and parents find themselves being pulled along from one activity to another by their eager children. Visitors can also explore the outdoor area immediately surrounding the museum, where a Model T is one of the play structures. For those who are caught picnic-less, a cafe serves appropriate fare, and outdoor picnic tables afford a magnificent close-up view of the Golden Gate Bridge. Special programs, festivals, and workshops are scheduled regularly.

The Marine Mammal Center *(415) 289-7325. Daily 10-4. Free.*

Staffed by volunteers, this is one of the largest wild animal hospitals in the world. A variety of injured, sick, or orphaned marine mammals (seals, dolphins, porpoises, whales) are brought here to be nursed back to health. When ready, they are released back into their natural habitat. Docent-led tours are available on weekends, self-guided tours during the week.

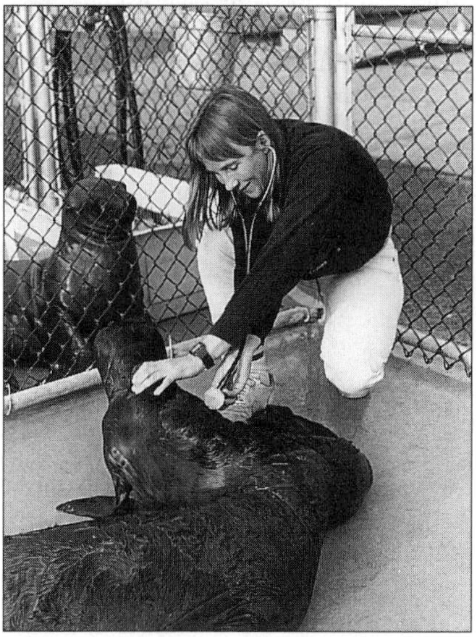

Point Bonita Lighthouse *(415) 331-1540. Trail open Sat & Sun 12:30-3:30; call for tour schedule.*

This lovely old light was the last on the Pacific Coast to be automated. The mostly dirt, 1/2-mile trail can be scary: It includes going through a tunnel and crossing a 120-foot suspension bridge. Full moon walks are sometimes scheduled.

WHERE TO STAY

Marin Headlands Hostel *Bldg. 941, (415) 331-2777, fax (415) 331-6943. 103 beds; private rooms. Tennis court.*

On the National Historic Register, this spacious, homey hostel operates in two charming turn-of-the-century buildings at historic Fort Barry. See also page 417.

Sausalito

A LITTLE BACKGROUND

People come from all over the world to stroll Bridgeway, the main street of this warm and sunny town. A former fishing village, Sausalito is often referred to as California's Riviera and is now a magnet for both artists and tourists and remains a pleasure for both. Restaurants and boutiques abound, and the view across the bay to Tiburon and San Francisco is superb. It is interesting to note that Jack London wrote the opening chapters of *The Sea Wolf* here.

Be careful. The largest source of income for the city is parking fines. In summer, a **shuttle** *((415) 331-7262. Daily 11-5:30. Round trip $2.)* runs between the Ferry Terminal, the Bay Model, the Discovery Museum, and the Golden Gate Bridge.

VISITOR INFORMATION

Sausalito Chamber of Commerce *29 Caledonia St., (415) 331-7262, fax (415) 332-0323; www.sausalito.org.*

GETTING THERE

Take the first exit (Alexander Avenue) off Highway 101 after crossing the Golden Gate Bridge. Another exit marked "Sausalito" is 3 miles farther north. Sausalito can also be reached from San Francisco via ferry.

ANNUAL EVENTS

Floating Homes Tour *Date varies. (415) 332-1916; www.floatinghomes.org. Tickets $20.*

Approximately ten houseboats open their premises for tours during this exciting event at Kappas Marina. A portion of the proceeds benefits a local non-profit organization.

Sausalito Art Festival *September, on Labor Day weekend. (415) 332-3555, fax (415) 331-1340; www.sausalitoartfest.org. Adults $10-$12, 62+ & 6-12 $5.*

This juried exhibit of over 200 artists—all of whom attend in person—includes live music, international cuisine, and plenty of wine, and the waterfront setting provides magnificent bay views. It is the top-rated non-profit fine arts festival in the U.S.

WHAT TO DO

Bay Model Visitor Center *2100 Bridgeway, (415) 332-3870, (415) 332-3871. Tu-F 9-4, Sat 10-3; in summer Tu-F 9-4, Sat & Sun 10-6. Free.*

Located on the outskirts of town, on the site of a shipyard that produced World War II Liberty Ships and tankers, this is a working hydraulic scale model of the Bay Area and Delta estuary systems. As big as two football fields, it was built to simulate bay water conditions for research. A computerized slide show and interpretive displays help make this complex scientific project understandable to the layman. The model operates irregularly; call for upcoming dates.

The Hawaiian Chieftain *3020 Bridgeway #266, (415) 331-3214, fax (415) 331-9415; www.hawaiianchieftain.com. Call for schedule. $25-$50. Reservations required.*

Take a jouney back in time on this 18th-century-style sailing tall-ship. Constructed in Maui, Hawaii to carry inter-island cargo, she now offers sunset sails, as well as Sunday brunch sails with jazz, reggae, or calypso music.

Heath Ceramics *400 Gate 5 Rd., (415) 332-3732; www.heathceramics.com. Daily 10-5.*

Seconds of this classically simple contemporary ceramic dinnerware, which is used at both Chez Panisse in Berkeley and at nearby Lark Creek Inn in Larkspur, are sold here at reduced prices. Teapots and tiles are also produced, some using recycled glazes developed by the chemist owner.

Sea Trek Ocean Kayaking Center *(415) 488-1000, fax (415) 488-1707. Rentals $15-$30/hr., $55-$70/day.*

Rent a kayak for just an hour or the entire day, or sign up for one lesson or a series. Special children's classes are available, and a customized Take the Kids Sea Kayaking program includes wet suits for the whole family.

Waldo Point *At north end of town.*

This private houseboat colony contains both the funky and exquisite. Visitors are not particularly welcomed by residents but are legally permitted to view the area if they respect posted no-trespassing signs. It is interesting to note that in 1967 singer Otis Redding rented a houseboat on the main dock here, which is said to have been the inspiration for his well-known song titled "(Sittin' On) The Dock of the Bay."

WHERE TO STAY

Casa Madrona Hotel *801 Bridgeway, (800) 567-9524, (415) 332-0502, fax (415) 332-2537; www.casam.com. 36 units; $$-$$$+; 2-night min. on weekends. Some kitchens & fireplaces. Hot tub. Evening snack, full breakfast; restaurant. Parking $7.*

Nestled against a picturesque hill above Bridgeway, this hotel offers lodging in either a converted Victorian house in back or in newer, individually decorated contemporary rooms sprinkled down the hillside and featuring water views. One of the most popular rooms is the uniquely decorated "Artist's Loft." Arrangements can also be made to stay on a local houseboat. Breakfast is served to guests in the hotel's elegant restaurant.

Romantic **Mikayla** *((415) 331-5888, fax (415) 332-2537; www.mikayla.com. D daily, SunBr; $$$. Highchairs, boosters, child portions. Reservations advised. Valet parking.)* serves innovative cuisine in an elegant atmosphere with expansive bay views. Local resident, artist Laurel Burch, who has a gallery in town, designed a hand-painted 12-foot mural for the restaurant telling a playful story about a mythical sea goddess, Mikayla. Main courses have included succulent roasted lobster with ricotta-mustard gnocchi and roasted chicken breast with risotto. Small appetizers, or "tastings," which consist of the chef's own favorite dishes, are noteworthy, especially roasted banana risotto topped with one perfect scallop, and American foie gras.

Hotel Sausalito *16 El Portal/Bridgeway, (888) 442-0700, (415) 332-0700, fax (415) 332-8788; www.hotelsausalito.com. 16 rooms; $$-$$$+; 2-night min. on weekends. Continental breakfast. No pets.*

Well-located next to the ferry landing, this small European-style boutique hotel was built in 1915 in Mission Revival style. In the past it has served as a bordello. In his heyday Baby Face Nelson was a regular guest, and writer Sterling Hayden once lived here. Now it is renovated into a bit of the French Riviera, with a sunny decor, colorful commissioned art decorating the halls, and handmade furniture and accents throughout. Most of the rooms retain their original stained-glass windows, and some rooms overlook Bridgeway, others tiny Vina del Mar Park.

The Inn Above Tide *30 El Portal, (800) 893-TIDE, (415) 332-9535, fax (415) 332-6714. 30 rooms; $$$-$$$+. Most gas fireplaces. Evening snack, continental breakfast.*

At the only hotel *on* San Francisco Bay (some rooms jut out over the water), all rooms have spectacular views of San Francisco and of a continuous parade of vessels. Some have a private decks with glass walls for even better, unobstructed gazing. Amenities include robes and binoculars. Evening wine and hors d'oeuvres and breakfast are served in the parlor; optionally, they can be delivered to guest rooms. The ferry from San Francisco docks immediately adjacent.

WHERE TO EAT

Alta Mira Hotel *125 Bulkley Ave., (415) 332-1350, fax (415) 331-3862. B,L,&D daily. Closed Jan. Highchairs, boosters, child menu. Reservations advised. Valet parking.*

Situated in the hills above town, this refined spot serves traditional continental cuisines. Its terrace, which commands an excellent bay view, is a particularly choice spot to enjoy a leisurely breakfast, lunch, or Sunday brunch.

Guest rooms and cottages *(35 units; $-$$$. Closed Jan. Some gas fireplaces. Restaurant, room service.)*, many with bay views, are also available.

Margaritaville *1200 Bridgeway, (415) 331-3226. L&D daily; $-$$. Highchairs, boosters, child portions. No reservations.*

Dining here can pass for a tropical mini-vacation. Most inside tables have some view of the water, but the outside deck is the place to be in warm weather. The bar takes up almost half the premises—a clue that this spot is popular with singles—and dispenses strong, tasty drinks, including fruit margaritas and smoothies as well as some unusual Caribbean concoctions. The decor is tropical, the menu is almost exclusively Mexican, and the music is Caribbean reggae. Generous portions of well-prepared, tasty items are served on gigantic plates and platters, and fajita plates arrive sizzling. Many vegetarian selections and smaller "platillos" for the lighter eater are available, and on Kids Night *(W after 5.)*, children under 13 eat free from a menu designed especially for them.

No Name Bar *757 Bridgeway/El Portal, (415) 332-1392. Daily 10am-2am.*

Famous for its low profile, this is where to stop and relax over a pitcher of Ramos fizzes in the garden-like back room. Live Dixieland jazz is performed every Sunday afternoon, and live jazz and blues are scheduled Wednesday through Saturday evenings.

Mill Valley

A LITTLE BACKGROUND

Thought of by many as the quintessential Marin, this tiny, laid-back town originated as an enclave of vacation cabins built by San Franciscans eager to escape the city's notoriously cool summers. It is said more professionals per capita live here than in any other community in the country. The town rests at the base of Mount Tamalpais, the county's principal landmark.

The unofficial center of town seems to be the **Depot Bookstore and Cafe** *(87 Throckmorton Ave. Daily 7am-10pm.)*. Once the town's Northwestern Pacific Railroad depot, it offers both indoor and outdoor seating and a plethora of reading material.

Mill Valley is also home to the original **Banana Republic** store—now a nationwide chain; its current location *(59 Throckmorton Ave.)* is not the original site. The town is also home to the modest original location of the **Smith & Hawken** garden-supply store *(35 Corte Madera Ave.)*.

VISITOR INFORMATION

Mill Valley Chamber of Commerce *85 Throckmorton Ave., (800) 388-9701, (415) 388-9700, fax (415) 388-9770; www.millvalley.org.*

GETTING THERE

Located approximately 5 miles north of Sausalito. Take exit off Highway 101 and follow signs to intersection of Miller and Throckmorton avenues.

ANNUAL EVENTS

Mill Valley Film Festival *October. (415) 383-5256, fax (415) 383-8606; www.finc.org. Screenings $6-$8.50.*

Running for 11 days, this well-established festival offers screenings of both American independent cinema and foreign films, major film premières, and tributes to top filmmakers and industry leaders. Seminars are scheduled for both aspiring filmmakers and the layman in search of enlightenment. A **Children's FilmFest**, with special screenings and workshops, is held at the same time.

WHAT TO DO

Old Mill Park *Throckmorton Ave./Old Mill Rd., (415) 383-1370.*

Holding the town's namesake 1834 sawmill, this park is sheltered by an old-growth redwood grove and offers idyllic stream-side picnicking. A rustic sun-speckled playground area has picnic tables, some of which are situated inside a circle of giant redwoods.

Sweetwater *153 Throckmorton Ave., (415) 388-2820; www.sweetwatersaloon.com.*

This locally legendary nightclub schedules intimate evening performances by an array of noteworthy rock and blues musicians. Bay Area residents Robert Cray and John Lee Hooker have been known to drop in to jam. Call for current lineup and show times.

WHERE TO STAY

Mill Valley Inn *165 Throckmorton Ave., (800) 595-2100, (415) 389-6608, fax (415) 389-5051; www.millvalleyinn.com. 16 rooms, 2 cottages; $$$-$$$+. 2-night min. on weekends. Some fireplaces. Continental breakfast; room service.*

Conveniently situated downtown, this circa 1994 European-style pension is tucked against a redwood-covered hill. Rooms are stylishly furnished with attractive handcrafted pieces from Northern California artists. Some have a balcony with views of the redwoods and Mt. Tamalpais, and two cottages offer privacy in a creekside forest setting. Breakfast in the morning is a buffet taken around the corner at Piazza D'Angelo; it includes an espresso bar and newspaper.

WHERE TO EAT

Avenue Grill *44 E. Blithedale Ave., (415) 388-6003. D daily; $$. Highchairs, boosters, child portions. Reservations advised.*

This noisy, yet cozy contemporary spot features an open dining room and is usually packed. The eclectic dinner menu offers everything from meatloaf to portobello mushrooms on polenta. For dessert, the light crème brulee pairs beautifully with coffee served in one of the restaurant's oversized cups. A large selection of unusual beers is available.

Buckeye Roadhouse *15 Shoreline Hwy., at Mill Valley/Stinson Beach exit off Hwy. 101, (415) 331-2600, fax (415) 331-6067. L&D daily, SunBr; $-$$. Highchairs, boosters, booths, child menu. Reservations advised.*

Situated inside a Bavarian-style chalet dating from 1937, but updated to the tune of $1 million, this unfussy restaurant features generous portions of tasty American-style food at reasonable prices. The main dining room has high peaked ceilings, a large stone fireplace, and dark mahogany accents. Some tables have a pleasant view over the freeway to Strawberry Point. Mixed drinks are on the menu, among them a spicy, delicious Bloody Mary. Winners on the interesting lunch menu include a well-seasoned coleslaw, an ahi sandwich served with pesto mayo and crisp housemade potato chips, and great onion rings—sliced very thin and served with housemade ketchup. Several salads, a pizza, a hamburger, and beer sausages with garlic mashed potatoes are also on the menu. Dinner items are more pricey and include steaks and chops, fresh fish, and assorted game. If the dining room is crowded, a snack can be ordered in the bar.

The Cantina *651 E. Blithedale Ave./Camino Alto, in Blithedale Plaza, (415) 381-1070. L&D daily; $$. Highchairs, boosters, booths, child menu. Reservations advised.*

It is not unusual in Marin County to find a very good restaurant, such as this one, located in a shopping center. Popular at lunch, it becomes more crowded at dinner, when waits can be long, but a variety of tangy margaritas and fresh fruit daiquiris can be ordered, with or without alcohol, to help pass the time. The predictable Mexican items and combination plates are on the large menu, as are a few more unusual ones—green enchiladas topped with a tart tomatillo sauce, an outstanding deep-fried chimichanga topped with guacamole. Chicken mole, fajitas, sandwiches, hamburgers, and steaks are also available. The patio is choice for lunch on warm days; in the evening it is open for drinks only.

Gira Polli *590 E. Blithedale Ave., (415) 383-6040.*

For description, see page 68.

Jennie Low's Chinese Cuisine *38 Miller Ave., in Mill Creek Plaza, (415) 388-8868. L M-Sat, D daily; $. Highchairs, boosters. Reservations advised.*

All items here are prepared without MSG. Co-owner, cooking teacher, and cookbook author Jennie Low has designed a menu making use of her own sauces, available bottled to take home. The menu stresses simple, home-style food that is easy on the spicing, with many low-fat options. Diners can also request dishes prepared with broth instead of oil and with Chinese brown sugar instead of white sugar. Among the best dishes are velvety Snow White Chicken with snow peas and large mushrooms, and Hot Spicy Eggplant accented with earthy wood ear mushrooms. Most of the noodle dishes are also very good, especially the noodle soup. The house tea is a fragrant lychee and black leaf blend that can also be purchased to take home. Because Low's favorite color is lavender, it is used on everything from the menu's type to the servers' uniform, and it is the color of everything she herself wears. And because her lucky number is eight, all menu prices end in eight. Working behind a large glass window, the busy chefs can be observed from the modern, clean-lined dining room.

La Ginestra *127 Throckmorton Ave./Miller Ave., (415) 388-0224, fax (415) 388-7420. D Tu-Sun; $$. Closed 2 weeks in summer. Highchairs, boosters, booths, child portions. No reservations.*

Named for the Scotch Broom flower that is native to both Mount Tamalpais and Sorrento, Italy, this popular, casual spot specializes in Neapolitan cuisine. The ample menu includes a large selection of pastas, pizzas, and veal dishes as well as minestrone soup made with fresh vegetables, and an excellent eggplant Parmesan. All are cooked to order and served with French bread and butter. Veal, chicken, and seafood entrees come with a choice of ravioli, spaghetti, French fries, or fresh vegetables. Fried or sautéed fresh squid is always on the menu along with potato gnocchi, saltimbocca. and housemade ravioli. Desserts include a rich housemade cannoli and a frothy white-wine zabaglione.

Piazza D'Angelo *22 Miller Ave., (415) 388-2000. L&D daily; $-$$. Highchairs, boosters. Reservations advised.*

Designed to resemble an Italian town square, this comfortable restaurant has a retractable skylight over its main dining room and two al fresco patios. Terra cotta floors, original modern art, and contemporary Italian music all help set the mood. Rotisserie-grilled meats are excellent, as are the antipastos, pastas, risotti, and innovative pizzas baked in a wood-burning oven. A rich tiramisu dessert, served in an oversize stemmed glass, is ample for two.

Picnic Pick-Ups.

• **Mill Valley Market** *12 Corte Madera Dr./Throckmorton, (415) 388-3222. M-Sat 7-7:30, Sun 9-7.*

Family-owned since 1929, this small but well-stocked grocery sells everything required for a fabulous picnic. An extensive selection of honeys, mustards, green olives, vinegars, salad dressings, and jams are available, and a deli/bakery tucked in the back dispenses prepared salads and baked goods.

Tiburon

A LITTLE BACKGROUND

Smaller and less well known than Sausalito, Tiburon's tiny Main Street is lined with boutiques, galleries, and restaurants. Its history is actually longer than San Francisco's, because the first explorers who sailed into the bay achored at Ayala Cove. Nearby **Belvedere**, which is Italian for "beautiful view," is Marin's smallest and most exclusive community and is filled with expensive homes.

VISITOR INFORMATION

Tiburon Peninsula Chamber of Commerce
96 Main St., (415) 435-5633, fax (415) 435-1132.

GETTING THERE

Take the Tiburon Boulevard exit off Highway 101. Follow Tiburon Boulevard 4 miles east into town.

WHAT TO DO

Angel Island State Park.

For description, see page 30. A ferry leaves from a dock behind Main Street's restaurants.

Ark Row. *West end of Main St.*

In times past, this street was a lagoon lined with arks and houseboats. Now boutiques operate from within land-bound houseboats, or "arks," that are more than 100 years old. The **Windsor Vineyards tasting room** *(72 Main St.)* dispenses samplings of wines available only here; they also sell their wines with custom messages on the labels.

Bay Audubon Center & Sanctuary *376 Greenwood Beach Rd./Tiburon Blvd., (415) 388-2524. W-Sun 9-5. Adults $4, under 18 $2.*

The 11 acres of land and 900 acres of bay that comprise this National Audubon Society wildlife sanctuary reflect grassland, coastal scrub, freshwater pond, and marsh habitats. A self-guided nature trail leads to a rocky beach and to a lookout spot with sweeping views of Richardson Bay and San Francisco. Except in summer, special programs are scheduled each Sunday.

Also on the property, the yellow 1876 **Lyford House** *(Ext. 103. Sun 1-4; Nov to mid-Apr only.)* is the first and oldest Victorian home in Marin County. Once part of a dairy farm, it was barged across Richardson Bay to this location.

Blackie's Pasture *On Greenwood Beach Rd., off Paradise Dr.*

Blackie was a legendary local horse that grazed here from 1938 to 1966. He was beloved by children in the area, who would feed him goodies from their lunch bags on the way to school. His former pasture is paved over now and is a parking lot. Thankfully, his charming gravesite was spared and can be visited at the edge of the lot, and a metal statue in his likeness now stands here.

A short walk away is **McKegney Green**, an expanse of grass overlooking the bay that is perfect for picnicking and kite-flying. A bike trail runs the 3 miles from here into town.

China Cabin *52 Beach Rd./Tiburon Blvd., Belvedere, (415) 435-1853. W & Sun 1-4; Apr-Oct only. Free.*

This exquisitely restored Victorian social saloon from the side-wheel steamer *SS China*, which provided transpacific mail and passenger service between 1866 and 1886, features 22-karat gold-leaf trim, cut-glass accents, walnut woodwork, and crystal and oil-burning brass chandeliers.

Old St. Hilary's Historic Preserve *1600 Juanita Lane, at Esperanza & Mar West sts., (415) 435-1853. W & Sun 1-4; Apr-Oct only. Free.*

Two rare wildflowers grow in the fields surrounding this also-rare 1888 Carpenter Gothic church. The Black Jewel and the Tiburon Paintbrush are found nowhere else in the world. When the spring wildflowers are blooming, this church displays these two and others from the 217 species protected here, all labeled for easy identification. An exhibit of wildflower photographs is also displayed.

Paradise Beach Park *On Paradise Dr., 1 mi. from town, (415) 435-9212. Daily 7-sunset. $7/vehicle.*

This sheltered, 19-acre bay-front park has a large lawn area and barbecues. The small, quiet beach is nice for wading, and license-free fishing is permitted from the pier. On warm days, the small parking lot fills early.

WHERE TO STAY

Tiburon Lodge *1651 Tiburon Blvd., (800) TIBURON, (800) 762-7770, (415) 435-3133, fax (415) 435-2451. 100 rooms; $$-$$$+. Children under 12 free. Some VCRs & kitchens. Heated pool. Full breakfast.*

The only overnight accommodation in town, this is just 1 block from Main Street. Some rooms have private whirlpool hot tubs; the most unusual is located in a black-tiled bathroom with piped-in music and underwater lights.

WHERE TO EAT

Guaymas *5 Main St., (415) 435-6300. L&D daily, SunBr; $$. Highchairs, boosters. Reservations advised.*

Authentic regional Mexican fare is the specialty at this always-bustling spot. In pleasant surroundings of bleached-wood furnishings and adobe-style decor, diners enjoy sweeping views of San Francisco. On warm days, two outdoor decks are also available. Three styles of margarita and a variety of Mexican beer are on the menu, and approximately 20 different tequilas can be ordered—with a complimentary sangrita chaser (a blend of tomato and orange juices spiked with chilies) if desired. All go well with the delicious complimentary house salsas and tortillas. Though a light meal can be made of just the appetizer platter, save room for the imaginative menu offering a large selection of tantalizing seafood items, the kitchen's forte—spit-roasted meats, and three kinds of delightful tamales. Even desserts are intriguing: a creamy coconut custard flan, a spectacular deep-fried pouch filled with "drunken" bananas and rich vanilla bean ice cream, and delicate Mexican wedding cookies. Everything is made in-house from scratch, and it seems there isn't a loser on the menu.

Picnic Pick-Ups.

- **Let's Eat** *1 Blackfield Dr., in Cove Shopping Center, (415) 383-FOOD, fax (415) 388-3656. Daily 10-7.*

Choose from a continuously changing menu of delicious salads—perhaps a wild rice with smoked cheese and grapes, or a flavorful Mexican chicken sprinkled generously with cilantro. Sandwiches are made to order, and a delicious "panhandle pastry" is sometimes available.

- **Sweet Things** *(415) 388-8583. M-F 8:30-7, Sat 8:30-6, Sun 9:30-6.*

A few doors away from Let's Eat, this spot specializes in great desserts that include a weighty carrot cake, a variety of interesting cookies, and the intriguingly named Fallen Angel Torte and Black Magic Cake.

Sam's Anchor Cafe *27 Main St., (415) 435-4527. L&D daily, Sat & SunBr; $-$$. Highchairs, boosters, child menu. No reservations.*

When the sun is shining, sitting outside on the deck here, watching the boats and seagulls, can be sublime. Dress is casual, and a typical weekend morning finds the rich and famous dining happily right alongside everyday people. Singles make their connections here at brunch, while parents relax with Sam's famous Ramos gin fizz. Cranky sounds from children don't travel far, but seem instead to magically vanish in the air. The brunch menu offers a variety of egg dishes, sandwiches, and salads, as well as a popular burger and fries. Unfortunately, the wait to get in can be long.

Sweden House Bakery *35 Main St., (415) 435-9767. M-F 8-6, Sat & Sun 8-7; $. 1 highchair, boosters.*

This cozy bakery is a good choice for a casual breakfast or lunch enjoyed either in the cozy interior or out on a small deck with a great bay view. For lunch, open-face sandwiches are made with a choice of either German six-grain bread or Swedish Limpa—a rye bread made with molasses and grated orange peel. Soups and salads are also available. Walk-away goodies can be selected from a tantalizing housemade array that includes chocolate tortes, fruit tarts, raspberry shortbread, and chocolate chip cookies.

San Anselmo

A LITTLE BACKGROUND

With more than 130 antique dealers, this sunny town is Northern California's antique capital. And it has no parking meters.

VISITOR INFORMATION

San Anselmo Chamber of Commerce *P.O. Box 2844, San Anselmo 94960, (415) 454-2510, fax (415) 258-2844; www.sananselmo.com.*

GETTING THERE

Located approximately 20 miles north of San Francisco. Take San Anselmo/Sir Francis Drake Boulevard exit off Highway 101 and continue west for approximately 5 miles.

ANNUAL EVENTS

Outdoor Antiques Faire *May. (415) 454-6439 or (415) 457-1241.*

WHAT TO DO

Marin Art and Garden Center *30 Sir Francis Drake Blvd., (415) 454-5597. M & Thur 10-3; Tu, W, F, & Sat 11-4.*

Operated by local volunteers, this historic 10-acre facility is planted with birch, laurel, holly, and rhododendrons and is also home to a rare dawn redwood, an unusual domed sequoia, and a spectacular magnolia tree planted in 1870. **Laurel House Antiques** *((415) 454-8472, fax (415) 454-0550)* operates adjacent selling consignment antiques. Proceeds benefit the center.

WHERE TO EAT

Bubba's Diner *566 San Anselmo Ave./Tunstead, (415) 459-6862. B,L,&D W-M; $. Boosters, booths. No reservations.*

Choose a comfy booth or swivel-stool at the long counter, where a collection of books invites single diners to browse. Breakfast items include buttermilk waffles, honey-whole wheat flapjacks, and brioche French toast as well as sides of grits, oatmeal, and acclaimed housemade biscuits and gravy. Lunch brings on a veggie burger and hamburger (made with fresh house-ground chuck), a portobello mushroom sandwich, and a flavorful open-face roasted turkey breast sandwich with gravy. Sides of a beautifully presented iceberg lettuce salad and housemade pickles should not be overlooked. Beginning at 5:30 p.m. the dinner menu offers baked meatloaf, chicken-fried steak, and a flavorful vegetable-bean chili. Blue-plate specials include buttermilk-marinated fried chicken on Wednesday and pot roast on Saturday. Do leave room for dessert, most especially the banana-butterscotch pie and tapioca pudding. With food this good, prices this low, and space this tight, there is usually a wait to get in. Pass the time checking out the local scene while lounging on one of the sturdy benches out front.

Cucina Jackson Fillmore *337 San Anselmo Ave./Ross Ave., (415) 721-4339. D Tu-Sun; $$.*

For description, see page 70.

Insalata's *120 Sir Francis Drake Blvd./Barber Ave., (415) 457-7700, fax (415) 457-8375. L M-Sat, SunBr, D daily; $$. Reservations recommended.*

The airy, open interior here is filled with good tables and even a few secluded booths. Walls are decorated with large French pastels of fruits done by San Francisco artist Laura Parker. Mediterranean fare dominates the menu, with lunch offerings including pastas, an unusual Tunisian seven-vegetable tagine with preserved lemons, and braised beef cheeks in a cabbage wrap zested up with horseradish cream. At dinner, delicious Spanish-style short ribs flavored with chocolate, sherry, and orange are sometimes available. All breads and desserts are made in-house. At brunch, try the tasty egg scramble with a side of perfectly browned and spiced homefries, or a Syrian chicken Fattoush salad tossed with toasted pita and a lemon-herb vinaigrette. But don't miss the to-die-for pecan sticky buns. Desserts are exotic: blood orange granita with vanilla bean madeleines; creamy risotto pudding with Chianti-soaked figs and a crisp almond twist. By the way, Insalata is chef-owner Heidi Krahling's maiden name. This restaurant is situated in an area filled with prime antique shops, making for great after-dining browsing.

Taqueria Mexican Grill *1001 Sir Francis Drake Blvd./College, in Kentfield, (415) 453-5811. L&D daily; $. Highchairs. No reservations. No cards.*

Nestled under tall redwoods, this fast-food spot is decorated with tile floors, massive wooden benches and tables, a jukebox playing Mexican tunes, and piñatas. All help set the mood for the burritos, chimichangas, and tacos that are the menu mainstays. A hamburger is also on the menu.

Larkspur & Corte Madera

A LITTLE BACKGROUND

The downtown area of charming Larkspur is listed on the National Register of Historic Places.

VISITOR INFORMATION

Larkspur Chamber of Commerce *P.O. Box 315, Larkspur 94977, (888) 800-5655, (415) 925-0759, fax (415) 925-0759.*

GETTING THERE

Take the Paradise exit off Highway 101. Follow Tamalpais Drive west until it becomes Redwood.

WHAT TO DO

Book Passage *51 Tamal Vista Blvd., Corte Madera, (415) 927-0960, fax (415) 927-1502; www.bookpassage.com.*

This very browsable shop has the best collection of travel books and mysteries around. A cafe serves coffees and simple foods, and very special author events are scheduled regularly.

WHERE TO EAT

Chai of Larkspur *25 Ward St./Magnolia, Corte Madera, (415) 945-7161, (415) fax 945-7164; www.chaioflarkspur.com. B,L,& tea Tu-Sun; tea $18-$20. Reservations advised.*

Offering a tranquil respite from the bustle of everyday life, this tea salon has a variety of tea services. Amid persimmon walls and chintz-covered chairs, tea-lovers sit and select perhaps a Mediterranean or Asian service, or maybe a traditional British high tea. Over 70 imported loose teas, tea accouterments, and tea-related gifts are also for sale. Live music—harp, blues, jazz, opera—is scheduled regularly.

El Quijoté *125 E. Sir Francis Drake Blvd., near Larkspur Landing, Larkspur, (415) 925-9391, fax (415) 925-1804. D daily; $$. Reservations advised. Free valet parking.*

Situated within former brick kilns, this unusual restaurant exudes a romantic atmosphere. A selection of tapas followed by a shared paella and dessert seems the way to go, but more substantial entrees are also available. Particularly tasty tapas include cool, Spanish-style ceviche and warm, seafood-stuffed Spanish piquillo red peppers. For those who thrive on the unusual, there is poached octopus and sautéed tripe. Live flamenco dancing is scheduled on weekends in the cozy bar, where choice dining tables are also available.

Lark Creek Inn *234 Magnolia Ave., Larkspur, (415) 924-7766, fax (415) 924-7117. L M-F, D daily, SunBr; $$-$$$. Highchairs, boosters, child menu. Reservations advised.*

Situated beneath a cluster of tall redwoods within an 1888 Victorian historical landmark, this destination restaurant is known for its seasonal farm-fresh American fare created by owner-chef Bradley Ogden. Seating is in the airy main dining room, in a smaller upstairs room, and on a brick patio—the spot of choice in warm weather. One dinner enjoyed on the patio here, out under the stars on a night of perfect temperature, started with a salad of heirloom tomatoes and local goat cheese. It was followed by an oak-grilled salmon entree with a variety of baby vegetables, and the memorable housemade dessert conclusion was coconut cake with blackberry swirl ice cream. Ingredients are secured from local sources when possible.

Pasticceria Rulli *464-470 Magnolia Ave., Larkspur, (415) 924-7478. Daily 7-7, F & Sat to 11; $. No cards.*

Offering what must be the most mouth-watering selection of sweets found this side of Milan, and displaying them in gleaming mahogany-and-glass cases worthy of jewels, this treasure chest is an authentic Italian pasty shop offering exquisite confections, including an enormous selection of chocolates and candies and ten kinds of gelato, plus seasonal specialties. It is possible to select and indulge in-house, along with an espresso or other beverage, and an extensive hot panini (sandwich) menu is also available.

World Wrapps *208 Corte Madera Town Center, Corte Madera, (415) 927-3663, fax (415) 927-3569.*

For description, see page 82.

Yet Wah *2019 Larkspur Landing Circle, Larkspur (415) 461-3631. L&D daily.*

For description, see page 82.

San Rafael

A LITTLE BACKGROUND

The oldest and largest city in Marin, San Rafael also has the best weather. It is located in Marin County's sunbelt and is an enchanting place to dine outdoors on a warm summer evening. A lot of artists and performers hide away here. A further claim to fame is that many silent films were shot here, and Fourth Street was the setting for George Lucas's *American Graffiti*. Take a walking tour of the historic downtown area by obtaining a guide from the chamber of commerce, and then following the plaque markers embedded in the sidewalk across the street from each site.

VISITOR INFORMATION

San Rafael Chamber of Commerce
817 Mission Ave., (800) 454-4163, (415) 454-4163, fax (415) 454-7039; www.sanrafael.org.

ANNUAL EVENTS

Marin County Fair *July. At Civic Center Fairgrounds; (415) 499-6400; www.marinfair.org. Adults $9, seniors & under 13 $7.*

Five days of fun include evening performances by big name entertainers and a low-level fireworks display. All entertainment and carnival rides are included in the admission fee. This fair is highly regarded for its innovation and creativity.

Marin Shakespeare Festival *July-Sept. At Forest Meadows Amphitheatre, Dominican College; (415) 456-8104, fax (415) 499-1492; www.marinShakespeare.org. Adults $20, 65+ $18, under 19 $12.*

This summer-long festival is presented in an intimate 600-seat outdoor theater.

WHAT TO DO

China Camp State Park *Take Civic Center exit off Hwy. 101, follow N. San Pedro Rd. east for 3 mi., (415) 456-0766. Daily 8-sunset. Free. Parking $3.*

Once the largest fishing settlement along this shore, this fishing village was home to hundreds of Chinese fishermen in the late 1800s.

Now visitors see the rustic, weathered remains of the pier and buildings. A Visitors Center displays period photographs and artifacts documenting the shrimping and fishing that occurred here until a 1911 ordinance outlawed the camp's primitive shrimp-trapping method. A charming small beach invites sunbathing and picnicking, and an old-time snack bar with a counter and swivel stools dispenses fast fare on weekends. In addition to the village, this 1,640-acre park has hiking trails through the hills, and campsites are available.

Downtown Art Center *1337 4th St./C St., (415) 451-8119. Tu-Sat 11-6.*

Housed in an historic 1870 opera house, **The Gallery Store** sells many of the unique items made by artists working in 30 studios in the back. Visitors are welcome to view these artists at work. The **Underground Gallery** *((415) 451-1815.)* hangs changing exhibits on its natural brick walls, and art classes are regularly scheduled for both adults and children.

Falkirk Cultural Center *1408 Mission Ave./E St., (415) 485-3328, fax (415) 485-3404; www.falkirkculturalcenter.org. Tu-F 10-5, Thur 10-9, Sat 10-1.*

This 17-room Queen Anne Victorian mansion, built in 1888 atop a hill just a few blocks from town, features original coffered ceilings, rich redwood paneling, decorative fireplaces, and stunning floor-to-ceiling stained-glass windows. Named for the lumber baron-owner's birthplace in Scotland, it now displays contemporary art in upstairs galleries. Eleven acres of formal gardens surround the house. Special events include a haunted house in October, an Alice-in-Wonderland egg hunt at Easter, and a Christmas program.

Guide Dogs for the Blind *350 Los Ranchitos Rd., (800) 295-4050, (415) 499-4000; www.guidedogs.com. Tours M-Sat at 10:30 & 2. Free.*

Formed to help servicemen blinded in World War II, this school for guide dogs presents new graduates to their visually-impaired partners at a monthly graduation ceremony. Tours include the kennels, dorms, and 11-acre campus. It is possible to become a foster home to one of the dogs in transition, or to raise a puppy for this service.

Marin County Civic Center *N. San Pedro Rd./Civic Center exit off Hwy. 101. Self-guided tours: M-F 9-6. Guided tours: (415) 499-6646; W at 10:30am; $3 donation.*

The last building designed by Frank Lloyd Wright before he died, this "bridge between two hills" is a national and state historic landmark. It also is where local resident George Lucas filmed his first big movie in 1971—*THX11380*—and houses various city offices and a performing arts and convention center. A 14-acre lagoon is surrounded by grassy areas perfect for picnicking and strolling.

Marin County Historical Society Museum *1125 B St., in Boyd Park, (415) 454-8538, fax (415) 454-6137; www.marinweb.com/marinhistory. Thur-Sat 1-4, 1st Thur of month to 7. Free.*

Situated within the Victorian Gothic **Boyd Gate House**, built in 1880, this museum is filled with area memorabilia. It commemorates the life and travels of Louise Boyd, an Arctic explorer and the first woman to fly over the North Pole.

McNears Beach Park *201 Cantera Rd., (415) 499-6387. Daily 8-8 in summer; call for off-season schedule. Admission $2 for walk-in, bike-in, or boat-in; $7/vehicle.*

A former country club, this very popular spot is equipped with a heated swimming pool, concession stand, fishing pier, picnic area with barbecue pits and tables, and two tennis courts. A terrific sandy wading beach fronts San Pablo Bay.

Mission San Rafael Archangel *1104 5th Ave., (415) 454-8141, fax (415) 454-8193. Daily 11-4. Free.*

Founded in 1817, this was the 20th mission. It was replicated in 1949 on the approximate site of the original mission and embodies some of the characteristics of the original mission church—star windows modeled after those at the Carmel Mission and a bell hung from cross beams. Visitors can take a self-guided audiotape tour. A tiny adjoining museum displays vintage photos of its reconstruction and original furniture.

Rafael Film Center *1118 4th St./B St., (415) 454-1222; www.finc.org. Adults $7, 60+ & under 13 $4.75.*

Built in 1938, this old film palace has been been renovated into a three-screen theater featuring first-run, independent, and vintage films. Each theater is equipped with the very best in sound and image projection, featuring THX and Dolby sound systems, and each has its own personality. The lobby and richly colored main theater reflect the original art deco style, with blue velvet drapes and marvelous period chandeliers. On the second floor, theater Two has the posh feel of the '20s, and the more streamlined decor of theater Three portrays a futuristic sense. Everything used in construction is non-toxic, so patrons don't have to fear the headaches and other health problems associated with off-gassing in most new construction. A special program for kids features obscure European films.

WildCare: Terwilliger Nature Education and Wildlife Rehabilitation *76 Albert Park Ln./B St., (415) 456-7283, fax (415) 456-0594. Daily 9-5. Free.*

Ill and orphaned animals are nursed back to health at this emergency veterinary hospital. When recovered, they are returned to their natural habitat. Visitors can view the animals, and a nature center has wildlife displays and hands-on exhibits. And this is where to sign up for "something special"—a nature discovery walk led by Mrs. Terwilliger herself. This organization also operates the Living with Wildlife Hotline, which provides tips on how to persuade various wild animals to take up residence elsewhere.

WHERE TO STAY

Embassy Suites *101 McInnis Pkwy., (800) EMBASSY, (415) 499-9222, fax (415) 499-9268; www.embassymarin.com.*

Situated just a footbridge away from the Marin Civic Center, this hotel often runs a special package with the Marin County Fair. For more description, see page 364.

WHERE TO EAT

Erik's Downtown Drive-In *836 2nd St., (415) 454-6605. B,L,&D daily; $. No cards.*

This is a great place to stop for a quick snack or meal. The car hops are gone, so it's park the car, order at the window, and then sit in a small inside dining area or outside at tables resembling Coke bottle tops. The fare is simple—burgers (including veggie burgers and ostrich burgers), dogs, cheese steaks, and chicken. Italian sodas, fresh fruit shakes, and coffee specialties are also available.

Lundy's Home Cooking *1143 4th St./B St., (415) 456-7669. B&L daily; $. No reservations. No cards.*

The usual breakfast items are available along with crumbly-good corn muffins, made fresh in the kitchen, and a variety of coffees and fresh-squeezed orange and grapefruit juices. Lunch items include an excellent hamburger, a frankfurter on a French baguette, and a grilled Swiss on rye—all served with a side of French fries or salad. The wonderful jams, soups, and desserts—even the mayonnaise—are all made from scratch. Seating is at tiny tables or at a long counter with swiveling stools.

Mayflower Inne *1533 4th St./E St., (415) 456-1011. L&D daily; $-$$. Highchairs, boosters, child portions. Reservations advised.*

This place offers the chance to experience the cozy ambiance of an English pub without leaving the country. Waitresses have been known to greet customers with a cheery "Hello, lovies" when presenting the menu. Among the traditional bland-but-hearty English items: steak and kidney pie, Cornish pasties (beef stew wrapped in a crescent pie pastry), bangers (English sausages), and fish & chips. Appetizers are a tad more interesting: a sausage roll (sausage baked in a pastry), a Scotch egg (hard-boiled egg rolled in sausage meat and bread crumbs and then deep-fried). English ales and beers are on tap, and dessert is a choice of fresh rhubarb pie, sherry trifle (a pudding), or chocolate cake. It is possible to relax in the English manner by indulging in a friendly game of darts or Ping-Pong.

Panama Hotel *4 Bayview St., (800) 899-3993, (415) 457-3993, fx (415) 457-6240; www.panamahotel.com. L M-F, D Tu-Sun, SunBr; $-$$.*

This charming dining room, with colorfully washed walls and eclectic decor, serves delicious, full-flavored renditions of Mexican-, Italian-, and Asian-influenced cuisines. Don't miss the stuffed pasilla pepper appetizer and Tuscan toast with relish. Fresh seafood and pastas are primo. Music is on the menu Tuesday and Thursday nights, and a tropical garden patio, reminiscent of something found in Key West or South America, is the way to go in warm weather.

Guest rooms *(15 rooms; $-$$$. Some kitchens; some shared baths. Continental breakfast; room service.)* are also available. Some rooms have clawfoot tubs, others have canopy beds, and yet others have vine-covered private balconies. The late Jerry Garcia is said to have kept a girlfriend lodged here for months and months. About the name. A former owner thought every town should have a Panama Hotel, and so this rambling structure, consisting of two 1910 homes connected by a patio, became San Rafael's.

The Rice Table *1617 Fourth St./G St., (415) 456-1808, same fax. D W-Sun; $$. Highchairs, boosters, booths. Reservations advised.*

The Indonesian islands were once also known as the "Spice Islands," as that area is where many spices originate. During their domination of Indonesia, the Dutch served some of the best native dishes at huge feasts called "rijsttafel" or "rice table." A West Java version of this elaborate dinner is served in this cozy, atmospherically decorated room. The rice table dinner begins with shrimp chips and several dipping sauces, green pea vegetable soup, deep-fried lumpia (like Chinese spring rolls), a salad with lemon dressing, both white and saffron-yellow rice, pickled vegetables, and roasted coconut. Then come marinated chicken satay, shrimp sautéed in butter and tamarind, a mild chicken curry, beef sautéed in soy sauce and cloves, fried rice noodles, and fried bananas for dessert. Less elaborate meals and vegetarian meals are also available. Beer, which perfectly compliments the food, is available along with Indonesian-style coffee, fresh tamarind juice, and several kinds of tea.

Tea-n-Crumpets *817 4th St., (415) 457-2495; www.tea-n-crumpets.com. M-F 7:30-6, Sat 9-5:30; $. No cards.*

Light, house-baked, fat-free crumpets are always on the menu here and can be purchased in quantity to take home. Sometimes it is possible to see them being prepared through the front windows. Scones, real Devonshire cream, and an enormous selection of teas are also available. The narrow, deep dining room is comfortable, with exposed brick walls and seating at informal tables.

Novato

VISITOR INFORMATION

Novato Chamber of Commerce *807 DeLong Ave., (415) 897-1164, fax (415) 898-9097; www.novato.org.*

WHAT TO DO

Marin Museum of the American Indian *2200 Novato Blvd., in Miwok Park, (415) 897-4064. Tu-F 10-3, Sat & Sun 12-4; tour Sun at 1:30. By donation.*

Marin County's earliest residents, the Miwok and Pomo Indians, are honored at this interactive museum. Exhibits and artifacts include tools, baskets, boats, and animal skins. Visitors can learn traditional Native American games, grind acorns with an authentic mortar, and visit a native plant garden. The 35-acre park has hiking trails, playing fields, and picnic facilities.

Novato History Museum *815 DeLong Ave., (415) 897-4320. W, Thur, Sat 12-4. Free.*

Built in 1850, the Victorian house this museum operates within is now home to a collection of antique dolls, toy trains, and pioneer tools that reflect the town's history.

WHERE TO EAT

Jennie Low's Chinese Cuisine *In Vintage Oaks Shopping Center, (415) 892-8838. L M-Sat, D daily; $.*

For description, see page 194.

Petaluma

A LITTLE BACKGROUND

Located less than an hour's drive north of San Francisco, Petaluma offers an old-fashioned small town atmosphere. Perhaps this is why it was chosen as the filming location for both *American Graffiti* and *Peggy Sue Got Married.* In fact, director Francis Ford Coppola is quoted as saying, "You can find any decade you want somewhere in Petaluma."

Once known as the "World's Egg Basket," this area still produces plenty of eggs but is currently better known as a dairy center.

It's pleasant to spend a day here, just walking around the downtown area. Noteworthy among the numerous antique shops is the architecturally magnificent **Vintage Bank Antiques** *(101 Petaluma Blvd. N., (707) 769-3097. Daily 10-5:30.),* located inside a former Wells Fargo bank. Also an antique of sorts is an old-time barbershop with a swirling pole at 152 Kentucky Street. The residential area is also worth checking out for its large collection of Victorian homes.

VISITOR INFORMATION

Petaluma Visitor's Program *799 Baywood Dr. #1, (877)-2-PETALUMA, (707) 769-0429, fax (707) 762-4721; www.petaluma.org.*

GETTING THERE

Located approximately 50 miles north of San Francisco.

ANNUAL EVENTS

Butter & Egg Days *April. (707) 769-0429. Free.*

In the past the hometown parade that kicks off this celebration has been populated with giant papier-mâché cows, huge dairy trucks converted into floats, and flocks of children dressed as chickens. Other events have included an Egg Toss, a Team Butter Churning Contest, and the Cutest Little Chick in Town Contest—when the imaginative costumes of those marching chickens, limited to ages 1 through 8, are judged,

The **Petaluma Outdoor Antique Faire** *((707) 763-9177)* takes place the next day on a street that is blocked off to traffic.

Ugly Dog Contest *June. (707) 763-0931. Fair admission: adults $6.50, 7-12 $3, free to those who enter a dog.*

Just one of the many events scheduled at the annual **Sonoma-Marin Fair,** this good-spirited contest has three divisions: Pedigree Class, Mutt Class, and Ring of Champions. Every dog wins a prize, and losers get a certificate stating they "are just too beautiful to be considered ugly."

Petaluma River Festival *August. (707) 762-5331. By donation.*

Once home to the third-busiest river in the state, this town celebrates its steamboat heyday with an old-fashioned pancake breakfast and boat rides galore. Usually the *Alma,* an 1891 scow schooner berthed at San Franciso's Hyde Street Pier, is on hand for tours and sea chantey sing-alongs led by park rangers.

Petaluma Summer Music Festival *August. (707) 763-8920, fax (707) 763-8929. $14-$20.*

This festival features diverse musical events that appeal to all ages. Many are scheduled in locations of historical interest.

World Wrist Wrestling Championships *October. (707) 778-1430; www.armwrestling.com. $10.*

Begun in a local bar, this contest became a world's championship in 1962. Anyone who pays the $25 entry fee can vie for the titles of right-handed and left-handed heavyweight, middleweight, lightweight, featherweight, and bantamweight.

WHAT TO DO

Garden Valley Ranch *498 Pepper Rd., 3 mi. north of town (call for directions), (707) 795-0919, fax (707) 792-0349; www.gardenvalley.com. W-Sun 10-4. Closed late Dec to mid-Jan. Adults $4, under 12 $2.*

This 8-acre ranch is the largest commercial grower of garden roses in the U.S. Among their well-known customers are the late Jacqueline Onassis (for daughter Caroline's wedding), Elizabeth Taylor, Whitney Huston, Barbra Streisand, and Martha Stewart. In one garden, over 4,000 rosebushes are cultivated for cuttings. In another, plants are grown for their perfume, and some are used for potpourri. The best time for viewing is May through October, when the roses are in full bloom. The admission fee includes a self-guided tour brochure. When a private party is scheduled, the gardens are closed to the public, but the nursery and test garden remain open; call ahead to verify.

The Great Petaluma Desert *5010 Bodega Ave., (707) 778-8278, fax (707) 778-0931; www.gpdesert. com. F-Sun 10-5, in winter to 4. Free.*

Featuring one of the largest selections of rare and exotic cacti and succulents in the country, this dramatic back roads nursery boasts nine greenhouses. Most of the stock is propagated on site. A few of the greenhouses are off-limits except to collectors who call ahead, but those that are accessible should satisfy most people. Among the most popular plants are tillandsia, also known as "air plants" because they require no soil.

Marin French Cheese Co./Rouge et Noir *7500 Red Hill Rd. (also known as Petaluma-Point Reyes Rd.), (800) 292-6001, (707) 762-6001, fax (707) 762-0430. Sales room daily 9-5; tours daily 10-4, on the hour. Free.*

Located way out in the country, this cheese factory has been operated by the Thompson family since 1865. By now, they have perfected the art of making Camembert cheese. They also make good Brie, schloss, and breakfast cheeses —all from milk produced by a local herd of Jersey cows. Tours take visitors through the factory and explain how these special cheeses are produced, and cheeses are sampled at the end. Picnic supplies are available in an adjoining store, where these house cheeses are on sale along with salami, French bread, sandwiches, crackers, soft drinks, juices, and ice cream. Two expansive grassy areas, one with a large pond, beckon for picnics. Some picnic tables are also available.

Petaluma Adobe State Historic Park *3325 Adobe Rd., 5 mi. east of town, (707) 762-4871. Daily 10-5. Adults $2, 6-11 $1.*

The boundaries of General Vallejo's vast 66,000-acre land grant once stretched from the Petaluma River on the west, to San Pablo Bay on the south, to Sonoma on the east, to Cotati and Glen Ellen on the North. This rancho, which was part of the estate, has been restored to reflect life as it was here in 1840. The living quarters, a weaving shop, and a blacksmith's forge display authentic furnishings and are all seen on the self-guided tour. An assortment of animals, including sheep and goats, roam freely. Shaded picnic tables are located by Adobe Creek.

The most interesting times to visit are for the annual events, including **Sheep Shearing** in April, **Living History Day** in May, and the **Old Adobe Fiesta**—with demonstrations of early California crafts and the chance for visitors to weave baskets and make hand-dipped candles—in August.

WHERE TO STAY

Cavanagh Inn *10 Keller St., (888) 765-4658, (707) 765-4657, fax (707) 769-0466; www.cavanaghinn.com. 7 rooms; 100% non-smoking;*

$-$$. Some shared baths. Evening snack, full breakfast.

The town's very first B&B, this large 1902 Georgian Revival mansion is just a few blocks from the historic downtown. It features gorgeous, rare, heart redwood paneling. Guest rooms are in both the main house and an adjacent cottage. Homemade cookies appear in each room at turndown, and breakfast is served in a beautifully appointed formal dining room.

KOA Kampground *20 Rainsville Rd., (800) KOA-1233, (707) 763-1492.*

For description, see page 415.

Quality Inn *5100 Montero Way, (800) 228-5151, (707) 664-1155, fax (707) 664-8566; www.lokhotels.com. 110 rooms; $$; 2-night min. May-Oct. Children under 19 free. Heated pool (unavail. Oct-Apr), hot tub, sauna. Continental breakfast. Dogs welcome.*

Located on the outskirts of town, this is a link in a chain known for its attractive Cape Cod-style of architecture and comfortable modern rooms. A generous buffet breakfast of hot drinks, pastries, cereals, and fresh fruit is served in the lobby.

WHERE TO EAT

McNear's Saloon & Dining House *23 Petaluma Blvd. N., (707) 765-2121, fax (707) 765-4671. L&D daily, Sat & SunBr; $-$$. Highchairs, boosters, booths, child menu.*

Located inside the historic 1886 McNear Building, this casual restaurant and sports bar serves an extensive eclectic menu. Diners can get great bar food, such as spicy buffalo wings and beer-batter mushrooms, as well as housemade soups, salads, sandwiches, hamburgers, barbecued chicken and ribs, pastas, and steaks. On fair weather days, windows are opened wide in the front dining area near the sidewalk, allowing for pleasant people-watching. The attached **McNear's Mystic Theatre** presents live music on Friday and Saturday nights.

Sonoma Taco Shop *953 Lakeville St., in Gateway Shopping Ctr., (707) 778-7921.*

For description, see page 208.

Santa Rosa

A LITTLE BACKGROUND

Believe it or not!, Robert Ripley was born, raised, and buried in Santa Rosa! Unfortunately, the museum that once honored him here has been dismantled.

VISITOR INFORMATION

Santa Rosa Convention & Visitors Bureau
9 Fourth St., (800) 404-ROSE, (707) 577-8674, fax (707) 571-5949; www.visitsantarosa.com.

Sonoma County Tourism Program
520 Mendocino Ave. #210, (800) 5-SONOMA, (707) 565-5383, fax (707) 565-5385; www.sonomacounty.com.

Sonoma County Farm Trails *(800) 207-9464, (707) 571-8288, fax (707) 571-7719; www.farmtrails.org.*

Call for a free map of area farms that sell directly to the consumer. The map pinpoints the location of u-pick farms as well as of farms selling more unusual items such as fresh rabbits, pheasants, herbs, and mushrooms—even feather pillows and earthworms.

GETTING THERE

Located approximately 10 miles north of Petaluma, and 60 miles north of San Francisco.

ANNUAL EVENTS

Luther Burbank Rose Parade Festival *May. (707) 542-7673, fax (707) 545-6914. Free.*

Some variation of this parade has been a tradition in town for over 100 years. It began in 1894 as a Rose Carnival and has continued most years since as some sort of parade. The current version hasn't missed a year since 1950.

Santa Rosa DixieJazz Festival *August. (707) 539-3494, same fax. $15-$50.*

WHAT TO DO

California Welcome Center *5000 Roberts Lake Rd., in Rohnert Park, 3 mi. south of town, (800) 939-7666, (707) 586-3795, fax (707) 586-1383; www.sonomawine.com. Daily 9-5.*

Get oriented to this area's attractions and do some free wine tasting here. Local wines and foods are for sale, and special events are often scheduled.

Howarth Memorial Park *Summerfield Rd., access from Sonoma Ave. & Montgomery Dr., (707) 543-3282. Rides: in summer, Tu-Sun 11-4; in spring & fall, Sat & Sun only. Closed Nov-Jan. $1-$1.50.*

There is something for everyone in this scenic park. Children especially enjoy the free playground but, of course, also love the attractions with an admission fee: miniature train, animal barn, pony rides, and merry-go-round. Paddleboat, rowboat, and sailboat rentals are available by Lake Ralphine, and hiking trails and tennis courts round out the facilities.

Luther Burbank Home & Gardens *Santa Rosa Ave./Sonoma Ave., (707) 524-5445, fax (707) 543-3030. Gardens: Daily 8-7; Nov-Mar to 5; free. Museum & House Tours: Tu-Sun 10-3:30; closed Oct-Mar. Museum free; house tours: adults $3, under 12 free.*

During his 50-year horticultural career, Luther Burbank developed over 800 new plants. This memorial garden displays many of his achievements, including a plumcot tree, the ornamental Shasta daisy, and a warren of spineless cacti. (He also developed the Santa Rosa plum and elephant garlic.) Burbank is buried here in an unmarked grave. Tours of his charming greenhouse and modified Greek Revival-style home, which retains its original furnishings, last 1/2 hour. The adjacent **Carriage House Museum** offers annual exhibits related to Burbank's life and work.

Railroad Square *Centered at 4th St./Davis St., (707) 578-8478.*

Now a national historic district, this area is thick with antique stores, restaurants, and specialty shops.

Redwood Empire Ice Arena *1667 W. Steele Lane, (707) 546-7147; www.snoopygift.com. Open daily; call for schedule. Adults $7.50, under 12 $6.50, skate rental included.*

Built in 1969, this ice-skating rink has been called "the most beautiful ice arena in the world." Since it was owned by the late cartoonist Charles Schulz, the Alpine decor is unexpected. However, the fast-food coffee shop does have a few stained-glass windows depicting Snoopy.

Located adjacent, **Snoopy's Gallery and Gift Shop** *((707) 546-3385. Daily 10-6.)* purveys the largest selection of "Peanuts" merchandise in the world. Cuddly Snoopys are available in sizes ranging from 4 inches to 5 feet. Copies of original "Peanuts" columns, matted and framed, are also available. Above the shop is a small museum containing Schulz's awards and some of his favorite drawings, as well as an assortment of other interesting items.

Each December the rink is converted into a theater for a special **Christmas Show**, when Snoopy always makes an appearance on ice skates. Some ice-side tables are available, and tickets sell out fast *((707) 546-3385).*

Sonoma County Museum *425 Seventh St., (707) 579-1500, fax (707) 579-4849. W-Sun 11-4; www.pressdemo.com/scmuseum. Adults $2, 65+ & 13-19 $1.*

Located inside the city's beautifully restored 1910 post office building, this museum exhibits material relating to the county's history.

Victorian Homes.

To view lovely Victorian mansions, drive along MacDonald Avenue in the older part of town.

WINERIES

Kendall-Jackson Wine Center *5007 Fulton Rd., north of town, in Fulton, (707) 571-8100, fax (707) 569-0105. Tasting daily 10-5 (fee $2; keep logo tasting glass); tours at 11, 1, & 3.*

Set amidst a mature walnut orchard and surrounded by 120 acres of vineyards, this château-like tasting room features new releases that often are not yet available in retail outlets. A large, educational Organic Demonstration Garden is planted with the herbs and vegetables representing Asia, South America, France, and Italy, demonstrating the diversity as well as the similarities of these cultures. The unique Wine Sensory Gardens permit visitors to wander, wine glass in hand, smelling and tasting the various vegetables, herbs, fruits, and flowers that compose wine tasting descriptors, and a Viticulture Exhibit permits a self-guided tour of a 1-acre vineyard identifying 26 distinct types of grapes and illustrating the 19 grapevine trellising systems most commonly used in California.

Martini & Prati Winery *2191 Laguna Rd., (800) 955-9585, (707) 823-2404 or (707) 829-6150, fax (707) 829-6151; www.martiniprati.com. Tasting daily 11-4; tour daily at 11.*

Founded in 1881, this rustic winery was purchased in 1902 by Rafael Martini, who hailed from Lucca, Italy and is the ancestor of today's owners. It was one of the few wineries to stay open during Prohibition, when it had a license to make sacramental wines, and is one of the oldest continuously operating wineries in California. Sort of a living museum of California wine-making, today's winery is state of the art 1938-style, when it was built. The specialty is classic Italian varietals—Sangiovese, Pinot Bianco, Barbera—and labels feature vintage photos from the family album. The facility holds enormous redwood tanks, some almost a century old, and still uses its original crush-pad pump, a 1948 Chevrolet Loadmaster truck, and a 1946 red military jeep. And the wine is still fermented in big concrete tanks, seen on the tour. Visitors can purchase a jug from the winery and fill it right from the tank with an unfiltered blend of Zinfandel, and an inviting shaded picnic area is available.

Matanzas Creek Winery *6097 Bennett Valley Rd., 5 mi. east of Hwy. 101 (call for directions), (800) 590-6464, (707) 528-6464, fax (707) 571-0156; www.winery.com. Tasting (fee $2) & tours daily 10-4:30.*

Located way off the beaten track, back in some rolling foothills far away from other enterprise, this winery is the state's largest producer of lavender, growing both the Provence variety for cooking and the Grosso variety for scenting soaps and oils. Peak bloom is in June, and an assortment of products made with the bounty, including handmade soaps and sachets, are sold in the gift shop. Additionally, the winery tasting room is surrounded by a beautifully maintained garden dotted with modern sculpture and several fountains, and two llamas are housed off the parking lot. A picnic area is available.

WHERE TO STAY

Flamingo Resort Hotel & Conference Center *2777 4th St./Hwy. 12, (800) 848-8300, (707) 545-8530, fax (707) 528-1404; www.flamingoresort.com. 170 rooms; 100% non-smoking; $$-$$$; 2-night min. on summer weekends. Children under 12 free. Heated pool, children's wading pool, hot tub, fitness center (fee), 5 tennis courts (fee). Restaurant, room service.*

When this spacious, unpretentious resort was originally built, it was out in the country. Now, due to urban sprawl, it is right in town. Providing all the comforts of a full-service resort, it also gives guests the convenience of a motel—parking just outside their room; not having to walk through a lobby—with the amenities of a hotel—a piano bar with live entertainment and dancing. Facilities include a children's playground, shuffleboard, Ping-Pong, and a lighted jogging path. The Olympic-size pool is heated year-round, and a state-of-the-art fitness center features sauna and steam rooms, basketball and volleyball courts, and massage service. Packages are available.

The Gables *4257 Petaluma Hill Rd., (800) GABLES-N, (707) 585-7777, fax (707) 584-5634. 7 rooms, 1 cottage; 100% non-smoking; $$$-$$$+; 2-night min. on Sat. Unsuitable for children under 12. No TVs; 1 kitchen; some wood-burning & gas fireplaces. Afternoon snack, full breakfast.*

Named for the 15 gables that crown this 1877 High Victorian Gothic Revival house, this inn welcomes guests with spacious rooms furnished with antiques and clawfoot tubs. Among its unusual features are three Italian marble fireplaces that were shipped around the Horn, a steep mahogany spiral staircase, keyhole-shaped windows, and 12-foot ceilings. In the horse-and-buggy days, governors and legislators stopped their wagons here for country hospitality. More house history is found in the parlor, where historical photos of the house and a copy of a thesis about the house written by a Sonoma State professor are available for perusal; quilt pieces made by the original owner are displayed here as wall decorations. The house is set on 3 1/2 acres in a rural area reminiscent of the south of France. The original outhouse and a 150-year-old barn remain, and a bucolic deck invites sun worship. All this and one of Northern California's best inn breakfasts, too.

Hilton *3555 Round Barn Blvd., (800) HILTONS, (800) 321-3232, (707) 523-7555, fax (707) 569-5555; www.sonomacounty.hilton.com. 246 rooms; $$. Children under 18 free. Pool (heated in summer only), hot tub, fitness center. Restaurant, room service.*

Sprawled across one of the few hills in town, this comfortable contemporary lodging offers guests a 7.5-mile jogging trail and sand volleyball court as well as access to golf and tennis facilities at a nearby country club.

Hotel La Rose *308 Wilson St., in Railroad Square, (800) LAROSE-8, (707) 579-3200, fax (707) 579-3247; www.hotellarose.com. 4 stories; 49 rooms; $$$-$$$+. Children under 13 free. Hot tub. Continental breakfast; restaurant, room service. Free valet parking.*

This well-located, European-style small hotel was built in 1907 of cut stone quarried from the nearby area now known as Annadel State Park. On the National Register of Historic Places, it combines turn-of-the-century charm with modern conveniences. Rooms are stylishly decorated and furnished with English country antiques and reproductions and feature nice touches like shiny marble floors and floral wallpapers. Many on the top floor have pitched ceilings, and some have private balconies. Twenty of the rooms are in a more modern annex across the street from the main hotel. A communal sun deck equipped with a hot tub is available for relaxation, and a continental breakfast is served each morning in a cheery, high-ceilinged room but can also be delivered to the room. All this and a handmade candy on the pillow at turndown each night, too!

Josef's *((707) 571-8664, fax (707) 571-8760. L Tu-F, D M-Sat. Reservations advised.)* cozy French restaurant operates off the lobby.

Vintners Inn *4350 Barnes Rd., (800) 421-2584, (707) 575-7350, fax (707) 575-1426; www.vintnersinn.com. 44 rooms; 100% non-smoking; $$-$$$+; 2-night min. on Sat. Children under 5 free. Some wood-burning fireplaces. Hot tub. Continental breakfast; restaurant, room service.*

This elegant country inn is surrounded by a 45-acre working vineyard. Spread through three separate buildings, the rooms are all decorated with European antiques.

The inn's restaurant is the highly acclaimed **John Ash & Co.** *((707) 527-7687; L Tu-Sun, D daily; $$$. Highchairs. Reservations advised.)*, featuring vineyard views and dishes highlighting local products.

WHERE TO EAT

Santa Rosa is where John A. McDougall, author of *The McDougall Plan for Super Health and Life-Long Weight Loss* and promoter of heart-healthy eating, makes his home. It is interesting to note his influence on this area. Most, if not all, of the restaurants have at least one heart-healthy item on the menu. Many have more. Surprisingly, even small fast-food spots such as the **Sonoma Taco Shop** *(100 Brookwood St., in Creekside Ctr., (707) 525-8585.)*, with its impressive 33 heart-healthy options (a complete nutrient breakdown of each item is available), can be counted on to satisfy this need.

The Cantina *500 4th St., in Courthouse Square, (707) 523-3663.*

For description, see page 194.

Chevys Fresh Mex *24 4th St., in Railroad Square, (707) 571-1082. L&D daily.*

This branch of the popular chain is located within an atmospheric old building. For description, see page 62.

Flying Goat Coffee *10 4th St., (707) 575-1202. M-F 7-6, Sat & Sun 8-6.*

Fresh-roasted specialty coffees can be sipped either in the laid-back atmosphere of a tall-ceilinged shop, or outside, where the sport is train-watching. Housemade pastries are also available.

Mixx *135 4th St., in Railroad Square, (707) 573-1344, same fax. L M-F, D M-Sat; $$. Highchairs, boosters, booths, child menu. Reservations advised.*

This restaurant is oversize in every way: seating, ceiling (20 feet high), wine glasses, food seasoning. Sitting beneath the drooping lily light fixtures at one of the substantial tables here feels great. Drinks can be ordered from a full bar, which as it happens is not just any bar. Built in the late 1800s in Italy, it was shipped around Cape Horn in 1904 and has been here ever since. In fact, the building has been either a bar or restaurant since that opening date. And then there is the food. Prepared by owner-chef Dan Berman and his wife Kathleen, who is the pastry chef, the delightful eclectic menu satisfys all stages of hunger. Appetizers include a spicy, complexly flavored purèed soup of guajillo chili, roasted tomato, and smoked chicken, and a perfect house salad composed of local greens accented colorfully with edible flowers. With preference given to ingredients available locally, the dinner menu features some relatively unusual items such as venison and free-range veal, the latter prepared memorably with a whole-grain mustard sauce and garnish of garlicky, crisp Yukon gold potatoes. The restaurant is deservedly famous for its housemade ice creams and sorbets, and the crème brulee just might be the world's best.

Omelette Express *112 4th St., in Railroad Square, (707) 525-1690. B&L daily; $. Highchairs, boosters, child items. No reservations.*

This airy, popular cafe seats diners at old-fashioned oak tables on pressed-back chairs. All omelettes are available with egg whites only, and hamburgers, sandwiches, and a variety of salads are also on the menu.

Peter Rabbit's Chocolate Factory
2489 Guerneville Rd./Fulton Rd., (800) 4-R-CANDY, (707) 575-7110, fax (707) 579-5663. M-Sat 10-6.

Located on the outskirts of town, in a building that belies the cute name, this candy store is worth seeking out. Visitors can usually observe some yummy or other being whipped up on huge marble slabs located adjacent to the retail area. Among the over 120 goodies produced are nut brittles, salt water taffy, and caramel corn that seems to get better with age. There are even chocolate-dipped prunes. Should addiction occur, everything is available by mail order.

Wednesday Night Market *On 4th St. & B St. W 5-8; June-Sept only. Free.*

At this festive event, local restaurants serve up inexpensive portions of barbecued turkey legs, sausage, kebobs, burgers, and oysters along with salads, calzone, chili, and burritos. Farmers are on hand with fresh produce, arts and crafts people display their wares, and plenty of street entertainers also do their thing.

Willie Bird's Restaurant *1150 Santa Rosa Ave., (707) 542-0861. B,L,&D daily; $-$$. Highchairs, boosters, child menu.*

This casual, old-time restaurant celebrates Thanksgiving every day by serving their own tasty, natural brand of turkey in varied forms. Try the Willie Bird Special—a traditional turkey feast—or something more unusual, such as turkey scallopini or turkey sausage. Children's portions include a turkey hamburger and turkey hot dog. Plenty of non-turkey items are also available.

Guerneville and Russian River Area

A LITTLE BACKGROUND

Once upon a time, in 1809, a party of Russians and Aleuts from the Russian-American Fur Company in Sitka, Alaska, landed at the mouth of what is now the Russian River. They named it "Slavianka," or "little beauty." In recognition of the Russian influence in the area, it was later referred to as the "Russian" River.

In the '20s and '30s the area became a summer resort favored by wealthy San Franciscans who traveled here by ferry and train. Then it faded in popularity and became a pleasant and uncrowded retreat. Today, slowly recovering from a state of decay, it is regaining some of its former popularity and is known nationally for its resorts catering to gays. The atmosphere is easygoing, and it is acceptable to dine anywhere in casual clothing.

Guerneville, the hub of the Russian River resort area, is surrounded by many smaller towns. There are numerous public beaches, even more privately-owned ones, and also some unofficial nude beaches. Inquire in town about how to find, or avoid, them.

VISITOR INFORMATION

Russian River Region Visitors Bureau *14034 Armstrong Woods Rd., Guerneville, (800) 253-8800, (707) 869-9212, fax (707) 869-9215; www.russianriver.org.*

Russian River Wine Road *P.O. Box 46, Healdsburg 95448, (800) 723-6336, (707) 433-4335; www.wineroad.com.*

A free map provides details on wineries and lodgings stretching from Forestville to Cloverdale.

GETTING THERE

Located approximately 75 miles north of San Francisco. Exit Highway 101 at Highway 12 west, following it to Highway 116. For a more scenic route, take the River Road exit just north of Santa Rosa and follow it west. Located approximately 15 miles west of Santa Rosa.

ANNUAL EVENTS

Russian River Wine Road Barrel Tasting *March. (800) 723-6336, (707) 433-4335.*

Participants are permitted to get behind the scenes in wine-making and sample special wines that aren't normally available for tasting. Wineries provide tastes of wines still in the barrel as well as of some new vintages and old library treasures.

Apple Blossom Festival *April. In Sebastopol; (707) 824-0501, fax (707) 823-8439. Adults $5, 55+ $2, 6-12 $1.*

Scheduled each year to occur when the area's plentiful apple orchards are snowy-white with blossoms, this festival includes a parade down Main Street and plenty of booths purveying apple-related crafts and foods.

Bohemian Grove *Last 2 weeks of July.*

Many of the world's most powerful political, military, and corporate leaders get together at this 2,700-acre private resort. The public is not invited.

Gravenstein Apple Fair *August. In Sebastopol; (800) 207-9464, (707) 824-2060, fax (707) 996-2136; www.farmtrails.org. Adults $6, 60+ $4, 6-16 $2.*

Held on and off since the turn of the century, this old-time country fair is staged amid the large, shady oak trees and rolling hills of Ragle Ranch Park. The fair specifically celebrates the flavorful, crisp, early-ripening Gravenstein apple, an old German variety dating from 1790 that is indigenous to the area and well-known for making the best juices and pies. In fact, this area is known as the world's Gravenstein capital. Fun at the fair is of the down-home variety, with opportunities to taste apples, observe beekeepers in action, and pet a variety of farm animals. Apples and related foods and products are available for purchase directly from farmers. Proceeds fund the printing of the Sonoma County Farm Trails map.

Russian River Jazz Festival *September. In Guerneville; (707) 869-3940. $28-$37, under 11 free.*

Music festivals don't get much more casual than this one. Audience members can actually float in the placid river on an inner tube while listening to a range of jazz. It's a good idea to pack an ice chest and picnic basket, but food and drink are available for sale. Note that no bottles or cans are permitted.

WHAT TO DO

Armstrong Redwoods State Reserve *17000 Armstrong Woods Rd., (707) 869-2015. Daily 8am-1 hr. after sunset. $5/vehicle.*

A Visitors Center orients hikers to the trail system within this 700+-acre park of thousand-year-old redwood groves. A free parking lot is located just outside the toll gate, and no admission fee is charged for those who park their car and walk in.

The **Armstrong Woods Pack Station** (*(707) 887-2939; www.metro.net/ayers. Riders must be 10 or older or have guide's permission. Reservations required. $40-$100.)* offers trail rides and full-day lunch rides among the mammoth trees found here. Overnight trail rides and longer pack trips are available May through October.

Almost 4 miles farther, at the end of a narrow, steep, winding road, **Austin Creek State Recreation Area** offers 20 miles of hiking trails, plus rustic camping facilities and four hike-in campsites.

Duncans Mills *On Hwy. 116, 10 mi. west of Guerneville.*

Once a lumber village, this tiny town is now home to a collection of shops, a deli, a restaurant, a riverside campground with private beach, and a horseback-riding concession.

J's Amusements *16101 Neeley Rd., (707) 869-3102. Daily in summer; Sat & Sun only, Sept & Mar-June; closed in winter. $1.50-$3.75/ride.*

Various kiddie rides and entertainments await families in search of cheap thrills. Among them are a rickety mini-roller coaster, a tilt-a-whirl, a waterslide, and a 36-hole miniature golf course.

Kozlowski Farms *5566 Hwy. 116 N., Forestville, (800) 4-R-FARMS, (707) 887-1587, fax (707) 887-9650; www. kozlowskifarms.com. Daily 9-5.*

This scenic farm is planted with 25 acres of apple trees and assorted berries. In season, produce can be purchased in bulk. Homemade juices, berry vinegars, wine jellies, berry jams and fruit butters made without sugar, and much more are sold year-round at the farm's barn outlet. A mail-order catalogue is also available.

Pet-A-Llama Ranch *5505 Lone Pine Rd., Sebastopol, (707) 823-9395. Sat & Sun 10-4; closed Jan-Mar. Free; feed 50¢.*

Spread over 15 acres, this ranch is home to a herd of about 20 llamas. They love being petted and love it even more when someone purchases a cup of feed for them. Picnic tables are set up under trees adjacent to their pens. The farmhouse garage doubles as a crafts shop, with handmade llama wool items for sale (shawls, blankets, hats). Sometimes fleece collected from a favorite llama is also available, and spinning wheels and drop spindles are displayed.

Swimming.

Anywhere along the banks of the Russian River is bound to be nice to lay a blanket. A prime spot is under the **Monte Rio bridge**, where parking and beach access are free. Another choice spot is **Johnson's Beach** (see page 213). Canoe and paddleboat rentals and snack stands are available at both. The riverbed and beaches are covered with pebbles, so waterproof shoes are advised.

A good game to play with children here is "Find the Siamese Twin Clam Shells." Be prepared with a special prize for the kid who finds the most intact pairs.

WINERIES

Korbel Champagne Cellars *13250 River Rd., (707) 887-2294, fax (707) 869-2981. Tasting daily 10-4; tours daily 10-3, on the hour. Rose garden tours Apr-Oct only, Tu-Sun at 11 & 3; free.*

The nation's oldest producer of methode champenoise champagne, this century-old winery also produces brandy and wine. Eight kinds of champagne can be tasted, and chilled splits and deli items can be purchased for impromptu picnics.

The grounds are landscaped with beautifully maintained flower gardens. An **Antique Rose Garden**, faithfully restored to its turn-of-the-century beauty, is filled with old-time flowers such as coral bells, primroses, and violets, as well as some more unusual plants. Among the more than 250 varieties of rose are rare specimens such as the original Burbank Tea, the Double Musk celebrated in Shakespeare's plays, and the True Ambassador, which was once thought to be extinct.

Mark West Estate Winery *7010 Trenton-Healdsburg Rd., off River Rd., Forestville, (800) 955-9585, (707) 836-9647, fax (707) 836-0147; www.markwestwinery.com. Tasting daily 10-5:30; tours by appt.*

Located off the beaten path, back among some scenic vineyards and up on a little hill, this winery can be difficult to find. Do call ahead for directions. Named for the creek that surrounds the property, the winery is known for its use of only organic grapes and produces an unusual dry Gewurztraminer and some delicious Chardonnay and Pinot Noir. Picnic tables are provided on a shaded lawn, and limited deli items are available for purchase.

Just behind the tasting room, **California Carnivores** *(7020 Trenton-Healdsburg Rd., Forestville, (707) 838-1630, fax (707) 838-9899; www.californiacarnivores.com. Daily 10-4; call ahead in bad weather. Free.)*, which is the world's largest seller of carnivorous plants, operates their unusual business out of a single greenhouse. Over 400 varieties of insect-eating plants are displayed and sold here, including inexpensive Venus fly traps as well as more exotic varieties, one of which resembles the star of the movie *The Little Shop of Horrors*. They have the largest collection of butterworts on earth, and some plants so new that they haven't been named yet. According to the *New York Times* it is "a botanical museum." The *San Francisco Examiner* calls it an "arresting assemblage." For those who want to feed the plants, the policy is B.Y.O.B. (bring your own bug). They'll provide the tweezer.

WHERE TO STAY

Applewood Inn and Restaurant *13555 Hwy. 116, (800) 555-8509, (707) 869-9093, fax (707) 869-9170; www.applewoodinn.com. 16 rooms; 100% non-smoking; $$-$$$+; 2-night min. on weekends. Unsuitable for children under 21. Some gas fireplaces. Heated pool (May-Oct only), hot tub. Full breakfast; restaurant.*

Built in 1922 as a private home, this Mission Revival-style mansion, now a county historical landmark, is situated on 6 acres and features an idyllic pool area surrounded by mature vineyards and tall redwood trees. The hot tub is wonderful at night, especially when all the stars are out. Public tennis courts, located adjacent to the property, are reached via a short walk through a valley still populated with apple trees that once comprised an orchard. The inn's decor is tasteful and unfussy, and rooms are spacious and comfortable, with aesthetically pleasing touches. Some rooms have private patios or balconies overlooking the vineyards and peaceful pastures beyond. Breakfast is simple, yet special—perhaps a sectioned grapefruit topped with a perfect red maraschino cherry, followed by beautifully presented eggs Florentine prepared with tender baby spinach fresh from the inn's own garden—and on warm days can be enjoyed outdoors by the pool.

Enticing, sophisticated California-Provençale dinners are served in the new **restaurant** *(D Tu-Sat; $$. Reservations advised.)* designed to resemble a French Barn, with two river rock fireplaces, lofty beamed ceilings, and windows looking out over tall redwoods.

Creekside Inn & Resort *16180 Neeley Rd., (800) 776-6586, (707) 869-3623, fax (707) 869-1417; www.creeksideinn.com. 16 units; $-$$$+; 2-night min. on weekends. Children under 2 free. Some VCRs, kitchens, & wood-burning fireplaces; some shared baths. Unheated pool (unavail. Nov-Mar). Full breakfast (B&B rooms only). Pets welcome in 2 cottages.*

Located a short stroll from town, just across the historical bridge, this quiet resort dates back to the '30s. Guests have a choice of lodgings. The main house operates as a B&B, with six rooms sharing two bathrooms. Nine modernized housekeeping cottages feature attractive half-timbered exteriors. One of the nicest is the Tree House, which derives its name from the fact that trees can be observed from every window. RV spaces are also available. Facilities include a large outdoor pool area with a barbecue, horseshoe pit, pool table, Ping-Pong table, croquet lawn, and lending library. When rains are normal, Pocket Canyon Creek provides the soothing sound of running water as it meanders through the property.

The Inn at Occidental *3657 Church St., Occidental, (800) 522-6324, (707) 874-1047, fax (707) 874-1078; www.innatoccidental.com. 17 rooms; 100% non-smoking; $-$$$. Unsuitable for children under 10. Some fireplaces. Afternoon & evening snack, full breakfast.*

Not your average B&B, this exquisite, yet cozy beauty of an inn presents guests with the very best in food and hospitality. This restored Victorian, the town's oldest residential structure, sits tucked among tall redwoods on a hillside just above town. Outside it has covered porches furnished with wicker, plus a walled courtyard and a garden with a fountain. Inside it has fir floors, wainscotted hallways, and themed guest rooms—one with a private hot tub. It is delightfully furnished with the owner's vast and ever-growing antique and art collection. (Is that why this inn recently doubled in size, adding a new wing in the back? Or is it because they are always filled to the gills?) Sonoma Tastemaker Dinners are scheduled irregularly and held in the formal dining room. These multi-course dinners provide the chance to dine with some of the area's local food providers, whose products are featured in the meal. Best of all, the owner's collection of beautiful china, which must rival that of Martha Stewart, is put into use.

Johnson's Beach & Resort *16241 First St., (707) 869-2022. 10 rooms; ¢. Closed Nov-Apr. Some kitchens.*

These bargain old-time hotel rooms are adjacent to the river. Only week-long rentals are reservable; shorter stays are first-come, first-served. Facilities include two rustic wooden swings, a large tire sandbox, pool and Ping-Pong tables, and access to a beach with a snack bar and both boat and beach paraphernalia rentals. Campsites are also available.

Ridenhour Ranch House Inn *12850 River Rd., (888) 877-4466, (707) 887-1033, fax (707) 869-2967; www.ridenhourranchhouseinn.com. 8 rooms; 100% non-smoking; $$-$$$; 2-night min. on weekends. Children under 5 free. Some TVs; 1 gas fireplace & 1 wood-burning stove. Hot tub. Afternoon snack, full breakfast.*

Built of redwood in 1906, this canary-yellow ranch house was constructed by the first settlers in the area. Decorated with English and American antiques, the house has six guest rooms. Two more rooms are available in an adjacent cottage dating from 1934. Recreational facilities include a hot tub pleasantly situated beneath sheltering trees, a badminton area, and a croquet lawn. Across the highway, secluded beaches can be reached via a short walk down a lane lined with blackberry bushes. An expansive breakfast is prepared each morning in a restaurant-style kitchen by the Austrian owner-chef, who warns his guests, "If you don't eat well in the morning, you don't look well at the wineries." So he offers wonderful treats such as homemade Gravenstein applesauce and fruit preserves, gigantic croissants, a fruit smoothie with a touch of brandy from neighboring Korbel winery, a wonderfully light bread pudding, and some sort of egg dish—perhaps eggs Florentine—made with eggs collected from the ranch's own hens. Fresh cookies and sherry are always available in the living room, which is also well-equipped with games and reading matter.

Rio Villa Beach Resort *20292 Hwy. 116, Monte Rio, (707) 865-1143, fax (707) 865-0115; www.riovilla.com. 12 rooms, 2 cabins; $-$$$; 2-night min. on weekends May-Oct. Children under 2 free. Some VCRs, kitchens, & wood-burning fireplaces. Continental breakfast on weekends.*

Some of the rooms at this peaceful spot have private balconies with river views. Guests can relax on a large deck area surrounded by manicured grounds overlooking the river and enjoy a private beach.

Riverlane Resort *16320 First St., (800) 201-2324, (707) 869-2323; www.riverlaneresort.com. 12 cabins; ¢-$$; 2-night min. on weekends. Children under 3 free. All kitchens; some wood-burning fireplaces & stoves. Heated pool (unavail. Oct-Apr), hot tub.*

Located by the river, this pleasant enclave of cabins offers river access.

Village Inn *20822 River Blvd., Monte Rio, (800) 303-2303, (707) 865-2304; www.village-inn.com. 15 rooms; $-$$; 2-night min. on weekends July-Sept. Some rooms suitable for children; children under 2 free. Some TVs; 1 kitchen; some shared baths. Continental breakfast; restaurant, room service.*

Built as a summer home in 1906, this rustic structure was turned into a hotel in 1908 and has remained one ever since. A worthy claim to fame is that *Holiday Inn*, starring Bing Crosby, was filmed here. Lodging facilities vary from small sleeping rooms to suites with a riverfront deck. In summer the restaurant serves a popular Sunday brunch outdoors on a pleasant deck overlooking the river.

House Rentals.

Call the Visitors Bureau for the names of realty companies that rent private homes to vacationers.

WHERE TO EAT

Ace-In-The-Hole Pub *3100 Hwy. 116 N., Sebastopol, (707) 829-1101, fax (707) 829-1157; www.acecider.com.*

Taste refreshing hard ciders made from local ingredients at America's very first cider pub. They're made from fermented apple juice (5 percent alcohol), are said to be an "exhilarating" alternative to the heaviness of beer and the high alcohol content of wine, and come in four flavors: apple, pear, apple honey, and berry. Can't decide? Try a sampler. The large, open interior is welcoming on dreary days, while the ample patio is prime in sunny weather. Tours of the cider mill behind the pub are available upon request.

Burdons *15405 River Rd., (707) 869-2615. D W-Sun; $$. Closed Jan. Boosters, child menu. Reservations advised on weekends.*

The American-continental menu here features reliably well-prepared steaks, chops, and prime rib—the house specialty. Pastas and fresh local fish are also on the menu, as is a particularly tender rack of lamb consisting of tiny chops garnished with green mint sauce and a side of creamy scalloped potatoes. All dinners come with housemade soup and a crisp tossed green or spinach salad. Dessert choices change daily and sometimes include a delicious strawberry shortcake made with tasty berries, a homemade biscuit, and the lightest whipped cream imaginable. Further enhancing the dining experience, the walls of the simple dining room are decorated with colorful, whimsical paintings by the chef.

Cazanoma Lodge *1000 Kidd Creek Rd., Cazadero, 3 mi. west of town, (888) 699-8499, (707) 632-5255, fax (707) 632-5256. D (seasonal), SunBr; $-$$; Closed Dec-Feb. Highchairs, boosters, child portions. Reservations advised.*

Nestled between two creeks in a protected valley, this 1926 lodge is reached via a 1-mile-long dirt road. German specialties—barbecue spareribs, several schnitzels, a sausage platter with sauerkraut—are on the menu along with American fare. But the really unusual item here is "catch your own trout." That's right. To make sure it's really *fresh*, diners here can catch it themselves from a well-stocked spring-fed trout pond. For the unimpressed, the kitchen will do the job with a net. The dining room offers great views of the tranquil forest setting, and in warm weather a large deck under the redwoods is irresistible. Live music is usually scheduled on weekends.

Cabins and lodge rooms *(4 rooms, 2 cabins; $-$$; 2-night min. on Sat May-Sept. Children under 12 free. No TVs; some kitchens & wood-burning fireplaces. Unheated pool (unavail. Oct-May). Evening snack, continental breakfast. Dogs welcome in cabins.)* are also available. Among the features on the 147 acres are a man-made waterfall, a swimming pool, and 2 miles of hiking trails.

Mom's Apple Pie *4550 Hwy. 116 N., Sebastopol, (707) 823-8330, fax (707) 823-5482. Daily 10-7; $. 1 highchair.*

Located near the intersection of Highways 12 and 116, this little lunch counter is worth a stop for the tasty homemade soup and pie. Fried chicken and sandwiches are also available.

The Occidental Two *In Occidental.*

Both of these restaurants serve bountiful multi-course, family-style Italian dinners. They have highchairs, boosters, and a reasonable plate charge for small children. Prices are moderate, and inexpensive ravioli and spaghetti dinners with fewer side dishes are also available. Reservations are advised at prime dining times during the summer, and on weekends and holidays year-round. People come to these restaurants to eat BIG. Picking a favorite can prove fattening.

• **Negri's** *3700 Main St., (707) 823-5301, fax (707) 874-2158. L&D daily.*

Meals here start with a steaming bowl of minestrone soup, rounds of moist salami, and a hunk of crusty Italian bread. Then come more plates bearing pickled vegetables, marinated bean salad, creamy large-curd cottage cheese, and a salad tossed with Thousand Island dressing. When tummies begin to settle, the ravioli arrives—stuffed with spinach and topped with an excellent tomato-meat sauce. Then the entree arrives: a choice of crispy, moist fried chicken, saucy duck, or grilled porterhouse steak. (Seafood entrees are available on weeknights.) Entrees are served with a side of thick French fries and heavy zucchini pancakes. Then come the doggie bags. For those with room, apple fritters are available at additional charge.

• **Union Hotel** *3731 Main St., (707) 874-3555, fax (707) 874-3662. L&D daily.*

In operation since 1876, this restaurant seats 400 people in three enormous dining rooms and on an outdoor patio. Simplicity seems to be the key to its success. The entree choice is limited to roasted chicken, chicken cacciatora, duck, or steak. Side dishes include an antipasto plate of marinated kidney beans, cheese, and salami, plus minestrone soup, a delicious salad with light Thousand Island dressing, hand-rolled ravioli, zucchini fritters, potatoes, a fresh vegetable, and bread and butter. Dessert—apple fritters, spumoni ice cream, or apple pie—and coffee are extra. A bakery, pizzeria, and cafe adjoin.

River Inn Restaurant *16141 Main St., (707) 869-0481. B,L,&D daily; $-$$. Closed Nov-Mar. Highchairs, boosters, booths, child portions. No reservations.*

Extensive menu choices at breakfast include crisp waffles, thin Swedish pancakes, perfect French toast, omelettes, oatmeal, and fresh fruit. At lunch and dinner, just about everything imaginable is available. All this in a casual coffee shop atmosphere with many comfy booths.

Topolos at Russian River Vineyards Restaurant *5700 Hwy. 116 N., Forestville, (800) TOPOLOS, (707) 887-1562, fax (707) 887-1399. L&D daily in summer, SunBr; closed M & Tu rest of year; $$. Highchairs, boosters, child portions. Reservations advised.*

In good weather, diners are seated outdoors in an attractive area shaded by grape arbors and umbrellas. In colder weather, tables are available inside the century-old farmhouse that is now the restaurant. Greek dishes are the specialty but a hamburger is on the lunch menu, and extensive use is made of local products as well as of fresh organic herbs and vegetables grown on-site. A large selection of the winery's own vintages are available by the glass. This is the only family-owned and -operated winery/restaurant in the state.

Do stop in at the adjacent tiny **Topolos at Russian River Vineyards Winery** tasting room *((707) 887-1575. Tasting daily 11-5; tours by appt.)*. Of special interest among these organically grown wines are the Zinfandel—which winemaker Michael Topolos describes as "very American. It's forward and gutsy just like we are."—and the unusual, rich Alicante Bouschet varietal. Children are served sparkling apple cider while their parents taste.

Healdsburg

A LITTLE BACKGROUND

Small town America is alive and well in Northern California. When visitors arrive in this charming old-fashioned town, they sometimes are shocked to find cars stopping *willingly* as they wait in a crosswalk to cross the street. Even the cars in the far lane are known to wait! And parking places are usually easy to find, even around the popular town square. All this plus the weather is generally sunny.

The surrounding area is home to over 50 premium wineries, a few of which have tasting rooms right in town. Visitors can spend the day driving or biking the back roads, happily hopping from winery to winery, or can opt to just stay in town antiquing and shopping.

Healdsburg was incorporated in 1867 and then slowly rose around a central Spanish-style plaza. It is one of the few examples remaining of a planned early California town. The plaza was given to the town as a gift by its original owner, to be used forever as a "pleasure ground" free from public buildings. Nowadays, a free **Summer Sunday Concert Series** is scheduled on the plaza June through August.

Historic homes and buildings are sprinkled around the square and throughout the surrounding neighborhood, adding greatly to the turn-of-the century flavor.

VISITOR INFORMATION

Healdsburg Chamber of Commerce & Visitors Bureau *217 Healdsburg Ave., (800) 648-9922, (707) 433-6935, fax (707) 433-7562; www.ci.healdsburg.ca.us.*

GETTING THERE

Located 75 miles north of San Francisco, and 12 miles north of Santa Rosa.

ANNUAL EVENTS

World Croquet Championship Finals *May. In Windsor; (707) 528-1181. Free, except day of the tournament when tickets cost approx. $175.*

Spectators are welcome to view the championships, held at **Sonoma-Cutrer Vineyards** *(4401 Slusser Rd. Tasting & tours by appt.)*, and picnics are de rigueur.

Pumpkin Festival *Last 3 weekends in October. At* ***Westside Farms****, 7097 Westside Rd., 7 mi. south of town; (707) 431-1432, fax (707) 431-9433.*

Visitors to this especially family-friendly event, held on a scenic old-time farm, enjoy hayrides and other down-home activities. A variety of farm animals are on hand, and a picnic area is provided. In addition to several varieties of pumpkin, both gourds and Indian corn are available for purchase. The farm is also open the entire month of June for U-pick olallieberries and boysenberries.

WHAT TO DO

Healdsburg Veterans Memorial Beach *13839 Old Redwood Hwy., (707) 433-1625. Daily 7am-8pm; June-Sept only. $3/vehicle.*

This is a choice spot to swim in the warm Russian River, which in summer has an average water temperature of 70 to 75 degrees. A lifeguard is on duty from 10, and canoe and inner tube rentals are available. Facilities include a diving board, children's wading area, a picnic area with barbecues, and a snack bar. Sunbathers have a choice of a large sandy beach or a shady lawn area.

Timber Crest Farms *4791 Dry Creek Rd., (707) 433-8251, fax (707) 433-8255; www.timbercrest.com. M-F 10-5, Sat 10-4.*

The high-quality dried fruits and tomatoes available here are made without sulfur, preservatives, or additives. The usual are available as well as the unusual—pitted Bing cherries and mission figs. A bottled mixture of Dried Tomato Spice Medley is particularly delicious on crackers. Sometimes it is possible to observe produce being harvested or prepared for packaging.

W.C. "Bob" Trowbridge Canoe Trips *20 Healdsburg Ave., (800) 640-1386, (707) 433-7247, fax (707) 433-6384. Check-in daily 8-12:30, Apr-Oct only. $39/canoe/day. Children must be 6 or older. Reservations necessary. Dinner: Adults $7.95, under 13 $5.95.*

The canoe fee for these unguided trips includes life jackets, paddles, and canoe transport. An after-canoeing barbecue takes place from 4 to 7 p.m. each weekend and includes steak or chicken, vegetable, baked beans, salad, garlic bread, and beverage. Trowbridge has five other rental sites along the river. A 2-day trip is also available.

Windsor Waterworks & Slides *8225 Conde Lane, Windsor, 6 mi. south of town, (707) 838-7760, fax (707) 838-7690. Daily 11-7, June-Aug; weekends only May & Sept.; closed Oct-Apr. Age 3+ $13.25.*

In addition to several waterslides, this water-oriented facility holds a swimming pool, a wading pool, a volleyball court, a snack bar, and shaded picnic facilities.

WINERIES

Dry Creek Vineyard *3770 Lambert Bridge Rd., 3 mi. west of Hwy. 101, (707) 433-1000, fax (707) 433-5329; www.drycreekvineyard.com. Tasting daily 10:30-4:30; no tours.*

Known for its Fumé Blancs and Chenin Blancs, this winery has a cool, shady picnic area under a canopy of old pine and maple trees. An annual June **Open House** *($20-$40.)* celebrates the season with live music, wine tasting, and plenty of good food.

Foppiano Vineyards *12707 Old Redwood Hwy., (707) 433-7272; www.foppiano.com. Tasting daily 10-4:30; self-guided tour.*

Established in 1896, this family-owned winery offers a self-guided tour through its Chardonnay, Cabernet Sauvignon, and Petite Sirah vineyards. It takes about 30 minutes, and a free explanatory brochure is available in the tasting room.

Hop Kiln Winery *6050 Westside Rd., (707) 433-6491, fax (707) 433-8162. Tasting daily 10-5; no tours.*

This unique winery is reached by taking a quiet back road through miles of scenic vineyards. Wine tasting occurs inside a landmark 1905 hops-drying barn built by Italian stonemasons (it was once used to supply San Francisco breweries). Known for its big Zinfandels, the winery also produces unique Big Red and A Thousand Flowers blends. Two appealing picnic areas are available: One overlooks a duck pond and vineyards; the other is situated in the shade of a gigantic Kadota fig tree planted in 1880.

J Wine Company *11447 Old Redwood Hwy., (888) J WINE CO, (707) 431-5400, fax (707) 431-5410; www.jwine.com. Tasting W-Sun 11-5 (fee $3-$8); tours by appt.*

The lines of this ultra-modern winery are softened with attractive landscaping and a lily pond. Now producing an array of sparkling wines, this winery has plans for adding still wines soon. At a bar backed by a massive sculpture certain to provoke discussion, tasters can try wines by the glass or sample an entire flight accompanied by foods designed to complement them. A stop here allows killing the proverbial two birds with one stone. Park once, taste twice: Rodney Strong Vineyards is located just across the way.

The Meeker Vineyard *9711 W. Dry Creek Rd., (707) 431-2148. Tasting daily 10:30-5; no tours.*

Located at the very end of a scenic, rural road, this winery's unusual tasting room operates within a huge tepee. Inside, it's party time, with rock & roll music and a ceiling mister intermittently cooling things off. Call ahead, as the tasting room is scheduled to move to a historic bank vault in downtown Geyserville during winery construction.

Preston Vineyards *9282 W. Dry Creek Rd., (800) 305-9707, (707) 433-3372, fax (707) 433-5307, bread hotline (707) 433-4720; www.prestonvineyards.com. Tasting daily 11-4:30; no tours.*

This small family-owned winery produces terrific Rhone-style wines and good Fumé Blancs. Outside the tasting room, a shaded brick patio offers comfy wicker chairs and numerous resident cats. Bread baked on the premises in an Italian-style forno oven can be purchased; call ahead to find out what Lou, the winery owner, is baking and when it's available for sale. Picnic tables are shaded by an old walnut tree, and courts for Italian bocce ball and French petanque are available. On the way in or out, an inviting road-side creek invites frolicking.

Rodney Strong Vineyards *11455 Old Redwood Hwy., (800) 678-4763, (707) 431-1533, fax (707) 433-0939; www.rodneystrong.com. Tasting daily 10-5; tours daily, call for schedule.*

Do sample the winery's Chardonnays and Cabernet Sauvignons. Picnic tables are available.

Simi Winery *16275 Healdsburg Ave., (707) 433-6981, fax (707) 433-6253; www.simiwinery.com. Tasting daily 10-4:30; tours at 11, 1, & 3.*

Opened in 1890, this friendly winery pours samples of reserve wines for a small fee. An inviting redwood-shaded picnic area is available.

WHERE TO STAY

Camellia Inn *211 North St., (800) 727-8182, (707) 433-8182, fax (707) 433-8130; www.camelliainn.com. 9 rooms; 100% non-smoking; $-$$$; 2-night min. on Sat. Children under 2 free. No TVs; some gas fireplaces. Heated pool (unavail. Nov-Apr). Afternoon snack, full breakfast.*

Situated just 2 blocks from the town square, this 1869 Italianate Victorian townhouse offers a quiet retreat. The grounds surrounding the inn are planted with over 50 varieties of camellia, some of which were given to the original owner by Luther Burbank. In keeping with the theme, each room is named for a camellia variety. The tastefully furnished, high-ceilinged Royalty Room, originally the home's dining room, boasts an antique Scottish high bed with a ceiling-hung canopy and step stool as well as an unusual ornate antique brass sink fitting. Several rooms have whirlpool bathtubs for two. An afternoon out by the oak-shaded, villa-style pool area is incredibly relaxing. Breakfast is served buffet-style in the dining room, where guests are seated at a large claw-foot mahogany table.

Dry Creek Inn *198 Dry Creek Rd., (800) 222-5784, (707) 433-0300, fax (707) 433-1129; www.drycreekinn.com. 102 rooms; $-$$. Children under 12 free. Heated pool (unheated Nov-Mar), hot tub, fitness center. Continental breakfast; restaurant. Pets welcome ($10).*

Part of the Best Western chain, this is an attractive contemporary motel. All guests are greeted with a complimentary bottle of wine in their room.

Madrona Manor *1001 Westside Rd., (800) 258-4003, (707) 433-4231, fax (707) 433-0703; www.madronamanor.com. 21 rooms; 100% non-smoking; $$$-$$$+; 2-night min. Apr-Nov. Children under 12 stay free. No TVs; some wood-burning & gas fireplaces. Heated pool (unavail. Dec-March). Full breakfast; restaurant. Dogs welcome in some rooms.*

Featuring an unusual mansard roof, which makes it look moody in spite of its cheery cream-and-baby blue exterior, this majestic mansion is situated off a sideroad running through rural vineyards. An imposing archway frames a long driveway leading up to the 8-acre estate, built in 1881 as a country retreat and now a protected historic site operating as an inn. Five rooms feature furniture original to the house, and a public music room boasts an unusual square rosewood piano. Room number 202 has a particularly charming decor of floral wallpaper with mint green trim, a dark-wood dresser and matching cozy double bed, and a very high ceiling. Its spacious bathroom holds a dramatic, unexpected giant cactus and an old-fashioned deep clawfoot tub. Four newer outer structures hold more rooms. Breakfast here is reminiscent of a typical European morning spread, with juice, coffee, breakfast breads, housemade jams, seasonal fruits, meats and cheeses, soft-boiled eggs (in a chicken-shaped basket), a vegetable frittata, a fabulous light bread pudding, and housemade granola among the choices.

For dinner, guests need just enter the elegant dining rooms known as **Restaurant at Madrona Manor** *(D daily. Highchairs, boosters, child portions. Reservations advised.)*, where wonderfully complex dishes often feature produce from the estate's own gardens and orchards. Both a fixed-price, three-course dinner and an a la carte menu are offered. One dinner enjoyed here featured a delicious soft-shell crab tempura and a peachy-keen dessert sampler of peach shortcake, peach crisp, and peach ice cream. The wine list features local Sonoma vintages. Outside seating is available on a heated terrace.

WHERE TO EAT

Flying Goat Coffee *324 Center St., (707) 433-9081, fax (707) 433-0704.*

For description, see page 208.

Picnic Pick-Ups.

- **Costeaux French Bakery & Cafe** *417 Healdsburg Ave., (707) 433-1913, fax (707) 433-1955. B&L daily; $. Highchairs, child portions. No reservations.*

Family-owned and -operated since 1923, this spot is choice for picking up picnic supplies or ribbon-tied box lunches. Huge sandwiches are prepared on a choice of light deli rolls or other housemade breads, plus there are wonderful housemade soups, deli salads, sandwiches, and pizzas. The awe-inspiring selection of desserts includes a caramel-macadamia nut tart, several cheesecakes, and an assortment of fresh fruit tarts and French pastries. Seating is either in the airy, high-ceilinged interior or outside on a pleasant sidewalk patio. And don't miss seeing the bathroom, papered attractively with authentic wine labels.

- **Downtown Bakery & Creamery** *308-A Center St., (707) 431-2719, fax (707) 431-1579. M-F 6am-5:30, Sat 7-5:30, Sun 7-4.*

Co-owner Lindsey Shere did time in the kitchen at Berkeley's renowned Chez Panisse. She also wrote the best-selling cookbook *Chez Panisse Desserts.* So the exceptional hand-shaped breads, pastries, and ice creams produced in her kitchen here are not a complete surprise. When available, the focaccia, sticky buns, fruit turnovers, and fig newtons are not to be missed. And on warm Wine Country days, it is a refreshing pleasure to indulge in one of the shop's old-fashioned milkshakes or sundaes.

- **Dry Creek General Store** *3495 Dry Creek Rd., (707) 433-4171, fax (707) 433-0409. Daily 6am-6pm, in summer to 7.*

This old-fashioned general store/deli opened in 1881 and is now a state historical landmark. Claiming to be "the best deli by a dam site!", it *is* located by a dam site (the Warm Springs Dam) and it sure *does* dispense good picnic fare! Sandwiches are made to order, and there are plenty of housemade salads and garnishes.

- **Jimtown Store** *6706 Hwy. 128, (707) 433-1212, fax (707) 433-1252; www.jimtown.com. M-F 7-5, Sat & Sun 7:30-5. Closed 2 weeks in Jan.*

Dating back to the late 1800s, this landmark general store specializes in preparing great picnics that can be enjoyed right on their patio or taken along to a winery. Among the eclectic gourmet sandwiches: Brie with olive salad, lamb with fig tapenade, roast turkey with balsamic onions. But ham and cheese, chicken salad, and peanut butter & jelly are also available. Picnic hampers are available for loan, complete with suggestions about where to find the perfect picnic spot. Antiques, folk art, and local products are also for sale.

- **Oakville Grocery** *124 Matheson St., on the Plaza, (707) 433-3200.*

For description, see page 372.

Restaurant Charcuterie *335 Healdsburg Ave., (707) 431-7213. L M-Sat, D daily; $. No reservations. No cards.*

With a light, French-influenced menu, this casual spot is perfect for a quick meal. Particularly tasty salads—the item of choice in this generally warm area— include one with strips of blackened chicken breast served over a lightly dressed Caesar salad, and another with toasted walnuts, cubes of apple, golden raisins, and Gorgonzola over baby greens with poppy seed dressing. Sandwiches and pastas are available at lunch, and at dinner more substantial entrees—such as baked chicken and rabbit fricassée—are added.

Geyserville

GETTING THERE

Located approximately 8 miles north of Healdsburg.

ANNUAL EVENTS

Fall Colors Festival *October. (707) 857-3745.*

The whole town celebrates the end of the grape harvest with this festival.

WHAT TO DO

Lake Sonoma *3333 Skaggs Springs Rd., (707) 433-9483. Free.*

This scenic spot hosts all manner of water activities—fishing, boating, water-skiing, swimming. Everything from a canoe to a patio boat or houseboat can be rented from the **Lake Sonoma Resort** *(Stewarts Point Rd., (707) 433-2200.).* A Visitors Center displays the area's wildlife and provides a self-guided tour through the **Don Clausen Fish Hatchery**. When the steelhead trout and salmon run here, usually from November through April, they can be observed using a man-made fish ladder.

WINERIES

Geyser Peak Winery *22281 Chianti Rd., 1 mi. north of town at Canyon Rd. exit off Hwy. 101, (800) 255-WINE, (707) 857-9400; www.geyserpeakwinery.com. Tasting daily 10-5; no tours.*

Shaded patio picnic tables here overlook Alexander Valley.

Trentadue Winery *19170 Geyserville Ave., (707) 433-3104, fax (707) 433-5825; www.trentadue.com. Tasting daily 11-4:30; no tours.*

Don't miss a picnic here in the welcoming shade of a spacious grape arbor. Known for its spicy red Carignane and Sengoviese, this small family enterprise also sells some picnic supplies in its tasting room. Children get soft drinks, cookies, and candy to keep them happy while their parents taste.

WHERE TO STAY

The Hope-Merrill House *21253 Geyserville Ave., (800) 825-4BED, (707) 857-3356, fax (707) 857-3857; www.hope-inns.com. 12 rooms; 100% non-smoking; $$-$$$+; 2-night min. on Sat. Children under 2 free. 1 TV; some wood-burning & gas fireplaces. Heated pool (unavail. Oct-Apr). Full breakfast.*

This 1870 Eastlake Stick Victorian is exquisitely restored to that period with antique furnishings and authentic Bradbury & Bradbury silk-screened wallpapers. In fact, the owner's restoration efforts won a first place award from the National Trust for Historic Preservation. When the temperature permits, a dip in the attractively situated pool beckons, and in the morning a full breakfast is served in the formal dining room. Should this lovely inn be booked, opt for the charming Queen Anne Victorian **Hope-Bosworth House** located across the street. Under the same ownership, these two houses share some facilities. Guests at either house can reserve a gourmet picnic lunch for two featuring local foods.

A special two-part "Pick and Press Crushing Good Time" package is available for wannabe wine-makers. Participants check in at harvest time in September for a round of grape picking and pressing, plus, of course, some tasting and dining. They return in the spring for a bottling and labeling session, plus, of course, more tasting and dining, and then depart with two cases of their own wine sporting personalized labels. Call for details.

WHERE TO EAT

Château Souverain *400 Souverain Rd., at Independence Lane exit off Hwy. 101, (707) 433-8281. Closed first 2 weeks in Jan. Restaurant: L&D F-Sun; $-$$$. Highchairs, boosters. Reservations advised. Winery: Tasting daily 10-5; no tours.*

Tucked into a vineyard-covered hill and featuring distinctive towers reminiscent of the area's once-common hop kilns, this winery features a first-rate restaurant. Overlooking the scenic Alexander Valley, **Cafe at the Winery** presents a menu of refined cuisine designed to complement the wine list. The dining room features a beamed ceiling and oversize fireplace, with spectacular views of the vineyards and hills. In good weather, diners can be seated outdoors on the Garden Terrace.

Anderson Valley

A LITTLE BACKGROUND

Once famous for its apple orchards, this area is now better known for its grapes and wines. In Boonville, a town that has yet to install a stop sign or traffic light, the townspeople speak an unusual 19th-century slang known as "Boontling." Here public telephones are labeled "Buckey Walter" and quail are called—after the sound they make—"rookie-to."

VISITOR INFORMATION

Anderson Valley Chamber of Commerce *P.O. Box 275, Boonville 95415, (707) 895-2379; www.andersonvalleychamber.com.*

Anderson Valley Wine Association *(707) 895-9463; www.avwines.com.*

This organization provides free information on the valley's wineries.

GETTING THERE

Take Highway 128 north. Boonville, the valley's largest town, is about 50 miles north of Geyserville and 115 miles north of San Francisco. This spectacular winding route is a rural two-lane back road that follows the Navarro River through oak-wooded hills dotted with sheep peacefully grazing in meadows. After Philo, it passes through an 11-mile corridor of redwoods known as the "tunnel to the sea." Gas up before heading out, and avoid this route after dusk.

ANNUAL EVENTS

Floyd Johnson Memorial Sheep Dog Trials and California Wool and Fiber Festival *May. In Boonville; (707) 895-3011. Free.*

In addition to the sheep dog trails, visitors see sheep-shearing, wool spun into yarn, and related crafts. A barbecued lamb feast and sheep weight-guessing contest are also part of the fun.

California Wine Tasting Championships *July. In Philo; (707) 895-2002, fax (707) 895-2001. Free for spectators.*

Held at **Greenwood Ridge Vineyards** *(5501 Hwy. 128. Daily 10-5.)* this unique and festive event includes good food, live music, chocolate and cheese tasting contests, and novice, amateur, and professional wine tasting competitions.

WHAT TO DO

Anderson Valley Historical Museum *Hwy. 128/ Anderson Valley Way, Boonville, (707) 895-3207. F-Sun 1-4; from 11 in summer. Free.*

This old-fashioned, one-room red schoolhouse located just west of town is a worthwhile stop.

The Apple Farm *18501 Greenwood Rd., Philo, (707) 895-2461, same fax. Fruit stand: Daily 9-5; later in summer & fall.*

One part of this enterprise is a certified organic 30-acre farm with over 80 varieties of apples ripening at different times from August through October. The bounty and related products are for sale at the farm's fruitstand. The other part is a cooking school operated by the former proprietors of the highly acclaimed French Laundry in Yountville. The school strives to simplify everyday cooking and to get participants back in their kitchens preparing daily meals and enjoying it. On Farm Weekends everyone get hands-on experience, preparing and consuming Friday dinner, Saturday lunch and dinner, and Sunday brunch. According to owner Sally Schmitt, it is "like a house party with some cooking lessons thrown in." Schmitt teaches students to use what is already in their garden and panty and encourages using the best ingredients while doing the least possible to them. Participants get 3 hours off on Saturday afternoon to hike, bike, or visit local wineries on their own. Weekends run $225 per person and are limited to eight participants. Lodging is additional. Currently one guest room is available on the premises.

Picnic Spots.

- **Hendy Woods State Park** *On Greenwood Rd., off Hwy. 128, (707) 937-5804. $5/vehicle.*

  Situated along the Navarro River, this 850-acre park holds two groves of old-growth redwoods, a riverside picnic area with tables under a grove of sprawling walnuts, and a 1-mile self-guided nature Loop Trail. Campsites are available.

- **Indian Creek City Park** *Located just east of Boonville.*

- **Masonite Corporation Demonstration Forest** *Located just past Navarro.*

WINERIES

Navarro Vineyards *5601 Hwy. 128, Philo, (800) 537-9463, (707) 895-3686, fax (707) 895-3647; www.navarrowine.com. Tasting daily 10-5, in summer to 6; tours by appt.*

Known for its varied Gewurztraminers and varietal grape juices, which are offered to lucky children for sampling, this winery is situated within a striking Craftsman-style redwood building. Attractive picnic areas are provided on a deck overlooking the vineyard and under a trellis in the vineyard.

Roederer Estate *4501 Hwy. 128, Philo, (707) 895-2288, fax (707) 895-2120. Tasting daily 11-5 (fee $3; applies to purchase); tours by appt.*

Boasting state-of-the-art methode champenoise wine-making facilities, this winery has a tasting room with beautiful valley views.

WHERE TO STAY

Highland Ranch *18941 Philo-Greenwood Rd., Philo, (707) 895-3600, fax (707) 895-3702; www.highlandranch.com. 11 cabins; $$$+; 2-night min. Closed mid-Dec. Children under 2 free. No TVs; all wood-burning fireplaces. Unheated pool (unavail. Nov-May), 2 tennis courts. Full breakfast, lunch, & dinner included. Pets welcome.*

Guests at this secluded spot can enjoy the rural pleasures of fishing, swimming, and canoeing in three ponds, plus clay pigeon shooting, mountain biking, hiking, and horseback riding—all at no additional charge. Lodging is in modern redwood cabins.

Wellspring Renewal Center *8550 Rays Rd./ Hwy. 138, Philo, (707) 895-3893. 9 cabins; 100% non-smoking; ¢-$. Children under 3 free. No TVs; some kitchens & wood-burning stoves; some shared baths.*

Founded in 1979 as an interfaith center, this 50-acre facility located adjacent to Hendy Woods State Park offers programs focused on deepening spirituality and engendering creativity. Regularly scheduled programs include planting and harvesting weekends, meditation and healing retreats, an arts and crafts week, and storytelling workshops. A variety of lodging is available—lodge rooms, both rustic and improved cabins, and a campground at which guests can either pitch their own tent or rent a tepee or tent cabin. Prices vary from $8 to $28 per person per day, $3 to $10 for children ages 2 through 15. All guests are asked, but not required, to donate 1 hour of their time each day to a needed chore. Individuals, families, and groups are welcome.

WHERE TO EAT

Boonville Hotel *14050 Hwy. 128/Lambert Ln., Boonville, (707) 895-2210, same fax. L W-Sun, D W-Mon; closed 1st 2 weeks in Jan. Highchairs, boosters. Reservations advised for dinner.*

Owner-chef John Schmitt did his internship at his parent's former restaurant, the French Laundry in Yountville, and he displays his expertise in every dish. Here he uses the local bounty for salads, soups, upscale pizza, hearty entrees, and wonderful desserts, and he features local Anderson Valley wines. A "taqueria lunch" is served in the attractive dining area, and the all-inclusive regional dinners that are scheduled regularly are worth going out of the way for.

Lodging *(10 rooms; 100% non-smoking; $-$$$. Closed 1st 2 weeks in Jan. Children under 1 free. No TVs. Continental breakfast.)* is also available. The light, airy rooms are of a clean-lined contemporary style, with light woods and sumptuous tiled bathrooms, and are furnished with simple shaker furniture and handmade furnishings made by local craftspeople (many pieces are available for purchase). Beds are made with all-cotton sheets and boldly striped down comforters, and unusual, attractive floral arrangements (try white hydrangia balls mixed with wispy blue forget-me-nots on for size) add a touch of whimsy.

Buckhorn Saloon *14081 Hwy. 128, Boonville, (800) 207-BEER, (707) 895-BEER, fax (707) 895-2353; www.avbc.com. L&D daily in summer; Oct-Mar, call for schedule. Highchairs, boosters, child portions. No reservations.*

The casual and airy dining room here overlooks the scenic countryside and an outdoor beer garden with horseshoe pits. The inexpensive lunch menu features snack items—nachos, spicy chicken wings, sausages boiled in beer—as well as fish & chips and several kinds of hamburgers and deli sandwiches. At dinner, steaks and seafood are added. Breads are from the local Bruce Bread Bakery, and soups and desserts are housemade. Beers, brewed directly beneath the pub, include Poleeko Gold (light ale), High Rollers (wheat beer), Boont Amber (ale), Deependers Dark (porter), and Barney Flats (oatmeal stout). Fresh lemonade and an apple spritzer, made with local apple juice and sparkling mineral water, are also available. Brewery tours can sometimes be arranged on the spot by request.

Picnic Pick-Up.

• **Boont Berry Farm** *13981 Hwy. 128, Boonville, (707) 895-3576. M-F 9-6, Sat 10-6, Sun 12-6.*

This tiny health food store has a cozy, old-fashioned atmosphere and is well-stocked with deli items, locally-grown organic produce, pastries, breads (including the town's famous Bruce Bread), and homemade ice cream.

Hopland

A LITTLE BACKGROUND

Tiny Hopland is easy to overlook as a getaway destination. Located just 1 1/2 hours from the Bay Area and about 45 minutes north of Santa Rosa, this 3-block-long slow-down in the road seems too soon to stop for the night. But it is equipped to provide a satisfying weekend escape.

Prior to the arrival of white settlers in the mid 1800s, this area was home to Pomo Indians, who were accomplished basket weavers. Hopland was named after the hops that still grow wild here, and which have been cultivated since 1860 for brewing beer. Though hops were once the area's primary crop, they were displaced in the 1940s by fruits, and now wine grapes. And while this low-key area is slowly transforming from a farming community into a recreational destination, it has a long way to go.

VISITOR INFORMATION

Hopland Chamber of Commerce *P.O. Box 677, Hopland 95449, (707) 744-1379; www.hoplandchamber.org.*

GETTING THERE

Located approximately 25 miles north of Geyserville, and 110 miles north of San Francisco.

ANNUAL EVENTS

Redwood Run *June.*

This town's answer to the Rose Parade, this event finds thousands of motorcycles and their riders making the run from the Bay Area

Redwood Run

to the Garberville-Piercy area on the Eel River and back again. Most seem to stopover midday in Hopland, making for quite a sight. The group has a reputation for not causing trouble and is certainly exciting to witness.

WHAT TO DO

Real Goods Solar Living Center *13771 S. Hwy. 101, (707) 744-2100; www.realgoods.com. Open daily. Guided tours F, Sat, & Sun at 11 & 3.*

Pick up a self-guided tour brochure at the entrance to this surprising, impressive 12 1/2-acre complex, or coordinate your visit to include a guided tour. An especially refreshing stop on a hot day (it can soar to 110 degrees around here in summer, and the town claims 300 days of sunshine every year), this small oasis has an Agave Cooling Tower dispensing a refreshing mist, and a Children's Play Area with an optional pipe-tunnel entrance, a sandbox, and a water pump. The symbolic center of the site is formed by the Central Oasis, a sort of a mini-Yellowstone fountain of dancing geysers, and the Solar Calendar, a sort of mini-Stonehenge designed to reconnect visitors to the changing seasons. Once inside the cool store, double-entendre intended, browse the useful merchandise and check out a wall cutaway showing the building's unusual straw-bale construction. Upon leaving, a sign urges: "Turn inspiration into action."

Sho-Ka-Wah Casino *13101 Nokomis Rd., (707) 744-1395. Open 24 hours.*

Offering a tiny bit of night life, this Native American-run casino operates in a magical rural area just a few miles east of Highway 101.

WINERIES

Brutacao Vineyards *13500 S. Hwy. 101, (800) 433-3689, (707) 744-1664; www.brutacao cellars.com. Tasting daily.*

Scheduled to open soon an impressive new tasting room inside an historic building that formerly served as the town's high school, this winery also has an adjacent garden with 5,000 roses forming a rainbow, bocce ball courts, a concert area, and a deli as part of the package.

Fetzer Vineyards Tasting Room & Visitor Center *13601 Eastside Rd., (800) 846-8637, (707) 744-1250, (707) 744-7488; www.fetzer.com. Tasting daily 8-5. Unguided garden tours: daily 9-5; free. Cooking classes, (707) 744-7604.*

Fetzer Vineyards is reached by taking Highway 175 east about a mile through lush meadows. After driving down the elm-lined lane leading into this property, visitors can taste wine, take a tour of the extensive organic gardens, participate in a cooking class, and even spend the night. Fetzer is the industry leader in farming organic grapes, is heavy into recycling, and is the only U.S. winery that builds its own oak barrels on-site. The tasting room offers free samplings of all Fetzer wines, including their famously well-priced Sundial Chardonnay, and its **Valley Oaks Deli** dispenses freshly prepared salads, soups, sandwiches, and other picnic goodies. Guided tours of the impressive and beautiful 5-acre **Bonterra Organic Gardens**, filled with riotously colorful flowers and fragrant herbs and even mulberry trees, are scheduled daily (call for times). Special events and cooking classes are scheduled regularly in a well-equipped culinary center overlooking a bucolic pond.

Located in the property's converted carriage house, each of the contemporary-style rooms in the **Fetzer B&B** *(6 rooms; $$-$$$. Pool (seasonal). Continental breakfast.)* has a vineyard view; several have whirlpool tubs.

WHERE TO STAY

Thatcher Inn *13401 S. Hwy. 101, (800) 266-1891, (707) 744-1890; fax 707-744-1219; www.thatcherinn.com. 20 rooms; $-$$$. Unsuitable for children. Pool (seasonal). Full breakfast; restaurant.*

The Thatcher Inn has been around since 1890. It is authentically restored, down to its original exterior colors and the period furnishings sprinkled throughout. The large, high-ceilinged guest rooms feature coordinated wallpapers and bedspreads, and some have couches or large bathrooms with tubs. Each is named for a local pioneer family and decorated with fascinating historical black-and-white photos of the family. Though situated right on Highway 101, its back rooms are quiet, and as evening descends or as the sun rises, the crowing of a crazed rural rooster can often be heard somewhere beyond the busy-ness of the highway. Staying here permits walking just about anywhere in town. In warm weather, a small pool provides respite from the heat, and breakfast is served then on an outdoor patio under an enormous 500-year-old oak. A grand, marble-topped bar—featuring racks of liquor bottles on either side of a gargantuan mirror and a rolling ladder for reaching them—is original to the building and a gathering spot for evening refreshment (the bar is open only to inn guests). Then it is just a mosey on into the elegant **dining room** for a tasty dinner *(served W-Sat)* prepared by the skilled innkeepers.

WHERE TO EAT

Bluebird Cafe *13340 S. Hwy. 101, (707) 744-1633. B&L daily.*

Choose from five types of grape juice and five types of burger—ostrich, salmon, turkey, garden, or regular—as well as stir-frys, pastas, and salads. It's cool and comfortable inside, with lace curtains on the windows and attractive paintings (all for sale) and a stuffed moose head decorating the walls.

The Cheesecake Lady *13325 S. Hwy. 101, (800) CAKE-LADY, (707) 744-1441, fax (707) 744-1312; www.galaxydesserts.com. B&L daily; $. Child portions.*

The factory, which supplies restaurants and hotels throughout Northern California, has moved, but the cafe still serves over 30 different desserts, as well as premium Double Rainbow ice cream and drinks from an espresso bar. Cheesecakes can be shipped anywhere in the country through the mail-order division.

The Hopland Brewery *13351 S. Hwy. 101, (800) 733-3871, (707) 744-1015, fax (707) 744-1910. L&D daily; $. Highchairs, child portions. No reservations.*

Opened in 1983, this was the first brewpub in California since Prohibition. Ales are unpasteurized and unfiltered. Try a Blue Heron Pale Ale (like English bitter) or a sweeter Red Tail Ale. Seating is either inside the 100-year-old brick pub room, featuring vintage stamped-tin walls, or outside in a pleasant beer garden, where children can play in a large sandbox while adults sip suds in shade provided by hop vines. The simple pub fare includes juicy hamburgers, Red Tail Ale chili, burritos, salads, and chips with fresh salsa or guacamole. The don't-miss dessert is Blackhawk Stout double-chocolate cheesecake from their neighbor. The **Mendocino Brewing Company brewhouse** is located out back. Tours are available with 24-hour notice.

Clear Lake

A LITTLE BACKGROUND

Spring-fed Clear Lake is the largest natural fresh-water lake that is totally within California (Lake Tahoe is partially in Nevada). It measures 19 miles by 8 miles. The 90-mile drive around the perimeter takes 2 1/2 to 3 hours.

From the 1870s into the early 1900s, this area was world-famous for its health spas and huge luxury resort hotels. Then, for various reasons, it fell into a state of disrepair and slowly lost its acclaim. Now it is a reasonably-priced family resort area.

Lake County's first traffic light was installed in 1982. There are now seven, but it still has no parking meters.

Clear Lake is situated on volcanic terrain, giving it an unusual physical appearance and a profusion of hot springs. According to a Pomo Indian legend, when there is no snow on 4,200-foot Mount Konocti in April, the volcano will erupt. Those who heed legends should check the April snowfall before making vacation plans.

VISITOR INFORMATION

Lake County Visitor Information Center
875 Lakeport Blvd., Lakeport, (800) LAKESIDE, (707) 263-9544, fax (707) 263-9564; www.lakecounty.com.

GETTING THERE

Located approximately 19 miles east of Hopland via Highway 175. An alternate route follows Highway 29 north from St. Helena. This scenic route goes through the heart of the Wine Country. The rolling hills are strewn with blooming wild flowers during the spring, and with brilliantly colored foliage during the fall. Make the drive during daylight; this winding two-lane road is tedious to drive at night, and, of course, the lovely scenery cannot be enjoyed then.

ANNUAL EVENTS

Summer Concert Series *June-August. In Library Park in Lakeport. Free.*

A little bit of everything is on the bill at this casual event. In the past the mostly-California bands have included Joe Louis Walker and Country Joe and the Fish.

WHAT TO DO

Fishing, swimming, boating, rock hunting, golfing, and water-skiing are the big activities here. Fishing is the biggest. The lake is reputed to be the best bass-fishing spot in the West—

maybe even the best in the entire country. The lake's nutrient-rich waters are credited with producing plenty of 10-pounders, and the lake record is a 17.52-pounder!

Lakefront public parks and beaches are located in Lakeport and Clearlake.

Anderson Marsh State Historic Park *On Hwy. 53 between Lower Lake & Clearlake, (707) 994-0688. W-Sun 10-5. $2/vehicle.*

Acquired by the state in 1982, this 940-acre park contains an additional 470 acres of tule marsh. An 1855 ranch house is open to visitors during special events, and tree-shaded picnic tables are provided.

An annual **Blackberry Festival** *(August; (707) 995-BERY. $2-$3.)* features a variety of entertainment and plenty of homemade blackberry pie.

Clear Lake State Park *5300 Soda Bay Rd., Kelseyville, 3.5 mi. northeast of town, (707) 279-4293. Daily sunrise-sunset. $5/vehicle.*

Located on the shores of the lake, this park offers swimming, fishing, a boat-launching ramp, picnic facilities, campsites, and miles of hiking trails—including the 1/4-mile Indian Nature Trail and 3-mile Dorn Nature Trail. A Visitor Center provides a slide show introduction to the area and a Touch Corner for children. Displays include local wildlife dioramas, a native fish aquarium, an erupting volcano, and exhibits on the area's Pomo Indian history.

Homestake Mining Company Tour
26650 Morgan Valley Rd., 15 mi. southeast of Lower Lake, (800) 525-3743, (707) 263-9544. 1st & 3rd F & Sat of month at 10am; June-Sept only. Free. Reservations required. Strollers not permitted.

Visitors to this modern gold mine are treated to a 3-hour guided bus tour of the **McLaughlin Gold Mine**. Picnic facilities are available.

Lake County Museum *255 N. Main St., Lakeport, (707) 263-4555; www.lakecounty.com. W-Sat 11-4; also Sun, June-Sept.*

Formerly a courthouse, this brick building was built in 1871. It holds a renowned collection of Pomo Indian baskets, stone arrowheads and tools, and historical records.

Each year from mid-November through mid-January, this museum hosts a **Teddy Bear Exhibit**. Hundreds of bears, most loaned to the museum by area residents, are displayed in festive scenes complemented by traditional music.

Lower Lake Historical Schoolhouse Museum
16435 Morgan Valley Rd., Lower Lake, (707) 995-3565; www.lakecounty.com. W-Sat 11-3.

This restored Lower Lake Grammar School houses a reconstructed turn-of-the-century classroom. Museum exhibits include an extensive geological display, a scale model of the dam on Cache Creek, and collections from pioneer families.

WHERE TO STAY

Jules Resort *14195 Lakeshore Dr., Clearlake, (707) 994-6491. 18 units; ¢-$; 1-week min. July & Aug. All kitchens; 1 fireplace. Heated pool (unavail. Nov-Mar), hot tub, sauna.*

Lodging here is in pleasant vintage cabins.

Facilities include a lakefront pool, private beach, fishing pier, and launching ramp. This place is so popular in the summer that it is necessary to book at least 1 year in advance!

Konocti Harbor Resort & Spa *8727 Soda Bay Rd., Kelseyville, (800) 660-LAKE, (707) 279-8575, fax (707) 279-9205; www.konocti harbor.com. 248 rooms; $$-$$$+. Children under 12 free. Some kitchens. 2 heated pools, 2 children's wading pools, fitness center, health spa, 8 clay tennis courts (night lights). 2 restaurants.*

Nestled in the shadow of Mount Konocti on the rim of the lake, this beautifully landscaped resort enjoys a superb setting. Reminiscent of luxury resorts in Hawaii, it is a lot easier to reach and much less expensive. The list of facilities and services is extensive: pro tennis lessons, a children's playground, a recreation room, a jogging trail, a bar with live music in the evenings, a paddle-wheel boat cruise, a miniature golf course, and a marina that rents fishing boats, water-skiing equipment, and pedal boats. Babysitting can be arranged, and tennis, spa, concert, and fishing packages are available. For an added fee, the spa/fitness center offers an additional indoor pool and hot tub, a sauna and steam room, a gym, and a variety of pampering treatments.

The **restaurant** dining room has stunning lake views, offers an innovative American menu, and is comfortably equipped for children, while the **Classic Rock Cafe** offers fun and innovative American meals in a rock museum setting.

A **Classic Concerts by the Lake** series, which has both dinner and cocktail seatings, brings in big name entertainment year-round. In good weather, shows are held in an outdoor amphitheater. Packages are available.

Skylark Shores Resort Motel *1120 N. Main St., Lakeport, (800) 675-6151, (707) 263-6151, fax (707) 263-7733; www.skylarkshoresmotel.com. 45 rooms; 100% non-smoking; $-$$. Children under 1 free. Some kitchens. Heated pool (unavail. Oct-May).*

These modern motel units are located lakefront. The spacious, well-maintained grounds feature an expansive lawn, swings, and a wading area in the lake.

WHERE TO STAY NEARBY

Wilbur Hot Springs Health Sanctuary
3375 Wilbur Springs Rd., near intersection of Hwys. 16 & 20, 25 mi. east of lake, 22 mi. west of Williams, (530) 473-2306; www.wilburhot springs.com. 20 rooms; 100% non-smoking; $-$$$+; 2-night min. on weekends. Unsuitable for children under 3. No TVs; some shared baths. Pool, 4 hot tubs, sauna. Day use: $33/person; reservations required.

Soaking in one of the four tubs filled with hot sulfurous spring water and then plunging into the cool water of the outdoor pool are the main activities here. Clothing is optional in pool and tub areas only. Several styles of massage are available, and the more ambitious can take walks in the surrounding hills. Lodging is in both private rooms and dormitory-style shared rooms that have no electric light in the evening, plus campsites are available. A parlor is equipped with a pool table and piano for entertainment, and guests can prepare their own meals in a large communal kitchen.

WHERE TO EAT

Park Place *50 Third St., Lakeport, (707) 263-0444. L&D daily; $-$$. Highchairs, boosters, child portions. Reservations advised.*

Located lakefront and across the street from Library Park, this cafe offers incredible views from its outdoor rooftop dining area. For starters, don't miss the magnificent bruchetta—a baguette topped with pesto and sun-dried tomatoes and then grilled. The menu boasts a large selection of fresh pastas, including several kinds of tortellinis and raviolis, and fresh fish, steaks, and hamburgers are available.

Ukiah

GETTING THERE

Located approximately 15 miles north of Hopland.

WHAT TO DO

Grace Hudson Museum and **Sun House** *431 S. Main St., (707) 462-3370. W-Sat 10-4:30, Sun 12-4; tours of Sun House on the hour, 12-3. By donation: $2/person, $5/family.*

Named for the prominent painter who specialized in doing portraits of the area's Pomo Indians, this museum displays Native American games, musical instruments, and baskets as well as some of Ms. Hudson's personal paraphernalia. Her six-room home, the California Craftsman-style Sun House, is adjacent to the museum. Built of redwood in 1911, it still holds most of its original furnishings. Picnic facilities are available in a park area within the 4 1/2-acre complex.

WHERE TO STAY

Orr Hot Springs *13201 Orr Springs Rd., 13 mi. west of Hwy. 101, (707) 462-6277, fax (707) 463-2516. 3 rooms, 14 cottages; 100% non-smoking; $$-$$$; 2-night min. on Sat. Children under 3 free. No TVs; some kitchens + communal kitchen; some wood-burning stoves; some shared baths. Unheated mineral water pool, natural hot springs pool, 4 private & 2 communal hot tubs, sauna. Day use: daily 10-10; $17/person, $10 on M.*

In the 1850s, when this mineral springs resort was built, patrons reached it via stagecoach. Now visitors get here by driving a scenic, winding, two-lane road. A natural rock swimming pool built into the hillside is filled with cool mineral spring water, and several underground springs are tapped to fill, with body-temperature water, four porcelain Victorian tubs in an 1863 bath house. A gas-fired sauna features a stained-glass window and a clear skylight. Note that this is a clothing optional establishment. Guests sleep either in dormitories, guest rooms, or cottages built in the 1940s from locally milled redwood, or in a dormitory, and must bring their own food. Campsites are also available. **Montgomery Redwoods State Park**, which offers two loop trails for hiking, is just 1 mile down the road.

Vichy Hot Springs Resort *2605 Vichy Springs Rd., 3 mi. east of Hwy. 101, (707) 462-9515, fax (707) 462-9516; www.vichysprings.com. 12 rooms, 3 cottages; 100% non-smoking; $$$. Children under 1 free. No TVs; some kitchens & gas fireplaces. Unheated pool & natural hot springs pool, hot tub, health spa. Full breakfast. Day use: $25/person.*

Founded in 1854, this 700-acre resort still has three cottages that were built then—two of which are the oldest still-standing structures in Mendocino County—and a hotel built of redwood in the 1860s. It was named after the famous French springs discovered by Julius Caesar and is said to have the only naturally carbonated warm mineral baths in North America. In its heyday the resort attracted guests from San Francisco, who had to endure a day's journey to get here—by ferry across the bay, by train to Cloverdale, then by stagecoach to the resort. They came in search of curative powers attributed to the waters found here. Among the famous guests were writers Mark Twain, Jack London, and Robert Louis Stevenson, and presidents Ulysses S. Grant, Benjamin Harrison, and Teddy Roosevelt. The resort's 130-year-old concrete "champagne" tubs—filled with 90-degree, tingling, naturally carbonated water—are situated in a shady area overlooking a creek. Swimsuits are required. Guests can hike to a 40-foot-tall waterfall, mountain bike over dirt roads, and swim in an un-chlorinated Olympic-size pool. Picnic lunches can be arranged, and the resort's own bottled Vichy Springs Mineral Water is available.

Willits

A LITTLE BACKGROUND

An old-time sign over Main Street welcomes visitors to the "Gateway to the Redwoods."

VISITOR INFORMATION

Willits Chamber of Commerce *239 S. Main St., (707) 459-7910.*

Mark Twain taking the waters

GETTING THERE

Located approximately 25 miles north of Ukiah, and 140 miles north of San Francisco. Heading north after here, it begins getting mountainous and scenic.

WHERE TO STAY

Emandal Farm *16500 Hearst Rd., 16 mi. northeast of town, (800) 262-9597, (707) 459-5439, fax (707) 459-1808; www.emandal.com. Open for 1-week stays during Aug; weekends in spring & fall. Rates vary according to age and include 3 meals per day. All shared bathrooms.*

On weekend visits to this 1,000-acre working farm, guests arrive for Friday night dinner. Families are assigned a table for the weekend and then spend some blissful hours there chowing down superb home cooking prepared with the farm's own organically grown produce. Days are filled with leisurely activities—perhaps a short hike down to a sandy beach on the magnificent Eel River for a swim, or maybe a hike up the steep mountain behind the barn to Rainbow Lake. Some folks just doze in the hammocks outside each of the rustic one-room redwood cabins dating from 1916. Others get involved with the farm chores: milking the goats, collecting eggs, feeding the pigs. In the fall, the farm's very special jams, relishes, and baking mixes are available by mail order for the holidays.

KOA Kampground *(800) KOA-8542, (707) 459-6179.*

For description, see page 415.

WHERE TO EAT

Fast Food.

It's all here. Families will favor **Burger King, Fosters Freeze**, and **McDonald's**—all of which have colorful playgrounds attached to their dining areas.

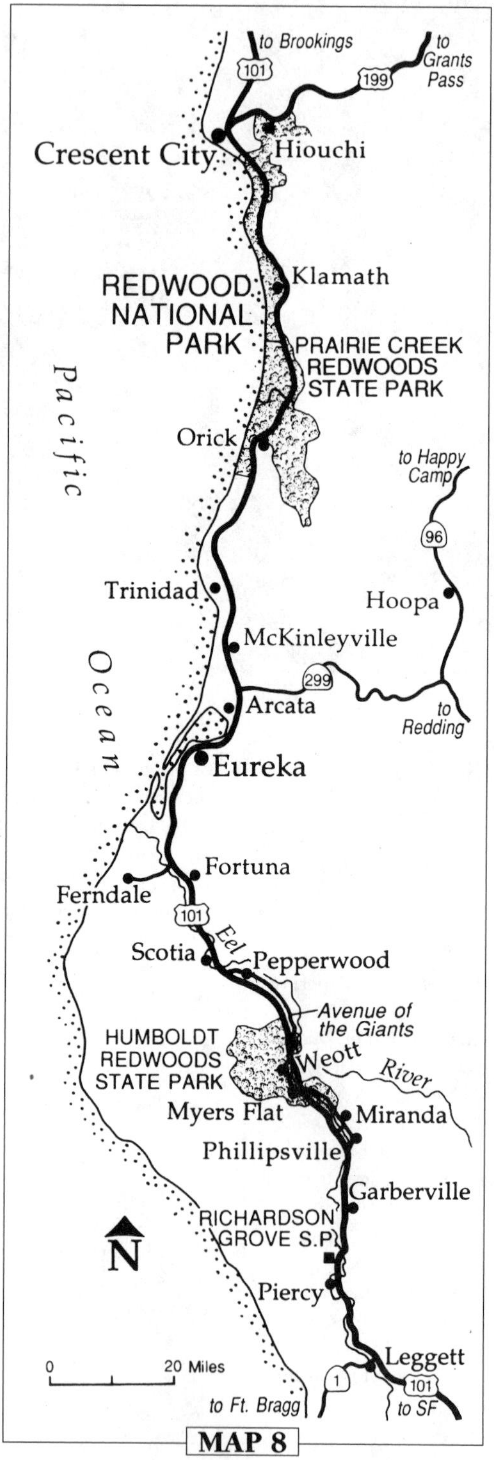
to Brookings
101
to
Grants
Pass
199
Crescent City
Hiouchi
Klamath
REDWOOD
NATIONAL
PARK
PRAIRIE CREEK
REDWOODS
STATE PARK
Pacific
Orick
to Happy
Camp
96
Trinidad
Hoopa
McKinleyville
Ocean
299
Arcata
to
Redding
Eureka
Fortuna
Ferndale
101
Eel
Scotia
Pepperwood
Avenue of
the Giants
HUMBOLDT
REDWOODS
STATE PARK
Weott
River
Myers Flat
Miranda
Phillipsville
Garberville
RICHARDSON
GROVE S.P.
N
Piercy
Leggett
0
20 Miles
1
101
to Ft. Bragg
to SF

MAP 8

The Avenue of the Giants

A LITTLE BACKGROUND

The redwoods, once seen, leave a mark or create a vision that stays with you always . . . It's not their stature nor the color that seems to shift and vary under your eyes; no, they are not like any other trees we know, they are ambassadors from another time.

—John Steinbeck, 1962

Actually the old Highway 101, this spectacularly scenic drive begins at Phillipsville. Paralleling the freeway and the Eel River, this breathtaking route winds through grove after grove of huge sequoia sempervirens redwoods. In fact, the route is home to 60 percent of the tallest trees in the world. It continues for 32 miles to Pepperwood, where it rejoins the busier new Highway 101. Unfortunately, in spots it juxtaposes nature's best and most majestic with humankind's most kitchy and trite. Fortunately, the number of shops displaying chainsaw-carved redwood souvenirs is small, with plenty of long stretches of uninterrupted tall trees in between.

Millions of years ago, when dinosaurs roamed the earth, gigantic redwood forests were plentiful. After the Ice Age, the redwood, which has a life span of 400 to 800 years but has been known to live beyond 2,000 years, survived only in a narrow 540-mile-long by 40-mile-wide strip along the northern coast of California. Before the logging days on the north coast, it is estimated this area contained 2 1/2 million acres of redwoods. Now only 100,000 acres of ancient old-growth redwoods remain—most preserved by the state park system and Redwood National Park. Approximately half of these huge old trees are found in **Humboldt Redwoods State Park** in Weott *(Daily dawn-dusk. $5/vehicle.)*. The park's **Visitor Center** *((707) 946-2409, fax (707) 946-2326. Daily 9-5, Mar-Oct; Thur-Sun 10-4, Nov-Feb.)* is located 2 miles south of Weott, next to Burlington Campground.

Unusual sights along this unique stretch of road are numerous. The 10,000-acre **Rockefeller Forest**—the world's largest grove of virgin redwoods—is near Weott. Also referred to as "the world's finest forest," it features hiking trails leading to the Flatiron Tree, the Giant Tree, and the 356-foot Tall Tree. Campsites are available. (**Richardson Grove State Park** *(8 mi. south of Garberville, (707) 247-3318.)* also has campsites.) The **Children's Forest**, located across the south fork of the Eel River, is a 1,120-acre memorial to children, and **Williams Grove** features picturesque picnic and swimming sites on the river. In Myers Flat, the 275-foot-tall **Shrine Drive-Thru Tree** *(13078 Avenue of the Giants. $1.50, under 10 free.)*, which is not part of the state park, has a circumference of approximately 64 feet and provides the opportunity to take an unusual picture in a natural fire cavity that has been widened to accommodate cars.

GETTING THERE

Phillipsville is 78 miles north of Willits, and 214 miles north of San Francisco.

ANNUAL EVENTS

Reggae on the River *August. In Piercy; (707) 923-3368.*

Held on the banks of the Eel River, this is

considered one of the best reggae music festivals in the U.S.

WHAT TO DO

Confusion Hill *75001 N. Hwy. 101, Piercy, (707) 925-6456. Daily 10-4; in summer 8-7. House: Adults $3, 6-12 $2. Train: Adults $3, 3-12 $2.*

Water runs uphill here, appearing to defy gravity, and a miniature train takes passengers on a ride through a tree tunnel to the crest of a hill in the redwoods.

Drive-Thru Tree Park *67402 Drive-Thru Tree Rd., Leggett, (707) 925-6363. Daily 8-dusk. $3/car.*

Most average-size cars can squeeze through the hole in this 315-foot high, 21-foot diameter, 2,400-year-old giant redwood known as the Chandelier Tree. Bring a camera. Nature trails and lakeside picnic tables are also available.

WHERE TO STAY

Benbow Inn *445 Lake Benbow Dr., Garberville, (800) 355-3301, (707) 923-2124, fax (707) 923-2897; www.benbowinn.com. 55 rooms; 100% non-smoking; $$-$$$+; 2-night min. on Sat. Closed Jan-Mar. Some TVs, VCRs, & wood-burning fireplaces. Afternoon tea; restaurant.*

This magnificent English Tudor inn, which opened to the public in 1926, offers a variety of rooms—all of which are furnished with antiques. Some rooms have lake views and private patios; all are equipped with a basket of mystery novels and a carafe of sherry. A majestic communal lounge with fireplace and library invites socializing, and game tables are set with chess boards and jigsaw puzzles. Interesting art prints decorate the walls throughout. This spot enjoys perfect summer temperatures. Outside pleasures that make the most of it include colorful English gardens with grassy expanses, a small private beach and lake, a putting green, lawn games, and free bicycles. Off premises, a 9-hole golf course and heated swimming pool are within walking distance. A complimentary tea is served each afternoon at 3 p.m. (non-guests may partake for a small charge), and classic films are screened each evening. Special events are often scheduled, and holiday festivities occur throughout December.

The elegant **restaurant** *(B,L,&D daily; $-$$$.)* serves an expansive menu, with both simple dishes and more sophisticated fare. In fair weather, a well-priced Sunday champagne brunch buffet is served outdoors on a large terrace overlooking the lake. Additionally, a cozy taproom bar dispenses good cheer and live entertainment on some evenings, and picnic baskets can be ordered by guests.

Miranda Gardens Resort *6766 Avenue of the Giants, Miranda, (707) 943-3011, fax (707) 943-3584; www.mirandagardens.com. 16 units; $-$$$. Some kitchens & fireplaces. Heated pool (unavail. Nov-Apr), 2 tennis courts. Pets welcome.*

Lodging here is a choice of either motel rooms or cottages. A children's playground and plenty of outdoor games— croquet, shuffleboard, and horseshoes—are available.

Scotia

A LITTLE BACKGROUND

Scotia is one of the last company-owned lumber towns in the United States. Owned by the Pacific Lumber Company, which has its headquarters here, the town was founded in 1869. Today it caters to workers offering them homes and facilities.

WHAT TO DO

Demonstration Forest *On Hwy. 101, 5 mi. south of town, (707) 764-2222. Daily 8-4; summer only. Free.*

To educate the public about modern forestry practices and permit seeing how a forest grows back after harvest, the Pacific Lumber Company offers self-guided tours through a part of its forest that was harvested in 1941. Picnic tables are available.

Pacific Lumber Company Mill Tour *125 Main St., (707) 764-2222, fax (707) 764-4396. M-F 7:30-2. Closed weeks of July 4th and Christmas. Free.*

Take a self-guided tour through the world's largest redwood lumber mill. Most visitors consider this an exciting and amazing experience, and a highlight of their visit to this area. Get a pass for the hour-long tour in the old Greek Revival-style First National Bank building, which is now a logging museum.

WHERE TO STAY

Scotia Inn *100 Mill St./Main St., (707) 764-5683; www.scotiainn.com. 10 rooms; 100% non-smoking; $-$$$. Children free. Some TVs. Continental breakfast; restaurant.*

The hotel that stood on this site in 1888 accommodated travelers waiting for the stage-coach south. The current hotel, built in 1923, greets guests with a magnificent lobby featuring walls of burnished redwood. Rooms are furnished with antiques, and bathrooms feature clawfoot tubs. A splurge on the Bridal Suite is worthwhile just for its impressive private Jacuzzi room. Dinner and Sunday brunch are served in grand style in the dining room.

Ferndale

A LITTLE BACKGROUND

Composed of well-preserved and restored Victorian buildings, this village was founded in 1852. It remains largely unchanged since the 1890s (except that then it had 9 churches and 9 saloons and now it has 6 churches and 3 saloons) and is now a State Historical Landmark. Of special note are the "Butterfat Palaces"—elaborate Victorian homes paid for by the rich local dairy industry.

Now, in addition to the dairy farming, the town prospers as an artists' colony and is filled with galleries and antique shops. Shops of particular interest include the old-time **Ferndale Meat Company** at 376 Main Street, which uses old-fashioned curing and smoking techniques and sells deli items, and the **Lentz Department Store** at 406 Main Street, which has creaky floorboards and dispenses vintage items associated with the good old days. It is so civilized here, that the town bookstore leaves bargain used books out at night in its entryway; anyone who wants to purchase one is on the honor system to slip a dollar through the mail slot.

The scenic pioneer cemetery on a hill behind the old Methodist church is also interesting to visit, and don't miss the circa 1860 gumdrop-shaped coast cypress trees on Ocean Avenue. A great way to get the lay of the land is via a horse-drawn carriage tour that is surprisingly well-priced.

In 1994, the whole town starred in the film *Outbreak.*

VISITOR INFORMATION

Ferndale Chamber of Commerce *P.O. Box 325, Ferndale 95536, (707) 786-4477, same fax; www.victorianferndale.org/chamber.*

GETTING THERE

Located approximately 15 miles south of Eureka, and 5 miles west of Highway 101. The exit that leads through Fernbridge permits crossing the Eel River over an historic 1911 bridge that is the oldest reinforced concrete bridge still in existence.

ANNUAL EVENTS

Cross Country Kinetic Sculpture Race *May; on Memorial Day Weekend.. (707) 786-9259. Free.*

In this unusual competition, bizarre and artistic people-powered sculptures race 38 miles over dunes and rivers from Arcata to Ferndale. Cheating is encouraged, and the prizes are questionable.

Fortuna Rodeo *July. In Fortuna; (707) 725-6921.*

The oldest professional rodeo in the West, this event includes a chili cook-off, street games, a parade, a carnival, and more.

Humboldt County Fair and Horse Races *August. (707) 786-9511.*

The oldest uninterrupted county fair in California, this event has happened annually since 1897 and includes contests, carnival rides, sheepshearing, and more.

America's Tallest Living Christmas Tree *December. (707) 786-4477.*

Heralding the Christmas spirit, this village annually rekindles its 125-foot Sitka spruce in a ceremony that has been a tradition since the 1930s.

Lighted Tractor Parade *December. (800) 346-3482, (707) 786-4116.*

Area farmers decorate their antique and modern tractors, trailers, and wagons with Christmas lights and holiday scenes.

WHAT TO DO

Ferndale Museum *515 Shaw Ave., (707) 786-4466. W-Sat 11-4, Sun 1-4.*

Exhibits here include Victorian room settings, a crosscut of a 1,237-year-old redwood, and a working turn-of-the-century seismograph. An annex displays farming, logging, and dairy equipment.

Historic Homes.

- **Fern Cottage** *(707) 786-4835, (707) 786-4735. Call for schedule. Adults $3, under 12 $2.*

This 19th-century settlement farmhouse is significant for its gracious, well-preserved architecture. The house's fabric and content have remained virtually unchanged for more than half a century.

- **Linden Hall** *(707) 786-4908. Call for schedule; Mar-Dec only. Adults $3, under 12 $2.*

Built in 1901 by a prominent dairyman, this large, 2-story Queen Anne Victorian features grand architectural details such as curly redwood moldings and parquet floors. The house contains many of its original furnishings as well as its original gas lighting fixtures and parlor wallpaper. A surrounding English country garden is being developed.

Kinetic Sculpture Museum *393 Main St., (707) 786-9259. Daily 9-5.*

Human-powered vehicles designed to travel over roads, mud, sand, and water are on display.

Loleta Cheese Factory *252 Loleta Dr., Loleta, (800) 995-0453, (707) 733-5470. M-F 9-5, Sat 10-4; also Sun 12-4, June-mid-Oct.*

Known for their Monterey Jacks and smoked salmon Cheddar, this factory has big windows through which the cheese-making process can be observed. Cheeses are made from the rich milk of cows grazed on the grass and clover pastures of the Eel River Valley. Sixteen different kinds of cheeses can be tasted, including smoked salmon and white cheddars. A note of interest is that part of *Halloween II* was filmed across the street in the Familiar Foods building.

Lost Coast.

Given this name because of its remoteness, the wildly scenic area of Cape Mendocino, the westernmost point in the continental U.S., is just south of town. It is reached via steep Wildcat Road, which dates back to the 1870s and begins off Ocean Avenue 1 block west of Main Street, and then twists and turns for 30 scenic miles to the treacherous waters of the ocean. Look for the sign to "Cape Town—Petrolia." Not many redwoods grow here, as they are repelled by salt air, but dense Douglas fir forests and unspoiled farm lands make up for that. Make a day of it by traveling all the way to Petrolia, which was the home of California's first oil well in 1865 and where there are campsites and a few inns, and on to Honeydew, to the Rockefeller Forest, and to Highway 101 for a return to Ferndale. Pack in food and fill the gas tank, as there are few if any concessions along the way, though campsites are available.

WHERE TO STAY

Gingerbread Mansion Inn *400 Berding St., (800) 952-4136, (707) 786-4000, fax (707) 786-4381; www.gingerbread-mansion.com. 10 rooms; 100% non-smoking; $$$-$$$+; 2-night min. on weekends. Unsuitable for children under 10. No TVs; some wood-burning & gas fireplaces. Afternoon tea, full breakfast.*

Originally built in 1899 as a doctor's home, this carefully restored, cheery peach-and-yellow Queen Anne-Eastlake Victorian mansion boasts gables and turrets and elaborate gingerbread trim. Rooms are furnished with Victorian antiques, and each has its own charm: The Gingerbread Suite features antique "his" and "hers" clawfoot tubs perched toe to toe right in the bedroom, with framed art of bathing babies hanging on the wall above; several others have spectacular spacious bathrooms equipped with wood-burning fireplaces and twin clawfoot tubs placed side by side. The third-floor attic is the opulent Empire Suite,

with a dramatic 12-foot ceiling and marble floor. Guests are pampered with bathrobes and bubble bath. Breakfast, served in the grand dining room, is enhanced by the use of the owner's collection of green cameo Depression glass, and a proper afternoon tea, with assorted sweets and savories, is served in the four guest parlors. All food is made on the premises, including the hand-dipped chocolates that announce bedtime. Guests can stroll or sit in the formal English garden and view its unusual topiaries, 2-story-high camellia bushes, and variety of fuchsias; they can also sit on the second-floor porch and watch the very limited street action.

Shaw House B&B Inn *703 Main St., (800) 557-SHAW, (707) 786-9958; www.shawhouse.com. 8 rooms; 100% non-smoking; $-$$$. Afternoon tea, full breakfast.*

Built in 1854 by the town founder, this white-and-blue gabled Carpenter Gothic Victorian farmhouse, set on park-like grounds way back from the street behind a white picket fence, is the oldest house in town. It is so old that it predates the town of Ferndale. In fact, its original name was Ferndale. Made entirely of redwood, with unusual paneled ceilings, it is listed on the National Register of Historic Places. Public spaces include a library, two parlors, a dining room, and balconies, and antique furnishings are used throughout. The expansive surrounding garden was carefully researched to reflect the house's era and includes vintage wildflowers, old roses, and fragrant wisterias.

Victorian Inn *400 Ocean Ave., (888) 589-1808, (707) 786-4949, fax (707) 786-4558; www.a-victorian-inn.com. 12 rooms; $-$$. Some fireplaces. Continental breakfast; restaurant.*

Built in 1890 of local redwood, this massive, high-ceilinged hotel features beautifully appointed rooms with vintage fixtures and furnishings. Some rooms have clawfoot tubs and window alcoves overlooking Main Street. **Silva's Fine Jewelry** salon operates in the former front parlor.

WHERE TO EAT

Curley's Grill *400 Ocean Ave., in the Victorian Inn, (707) 786-9696. L&D daily; $-$$. Highchairs, boosters. Reservations advised.*

Extremely popular with locals, this comfortable spot is known for generous servings of consistently good food at fair prices. The atmosphere is bright and cheery, and a collection of vintage salt-and-pepper shakers adds a touch of whimsy to each table. Highly touted dishes include a tortilla-and-onion cake and the house Caesar salad. More sure things include the housemade soup of the day and the delicate fresh snapper sautéed with lemon and white wine. In addition to full dinners, a hamburger, a vegetarian burger, and several sandwiches and salads are also available.

Ferndale Emporium *344 Main St., (707) 786-9877, fax (707) 786-9882. High tea Thur, F, & Sat 11:30-4; $. Unsuitable for children under 6. Reservations advised.*

The three-tiered high tea served here on the mezzanine level is extensive enough to pass for lunch or an early dinner. All the accouterments that make this ritual so enjoyable are provided along with a big pot of tea and an array of edibles. A special children's tea includes lemonade and peanut butter sandwiches. After muching on tiny sandwiches and tea cakes and sipping a refreshing brew from china cups, a shop filled with tea-related paraphernalia awaits browsing.

Ferndale Pizza Company *607 Main St., (707) 786-4345. L&D Tu-Sun; $. Highchairs, boosters.*

Operating out of a converted service station, this modest, cozy spot serves up delicious hand-thrown pizza as well as sandwiches served on homemade rolls and a good salad bar. The owner grinds his meats and hand-forms the meatballs.

Eureka

A LITTLE BACKGROUND

Eureka was founded in 1850 as a gold rush supply base for inland mines. By 1865 it had shifted into harvesting lumber for shipbuilding and housing. Ambitious logging activity has, over time, changed the scenery here quite a bit. The best of the remaining virgin redwoods are in this area's state parks, all of which were established in the 1920s.

A small town with a welcoming attitude and atmosphere, Eureka is known as "the coolest city in the nation." The average temperature in July ranges from 52 to 60 degrees. In January it drops to between 41 and 53 degrees. In fact, the highest temperature ever recorded in Eureka was 87 degrees on October 26, 1993. The average annual rainfall is 37 inches, and fog can sometimes be heavy even in summer.

The winter off-season is an uncrowded time to visit the north coast redwood country around Humboldt Bay. Visitors then should pack warm clothing and kiss the sunshine good-bye as they prepare to enjoy the stunning beauty of this quiet, often misty area.

Eureka and nearby Arcata are both known for their brightly painted, well-preserved Victorian homes. In fact, Eureka has more Victorian buildings than any other city in the U.S. See an interesting variety by driving down Hillsdale Street between E and C streets.

Be warned that gas is expensive here. That's because it is brought up by barge.

VISITOR INFORMATION

Humboldt County Convention & Visitors Bureau *1034 2nd St., (800) 346-3482, (707) 443-5097, fax (707) 443-5115; www.redwoodvisitor.org.*

The Greater Eureka Chamber of Commerce *2112 Broadway, (800) 356-6381, (707) 442-3738.*

GETTING THERE

Located approximately 130 miles north of Willits, and approximately 280 miles north of San Francisco.

ANNUAL EVENTS

Independence Day Humboldt Bay 4th of July Festival *July. (707) 444-8817.*

For this old-fashioned celebration, a street festival takes over four city blocks with live entertainment, train rides, and children's activities. It culminates with a fireworks extravaganza over Humboldt Bay.

A Coastal Christmas *November-December. (800) 346-3482.*

The whole town is elaborately decorated for the season, and lodgings book up fast. Call for a brochure describing seasonal activities.

Truckers Christmas Light Convoy *December. (800) 346-3482, (707) 444-2323, (707) 442-5744.*

Each year over 150 18-wheel big rigs—decorated with thousands of twinkling lights and loaded with "candy cane" logs—are seen truckin' on through town in a slow procession. A manger scene is carried by a crane, carolers sing from a hayhauler, and Santa's sled is pulled by cows.

WHAT TO DO

Blue Ox Millworks *Foot of X St., 3 blocks north of 4th St., (800) 248-4259, (707) 444-3437, fax (707) 444-0918; www.blueoxmill.com. Tours M-Sat 9-5, Sun 11-4; closed Sun in winter. Adults $5, seniors $4, 6-12 $2.50.*

Dozens of antique woodworking machines can be viewed in this working museum on a self-guided, 1-hour tour. The oldest dates back to 1860 and the newest to 1948. Many of the Victorian-era machines are pedal-powered and currently used to reproduce gingerbread trim for renovated Victorian homes. Of special interest are several "skid" buildings. Built on sleds, or "skids," these structures were once pulled through the snow to each new logging site. Kids particularly enjoy meeting the two blue oxen, weighing in at 2,000 pounds each, and the assortment of farm animals.

Carson Mansion *143 M St./2nd St..*

Built between 1884 and 1886, this is said to be the most photographed Victorian house in the world and is the "queen" of Victorian architecture. A mixture of several building styles—including Queen Anne, Italianate, and Stick-Eastlake—it took 100 men more than 2 years to build. Built during a depression, it was privately financed by pioneer lumber baron William Carson, a failed gold miner, in order to avoid laying off his best men. It now houses a private club and can be viewed only from the exterior.

Carson Mansion

Clarke Memorial Museum *240 E St./3rd St., in Old Town, (707) 443-0290. Tu-Sat 12-4. By donation.*

An important collection of local Indian baskets and ceremonial regalia is on display here along with an extensive collection of 19th-century regional artifacts and pioneer relics. The palatial 1912 building is also the backdrop for displays of antique weapons and Victorian furniture and decorative arts.

Covered Bridges *Take Hwy. 101 south to Elk River Rd., then follow Elk River Rd. to either Bertas Rd. (2 mi.) or Zanes Rd. (3 mi.).*

These two all-wood covered bridges were constructed of redwood in 1936. **Berta's Ranch bridge** is the most westerly covered bridge in the U.S. **Zane's Ranch bridge** is the second-most westerly covered bridge in the U.S. Both are 52 feet long.

Fort Humboldt State Historic Park *3431 Fort Ave., at south end of town, (707) 445-6567. Daily 9-5. Free.*

U.S. Grant was posted here in 1854. The hospital, which dates to 1863, has been restored and is now used as a museum. Exhibits within

Dolbur steam donkey

the park include some locomotives, a restored logger's cabin, and displays of pioneer logging methods. An excellent view of Humboldt Bay makes this a nice spot for a picnic.

At the annual **Steam Donkey Days**, held in April, antique equipment is put into action. Steam donkeys are operated and logging techniques are demonstrated. Train rides are also part of the fun.

Golden Angels Cellars *333 1st St./E St., in Old Town, (888) 4GAMEAD, (707) 443-6323, fax (707) 444-7863; www.goldenangels.com. Daily 11-5.*

Mead is the oldest fermented drink known to man. Several styles are made here, including plain honey, honey-apple, and honey-cherry. Sample them in the tasting room located inside the town's former Opera House. Cider made from area heirloom apples and other locally-made foods are also available.

Humboldt Bay Harbor Cruise *Foot of C St., (707) 445-1910, fax (707) 445-0249. Daily at 1, 2:30, 4, & 5:30. Closed Nov & Jan-Feb. Adults $9.50, 60+ $8.50, 4-12 $6.50.*

The 75-minute cruise aboard the tiny *M/V Madaket*, which once ferried workers to the lumber mills across the bay in Samoa, allows a view of the bustling activity and native wildlife of the bay. Built in 1910 in Fairhaven, California, it is the oldest operating passenger vessel in the U.S. and has the smallest licensed bar in the state. A dinner cruise sails on Saturdays at 7:30, and a Sunday brunch cruise sails at 11; both have an additional charge.

Morris Graves Museum of Art *636 F St./7th St., (707) 442-0278, fax (707) 442-2040; www.thepalette.com. W-Sun 12-5, Thur to 8. Free.*

Located within the historic Carnegie Library building, which was the state's first free public library in 1904, this new museum features beautifully restored woodwork and a magnificent tile floor. It displays local and traveling exhibitions, and an outdoor sculpture garden and a small performance space are part of the facilities.

Old Town *1st St./2nd St./3rd St., from C St. to G St., (707) 443-5097.*

This waterfront area consists of restored commercial and residential Victorian buildings. Many restaurants, boutiques, and antique shops are located here, including the original **Restoration Hardware.** The **Romano Gabriel Sculpture Garden**—a folk art garden constructed from vegetable crates by the late artist Romano Gabriel—can be viewed at 315 2nd Street.

Sequoia Park Zoo *3414 W St./Glatt St., (707) 442-6552. Tu-Sun 10-5; May-Sept to 7. Free.*

The backdrop for this combination zoo/playground/picnic area is a 52-acre grove of old-growth redwoods. Hiking trails, gardens, and a duck pond are also within the zoo, and a petting zoo is open during the summer.

WHERE TO STAY

Carter House *1033 3rd St./L St., (800) 404-1390, (707) 444-8062, fax (707) 444-8067; www.carterhouse.com. 4 stories; 6 rooms; 100% non-smoking; $$$-$$$+. Children under 12 free; unsuitable for toddlers. 1 TV & VCR; 1 fireplace. Afternoon & evening snack, full breakfast; room service.*

Looking like it has been here forever, this weather-darkened redwood inn was actually built by owner Mark Carter in 1982. It is a re-creation of the 1884 design of two San Francisco architects, one of whom designed Eureka's famous Carson Mansion. (The original house stood on the corner of Bush and Jones in San Francisco and was destroyed in the fire following the 1906 earthquake.) Rooms are all oversize and elegantly furnished. Evening wine and hors d'oeuvres are served in a pleasant parlor, and at bedtime cookies and cordials appear. Dinner is available in the dining room on weekends by reservation.

Across the street, the even newer **Hotel Carter** *(301 L St. 24 rooms; 100% non-smoking; $$$-$$$+. Children under 12 free. Some VCRs & gas fireplaces. Afternoon & evening snack, full breakfast; restaurant, room service.)* provides casual, tasteful lodging amenable to families. Some large suites have showers built for two and in-room hot tubs large enough for a family of four, and a video library of almost 300 films is available to guests at no charge. An impressive **wine shop** operates off the lobby; a mail-order service is available in which two featured wines per month are sent to participants.

Also just off the lobby of the Hotel Carter, **Restaurant 301** *(B&L daily. Highchairs, boosters, child portions. Reservations advised.)* produces elegant meals showcasing the region's finest seasonal delicacies, including Kumamoto oysters and Pacific salmon. Designed to please both the eye and the palate, entrees are artistically arranged on oversize plates and garnished with such delights as fresh flowers and herb sprigs. Selections from a recent menu included flavorful squash cakes, chicken cacciatora with creamy polenta, and grilled pork loin with both housemade chutney and applesauce. A well-priced five-course, fixed price dinner is available with optional selected wine pairings. In addition to an extensive, carefully chosen wine list, bar drinks are also available. Breakfast for the four inns is served here and includes a pastry buffet and hot entree.

Continuing the empire-building, **Bell Cottage** *(1023 3rd St. 3 rooms. All VCRs; shared kitchen; some wood-burning & gas fireplaces. Room service.)*, which is adjacent to the Carter House, has recently been added to the holdings, as has a vintage Victorian house.

Throughout all four inns, the owner's substantial collection of original local art can be viewed. Guests who are interested may visit the herb and vegetable garden that supplies the restaurant. It is the most extensive inn kitchen garden on the West Coast.

Daly Inn *1125 H St., (800) 321-9656, (707) 445-3638. 5 rooms. Unsuitable for children under 12. Full breakfast.*

Built in 1905, this Colonial Revival mansion is elegantly restored, furnished with interesting antiques, and decorated with an array of exquisite wallpaper patterns. Among the several public spaces are a sun porch and a TV room.

"An Elegant Victorian Mansion" *1406 C St., (707) 444-3144, (707) 442-5594. 4 rooms; 100% non-smoking; $$-$$$. Unsuitable for children. Some shared baths. Sauna. Afternoon snack, full breakfast.*

The Eureka Inn

A National Historic Landmark, this spectacular 1888 Queen Anne-influenced Eastlake Victorian was originally built for the town mayor. It is located in a residential neighborhood overlooking Humboldt Bay. Opulently decorated with many of the innkeeper's family heirlooms, its public spaces include two parlors, a library, and a sitting room. Guests are entertained by such nostalgic pleasures as listening to the Victrola and watching silent movies. Each guest room is unique, but the Van Gogh Room is exceptional in that it displays an original watercolor by the artist as well as several original works by Dali. The afternoon snack here is old-time lemonade, or maybe an ice cream soda, but certainly *not* contemporary wine and cheese. The house is set on a tranquil, park-like estate complete with manicured Victorian flower gardens and a croquet lawn, and bicycles can be borrowed. Perfectly accenting the inn's splendor is the spirited innkeepers' enthusiasm for sharing information about anything that might intrigue a guest. Town tours from the rumble seat of a lovingly restored Model T can be arranged, with the dramatic innkeeper dressed in charming era garb and donning a straw hat. A visit here offers a step back in time to a more gracious era; it is a sort of Victorian living history experience. A lavish, formal breakfast is served at an elegantly set table and includes the house coffee—a fragrant blend with hints of chocolate and hazelnut.

The Eureka Inn *518 7th St., (800) 862-4906, (707) 442-6441, fax (707) 442-0637; www.eurekainn.com. 4 stories; 105 rooms; $$-$$$. Children under 16 free. 1 kitchen; 1 woodburning & 1 gas fireplace. Heated pool, hot tub, 2 saunas. 2 restaurants, room service. Dogs welcome.*

Built in Tudor Revival style in 1922 and now a National Historic Landmark, this stately hotel covers an entire block and is within easy walking distance of Old Town attractions. It has what is perhaps the oldest drive-up entrance in the state, and its large, high-ceilinged lobby features redwood beams and a massive fireplace trimmed in oak and redwood and crowned with a brass mantle.

The mellow **Bristol Rose Cafe**, paneled with oak (rare in this area) and featuring comfy booths and a high beamed ceiling, is a delightful spot for breakfast or lunch. Dinner in the clubby **Rib Room and Wine Cellar**, which is lined with warm redwood paneling and has comfortable booths surrounding its narrow room, features three cuts of prime rib as well as other meat and fresh fish items. Desserts are theatrical—Cherries Jubilee, Bananas Foster—and prepared tableside with liberal amounts of flame.

An elaborate **Christmas Celebration** is scheduled here throughout December in the grand wood-paneled lobby, including the unveiling of an elaborate 28-foot-tall Christmas tree and a variety of complimentary special events each night in the lobby.

KOA Kampground *4050 N. Hwy 101, 4 mi. north of town, (800) KOA-3136, (707) 822-4243.*

This branch has Kamping Kottages. For description, see page 415.

Motel Row.

Last-minute accommodations can usually be found along both 4th and 5th streets and Broadway.

WHERE TO EAT

Bon Boniere *215 F St., in Old Town, (707) 268-0122. M-F 11-9, Sat & Sun to 11.*

For description, see page 242.

Café Waterfront *102 F St., in Old Town, (707) 443-9190; www.cafewaterfront.com. B,L,&D daily; $-$$.*

Operating within a Queen Anne Victorian, with one cozy room and a very high ceiling, this restaurant serves up some tasty fresh seafood dishes as well as simpler soups, salads, and burgers. A high bar offers additional seating. Two beautifully decorated **guest rooms** are available upstairs.

Los Bagels *403 2nd St., in Old Town, (707) 442-8525. B&L W-M.*

This is the spot for a quick and cheap snack or meal of house-made bagels and other freshly baked goods. Mexican hot chocolate, fresh juices, and smoothies are also on the limited menu. Seating is available in the attractive, high-ceilinged building.

Lost Coast Brewery & Cafe *617 4th St., in Old Town, (707) 445-4480, fax (707) 445-4483. L&D daily; $.*

Situated within an historic building, this is the first brewery in the U.S. founded and operated by women. Among the several kinds of hand-crafted micro-brews, the hands-down favorite seems to be the Downtown Brown Ale. Inexpensive pub fare is available—some use the house beers in their recipes—and goes well with a pint.

Samoa Cookhouse *On Cookhouse Dr. (from Hwy. 101 take Samoa Bridge to end, turn left on Samoa Blvd., then take first left turn), (707) 442-1659, fax (707)442-0864; www.humboldtdining.com/cookhouse. B,L,&D daily; $. Highchairs, boosters, child prices. No reservations.*

Originally built in the 1890s by the Georgia-Pacific Corporation to feed its loggers, this is the last surviving cookhouse in the West. There is no menu. Just sit down at one of the long, boarding house-style tables and the hearty, delicious, family-style meal starts arriving. Though the menu changes daily, a typical breakfast consists of biscuits and gravy, fluffy scrambled eggs, pancakes, sausage, and coffee or tea. Lunch might consist of marinated three-bean salad, long-simmered and flavorful vegetarian tomato Florentine soup, fresh-baked bread with butter and assorted jams, green salad with ranch dressing and croutons, rice pilaf, lemon-pepper chicken, saucy beans, peas, chocolate cake with chocolate pudding frosting and whipped cream topping, and coffee or tea. A fantastic value! Most dishes are prepared from scratch with fresh ingredients. The only items not included in the fixed price are milk and sodas.

After dining, wander through the logging mini-museum of artifacts and historic photos. To work up an appetite before, or to work off some calories after, take a walk along the area's driftwood-strewn beaches. To find them, follow any of the unmarked turnoffs from Samoa Boulevard.

Tomaso's Tomato Pies *216 E St., in Old Town, (707) 445-0100. L M-Sat, D daily; $-$$. Highchairs, boosters, child menu. No reservations.*

Menu items in this casual spot include a square Sicilian-style pizza with whole-wheat crust, spinach pies, calzone, housemade soups, and hot pasta items. Portions run large, and delicious housemade breadsticks are served with all dinners. For dessert there are cakes, a variety of coffees, and hot chocolate made with milk. A dumbwaiter, which delivers orders to the loft dining area, provides free entertainment.

Arcata

A LITTLE BACKGROUND

Home to Humboldt State University, this small city is centered around an old-fashioned town square lined with bookstores, coffeehouses, and inexpensive restaurants. A birders paradise, enthusiasts can call (707) 822-LOON for a rundown on the current rare-bird sightings in the area.

VISITOR INFORMATION

Arcata Chamber of Commerce *1062 G St., (707) 822-3619, (707) 822-3515; www.arcata.com/chamber.*

ANNUAL EVENTS

Godwit Days *April. (800) 908-WING, (707) 822-3619; www.godwitdays.com. $15-$30.*

Named for the Marbled Godwit—a large brown shorebird with a long, slightly upturned bill—this fair celebrates the spring bird migration with seminars and exhibits.

Arcata Bay Oyster Festival *June.*

Humboldt Bay produces 90 percent of California's oysters. Most local restaurants feature them on their menus, and this annual festival celebrates the bounty.

Bigfoot Daze *September; in Willow Creek, 40 mi. east of town.*

Numerous reported sightings of the man-like, hairy creature known as Bigfoot have occured in this area. Look for a foul-smelling creature standing 7 to 8 feet tall and weighing from 350 to 800 pounds.

WHAT TO DO

Arcata Marsh and Wildlife Sanctuary
600 S. G St., (707) 826-2359. Interpretive center: Daily 1-5; guided tours Sat at 2.

Home and temporary refuge to over 200 species of bird, this is a breeding area for ducks and other waterfowl and a feeding area for fish-eating birds such as osprey, herons, grebes, and egrets. At low tide, people flock here to view the thousands of shore birds foraging on the mud flats of Humboldt Bay. Though birds are here year-round, the largest variety can be seen during the fall and spring migrations. Facilities include 4.5 miles of trails, observation blinds, an interpretive center, and a picnic area. After that description, it is amazing to learn that this thriving, scenic wetlands preserve is positioned over the former city dump and currently treats and recycles the city's waste water and sewage.

Fire & Light *1499 10th St., (800) 844-2223, (707) 825-7500, fax (707) 825-7700; www.fireandlight.com. Tours Tu & Thur at 10. Reservations required.*

The people in the U.S. throw away enough glass to fill both towers of the World Trade Center in Manhattan every 2 weeks. Doing their bit to stem that tide, this unusual business makes beautiful, high quality tableware from hand-poured recycled glass.

WHERE TO EAT

Jacoby's Storehouse *791 8th St., on the Plaza.*

Built in 1857, this fireproof stone storehouse once supplied the mule trains headed to the gold mines. It is the oldest masonry building in Humboldt County. Interesting features include pressed-tin ceilings and unusual stained-glass light fixtures.

On the first floor, **Abruzzi** *((707) 826-2345; www.abruzzicatering.com. $$-$$$.)* is a popular spot to celebrate a special occasion. With crisp white nappery and a romantic atmosphere, the restaurant specializes in housemade breads and pastas and fine Italian cuisine.

On the second floor, amid a pathway of interesting boutiques, the **Bon Boniere** ice cream parlor *((707) 822-6388. Daily 10-10.)*, dishes up everything cold and creamy. A large variety of sandwiches and snacks are also on the menu.

On the third floor, the **Plaza Grill** *((707) 826-0860. D daily; $. Child menu.)* is a casual spot that is good with kids. A barkeep mixes up cocktails, and the menu offers sandwiches, salads, and grilled items, including steaks and fresh fish. The fireplace here came from actor Humphrey Bogart's house in Los Angeles, and beautiful etched glass and grillwork windows came from the Plaza Hotel in New York City.

Los Bagels *1061 I St., (707) 822-3150.*
For description, see page 241.

Trinidad

A LITTLE BACKGROUND

Older than Eureka by about 4 months, this scenic fishing village was a supply port for gold miners in the 1850s and later became a whaling port. It has a circa 1860 lighthouse that is still in operation and a very nice beach.

VISITOR INFORMATION

Trinidad Chamber of Commerce *P.O. Box 356, Trinidad 95570, (707) 677-0591.*

GETTING THERE

Located 23 miles north of Eureka.

WHAT TO DO

Humboldt State University Marine Laboratory *570 Ewing St., (707) 826-3671. M-F 8-5; also Sat & Sun during school year. Free.*

This research facility has a small aquarium exhibit and a touch tank that are open to the public. A 30-minute guided tour is available by reservation.

Patrick's Point State Park *4150 Patrick's Point Dr., 6 mi. north of town, (707) 677-3570. $5/vehicle.*

Whale-watching and weddings are both prime at Wedding Rock here. A few years ago star-gazing was part of the scene, too, when *The Lost World* was filmed here. Some grey whales have become residents, living here year-round. Agate Beach is reached via a steep, winding trail with lots of stairs, and Octopus Trees Trail passes by Sitka spruces, whose odd roots cause them to resemble octopuses. This 632-acre park is also home to an authentically re-created Yurok Indian village, and a Visitor Center has relevant displays. Campsites are available, as are a **yurt and cabin** *($40 & $65/night).*

WHERE TO STAY

Bishop Pine Lodge *1481 Patrick's Point Dr., (707) 677-3314, fax (707) 677-3444. 12 cabins; $. Some kitchens. Hot tub. Pets welcome.*

These cozy, secluded cabins are situated among redwoods. A playground, complete with a rustic tree house, is on the spacious, well-maintained grounds, and the helpful owner knows where to find both the Roosevelt elk and the best restaurants.

The Lost Whale Bed & Breakfast Inn
3452 Patrick's Point Dr., (800) 677-7859, (707) 677-3425, fax (707) 677-0284; www.lostwhaleinn.com. 8 rooms; 100% non-smoking; $$-$$$; 2-night min. on weekends & nightly in summer. Children under 3 free. No TVs. Hot tub. Afternoon tea, full breakfast.

Located on 4 acres of coastal property, this Cape Cod-style farmhouse inn features spacious suites, five with spectacular ocean views. Guests often wake up to the sound of sea lions barking out on Turtle Rock, and migrating whales can sometimes be observed from the dining room or deck while eating breakfast. A scenic, wooded trail leads to the inn's private beach, and Patrick's Point State Park is just down the road. Children, who are especially well cared for here, can look forward to picking berries, fantasizing in a playhouse, frolicking on an enclosed playground, and feeding the inn's ducks and goats. Two of the suites have special sleeping lofts for children.

Klamath

GETTING THERE

Located approximately 60 miles north of Eureka.

WHAT TO DO

Klamath River Jet Boat Tours *On Hwy. 101 S., (800) 887-JETS, (707) 482-7775. May-Oct only; departure times and prices vary.*

This invigorating journey begins at the Klamath estuary called "Rekwoi"—the Native American word for where fresh water meets the Pacific Ocean. From there, the boat turns upriver for a closer look at the area's natural wildlife. With flat bottoms and no rudder or propeller, jet boats provide a smooth and safe, yet fast and exciting ride. Some trips include a barbecue dinner.

Prairie Creek Redwoods State Park *On Hwy. 101, 6 mi. north of Orick, (707) 488-2171. Daily 9:30-5. $5/vehicle.*

The 8-mile unpaved gravel road to Gold Bluffs Beach and Fern Canyon—where a short and easy trail awaits—passes through a beautiful forest into an area of fern-covered cliffs. This 14,000-acre park is a refuge for one of the few remaining herds of native Roosevelt elk. Campsites are available.

Redwood National Park *Visitor Centers in Orick, Crescent City, and Hiouchi, (707) 464-6101, fax (707) 464-1812; www.nps.gov/redw. Daily 9-5; in summer 8-6. $5/vehicle.*

This magnificent national park encompasses 105,000 acres. Ranger-led interpretive programs are scheduled daily June through August. Inquire at the Visitors Center about borrowing Family Adventure Packs to use with children. Permits are required for visiting the Tall Trees Grove, which contains the world's tallest tree (367.8 feet) as well as the second, third, and fifth tallest trees. The permits are free and can be obtained from the Orick Visitor Center. The walk takes about 4 hours and covers 3.2 miles.

Trees of Mystery *15500 Hwy. 101, (800) 638-3389, (707) 482-2251, fax (707) 482-2005. Daily dawn-dusk. Adults $6.50, 61+ $5, 6-12 $4.*

As visitors approach this privately-owned grove of redwoods, they are greeted by a 50-foot-tall Paul Bunyan and a 32-foot-tall Babe. This is really fun for kids, and they can pose for a picture on Paul's boot without entering the park. The trail inside, which is steep in parts, passes through a tunnel made from a hollowed-out log and continues on past a well-maintained group of unusual trees. In a setting at times reminiscent of Disney meets Ripley's Believe It of Not!, visitors see the Candelabra Tree with new trees growing off its fallen trunk, the famous Cathedral Tree with nine trees growing from one root structure, and similar natural wonders. The world's largest private collection of Native American artifacts is displayed in the back of the gift shop in the **End of the Trail Indian Museum**. Admission is free. Two snack bars and picnic facilities are available.

WHERE TO STAY

Redwood National Park Hostel *14480 Hwy. 101, 7 mi. north of town, 12 mi. south of Crescent City, (800) 909-4776 ext. 74, (707) 482-8265, fax (707) 482-4665. 8 beds; 1 private room.*

This northernmost link in the California coast hostel chain is located within national park boundaries. Operating within the historic circa 1890s pioneer DeMartin House, it has a full kitchen and spectacular ocean views. See also page 417.

Requa Inn *451 Requa Rd., (707) 482-8205, fax (707) 482-0844. 10 rooms; 100% non-smoking; $. Closed Jan. Children free. No TVs. Full breakfast; restaurant.*

Comfortable, pleasantly decorated rooms are available in this restored historic hotel dating from 1885, and a surf & turf menu is served in the dining room. Fishermen particularly favor the location at the scenic mouth of the Klamath River in the center of Redwood National Park.

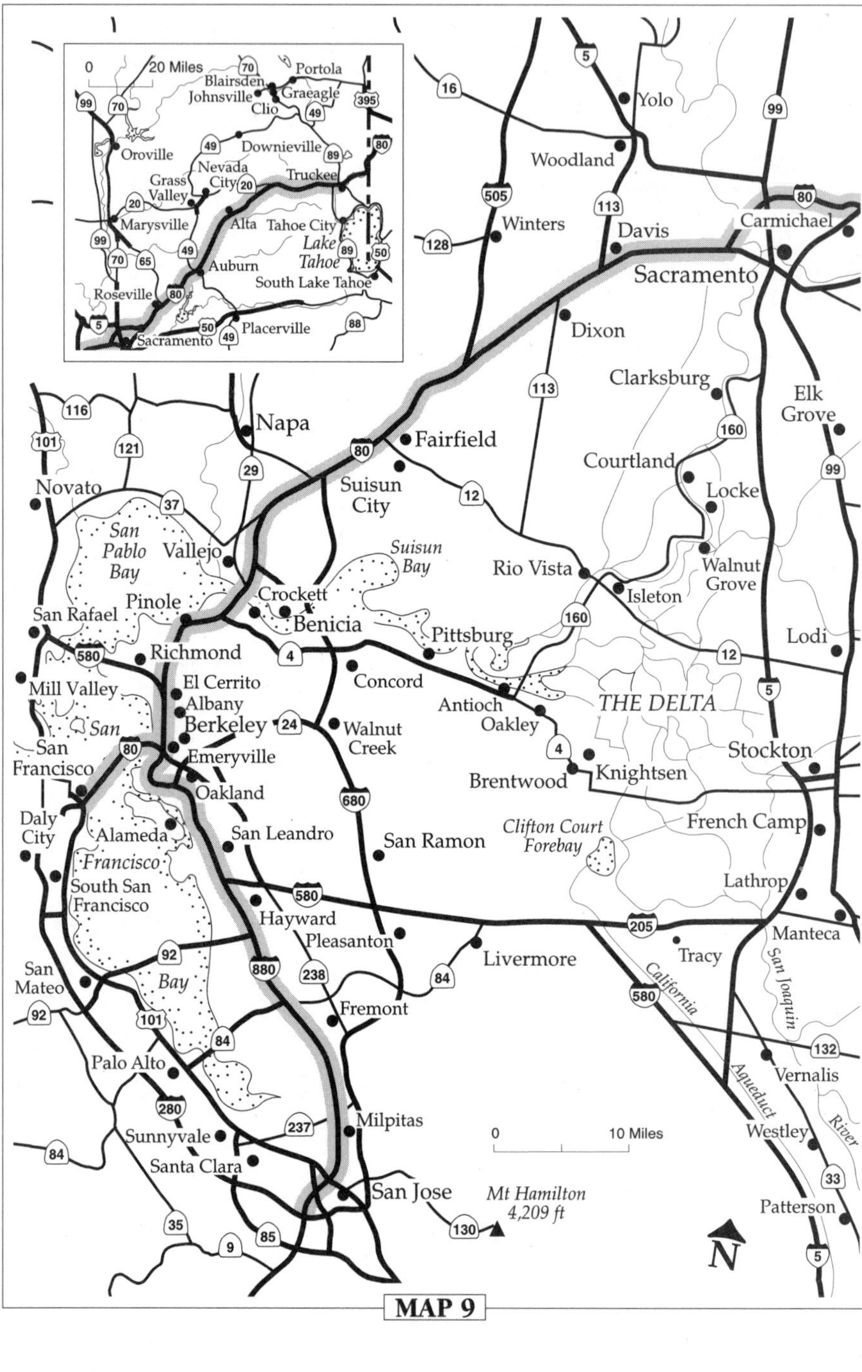
Portola
Blairsden
Johnsville
Graeagle
Clio
Downieville
Oroville
Nevada City
Grass Valley
Truckee
Marysville
Alta
Tahoe City
Lake Tahoe
Auburn
South Lake Tahoe
Roseville
Sacramento
Placerville
20 Miles
Yolo
Woodland
Winters
Davis
Carmichael
Sacramento
Dixon
Clarksburg
Elk Grove
Napa
Fairfield
Courtland
Novato
Suisun City
Locke
San Pablo Bay
Vallejo
Suisun Bay
Rio Vista
Walnut Grove
Isleton
Pinole
Crockett
San Rafael
Benicia
Pittsburg
Lodi
Richmond
Mill Valley
El Cerrito
Concord
Albany
Antioch
THE DELTA
Berkeley
Walnut Creek
Oakley
San Francisco
Emeryville
Stockton
Oakland
Brentwood
Knightsen
Daly City
Alameda
San Leandro
San Ramon
Clifton Court Forebay
French Camp
San Francisco Bay
South San Francisco
Lathrop
Hayward
Pleasanton
Manteca
Livermore
Tracy
San Mateo
California Aqueduct
San Joaquin River
Fremont
Palo Alto
Vernalis
Milpitas
Sunnyvale
Santa Clara
10 Miles
Westley
San Jose
Mt Hamilton 4,209 ft
Patterson
N
MAP 9

Emeryville

WHERE TO EAT

EmeryBay Public Market *5800 Shellmound St. M-F 10-7, Sat 9-9, Sun 10-5.*

In a cavernous building, just about every ethnic cuisine imaginable is purveyed at bargain prices. The people-watching is prime, and a Borders bookstore and a movie multi-plex are adjacent.

Hong Kong East Ocean Seafood Restaurant *3199 Powell St., (510) 655-3388 or (510) 655-3389, fax (510) 654-5349. L&D daily; $-$$. No reservations accepted for L.*

Surprisingly, this out-of-the-way restaurant, reached via a scenic waterfront drive, serves up dim sum every bit as good as that found in San Francisco's Chinatown and has waits almost as long. Except here, a gorgeous bay view can be enjoyed while waiting and dining. Light Cantonese seafood and vegetable dishes are also available. Note that dim sum is not brought around on carts or trays here. Instead, diners mark their selections on a menu form.

Berkeley

A LITTLE BACKGROUND

The always fascinating community of Berkeley is a study in contrasts. Visitors arrive with a variety of expectations. Some seek the intellectual climate associated with a community built around the University of California, the state's most prestigious public university. Others expect to see weird people and hippie communes. Those who know their food come seeking the acclaimed restaurants, and those who know one of the town's nicknames, Berserkeley, expect to see a bit of that. Then there is the well-known ultra-liberal political climate, in which someone who would be thought a liberal elsewhere is here considered to be a conservative, which explains another nickname—the People's Republic of Berkeley. In reality, Berkeley is all these things, and, making any stereotype impossible, it is also the place where the word "yuppie" was coined. Berkeley has also pioneered many frontiers. It was the first city in the nation with a public health department, the first to have a lie-detector machine, the first with curbcuts for wheelchairs, the first to ban Styrofoam, and the first to rename Columbus Day the more politically correct "Indigenous Peoples Day" (it's listed that way under "holidays" on parking meters). Most recently, it is the first to have all-organic school lunches. And it is the place where plutonium and berkelium, the 97th element, were discovered.

VISITOR INFORMATION

Berkeley Convention & Visitors Bureau *2015 Center St., (800) 847-4823, (510) 549-7040, fax (510) 644-2052; www.berkeleycvb.com.*

GETTING THERE

Cross the Bay Bridge and follow the signs to I-80 north. The central Berkeley exit is University Avenue.

ANNUAL EVENTS

Spring House Tour *April. (510) 841-2242. $32.*

Sponsored by the Berkeley Architectural Heritage Association, this tour provides acess to some of the city's many architectually interesting homes. Related talks are usually scheduled.

Live Oak Park Fair *June. (510) 986-9337. Free.*

Among the festivities are juried arts and crafts booths, live entertainment, and multiethnic foods. The park itself—with its mature shade trees, rolling lawns, and meandering creek—is inviting to visit any time.

Open Studios *June. (510) 763-4361, fax (510) 763-9470; www.proartsgallery.org. Free.*

For this combination gallery exhibit and self-guided tour of artists' workplaces throughout the East Bay, more than 400 artists open the doors to their studios, workshops, lofts, and homes so that they can meet with the public. Many works are for sale.

Solano Avenue Stroll *September. (510) 527-5358. Free.*

This mile-long block party is the oldest and largest free street festival in the East Bay. It is possible for strollers to munch their way from one end to the other.

International Taiko Festival *November. At U.C. Berkeley, Zellerbach Hall. (510) 642-9988. $20-$30.*

It's hard to imagine something more exhilarating than witnessing one muscle-bound taiko drummer after another beating out an intoxicating primal rhythm. Dating back 2,000 years, the thunderous sound of these drums was once used to stimulate rain and then to signal Japanese armies into battle. It is said to be the heartbeat of the Japanese people. San Francisco's internationally acclaimed Taiko Dojo usually performs on a 1-ton, 12-foot-high drum—the largest in the western hemisphere.

WHAT TO DO

Adventure Playground *160 University Ave., next to Cal Sailing Club, (510) 644-8623. Sat & Sun 11-4; in summer M-F 9-5, Sat & Sun 11-5. Free.*

The story goes that in Europe after World War II a designer built a series of modern playgrounds. But the children continued, indeed *preferred*, to play in bombed-out buildings and to construct their own play equipment from the plentiful rubble and debris. Taking that cue, he designed the first Adventure Playground. This U.S. version offers a storage shed full of tools and scrap wood that children can use to build forts and clubhouses and other things, and then leave them up or tear them down when they are done. The playground also has a tire swing, climbing net, and fast-moving trolley hanging from a pulley. Outside the fence is a par course and a large grassy area with a more traditional tiny-tot play area.

Across the street, **Shorebird Nature Center** *((510) 644-8623; Tu-F 2-5, Sat 9-5.)* has a 100-gallon aquarium. Special family programs are often scheduled, as are marina tours and walks.

Nearby, at the bay end of University Avenue near the Berkeley Pier, is a bow-and-arrow-wielding sculpture by artist Fred Fierstein. The artist is said to have plopped it there himself in 1985 when he got tired of waiting for Berkeley politicians to decide to do it for him. He had offered "The Guardian" to the city at no cost, but after long deliberation it was rejected as too aggressive (not to mention that the animal appears to urinate when it rains). Berkeley residents then voted to keep it there, but their decision might not be final. See it now.

Audubon Cellars Winery *600 Addison St./2nd St., (510) 540-5384. Tasting & tours M-F by appt.*

A winery in Berkeley? Yes, that's right, but don't expect to see vineyards. This winery buys its grapes from growers in the Sonoma and Napa valleys.

Berkeley Iceland *2727 Milvia St./Derby St., (510) 843-8800. Tu-Sun; schedule varies. Adults $6, under 17 $5-$6, skate rental $2.*

Measuring 100 by 200 feet, this rink ranks as one of the largest ice skating surfaces in the country.

Berkeley Rose Garden *On Euclid Ave./Buena Vista Way, (510) 644-6530. Daily sunrise-sunset. Free.*

Planted at the turn of the century, this garden was originally conceived as a classical Green arboretum. It is a particular delight in late spring and summer, when the roses are in full bloom. Benches sheltered by arbors covered with climbing roses make for pleasant picnicking with gorgeous views of the bay and San Francisco. Tennis courts adjoin. The garden is a popular spot for weddings, and a knot of people can be found at the top most evenings watching the sun set. Across the street, **Codornices Park** is equipped with a playground, a basketball court, and a long, exciting, and potentially dangerous concrete slide.

Fourth Street *1800 block. Stores generally open M-Sat 10-6.*

Surprisingly, in a city of Berkeley's size and income level, there are no department stores or traditional shopping malls. This trendy block featuring a 1920s industrial style of architecture is as close to one as the city comes. It is a shopping mall done Berkeley-style. Designed, built, and owned by a Berkeley developer/architectural firm, the street's buildings are kept at 2 stories. The owner controls leasing of the entire block and hand-picks the unusual, mostly home-oriented stores. Many outdoor cafes offer delicious fare and spectacular people-watching.

- **Builders Booksource** *(#1817, (510) 845-6874)* stocks books on architecture and design.
- **The Gardener** *(#1836, (510) 548-4545)* specializes in elegant accessories for the garden.
- **Hear** *(#1809, (510) 204-9595)* is an upscale music store that permits listening before buying.
- **Lighting Studio** *(#1808, (510) 843-3468)* displays the very best and latest in lighting fixtures.
- **Miki's Paper** *(#1801, (510) 845-9530)* has an impressive selection of handmade Japanese papers.
- **The Pasta Shop** *(#1786, (510) 528-1786)* is a spacious branch of the mother ship in Oakland (see page 289).
- **Sur La Table** *(#1806, (800) 221-5786, (510) 849-2252, fax (510) 849-1980)* purveys fine kitchen equipment at fair prices.

Judah L. Magnes Museum *2911 Russell St./College Ave., (510) 549-6950. Sun-Thur 10-4; tours on W & Sun. By donation.*

The first Jewish museum established in the western U.S., this institution exhibits Jewish ceremonial and fine arts from communities around the world. It is housed in a converted 1908 mansion, the gardens for which were landscaped by John McLaren, designer of San Francisco's Golden Gate Park.

Ohlone Dog Park *Hearst St./Grant St., (510) 644-6943. Daily 6am-10pm. Free.*

Established as an experiment in 1979, this was the first leash-free dog park in the nation. Located within Ohlone Park, this small dog park has 4-foot-high fences that foil even the most gifted jumpers. A concrete walkway is equipped with seating areas alongside, and a lawn with wood chips is on either side of the walkway. Two water taps are provided at both ends of the park. Because it is partially paved, the park is a particularly good choice in wet weather, and dogs like to run here. Owners must clean up after their dogs, and plastic bags are provided.

Takara Sake USA Tasting Room and Museum *708 Addison St./4th St., (800) 4-TAKARA, (510) 540-8250. Tasting M-F 1-5, Sat & Sun 12-6. Free.*

Sample several kinds of sake and plum wine in the spacious tasting room of this nation's largest sake brewery. A raised tatami room invites removing shoes and relaxing for a bit. Upon request, an informative video tells about the history and making of sake. The country's only sake museum displays artifacts related to this subtle beverage.

Telegraph Avenue *4 blocks between Bancroft Way & Dwight Way, south of campus.*

Fondly referred to as "the Ave" or "Tele" by locals, this famous, or perhaps infamous, avenue is probably best known for its role as a gathering spot and point of confrontation during the 1960s Free Speech Movement. It has now slipped into a more peaceful state, but still appears stalled in the '60s. On weekdays rushing students crowd the sidewalks, and on weekends shoppers crowd its many boutiques. A stroll here passes a street bazaar of crafts stalls selling souvenirs such as colorful tie-dyed t-shirts and peace symbol jewelry. Thoroughly modern chain stores are also well represented.

People's Park *(bounded by Telegraph Ave., Haste St., Hillegass Ave., & Dwight Way)* was the rallying place for some of the anti-war and free speech protests in the '60s and '70s. Recently, in an attempt to make the park truly accessible to all people, the University of California-owned site was cleared of its homeless residents and refurbished with two sandy volleyball courts. The clearing was not accomplished without new resistance and protest, but the volleyball courts remain.

• **Annapurna** *(#2416, (510) 841-6187)* is a psychedelic "head shop" left over from the turbulent 1960s.

• **Bookstores** in the 2400 block include **Cody's**, which stocks new obscure tomes along with the latest best-sellers and holds Wednesday evening poetry readings, and **Moe's**, which is said to be the biggest used bookstore west of the Hudson, and **Shakespeare & Co.**, which sells unusual used editions.

Tilden Regional Park *Off Grizzly Peak, below Wildcat Canyon Rd.; www.ebparks.org.*

This beautiful, well-developed 2,058-acre park has 35 miles of hiking trails as well as numerous picnic spots, many with tables and barbecues.

• **Environmental Education Center** *(510) 525-2233, fax (510) 526-2393. Tu-Sun 10-5. Free.*

This is a good place to get oriented and obtain current information about park attractions. Exhibits stress local natural history. Educational programs and naturalist-guided walks, many designed especially for families and children, are scheduled regularly.

• **Golf Course** *(510) 848-7373. Daily sunrise-sunset. M-Thur $25, F $35, Sat & Sun $40; special twilight rates.*

This scenic 18-hole course has all types of holes permitting all types of shots.

• **Lake Anza** *(510) 848-3028. Daily 11-6, May-Oct. Adults $2.50, 62+ & 1-15 $1.50.*

This low-key swimming area has lifeguards on duty, and a snack bar is available. It is also open in off-season at no charge, but without lifeguards.

• **Little Farm** *(510) 525-2233. Daily 8:30-5. Free.*

This brightly painted, well-maintained farm is home to cows, donkeys, sheep, ducks, chickens, goats, rabbits, pigs, and assorted other barnyard animals.

• **Merry-Go-Round** *(510) 524-6773. Sat & Sun 11-5; daily in summer. $1.*

One of only four classic four-row carousels remaining in Northern California, this antique gem is located in the center of the park. Built in 1911 by the Herschel-Spillman firm in New York, it spent time at Urbita Springs Park in San Bernardino, at Ocean Beach in San Diego, and at Griffith Park in Los Angeles before it settled here. It was restored in 1978. In addition to horses, it sports an assortment of colorful animals, including a stork, a dragon, and a frog. Its large band organ, which operates like a player piano, is regarded as one of the finest examples of its kind.

• **Pony Rides** *(510) 527-0421. Sat & Sun 11-5, spring & fall, weather permitting; daily in summer. $2.50.*

Children age 2 and older are strapped securely into a saddle with a back support and given an exciting ride in the pony wheel. Children 5 and older can ride horses on the fast track in a larger ring.

• Regional Parks Botanic Garden *(510) 841-8732. Daily 8:30-5. Free.*

Located across from the carousel, this 10-acre garden was begun in 1940. It offers the opportunity for a leisurely, quiet walk. Over 3,000 drought-resistant species and subspecies are displayed, and native plants are also featured.

• Tilden Steam Train (Redwood Valley Railway) *Grizzly Peak Blvd./Lomas Cantadas, (510) 548-6100. Sat & Sun 12-5, weather permitting; daily in summer. $1.50.*

This 15-inch gauge, 5-inch scale narrow-gauge, oil-burning miniature steam train (whew!) follows a scenic route that includes one tunnel and two trestles. The ride covers 1/4 mile and lasts 12 minutes.

U.C. Theatre *2036 University Ave./Shattuck Ave., (510) 843-FILM. Adults $7, 62+ & under 13 $5.*

Berkeley's last single-screen cinema, this gargantuan 1,250-seat, 1917-vintage theater shows something new (really something *old*) every day on its giant 40-foot-wide by 27-foot-high screen. It is almost worth the price of admission just to see the campy "no smoking" spot starring director John Waters that is usually shown before every film. Also noteworthy are the snackbar items: fresh popcorn topped with *real* butter, made-from-scratch herbal ice tea, fresh-baked cookies, and pretzels for vegans! This theater was the first to present *The Rocky Horror Picture Show* every Saturday at midnight. Though the run lasted for 20 years, it is history now.

University of California *Telegraph Ave./Bancroft Way, (510) 642-6000; www.berkeley.edu.*

The foremost attraction here is, of course, higher learning. Known for academic excellence, U.C. Berkeley boasts a faculty distinguished by 16 Nobel Prize winners. Many noteworthy facilities on this 1,232-acre campus are open to the public.

• Berkeley Art Museum *2626 Bancroft Way/College Ave., (510) 642-0808, fax (510) 642-4889; www.bampfa.berkeley.edu. W-Sun 11-5, Thur to 9. Adults $6, 65+ & 12-17 $4; free Thur 11-noon & 5-9.*

Many visitors think that this building itself is as interesting and unusual as its contents. Built in a cubist style of architecture, this striking museum is reminiscent of New York's Guggenheim—except that it is angular instead of circular. The permanent collection stresses modern and Asian art and includes a large collection of paintings by Modernist Hans Hofmann.

In the basement, the casual cafeteria-style **Cafe Grace** *(2625 Durant Ave., (510) 548-4366. Tu-Sun 11-4; $. 1 highchair. No reservations. No cards.)* dispenses high quality, delicious California-style deli fare as well as coffees and pastries. Seating is in an attractive interior space, with large windows looking out into the museum's sculpture garden, and in a sunny courtyard.

Also in the basement, the **Pacific Film Archive** *((510) 642-1124; www.uampfa.berkeley.edu. Adults $6, 65+ & under 13 $3.50.)* is known internationally for its film exhibitions

Teddy Bear Film Festival

and scholarship. It is one of five world-class public archival film collections in the U.S. It has the largest collection of Japanese titles outside of Japan and one of the world's largest collections of silent and early films from the former Soviet Union and pre-1960 Eastern Europe, plus hundreds of experimental movies by West Coast filmmakers. Daily public programs are filled with gems for film buffs. The theater is clean, the sound system excellent, and the audience well-mannered. No snacks are available. A **Children's Film Festival** held annually in January and February provides the chance for young people to see the world. A charming **Teddy Bear Parade and Film Festival** is held annually in November. Children are invited to bring their teddies and join in an informal parade that precedes the screening. To avoid unbearable disappointment, purchase tickets in advance.

• **Botanical Garden** *200 Centennial Dr., (510) 643-2755 or (510) 642-3343; www.mip.berkeley.edu/garden. Daily 9-4:45, in summer to 7; tours Thur, Sat, & Sun at 1:30. Adults $3, 65+ $2, 3-18 $1; free on Thur.*

Located behind the campus in lush Strawberry Canyon, this "library of living plants" covers 34 acres and contains over 13,000 different types of plants organized by continent of origin. Of special interest are the herb garden, rhododendron dell, redwood grove, California native plants area (which includes more than 1/4 of the state's native species), old rose garden, and Chinese medicinal herb garden stocked with over 90 rare plants. Children particularly enjoy the greenhouse filled with carnivorous plants and the lily pond stocked with colorful koi. Grassy areas perfect for picnicking are scattered throughout this peaceful spot.

• **Cal Day Open House** *Annually in April. (510) 642-5215; www.urel.berkeley.edu/calday. Free.*

Most of the university departments sponsor exhibits and events.

• **Cal Performances** *(510) 642-9988, fax (510) 643-2359. Tickets $20-$52.*

Acclaimed internationally for presenting extraordinary talent, this series is famous for showcasing the latest works of established artists and the debuts of new talent.

• **Campanile** *In center of campus, (510) 642-3666. Elevator: M-F 10-4, Sat & Sun 10-5. $2.*

Modeled after the slightly taller campanile in St. Marks Square in Venice, this campus landmark stands 307 feet tall—the equivalent of 30 stories. When classes are in session, 10-minute mini-concerts are hand-played on its 61-bell carillon three times each weekday at 7:50 a.m., noon, and 6 p.m. On Sundays a 45-minute recital is performed at 2 p.m.—the perfect time to enjoy a picnic on the surrounding lawn. An elevator takes visitors up 200 feet to an observation platform for a 360-degree view of the area.

• **Campus Tour** *Meet at Visitors Center in University Hall, room 101, 2200 University Ave./Oxford St., (510) 642-5215. M-F at 10 & 1; call to confirm Sat tour at 10. Free.*

This guided tour is a good way to get an overview of the campus. A self-guiding tour brochure is also available here.

• **Lawrence Hall of Science** *On Centennial Dr., below Grizzly Peak Blvd., (510) 642-5132; www.lhs.berkeley.edu. Daily 10-5. Adults $7, 62+ & 5-18 $5, 3-4 $3; planetarium $2, under 6 not admitted; parking 50¢/hr.*

Located high in the hills behind the campus, this participatory museum was established by the university in 1958 as a memorial to

DNA Model at Lawrence Hall of Science

Ernest Orlando Lawrence, who developed the cyclotron and was the university's first Nobel laureate. Of special interest to school-age children, this button-pusher's paradise holds educational games, an Earthquake Information Center, a seismic recorder, and a mini-planetarium. The hall's permanent exhibits include the popular "Within the Human Brain" (an assortment of intriguing activities that explain how our brains function) and "Math Rules" (puzzles and mathematical challenges that defy the popular notion that math isn't fun). On weekends, a Biology Lab permits experimenting with mazes and learning about a variety of small animals.

The short-order **Small Planet Cafe** provides a magnificent panoramic view of the bay and San Francisco.

• **Museum of Paleontology** *Near Oxford St./University Ave., 1101 Valley Life Sciences Bldg., (510) 642-1821, fax (510) 642-1822; www.ucmp.berkeley.edu. M-F 8-5, Sat & Sun 12-5. Free.*

Initiated in the 1860s, this collection of fossils is one of the largest and oldest in North America. Among the displays are a complete Tyrannosaurus rex skeleton, the largest Triceratops skull ever found, a frozen mammoth, ancient bacteria, and the skeleton of a saber-toothed tiger—California's state fossil.

In the same building, the **Museum of Vertebrate Zoology** *(Room 3101; (510) 642-3059, fax (510) 643-8238.)* holds one of the largest and most important collections of vertebrates in the world.

• **Phoebe Apperson Hearst Museum of Anthropology** *At Bancroft Way/College Ave., 103 Kroeber Hall, (510) 643-7648. W-Sun 10-4:30, Thur to 9; in summer, W-Sun 10-4. Adults $2, seniors $1, 3-16 50¢; free on Thur.*

Part of the campus since 1901, this museum stores the largest anthropological research collection (over 4 million artifacts) in the western U.S.

WHERE TO STAY

Bancroft Hotel *2680 Bancroft Way/College Ave., (800) 549-1002, (510) 549-1000, fax (510) 549-1070. 3 stories; 22 rooms; 100% non-smoking; $-$$. Children under 12 free. Continental breakfast. Parking $6.*

Located directly across from the campus, this 1928 landmark arts and crafts-style hotel, designed by Walter T. Steilberg, an associate of Julia Morgan, offers peaceful, airy rooms with sweeping views of San Francisco Bay and the Berkeley hills. Many also have large balconies or decks

Berkeley City Club *2315 Durant Ave./Dana St., (510) 848-7800, fax (510) 848-5900; www.berkeleycityclub.com. 6 stories; 40 rooms; $-$$. No TVs. Indoor heated pool, fitness room. Continental breakfast; restaurant. Free parking.*

Founded in 1927 and opened in 1930 as the Berkeley Women's City Club, this magnificent building, an historical landmark, was designed by Julia Morgan—the well-known architect who designed Hearst Castle. With

Moorish and Gothic elements, it is beautifully appointed with oriental rugs and tasteful vintage furniture that enhance the Old World beauty of the lead-paned windows and aged redwood trim. Rooms are comfortably furnished, and all have good views of either the San Francisco Bay or the campus and hills. A bar and restaurant are available for guests only, and a beauty salon and massage service operate on site.

Claremont Resort & Spa *41 Tunnel Rd., at Ashby Ave./Domingo Ave., (800) 551-7266, (510) 843-3000, fax (510) 843-6239;www.claremontresort.com. 6 stories; 267 rooms; $$$+. Children under 18 free. 2 heated pools, hot tub, 4 saunas, 2 steam rooms, health spa, fitness center, 10 tennis courts (fee; 6 with night lights). Restaurant, room service. Valet parking $12.*

Built originally by a Kansas farmer who struck it rich and wanted to fulfill his wife's dream of living in a home resembling an English castle, the first incarnation of this hotel burned to the ground in 1901. The current Victorian hotel, built in 1915, once charmed architect Frank Lloyd Wright into describing it as ". . . one of the few hotels in the world with warmth, character and charm." The hotel now provides all the amenities of a resort in an urban setting. Lobby and hallways are decorated with a collection of contemporary art (the largest private collection of contemporary Pacific Northwestern artists in the U.S.), and wine tastings and food samplings occur there on Saturday afternoons.

Forty luxurious new North Wing rooms are the first in the country to offer guests the opportunity to try high-speed internet access. CD and video players are also available (the concierge maintains a free library), and these rooms boast Jacuzzi tubs for two and views of San Francisco. Most unique is that guests can pick and choose amenities before arriving, and upon check-in find their snack and magazine of choice awaiting.

The hotel's two pools and a hot tub are surrounded by several long rows of chaise lounges—looking like something out of sunny Southern California or Hawaii, but certainly not Berkeley. A full-service European-style spa offers a variety of revitalizing treatments and packages, and a kids activity center permits dropping them off for a few hours of fun and games.

Romantic **Jordan's** *((510) 843-3000. B,L,&D daily; SunBr; $$$. Highchairs, boosters, reduced child price. Reservations advised. Valet parking.)* provides a menu of Lifestyle

Cuisine—California fare with a touch of the Pacific Rim a la celebrity Chef Hans Wiegand. Examples are grilled salmon with teriyaki glaze served with baby bok choy and black Thai rice, and grilled breast of free-range chicken with Thai curry and mashed taro root. Black Angus beef dishes are also on the menu, and a fixed-price four-course tasting menu is available. In addition to a good selection by the glass, wines can also be ordered by the half-glass, allowing the sampling of several different kinds. Desserts include a divine green tea-flavored crème brulee and a playful rice pudding sushi consisting of sweet rice surrounding a fresh fruit center that is rolled in a nutty outer crust and served with thin chocolate cookie "chopsticks." Comfortable chairs invite sitting back and enjoying the spectacular bay view. Live entertainment is scheduled on Friday and Saturday evenings after 8:30. Sunday brunch here is an extravagant buffet of salads, fresh fruit, seafood, and meats. It includes a design-your-own-omelette station and a dessert table laden with fine cakes, chocolate eclairs, chocolate fondue, and several flavors of mousse. Of special interest at lunch and dinner is the low-fat spa cuisine, which can be satisfyingly tasty.

The **Terrace Bar** is the first in the state in a major hotel to become 100 percent smoke-free. In addition to more common drinks, healthy "smart drinks"—made with amino acids and other natural ingredients and bearing names that include Berry Brain Blaster and Cosmic Coconut—can be ordered.

The French Hotel *1538 Shattuck Ave./Cedar St., (510) 548-9930, same fax. 18 rooms; $-$$. Cafe, room service.*

In this European-modern hotel situated just across the street from Chez Panisse, all rooms have a private patio. Just off the lobby, the hotel's coffee house has sidewalk tables that in good weather are popular with locals.

Hotel Durant *2600 Durant Ave./Bowditch St., (800) 2-DURANT, (510) 845-8981, fax (510) 486-8336; www.hoteldurant.com. 6 stories; 140 rooms; $$-$$$. Children under 12 free. Restaurant, room service. Parking $7.*

Particularly popular with parents in town to visit their children at the university, this atmospheric hotel's hallways are decorated with historic photographs of the campus. It is located just 1 block from the university, and some of the attractively appointed rooms feature campanile views.

Henry's Publick House & Grille has a cozy, comfortable pub atmosphere and authentic Tiffany lamp fixtures. Food is well-prepared and includes a very good hamburger, fresh fish items, and a variety of inexpensive sandwiches and salads.

Radisson Hotel Berkeley Marina *200 Marina Blvd., (800) 333-3333, (510) 548-7920, fax (510) 548-7944; www.radisson.com. 375 rooms; $-$$$. Restaurant. Indoor heated pool & hot tub; fitness center. Restaurant.*

Situated in a tranquil setting on the marina, this comfortable low-rise lodging provides easy parking and rooms with marina views. All rooms have either a patio or balcony.

Rose Garden Inn *2740 Telegraph Ave./Ward St., (510) 549-2145, fax (510) 549-1085. 40 rooms; 100% non-smoking; $-$$. Children under 4 free. 1 kitchen; some wood-burning & gas fireplaces. Evening snack, continental breakfast. Pets welcome.*

Situated 7 blocks from the university, this charming lodging complex includes two landmark Tudor-style mansions, a carriage house, and a garden house. Rooms are attractively decorated and comfortable, and some have views of San Francisco. The buildings open onto a central garden oasis filled with fountains, patios, and hundreds of rose bushes, and the cookie jar is always full for snacking. Families are accommodated comfortably in the larger junior suites.

WHERE TO EAT

Berkeley was the first city in the state to introduce legislation regulating smoking in public places. It was also the first city to require non-smoking sections in restaurants. Now California is the first state in the nation to require that all restaurants and bars in the state are 100 percent non-smoking. Smoking in workplaces is also prohibited.

Ajanta *1888 Solano Ave./The Alameda, (510) 526-4373, fax (510) 526-3885. L&D daily; $$. Highchairs, boosters. Reservations advised.*

With an ever-changing menu of creative, complex regional Indian dishes, this simple restaurant is always a delight. Complete dinners are well priced, but ordering a la carte doesn't cost much more and offers the opportunity to try some unusual items. Presentation is part of the pleasure. All dinners begin with papadam—a crisp lentil wafer served with dipping sauce—chewy nan bread, and condiments of mango chutney, housemade carrot relish, and lime pickles. Appetizers include alu tikki—deep-fried potato-and-pea patties. Entrees include various curries, tandoori meats (including their signature lamb rib chops) and fish, plus a good selection of vegetarian and vegan dishes; all can be ordered in any degree of spiciness. Entrees are served on an attractively arranged plate bearing three scoops of saffron-laced rice anchored in the middle by a mound of spinach purée. The light mango mousse and liquidy kulfi rice pudding are especially delightful desserts. This restaurant is named for the site of ancient Buddhist cave temples that is a famous tourist attraction in western India. Reproductions of some of the cave paintings appear on wall murals that were painted in India.

Ambrosia Garden *843 San Pablo Ave./Solano Ave., Albany, (510) 528-5388. L&D W-M; $.*

Operating within a pleasant room with high ceilings, this all-vegetarian Taiwanese restaurant serves up delicious meatless fare. Many dishes are made with mock meats composed from soy protein, gluten, and bean curd. Personal favorites include green dumplings (pot stickers stuffed with soy protein, diced mushrooms, and cabbage) and General Chou's chicken (crispy deep-fried wheat gluten with a tangy sweet & sour sauce). Very little oil and no MSG are used. Surprisingly, no onion or garlic are used either because the chef considers them difficult to digest. Dishes are spiced instead with ginger, ginseng, and dong quai—Chinese herbs and roots that boost energy and the circulatory system. For dessert, experience the infamous Asian durian fruit, with its undertone of rot, in a pretty lemon-colored ice cream. Taro flavor is also available. Adding to the good experience here is an extremely polite wait-staff.

Berkeley Thai House *2511 Channing Way/Telegraph Ave., (510) 843-7352. L&D daily; $. Highchairs, boosters. Reservations advised at D.*

In good weather, a table on the wooden deck here is a choice spot to relax with a cooling, sweet Thai iced tea. On nippier days, or in the evening, the cozy inside dining room, decorated with Indonesian artifacts, is an inviting option. Specials chalked on a board by the entrance are usually a good bet. Favorite dishes include spicy-hot basil chicken; full-flavored cashew nut chicken; moo-prik-khing—a superb stir-fry with pork and fresh green beans in a spicy sauce; panang neur—beef and sweet basil in a spicy red curry sauce with a coconut milk base; and pad thai—a sweet, orange-colored noodle dish accented with ground peanuts, bean sprouts, bean cake, and a few tiny shrimp.

Bette's Oceanview Diner *1807 4th St./Hearst Ave., (510) 644-3230. B&L daily; $. Boosters, booths. No reservations.*

It's fun to sit on a counter stool and watch the cooks hustle in this casual, noisy diner featuring a 1950s truck-stop decor and a menu of traditional American food. More entertainment is provided by the jukebox and its eclectic mix of everything from '50s classics to reggae. Breakfast choices are available all day and include spicy scrambled eggs, steak and eggs, omelettes, griddle cakes with real maple syrup, French toast, and some combination plates—The New York (smoked salmon, bagel, cream cheese, red onion, and tomato) and The Philadelphia (scrapple, poached eggs, toast, and grilled tomato). Blintzes are also sometimes available. Lunch is a satisfying assortment of well-prepared classic sandwiches, housemade soups, and homey items such as meatloaf, grilled bockwurst, and potato pancakes. Thick old-fashioned milkshakes are available, too, but oddly no hamburger or fries. By the way. About that ocean view. There is none. Oceanview is the name of the neighborhood in which the restaurant is located.

Next door, **Bette's To Go** *((510) 548-9494. M-F 6:30-5, Sat & Sun 8-5.)* has take-out pastries, sandwiches, salads, pizza by the slice, and other goodies.

Blakes *2367 Telegraph Ave./Durant Ave., (510) 848-0886. L&D daily; $. Highchairs, boosters, booths. Reservations accepted.*

A campus hangout since 1940, this restaurant serves a large variety of hamburgers and snacks. Weekdays, lunch is served both downstairs in the funky rathskeller, with its sawdust-covered floor and old wooden booths, and upstairs, where diners get excellent views of the sidewalk parade outside. A cover charge is levied on the live music scheduled most evenings.

Blue Nile *2525 Telegraph Ave./Dwight Way, (510) 540-6777. L Tu-Sat, D Tu-Sun; $. Reservations suggested on Sat & Sun.*

Delicious, spicy Ethiopian stews (wat) are served here on traditional spongy bread (injera). A favorite is chicken tibs served with sides of steamed carrots and green salad. Diners may eat in the traditional Ethiopian manner, with fingers, but plastic forks are available for those who prefer the traditional American way. Sweet honey wine and house-made fruit drinks perfectly complement the cuisine. Downstairs seating, within beaded-curtain alcoves, is prime.

Boran Thai *1892 Solano Ave./The Alameda, (510) 525-3625. L M-F, D daily; $.*

After selecting seating in either the front area, where diners remove their shoes and sit on floor cushions with feet dangling under the table, or at regular tables in the back, complimentary shrimp chips and dipping sauce are brought for munching on while perusing the menu. Winners include delicate basil chicken, tasty cashew nut chicken, crispy-fried fresh red snapper glazed with a hot-and-sweet tamarind sauce, and flavorful Panang beef in peanut-curry sauce. A good selection of vegetarian options is available, and all entrees are served with a cabbage soup, steamed rice, and fresh steamed vegetables.

Breads of India *2448 Sacramento St./Dwight Way, (510) 848-7684. L M-Sat, D daily; $. No reservations. No cards.*

In spite of having only seven tables and almost no ambiance, this popular spot usually has a line waiting to get in. A sign-up sheet outside provides the option of sharing a table—an option it is wise to take to avoid a long wait. Once inside, it is simply amazing what feasts the teeny kitchen stuffed with cooks can produce: jumbo prawns in a complexly spiced, tomato-based masala sauce; organic Yukon gold potatoes in a mild fresh spinach purée; fabulous garlic naan. More exotic bread options include roomali roti—a thin unleavened bread prepared with a blend of white and wheat flours—and tawa daal paratha, stuffed with spicy chickpeas. Entrees are served on one American-style plate with trimmings of basmati rice and dahl. The kitchen uses the best ingredients, blends their own spices, and never freezes or microwaves anything (indeed, there doesn't seem to be any room for these appliances in the tiny kitchen). Only olive oil is used—none of that fattening Indian ghee. The menu changes daily, and always among the choices are a tandoori-cooked meat item and two vegetarian dishes. With 300 recipes for entrees and 140 for breads, this restaurant aims to surprise.

Brennan's *720 University Ave./4th St., (510) 841-0960. L&D daily; $. 1 highchair, boosters. No reservations.*

Reminiscent of a shamrock, with its dark green exterior and bright green interior, this Berkeley institution's hall-like dining room is dominated by an enormous rectangular bar. Two large-screen TVs are perpetually tuned to sporting events. Always crowded and boisterous, it has a variety of beers and microbrews on tap and is furnished with simple Formica tables. The hofbrau-style food is basically meat and potatoes, and each night has its special. Hot sandwiches are served with made-from-scratch mashed potatoes smothered in gravy, and side dishes include tasty stuffing, macaroni salad, potato salad, and coleslaw.

Cactus Taqueria *1881 Solano Ave./The Alameda, (510) 528-1881. L&D daily; $. Highchairs, boosters. No reservations.*

Mexican fast food at its best is served cafeteria-style in this popular taqueria. Burritos are custom made, with a choice of several kinds of tortillas (chili- or tomato-red, spinach-green, plain), black or pinto beans, and a variety of well-seasoned fillings. Tacos and tamales are also available. Tortillas are lard-free, meats are the best, and tortilla chips are fried in safflower oil. Housemade drinks include several fresh fruit agua frescas and horchata (a sweet rice drink), and two kinds of addictive salsa are on each table—a tangy green tomatillo and a smoky mole. Seating is at colorfully-stained wooden tables, and an indoor water fountain provides restive background sound.

Cafe de la Paz *1600 Shattuck Ave./Cedar St., upstairs in Cedar Center, (510) 843-0662, fax (510)843-0669; www.cafedelapazberkeley.com. D daily; $$. Highchairs, boosters. Reservations advised.*

Wildly popular with locals, this exciting spot serves authentic interpretations of traditional and contemporary Latin American cuisine with many vegetarian and vegan options. Specialties include cachapas from Venezuela (corn pancakes topped with a sweet pepper sauce), tamal de pollo from Guatemala (corn masa with chicken mole and a spicy chili sauce), and carne asada fajitas con salsa barbacoa (beef topped with a spicy smoky-sweet sauce). Personal favorites are the chicken and vegetable enchiladas topped with either a rich mole sauce or piquant tomatillo sauce, and fabulous corn bread made with whole corn kernels. The welcoming dining room, with its large windows and soothing water fountain, add to the experience.

Cafe Fanny *1603 San Pablo Ave./Cedar St., (510) 524-5447. B&L daily; $. No reservations.*

Operated by the venerable Alice Waters, this simple spot, named for her daughter, is an outpost of tonier Chez Panisse. Breakfasts are simple, but the boiled egg is perfect and the toast is, too. Lunch is a selection of several sandwiches. Limited seating is available outside, beside a noisy parking lot, but no one seems to mind.

Cafe Panini *2115 Allston Way/Shattuck Ave., in Trumpetvine Court, (510) 849-0405. M-Sat 9-4; $. No reservations. No cards.*

Popular with university students and staff, this tiny spot produces divine gourmet sandwiches. Diners order at the counter, pay, and then select a seat either in the brick-walled interior or out in a courtyard—the supreme choice on a sunny day. Sandwiches are made with magnificent sourdough baguettes from Semifreddi Bakery and topped with enticing combinations. A personal favorite is the mushroom-sun-dried tomato-pesto with melted mozzarella. As at Chez Panisse—where this cafe's owner was once a waitress and then a wine buyer—all ingredients are fresh. Tuna is not from a can. Meats are cooked in-house. Mayonnaise is made from scratch. Herbs are fresh. A soup, a pasta salad, and some great housemade desserts are also available.

Cancun Taqueria *2134 Allston Way/Shattuck Ave., (510) 549-0964. L&D daily; $. No reservations.*

Meats here are broiled over open flames, and seafood is grilled. Lard and MSG are not used, but purified water is. Everything—soft and crispy tacos, burritos, quesadillas, tostadas—is super tasty, especially when tarted up with delicious selections from the extensive complimentary salsa bar, and there are plenty of vegetarian specials.

César *1515 Shattuck Ave./Cedar St., (510) 883-0222. Open 3pm-midnight daily; $-$$. No reservations.*

Casual and cozy, this tapas bar is operated by a group that includes Alice Waters' husband and is located in the Gourmet Ghetto next door to Chez Panisse. A true bar, its menu offers a large selection of spirits—Cognacs, single-malt and blended Scotches, American whiskeys, gins, tequilas, and vodkas—and wines, and it serves food until 11 p.m. The short menu changes daily but always includes some delicious options: a tiny plate of two tasty red piquillo peppers filled with melted cheese; a more substantial stack of flat, thin fried potatoes seasoned with rosemary and whole sage leaves; rock cod with a spicy red romesco sauce; a bocadillo (sandwich) of spicy tuna and egg. A small bowl of olives and spartan basket of bread are served compliments of the house, and chewy Catalan almond cookies and dessert wines provide fine finishes. The open room has a large communal table in the center made from floorboards brought in from an old London warehouse.

Cha-Am *1543 Shattuck Ave./Cedar St., (510) 848-9664. L M-Sat, D daily; $. Highchairs, boosters. Reservations advised.*

The current leader in the informal ranking of this city's best Thai restaurants, this gem features a festive atmosphere, an attentive staff, and chefs who produce complex flavors and interesting combinations. Among the winners on its exciting menu are: laap-gai (a chopped chicken salad tossed with fresh mint and coriander), pad-makua-yao (chicken sautéed with basil, chili, and eggplant), and pad-ped-gung (prawns sautéed with sweet curry sauce, fresh Thai herbs, and green beans).

Chez Panisse *1517 Shattuck Ave./Cedar St. L&D M-Sat; $$-$$$. Boosters, booths, child menu M-Thur. Cafe: L or D reservations accepted after 9am on the same day; (510) 548-5049. Downstairs: Reservations essential; can be made up to 1 month in advance; (510) 548-5525.*

Opened in 1971 by U.C. graduate Alice Waters as a hangout for her friends, this fabulously famous restaurant features the definitive California cuisine—simply prepared food made with the freshest ingredients. A different fixed-price menu *(M $39, Tu-Thur $59, F & Sat $69)* is served each night in the legendary downstairs dining room. A less expensive upstairs cafe serves a seasonal menu of simple items such as baked goat cheese salad, Spanish-style grilled chicken with lentils, and strawberry shortcake. Meals in both venues are almost always a perfect 10. A 15 percent service charge is automatically added to the bill and divided by the entire staff. The area surrounding this restaurant is known as the "Gourmet Ghetto." Allow time to explore.

The Counter *1901 University Ave./Martin Luther King Jr. Way, (510) 849-4165. L M-F, D M-Sat; $.*

This tiny space offers only a few cramped tables and the promised counter, but people come here for the international menu of vegetarian and vegan cuisine. A few dishes for hard-core carnivores are also available. Soups, salads, sandwiches, and meatless burgers dominate the lunch menu. Dinner choices include French onion soup, spring rolls, Thai vegi-chicken, tofu chili, and several meatless burgers.

FatApple's *1346 Martin Luther King Jr. Way/Rose St., (510) 526-2260. B,L,&D daily; $-$$. Highchairs, boosters. No reservations.*

This popular restaurant's forte is good food made from scratch using basic ingredients: The lean ground chuck used for hamburgers is ground on the premises; soup is made fresh; blue cheese salad dressing is made with the real stuff; robust Peet's coffee is freshly ground and served with heavy whipping cream. The famous hamburger is served on a toasted housemade wheat or white bun, and just-right milkshakes are served in the metal mixing canister. For dessert, it's impossible to go wrong with a slice of the puffy apple pie the restaurant is named for, but the chocolate velvet and lemon meringue pies are also delicious. Breakfast features fresh-squeezed orange juice, crisp waffles served with pure Vermont maple syrup, omelettes, buckwheat or whole-wheat pancakes, and freshly baked pastries.

Ginger Island *1820 4th St./Hearst Ave., (510) 644-0444. L M-F, D daily, Sat & SunBr; $$. Highchairs, boosters, child items (ask server). Reservations advised.*

Operating in the inviting contemporary space where celebrity chef Mark Miller first dished out his Southwestern Cuisine (he's gone on to the Coyote Cafe in Santa Fe and Red Sage in Washington, D.C.), this exciting restaurant now serves up American cuisine with an Asian flair. Dinner menu favorites include sensuously soft won tons exploding with flavor, a salmon "napoleon" consisting of an alternating stack of house-smoked salmon and crisp taro rounds colorfully splashed with tiny orange caviar, delicious and tender sweet-sauced baby back ribs served with potato, yam, and taro fries, and the dessert every meal should end with—gingery ginger cake. At lunch, delightful salads and sandwiches are among the selections. Drinks include a potent Singapore "Sting" served in a tall glass, iced lychee tea, and housemade ginger ale and limeade.

Kathmandu *1410 Solano Ave./Santa Fe Ave., Albany, (510) 526-3222. D daily; $$. Reservations advised.*

Tibetan and Napalese cuisine—a cross between Chinese and Indian cuisines—is served in this tiny space. A good selection of vegetarian items is available, and various kinds of sprouted beans add a pleasing crunch to many dishes. Lamb items are a specialty, and khashi ya chhwela, a spicy stew served at room temperture, is choice. Though entree dishes come with condiments, rice, and bread, do also try chatmari, a soft rice-flour bread stuffed with curried chicken. Beer and either cinnamon or banana lassi yogurt drinks are good accompaniments. A pot of chia, a spiced tea served with milk, makes a nice ending. Careful, the bill here grows quickly.

King Tsin *1699-1701 Solano Ave./Tulare Ave., (510) 525-9890. L&D daily; $$. Highchairs, boosters. Reservations advised.*

The first Mandarin Chinese restaurant in town, this popular spot serves a consistently well-executed menu. No MSG is used in preparing the tasty items that include hot and sour soup, spiced prawns (coated with batter, deep-fried, and served in a spicy-sweet sauce), Mongolian beef (smothered in green onions and served on a bed of crisp rice noodles), vegetarian green beans, and dramatic sizzling meat and fish plates. Mixed drinks can be ordered from a full bar.

King Yen *2995 College Ave./Ashby Ave., (510) 845-1286. L&D daily; $-$$. Highchairs, boosters. No reservations.*

Three brothers are the exclusive cooks here, which translates into no bad nights when the main cook is off. Among the best items are tasty Szechwan beef (batter-dipped meat is deep-fried, then stir-fried with a spicy-sweet sauce) and delicately seasoned mu shu pork. Exotic beggar's chicken and Peking duck can be ordered in advance. Good vegetarian items include crispy spring rolls, dry-braised long green beans, and bean curd with black bean sauce; chow mein and hot and sour soup also can be requested without meat. Both white and brown rice are available, and no MSG is used in the kitchen. The high-ceilinged main dining room, with its generous flower arrangements and potted plants, is as delightful as the food.

La Mediterranee *2936 College Ave./Ashby Ave., (510) 540-7773, fax (510) 540-0665. B,L,&D daily. Highchairs, boosters.*

This is the perfect place for refreshment during a shopping spree in this low-key neighborhood. If unfamiliar with Middle Eastern cuisine, try a sampler plate. Cinnamony chicken cilicia in phyllo dough and succulent chicken pomegranate are both outstanding. Soups and salads are available for lighter appetites, and a selection of coffees and sweets are perfect for a snack.

La Note *2377 Shattuck Ave./Channing Way, (510) 843-1535. B&L daily, D F & Sat; $. Highchairs, boosters. No reservations for Sat & SunBr.*

Touching just the right culinary notes, this charming restaurant delivers the French Provence dining experience—without the negatives of small dogs and smoking in its cheery dining room. On a warm, sunny day, while sipping a cafe au lait out of a big bowl as they do in France, it's possible to imagine actually being in Provence. Winning items on the breakfast menu include lemon-gingerbread pancakes with poached pears, fluffy scrambled eggs, and perfectly fried rosemary potatoes. Omelettes, hot cereals, and French toast made with cinnamon brioche soaked in orange water batter and drizzled with lavender honey are also available. Lunch brings on les sandwiches, and dinner les entrees, les bagnats (traditional provençale sandwiches), les poissons (fish), and les viandes (meats)—plus a three-course fixed-price menu. Bon appetit!

La Val's *1834 Euclid Ave./Hearst Ave., (510) 843-5617. L&D daily; $. Highchairs, boosters, booths. No reservations.*

Located on the quieter north side of the U.C. campus, this long-popular student hangout has good pizza, pastas, and brew—all at great prices. The super-casual seating inside is sometimes enhanced with overhead TVs broadcasting sporting events, and a courtyard beer garden with picnic tables is inviting on warm afternoons. Older children can spend waiting time playing video games; younger ones can ride in a miniature moving car. A cover charge is levied on the live music and plays scheduled downstairs in the **Subterranean**. Food can also be ordered there, and children are welcome.

Mazzini *2826 Telegraph Ave./Oregon St., (510) 848-5599. L&D daily; $$. Reservations accepted.*

Located on the quiet end of the town's most frenetic thoroughfare, this neighborhood trattoria is co-owned by the sister of Alice Waters of Chez Panisse fame. The authentic, hearty Tuscan and Umbrian fare, described by the owners as "Italian farmhouse cooking," includes appetizers—a light fritto misto (with fennel, artichokes, mushrooms, and unexpected piquant lemon rounds) and a satisfying Tuscan bread soup made with lots of chard and cannellini beans. Entrees include fish items (a moist swordfish topped with a delicious green sauce) and meat items (braised rabbit, roasted chicken, pork chop, steak) as well as pizzas and pastas. A menu of cocktails includes several non-alcoholic possibilities—the citrusy pink Mazzini Cocktail is particularly tasty—and can be ordered from a full bar in the entry, and many good wines are available by the glass. Desserts are a selection of housemade tarts, tortas, and gelati. The marble-topped tables and bar and the Florentine-style woodwork were designed by Berkeley Mills.

The Med (iterraneum Caffe) *2475 Telegraph Ave./Haste St., (510) 549-1128. Daily 7am-midnight; $. No reservations. No cards.*

With a casual atmosphere and untidy decor, this coffeehouse seems to have been serving students forever. It catered the Free Speech Movement activists back in the '60s as they planned their moves, including Jerry "You can't trust anybody over 30" Rubin. Don't miss the Berliner—a sort of coffee ice cream float—and the fabulous moist chocolate layer cake with rum custard filling.

North Beach Pizza *1598 University Ave./California St., (510) 849-9800. Daily 11am-midnight.*

For description, see page 75.

O Chame Restaurant & Tea Room *1830 4th St./Hearst Ave., (510) 841-8783. L&D M-Sat; $$. 1 highchair. Reservations advised.*

Reminiscent of Chez Panisse in its simplicity and use of the freshest ingredients, this soothing, tranquil spot has a refined menu that changes weekly. Among the offerings are some whimsical presentations (a "tower" salad composed of stacked slices of daikon radish, smoked salmon, and mango) as well as more traditional presentations (soup prepared with king salmon, mustard greens, fresh shitake mushrooms, and soba noodles). The restaurant is known for its noodle dishes, one of the most popular being udon noodles with smoked trout. A variety of sakes, including the Hakusan brand produced domestically in the Wine Country, and an extensive list of teas are also available. Dessert can be simple but exquisite: fresh sweet cherries served chilling amid ice cubes. Beautiful bento box lunches are available to go.

Peet's *2112 Vine St./Cedar St., (510) 841-0564; www.peets.com. M-Sat 7-7, Sun 8-7.*

It was here in 1966 that now-retired owner Alfred Peet, a Dutch émigré, became the first in the trade to import specialty varieties of coffees and to dark-roast whole coffee beans—a radical move at the time that touched off a revolution among coffee drinkers. A Berkeley institution, this coffee boutique dispenses an impressive variety of coffee beans and teas and, though it has no place to sit down, is the gathering spot each morning for great numbers of coffee freaks. Holding their hot cups of java, they spill right into the street. Professionals in three-piece suits mingle here with blue-collar workers, all chatting happily. Sometimes it seems that almost everyone in this town, no matter what kind of work they do, has a curious, educated mind. Perhaps they would like to mull this over: Starbucks owned Peet's from 1984 to 1987. Fortunately, Peet's is now an independent company once again, with a plethora of outlets throughout the Bay Area.

Picante Cocina Mexicana *1328 6th St./Gilman St., (510) 525-3121. L&D daily, SunBr; $. Highchairs, boosters, booths, child menu. No reservations.*

Claiming to be the largest taqueria in the Bay Area, this casual spot has two large indoor dining rooms and a pleasant outside area boasting a soothing wall fountain. Menu choices include the expected burritos, tamales, tacos, quesadillas, and tostadas. Especially good fillings include carnitas (slow-cooked pork), pollo asado (grilled chicken with fresh salsa), rajas (roasted Poblano chilies with sautéed onions and Mexican cheese), and chorizo y papas (spicy Mexican sausage and potatoes). Special vegetarian and vegan items are also available. Among the drinks are several aguas frescas (fresh fruit drinks), margaritas made with agave wine, and a large selection of Mexican beers.

Picnic Pick-Ups.

• **Andronico's Market** *1550 Shattuck Ave./Cedar St., (510) 841-7942. Daily 7-11.*

This upscale supermarket carries delicious take-out fare and locally made gourmet treats, and boxed lunches are available by 24-hour advance reservation. It is located within what was once the consumer-owned Co-op, a supermarket that operated here from 1938 to 1988 and was the country's largest urban cooperative.

• **Food Stalls** *At the campus entrance, on Bancroft Way/Telegraph Ave. M-F 11-3, more or less; $. No cards.*

These informal stands offer simple fast foods such as donuts, soft pretzels, fresh juices and smoothies, falafel (a Middle Eastern vegetarian sandwich made with pocket bread), and other ethnic dishes. Nearby benches, steps, and grassy areas offer impromptu picnic possibilities. And because this famous intersection attracts all kinds of entertainers—jugglers, musicians, revivalists, you-name-it—an amazing floor show is free.

• **Made to Order** *1576 Hopkins St./Monterey Ave., (510) 524-7552. M-Sat 9:30-6.*

Wonderful deli fare, including freshly prepared salads and sandwiches, is found here. Favorites include meat pies and the rarely-available Grandma's potatoes.

• **Monterey Market** *1550 Hopkins St./Monterey Ave., (510) 526-6042. M-Sat 9-6. No cards.*

This low-key, much-heralded produce market caters to the sophisticated Berkeley palate with an amazing assortment of produce, including tender baby vegetables, unusual melons, and exotic wild mushrooms. The market also supplies the area's fine restaurants, and prices are unexpectedly low.

• **Noah's Bagels** *1883 Solano Ave./The Alameda, (510) 525-4447, fax (510) 525-4408. M-F 7-6:30, Sat 7-6, Sun 7-5.*

The very first Noah's store opened in nearby Emeryville. This branch was among the first in what has now become a very large chain. Promising "a taste of old New York," this shop delivers a bagel that is described by the founder as "crusty outside, chewy inside, tasty and big." They come in many flavors, including "super onion" and "multi-grain," and a variety of freshly-made cream cheese "shmears" make the perfect topping. Bagel sandwiches are made to order, and plenty of supporting items and cold drinks are also available. Noah says, "Protect your bagels . . . put lox on them!"

• **Whole Foods Market** *3000 Telegraph Ave./Ashby Ave., (510) 649-1333. Daily 9am-10pm.*

This Texas-based natural foods retailer purveys an amazing selection of good-for-you foods, and its busy bakery and deli-coffee bar have the makings for a great picnic. Seating is also available in comfortable booths inside and at sheltered tables outside. Special child-size shopping carts are fun for children.

Plearn *2050 University Ave./Shattuck Ave., (510) 841-2148. L&D M-Sat; $-$$. 1 highchair, boosters. No reservations.*

Very popular and with a "Thai-tech" decor, this restaurant's best dishes include: yum-nua (a yummy mixture of beef slices seasoned with onion, ground chilies, fragrant fresh mint, and lime juice), him-ma-pan (chicken with cashew nuts and chilies), and pat-prik-king (pork with chilies and string beans). For a pittance more, an entree is served with both rice and an iceberg lettuce salad topped with an exotic bright yellow, tangy-sweet dressing. For dessert, a crispy deep-fried banana topped with a light coconut sauce can be pleasant.

Pyramid Brewery & Alehouse *901 Gilman St./6th St., (510) 528-9880; www.PyramidBrew.com. L&D daily; $-$$. Booths, child menu. Reservations taken for L only.*

Situated within one gargantuan room, this massive, very noisy operation can still feel cozy for diners seated in one of the comfy, private booths. But for those in the mood to mingle, tables and chairs and bar-tables abound. Fifteen beers are on tap, all brewed on the premises in huge brewery vats visible from the dining room. Try the popular traditional Amber Lager, the Hefeweizen wheat beer served with a lemon wedge, or the Weizen Berry—Hefeweizen flavored with raspberry. Can't decide? Get a sampler of four. Nice for light drinkers is the fact that single 4-ounce sample sizes can be ordered. The expansive, eclectic menu offers snacks, soups, pizzas, sandwiches, burgers, and salads, as well as heftier entrees of fish & chips, baby back ribs, and assorted steaks. The chicken-fried steak pub plate is particularly good. A tasty spicy-sweet housemade mustard is served with many items. For dessert, be daring and order up an Espresso Stout float. **Brewery tours** are scheduled Monday through Friday at 2 and 4 p.m., and Saturday and Sunday at 1, 2, and 4 p.m. In summer, evening movies are scheduled outdoors in the parking lot.

Raja Restaurant *2160 University Ave./Oxford St., (510) 848-7252. L M-Sat, D daily; $$. Reservations accepted.*

One of the best Indian restaurants in town, this sedate spot is particularly strong in its vegetarian offerings. Crisp vegetable samosa appetizers are stuffed with a spicy filling of potatoes and peas and served with a tart green cilantro sauce and a sweet tamarind sauce. Bread dishes include a perfect garlic naan, onion kulcha (stuffed with onion and fresh cilantro), and aloo paratha (stuffed with potatoes, onion, ginger, and peas). Among the entrees are a superb dry aloo gobi (cauliflower and potatoes), a delightful channa masala (garbanzo beans), and a spicy aloo vindaloo (dumpling-like potaoes in a creamy hot sauce). Delicious dishes for carnivores include a garlic chicken kebab and a tasty chicken curry masala.

Restoran Rasa Sayang *977 San Pablo Ave./Marin Ave., Albany, (510) 525-7000. D Tu-Sun; $$. Highchairs.*

The only restaurant in the Bay Area serving spicy, delectable Malaysian cuisine, this spot presents a wonderfully light roti chanai flat bread (also available stuffed with meat as murtabak), a delicious long-simmered rendang chicken, and really good kuey teow goreng rice noodles with shrimp, eggs, and bean sprouts. Complet thali dinners are available for a small additional fee, and all stir-fried dishes can be made vegetarian.

Rick & Ann's *2922 Domingo Ave./Ashby Ave., (510) 649-8538. B&L daily, D Tu-Sun; $. Highchairs, boosters, child portions. No reservations.*

The extensive breakfast menu at this cozy neighborhood restaurant is served until 2:30 p.m. and features both the usual and the unusual—gingerbread waffles, hash prepared with beets, lacy corn cakes, French toast made with challah dipped in orange-cardamom batter. The superb homefries are made from fresh potatoes fried until they are *done* and served topped with sour cream and chopped green onions. At lunch, hamburgers, salads, and a variety of sandwiches are added to the menu. Banquettes along the wall, Shaker-style chairs, and tables with hammered metal tops lend a solid feeling. Kids get a coloring place mat and a basket of crayons to keep them occupied.

Santa Fe Bar & Grill *1310 University Ave., (510) 841-4740, fax (510) 841-5585. L M-F, D daily; $$$. Reservations advised.*

Berkeley's circa 1904 Santa Fe railroad depot was first remodeled and used as a restaurant in 1969 by Jeremiah Tower. Now under different ownership and completely redesigned, the basically circular interior features several comfortable rooms opening onto a center room dominated by a grand piano (live music nightly). An inviting bar area serving complimentary housemade potato chips also opens off of this main room, and in good weather outside dining is available. The menu centers on regional American items with a Mediterranean accent, such as broiled salmon served on a bed of fresh sautéed spinach with oyster mushrooms, or a house-cured smoked pork chop served with Comice pear-Granny Smith applesauce and mashed potatoes. Meats and game are smoked in-house, and breads, pizzas, and desserts are made from scratch. Vegetables, lettuces, and herbs are grown in the restaurant's own organic garden located adjacent. Garden tours are available upon request, and a box of salad greens can be purchased off the menu to take home.

Saul's Restaurant & Delicatessen *1475 Shattuck Ave./Cedar St., (510) 848-DELI, fax (510) 848-8366; www.saulsdeli.com. B,L,&D daily; $. Highchairs, boosters, booths, child menu. No reservations.*

With a N.Y.C. deli feel and some very comfortable booths, this casual spot presents popular traditional Jewish deli dishes: chicken soup with matzo balls or noodles, long-simmered brisket with carrots and onions, tasty coleslaw and potato salad, crispy latkes, delicious egg creams, and creamy rice pudding. A complimentary bowl of addictive whole, crisp cucumber pickles are brought to munch on while perusing the menu. The deli prepares everything to go.

Skates *100 Seawall Dr., at foot of University Ave., (510) 549-1900. L&D daily, SunBr; $$. Highchairs, boosters, booths, child portions. Reservations advised.*

The dining room here has thick carpeting, ceiling fans, and oversize booths and tables. Window tables take best advantage of the stunning three-bridge view. Brunch items include an omelette and frittata, French toast, a shellfish Benedict with lemon-dill scones, and macademia nut-banana sourdough pancakes. The extensive lunch menu offers deep-fried Cajun shrimp in coconut beer batter, a hamburger on focaccia bun, and a variety of soups, salads, and pastas. The dinner menu brings on more fresh fish items. Desserts are traditional and include a hot fudge sundae, a burnt cream custard, and, in season, a giant strawberry shortcake.

Smokey Joe's *On Shattuck Ave./Cedar Ave., no phone. B&L daily, D F & Sat. No cards.*

The owner of this tiny hole-in-the-wall diner—basically a counter with stools plus several small tables—has been dishing up noteworthy breakfasts since 1973. Smokey is famous for his homefries and delicious omelettes. Everything is made to order, and the o.j. is squeezed *after* it is ordered. The all-vegetarian menu states this is "where the elite meet to eat no meat." Decor consists of '60s memorbilia—tie-dyed things, a large peace symbol brick. Live music is often scheduled evenings from 7 to 9 p.m.

Spenger's Fresh Fish Grotto *1919 4th St./ University Ave., (510) 845-7771, fax (510) 845-7778; www.mccormickandschmicks.com. L&D daily; $$-$$$. Highchairs, boosters, child menu. Resrvations advised.*

Begun in 1890 as a country store, Spenger's then became a fish market, evolving after Prohibition into a bar and restaurant. Recently taken over and renovated by the McCormick & Schmick seafood chain, it now serves the very freshest fish in a vast variety of styles. The menu changes daily and includes everyone's favorite standards as well as some more unusual items. The restaurant remains one of Berkeley's most popular. Seating includes comfy boothes and "snugs" (semi-closed-off private areas) in a warren of rooms decorated with everything sea-related—it's a veritable maritime museum. Don't miss seeing the extensive collection of model ships and the huge 34-carat canary Star of Denmark diamond, once owned by Hawaii's Queen Kapiolani, displayed in the Diamond Bar. A well-stocked fish market adjoins.

Taiwan *2071 University Ave./Shattuck Ave., (510) 845-1456. B Sat & Sun, L&D daily; $. Highchairs, boosters. No reservations.*

Representative dishes from most of the Chinese provinces, including Taiwanese specialties, are among those served here. Portions are generous. Favorites include spinach with garlic, dry-braised green beans, General Tsao's chicken, spicy fish-flavored chicken, beef a la Shangtung (deep-fried pieces of battered beef in a tasty sauce), showy sizzling beef and sizzling chicken platters, Mongolian beef, and spicy prawns. More exotic items include Taiwan pickle cabbage with pork tripe soup, boneless duck web, and numerous squid dishes. Beggar's chicken and Peking duck are available when ordered one day in advance. On weekends, a Chinese breakfast is served. The fortune cookies here are unusually prophetic. The strip inside mine once read, "You would make an excellent critic."

Top Dog *2503 Hearst Ave./Euclid Ave., (510) 843-1241. L&D daily; $. No reservations.*

Hot dogs are the extent of the menu at this atmospheric hole in the wall. Twelve different kinds are available, but, surprisingly, not a veggie version is among them. Topped off with sauerkraut and mustard, it's one of the best dogs on the West Coast. To dine, grab one of the few counter stools, sit on the bench outside, or just stomp and chomp.

VIK's Chaat Corner *726 Allston Way/6th St., (510) 644-4412. L Tu-Sun; $. No reservations.*

Operating within a one-room garage-warehouse, this casual Indian cafe is said to be reminiscent of a New Delhi bazaar. Addicted diners line up out the door waiting to order at the counter and then volley for space at the charmless tables. The limited menu is handwritten on a board and changes daily. Food is served unceremoniously on paper plates with plastic untensils. Chaat translates as "small snacks," and deliciously spiced choices include a variety of appetizer-sized items that make a nice meal when shared. Consider pakori chaat (lentil dumplings with tamarind chutney), sev puri (potatoes and onions with garlic chutney), and samosas topped with spicy garbanzo curry. Both a meat and a vegetarian plate complete with rice and bread are also available. Drinks include a delicious creamy mango lassi and a thick guava nectar, and for dessert Indian sweets can be selected from a glass case. Next door, a related shop sells exotic Indian cooking staples.

Walker's Restaurant and Pie Shop *1491 Solano Ave./Curtis St., Albany, (510) 525-4647. B&L Tu-Sat, D Tu-Sun; $$. Highchairs, boosters, child portions. No reservations.*

Most everyone in these parts has been here at some point for one of the famous home-style meals. Complete dinners include housemade soup, either a green salad or a gelatin salad, popovers, an entree with a fresh vegetable and either baked or scalloped potato, and a slice of their celebrated flaky-crusted pie (the banana cream and sour cherry are fabulous). Entrees include fish, fried chicken, ham, New York steak, prime rib, and daily specials. Lunch is a similar menu, but also with lighter options such as sandwiches and hamburgers. For a take-out pie, it is wise to reserve a favorite a day in advance.

Xanadu *700 University Ave./6th St., (510) 548-7880, fax (510) 548-7882. L&D M-Sat; $$-$$$. Reservations advised.*

That an exotic space has been entered is apparent in the waiting area, where diners are treated to the sight of water-filled crocks holding fragrant floating flowers and where an antique chest with drawers displays some of the exotic ingredients used in preparing this restaurant's unusual dishes. Even the dining rooms are made mysterious with deep-hued tones of reds and greens. However, the ambiance is far from peaceful, as diners literally roar with enthusiasm—so loud, in fact, that when trains fly by on the tracks outside this former Southern Pacific train station, no one even notices. The aim of the "RestorAsian" cuisine here is to balance the yin and yang of the qi, which is central to the energy and fundamental health of the human body. Many of the dishes here are available nowhere else in the U.S. Particularly tasty and healthful items include flavorful roasted chicken with ginger sauce and lettuce leaves for wrapping (the ginger provides a warming effect—yang—aiding the heart and liver and acting as an antidote to colds and flus); dramatic Szechwan-style lacquered quail buried in a mountain of sun-dried chilies and fried garlic (the dry-wok preparation allows oils from the peppers to season the tiny birds, chasing away many ailments); and luscious galanga-spiced beef served with crispy yams and watercress salad (the beef is warming, the yams neutral, and the watercress cooling). But don't overlook the stunning crispy-fried whole fish, served upright and in an "S" shape, and do try any noodle dish offered on the ever-changing menu. Those who don't leave here healthier, do leave sated and content.

Crockett

WHERE TO EAT

The Nantucket *Foot of Port St., (510) 787-2233. L&D daily; $$. Highchairs, boosters, child portions. Reservations advised.*

Situated at the end of a twisting road under the Carquinez Bridge, on the other side of the tracks, this unpretentious, popular restaurant specializes in serving New England-style fresh fish items. Most are available either charcoal-broiled or pan-fried. Shellfish is lightly breaded and deep-fried Cape Cod-style and is also available in casseroles with Newburg or Mornay sauce. Shellfish cioppino, a house specialty, is either old-fashioned style (in the shell) or lazy man's style (out of the shell). Lobster and steak comprise the higher-priced end of the menu. All dinners are served with a choice of either creamy white clam chowder or a green salad topped with shrimp, with Parmesan cheese-topped French bread, with a fresh vegetable prepared with flair, and with a choice of either French fries or seasoned rice. Cheesecake in several unusual flavors is available for dessert. All tables have a view of the water and, if there is a wait to be seated, drinks and seafood appetizers can be ordered from the bar and enjoyed either indoors or out on the pier.

Crockett is the major center for sugar production on the West Coast. Driving back to the freeway, the large red brick building seen to the east is the circa 1906 C & H Sugar refinery.

Benicia

A LITTLE BACKGROUND

Founded in 1847 by General Vallejo and named for his bride, this low-key town was the state capital for a short time in 1853. Situated on the Carquinez Strait, about 30 miles northeast of San Francisco, it was also a very busy port. Now it is known for its many antique shops (located along First Street) and the Benicia Glass Studios consortium of glass-blowing factories (located on H Street). Note that many of the shops are closed on Mondays and Tuesdays.

VISITOR INFORMATION

Benicia Chamber of Commerce *601 First St., (800) 559-7377, (707) 745-2120, fax (707) 745-2275.*

GETTING THERE

Located 7 miles east of Vallejo via I-780.

WHAT TO DO

Benicia Capitol State Historic Park *115 W. G St., (707) 745-3385. Daily 10-5; house tours on 3rd Sun 12-4. Adults $3, 6-13 $2.*

Historic information and artifacts await visitors inside this restored 2-story, red brick Greek Revival building that served as the state capitol from February 4, 1853 to February 25, 1854. It is furnished with period pieces. Also in the park, the 1858 Federal-style Victorian **Fischer-Hanlon House**, a renovated Gold Rush hotel, holds an impressive collection of period furniture.

WHERE TO STAY & EAT

Union Hotel *401 First St., (707) 746-0100, fax (707) 746-6458. 21 rooms; $$-$$$. Unsuitable for children under 12. 1 VCR. Continental breakfast; restaurant.*

Located right on the main street, in the part of town reflecting the ambiance of a quieter era, this 1882 Victorian hotel offers 12 individually decorated rooms. For example, the Victoriana Room is decorated with rich, dark floral wallpaper and furnished with an assortment of antiques, among them a substantial armoire. A nine-room annex, the **Union Gardens**, is located down the street.

For dinner, hotel guests just catch the elevator down to the attractive **restaurant** *(L&D daily, Sat & SunBr. Highchairs, boosters, child portions. Reservations advised.)* serving gourmet meals. Then it's just a few steps over to the cozy **lounge** for a relaxing after-dinner drink. Featuring an impressive 110-year-old mahogany bar and faux tin walls, it is a showcase for live jazz.

Vallejo

VISITOR INFORMATION

Vallejo Convention & Visitors Bureau *495 Mare Island Way, (800) 4-VALLEJO, (707) 642-3653, fax (707) 644-2206; www.visitvallejo.com.*

This bureau also provides information on Benicia.

GETTING THERE

Located 30 miles northeast of San Francisco.

WHAT TO DO

Six Flags Marine World *Marine World Parkway/ Hwy. 37, (707) 643-ORCA; www.sixflags.com. W-Sun 9:30-5; in summer daily 9:30-6; closed Nov-Apr. Adults $34, 60+ $25, 4-12 $17. Parking $6. Dolphin-shaped stroller rentals available.*

Just a few years ago this theme park completely reinvented itself, adding rides to its world-famous collection of wildlife shows. It is now the nation's only combination wildlife park, oceanarium, and theme park. The exciting animal shows feature killer whales, dolphins, sea lions, elephants, chimpanzees, tigers, and exotic birds, and a spectacular water-skiing show is put on by daredevil humans. Visitors can walk through animal habitat areas to see African animals and ride an Asian elephant *($5)*. The Gentle Jungle petting area, and the Looney Tunes Acme Foam Factory, with slides and climbing structures and hundreds of orange foam balls for kids to toss or shoot from air cannons, are particularly popular with young children. Butterfly Habitat is the first

walk-through free-flight butterfly enclosure in the western U.S., and the walk-in Lorikeet Aviary provides up-close observation of these brightly colored birds and the opportunity to feed them. Now adding thrills to the mix are three monster roller coasters, the world's first 3-D motion simulator ride, and an assortment of other wild rides. Consider taking the ferry from San Francisco—the Blue & Gold Fleet *((415) 705-5555)* departs from Pier 39—or BART *((415) 992-2278; runs M-Sat.).*

Fairfield

WHAT TO DO

Anheuser-Busch Brewery Tours *3101 Busch Dr., (707) 429-7595. Tu-Sat 9-4, on the hour; also M June-Aug. Free.*

The tour here starts with a short video explaining how a Bud is made. Then visitors don plastic safety glasses and head out to see the beer bottled and capped—or canned—and then boxed. Back in the Hospitality Room everyone gets free samples. Snacks and soft drinks are also provided.

Herman Goelitz Candy Company *On Jelly Belly Lane, in Solano Business Park, (800) 9-JELLY-B, (707) 428-2838; www.jellybelly.com. Tours: Daily 9-5; free; strollers permitted. Store: (707) 447-4821; M-Sat 10-8, Sun 10-6.*

Family-run since 1898, this company is credited with inventing candy corn in 1900 and the famous, and flavorful, Jelly Belly® jelly bean in 1976. After taking the quarter-hour Candyland Tour, everyone gets a souvenir bag of the company's jelly beans. When available, the gift shop sells Belly Flops™—sometimes called rejects—at bargain prices; and a cafe offers Jelly Belly-flavored ice cream. A picnic area and a dogwalk are also available.

Western Railway Museum *5848 Hwy. 12, Suisun City, between Fairfield & Rio Vista (exit Hwy. 80 at Hwy. 12, then drive east), (707) 374-2978; www.wrm.org. Sat & Sun 11-5; W-Sun in July & Aug. Adults $7, 65+ $6, 3-14 $4.*

Located between two sheep pastures in the middle of a flat, arid no-man's land, this very special museum displays and actually operates its collection of historic electric streetcars and steam train engines. Among the dozen or so operating electric cars are both an articulated car (hinged so it can go around corners), which ran on the Bay Bridge from 1939 to 1958, and a bright red car from the Peninsular Railway. Several cars operate each weekend, running along a 1.5-mile stretch of track with overhead electric trolley wires. Cars are operated by the same volunteers who spent countless hours lovingly restoring them. Stationary cars, waiting for repairs, can be viewed in several large barns. An oasis-like picnic and play area is available to visitors, and a bookstore with a past (check out the plaque above the bench in front) offers a large collection of railroad books and paraphernalia. All fees collected are used to restore and maintain the streetcars. (It costs between $25,000 and $50,000 to restore a car and, because the labor is volunteer, it can take as long as ten years!)

The museum also operates theme trains over the Sacramento Northern Railway. Pumpkin Patch Trains run at Halloween and Santa Claus Specials during December.

Sacramento

A LITTLE BACKGROUND

It is fiery summer always, and you can gather roses, and eat strawberries and ice-cream, and wear white linen clothes, and pant and perspire at eight or nine o'clock in the morning.

— Mark Twain

Gold was discovered in 1848 just 30 miles east of Sacramento, and the rest is history. As news of the discovery spread like wild-fire around the globe, fortune hunters came here before setting out for the mining fields. Sacramento has been the state capital since 1854. In 1866, Mark Twain was a special news correspondent with the *Sacramento Union Newspaper.*

Like New York City, the streets here are almost empty on Sunday and prettty quiet on Saturday. Surprisingly, on weekends it is a great destination for avoiding crowds. Most of the major historic attractions are concentrated in the downtown area. This flat, central part of

town was laid out in a grid of lettered and numbered streets by town founder John Sutter's son, John Sutter, Jr., making it easy to get around even now.

VISITOR INFORMATION

Sacramento Convention & Visitors Bureau *1303 J St. #600., (916) 264-7777, fax (916) 264-7788; www.sacramentocvb.org.*

GETTING THERE

Located approximately 90 miles northeast of San Francisco.

— By Cruise Ship —

Clipper *((800) 325-0010, (314) 727-2929)* offers a 6-day, 5-night cruise.

— By Train —

Amtrak *((800) 872-7245)* trains leave for Sacramento daily from San Jose, San Francisco (via bus connection to Oakland), and Oakland. Special family fares are available. Overnight train-hotel packages can be reserved through **Amtrak Vacations** *((800) 440-8202)*. Call for fare and schedule information and to make reservations.

— Scenic Route by Car —

Take Highway 160 through the Delta (see page 345).

ANNUAL EVENTS

Sacramento Jazz Jubilee *May; on Memorial Day weekend. (916) 372-5277. Tickets $10-$70.*

This is the world's largest traditional jazz festival.

California State Fair *August. (916) 263-FAIR; www.bigfun.org. Adults $7, 62+ $5, 5-12 $4. Parking $4.*

There's something for everyone at the oldest state fair in the West, which is also the largest agricultural fair in the U.S. Pleasures include monorail and carnival rides, thoroughbred racing, educational exhibits, and live entertainment. Special for children are a petting farm, pony rides, and a nursery where baby animals are born each day.

Waterworld USA Family Waterpark *(1600 Exposition Blvd., (916) 924-0556. Daily 10:30-6; June-Aug only. Over 4' tall $16.97, under 4' $9.95, under age 3 free.)* operates adjacent to the fair site. It features the largest wave pool in Northern California, the highest waterslides in the West, and an assortment of other attractions.

WHAT TO DO

American River Parkway *(916) 366-2072, fax (916) 855-5932. Daily dawn-dusk. $4/vehicle.*

This is basically 23 miles of water fun. Call for a free map and more information about facilities.

- **Bike Trail.**

The paved Jedediah Smith National Recreation Trail runs for 23 miles along the American River.

- **Fishing.**

The best month for salmon and steelhead is October. Favorite spots are the Nimbus Basin below the dam and Sailor Bar. A state license in required.

- **Nature Walks.**

The **Effie Yeaw Nature Center** *(6700 Tarshes Dr., in Ancil Hoffman County Park, Carmichael, (916) 489-4918, fax (916) 489-4983; www.effieyeaw.org. Daily 10-5. Free. Parking $4.)* features displays and hands-on exhibits of the area's natural and cultural history. A Maidu Indian Demonstration Area and a 77-acre Nature Area with three self-guided nature trails are also part of the center.

- **Raft Trips.**

Trips begin in the Upper Sunrise Recreation Area, located north of the Sunrise Boulevard exit off Highway 50. In summer several companies rent rafts and provide shuttle bus return.

Bridges.

Located near Old Sacramento, the Tower Bridge, a liftspan drawbridge, sometimes can be observed going up. To the right of it, the I Street Bridge is one of the few remaining pedestal bridges in the country; sometimes it can be observed turning.

The B Street Theatre *2711 B St./27th St., (916) 443-5300, fax (916) 443-0874; www.sna.com/bstreet. Tickets $15.50-$19.50.*

Founded by actor Timothy Busfield, who starred in TV's memorable *Thirty-Something*, and his brother Buck, this small non-profit professional theater company presents only world premieres. Nothing has been performed anywhere else. The theater itself is small, and seating in the round means performances are in-your-face intimate. The audience is close enough to the actors to see their warts, wrinkles, and other imperfections. Everything is in place for a satisfying night of theater.

California State Capitol Museum *10th St./L St., (916) 324-0333; www.assembly.ca.gov. Tours daily 9-4. Free.*

Restored now to its turn-of-the-century decor and earthquake-safe—a job that cost $68 million and is said to have been the largest restoration project in the history of the country—the Capitol is quite a showcase. Free tickets can be picked up in the basement a half-hour before each tour, and a small museum with a 10-minute orientation film entertains visitors during any wait.

A short-order cafeteria operates in the basement for meals and snacks, and the full-service **Capitol Cafe** is open weekdays on the sixth floor.

Tours of the surrounding park, which is the largest arboretum west of the Mississippi and home to over 300 varieties of trees and flowers from all over the world as well as one of the largest camellia groves in the world, are scheduled daily in summer at 10:30 a.m. The circular **California Vietnam Veteran's Memorial** is located by the rose garden at the park's east end *(15th St./Capitol Ave.)*. The 22 shiny black granite panels of this privately funded monument are engraved with the 5,822 names of California's dead and missing.

California State Indian Museum *2618 K St./26th St., (916) 324-0971. Daily 10-5. Adults $3, 6-12 $1.50.*

Established in 1940, this museum displays especially interesting samples of bark clothing and a permanent basket collection featuring colorful Pomo feather baskets. Films are presented throughout the day. Picnicking is particularly pleasant beside a duck pond across from the museum.

Crocker Art Museum *216 O St./3rd St., (916) 264-5423, fax (916) 264-7372; www.sacto.org/crocker. Tu-Sun 10-5, Thur to 9. Adults $5.50, 65+ $4.50, 7-17 $3.*

Located within a magnificent Italianate building dating from 1874, this is the oldest public art museum west of the Mississippi. Collection highlights include Master drawings, 19th-century American and European paintings, and contemporary Northern California art in all media. Family activities occur every weekend, and lectures, films, and Sunday afternoon concerts are often scheduled. Picnic tables are available across the street in lovely Crocker Park.

Dial A Story *(916) 441-1234.*

A new story is recorded each week especially for 3- to 6-year-olds.

Dial A Book *(916) 442-2442.*

A new chapter of a book is recorded weekly especially for 7- to 12-year-olds.

Golden State Museum *1020 O St./10th St., (916) 653-7524, fax (916) 653-7134; www.goldenstatemuseum.org. Tu-Sat 10-5, Sun 12-5. Adults $6.50, 55+ $5, 6-13 $3.50.*

Arranged by topics, this new museum tells the state's story in four exhibit galleries: the Place, People, Promise, and Politics of California. The collection includes authentic documents, films, an inviting reconstructed cafe, a ghostly hologram, and the occasional car and bus. All visitors are loaned an audio guide for self-touring. The museum occupies the first two floors of the California Archives building. Before leaving, visit the interior courtyard sculpture known as "Constitution Wall."

Governor's Mansion State Historic Park *1526 H St./16th St., (916) 323-3047. Tours daily 10-4, on the hour. Adults $3, 6-12 $1.50.*

Built in 1877, this 30-room Victorian mansion was bought by the state in 1903 for $32,500. During the next 64 years it was home to 13 governors and their families. It remains just as it was when vacated by its last tenant—Governor Reagan. Now serving the public as an interesting museum, it displays 15 rooms of furnishings and personal items left behind by each family. Visitors see Governor George Pardee's 1902 Steinway piano, Earl Warren's hand-tied Persian carpets, and Hiram Johnson's plum velvet sofa and chairs. Among the interesting artifacts are marble fireplaces from Italy and gold-framed mirrors from France. The official State of California china, selected by the wife of Goodwin Knight in the late 1950s, is also on display.

Music Circus *1419 H St., adjacent to the Sacramento Convention Center, (916) 557-1999. Daily in July & Aug. Tickets $19-$35, children half-price at some performances.*

Said to be the only tent theater west of the Mississippi, this 2,500-seat facility presents summer stock musicals suitable for the entire family.

Old Sacramento.

Situated along the Sacramento River, Old Sacramento was the kickoff point for the gold fields during the Gold Rush. It was the western terminus for both the Pony Express and the country's first long distance telegraph, and the country's first transcontinental railroad started here. Said to be the largest historic preservation project in the West, Old Sacramento is a 28-acre living museum of the Old West. Vintage buildings, wooden walkways, and cobblestone streets recall the period from 1850 to 1880. Restaurants, shops, and historic exhibits combine to make it both an entertaining and educational spot to visit.

Guided tours of the area *((916) 324-0040)* begin at the California State Railroad Museum on selected Saturdays. Information on self-guided tours can be obtained at the **Visitor Information Center** *(1101 2nd St./K St., (916) 442-7644. Daily 9-5.)*. Horse-drawn carriages can be hired for rides from Old Sacramento to the Capitol.

• California State Railroad Museum *111 I St./2nd St., (916) 445-6645; www.csrmf.org. Daily 10-5. Adults $6, 6-12 $3; ticket good on same day for admission to Central Pacific Passenger Depot.*

This gigantic 3-story building holds the largest interpretive railroad museum in North America. Inside, 21 beautifully restored, full-size railroad locomotives and cars representing the 1860s through the 1960s are on display. Among them are an apartment-size, lushly furnished Georgia Northern private car complete

with stained-glass windows, and a Canadian Pullman rigged to feel as if it is actually moving. A film, a 30-projector multi-image slide show, and assorted interpretive displays tell the history of American railroading. Docent-led tours are often available, and well-trained, railroad-loving volunteers, wearing historically authentic railroad workers' garb, are always on hand to answer questions. Upstairs, great views of the trains below are available from an oversize catwalk. A large collection of toy trains—including a 1957 pastel pink Lionel train designed especially for little girls—is also displayed.

Nearby the **Central Pacific Passenger Depot** *(930 Front St.)* displays nine more locomotives and cars. Visiting this reconstructed train depot provides the opportunity to step back in time to 1876—an era when riding the train was the chic way to travel. An audio tour wand that picks up recorded descriptions of displays is provided. On weekends April through September, the **Sacramento Southern Railroad** excursion steam train leaves the depot hourly from 11 a.m. to 5 p.m. for a 6-mile, 40-minute round-trip.

• **Discovery Museum History Center** *101 I St., (916) 264-7057, fax (916) 264-5100; www.thediscovery.org. Tu-Sun 10-5. Adults $5, 13-17 $4, 6-12 $3.*

This 3-story brick building is a replica of Sacramento's first public building—the 1854 City Hall. A 113-foot free-standing fiberglass flagpole in front is said to be the tallest in the entire country. The museum inside brings Sacramento's history and the 1849 Gold Rush to life with an extensive collection of gold specimens (worth $1 million), historical photos, and historic farm equipment. Among the exhibits are a 13-pound gold nugget and an antique poultry incubator. Children especially enjoy a kid-sized log cabin and story area with rocking chair, as well as coloring stations located throughout. The **Discovery Museum Science & Space Center** *(3615 Auburn Blvd., (916) 575-3941, fax (916) 575-3925. M-F 12-5, Sat & Sun 10-5. Adults $4, 6-12 $2.)* is nearby and has the area's only planetarium, plus live animals and a nature trail.

• **Eagle Theatre** *925 Front St./J St., (916) 323-6343, fax (916) 327-0953. F & Sat at 8pm. Tickets $10.*

A reconstruction of California's first theater building, built in 1849, the Eagle now presents Gold Rush-era plays and musicals. Children's programs are also sometimes scheduled. Call for current production information and for schedule of free tours.

• **Riverboat cruises.** *110 L St., (800) 433-0263, (916) 552-2933; www.oldsacriverboat.com. Call for schedule. Tickets $15-$30. Reservations required.*

Two paddlewheelers, the *Spirit of Sacramento* and the *Matthew McKinley*, ply the waters here offering sightseeing cruises, brunch and lunch and dinner cruises, and sunset and happy hour cruises.

• **Schoolhouse** *1200 Front St./L St., (916) 483-8818. M-F 10-4, Sat & Sun 12-4.*

Now a museum, this one-room schoolhouse has a play yard with old-fashioned board swings kids can use.

Sutter's Fort State Historic Park *2701 L St./27th St., (916) 445-4422. Daily 10-5. Adults $3-$6, 6-12 $1.50-$3.*

A reconstruction of the settlement founded in 1839 by Captain John A. Sutter, this is the oldest restored fort in the West. Exhibits include carpenter, cooper, and blacksmith shops as well as prison and living quarters. An audio tour is included with admission. Admission is higher in summer, when interpreters demonstrate crafts and daily life of the 1840s.

Towe Auto Museum *2200 Front St., (916) 442-6802, fax (916) 442-2646. Daily 10-6. Adults $6, 15-18 $2.50, 5-14 $1.*

Opened in 1987, this cavernous museum displays 150 antique cars depicting the history of the American automobile. In addition to the cars, the museum has a Mighty Wurlitzer Theater Pipe Organ with 1,200 pipes. Mini-concerts are presented on Sunday afternoons in the spring and fall. A shuttle bus from Old Sacramento operates daily in summer and on weekends the rest of the year. If driving, call for directions; this museum is difficult to find.

Victorian Houses.

Elaborate Victorian homes are found between 7th and 16th streets, from E to I streets. Don't miss the Heilbron house at 740 O Street and the Stanford house at 800 N Street.

William Land Park *On Freeport Blvd. between 13th Ave. & Sutterville Rd.*

This 236-acre park has a supervised playground, children's wading pool, 9-hole golf course, and fishing pond for children under 16. It also incorporates:

- **Fairytale Town** *1501 Sutterville Rd./Land Park Dr., (916) 264-5233. Daily 10-5; in summer 9-4. Admission $3-$3.50, under 2 free.*

Nursery rhymes and fairy tales come to life in this 2 1/2-acre amusement park.

- **Funderland** *Sutterville Rd./S. Land Park Dr., (916) 456-0115, fax (916) 383-7735. Daily 10-6, June-Aug; rest of year F-Sun only. Closed Dec & Jan. 85¢-$1/ride.*

In operation since 1948, this amusement park for young children delights them with nine rides. Pony rides are available adjacent.

- **Sacramento Zoo** *Land Park Dr./Sutterville Rd., (916) 264-5166 or (916) 264-5888, fax (916) 264-5887; www.saczoo.com. Daily 10-4; in summer 9-4. Adults $4.50-$5, 3-12 $3-$3.50. Stroller rentals avail.*

This modest 15-acre zoo is home to over 150 exotic and native species, 40 of which are endangered or threatened. It holds just enough exhibits to keep visitors busy for a pleasant few hours. A snack bar dispenses a limited, but appropriate and satisfying, menu of hot dogs, sodas, cookies, etc.

WHERE TO STAY

Motels abound. Call a favorite chain for reservations, or contact the Convention & Visitors Bureau for a list of lodgings.

Delta King *1000 Front St., in Old Sacramento, (800) 825-KING, (916) 444-KING, fax (916) 444-5314; www.deltaking.com. 5 stories; 44 rooms; 100% non-smoking; $$-$$$. Children under 6 free. Continental breakfast; restaurant. Parking $6.*

Launched in 1927, this flat-bottomed riverboat plied the waters between Sacramento and San Francisco in the late 1920s and '30s. After having spent 15 months partially submerged in the San Francisco Bay, she was treated to years of restoration work costing $9.5 million. Now appropriately moored dockside in Old Sacramento, her rooms are furnished with brass beds and wicker accent pieces. All have private bathrooms with an old-fashioned pedestal sink and pull-chain, tall-tank toilet, and a few have clawfoot tubs. The vessel's wheelhouse has been converted into a room with a private second-story observation deck.

An elegant dinner with a river view can be enjoyed in the **Pilothouse Restaurant** *(L M-Sat, D daily, SunBr. Highchairs, boosters, child menu. Reservations advised.)*, located on the Promenade Deck. Entrees include luxury items such as prawns, steak, and rack of lamb. A well-executed Caesar salad is dramatically prepared table-side and not to be missed, and an enticing dessert tray is also available. Live music is performed on a grand piano most evenings in a cozy lounge-style bar adjoining the restaurant. On Friday and Saturday nights the **Paddlewheel Saloon**, a lively bar overlooking the boat's 17-ton paddle wheel, presents an interactive murder mystery dinner show. Live performances are also scheduled on weekends in an intimate theater down on the Cargo Deck. Intermissions are long, allowing plenty of time to visit the lobby bar. Dinner-theater and overnight packages are sometimes available.

Hyatt Regency Sacramento *1209 L St./12th St., (800) HYATT-CA, (916) 443-1234, fax (916) 321-6699; www.hyatt.com. 15 stories, 500 rooms; $$. Heated pool, hot tub, fitness center. 2 restaurants, room service. Parking $10-$15.*

Situated across the street from the Capitol and adjacent to both the convention center and the pedestrian K Street Mall, this extremely well-located luxury hotel features a Mediterranean architectural style, with an atrium lobby and marble floors. A charming topiary hedge fence in the shape of people and animals defines its front entrance.

KOA Kampground *3951 Lake Rd., West Sacramento, (800) KOA-2747, (916) 371-6771, fax (916) 371-0622.*

For description, see page 415.

Radisson Hotel Sacramento *500 Leisure Ln., (800) 333-3333, (916) 922-2020, fax (916) 649-9463; www.radisson.com/sacramentoca. 309 rooms; $-$$$+. Children under 18 free. Heated pool, hot tub, fitness center, parcourse. Restaurant.*

Located on the outskirts of downtown, this low-rise hotel complex is run much like a vacation resort. Rooms are spacious and comfortable, and some overlook a natural spring-fed lake and koi pond. On weekends throughout the summer, jazz and orchestra performances are scheduled in the property's own amphitheater and are free to guests. Bicycle rentals are available for rides along the scenic Jedediah Smith bike trail, which runs along the American River Parkway adjacent to the hotel. (The 35-mile trail runs along the river from Old Sacramento to Folsom. The hotel is about 5 miles from the Old Sacramento end.) A courtesy shuttle takes guests to the grand indoor Arden Fair Shopping Mall located nearby.

Sacramento Hostel *900 H St./9th St., (916) 443-1691, fax (916) 443-4763. 70 beds; private rooms.*

Operating within an 1885 Victorian mansion, this jewel is centrally located and convenient to major attractions. It features a restored drawing room, luxurious parlor, recreation room, and patio with barbecue as well as verandahs and gardens. See also page 417.

Sterling Hotel *1300 H St./13th St., (800) 365-7660, (916) 448-1300, fax (916) 455-6102. 16 rooms; 100% non-smoking; $$$-$$$+. Continental breakfast M-Sat, SunBr; restaurant.*

Located just 3 blocks from the Capitol, this converted Victorian mansion claims to be the only hotel in the country with private, oversize Jacuzzis in each all-marble bathroom. Room 303, furnished with a posh oriental carpet and with a balcony overlooking the front yard's magnolia trees, is especially nice.

The hotel's highly rated restaurant, **Chanterelle**, serves California cuisine.

WHERE TO EAT

Buffalo Bob's Ice Cream Saloon *110 K St., in Old Sacramento, (916) 442-1105. Daily 10-6; $. Highchairs, boosters. No cards.*

A variety of sandwiches and hot dogs are available here, as is old-time sarsaparilla to wash it all down. Ice cream concoctions dominate the menu and include exotic sundaes such as Fool's Gold (butter brickle ice cream topped with butterscotch and marshmallow, whipped cream, almonds, and a cherry) and Sierra Nevada (peaks of vanilla ice cream capped with hot fudge, whipped cream, almonds, and a cherry).

Chevys *1369 Garden Way, (916) 649-0390; also at 1234 Howe Ave./Hurley, (916) 923-6574.*

Situated on the river at Riverside Marina north of Old Sacramento, this popular Tex-Mex restaurant has waterside tables. For description, see page 62.

Fanny Ann's Saloon *1023 2nd St., in Old Sacramento, (916) 441-0505. L&D daily; $. No reservations.*

This narrow, four-level restaurant has a raucous ambiance and funky decor that provide the makings for instant fun. Children and adults alike enjoy the casual atmosphere and American-style fare: good half-pound hamburgers, assorted styles of 9-inch hot dogs, curly French fries, and large bowls of house-made soup. A variety of sandwiches and salads are also available. After orders are placed with the cook at the window in back, diners can relax with a game of pinball or get a downright cheap drink at the old bar. When one mother inquired whether there were booster seats, the cheerful hostess replied, "I'll hold the kids on my lap."

Fat City Bar & Grill *1001 Front St., in Old Sacramento, (916) 446-6768. L&D daily, SunBr; $$. Child menu.*

Located within a high-ceilinged brick warehouse dating from 1849, this popular spot features Tiffany-style lamps, stained-glass windows, and Victorian-style furnishings. Delicious specialty drinks can be enjoyed at an ornate old mahogany bar, or with meals at dining tables overlooking sidewalk traffic. Appetizer items such as Southern fried chicken strips and French onion soup are on the menu along with a variety of pasta dishes and hamburgers. Old-fashioned desserts such as strawberry shortcake and hot fudge sundaes wind things up.

Fox & Goose Public House *1001 R St./10th St., (916) 443-8825. B&L daily, D M-F; $. Highchairs, boosters, booths, child menu. No reservations.*

Located within a 1913 building that was once the Fuller Paint and Glass Company, this English-style pub features high ceilings, rustic unfinished floors, multi-paned windows, and roomy booths. Breakfast doesn't get any better. The menu then offers British-style grilled tomatoes, bangers, and crumpets, as well as American standards and a large variety of omelettes. Many items are made on the premises—granola, scones, muffins, and thoroughly cooked homefries—and free-range chicken eggs are available. Lunch items include Cornish pasties, Welsh rarebit, English tea sandwiches, and a classic ploughman's lunch, plus desserts of rich burnt cream custard and layered trifle. Live music is scheduled most evenings, when pub grub is served until 9:30. Over 15 English and Irish beers are on tap, and a good selection of California wines is available.

Hamburger Mary's *1630 J St./17th St., (916) 441-4340.*

For description, see page 69.

Hard Rock Cafe *7th St./K St., in Downtown Plaza, (916) 441-5591. L&D daily.*

For description, see page 69.

Jammin' Salmon *1801 Garden Hwy., (916) 929-6232. L M-F, D daily, Sat & SunBr; $$. 1 highchair, 1 booster. Reservations advised.*

A table on the peaceful deck here overlooking the placid Sacramento River is a great idea in warm weather. The eclectic lunch menu offers a variety of salads and sandwiches, as well as some more substantial fish entrees. Dinner is more pricey.

Down-river, the funkier, rowdier **Virgin Sturgeon** *(1577 Garden Hwy., (916) 921-2694. B Sat & Sun, L&D daily; $-$$. Boosters, child portions. No reservations.)*, reached via a ramp through a converted truck rig, is popular with politicians and "river rats" (people with boats). Situated atop a barge, it has outdoor deck seating as well as cozy interior seating and is known for serving great Cuban black beans and rice, steamed clams, barbecued pork ribs, and mushroom cheeseburgers.

Several other wildly popular restaurants can also be found in this area.

Los Nopales *106 J St., in Old Sacramento, (916) 443-6376, fax (916) 443-6998. L&D daily; $-$$. Highchairs, boosters, booths, child portions. No reservations.*

The lovely old brick walls of this festively appointed restaurant are decorated with paintings of the California missions. Mexican fare includes nachos, quesadillas, and homemade tamales and sopes. Both full meals and less expansive, and expensive, a la carte items are available. For dessert try the deep-fried ice cream. Live music is scheduled on Friday and Saturday nights.

Max's Opera Cafe *1735 Arden Way, in Market Square Plaza at Arden Fair Shopping Mall, (916) 927-6297.*

For description, see page 73.

Old Spaghetti Factory *1910 J St., (916) 443-2862, fax (916) 443-4354.*

Located within a former Western Pacific Depot outside the main tourist area, this is a link in the popular noodle chain. For description, see page 179.

Pizza & Pipes *2911 Arden Way, (916) 488-5470.*

A 1,400-pipe theater organ entertains with popular songs as diners down pizza. For description, see page 162.

Ristorante Piatti *571 Pavilions Lane, (916) 649-8885. L&D daily.*

For description, see page 356.

T.G.I. Fridays *1229 Howe Ave., (916) 925-5766. L&D daily, SunBr.*

For description, see page 161.

Virga's *14th St./O St., (916) 442-8516. L Tu-F, D Tu-Sat; $$.*

With seating both indoors and out, this small venue injects some really big flavors in its Italian cuisine. Lunch finds items such as artichoke cheese fondue, a house-smoked salmon salad, and assorted panini on the menu along with a burger on focaccia. At dinner, the house-made soups are always interesting, but the Italian potstickers and crispy olives stuffed with an anchovy-cheese mix are also alluring. Pastas, including an oversize handstuffed ravioli of the day, and risottos share the entree selections along with unusual meat and fresh fish items. It is difficult to order wrong here.

World Wrapps *2912 Fulton Ave., in Town & Country Center, (916) 489-9727, fax (916) 489-9733; also at 2449 Fair Oaks Blvd., in Loehmann's Plaza, (916) 488-7300, fax (916) 488-7034.*

For description, see page 82.

Truckee

A LITTLE BACKGROUND

Much of the original architecture in this old mining town is well preserved, and many shops and restaurants on the main street operate within interesting, sometimes beautifully restored, historic buildings. The town's yellow Victorian Southern Pacific Depot dates from 1896 and is now the Amtrak and Greyhound station as well as the Visitors Center.

VISITOR INFORMATION

Truckee Donner Chamber of Commerce
12036 Donner Pass Rd., (530) 587-2757, fax (530) 587-2439.

Truckee-Donner Visitor Information Center
10065 Donner Pass Rd., in the train depot, (800) 548-8388, (530) 587-2757; www.truckee.com.

This service assists with lodging reservations.

GETTING THERE

Located approximately 185 miles northeast of San Francisco, and 100 miles northeast of Sacramento. Located approximately 55 miles northwest of North Lake Tahoe via Highway 267.

WHAT TO DO

Donner Memorial State Park *12593 Donner Pass Rd., off Hwy. 40, 2 mi. west of town, (530) 582-7892. Daily 8-dusk. $5/vehicle. Museum: Daily 9-4; in summer to 5. Adults $2, 6-12 $1.*

Located on Donner Lake, this park is a monument to the tragic Donner Party stranded here by blizzards in 1846. Picnic facilities, lake swimming, hiking trails, nature programs, and campsites (June through September only) are available. The **Emigrant Trail Museum** features exhibits on the area's history.

WHERE TO STAY

The Truckee Hotel *10007 Bridge St., (800) 659-6921, (530) 587-4444, fax (530) 587-1599; www.thetruckeehotel.com. 4 stories; 36 rooms; 100% non-smoking; $-$$. Children under 4 free. Some TVs; some shared baths. Afternoon tea on weekends, continental breakfast.*

Originally built as a stage coach stop in 1868, this beautifully renovated Victorian offers stylish period lodging.

WHERE TO EAT

Squeeze In *10060 Commercial Row, (530) 587-9814. B&L daily; $. Highchairs, boosters. No reservations. No cards.*

At breakfast in this long, narrow cafe, diners have a choice of 57 kinds of omelettes. A variety of other breakfast dishes and sandwiches are also on the menu.

Plumas County

A LITTLE BACKGROUND

Boasting an abundance of national forest land, this area is noted for its outdoor recreation. Visitors can fish, ride horses, take pack trips, hike, camp, ride bikes, white water raft and kayak, and golf on five courses (including Whitehawk Ranch, the only course in the country that permits players to wear jeans). Birdwatching is prime on man-made Lake Davis, where campsites are also available, and wildlife spotting is generally good throughout the area. The Lakes Basin Recreation Area, a former gold mining hideaway, now offers all the sports mentioned above plus stays in historic, rustic lodging; over 30 natural mountain lakes are hidden in this remote, unspoiled terrain located within the Plumas National Forest. Frenchman Lake, is located north of Chilcoot and old-time **Wiggin's Trading Post** *((530) 993-4721)*, where everything from worms to chapstick to Daniel Boon fur hats are for sale. It is reached via a senic drive through Little Last Chance Creek canyon, featuring unique geological formations of vocanic rock, and is known for giving up trophy trout. In October and November, the entire area puts on a dazzling fall foliage display of color.

The charming town of Graeagle, with its line of red cottages that were once the homes of lumber mill workers and are now coverted into shops, is one of the area's larger towns and a convenient spot to settle in. The town's Mill Pond has kayak and paddleboat rentals, and its main drag holds several interesting antique shops. Claiming to be the birthplace of winter sports, it is also a good destination in winter.

VISITOR INFORMATION

Eastern Plumas Chamber of Commerce *73136 Hwy. 70, Portola, (800) 995-6057, (530) 832-5444, fax (530) 832-1938; www.psln.com/epluchmb.*

Plumas County Visitors Bureau *550 Crescent St., Quincy, (800) 326-2247, (530) 283-6345, fax (530) 283-5465; www.plumas.ca.us.*

GETTING THERE

Follow Highway 89 north for 50 miles into Graeagle, passing through the Sierra Valley—the largest alpine valley in North America, with scenery varying from conifer and aspen forests to pastures and wildflowers. Alternatively, travel here via Highway 5, to Highway 99, to Highway 70, following Highway 70 to the north of Oroville and then along the 130-mile Feather River National Scenic Byway through the spectacularly scenic Feather River Canyon, and on to Hallelujah Junction at Highway 395, just east of Chilcoot. The route crosses antique railroad bridges and passes through tunnels. This area is 240 miles northeast of San Francisco.

ANNUAL EVENTS

Mohawk Valley Independence Day Celebration *July. In Graeagle; (530) 832-5444.*

Festivities include a small parade with marching bands and bagpipers, fireworks over the town pond, a pancake breakfast, live music in the park, and line dancing lessons.

Charming cottage shop in Graeagle

Railroad Days *August. In Portola; (530) 832-5444.*

This festive event celebrates the railroad, mining, and logging industries that shaped Portola's past. Train rides, music, arts and crafts, and kids' activities are part of the fun.

WHAT TO DO

Jim Beckwourth Museum *On Rocky Point Rd., east of Portola, (530) 832-4888.*

Also known as the Beckwourth Cabin, this refurbished 1850s log cabin was once a trading post and hotel. It now honors African-American frontiersman James P. Beckwourth, who discovered in 1851 the lowest pass through the Sierra Nevada. The trail named for him begins in Reno, runs through this area, and ends in Oroville.

Plumas-Eureka State Park *In Johnsville, (530) 836-2380.*

Situated on the site of one of the region's largest quartz mining operations, the museum here is located in a former bunkhouse. It features a display on longboard ski racing, which originated nearby. An outdoor complex includes a restored stamp mill, miner's home, blacksmith shop, and assayer's office. A supervised gold-panning program with the equipment included is offered here during the summer, as is a Junior Ranger Program (see page 417). Also in summer, Living History Days, featuring costumed docents and hands-on pioneer activities, are held on the last Saturday of each month. Campsites and ranger programs are available.

Nearby, Ski Gold Mountain (see page 400) is the birthplace of ski racing and annually stages the Historic Longboard Revival Series races.

Portola Railroad Museum *Off Commercial St., Portola, (530) 832-4131. Open Mar-Oct 10-5. By donation. Train rides: $2, family $5; Sat & Sun June-Aug. Rent-a-Locomotive $95+.*

Housed in the former Western Pacific diesel shop, this hands-on museum features one of the largest and most historic collections of diesel locomotives in the nation. It also has 95 freight and passenger cars, 12,000 feet of

track, and assorted photos and artifacts. Visitors can climb aboard the cars outside. A few rarer cars stored inside require guided tours. This facility is world-famous for its unique Rent-a-Locomotive program, allowing visitors to actually drive a diesel locomotive. A ride in a train of cabooses is offered on summer weekends along a 1-mile balloon track.

Reid Horse & Cattle Co. Graeagle Stables *On Hwy. 89, Graeagle, (530) 836-0430; www.reidhorse.com. 1 hr./$24.*

In addition to trail rides, horse-drawn wagon rides with a western cookout lunch or dinner are offered *((530) 836-4078. Reservations required.)* and pack trips can be arranged *((530) 283-1147)*. Stables are also located at Gold Lake and Bucks Lake.

WHERE TO STAY

Feather River Inn *On Hwy. 70, west of Blairsden, (530) 836-2623. 100+ rooms. Heated pool, tennis courts, 9-hole golf course. Restaurant.*

Built in 1914, this charmingly rustic Swiss-style resort was once a destination for the Bay Area's elite, who arrived by train and deboarded at the facility's own depot. It is now a private camp and conference center, with a golf course, communal cabins, and a chalet-style lodge and restaurant. A prime spot for family reunions, it also hosts a family camp and

Elderhostel program. Some rooms are available to the public, as are summer Friday night prime rib dinners and the extensive Sunday brunch. Recreation includes basketball, sand volleyball, and horseshoes.

Gray Eagle Lodge *On Gold Lake Road, in Lakes Basin Recreation Area, 5 mi. south of Graeagle, (800) 635-8778, (530) 836-2511; www.grayeaglelodge.com. 18 cabins; $$$. No TVs. Unheated swimming hole. Includes full breakfast and dinner; restaurant. Pets welcome ($10/day).*

Operating on the modified American plan, with rates including a four-course dinner and full breakfast, this rustic, remote, and very inviting complex includes a massive log lodge with an open, log-beam ceiling. Comfortably appointed cabins, with knotty pine interiors, are spread along Graeagle Creek & Falls, which provides Graeagle's drinking water and feeds into the town's Old Mill Pond. Some cabins have sleeping lofts or second bedrooms, making them particularly attractive to families. Others permit casting a fishing line right from their deck.

Fine dining is available to non-guests in **Firewoods** *($$$. Child menu. Reservations required.)*, which serves California mountain cuisine with housemade soups and breads. Anyone who catches a fish can arrange for the chef to clean and cook it.

Pullman House Inn *256 Commercial St., Portola, (530) 832-0107; www.psln.com/pullman. 6 rooms; $. 100% non-smoking. Full breakfast.*

Built in 1910 as a boarding house for railroad workers, this B&B sports a railroad theme. A model train runs on tracks attached to the perimeter of the breakfast room ceiling, and stunning locomotive paintings done by local artist Ken Roller hang on the walls. Pullman memorabilia is displayed throughout. A deck permits sitting and watching the arrivals and departures of trains on the nearby tracks.

River Pines Resort *8296 Hwy. 89, Blairsden, (800) 696-2551, (530) 836-0313, fax (530) 836-0815; www.riverpines.com. 65 units; $-$$. Continental breakfast in winter; restaurant.*

This old-fashioned motel is the kind of place where guests gather fallen pinecones and line them up in front of their cabin. Guests can park right in front of their unit, and rooms are paneled in knotty pine and feature soothing views of the surrounding pines. Housekeeping cottages require a three-night minimum stay.

The Coyote Grill *(530) 836-2002, fax (530) 836-0815. D Tu-Sun.)* features Southwestern-style cuisine.

Sardine Lake Resort *Summer (530) 862-1196; winter (916) 645-8882. 9 cabins; $-$$. Pets welcome ($10).*

This spectacularly scenic lake was called Emerald Lake once upon a time, until a mule named Sardine fell in and miners renamed it in her honor. It has a dramatic view of the craggy Sierra Buttes. Though the cabins here are so popular that it is neigh on impossible for new guests to get a reservation (there is a story that one family that was going through a divorce considered the annual reservation here more important than their dog), it *is* possible to come here and fish from the window of the open-air bar, or to rent a boat, or to have an elegant dinner in the cozy **dining room** *(D mid-May to mid-Oct. Reservations required.).*

White Sulphur Springs Ranch Bed & Breakfast *On Hwy. 89, Clio, 3 mi. south of Graeagle, (800) 854-1797, (530) 836-2387; www.graeagle.com/marketplace/whtssbb. 8 units; $-$$; 100% non-smoking. Pool. Full breakfast.*

A former stagecoach stop, this structure has remained in the family since it was built in 1852. It has been restored and is furnished with many antiques original to the house. In addition, the former dairy house and henhouse have been converted into private cottages. The spacious grounds feature an expansive view of the Mohawk Valley and sport an Olympic-size pool filled by warm mineral springs.

WHERE TO EAT

Alpine Moon *165 E. Sierra Ave., Portola, (530) 832-5360. L M-F, D Tu-Sun; $-$$.*

This comfy coffee shop offers roomy wooden booths with a view of the highway and mountains across the street. The specialty here is authentic Italian and American food, and at lunch the menu includes a large variety of sandwiches and pastas.

Grizzly Grill *250 Bonta St., Blairsden (530) 836-1300. D daily; closed M Apr-May; $$.*

Contemporary American cuisine is the specialty in this tasteful, upscale venue. A particularly good baby greens salad with honey-roasted walnuts and crumbled bleu cheese is among the appetizers, and assorted pastas, meats, and fish round out the offerings. An antique bar and comfortable lounge area furnished with lodgepole furniture invites lingering.

The Log Cabin *64 E. Sierra Ave., Portola, (530) 832-5243. D W-M; $$. Booths, child portions.*

German and American cuisine are the specialties, with particularly good schnitzel, sauerbraten, and steaks. The knotty pine interior is cozy, with china plates decorating the walls and comfortable wooden booths for seating.

The Village Baker *340 Bonta St., Blairsden, (530) 836-4064. Tu-Sat 6-3, Sun to noon.*

This spacious old-time bakery is definitely the place to go for delicious European-style pastries and breads, not to mention espresso drinks.

Oakland

A LITTLE BACKGROUND

Though this much-maligned city usually loses in the struggle with San Francisco for media attention, it does have a "there there." (Although Gertrude Stein, who lived here as a child, is often quoted as having said about this city, "There is no there there," in reality it seems that she was referring to what remained of her demolished childhood home.) Interesting facts about this surprising city: The Human Wave, the synchronized movement of sports fans in stadiums, was "invented" in Oakland during the seventh inning stretch of the final playoff game between the Oakland Athletics and New York Yankees on October 15, 1981; it is the most ethnically diverse city in the U.S., with at least 81 different languages and dialects spoken; Mother's Cake & Cookie Company, the largest cookie producer in the U.S., has been located here since 1914.

VISITOR INFORMATION

Oakland Convention and Visitors Bureau *475 14th St. #120, (510) 839-9000, fax (510) 839-5924; www.oaklandcvb.com.*

GETTING THERE

Located approximately 10 miles east of San Francisco. From San Francisco, cross the Bay Bridge, taking Highway 580 south into Oakland.

ANNUAL EVENTS

Woodminster Summer Musicals *June-September. (510) 531-9597. Tickets $15-$26, parking $2.*

It's difficult to imagine a more pleasant way to spend a balmy summer evening than at a live performance here. Witnessing the deepening of the evening and the slow appearance of the stars adds to the overall enjoyment of the production on stage. The amphitheater seats approximately 1,500 people on individually molded seats, all with good views. Pre-theater picnic tables are set up in redwood groves outside the theater. Children under 16 can attend free if they are with an adult paying full price and purchasing tickets within an hour of an 8 p.m. evening performance.

Dragon Boat Races *August. At Jack London Square; (510) 452-4272; www.dragon-boat.org. Free.*

Racing dragon boats is said to be the second most popular sport in the world. According to legend, the races began over 2,300 years ago, in 288 B.C., when fishermen rowed into the Mi Lo river to try to rescue an exiled poet as he drowned himself in protest against a corrupt government. Though the fishermen thrashed their oars in the water to scare away evil spirits, the poet died anyway. Nowadays, dragon boat racing commemorates the poet's heroic spirit.This traditional race attracts over 700 paddlers, many in traditional Chinese costume. The long, narrow, modern fiberglass boats are adorned with colorful dragon figureheads, and each holds a drummer to set the pace.

Black Cowboy Parade *October. On 14th St. near City Hall; (510) 531-7583. Free.*

The only such event in the U.S., this parade commemorates the contributions made by African Americans and other minorities to the building of the American West. A festival follows in Deremery Park.

Lighted Yacht Parade *December. At Jack London Square, (510) 814-6000. Free.*

Festivities include a parade of twinkling vessels plus holiday music and children's activities.

WHAT TO DO

Anthony Chabot Regional Park *9999 Redwood Rd., (510) 635-0138 ext. 2570 or ext. 2571; www.ebparks.org. Daily 7am-10 pm. Free. Lake Chabot: $2-3/vehicle, $1/dog.*

Located adjacent to Lake Chabot, this 5,000–acre park offers fishing, boating, and picnicking as well as 14 miles of biking trails and 46 miles of horseback riding and hiking trails. Facilities include a rifle range, equestrian center, golf course, and 75 campsites. Dogs can be off leashes unless otherwise posted.

Guided trail rides through the park can be arranged at **Chabot Riding Stables** *(14600 Skyline Blvd., (510) 638-0610. Daily 9-5. $25/1 hr., $35/ 1 1/2 hr., $45/2 hrs. Children must be 7 or older.)* Both English- and Western-style lessons are available. Children under 7 can take a pony ride, and a children's day camp operates in summer.

Chabot Space & Science Center *10000 Skyline Blvd., (510) 336-7300, fax (510) 530-3499; www.chabotspace.org. Call for hours and admission fee.*

Begun in 1883 as the Oakland Observatory, this facility was originally located downtown. For decades it served as the official timekeeping station for the entire Bay Area, measuring time with its transit telescope. Public planetarium programs include science demonstrations, a film, and the chance to view the heavens through the largest telescope in the nation regularly available to the public—a 20-incher. This center is in the process of reinventing itself and will re-open with a large-screen IMAX theater and an outdoor environmental education facility.

Dunsmuir Historic Estate *2960 Peralta Oaks Ct., near 106th St. exit off I-580 east, (510) 615-5555, fax (510) 562-8294; www.dunsmuir.org. House and grounds open 1st Sun 12-3, Easter-Sept; also house tours W at 11 & 12. Adults $5, 62+ & 6-13 $4. Grounds open for strolling Tu-F 10-4; free.*

Built in 1899, this 37-room Neoclassical Revival mansion has been renovated and furnished with period antiques. It features a Tiffany-style dome and ten fireplaces. Visitors can picnic and stroll on the 50 acres of grounds. Of special interest are the grotto, the drained but rustically beautiful swimming pool, and the peaceful duck and swan pond. The horror film *Burnt Offerings* and the James Bond thriller *A View to a Kill* were both filmed here.

On Family Sundays, badminton, croquet, and other lawn games are set up for children, and cultural entertainment is scheduled. Each December the grounds are transformed into a wonderland for **Christmas at Dunsmuir**, and the house is decked out in appropriate finery. Other annual special events include a **Spring**

Festival and Mother's Day Tea, and a **Scot's Faire** the first weekend in July with Highland games and more.

Fortune Cookie Factory Tour *261 12th St./ Harrison St., (510) 832-5552. M-F 10-3, Sat & Sun by appt. $1/person.*

This bakery makes unusual fruit-flavored fortune cookies and also permits customers to insert their own original messages. Drop-in tours last about 15 minutes and include a small bag of cookies.

Jack London Square.

Situated on the inlet of the Oakland Estuary, this shopping area borders the city's huge commercial shipping area. Come here to stroll the spacious modern walkways, closed to cars, and to browse in a variety of shops and dine in myriad restaurants. Boat-watching on the estuary is enjoyable, and trains regularly pass slowly on the tracks running at the northern edge of the area. **Jack London Village,** an atmospheric shopping complex, is at the square's eastern end.

- **Heinold's First and Last Chance Saloon** *56 Jack London Square, (510) 839-6761. Daily noon-midnight, Sun to 8. Age 21+only.*

Said to have been built more than a century ago from the remnants of a whaling ship, this informal, funky bar with a tilted floor pays tribute to the area's waterfront past. Jack London, a longtime Oakland resident, was a regular customer during the period when he was an oyster fisherman here. Though somewhat menacing in appearance (it is impossible to see in through the thick windows), this saloon makes a good spot to wet a dry whistle. While here, notice the still-fuctioning gas lamps and a clock that stopped at 5:18 a.m. in the 1906 earthquake.

Jack London's Cabin is across the way. Moved here in 1970, this rustic one-room hovel is believed to have housed London when he prospected in the Yukon Territory during the 1897 Klondike Gold Rush.

- **Port of Oakland Tours** *(510) 272-1188. May-Aug; call for schedule and reservations. Free.*

These 90-minute tours are sponsored by the Port of Oakland.

- **USS Potomac** *Berthed at FDR Pier, at north end of Jack London Square. Visitor Center at 540 Water St./Clay St., (510) 839-7533 or (510) 839-8256, fax (510) 839-4729. Dockside tour: W & F 10-2, Sun 12-4; adults $3, 60+ $2, 6-17 $1. Narrated history cruise: 1st & 3rd Thur, 2nd & 4th Sat of month, mid-April to mid-Nov, weather permitting; adults $30, 60+ $27, 6-17 $15; advance purchase advised.*

This 165-foot-long, all-steel vessel served as President Franklin Delano Roosevelt's "floating White House." Having undergone a 12-year, $5 million restoration, it is now a National Historic Landmark. The 2-hour ride begins ashore with a background video and the chance to study some historical photos, including one of Elvis Presley, who once owned the yacht, presenting it to his friend Danny Thomas for St. Jude's Hospital. More photos testify to its degeneration from its original purpose of chasing rum-runners into being used for drug-running, and its eventual sinking near Treasure Island. Ronald Reagan passed legislation to restore her and, happily, with the help of the Port of Oakland and many dedicated volunteers, she now operates as a public museum. FDR, who was confined to a wheelchair and suffered from sinusitis, preferred the *Potomac* to the White House on sulty summer days. He relaxed on this simple, but comfortable ship as he led the country through the Great Depression and World War II. Aboard, visitors can see his surprisingly small and simply furnished cabin and his private elevator mounted

within a false smokestack (it may be used by visitors in wheelchairs). The radio room, pilot house, and various guest rooms are also open for inspection. The cruise goes out past Treasure Island and then around Alcatraz. Complimentary snacks include coffee, soft drinks, and juices as well as cookies. A favorite spot to settle in is the lower fantail deck lounge in back, with a seat so deep legs must be stretched out straight.

Lake Merritt and Lakeside Park *Parking $2 on Sat & Sun.*

More than just a lake, this beautiful expanse of water is the hub of a variety of activities. In the evening a lovely necklace of lights encircles it.

• **Camron-Stanford House** *1418 Lakeside Dr./14th St., (510) 444-1876. Tours W 11-4, Sun 1-5. Adults $4, under 13 free.*

Restored and furnished in period fashion, this 1876 Italianate-style Victorian is on the western edge of Lake Merritt. A short film on Oakland's history is presented.

• **Children's Fairyland** *Grand Ave./Bellevue Ave., (510) 452-2259; www.fairyland.org. Daily in summer, W-Sun in spring & fall, F-Sun in winter 10-4; puppet shows at 11, 2, & 4. Admission $5; magic key $1.65.*

Designed especially for children age 8 and under, this was the country's first educational storybook theme park when it opened in 1950. Disneyland was patterned after it. Mother Goose rhymes and fairy tales come to life in more than 30 fantasy sets, some of which are inhabited by live animals. Among the attractions are a board maze, a variety of slides (including one down a dragon's back), and rides on a mini-carousel and -Ferris wheel. Kids can also steer a motor boat and watch an award-winning puppet show. A picnic area and a packaged birthday party are also available.

Very special programs are scheduled around holidays. For the annual **Jack-O-Lantern Jamboree**, everyone is encouraged to come in costume. Children must be accompanied by an adult, and tickets must be purchased in advance. After Christmas, **Thank You Santa Day** gives children the rare opportunity to spontaneously express their gratitude to St. Nick in person. The jolly one strolls the grounds, usually on the 26th and 27th.

• **Lakeside Garden Center** *666 Bellevue Ave., at north end of lake, (510) 238-3186. M-F 10-3, Sat & Sun 10-4:30. Free.*

This beautifully landscaped garden features acres of flowers, plants, and cacti. It includes fuchsia and bulb gardens, a Japanese garden, a citrus garden, an herb garden for the blind and disabled, and a new bonsai garden with a 400-year-old Japanese black pine that was brought to the U.S. for the 1915 Panama Pacific International Exposition in San Francisco. Free use of a community garden is available to anyone who wants to grow their own pesticide-free produce.

• **Rotary Nature Center/Lake Merritt Wildlife Refuge** *552 Bellevue Ave./Perkins St., at north end of lake, (510) 238-3739. Center open daily 10-5. Free.*

The nature center has a nature/science library and computers for children to use when researching school reports. The wildlife refuge dates to 1870 and is the first and oldest in the country. Among the birds seen here regularly are egrets, mallards, Canada geese, and herons. Daily feedings are at 3:30 p.m.

• **Sailboat House** *568 Bellevue Ave./near Grand Ave., (510) 444-3807. Daily 9-3:30, later in summer. Boat rentals $4-$10/hr.*

A variety of vessels can be rented here, including rowboats, sailboats, and pedal boats. The replica Mississippi stern-wheeler ***Merritt Queen*** *(Sat & Sun; daily in summer; call for* *hours. Adults $1, under 12 50¢.)* can be boarded for a 30-minute tour of the lake. During December, she totes carolers around the lake on **caroling cruises**; reservations are necessary.

Morcom Amphitheater of Roses *700 Jean St./Grand Ave., (510) 597-5039. Daily dawn-dusk. Free.*

Not far from Lake Merritt, this peaceful garden is designed in traditional Florentine style, with terraces and a classic reflecting pool. Special sections are devoted to pastel roses and antique roses, and a children's garden is planted with miniature roses. A wedding site designed with a color scheme of white, beige, and pink is reputed to bring good luck. Bloom is best June through October, and benches positioned throughout invite picnicking.

Museum of Children's Art (MOCHA) *538 Ninth St./Washington St.,(510) 465-8770, fax (510) 465-0772; www.mocha.org. Tu-Sat 10-5, Sun 12-5. Free; fee for classes.*

This gallery shows East Bay children's art as well as the occasional national and international exhibit. Drop-In Art is scheduled on weekends from 2 to 4 p.m. Kids age 5 and older can stay alone while their parents shop or relax in the area. Special classes for parents and kids together are scheduled on Saturdays.

Oakland Ice Center *519 18th St./San Pablo Ave., (510) 268-9000. Daily noon-5; call for evening hours. Adults $8, 55+ & under 13 $7, skate rental included.*

This Olympic-size rink has lockers and secure parking.

Oakland Museum of California *1000 Oak St./10th St., (888) OAK-MUSE, (510) 238-2200; www.museumca.org. W-Sat 12-5, Sun 10-9; free 2nd Sun of month. Adults $6, 65+ & 5-18 $4.*

This beautifully designed tri-level museum is the only one in the state focusing on the art, natural sciences, and history of California. Built in 1969, it is celebrated both for its architecture and its innovative shows. One permanent exhibit walks visitors across a miniature representation of the state, complete with appropriate plant and animal life. Near the gift shop, visitors can rest in a surprisingly comfortable chair fashioned from one large slice of a giant redwood burl and also view multi-colored koi in a lily pond outside. An airy cafe has huge picture windows overlooking the gardens and serves reasonably priced lunches and snacks.

Each March the museum is benefitted by a **White Elephant Sale** *((510) 273-3401. Free.)*. This truly mammoth rummage sale offers just about anything imaginable, as well as many things unimaginable. In April or May, volunteers collect hundreds of California wildflowers for display at the annual **California Wildflower Show**.

Oakland Zoo *9777 Golf Links Rd., off Hwy. 580, in Knowland Park, (510) 632-9525. Daily, 10-4, weather permitting; rides open at 11. Adults $6.50, 55+ & 2-14 $3.50; parking $3.*

Be sure to see the state-of-the-art Malayan sun bear exhibit (the largest in the U.S.). The Skyride chairlift offers a good view of the outstanding African Veldt enclosure, with its watering hole for giraffes and several species of crane, and provides at its crest a magnificent panoramic view of the bay. Children can feed and pet small animals in the Children's Zoo, and a kiddie ride area includes a carousel and train. Special events are scheduled regularly.

Paramount Theatre *2025 Broadway/21st St., (510) 465-6400. Tours: (510) 893-2300; 1st & 3rd Sat at 10am; $1; children must be age 10 or older.*

Built in 1931, this magnificently renovated, ravishingly beautiful landmark is at its best during an actual performance. Try to come for the Organ Pops series, when silent films are accompanied live by a magnificent old Wurlitzer organ (the second largest west of the Mississippi), or for the Hollywood Movie Classics series, which features the best of the old movies.

Spectator Sports.

- **Baseball.**

Oakland Athletics *Oakland Coliseum, Hegenberger Rd. exit off I-880, (510) 638-GOAS; www.oaklandathletics.com.*

- **Basketball.**

Golden State Warriors *Oakland Coliseum, Hegenberger Rd. exit off I-880, (888) GSW-HOOP; www.warriors.com. Nov-Apr.*

• **Football.**

Oakland Raiders *Oakland Coliseum, Hegenberger Rd. exit off I-880, (510) 864-5000.*

Yoshi's *510 Embarcadero West/Washington St., (510) 238-9200. www.yoshis.com.*

Though this contemporary space holds a California-Japanese restaurant complete with a tatami room and separate sushi bar, the music in the jazz club far eclipses the food. In the club, which attracts the circuit elite, the audience can order light snacks and sushi.

WHERE TO STAY

Dockside Boat & Bed *419 Water St./Franklin St., at Jack London Square, (800) 436-2574, (510) 444-5858, fax (510) 444-0420; www.boatandbed.com. 7 yachts; $$-$$$+. Some accommodate children. Continental breakfast.*

Find out what it's like to sleep on a luxury yacht here without ever setting sail. These vessels, ranging in length from 32 to 68 feet, are anchored in the estuary and rented out when not being used by their owners. A personal favorite is *The Arnie*, which at 35 feet is small, but it sports a nice teakwood trim and permits snuggling in a bed with a skylight view of the stars. Galleys can be interesting to prepare a meal in, or arrangements can be made for dinner to be delivered on board. The breakfast basket can be enjoyed on deck, basking in the sun's warmth and perhaps reading the paper or tossing leftovers to an assortment of fat ducks and quick gulls. Watching neighbors busy doing chores on their yachts underscores a decided advantage of renting over owning. Arrangements can be made for a captain to take the yacht out for a cruise.

Oakland Marriott City Center *1001 Broadway, (800) 228-9290, (510) 451-4000, fax (415) 835-3466. 21 stories, 479 rooms; $$-$$$. Children 18 & under free. Lap pool, hot tub, fitness center. Restaurant. Parking $12-$20.*

Casting a dramatic profile on the downtown skyline, this centrally located, angular building is Oakland's only high-rise, full-service luxury hotel. Its roof-top restaurant has a spectacular panoramic view.

Waterfront Plaza Hotel *10 Washington St., at Jack London Square, (800) 729-3638, (510) 836-3800, fax (510) 832-5695; www.waterfrontplaza.com. 5 stories; 144 rooms; $$$-$$$+. Heated pool, sauna, fitness center. Restaurant, room service. Valet parking $12.*

Situated right next door to the ferry to San Francisco, this contemporary hotel offers an atmosphere of casual luxury and features a glass-enclosed swimming pool deck overlooking the estuary. More than half of its rooms have water views.

The hotel restaurant, **Jack's Bistro**, offers moderately priced meals, patio dining, and more splendid water views.

WHERE TO EAT

Bay Wolf *3853 Piedmont Ave., (510) 655-6004, fax (510) 652-0429; www.baywolf.com. L M-F, D daily; $$. Reservations advised.*

One of the region's very best restaurants, this veteran bistro has been around for more than 25 years now. It serves a Mediterranean-inspired menu and operates out of a simple but cozy remodeled Victorian house sporting paintings by internationally recognized local artists. The menu changes every 3 weeks, highlighting the food of a different region, and making use of the season's bounty. Selections might include a subtly-spiced, puréed cauliflower soup or a vibrantly colored citrus-beet salad as starters. The sublime, silky duck liver flan that is the kitchen's signature is always available. Entrees have included a satisfying swordfish steak served with French lentils, and a magnificent ravioli stuffed with butternut squash purée and topped deliciously with sautéed onions, bacon, and fresh sage leaves. Desserts here are worth saving space for, but when there is little room left, try a nice plate of sweets that might include a liquour-soaked, chocolate-covered cherry and a tiny gingerbread angel. Brunch is served only once each year, on Mother's Day.

Cactus Taqueria *5525 College Ave., (510) 547-1305.*

For description, see page 257.

Caffe 817 *817 Washington St./9th St., (510) 271-7965. B&L M-Sat; $.*

This slick, modern paninoteca, or Italian sandwich bar, prepares a perfectly poached blue Aracauna hen egg for breakfast and superb coffees using Illy beans imported from Trieste and a state-of-the-art espresso machine. Lunch items include assorted housemade soups, polentas, salads, and panini. Add to these choices sun-brewed iced tea, Tuscan wines, fresh juices, and Italian Moretti beer from the Tyrolian area of Udine, and life is good. A picnic box can be prepared with a call by 4 p.m. the day before needed.

The Cantina *4239 Park Blvd./Wellington St.; (510) 482-3663, fax (510) 482-3073.*

For description, see page 194.

Emil Villa's *1982 Pleasant Valley Rd./Broadway, in Rockridge Shopping Center, (510) 654-0915. B,L,&D daily; $. Highchairs, boosters, booths; child menu. No reservations. No cards.*

The fare here is barbecued meats—pork and ham ("from pigs that made hogs of themselves"), beef, turkey, chicken, and especially ribs—served in hot or cold sandwiches or as dinner plates. A hamburger and grilled cheese sandwich are also on the menu. Dessert is a hunk of freshly-baked pie chosen from an always tempting array. And service is fast.

Everett & Jones Barbeque *126 Broadway/2nd St., near Jack London Square, (510) 663-2350, fax (510) 663-8856. L&D daily; $.*

This branch of a popular take-out store is also a full-service restaurant. Lunch portions of chicken, ribs, homemade beef links, and the house specialty beef brisket come with potato salad, wheat bread, and the award-winning house sauce in a choice of mild, medium, or hot. Dinner portions are bigger and include a choice of fresh homemade greens, yams, potato salad, and baked beans plus either corn bread or wheat bread. Desserts include sweet potato, pecan, and peach pies, and lemon, chocolate, and sock-it-to-me cakes.

Fentons Creamery *4226 Piedmont Ave./Entrada Ave., (510) 658-7000. M-Sat 11am-11pm, Sun from noon; $. Highchairs, boosters, children's menu. No reservations.*

Enormous portions of housemade 14 percent butterfat ice cream is the name of the game at this well-established ice cream parlor, in business here since 1922. Favorite flavors are toasted almond and Swiss milk chocolate. Many of the sundaes are of a size appropriate for sharing among several people. If all those people eating out of one bowl is unappealing, ask for extra bowls. Drinks include milkshakes served in old-fashioned metal containers as well as sodas, floats, and sherbet freezes. Fizzes are made with juice, sherbet, carbonated water, and an egg blended into a froth. The menu also offers soups and salads, a hamburger, and an assortment of sandwiches, including the excellent house specialty—fresh crab salad on grilled sourdough.

Il Pescatore *57 Jack London Square, (510) 465-2188, fax 510-465-0238. L&D daily; $$. Reservations advised.*

This atmospheric, bustling, remotely ark-shaped restaurant serves a variety of garlic-laden Italian seafood dishes. Though waiters don spiffy white shirts with black vests and ties, customers dress casually. Garlicky baked Dungeness crab, positioned attractively on large clam shells, is a great appetizer. Entrees include a delicious, delicate fresh filet of sole covered in a light egg batter and sautéed with white wine, lemon juice, and capers. The extensive, mouth-watering menu also offers plenty of other seafood choices, plus meats, pastas, and vegetarian items, all accompanied by steamed fresh chard and pasta tubes in a light tomato sauce. A slab of liquor-soaked housemade tiramisu provides a just right, not-too-sweet ending.

Italian Colors *2220 Mountain Blvd./Park Blvd., in Montclair area, (510) 482-8094. L M-F, D daily; $$. Highchairs, boosters, child portions. Reservations advised.*

Italian-style California cuisine is served in this attractively decorated neighborhood restaurant featuring warm peach-colored walls and a high-ceilinged, open dining room. Outdoor patio dining, with a view of the hills, is available in warm weather. Menu items include pastas, pizzas, a signature smoked-chicken, and housemade desserts. Though the menu changes seasonally, particularly nice items have included a delicious bruchetta starter topped with a variety of mushrooms, delicate green scarves lasagna made with thin layers of pasta atop a cheese-cream sauce, and a perfect sea bass. Sicily is the focus of the menu specials every Monday night. Diners young and old alike are given crayons with which to express themselves on the white butcher-paper-covered tables (after all, this *is* California).

A second location is at Jack London Square *(101 Broadway, (510) 267-0412, fax (510) 267-0416).*

Jade Villa *800 Broadway/8th St., (510) 839-1688. Dim sum daily 9:30-3, D daily; $. Boosters. Reservations advised for dim sum M-F, not taken for Sat & Sun.*

There are many excellent dim sum restaurants in San Francisco's Chinatown, however difficult parking and long waits for seating can be a deterrant. This spot in Oakland's smaller Chinatown combines enjoying a meal of these tasty appetizers with easier parking and a shorter wait. Especially good among the 70 to 120 kinds of dim sum served are deep-fried sweet taro balls, nicely spiced pork-filled bows, delicate steamed shrimp dumplings, and exquisite deep-fried shrimp toasts topped with a pea. The Cantonese-style dinner menu features fresh fish dishes and several family-style dinners.

Just Desserts *4001-B Piedmont Ave./40th St., (510) 601-7780.*

For description, see page 70.

King Yen *4080 Piedmont Ave./41st St., (415) 652-9678.*

For description, see page 260.

Kinkaid's Bayhouse *1 Franklin St., at Jack London Square, (510) 835-8600, fax (510) 835-2032. L M-Sat, D daily, SunBr; $-$$. Highchairs, boosters, child menu.*

The ideal spot for lunch here is at a waterside table in the room fitted with a magnificent 15-foot-tall teak bar. Kayakers, canoers, and motorboaters provide constant entertainment. Delicious wedges of housemade sesame pan bread come with meals.

Max's Diner *500 12th St./Broadway, (510) 451-MAXS.*

For description, see page 73.

Nan Yang *6048 College Ave./Claremont Ave., (510) 655-3298. L&D Tu-Sun; $. Highchairs, boosters.*

The Bay Area's first Burmese restaurant (opened in 1983), this restive spot includes the refined touch of cloth napkins. The particularly good selection of vegetarian items includes a crunchy Burmese ginger salad composed of 16 ingredients—among them shredded ginger and cabbage, toasted yellow split peas, fava beans, and peanuts—all mixed together at table by the server. Also exceptional on the enticing menu are a green papaya salad with Burmese dressing, a savory curried smoked eggplant, an appetizer of batter-fried tropical squash served with a tomato-garlic sauce, and flavorful curried garlic noodles served with succulent chicken and crisp lettuce.

Oakland Grill *301 Franklin St./3rd St., near Jack London Square, (510) 835-1176, fax (510) 835-1804. B,L,&D daily; $.*

Situated in the town's produce district, this down-to-earth spot is a cheery haven for a satisfying meal and a good cup of coffee. The excellent breakfasts are served all day. Three-egg omelettes and two-egg "scramlets" can be combined with any of an extensive list of fillings, and are prepared with egg whites upon request. They come with a side of baking powder bisuits and home-fried potatoes. Hot cakes, French toast, crêpes, and eggs Benedict are also among the choices. Lunch brings on a hamburger and veggie burger, a French dip, and other sandwiches and salads. Dinner concentrates on steaks and a few chicken and fish dishes. Being selected by *Travel & Leisure* magazine as one of the country's top 100 restaurants in 1995 obviously refers to the food, not the ambiance.

The Old Spaghetti Factory *62 Jack London Square, (510) 893-0222. L M-F, D daily; $.*

For description, see page 179.

Oliveto *5655 College Ave./Shafter Ave., (510) 547-5356. L M-F, D daily; $$$. Reservations advised.*

Preparing delicious, simple dishes made with the freshest seasonal ingredients is the creed of the kitchen here. Perhaps that shouldn't be a surprise, since the well-known chef, Paul Bertolli, honed his skills at Chez Panisse. Meals are a la carte. Sample dishes include a salad of blood orange, avocado, and butter lettuce, and an entree of flavorful pan-roasted halibut. A seasonal soup, freshly made pastas, and an assortment of side dishes are always available at dinner. Do leave room for dessert, as they are exceptional: a warm rhubarb and candied-orange pastry, Meyer lemon eclairs with lemon-caramel sauce and pistachios, a simple tangelo sherbet. Should the classy upstairs restaurant be completely booked, as it often is, opt for a less expansive, and less expensive, meal in the cozy downstairs cafe.

Picnic Pick-Ups.

• **G. B. Ratto & Co. International Grocers** *821 Washington St./9th St., (510) 832-6503. M-Sat 8-5.*

Don't expect to just dash in and out of this Old World-style wonderland of international foods. Family-operated since 1897, this turn-of-the-century brick building is literally stuffed to the rafters with goodies. There are bins of grains and pastas, bulk spices, hanging sausages, garlic braids, and fresh breads. There is sauerkraut from Germany, pepper from India, and morel mushrooms from France. A long deli counter provides countless sandwich possibilities, and a picnic box can be pre-packed by reservation.

• **Rockridge Market Hall** *5655 College Ave., (510) 655-7748; www.rockridgemarkethall.com. Open daily.*

Specialty shops include **Grace Baking** for fabulous breads and fancy pastries and the **Pasta Shop** for deli foods and a vast variety of fresh pastas, as well as a produce shop, wine shop, and flower shop.

Scott's Seafood Grill & Bar *73 Jack London Square, (510) 444-3456. L&D daily; $$$. Boosters, booths. Reservations advised. Valet parking.*

With window tables overlooking the estuary and live background music emanating from the bar, this upscale spot is a great place for a celebration. The extenseive menu of fresh seafood also offers some pastas and steaks.

Szechwan Restaurant *366 8th St./Franklin St., (510) 832-7878, (510) 832-9888. L M-F, D daily, Sat&SunBr; $. Highchairs, boosters. Reservations accepted.*

All the usual suspects can be found on this extensive menu: crispy fried won tons, noisy sizzling rice soup, spicy hot-and-sour soup, Chinese burrito-like mu shu dishes, and dramatic sizzling iron platters. Personal favorites include crispy dry-braised green beans in a garlicky sauce with minced pork, and the house special chow fun—a wonderful, colorful, fragrant hodgepodge of meats and vegetables mixed with addictive wide, flat rice noodles. The weekend Chinese brunch is different than the more common dim sum breakfast, with items such as Chinese-style donuts, onion pancakes, and almond jelly on the menu.

T.G.I. Friday's *450 Water St., at Jack London Square, (510) 451-3834. L&D daily.*

For description, see page 161.

TJ's Gingerbread House *741 5th St./Brush St., (510) 444-7373, fax (510) 444-2204. B,L,&D & afternoon tea Tu-Sat; $$-$$$. Child portions. D reservations required.*

The first step to enjoying a Cajun-Creole dinner at this unique restaurant is requesting that a menu be faxed or mailed. Then diners call to reserve a date and place their entree order—an unusual procedure that leaves one anticipating the experience. Arrival at the colorful little empire that is TJ's meets expectations. The three dining rooms include two delightful rooms in the original Victorian house, each boasting an extensive doll collection, plus a newer gazebo annex. Appetizers include shrimp rémoulade and escargots. Among the 20-plus main courses is the house specialty—a tasty, mildly spicy "spoon" jambalaya heavy with ham, Louisiana hot sausage, and prawns. Other entrees include Bayou catfish Étouffée, whiskey-stuffed lobster, and sautéed quail. Complete dinners include "sassy" corn bread, marinated steamed vegetables, and Cajun "come back" dirty rice, and a dessert bowl of vanilla ice cream with a tiny frosted gingerbread man and a large ginger cake cookie studded with walnuts, raisins, and chocolate chips. A teeny, tiny shop tucked under the front porch purveys everything gingerbread: dolls, bubble bath, fresh cookies.

Fremont

A LITTLE BACKGROUD

In its heyday, from 1912 to 1916, the Niles district of town was once the largest film studio in Northern California. Charlie Chaplin made some of his earliest films here—*The Champion* and *The Tramp*. More recently, Fremont has been declared the best city in America to raise a child.

ANNUAL EVENTS

Broncho Billy Film Festival *June. (510) 742-9868. Tickets $2.50-$12.*

Screenings of movies filmed in the area are combined with film seminars and tours of historic Niles.

WHAT TO DO

Ardenwood Historic Farm *34600 Ardenwood Blvd., off Hwy. 84, (510) 796-0663. Thur-Sun 10-4, also open Tu & W with no special activities; closed Nov-Mar. Adults $6, 62+ $4, 4-17 $3.50; on Tu & W adults $1, 4-17 50¢. House tours: Thur-Sun 11:30-4; get tickets at train station; no additional fee; under 6 not admitted except on Thur & F family tours.*

Situated in a fragrant eucalyptus grove, this 205-acre farm was named after a forested area described in Shakespeare's *As You Like It*. It is one of the few historic farm parks in the West to allow visitors to step back in time for a view of 1880s farm life. The old farm buildings, crop fields, and antique farm equipment have all been restored, and the admission fee includes rides on a novel horse-drawn narrow-gauge railroad as well as on several haywagons and surreys. Hourly tours are scheduled of the restored **Patterson House**—a white gingerbread Victorian farmhouse furnished with period antiques. Throughout the property, staff in period costumes demonstrate typical Victorian farm chores, which vary with the season but might include shoeing a horse, shearing a sheep, constructing a barrel, thrashing wheat, milking a goat, washing clothes, or making cheese. Visitors are encouraged to pitch in. A blacksmith demonstrates his craft daily. Children especially enjoy rolling around on the grassy expanses. Sometimes they can see baby farm animals, and sometimes rugs are hung out on the line for them to beat clean.

Coyote Hills Regional Park *8000 Patterson Ranch Rd., (510) 795-9385. Daily 8-8 Apr-Oct, 8-6 rest of year. $3/vehicle, $1/dog.*

The Visitors Center features an Ohlone Indian display, and an Indian archaeological site is sometimes accessible. The park has 15 miles of trails, plus a boardwalk trail through a freshwater cattail marsh. Picnic tables are available, and dogs can be off leashes unless otherwise posted.

Dreyer's Grand Ice Cream Factory Tour *1250 Whipple Rd./Hwy. 880, Union City, (510) 471-6622. Tours M-F at 9:15, 11:15, & 2. Reservations required. $2/person.*

Learn how ice cream is made on this cool 90-minute tour. It begins with a brief video, shown to participants seated at ice cream parlour tables in the Double Scoop Depot tasting room. Then a tour above the production floor takes in the assembly line, where it is possible to produce 75,000 gallons of ice cream every 24 hours. Participants can sample ice cream fresh from the production line. But save room, because later, back at the Depot, everyone gets to choose two scoops of ice cream from a choice of about a dozen. Favorite flavors are vanilla (#1) and chocolate chip cookie dough (#2). Book the weekday tour at least 3 months in advance; call Monday through Friday between 8 and 9 a.m. or after 3:30 p.m. For safety reasons, children must be at least age 5.

Iceoplex *44388 Old Warm Springs Blvd., (510) 490-6621; www.iceoplex.com. Call for schedule. Admission $6, skate rental $2.50; Sunday family pass $22 for 2 adults and 2 children, skates additional.*

The innovative programs at this state-of-the-art ice arena include a skating school and ice hockey. It provides the perfect spot to beat the summer heat.

Mission San Jose De Guadalupe *43300 Mission Blvd./Washington Blvd., (510) 657-1797. Daily 10-4:30. By donation.*

Marking the center of the oldest community in the East Bay, this mission was founded in 1797 and is 14th in the chain of California missions. It was the only mission built in the East Bay. Though little remains of the original structure, part of the original adobe monestary wing now holds exhibits. Of particular note are the quiet graveyard and the beautifully decorated interior of the 1809 New England Gothic-style St. Joseph's Church.

Niles Canyon Railway Museum *Main St./Kilkare Rd., Sunol, (925) 862-9063; www.ncry.org. 1st & 3rd Sun, 10-4. Suggested donation: adults $7, 3-12 $3.*

Operating on abandoned Southern Pacific Lines rail, refurbished oil-burning and steam engines and World War II-era diesel locomotives follow the original route of the 1869 transcontinental railroad. They hiss and chug through a woodsy gorge while pulling a variety of vintage cars between Sunol and Niles. The 12 1/2-mile round trip takes 1 hour and 45 minutes. Just a caboose or the entire train can be chartered for a special occasion.

WHERE TO EAT

Cloverdale Creamery *37085 Fremont Blvd., (510) 797-1303. M-Thur 10-9, F & Sat to 11.*

This cozy ice cream parlor dates from 1938. A bit of a time capsule, it has vintage milk trucks in the back, kept there by the owners "just because." The waitresses have worked here forever, serving ice cream goodies and lunch plates. It's so retro, it's cool.

Fellini-O *3900 New Park Mall Rd., Newark, (510) 792-6600, fax (510) 713-0501. L M-F, D daily; $$. Highchairs, boosters. Reservations suggested.*

The Italian arias play at just the right decibel, the attentive servers have Italian accents, and the food is European Italian. It is, in fact, reminiscent of dining beside Lake Como, except the view is of a shopping mall. Oh well, back to that food. The kitchen is accommodating about splitting orders, so try sharing a fabulous housemade pasta and perhaps a meat or fish dish.

Pearl's Cafe *4096 Bay St., (510) 490-2190. L Tu-F, D Tu-Sat; $$. Reservations advised.*

When you finally find this enticing spot in sprawling Fremont, which is one of the ten largest cities in square miles in the country, the sense of euphoria is much the same as that experienced when finding a rare pearl in an oyster. No wonder Clint Eastwood hangs here after hours, though he is probably also influenced by the fact that his wife is a friend of the owner. A sample menu might offer up delicious deep-fried artichoke and sweet potato fritters with a garlicky aioli dip as a starter, and pork loin with a tasty balsamic vinegar-strawberry sauce or a pan-roasted salmon with lemon-scented mashed potatoes as main courses. Desserts are killers, and the best way to die is eating the Snickers ice cream pie.

Tyme for Tea *37501 Niles Blvd., (510) 790-0944. F 12-3, Sat & Sun 11-5; $. Reservations advised.*

Henry James once said, "There are few hours in life more agreeable than the hour dedicated to the ceremony known as afternoon tea." True. Sydney Smith said, "Thank God for tea! What would the world do without tea?—how did it exist? I am glad I was not born before tea." True again. Operating in an alcove within an antique shop and making good use of doilies, mismatched vintage silverware, and charming bone china tea cups, this tea room offers respite from the day's tribulations. The full Victoria Tea includes loose leaf tea (herbals and decafs available) or coffee (this *is* the U.S., *not* England), a scone with crème fraîche plus lemon curd and preserves, and assorted tea sandwiches and pastries. Smaller spreads are also available. Should there be wait, browsing the shop's well-priced collection is time well spent.

World Wrapps *3954 Mowry Ave., (510) 795-9727.*

For description, see page 82.

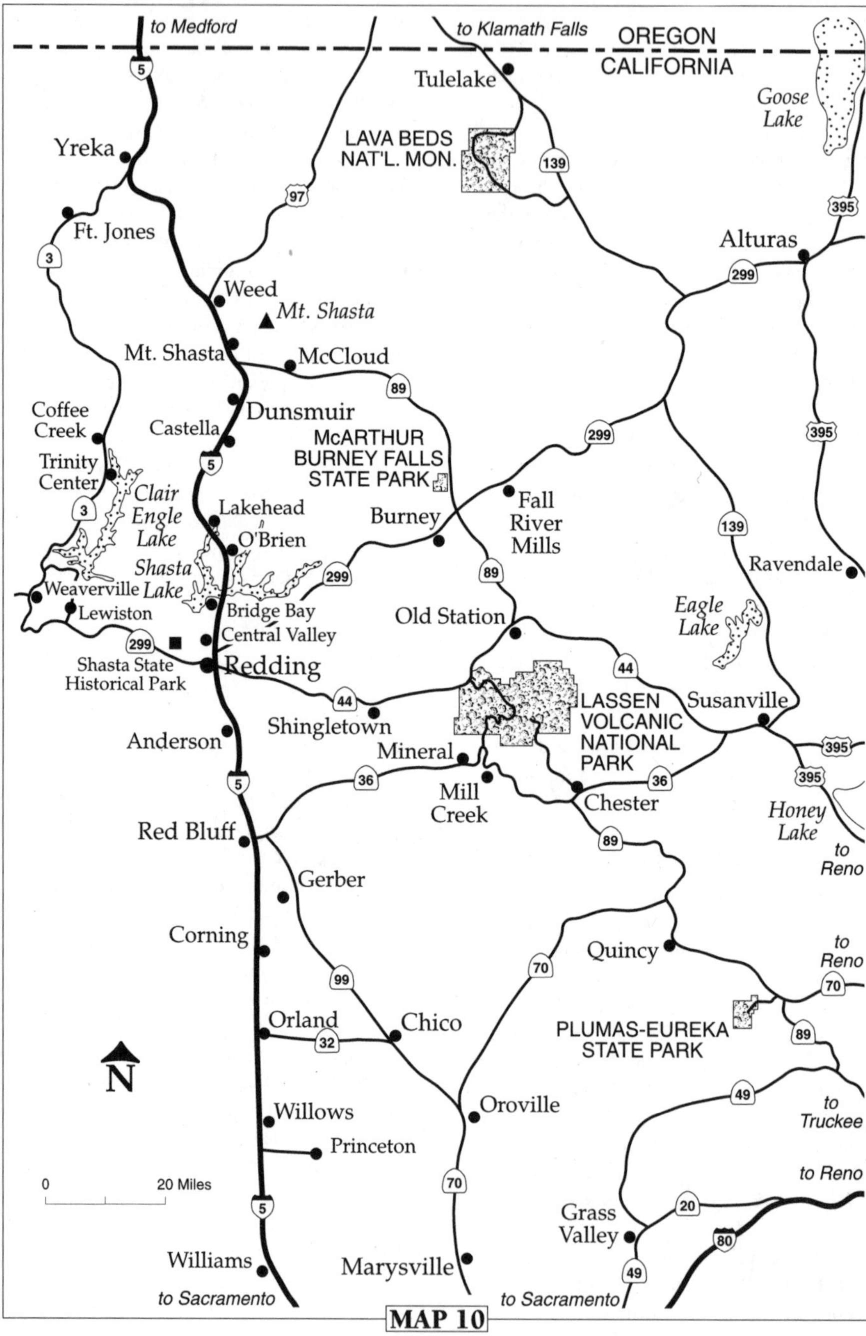
to Medford
to Klamath Falls
OREGON
CALIFORNIA
Tulelake
Goose Lake
LAVA BEDS NAT'L. MON.
Yreka
Ft. Jones
Alturas
Weed
Mt. Shasta
Mt. Shasta
McCloud
Coffee Creek
Castella
Dunsmuir
McARTHUR BURNEY FALLS STATE PARK
Trinity Center
Clair Engle Lake
Lakehead
Burney
Fall River Mills
O'Brien
Shasta Lake
Ravendale
Weaverville
Lewiston
Bridge Bay
Central Valley
Old Station
Eagle Lake
Shasta State Historical Park
Redding
LASSEN VOLCANIC NATIONAL PARK
Susanville
Shingletown
Anderson
Mineral
Mill Creek
Chester
Honey Lake
Red Bluff
to Reno
Gerber
Corning
Quincy
to Reno
Orland
Chico
PLUMAS-EUREKA STATE PARK
N
Willows
Oroville
to Truckee
Princeton
0
20 Miles
to Reno
Grass Valley
Williams
Marysville
to Sacramento
to Sacramento
MAP 10

Princeton

WHAT TO DO

Princeton Ferry *50¢/car.*

This cable-pulled ferry, the last ferry on the Sacramento River, has been operating since 1854. Taking about 4 minutes to cross the river, it is said to be "too slow for the farmers and too fast for the tourists." To get here, approximately 5 miles south of Willows take the Norman Road exit east for 10 miles to the ferry. On the way, the route passes through the **Sacramento National Wildlife Refuge** *((916) 934-2801)*; the Visitors Center is open daily during migration from 7:30 a.m. to 4 p.m. Alternatively, do a loop by exiting onto Highway 20 about 15 miles south of Willows and just north of Williams, following Highway 20 for 7 miles to the **Colusa National Wildlife Refuge** (which has a 3 1/2-mile gravel loop drive), and then into Colusa, turning north on River Road and following it through the area's rice country to the ferry. Then take Norman Road west back to Highway 5.

Corning

GETTING THERE

This small town is 170 somewhat flat, dreary miles from San Francisco, punctuated only by the occasional sighting of an unusual migrating bird.

WHAT TO DO

Olive Pit *2156 Solano St., (530) 824-4667; mail order (800) OLIVE-PIT.*

Everything olive is here. Taste a vast variety of flavored olives (the best being the greens stuffed with pimento and almond), pick up some car snacks, or chow down on fast food.

Red Bluff

VISITOR INFORMATION

Red Bluff Chamber of Commerce *100 Main St., (530) 527-6220.*

ANNUAL EVENTS

South Shasta Model Railroad *April & May; on Sundays. In Gerber, 12 mi. south of town, (530) 385-1389. Adults $4, 5-12 $3.*

This miniature 1/4-inch O-gauge reproduction of the 100-mile Southern Pacific Railroad line from Gerber to Dunsmuir operates in the basement of a private farmhouse. It includes 16 handmade steam locomotives, 100 cars, and over 900 feet of track. Visitors can also ride on a 2-foot-gauge steam train and visit a museum of antique farm equipment.

WHAT TO DO

Kelly-Griggs House Museum *311 Washington St., (530) 527-1129. Thur-Sun 2-4. By donation.*

This restored 1880s Victorian is just off the freeway. While here, pick up a self-guiding map of local Victorian homes.

William B. Ide Adobe State Historic Park *21659 Adobe Rd., (530) 529-8599. Daily 8-5. $3/car.*

Located on the outskirts of town by the Sacramento River, this authentically furnished one-room adobe house was the home of early California settler William B. Ide—the Republic of California's first and only president. Other buildings in the 3-acre park are an adobe smokehouse, a carriage shed for old buggies, and a small corral. This is a great spot for a picnic.

Lassen Volcanic National Park and Area

A LITTLE BACKGROUND

Now a dormant volcano, imposing 10,457-foot Lassen Peak last erupted in 1915. It is thought to be the largest plug dome volcano in the world. The best time to visit is July through September, when the 35-mile road through the park is least likely to be closed by snow. Visitors can take several self-guided nature walks, and guided hikes and campfire talks are scheduled in the summer. Wooden catwalks supplement the trail through popular Bumpass Hell, an area featuring geological oddities such as boiling springs and mud pots, pyrite pools, and noisy fumaroles. The trail covers 3 miles and takes about 3 hours round trip. The park also offers over 150 miles of back country trails, including a 17-mile section of the Pacific Crest Trail. A free park newsletter/map orients visitors and lists daily activities. Eight campgrounds are available on a first-come, first-served basis. For skiing information, see page 400. Park admission is $10 per vehicle.

VISITOR INFORMATION

Park Headquarters *38350 Hwy. 36, Mineral, (530) 595-4444, fax (530) 595-3262.*

Lassen County Chamber of Commerce *84 N. Lassen St., Susanville, (530) 257-4323, fax (530) 251-2561.*

GETTING THERE

Take Highway 36 east from Red Bluff, or Highway 44 east from Redding.

WHAT TO DO

Fort Crook Museum *43030 Fort Crook Museum Rd., on Hwy. 299, Fall River Mills, (530) 336-5110. Tu-Sun 12-4, May-Oct only. Free.*

Composed of a 3-story main building and five outer buildings, this large museum complex displays six rooms of antique furniture, a collection of early farm implements and Native American artifacts, the old Fall River jail, a one-room school house from Pittville, and a pioneer log cabin.

McArthur-Burney Falls Memorial State Park *24898 Hwy. 89, Burney, (530) 335-2777. Daily 8-4; Apr-Sept to 10. $5/vehicle.*

A lovely 1-mile nature trail winds past the soothing rush of the 129-foot waterfall here, allowing for closer inspection of the volcanic terrain for which this area is known. Paddle

boats can be rented at man-made Lake Britton, where facilities include picnic tables, a sandy beach, and a wading area for children. Swimming is allowed only in designated areas, as the lake has a steep drop-off. Campsites are available.

A boat is needed to reach isolated **Ahjumawi Lava Springs State Park**, which features one of the largest systems of freshwater springs in the world. Descendants of the Native American Ahjumawi tribe reside in the area. Call for maps and information.

Twelve miles away, the town of Burney offers modern motels and supermarkets.

Spattercone Crest Trail *1/2 mi. west of Old Station, across from Hat Creek Campground. Free.*

This 2-mile, self-interpretive trail winds past a number of volcanic spattercones, lava tubes, domes, and blowholes. It takes about 2 hours to walk and is most comfortably hiked in early morning or late afternoon.

Subway Cave *1 mi. north of Old Station, near junction of Hwys. 44 & 89, (530) 335-2111. Free.*

Lava tubes were formed here about 2,000 years ago, when the surface of a lava flow cooled and hardened while the liquid lava beneath the hard crust flowed away. This cave, which is actually a lava tube, winds for about 1/4 mile. Always a cool 46 degrees, it makes a good place to visit on a hot afternoon. However, it is completely unlighted inside, so visitors are advised to bring along a powerful lantern. Allow time for a picnic in the lovely surrounding woods.

WHERE TO STAY

Little lodging is found here, but many forest campsites are available on a first-come, first-served basis. Visitors should bear in mind that this area is remote and does not offer big-city facilities such as supermarkets.

Drakesbad Guest Ranch *At end of Warner Valley Rd., 18 mi. from Chester, (530) 529-1512, fax (530) 529-4511. 19 units; $$$+. Closed Oct-May. Special children's rates; under 2 free. No TVs. Natural hot springs pool. Includes 3 meals; restaurant. Dogs welcome.*

Located at the end of the road in a secluded, scenic mountain valley within the national park, this rustic resort was a hot springs spa in the mid-1800s. It has been a guest ranch since the turn of the century and is now the only guest ranch located within a national park. Most of the rustic cabins, bungalows, and lodge rooms have no electricity, so kerosene lanterns are used for light. The ranch is close to some of Lassen's thermal sights: 1 mile from the steaming fumaroles at Boiling

Springs Lake; 2 miles from the bubbling sulfurous mud pots at Devil's Kitchen. Guests can rent horses from the ranch stables and take guided rides into these areas. All this and a good trout-fishing stream, too! Day visitors should call ahead for horse or dining reservations. Overnight guests should book 1 year in advance.

Hat Creek Resort *On Hwy. 89 just north of Hwy. 44, Old Station, 11 mi. from north entrance to Lassen Park, (530) 335-7121. 17 units; $; 2-night min. in cabins. Some kitchens.*

These bargain motel units and old-time housekeeping cabins, with linoleum floors and homemade curtains, are located beside rushing Hat Creek. Guests can fish in the creek, roast marshmallows over an open fire, and check out the stars at night.

WHERE TO STAY FARTHER AWAY

Spanish Springs Ranch *Ravendale, east of Lassen on Hwy. 395, 40 mi. north of Susanville, (800) 272-8282, RAVENDALE-30, fax (530) 234-2041. $125/day, 13-17 $100, 3-12 $60, under 3 free. All meals included.*

Located in the remote northeast corner of the state, this 70,000-acre working cattle ranch offers a variety of vacation options as well as plenty of horseback riding. Guests can opt for the main lodge—where the luxurious amenities congregate—or for the less luxurious, and less expensive, bunkhouse. In spring and fall, 5-day horse drives are scheduled, and weekly rates and special packages are also available.

Wild Horse and Burro Sanctuary *On Wilson Hill Rd., Shingletown, 5 mi. south of Hwy. 44, 21 mi. from Lassen, (530) 474-5770, fax (530) 474-5728. 5 cabins; 1 night/$235/person, 2 nights/$335/person; Apr-July & Sept-Oct only. Unsuitable for children under 14. No TVs; shared bath house. All meals included.*

This protected preserve for wild mustangs and burros is the only wild horse sanctuary in the nation. Guests ride out of a base camp to observe the 300-plus population in their natural habitat. Meals are served by an open campfire, and overnight accommodations are in new, but rustic, cabins overlooking Vernal Lake. Prices include everything.

WHERE TO EAT

Uncle Runt's Place *On Hwy. 44, Old Station, (530) 335-7177. L&D Tu-Sun, Apr-Jan; Thur-Sun rest of year; $. Highchairs, boosters, child portions. Reservations advised. No cards.*

Located right on Hat Creek, this cozy restaurant caters to locals and has a short-order menu of sandwiches, hamburgers, and dinner specials.

Lava Beds National Monument

A LITTLE BACKGROUND

It doesn't hurt to be warned ahead of time that this 46,000-acre national monument is located in the middle of nowhere. Perhaps you've heard the expression "out in the tules." This could be where it originated.

The monument has a campground, but the nearest motels and restaurants are far away in Tulelake. It's a good idea to pack-in picnic supplies as there is nowhere to buy food within many miles of the monument. The area also buzzes with insects, is a haven for rattlesnakes, and sometimes has plague warnings posted. Still, it is an unusual place that is well worth a visit.

The Visitors Center at the southern entrance offers a good orientation. Historically this area is known as the site of the 1872 Modoc War—the only major Indian war to be fought in California. Geologically the area is of interest because of its concentration of caves.

Park admission is $4 per vehicle.

VISITOR INFORMATION

Monument Headquarters *(530) 667-2282.*

GETTING THERE

Go north from Lassen Park to Highway 299. Continue north on Highway 139 through sparsely populated forest and farmland. The monument is approximately 115 miles northeast of Mt. Shasta city on Highway 5.

WHAT TO DO

Caves.

Located in the parking lot of the **Visitors Center** *(9-6 in summer, 8-5 rest of year.)*, Mushpot Cave has interpretive displays and is the only lighted cave here. A 2-mile loop road provides access to most of the other 19 caves that are open without passes, including some with descriptive names such as Blue Grotto, Sunshine, and Natural Bridge. The 71-step staircase at Skull Cave drops 80-feet to an ice floor, and Catacombs must be crawled through. To explore other caves (there are over 400), it is required that visitors register at the Visitors Center . . . just in case. Lanterns are available to borrow.

Tule Lake and **Lower Klamath Basin National Wildlife Refuges** *4 mi. south of Oregon state line, (530) 667-2231, fax (530) 667-3299; www.klamathnwr.org. Visitor Center: Located west of Tulelake; M-F 8-4:30, Sat & Sun 10-4; free.*

The gravel road north out of the monument passes through the Tule Lake portion of this scenic area, which is the largest wetlands west of the Mississippi. These refuges are home to a variety of interesting birds that can easily be viewed from a car. In winter they have the densest concentration of bald eagles in the U.S. south of Alaska.

Redding

VISITOR INFORMATION

Redding Convention & Visitors Bureau
777 Auditorium Dr., (800) 874-7562, (530) 225-4100, fax (530) 225-4354.

WHAT TO DO

Shasta State Historic Park *On Hwy. 299, 10 mi. west of I-5, in Old Shasta, (530) 243-8194. Free. Courthouse Museum: W-Sun 10-5; adults $2, 6-12 $1; includes same-day admission to Weaverville Joss House State Historic Park* *(see page 298).*

Prosperous and bustling during the Gold Rush, this gold-mining ghost town is now an interesting museum of restored buildings and picturesque ruins located on either side of the highway. In the 1861 **Courthouse Museum**, a lovely eclectic collection of early California art is displayed Louvre-like, all crowded together tightly on the walls. A collection of Modoc Indian baskets can also be viewed. The courtroom is completely restored and features a basement jail with heavy-duty ironwork and a gallows just outside. A large picnic area with tables and grassy expanses is adjacent, and across the highway the old bakery, though no longer operating, serves up some inexpensive baked goods and drinks.

Turtle Bay *800 Auditorium Dr. (call for directions), (530) 243-8850, fax (530) 243-8898; www.turtlebay.org. Tu-Sun 10-5. Adults $5, 4-17 $3; free on 1st Tu; includes admission to* ***Redding Museum of Art & History*** *((530) 243-8801) and* ***Carter House Natural Science Museum*** *((530) 243-5457), both in nearby Caldwell Park.*

Resembling a 19th-century logging mill, the Paul Bunyan Forest Camp center has exhibits about the region's logging days plus an extensive collection of California snakes. A creative outside play area has a walk-through tree stump maze, an osprey nest climbing structure, and a giant log slide. A new Visitor Center provides an orientation to this spread-out facility.

Trinity Alps

A LITTLE BACKGROUND

Densely forested and home to 55 alpine lakes, this is prime camping country. There really isn't much to do here except relax and perhaps fish, boat, or hike.

VISITOR INFORMATION

Trinity County Chamber of Commerce
317 Main St., Weaverville, (800) 421-7259, (530) 623-6101.

WHAT TO DO

Jake Jackson Memorial Museum and **Trinity County Historical Park** *508 Main St., Weaverville, (530) 623-5211. Daily 10-5, May-Oct; 12-4 Apr & Nov; closed Dec-Mar. By donation.*

Trinity County's history is traced here through mining equipment, old bottles, and photographs. A reconstructed blacksmith shop and miner's cabin are also displayed. Outside, a creekside picnic area beckons. A full-size steam-powered stamp mill, located on the block just below the museum, is operated on holidays.

Weaverville Joss House State Historic Park
412 Main St., Weaverville, (530) 623-5284. Tours on hour 10-4; call for days open. Adults $2, 6-13 $1. Includes same-day admission to Courthouse Museum at Shasta State Historic Park (see page 297).

Located in a shaded area beside a creek, this Chinese Taoist temple provides cool respite on a hot summer day. It was built in 1874 on the site of a previous temple that burned to the ground. Still used for worship, it is the oldest continuously used Chinese temple in the state.

WHERE TO STAY

Cedar Stock Resort and Marina *45810 Hwy. 3, Trinity Center, 15 mi. north of Weaverville, (800) 982-2279, (530) 286-2225. 12 cabins; $; 1-week min. in summer. Closed Nov-Feb. No TVs; all kitchens. Restaurant. Dogs welcome.*

This quiet spot offers lodging in a cabin in the woods or on a houseboat on Trinity Lake. Guests provide their own bedding and linens. The marina also rents boats and slips, and the bar and restaurant offer a terrific view of the lake.

Coffee Creek Ranch *Off Hwy. 3, Coffee Creek, 40 mi. north of Weaverville, (800) 624-4480, (530)266-3343, fax (530) 266-3597. 15 cabins; 100% non-smoking; $$$+; 2-night min. in spring & fall, 3-night min. June-Aug. Special rates for children. No TVs; wood-burning fireplaces & stoves. Heated pool (unavail. Nov-Mar), children's wading pool, hot tub, fitness center. All meals included; restaurant.*

The private one- and two-bedroom cabins here are surrounded by trees. Activities include horse-drawn hayrides, movies, steak-frys, outdoor games, square and line dancing, archery, gun practice on a rifle range, panning for gold, and supervised activities for children 3 to 17. Horseback riding is included in the price in spring and fall; in summer, there is an additional charge. Cross-country skiing, sleigh rides, and dog-sled rides are available in winter.

Trinity Alps Resort *1750 Trinity Alps Rd., Trinity Center, 12 mi. north of Weaverville, (530) 286-2205, same fax. 43 cabins; $$-$$$+; 1-week min. June-Aug, 3-night min. May & Sept. Closed Oct-Apr. No TVs; all kitchens. 1 tennis court. Restaurant. Pets welcome.*

Arranged especially to please families, this 90-acre resort is composed of rustic 1920s brown-shingle cabins with sleeping verandas—all scattered along rushing Stuart Fork River. Guests provide their own linens or pay additional to rent them. Simple pleasures include crossing the river on a suspension bridge, hanging out at the general store, and enjoying dinner at the riverside **Bear's Breath Bar & Grill**. Scheduled activities include square dancing, bingo, and evening movies. Horseback riding is available at additional cost, and kids can ride their bikes endlessly.

Shasta Lake Area

VISITOR INFORMATION

Shasta-Cascade Wonderland Association
1699 Hwy. 273, Anderson., 7 mi. south of Redding, (800) 474-2782, (530) 365-7500, fax (530) 365-1258; www.shastacascade.org.

GETTING THERE

Located approximately 235 miles north of San Francisco.

WHAT TO DO

Lake Shasta Caverns *In O}Brien, (800) 795-CAVE, (530) 238-2341, fax (530) 238-2386; www.shastacascade.org/shastacaverns. Tours daily; call for schedule. Adults $15, 4-12 $7.*

Discovered in 1878, these caverns weren't opened for tours until 1964. The 2-hour tour begins with a 15-minute catamaran cruise across the McCloud arm of Lake Shasta. Then visitors board a bus for a scenic, winding ride up the steep mountainside to the caverns. In this case, getting there really is half the fun. Nature trails, picnic facilities, and a snack bar are also available.

Shasta Dam *16349 Shasta Dam Blvd., Shasta Lake City, 5 mi. off Hwy. 5, (530) 275-4463. Daily 9-4; in summer, tours on the hour; call for winter schedule. Free.*

Built in 1945, this is the second largest dam in the U.S. and the highest center-overflow dam in the world (it's three times higher than Niagara Falls!). The guided tour includes a bus ride to the base of the dam, a film showing how dams are built, and a walk through a power plant and exhibit room.

WHERE TO STAY

Houseboats. See page 414.

Motel Row.

Inexpensive motels are located at Bridge Bay and in the Lakehead area.

Dunsmuir

A LITTLE BACKGROUND

Surrounded by a million acres of forest and wilderness areas, this wildly scenic town is known as "the home of the best water on Earth." And, indeed, pure spring water from glaciers on Mt. Shasta is delivered to the city via lava tubes and then piped to every tap in town. One of the hamlet's ten always-flowing public drinking fountains is in a sheltered spot by the side of the two-lane road through town. It is reminiscent of restorative fountains seen in small spa towns in Germany's Black Forest.

The town's history is the railroad. At the turn of the century, it was a division point on the railroad and a popular resort area. By the 1920s things were really booming. Celebrities stopped here by the train-load, including Clark Gable and Babe Ruth, and the town's California Theatre was a movie palace. Then, in the 1950s steam locomotives were phased out, drastically hurting the area's economy. And in 1961, the I-5 bypassed Dunsmuir—a mixed blessing that allowed the town to retain its charm.

VISITOR INFORMATION

Dunsmuir Chamber of Commerce
(800) DUNSMUIR, (530) 235-2177; www.snowcrest.net/dunsmuir.

WHAT TO DO

Castle Crags State Park *Castle Creek Rd., Castella, 10 mi. south of town; (530) 235-2684, fax (530) 235-2684. Daily sunrise-sunset. $5/vehicle.*

Mile-high, snaggle-tooth granite peaks dominate this 6,000-acre park. Hiking trails, picnic areas, and swimming holes are available. For a smashing picnic spot with a view of the crags and Mt. Shasta, drive up the narrow one-lane road leading to Vista Point. The 1-mile Indian Creek Nature Trail loop has gentle slopes and provides an easy leg-stretch. Campsites are available.

Enchanted Forest Porcelain Doll Factory
4100 Pine St., (916) 235-0441; www.snowcrest.net/enchantedforest. Tu-Sat 10-4.

Between them, Marian and Loren Anderson make about 1,600 expensive dolls each year for collectors. Marian sews all the outfits and will duplicate a wedding dress.

Hedge Creek Falls *On Dunsmuir Ave. at north end of town.*

The short, easy path leading to the falls follows the Sacramento River. Once there, it is possible to walk behind the base of the falls, and picnicking is lovely (a table and gazebo are provided at the trail head). It is said that the notorious Gold Rush-era bandit Black Bart once used the area as a hideout.

Upper Sacramento River Center
5819 Sacramento Ave., (530) 235-2012, fax (530) 235-2439; www.riverexchange.org. Tu-M 9-5. Free.

A 1991 Southern Pacific tanker car derailment here spilled 18,000 gallons of pesticide into the Sacramento River, killing everything in its path for 40 miles. It was the worst inland water spill in the state's history. After a lot of effort, the river is back to normal, and this center was built as part of a resulting settlement. Part hands-on museum and part river information center for those who want to fish, raft, hike, or mountain bike in the area, it has a variety of river-related exhibits. Among them are a 6- by 16-foot map of the Upper Sacramento River watershed, a stuffed black bear, and great activities for kids.

WHERE TO STAY

Castle Rock Inn *5827 Sacramento Ave., (530) 235-0100, fax (530) 235-0600. 7 rooms; $. Continental breakfast; restaurant.*

Situated in the town's historic district, this rustic vintage hotel has been comfortably restored. Rooms in front allow tenants to "look down on the Dunsmuir turntable, see Amtrak pull in, and be lulled to sleep by the lumbering locomotives." The downstairs cafe serves baked goods and coffees, and the adjacent pub schedules live music on weekends..

A few doors down, the **Brown Trout Gallery** *(5841 Sacramento Ave., (530) 235-0754; www.browntroutgallery.com. W-Sun.)* purveys some interesting crafts and art, but of special note is the stream running underneath that can be viewed and heard through a hole in the floor.

Castle Stone Cottage Inn *On Castle Loop Rd., Castella, 6 mi. south of town, (530) 235-0012; $; 2-night min. All kitchens & wood-burning stoves.*

Arriving here brings to mind Goldilocks' arrival at the Three Bears' cabin: It feels as if someone lives here and will be back shortly. Built in the 1920s for local railroad workers, these enchanting rural stone cottages have been lovingly renovated into cozy retreats furnished with fascinating bric-a-brac and equipped with fluffy beds and shelves of books. Front porch chairs face a charming garden, and the Upper Sacramento River across the way, where trout fishing is reputed to be quite fine, provides soothing background sounds. Occasionally a train sounding a haunting whistle rattles through the fields behind the cabin's tranquil backyard, where an old ski-lift chair has been ingeniously converted into a tree swing for two. What a joy to discover that this charmed spot right out of a fairy tale isn't make-believe but *real!*

Cave Springs Resort *4727 Dunsmuir Ave., (530) 235-2721. 25 units; ¢-$. All VCRs. Pool, hot tub, 1 tennis court. Restaurant.*

Situated on the outskirts of town, just above the river, this old-time mountain resort seems like something out of a time warp. It offers simple motel rooms, cabins, and RV accommodations, and facilities include a playground and bocce ball court on the spacious, cedar-sheltered grounds.

Railroad Park Resort *100 Railroad Park Rd., 1 mi. south of town, (800) 974-RAIL, (530) 235-4440, fax (530) 235-4470. 27 units; $. Some kitchens. Unheated pool, hot tub. Restaurant (closed Jan & Feb). Small pets welcome.*

Guests here can sleep in an authentic antique caboose or in a deluxe, handicapped-equipped box car unit. Each is furnished with antiques and a clawfoot tub, and family units have bunk beds. Three cabins and some creekside campsites are also available. The nearby Cascade Mountains and their granite Castle Crags Spires can be viewed while frolicking in the pool, and prime rib and seafood dinners are served inside an authentic McCloud River Railroad car that is converted into a restaurant.

WHERE TO EAT

Cafe Maddalena *5801 Sacramento Ave., (530) 235-2725, fax (530) 235-0639. D Thur-Sun; $$. Closed Jan-Mar. Highchairs, boosters.*

Located across the street from the old train station, this well-loved restaurant has a cozy interior lined with knotty-pine walls. The talented chef-owner hails from Sardinia and takes pride in whipping up authentic, well-executed Italian dishes that would be extraordinary anywhere, but seem especially so here, so far from a major city. Menu choices include housemade ravioli stuffed with ricotta and artichokes and topped with fresh tomato, and a superb pizza topped with a mixture of spinach, oyster mushrooms, garlic, eggplant, and mozzarella. (Sometimes the chef even makes *fresh* mozzarella.) Among the desserts are tiramisu and an unusual egg-less bitter lemon flan that is heaven for those watching their cholesterol.

McCloud

A LITTLE BACKGROUND

Set in the shadow of Mt. Shasta, this scenic mill town was owned by the McCloud Lumber Company from 1897 to 1965. It looks now much as it did then. The streets here are wide, with boardwalks fronting the commercial buildings, and there is little traffic and lots of trees.

GETTING THERE

From I-5, follow Highway 89 for 10 miles into town.

WHAT TO DO

Shasta Sunset Dinner Train *(800) 733-2141, (530) 964-2142, fax (530) 964-2250; www.mctrain.com. Feb-Aug. $75. Excursion train: May-Aug; adults $10, under 12 $5.*

Refurbished 1915 coach cars are used on the 3-hour dinner excursion, which includes a gourmet meal served on elegant white linen set with china and silver. On the scenic hour-long excursion to Signal Butte, passengers are seated in open-air cars.

WHERE TO STAY AND EAT

McCloud Guest House *606 W. Colombero Dr., (530) 964-3160. 5 rooms; 100% non-smoking; $-$$. Continental breakfast.*

Sitting on a hill above town amid 6 acres of gardens, this 1907 California Craftsman-style house has a large veranda and is furnished with antiques, including an ornate pool table in the lounge.

McCloud Hotel *408 Main St., (800) 964-2823, (530) 964-2822, fax (530) 964-2844; www.mchotel.com. 18 rooms; 100% non-smoking; $-$$$. Afternoon tea, full breakfast.*

A registered national landmark, this hotel was built in 1916 on the same foundation as a prior hotel that burned down that same year. It once had 93 rooms and provided housing for mill workers and teachers, and its basement was the town library until the 1960s. Now meticulously restored, its old-fashioned lobby invites lingering over a board game or book. The spacious rooms are individually decorated and furnished with rescued and restored pieces original to the hotel and area. Four suites are equipped with a canopy bed, whirlpool tub for two, and private balcony. Breakfast can be delivered to the room.

Across the yard, **The Dining Room** *(424 Main St., (530) 964-2225. D W-Sun; $$. Highchairs, boosters, child portions.)* operates in the historic Dance Country building, which has housed restaurants since 1915. It serves classics such as prime rib, New York steak, and fettucini Alfredo along with more unusual items such as chicken strudel. Outside, an enormous porch and yard provide seating for **The North Yard: Barbecue & Brew**, a more casual, inexpensive extension of the restaurant that is also open for lunch and specializes in barbecue. Especially inviting for families, it has baskets of peanuts on the table for munching on and feeding to the resident jays, and a large grassy expanse invites children to romp while parents finish their meals.

Mt. Shasta City

A LITTLE BACKGROUND

Mount Shasta, a14,161-foot-tall volcanic mountain that last erupted in 1786, holds five glaciers. It can be climbed in summer and skied in winter. Poet Joaquin Miller, who considered it the most beautiful mountain in the West, described it as "lonely as God and white as a winter moon." New Agers rank it up there with Stonehenge and the Egyptian pyramids, apparently because of its unusual energy fields. Peculiar stories, involving UFOs and Bigfoot, abound in this area.

VISITOR INFORMATION

Mt. Shasta Chamber of Commerce/Visitors Bureau *300 Pine St., (800) 926-4865, (530) 926-3696, fax (530) 926-0976.*

Siskiyou County Visitors Bureau *P.O. Box 1138, Mt. Shasta 96067, (530) 926-3850, fax (530) 926-3680.*

WHERE TO STAY

KOA Kampground *900 N. Mt. Shasta Blvd., (800) KOA-3617, (530) 926-4029.*

This picturesque campground has majestic Mt. Shasta as a backdrop. Recreational facilities include a swimming pool, volleyball courts, horseshoe pits, and a game room. For description, see page 415.

WHERE TO EAT

Fast-Food Row *At Central Mt. Shasta exit.*

Even with the various logo signs fighting it out amidst the trees, the view here is weepingly beautiful. On a clear day the mysterious mountain dominates the scene, and on a cloudy day it plays peek-a-boo, tantalizing the imagination. Alas, it seems the locals take this awesome sight for granted, so in the **Burger King** they often leave empty the corner tables boasting a million-dollar view.

Yreka

VISITOR INFORMATION

Yreka Chamber of Commerce *117 W. Miner St., (800) ON-YREKA, (530) 842-1649; www.yrekachamber.com.*

GETTING THERE

Located approximately 50 miles north of Mount Shasta, and 22 miles south of the Oregon border. This small town is also positioned halfway between San Francisco and Portland, Oregon.

WHAT TO DO

Siskiyou County Museum *910 S. Main St., (530) 842-3836; www.siskiyoucounty.com/museum. Tu-F 9-5, Sat 9-4. Adults $1, 6-12 75¢.*

Local artifacts and history are emphasized. Of special interest is the occasional exhibit on a local pioneer family, one of which was the Terwilligers. A 2 1/4-acre **Outdoor Museum** is located adjacent. Among its original and replica historic buildings are a schoolhouse, a Catholic church, a blacksmith shop, a miner's cabin, and an operating general store.

The Yreka Historic District *Along Miner St.*

More than 75 19th-century homes can be seen here, with most situated on the four blocks of Third Street located between Lennox and Miner. The Chamber of Commerce provides a descriptive tour brochure.

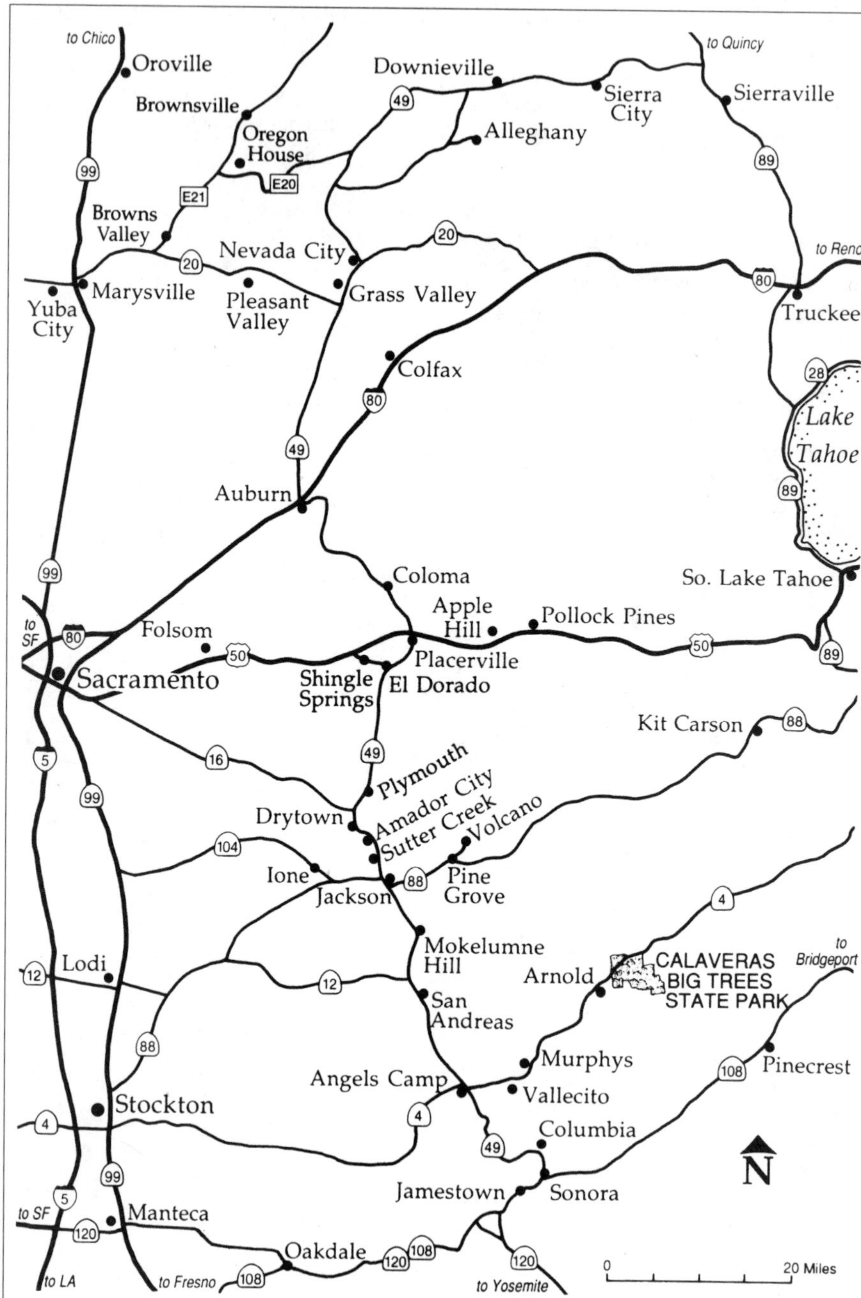
to Chico
Oroville
Brownsville
Oregon House
E20
E21
99
Browns Valley
Downieville
49
Alleghany
Sierra City
to Quincy
Sierraville
89
Nevada City
20
to Reno
80
Truckee
Marysville
Yuba City
Pleasant Valley
Grass Valley
Colfax
28
Lake Tahoe
49
Auburn
Coloma
So. Lake Tahoe
to SF
Folsom
Apple Hill
Pollock Pines
50
Sacramento
Placerville
Shingle Springs
El Dorado
5
16
Kit Carson
88
Plymouth
Amador City
Sutter Creek
Volcano
Drytown
104
Ione
Jackson
Pine Grove
4
Mokelumne Hill
12
Lodi
Arnold
CALAVERAS BIG TREES STATE PARK
to Bridgeport
San Andreas
Murphys
Angels Camp
Vallecito
Pinecrest
108
Stockton
Columbia
N
Jamestown
Sonora
Manteca
120
Oakdale
to LA
to Fresno
to Yosemite
0
20 Miles
MAP 11

A LITTLE BACKGROUND

The Mother Lode, as this area is sometimes referred to (a term that is derived from a Spanish word for "riches"), stretches along the entire route of Highway 49, south from Mariposa and north through Nevada City, ending in Downieville. (On the other hand the Mother Lode *veins*, which run from Northern California to South America, surface in the area between Jamestown and Auburn and again in Nevada City.)

All the main Gold Rush towns can be visited by driving along Highway 49. But many scenic side roads, leading to tiny hamlets with intriguing names such as Fiddletown and Rescue, invite exploration.

This area provides history, adventure, and scenic beauty. Not yet heavily promoted and packaged, it also provides many low-key and inexpensive vacation joys for the hype-weary traveler. A thorough visit could take weeks, but a satisfying visit takes only a few days. For a weekend visit, don't attempt to drive the entire route. Visit one portion and then go back another time to see the rest.

Because the area is steeped in history, consider doing some reading for more background information. Two classic books about the area that are also good for reading out loud are *The Celebrated Jumping Frog of Calaveras County* by Samuel L. Clemens (Mark Twain) and *The Luck of Roaring Camp* by Bret Harte.

Currently there is said to be another gold rush on. Many nervous people are staking claims, so caution is advised when doing any unguided panning or prospecting.

GETTING THERE

Located approximately 135 miles east of San Francisco. Take Highway 80 to Highway 580 to Highway 205 to Highway 120 to Highway 49.

Jamestown

A LITTLE BACKGROUND

Filled with architecturally interesting old buildings, this historical boom town's economy is now fueled by myriad antique shops.

WHAT TO DO

Gold Prospecting Expeditions *18170 Main St., (800) 596-0009, (209) 984-GOLD, fax (209) 984-0711; www.goldprospecting.com. Trips daily 10-5. 1-hr. trip $15/person, special family rates.*

Operating out of the town's old livery stable, this business organizes prospecting trips appropriate for children as well as adults. All equipment is supplied. Participants get down and dirty in a stream, where they are taught the basics. It is claimed gold has been found on every trip lasting 2 hours or more, and the rule is "finders, keepers." Trips by river raft or helicopter can also be arranged. Children can pan for free in a trough located in front of the shop.

Railtown 1897 State Historic Park *Fifth St./ Reservoir St., (916) 445-6645, store (209) 984-3953, fax (209) 984-4936; www.csrmf.org/rail town. Train: Sat & Sun, leaves on hr. 11-3; Apr-Oct only; adults $6, 6-12 $3. Roundhouse tours: Daily 9:30-4:30; adults $2, 6-12 $1.*

Be sure to allow time to watch the hubbub that surrounds preparing the train for departure, when the depot is full of excitement as the huge steam trains roll in and out, sounding their screaming whistles and belching a mix of fire, smoke, and steam. The Mother Lode Cannonball, an historic steam train, takes passengers on a 40-minute, 6-mile round trip to Woods Creek Siding. Several other special trips are sometimes available. A tour is given of the old six-stall roundhouse turntable and machine shop, where the trains are still serviced. If it all looks familiar, that could be because many TV shows and movies have been filmed here, including *Bonanza, Little House on the Prairie, The Virginian, High Noon,* and *Pale Rider.*

WHERE TO STAY

Jamestown Hotel *18153 Main St., (800) 205-4901, (209) 984-3902, fax (209) 984-4149; www.jamestownhotel.com. 11 rooms; 100% non-smoking; $-$$. Unsuitable for children under 7. No TVs. Continental breakfast; restaurant.*

Built in the 1850s, this hotel is furnished with Victorian antiques and has many spacious suites with sitting rooms. Guests are greeted in their room with a split of champagne and warm, fuzzy bathrobes. A communal TV room holds a big screen TV and VCR.

The **Cafe on the Patio** *(L M-Sat, D Tu-Sun, SunBr; $-$$. Highchairs, boosters, child portions.)* has indoor and outdoor seating and serves an eclectic lunch menu of soups, salads, wrapps, sandwiches, and pastas. Dinner brings on heartier entrees, including prime rib, scampi, rack of lamb, and several chicken dishes. A welcoming adjacent saloon specializes in fancy drinks, California wines, and tasty appetizers.

The National Hotel *77 Main St., (800) 894-3446, (209) 984-3446, fax (209) 984-5620; www.national-hotel.com. 9 rooms; 100% non-smoking; $-$$. Unsuitable for children under 10. TVs upon request. Full breakfast; restaurant, room service. Pets welcome.*

A sense of history awaits at this really *old* hotel. Built in 1859, it has been in continuous operation ever since. In fact, it is one of the ten oldest continuously operating hotels in the state and is now an official historical landmark. Until 1978 rooms were rented to men only and went for $4 a night. Indoor plumbing was added in 1981. Much of the antique furniture is original to the hotel, and that which isn't is right in tune with the era. A clawfoot tub for two ensconced in its own private room—sort of an 1800s hot tub—is available to all guests. Overall, everything is far more luxurious now than anything those gold miners ever experienced.

The hotel's **restaurant** *(L&D daily, SunBr. Highchairs, boosters, child menu. Reservations advised.)* is an especially inviting spot for dinner after the drive in. On warm evenings diners are seated outside on a pleasant patio. Strong points of the menu include fresh fish with creative sauces, a wine list with the largest selection of Gold Country wines available *anywhere,* and exceptional desserts. Located just off the parlor, an old-time saloon, featuring its original redwood long bar with brass rail and also an 1881 cash register, is the perfect spot for a nightcap.

WHERE TO EAT

Smoke Cafe *18191 Main St., (209) 984-3733. D Tu-Sun, L Sat & Sun in summer only; $-$$. Highchairs, boosters, child portions. No reservations.*

Located within a modern Santa Fe-style building with soft stucco edges and lots of tile, this popular upscale spot specializes in Mexican cuisine. Among the many items on the menu are pollo de mole poblano, chili verde, and a hamburger.

Sonora

A LITTLE BACKGROUND

Once known as the "Queen of the Southern Mines," when it was the richest and wildest town in the southern Mother Lode, this town still bustles and is a popular stopover spot for skiers and other travelers on their way to vacation cabins and recreation. Because it is a crossroads, it has been built up more than most Gold Rush towns and is far from quiet. But off the main thoroughfares, a taste of the old Sonora of Victorian homes and quiet streets can still be found. It is interesting to note that in Spanish "tuolumne" means "stone houses."

VISITOR INFORMATION

Tuolumne County Visitors Bureau *542 W. Stockton Rd., (800) 446-1333, (209) 533-4420, fax (209) 533-0956; www.thegreatunfenced.com.*

WHAT TO DO

Autumn Colors Drive.

Take Highway 108 about 30 to 35 miles east of town for a dazzling display of fall leaf colors. Populated with aspen, this entire area is usually vibrant with color after the first frost, which generally happens in early October. Beginning in late October, colorful leaves can be seen right in town.

Mark Twain's Cabin *Off Hwy. 49, midway between town & Angels Camp.*

Built on Jackass Hill, this replica of Twain's cabin is constructed around the original chimney. It can be viewed from the outside only. Twain lived here in 1864 and '65, when he wrote *The Celebrated Jumping Frog of Calaveras County* and *Roughing It.*

Tuolumne County Museum and History Center *158 W. Bradford Ave., (209) 532-1317. Sun-F 10-4, Sat 10-3:30. Free.*

Located inside a jail built in 1866, this museum displays Gold Rush-era relics that include pioneer firearms and gold samples. Picnic tables are available.

WHERE TO STAY

Gunn House Motel *286 S. Washington St., (209) 532-3421. 20 rooms; $-$$. Solar-heated pool. Continental breakfast on weekends; restaurant. Pets welcome.*

Built in 1850, this adobe house was once the residence of Dr. Lewis C. Gunn, and later the offices for the *Sonora Herald*—the area's first newspaper. Rooms are restored and furnished with antiques. The cozy office is staffed with helpful personnel, and a pool-side cocktail lounge is available to guests.

WHERE TO EAT

Good Heavens *49 N. Washington St., (209) 532-FOOD. L daily, D Thur-Sat; $$. 1 highchair.*

Operating within a restored historic brick building, this cozy, fussy little spot serves delicious freshly-made items. The lunch menu features made-from-scratch soups, inventive sandwiches and salads, and housemade desserts. The exceptional homemade jams can be purchased to go.

Columbia State Historic Park

A LITTLE BACKGROUND

In her prime, with over 6,000 people calling her home, Columbia was one of the largest mining towns in the southern Mother Lode. Her nickname, "Gem of the Southern Mines," was reference to the $87 million-plus in gold mined here (a figure calculated when gold was $35 an ounce).

Since 1945 this reconstructed Gold Rush town has been a state historic park. It is open daily from 9 to 5, and admission is free. Streets are blocked off to all but foot traffic and an occasional stagecoach. A museum introduces visitors to the town's history, and more exhibits are scattered among the many restored historic buildings.

In fact, the whole town is basically a living museum. Private concessionaires operate modern versions of businesses that would have been found here in the 1800s. Cold mugs of beer and old-fashioned root beer-like sarsaparilla are poured in the town saloon. A blacksmith ekes out a living practicing his craft in a ramshackle shed, and a candy kitchen uses 100-year-old recipes and antique equipment to turn out such old-time favorites as horehound, rocky road, and almond bark. Customers in the photography studio don Gold Rush-era clothing for portraits, which are taken with vintage camera equipment but developed with quick modern processes. Visitors can even tour a still-operating gold mine and learn to pan for gold in a salted sluice.

If it all looks familiar, note that *High Noon* and episodes of *Little House on the Prairie* were filmed here.

VISITOR INFORMATION

Columbia State Historic Park *22708 Broadway, (209) 532-0150.*

ANNUAL EVENTS

Victorian Easter Parade and Egg Hunt *March or April; on Easter Sunday.*

Fireman's Muster *May.*

A Miners Christmas *December; first 2 weekends.*

WHAT TO DO

Columbia Stage Line and Stable *(209) 532-0663. Daily 10:30-4:30, mid-May to Aug; Sat & Sun rest of year. Stage: Adults $4.50-$5.50, 65+ & under 13 $4-$5, under 5 free when held on adult's lap. Stable: pony rides $5, horse or pony trail rides $8-$50.*

Ride in an authentic stagecoach and experience what many gold-seekers did years ago. Or take a trail ride into the back woods through limestone canyons. Gentle ponies are available for small children.

Fallon House Theatre *(209) 532-3120, fax (209) 532-7270; www.sierrarep.com. W-Sat at 8pm, Sat & Sun at 2pm. Tickets $12-$17. Reservations advised.*

Located in the rear of the Fallon Hotel, this historic theater has been in operation since the 1880s. The second-longest continually operating playhouse in California, it stages first-run and classic dramas and musicals and employs both professional and student talent. The semi-professional repertory company does eight major productions each year.

WHERE TO STAY

City Hotel *On Main St., (800) 532-1479, (209) 532-1479, fax (209) 532-7027; www.cityhotel.com. 10 rooms; 100% non-smoking; $-$$. Children under 4 free. No TVs; all shared baths. Full breakfast; restaurant, limited room service.*

This 1856 hotel provides overnight lodging in keeping with the town's flavor. The restored rooms are furnished with Victorian antiques from the collection of the California State Parks Department. Eager-to-please students from the Columbia College Hospitality Management program dress in period clothing and supplement the full-time staff by perform-

ing such esoteric duties as fluffing pillows and, in the beautifully appointed restaurant downstairs, de-crumbing tables. Guests are encouraged to congregate in the parlor in the evening for sherry, conversation, and games. To make the trek down the hall to the bath more civilized, guests are loaned a wicker basket packed with shower cap, slippers, robe, soap, and shampoo.

The hotel **restaurant** *(D Tu-Sat, SunBr; $$. Highchairs, boosters, child portions. Reservations advised.)* prepares elegant regional cuisine, and fixed-price, seasonal four-course dinners are available. The cozy **What Cheer Saloon**, which retains its original cherry-wood bar that was shipped around the horn from New England, adjoins.

Columbia Gem Motel *22131 Parrotts Ferry Rd., 1 mi. from park, (209) 532-4508; www.columbiagem.com. 11 units; $-$$. Pets welcome.*

Typical motel-room decor greets guests inside tiny cabins scattered in an attractive pine tree setting.

Fallon Hotel *On Washington St., (800) 532-1479, (209) 532-1470, fax (209) 532-7027. 14 rooms; 100% non-smoking; $-$$. Closed M-W Oct-May. Children under 4 free. No TVs; many shared bathrooms. Continental breakfast.*

This historic hotel, dating from 1857, has undergone a $4 million renovation and is now beautifully restored to its Victorian grandeur. Many of the furnishings are original to the hotel. Several large second-floor rooms with balconies are perfect for families. The hotel is operated in similar style as the City Hotel and is under the same management. The **Fallon Ice Cream Parlor** dishes up goodies on the main floor, and packages that include lodging, dinner, and a theater performance are available.

Murphys

A LITTLE BACKGROUND

A map to the town's sights and buildings—many of which were constructed of lava stone and stucco after a tragic fire in 1859—is available from merchants and at the check-in desk in Murphys Hotel. It is believed that Joaquin Murieta began his outlaw ways here. Nicknamed "Queen of the Sierra," the town once was the source of goldstrike after goldstrike and made the founding Murphy brothers rich.

ANNUAL EVENTS

Bear Valley Music Festival *July. In Bear Valley; (209) 753-2574.*

Held high in the Sierra in a circus-style red-and-white-striped tent, this festival presents a musical smorgasbord.

WHAT TO DO

Black Bart Players *580 S. Algiers, (209) 728-8842. Weekends in Apr, Aug-Sept, & Nov only; 8pm. Tickets $7.50. Reservations advised.*

This little theater group performs musicals, melodramas, mysteries, comedies, and classics.

Calaveras Big Trees State Park *1170 E. Hwy. 4, Arnold, 15 mi. east of town, (209) 795-2334. Daily dawn-dusk. $5/vehicle.*

This ancient forest houses the mammoth, and now rare, giant sequoia variety of redwood. The Big Trees Nature Trail is a choice trek for families with young children. Other trails are also available, as are campsites and picnic and barbecue facilities. In warm weather, the Beaver Creek Picnic Area has a good wading area for children. (Picnic provisions can be picked up in Arnold, where there are delis, markets, and restaurants.) A cross-country ski trail is maintained in winter, and a horseback-riding concession operates in summer.

Mercer Caverns *1665 Sheepranch Rd., off Hwy. 4, 1 mi. north of town, (209) 728-2101; www.mercercaverns.com. Daily 9-6 June-Sept; rest of year Sun-Thur 10-4:30, F & Sat 10-8. Adults $7, 5-12 $3.50. Strollers not permitted.*

Discovered over 100 years ago in 1885, this well-lighted, 55-degree limestone cavern takes about an hour to tour. It is said to be the longest continually operating commercial cavern in the state. The tour involves descending stairs to a depth of 161 feet, stopping in ten rooms. New tours begin every 20 minutes.

Moaning Cavern *5350 Moaning Cave Rd., 5 mi. west of town in Vallecito, (800) 225-3764, (209) 736-2708, fax (209) 736-0330; www.caverntours.com. Daily 10-5; June-Aug 9-6. Adults $8.75, 65+ $6.75, 3-13 $4.50. Strollers not permitted.*

The 45-minute tour descends a 100-foot-high spiral staircase into the largest public cavern chamber in California. It is said to be big enough to hold the Statue of Liberty! The cavern was originally discovered by Native Americans, many of whom are thought to have fallen to their death here. In fact, the oldest human remains in the U.S. were found here. A more expensive **rappel tour** *(Must be age 12 or older. Reservations necessary.)* allows a 165-foot rope descent into the cave. Nature trails, picnic tables, and campsites are also available.

Old Timers Museum *On Main St., across street from Murphys Hotel, (209) 728-1160. F-Sun 11-4; in winter Sat & Sun only. Free.*

Dating from 1856, this is the oldest stone building in town. It is interesting to note that the stones were fitted together without mortar. The building now houses Gold Rush-era memorabilia.

Wineries.

- **Milliaire Winery** *276 Main St., (209) 728-1658; www.milliarewinery.com. Tasting & tours F-M 11-5.*

Operating out of a converted carriage house/gas station, this tiny winery is known for its intense, full-bodied wines. It also produces three delicious dessert wines: a late harvest Zinfandel, a Zinfandel Port, and Semillon.

- **Stevenot Winery** *2690 San Domingo Rd., 1 mi. past Mercer Caverns, (209) 728-3436; www.stevenotwinery.com. Tasting daily 10-5; tours by appt.*

Located in a canyon on the site of the first swimming pool in Calaveras County, this relatively big (40,000 cases annually), relatively old (circa 1978) winery is housed in a series of vintage buildings. The cool, rustic Alaska House tasting room is a replica Gold Rush cabin with a sod roof and split-log walls. The winery is famous for its Merlots and white Zinfandels. Picnic tables are sheltered under a grape arbor and have a view of the surrounding vineyards.

WHERE TO STAY

Dunbar House, 1880 Bed and Breakfast Inn *271 Jones St., (800) 692-6006, (209) 728-2897, fax (209) 728-1451; www.dunbarhouse.com. 4 rooms; 100% non-smoking; $$-$$$; 2-night min. on Sat. Unsuitable for children under 10. All VCRs & wood-burning stoves. Hot tub. Afternoon snack, full breakfast.*

This restored Italianate-style house was the filming location for the TV series *Seven Brides for Seven Brothers.* Rooms are decorated with antiques, lace, and down comforters. Guests are greeted each afternoon by an appetizer buffet, and a complimentary bottle of local wine awaits in each roomÆs private refrigerator. Horse-drawn buggy rides through town can be arranged.

Murphys Hotel and Historic Lodge *457 Main St., (800) 532-7684, (209) 728-3444, fax (209) 728-1590. 29 rooms; $; 2-night min. on some weekends May-Sept. Children under 12 free. Some TVs & shared baths. Continental breakfast; restaurant.*

Built in 1856 and a historical landmark since 1948, this very old hotel provided lodging for such Gold Rush-era luminaries as U.S. Grant, J.P. Morgan, Mark Twain, Horatio Alger, and Black Bart—each of whom has a room he actually stayed in named after him. Modern motel rooms, with no legends attached, are available adjacent to the hotel. Though the hotel rooms are immeasurably more interesting, they have one big drawback: The noisy hotel bar, reputed to be the best in the Mother Lode, is kept jumping until the wee hours by townspeople and travelers alike. Those who want to sleep should opt for a less interesting, but quiet, motel room. Special skier packages are available in winter.

The hotel **restaurant** *(B,L,&D daily; $-$$. Highchairs, boosters, child menu. Reservations advised.)* is popular with locals. Menu choices consist of hearty, made-from-scratch American country and continental fare, and portions tend to be large.

WHERE TO EAT

The Peppermint Stick *454 Main St., (209) 728-3570. Daily 11-8, June-Aug; Sun-Thur rest of year; $. Highchairs, boosters, child portions. No reservations. No cards.*

When it was built in 1893, this building served the town as an ice house. Now it is a cheerful ice cream parlor serving old-fashioned sodas and cleverly named sundaes. Sandwiches, soups, and candies are also available, and everything can be packed to go.

Angels Camp

A LITTLE BACKGROUND

Taking its name from George Angel, who founded it as a trading post in 1848, this bustling little burg is thought to be the town Bret Harte wrote of in *Luck of Roaring Camp.*

VISITOR INFORMATION

Calaveras County Chamber of Commerce *1211 S.. Main St., (209) 736-2580, fax (209) 736-2576.*

It is interesting to note that in Spanish "calaveras" means "skulls."

Calaveras Visitors Bureau *1211 S. Main St., (800) 225-3764, (209) 736-0049, fax (209) 736-9124; www.visitcalaveras.org.*

ANNUAL EVENTS

Jumping Frog Jubilee *May; third weekend. (209) 736-2561; www.frogtown.org. $5-$9.*

Visitors are invited to bring their own frog to enter in this historic contest, but rental frogs are available on site. In 1986, Rosie the Ribiter set the current world's record by landing, after three leaps, 21 feet 5 3/4 inches from the starting pad. She earned her jockey $1,500. The prize money is usually won by frog jockeys who are serious about the sport and bring 50 to 60 frogs. So far, a rental frog has never won. The **Calaveras County Fair** is part of the fun and features carnival rides, livestock exhibits, a rodeo, a destruction derby, headliner entertainers, and fireworks.

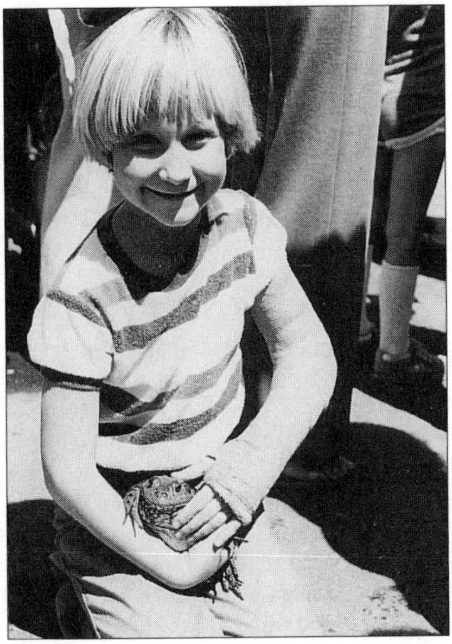

WHAT TO DO

Angels Camp Museum *753 S. Main St., (209) 736-2963. Daily 10-3, Apr-Nov; W-Sun rest of year. Adults $1, 6-12 25¢.*

A repository of Gold Rush memorabilia, this museum displays a blacksmith shop, an extensive rock collection, and a carriage barn filled with vintage wagons and buggies.

WHERE TO EAT

There is only one recommended restaurant for this town. Could this have something to do with Mark Twain's description of some coffee ("day-before-yesterday dishwater") and soup ("hellfire") suffered long ago at the Hotel Angels?

Picnic Pick-Up.

• **The Pickle Barrel** *1225 S. Main St., (209) 736-4704. M-Thur 8-4, F-Sun 8-8.*

This friendly Italian deli packs picnic supplies to go and provides tables for those who decide to stay.

Informal picnic areas can be found by the river. Scenic **Utica Park** has picnic tables and a children's play area.

San Andreas

A LITTLE BACKGROUND

Progress has stripped this town of most of its historic character. Now many locals work in a cement plant whose gravels just a century ago yielded gold to the town's original Mexican settlers. It is also home to the state's largest cashmere goat ranch, which is the only custom cashmere dehairer in the U.S.

WHAT TO DO

Calaveras County Historical Museum *30 N. Main St., (209) 754-3918. Daily 10-4. Adults 50¢ 6-13 25¢.*

Items on display upstairs in this restored 1867 courthouse include Miwok Indian and Gold Rush artifacts. Among the nicely organized exhibits is a full-size display of a Gold Rush-era general store. The jail cell Black Bart once occupied is downstairs in a rustic courtyard landscaped with native California plants and trees.

California Caverns *Off Mountain Ranch Rd., 10 mi. east of town, call for directions, (800) 225-3764, (209) 736-2708, fax (209) 736-0330; www.caverntours.com. Daily 10-5, June-Sept; 10-4 May & Oct-Dec; call for winter schedule; closed in winter. Adults $9, 65+ $7, 3-13 $4.75. Strollers not permitted.*

First opened to the public in 1850, this cavern is now a state historic landmark. The nearly level Trail of Lights tour, which takes 60 to 80 minutes, follows the footsteps of John Muir, Mark Twain, and Bret Harte. Another more strenuous **spelunking tour** *($75. Reservations required. Must be 16 or older.)* through the unlighted portion of the cavern "involves climbing rocks and a 60-foot ladder, squeezing through small passages, crossing 200-foot-deep lakes on rafts, and viewing breathtaking formations unequaled in any other cavern in the West."

WHERE TO STAY

Black Bart Inn and Motel *55 W. St. Charles St., (800) 225-3764 ext.331, (209) 754-3808, fax (209) 754-5755. 65 rooms; $; some shared baths. Pool (unavail. in winter). Restaurant.*

This lodging facility is named after the infamous highwayman, Black Bart, whose career ended in this town. He robbed 29 stagecoaches between 1875 and 1883, always using an unloaded gun. Rooms are available in both the old hotel and in a more modern motel located adjacent.

Mokelumne Hill

WHERE TO STAY

Hotel Leger *8304 Main St., (209) 286-1401, fax (209) 286-2105. 13 rooms; 100% non-smoking; $$. Some wood-burning fireplaces; some shared baths. Unheated pool. Restaurant.*

Once considered among the most luxurious of Gold Rush hotels, this 1879 lodging still provides comfortable rooms. Many have sitting areas, and all are furnished with tasteful period pieces. ("Leger" is now pronounced here "legger," although a while back French owners pronounced it "la-JAY.")

A **restaurant** *(D Thur-Sat, SunBr.)* and the old-time **Frontier Saloon** are located on the ground floor.

Jackson

A LITTLE BACKGROUND

Two important gold-bearing quartz mines are

located just north of this busy town. The Argonaut and Kennedy mines had some of the deepest vertical shafts in the world, extending over 5,000 feet into the ground.

VISITOR INFORMATION

Amador County Chamber of Commerce *125 Peek St., (800) 649-4988, (209) 223-0350, fax (209) 223-4425.*

It is interesting to note that in Spanish "amador" means "lover of gold."

ANNUAL EVENTS

Italian Picnic and Parade *June; first weekend. At Italian Picnic Grounds; (209) 267-0206. Admission.*

Since 1882 the public has been invited to this festive event sponsored by the Italian Benevolent Society of Amador County. The fun includes kiddie rides, dancing, a parade down Highway 49 in Sutter Creek, and an all-you-can-eat barbecue.

WHAT TO DO

Amador County Museum *225 Church St., (209) 223-6386. W-Sun 10-4. By donation. Scale models operate Sat & Sun on the hr.; $1, under 8 free.*

Located within an 1859 red brick house, this museum displays scale models of the Kennedy Mine tailing wheels and head frame and of the North Star Mine stamp mill. A brightly painted wooden train engine, which was once used as a prop on TV's *Petticoat Junction*, is permanently parked in front.

Kennedy Gold Mine *(209) 223-9542. Sat & Sun, mid-Mar to Oct. Adults $5, 6-12 $3.*

One of the richest gold mines in the world, this mine produced over $34.2 million worth of gold from 1880 to 1942. At 5,912 feet deep, it was once also the deepest mine in North America. During the guided surface tours, visitors can try panning for gold and see several mining buildings, the 125-foot-high metal head frame, and a display of mining equipment.

Kennedy Mine Tailing Wheels Park *On Jackson Gate Rd., 1 mi. north of town. Daily dawn to dusk. Free.*

Unique to the Gold Country, four huge 58-foot-diameter wheels—built in 1912 to lift waste gravel, or "tailings," into flumes so that they could be carried to a holding area—can be viewed by taking a short walk on well-marked trails on either side of the road. Two of the wheels have already collapsed. Better hurry to see this site before time takes its toll on the other two. The Kennedy Mine can be seen from here. Picnic tables are available.

Wine Tasting.

Many wineries are located in this area, with a heavy concentration occurring around the nearby town of Plymouth. Contact the Chamber of Commerce for a free map/brochure.

WHERE TO STAY

Country Squire Motel *1105 N. Main St., (209) 223-1657. 12 rooms; ¢-$. Continental breakfast. Dogs welcome.*

Located out in the country adjacent to the old Kennedy Gold Mine site, this comfortable motel housed one of the last private gambling casinos in California. (The casino was closed in 1952.) Gold panning can be practiced in the backyard "crick," and plenty of grass beckons children to romp.

National Hotel *2 Water St., (209) 223-0500, fax (209) 223-4845. 4 stories; 25 rooms; $. No TVs. Restaurant.*

This hotel claims to be the oldest in continuous operation (since 1862) in California. Room decor is modest, as are the prices. Prior guests have included every California governor since 1862, two Presidents (Garfield and Hoover), and John Wayne.

WHERE TO STAY NEARBY

The Heirloom *214 Shakeley Lane, Ione, 12 mi. from town, (888) 628-7896, (209) 274-4468; www.theheirloominn.com. 6 rooms; 100% non-smoking; $; 2-night min. on some Sat. Some wood-burning stoves. Afternoon snack, full breakfast.*

Being located in a town once known as Bed Bug could be a bit of a disadvantage for some lodgings. This B&B is so charming, however, that this history is easily overlooked. Resembling a colonial mansion, it is an 1863 red brick Greek Revival house situated on 1 1/2 acres of grassy, tree-rich grounds right on Sutter Creek. Two guest rooms are in an adjacent sod-roof adobe cottage. A full country-style breakfast is served on Limoges china either in the fireplace-warmed dining room or, in good weather, in the garden.

Roaring Camp Mining Co. *In Pine Grove, (209) 296-4100. 20 cabins; $400/week/couple for a prospector cabin, $135/extra person, $100/child under 18. Closed Oct-Apr. Shared modern bath house. Restaurant.*

Guests leave their cars behind and make the 1-hour trip into the remote canyon here via truck. They stay in this former mining camp in rustic prospector cabins without electricity and must bring all their own gear and food. Recreation consists of swimming, fishing, and panning for gold in the Mokelumne River, as well as hiking and perhaps collecting rocks. Guests may keep all found gold. A saloon, short order restaurant, and general store are available when guests get tired of roughing it. Weekly stays run Sunday to Sunday. For stays of less than a week, call the Monday before the anticipated date of arrival. Shorter 4-hour day tours are also available. On Saturday evenings a group of diners is trucked in for a riverside steak cookout; weekly guests are invited to join this event at no charge.

Sutter Creek

A LITTLE BACKGROUND

Seven gold mines were once located on this quiet Main Street. Now it is lined with modern gold mines—antique shops.

VISITOR INFORMATION

Sutter Creek Visitor Information *(800) 400-0305, (209) 267-1344.*

WHAT TO DO

Sutter Gold Mine *On Hwy. 49, toward Amador City, (888) 818-7462; www.suttergold.com. Sat & Sun 10-5:30, last tour at 4:30; daily in summer. Adults $14.50, 55+ $12.50, 5-12 $10. Children must be 4 or older for underground tour.*

Made up of 16 historic mines that produced over 1.3 million ounces of gold, this is the first active gold-mining operation in the area since the Central Eureka Mine closed in the late 1940s. A visit here lets visitors see both active and restored underground workings, pan for gold, and see gold bars being poured. After donning hard hats, a "boss buggy"—a jeep-like safari car shuttle—takes participants down about 450 feet for an underground walking tour, and later returns everyone to the surface. Picnic facilities are available.

WHERE TO STAY

Sutter Creek Inn *75 Main St., (209) 267-5606, fax (209) 267-9287. 17 rooms; 100% non-smoking; $-$$$; 2-night min. on Sat. Children under 4 free. Some TVs & wood-burning fireplaces. Afternoon snack, full breakfast.*

Opened as an inn in 1966, this 1859 Greek Revival structure was one of the first B&Bs west of the Mississippi. Rooms are available in the house as well as in an adjacent carriage house. As guests arrive each day, homemade lemonade and cookies are served in the garden. In the morning coffee is served by the fireplace, and then at 9 a.m. sharp a full sit-down breakfast is served family-style at long trestle tables in the dining room and kitchen. For those who have been longing to spend the night in a bed suspended from the ceiling by chains, this inn fulfills that and other yearnings. (The guests really swing here.) Some visitors have even seen a friendly ghost, although it has been 26 years since the last sighting. Croquet and hammocks beckon from the gardens, and handwriting analysis and both foot and body massage are available by appointment at an additional fee.

WHERE TO EAT

Sutter Creek Ice Cream *51 Main St., (209) 267-0543. Sun-Thur 10-8, F & Sat to 10; $. 1 highchair.*

This old-fashioned soda fountain sells ice cream specialties and over ten kinds of homemade fudge. Sandwiches, tamales, and corn dogs are also available.

Volcano

A LITTLE BACKGROUND

The scenic, rural drive here from Sutter Creek is ill-marked, poorly paved, and best maneuvered during daylight. And experience indicates that directions and information obtained around these parts are often vague or misleading, leaving plenty of room for error and making a good map worth its weight in gold.

Because this tiny town is built in a depression on top of limestone caves, it is green year-round. Sleepy and quiet now, during the Gold Rush it was a boom town well-known for its boisterous dance halls and saloons. It also opened the state's first public library.

ANNUAL EVENTS

Daffodil Hill *Mid-March until bloom is over in April. 18310 Rams Horn Grade, off Shake Ridge Rd., 3 mi. north of town, (209) 296-7048. By donation.*

Originally planted in the 1850s by a Dutch settler, then added to and maintained by Grandma McLaughlin, this 6-acre garden boasts more than 300 varieties of bulb. There are many, many daffodils, with a few tulips and hyacinths mixed in, too. More bulbs are planted every year by McLaughlin's grandchildren and great-grandchildren. Currently over 400,000 bloom together each spring, making for a spectacular display. Peacocks, chickens, and sheep wander the grounds, and there is a picnic area with tables. It is a pleasant surprise that this seasonal extravaganza of bloom is so non-commercial.

WHAT TO DO

Indian Grinding Rock State Historic Park *14881 Pine Grove-Volcano Rd., Pine Grove, southwest of town, (209) 296-7488. M-F 11-3, Sat & Sun 10-4. $5/vehicle.*

The largest of the grinding rocks—a huge flat bedrock limestone measuring 175 feet by 82 feet—has over 1,185 mortar holes and approximately 363 petroglyphs (rock carvings). All were made by Native Americans who ground their acorns and other seeds here with pestles. A reconstructed Miwok village contains a ceremonial roundhouse, a covered hand-game area, several cedar bark houses, and an Indian game field. Additional facilities include a self-guided nature trail and **Chaw se' Regional Indian Museum**, which orients visitors with a video show and interpretive displays. Picnic facilities and campsites are available. A **"Big Time" Miwok Celebration** is scheduled each September.

"Old Abe" Volcano Blues Cannon.

Located in the center of town in a protected shelter, this cannon helped win the Civil War without firing a shot! Cast of bronze and brass in Boston in 1837 and weighing 737 pounds, it somehow reached San Francisco and was smuggled to Volcano in 1863. It was used by the town to control renegades drawn here in search of quick wealth. For the complete story, ask around town.

Soldiers' Gulch Park.

Rocky terrain, a gurgling stream, and scenic stone ruins, including the façades of several ancient buildings, provide a picturesque backdrop against which to enjoy a picnic or just a few moments of quiet contemplation.

Volcano Theatre Company *(209) 223-4663. F & Sat at 8 & occasionally Sun. Closed Nov-Mar. Tickets $10. Reservations required.*

The first little theater group to form in California was the Volcano Thespian Society in 1854. Performances are held in the intimate 50-seat **Cobblestone Theater**, except in summer, when they occur in an outdoor amphitheater. Children are welcome.

WHERE TO STAY

St. George Hotel *16104 Main St., (209) 296-4458, fax (209) 296-4457; www.stgeorgehotel.com. 20 rooms; 100% non-smoking; $. Closed part of Jan. No TVs; some shared baths. Continental breakfast; restaurant.*

Rooms are available in either the solidly constructed main hotel, built in 1862, or in an annex built almost a hundred years later in 1961. For safety reasons families with children under 12 must stay in the newer and charmless, albeit comfortable, annex located around the corner, their consolation being a private bathroom. In the hotel, a cozy memorabilia-crammed bar and a parlor area with fireplace and games invite relaxing.

The hotel **restaurant** *(D Thur-Sun, SunBr; $-$$. Reservations advised.)* serves creative California cuisine.

Amador City

A LITTLE BACKGROUND

With a population of 202, this is said to be the smallest incorporated city in the state.

WHERE TO STAY

Mine House Inn *14125 Hwy. 49, (800) MINE-HSE, (209) 267-5900. 9 rooms; 100% non-smoking; $$-$$$; 2 night min. on Sat. No TVs; some gas fireplaces. Unheated pool (unavail. Oct-Apr), hot tub. Full breakfast.*

Built in 1881 as the headquarters for the Keystone Mine, this attractive restored brick building now houses guest rooms furnished with Gold Rush-era antiques. Each room is named for its original function: the Vault Room, the Retort Room, the Assay room. In the morning, guests just push a buzzer and breakfast is delivered to the door. One Easter, long ago, parents staying here arranged for an Easter basket to arrive in this same mysterious manner. The kid still hasn't figured out how they pulled off that one!

WHERE TO EAT

Buffalo Chips Emporium *14179 Hwy. 49, (209) 267-0570. B&L W- Sun; $. Highchair, booster. No cards.*

Some folks just buy a simple cone here and then sit outside on one of the weathered benches to leisurely watch the busy world drive by. Others prefer to sit inside what was once the town's Wells Fargo Bank and indulge in a fancy fountain item.

Drytown

A LITTLE BACKGROUND

Once home to 27 saloons, Drytown is now known for its equally abundant antique shops and not much else.

Shingle Springs

A LITTLE BACKGROUND

Named for a cool spring that surfaced near a shingle mill here in 1849, this rural area is now, just as it was then, the perfect spot to set up camp.

VISITOR INFORMATION

Shingle Springs/Cameron Park Chamber of Commerce *4065 Mother Lode Dr., (530) 677-8000, fax (530) 676-8313.*

WHERE TO STAY

KOA Kampground *4655 Rock Barn Rd., (800) KOA-4197, (530) 676-2267.*

For description, see page 415.

El Dorado

WHERE TO EAT

Poor Red's *6221 Main St., (530) 622-2901. L M-F, D daily; $. Highchairs, boosters, child portions. No reservations.*

Judging just from the outside, which looks to be an unsavory bar, this former Wells Fargo stage stop might easily be passed by. But then weary travelers would miss the experience of dining on exquisite ham, ribs, chicken, and steak—all cooked over an open oak wood pit and served in generous portions. Because this restaurant is very popular and also very small, weekend dinner waits can run over an hour. Some patrons pass that time downing Gold Cadillacs at the old-time horseshoe bar. (It is interesting to note that Poor Red's is the largest user of Galliano in North America, Galliano being the main ingredient in those Gold Cadillacs.) Some pass it studying the mural behind the bar that depicts the town as it appeared in the late 1800s. Others pass it feeding the jukebox. And some beat the wait by ordering take-out.

Placerville

A LITTLE BACKGROUND

Placerville, which in Spanish means "the golden one," was once known as Hangtown because hangings here were so common. This is where the Hangtown Fry—made with eggs, bacon, and oysters—originated. The town's **Hangman's Tree bar** *(305 Main St., (530) 622-3878.)* which is built on top of the legendary hanging tree's stump, sometimes has a controversial, lifelike dummy hanging from a rope out front.

Railroad magnate Mark Hopkins, meatpacker Philip Armour, and automobile-maker John Studebaker all got their financial starts here.

VISITOR INFORMATION

El Dorado County Chamber of Commerce
542 Main St., (800) 457-6279, (530) 621-5885, fax (530) 642-1624; www.eldoradocounty.org.

ANNUAL EVENTS

Apple Hill *September-December. Daily 9-6. (530) 644-7692; www.applehill.com.*

On a mountain ridge east of town, the Apple Hill tour route follows an historic path originally blazed out in 1857 by Pony Express riders. Each fall 42 apple ranches along this route sell 22 varieties of tree-fresh apples at bargain prices. And they're *crunchy*, because they're *fresh*! An impressive selection of homemade apple goodies can also be purchased: fresh-pressed apple cider, hard cider, apple wine, spicy apple butter, caramel apples, apple jelly, dried apples, apple cake, apple sundaes, apple syrup, and, of course, apple pie. Many of the farms have picnic facilities, and some have snack bars. A few also have hiking trails, fishing ponds, pony rides, train rides, and live jazz. Three wineries are also located here. Several apple varieties are available into December. Maps are available from the El Dorado County Chamber of Commerce.

Nine Christmas tree farms open the day after Thanksgiving. Cherry season begins on Father's Day weekend, when the **West Coast Cherry Pit-Spitting Championships** are held.

WHAT TO DO

El Dorado County Historical Museum
100 Placerville Dr., in El Dorado County Fairgrounds, 2 mi. west of town, (530) 621-5865. W-Sat 10-4; also Sun 12-4, Mar-Oct. By donation.

Historic exhibits in this "great hall" include a Wells Fargo stagecoach and a wheelbarrow made by John Studebaker in the days before he manufactured cars.

Gold Bug Mine *Off Bedford Ave., 1 mi. north of town, (530) 642-5232, fax (530) 642-5236. Daily 10-4 in summer; Sept-Apr, Sat & Sun only. Adults $2, 5-16 $1, cassette tour $1.*

Visitors here can take a self-guided tour through a cool 1/4 mile-long lighted mine shaft, see a working model of a stamp mill inside an authentic stamp mill building (once used to crush granite to get out the gold), picnic at creek-side tables, and hike in rugged 61-acre Gold Bug Park.

Wineries.

- **Boeger Winery** *1709 Carson Rd., Schnell School Rd. exit off Hwy. 50, (800) 655-2634, (530) 622-8094, fax (530) 622-8112; www.boegerwinery.com. Tasting daily 10-5; no tours.*

  The stone cellar tasting room here is part of the original winery that operated from the 1860s through the 1920s. During Prohibition the winery became a pear farm, becoming a winery again in the early 1970s. Shaded streamside picnic tables beckon, and a sandbox awaits children.

- **Sierra Vista Winery** *4560 Cabernet Way, (530) 622-7221; www.sierravistawinery.com. Tasting daily 10-5; tours by appt.*

  Enjoy a magnificent view of the entire Crystal Range of the Sierra Nevada while picnicking at this pleasant winery.

Coloma

A LITTLE BACKGROUND

This is where James Marshall, a sawmill foreman who worked for Captain John Sutter, discovered gold in 1848. The entire town is now a National Historic Landmark.

WHAT TO DO

Marshall Gold Discovery State Historic Park *On Hwy. 49, (530) 622-3470, fax (530) 622-3472. Park: Daily 8-sunset; $5/vehicle. Museum: Daily 10-5 in summer; shorter hours rest of year; free.*

This lovely 265-acre park encompasses 70 percent of the town. It contains a reconstruction of the original **Sutter's Mill** (where the Gold Rush began) as well as picnic facilities, nature trails, and Gold Rush-era buildings and artifacts. An exact replica of the piece of gold Marshall found is on display in the museum (the original is at the Smithsonian in Washington, D.C.). The **James W. Marshall Monument** is located on a hill overlooking the town. Marshall's grave is here, and a statue honoring him depicts him pointing to the spot where he discovered gold.

Whitewater Connection. *See page 414.*

The office and base camp for this white water rafting outfit is located adjacent to the state park. Participants on American River trips are permitted to camp out at the outfitter's riverside facility. Half- and full-day trips are offered daily from mid-April through September; longer trips are also available.

Auburn

VISITOR INFORMATION

Auburn Area Chamber of Commerce
601 Lincoln Way, (530) 885-5616.

Placer County Visitors Council *13464 Lincoln Way, (800) 427-6463, (530) 887-2111, fax (530) 887-2134; www.placer.ca.gov.*

It is interesting to note that in Spanish "placer" means "surface mining."

WHAT TO DO

Bernhard Museum Complex *291 Auburn-Folsom Rd., (530) 888-6891. Tu-F 10:30-3, Sat & Sun 12-4. Adults $1, 65+ & 6-16 50¢.*

Docent-led tours are available of the Greek Revival-style Bernhard Residence, a restored Victorian farmhouse built in 1851 and furnished with Victorian antiques.

Gold Country Museum *1273 High St., at Gold Country Fairgrounds, (530) 887-0690. Tu-F 10-3:30, Sat & Sun to 4. Adults $1, 65+ & 6-16 50¢.*

Located within a building constructed of logs and stones, this old-time museum emphasizes mining exhibits. Visitors can walk through a 48-foot-long mine shaft and view a working model of a stamp mill. Local Maidu Indian artifacts and an extensive doll collection are also on display.

WHERE TO STAY

KOA Kampground *3550 KOA Way, (800) KOA-6671, (530) 885-0990.*

For description, see page 415.

Motel Row.

Many motels are located at the top of the hill on Lincoln Way and across the freeway on Bowman Road.

WHERE TO EAT

Awful Annie's *160 Sacramento St., (530) 888-9857. B&L daily.*

Everything about this tiny spot is appealing: the lace-covered windows, outdoor deck, all-day breakfast menu. Truth be told, it's awful good.

Cafe Delicias *1591 Lincoln Way, (530) 885-2050. L&D daily; $. Highchairs, boosters, booths, child portions.*

Located in one of the town's oldest buildings, this casual Mexican restaurant serves especially good flautas and housemade tamales.

Ikeda's *13500 Lincoln Way, 1/4 mile east of Auburn Ravine-Foresthill exit off I-80, (530) 885-4243. Daily 10-7; to 9 in summer & on weekends; $. Highchairs, child portions. No cards.*

Since the 1950s, this casual snack bar has been serving travel-weary diners fast-food fare: fresh-ground hamburgers, corn dogs, burritos, deep-fried whole mushrooms, fruit pie, fresh fruit salad, frozen yogurt, ten flavors of hot chocolate, and thick fresh fruit milkshakes. An adjacent produce market sells some tempting car snacks, among them giant cashews and pistachios, both of which are grown in the area.

Shanghai Restaurant & Bar *289 Washington St., (530) 823-2613. L&D daily; $. Child portions. No cards.*

The oldest family-owned bar and restaurant in the state and the setting for the movie *Phenomenon*, this atmospheric spot has been serving Cantonese fare since 1906. The intriguing old building, with its very high ceilings and ancient interior, is reason enough to stop in. Vintage photos depict early Auburn and the Gold Rush, and colorful paper lanterns and fans add atmosphere. From the menu, family-style lunches and dinners are the way to go, but extensive a la carte items and a dinner steak are also available.

Grass Valley

A LITTLE BACKGROUND

It was here, in what was once the richest gold-bearing region in the state, that gold-mining became a well-organized industry. Many advanced mining techniques were developed and first used here.

VISITOR INFORMATION

Grass Valley/Nevada County Chamber of Commerce *248 Mill St., (800) 655-4667, (530) 273-4667, fax (530) 272-5440; www.gvncchamber.org.*

Because of its location inside a replica of the historic home once occupied by scandalous Gold Rush personality Lola Montez, this office is worth visiting in person.

ANNUAL EVENTS

Bluegrass Festival *June. (209) 293-1559. Admission.*

Cornish Christmas Celebration *December. (530) 272-8315. Free.*

Experience an old-time Christmas at this event celebrating the traditions of the Cornish miners who settled this Gold Rush town. Visitors can dance in the downtown streets, which are closed to traffic, and ride in a horse-drawn carriage.

WHAT TO DO

Bridgeport Covered Bridge *Take Hwy. 20 west 10 mi. to Pleasant Valley Rd., turn right (north) and follow south fork of Yuba River 9 mi. to Bridgeport; (530) 432-2546, fax (530) 432-4182.*

Built over the south fork of the Yuba River in 1862 and in use until 1971, this is the longest (256 feet) single-span wood-covered bridge in the world. It is now a State Historical Landmark and part of **South Yuba River State Park**. Not currently maintained and in shaky condition, it should be walked across with caution. A scenic picnic area is situated on the riverbank, and there are several hiking trails. Those who have witnessed it claim the wildflower display here in March is spectacular.

Empire Mine State Historic Park *10791 E. Empire St., (530) 273-8522. Daily 10-5, in summer 9-6. Adults $3, 6-12 $1, dogs $1.*

Once the largest and richest hard rock mine in the state, the Empire Mine was operated for over a century—from 1850 to 1956. Though it still holds millions of dollars worth of gold, the ore is too expensive to extract and the mine is now a 784-acre state park. Of special interest are the stone **Bourn Mansion** *(Tours Sat & Sun 12-3:30, May-Oct.)*, which was designed and built by Willis Polk in 1897 in the style of an English country lodge, and the surrounding 13-acre formal gardens featuring an antique rose garden and several reflecting pools. The mining area illustrates many facets of the business and allows visitors to look down a lighted mine shaft. There are also approximately 22 miles of self-guided back-country hiking trails. Picnicking is permitted only on the outskirts of the parking lot.

Grass Valley Museum *410 S. Church St./Chapel St., (530) 273-5509. Tu-F 12:30-3:30. By donation.*

Built in 1863 as Mount Saint Mary's Convent and Orphanage, this was the state's first orphanage for non-Indian children. The building now displays Gold Rush memorabilia and furnishings as well as a fully equipped doctor's office, classroom, parlor, and music room from that era.

North Star Mining Museum *On Allison Ranch Rd./south end of Mill St., (530) 273-4255. Daily 10-4; closed Oct-Apr. By donation.*

Once the power house for the North Star Mine, this rustic stone building houses a collection of old photographs, mining dioramas and models, and a 30-foot-diameter, 10-ton Pelton water wheel dating from 1896—the largest such wheel ever constructed. It also displays the largest operational Cornish pump in the country. A grassy picnic area is located across adjacent Wolf Creek.

Oregon House *Located 35 mi. west of town. Take Hwy. 20 west to Browns Valley, then Hwy. E21 north to Oregon House, then E20 east.*

- **Collins Lake Recreation Area** *On Collins Lake Rd., (530) 692-1600. Daily 5:30am-10pm, Mar-Aug; shorter hrs. rest of year. $5/vehicle, boat rentals $5-$12.50/hr.*

Popular with fishermen, this 1,000-acre lake also has lakefront campsites and RV hook-ups.

- **Renaissance Vineyard & Winery** *12585 Rices Crossing Rd., (800) 655-3277, (530) 692-2222, fax (530) 692-2497; www.renaissancewinery.com. Tasting & tours F & Sat at 11 by appt. ($3).*

The drive through the scenic Sierra Nevada foothills required to reach this isolated valley would be worthwhile even if this special winery weren't waiting at the end. Operated by the Fellowship of Friends, a non-denominational religious group, the winery is situated on a scenic hillside terraced with grapevines.

The Bistro *((530) 692-2938. L W-Sat; $. 1 highchair, 1 booster, 1 booth, child portions. Reservations advised.)*, which is also on the property, serves a seasonally changing menu of entrees designed to pair well with Renaissance wines. When the weather is warm, deck seating is available, and on hotter days the air-conditioned interior of the dining room brings welcome relief.

WHERE TO STAY

Holbrooke Hotel *212 W. Main St., (800) 933-7077, (530) 273-1353, fax (530) 273-0434; www.holbrooke.com. 28 rooms; $-$$. Some gas fireplaces. Continental breakfast; restaurant.*

Established in 1851, this meticulously restored Victorian grand hotel has hosted four presidents (Grant, Garfield, Cleveland, and

Harrison), stagecoach robber Black Bart, and author Mark Twain. Current guests can step back in time in beautifully appointed rooms featuring brass beds and the original clawfoot tubs. Most rooms hold only two people, but in a few larger rooms a child can be accommodated with a rollaway bed. A century-old wrought-iron elevator cage lifts guests from floor to floor. This lodging facility, which consists of both the hotel and the 1874 **Purcell House** behind it, is conveniently located in the center of town.

Both the **Golden Gate Saloon**, which is said to be the oldest continuously operating saloon in the Gold Country and which features an ornate bar that was shipped around the Horn, and an elegant **restaurant** *(L&D daily, SunBr.)* with full family amenities operate on the main floor.

Sivananda Ashram Yoga Farm *14651 Ballantree Lane, (800) 469-9642, (530) 272-9322, fax (530) 477-6054; www.sivananda.org. 8 rooms; 100% non-smoking; $. Children half price. No TVs; all shared bathrooms. Meals included.*

The bell rings here at 5:30 each morning to awaken guests. Attendance at scheduled meditation and yoga classes is mandatory. In between, guests dine on vegetarian meals and have plenty of free time to enjoy the natural surroundings of the 80-acre farm. Lodging is simple, almost austere, consisting of both dormitories and single and double rooms, and during the summer guests may bring their own tents.

WHERE TO EAT

Pasties.

These meat-and-potato turnovers were once popular lunch fare among the area's Cornish miners, who carried them down into the mines in their pockets. At lunchtime, they reheated their pasties on a shovel held over candles secured in their hard hats. How about a hasty tasty pasty picnic? (Actually, "pasty" rhymes with "nasty.") It was town resident William Brooks who invented the pasty-making machine now used throughout the world.

- **King Richard's** *217 Colfax Ave., (530) 273-9646.*

Pasties are made here using the Brooks machine, which can sometimes be observed in operation.

- **Marshall's Pasties** *203 Mill St., (530) 272-2844.*

They're made by hand here.

Tofanelli's *302 W. Main St., (530) 272-1468. B,L,&D daily; $. Highchairs, boosters, child portions.*

Every kind of breakfast item imaginable is on this menu, including design-your-own-omelettes, whole-wheat pancakes and waffles, and a large variety of teas. Salads, sandwiches, and several kinds of hamburgers—including a tofuburger and a veggieburger—join the menu at lunch. All this and an attractive brick and oak decor, too.

Nevada City

A LITTLE BACKGROUND

Said to be the best privately preserved and restored small city in the state, this picturesque mining town is also said to contain residential and commercial buildings representative of all the major 19th-century architectural styles. Scenically situated on seven hills, the town boasts a particularly fine assortment of lovely gingerbread-style Victorian homes, and the entire downtown district is on the National Register of Historic Places. It is interesting to note that in Spanish "nevada" means "snow-covered."

VISITOR INFORMATION

Nevada City Chamber of Commerce *132 Main St., (800) 655-NJOY, (530) 265-2692, fax (530) 265-3892; www.nevadacitychamber.com.*

ANNUAL EVENTS

International Teddy Bear Convention *April. (530) 265-5804, fax (530) 478-0728; www.teddybearcastle.com. Adults $5, seniors $3, under 12 $1, bears free.*

Bears from all over the world come out of hibernation for this warm, fuzzy event. Bearaphernalia and bear necessities and luxuries abound, and all kinds of bears are available for adoption.

4th of July Parade *July.*

Held in Nevada City on even years and in Grass Valley on odd, this old-fashioned celebration begins with a parade, followed by diversions—food stalls, competitions, entertainment—at the fairgrounds. As might be expected, it culminates in a fireworks extravaganza.

Constitution Day Parade *September.*

The signing of the U.S. Constitution is honored at this oldest and largest celebration in the West with marching bands, drill teams, floats, fire engines, and horsemen. Pre-parade activities include a re-enactment of the signing.

Fall Colors *Mid-October to mid-November.*

Victorian Christmas *December; on the three Wednesday evenings and usually all day on the Sunday before Christmas.*

WHAT TO DO

Firehouse Museum #1 *214 Main St., (530) 265-5468. Sat & Sun 11-4, daily in summer. By donation.*

Located inside a charming 1861 Victorian firehouse, this museum is said to be haunted. Among the intriguing pioneer memorabilia on display are a Chinese altar, snowshoes made for a horse, a noteworthy collection of Maidu Indian baskets, and relics from the Donner Party.

Nevada City Winery *321 Spring St., (800) 203-WINE, (530) 265-WINE, fax (530) 265-6860. Tasting daily 12-5; tour on Sat at 3.*

Housed now in an old foundry building, this winery is located only 2 blocks from where it originated a century ago. It is known for its Cabernets, Merlots, and Zinfandels.

Nevada Theatre *401 Broad St., (530) 265-6161, fax (530) 265-2294.*

Opened in September of 1865 and lectured in twice by Mark Twain, this is the oldest original-use theater building in California. It has been refurbished to appear as it did when it first opened and is used year-round for plays, concerts, films, and other performing arts events.

WHAT TO DO NEARBY

Independence Trail *Off Hwy. 49, 6 mi. north of town, (530) 272-3823. Free.*

Basically level and easy for both wheelchairs and baby strollers to navigate, this 4-mile nature trail was built in 1856 as the Excelsior Canal. It was used to run water through the mountains for hydraulic gold mining. One section of the trail permits hikers to cross flumes suspended over deep crevices and a waterfall. This area features an outstanding display of wildflowers in April and May.

Malakoff Diggins State Historic Park *23579 N. Bloomfield Rd., off Hwy. 49, 17 mi. northeast of town, (530) 265-2740, same fax. $5/vehicle. Museum: Daily 10-4, May-Sept; rest of year Sat & Sun only.*

Inhabited by over 1,500 people in the 1870s, when it was the largest hydraulic gold-mining operation in the world, North Bloomfield is now a ghost town. Several buildings have been restored, but there are no commercial stores. The park museum is in a former dance hall and has an interpretive display on hydraulic mining. Visitors can hike on numerous trails and fish in a small lake, and picnic facilities are available. Three primitive cabins, three walk-in campsites, and thirty regular campsites are available. Note that the drive from Nevada City takes just under an hour. Travelers with large RVs or trailers should enter the park via the Tyler-Foote route, located 11 miles north of Nevada City on Highway 49.

Oregon Creek Swimming Hole *On Hwy. 49, 18 mi. north of town.*

Located in the middle fork of the Yuba River, this popular spot has sandy beaches, both deep swimming and shallow wading spots, and picnic facilities.

WHERE TO STAY

Grandmere's Inn *449 Broad St., (530) 265-4660. 6 rooms; 100% non-smoking; $$-$$$; 2-night min. on weekends. Afternoon snack, full breakfast.*

This 1856 Colonial Revival home was built by Aaron Sargent, who wrote the 19th constitutional amendment granting women the vote. (The author of the 15th amendment, which freed former slaves, also lived in Nevada City.) On the National Register of Historic Places, it is beautifully decorated in French country style, with antique pine furnishings and gorgeous floral fabrics, and is conveniently located at the Top of Broad Street—one of the town's earliest residential areas.

National Hotel *211 Broad St., (530) 265-4551, fax (530) 265-2445. 42 rooms; $-$$. Children under 12 free. Some kitchens & 1 gas fireplace; some shared baths. Unheated pool. Restaurant, room service.*

Located on the town's main street, this claims to be the oldest continuously operating hotel west of the Rockies—maybe even west of the Mississippi. Luminaries who have been guests here include Herbert Hoover, who stayed here when he was a mining engineer for the Empire Mine, and Mark Twain. Built in 1856, it is a State Historical Landmark and features high ceilings, cozy floral wallpapers, and old-time furniture. Families of four can be accommodated in two separate rooms with a bath between.

The plush, old-fashioned **Victorian Dining Room** *(B,L,&D daily, SunBr; $-$$. Highchairs, boosters, child portions. Reservations advised.)* features a steak and lobster dinner menu.

Northern Queen Inn *400 Railroad Ave., (530) 265-5824, fax (530) 265-3720. 86 units; $. Some kitchens & wood-burning stoves. Heated pool, hot tub. Restaurant.*

Located on the outskirts of town beside Gold Run Creek, this pleasant lodging complex has modern motel rooms, cottages, and 2-story chalets. A small collection of full-size trains is displayed on the property, including a 1920s railbus, a 1910 wood-burning locomotive, and another engine that had roles in several classic western movies.

Piety Hill Cottages *523 Sacramento St., (800) 443-2245, (530) 265-2245. 9 cottages; 100% non-smoking; $-$$; 2-night min. on weekends. Children under 3 free. 1 kitchen; 1 wood-burning stove. Hot tub. Full breakfast.*

This 1930s auto court motel has one- and two-room cottages with antique furnishings.

Red Castle Inn *109 Prospect St., (800) 761-4766, (530) 265-5135. 7 rooms; 100% non-smoking; $-$$$; 2-night min. on Sat, Apr-Dec. Unsuitable for children under 10. No TVs. Full breakfast.*

Situated on a hilltop above town, this beautifully restored and plushly furnished Gothic Revival mansion was built in 1860. Said to be one of only two of this style left on the West Coast, it features gingerbread and icicle trim and has old-fashioned double brick walls. Some guests have reportedly seen the spirit of Laura Jean, who was once a governess here.

WHERE TO EAT

The Country Rose Cafe *300 Commercial St., (530) 265-6252. L&D daily, SunBr; $-$$. Boosters, booths, child portions. Reservations advised.*

An inviting country French menu is served in a charming inside area, with wooden booths and rose print tablecloths, and in a bucolic outdoor area with a creek running through it. Delicious housemade soup and sandwiches, French hot chocolate, and a great lemon chiffon pie are just a few of the menu gems.

Friar Tuck's *111 N. Pine St., (530) 265-9093; www.friartucks.com. D daily; $$. Highchairs, boosters, booths, child portions. Reservations advised.*

Operating in a building dating back to 1857, this cozy restaurant has many dining rooms and is furnished with large, comfortable wooden booths. The extensive menu offers a variety of casual fondue items—including a chocolate dessert version—as well as grilled fresh fish, rack of lamb, roasted duck, ribs, and steak. The wine list runs the gamut from inexpensive local labels to expensive rare vintages; varietals are available by the glass. Relaxing live guitar music is piped throughout, and an authentic 19th-century pub bar from Liverpool, England adds to the atmosphere.

Nevada City Grill *401 Commercial St., (530) 265-6138. L&D Tu-Sun; $-$$. Highchairs, boosters, booths, child menu. No reservations.*

Operating within a converted cottage tucked away on a back street, this spot is particularly nice in warm weather, when the sheltered outdoor patio and its gurgling fountain are especially inviting. The lunch menu offers salads, sandwiches, and hamburgers, plus soups and chili and the beer-batter fish & chips and hand-cut French fries for which the kitchen is well known. Dinner brings on pastas, seafood, and steaks.

Downieville

A LITTLE BACKGROUND

One of the Gold Country's best-preserved mining towns, this scenic mountain enclave is known as the gateway to the Lost Sierra and is a surprise to come upon as Highway 49 winds through, narrowing to one lane over the town's northern bridge. It is situated where the North Yuba River and the Downie River merge, and early miners are said to have found big gold nuggets here by the bucketful. The rustic town retains its 19th-century charm, with original buildings, including a white steepled church, wood plank sidewalks, and the ever-present soothing sound of the Downie River. Main Street still has a mining supply shop and saloon, and the 1885 town gallows, used only once, still stands outside the County Courthouse. Downieville is considered the least changed of all California's Gold Rush towns.

The best way to enjoy a quick stop is with a picnic among the Gold Rush artifacts in riverside Lions Memorial Park; sandwich and pizza shops are adjacent. And pick up a copy of *The Mountain Messenger* newspaper. It is the state's oldest continuously published weekly—since 1853. Nowadays the town is a popular destination with mountain bikers, who enjoy riding on the plentiful dirt roads.

VISITOR INFORMATION

Downieville Chamber of Commerce *(530) 289-3507; www.sierracounty.org.*

GETTING THERE

Located 60 miles northeast of Nevada City.

WHAT TO DO

Downieville Museum *(530) 289-3423. Daily 10-5, mid-April to mid-Oct. By donation.*

This small museum operates within a circa 1852 fire-repellant stone building, made with thick walls of mortarless schist and with iron shutters and doors. It was originally a Chinese store and gambling house. Displays include interesting historical photographs, artifacts, and clothing from the 1800s.

WHERE TO STAY

Sierra Shangri-La *On Hwy. 49, (530) 289-3455; www.sierrashangrila.com. 11 units; 100% non-smoking; $-$$; 1-week min. in cabins in summer. Children under 2 free. No TVs; some kitchens & wood-burning fireplaces & stoves.*

There is little to do here except commune with nature. Guests can relax, do some fishing and hiking, and enjoy the sight and sound of the Yuba River rushing past their cabin door. Some units are perched right over the river, allowing guests to fish from their deck. Eight housekeeping cottages and three B&B units are available.

Sierra City

VISITOR INFORMATION

Sierra County Chamber of Commerce
P.O. Box 436, Sierra City 96125, (800) 200-4949, (530) 862-0308; www.sierracounty.org.

GETTING THERE

Located 60 miles northeast of Nevada City.

WHAT TO DO

Sierra County Historical Park and Museum
100 Kentucky Mine Rd., off Hwy. 49, (530) 862-1310. W-Sun 10-5, June-Sept; Sat & Sun only in Oct. Mill tours at 11 & 2. Closed Nov-May. Adults $5, 7-17 $2.50. Museum only, $1; under 6 free.

A 45-minute guided tour through the reconstructed 1850s **Kentucky Mine Stamp**

Mill located here permits viewing the original machinery, which is still intact and operable. The museum is inside a reconstructed wood-frame hotel dating from the mid-19th century. Picnic tables and barbecue facilities are situated under a canopy of oak trees.

The eclectic **Kentucky Mine Concert Series** is held on Saturday evenings in July and August in an amphitheater within the complex.

WHERE TO STAY

Herrington's Sierra Pines Resort *On Hwy. 49, (800) 682-9848, (530) 862-1151. 21 units; $; 2-night min. on Sat. Closed Dec-Mar. Some kitchens & wood-burning fireplaces. Restaurant. Pets welcome.*

Located on the north fork of the Yuba River, this lodging facility consists of duplex units and one cabin. The **restaurant** *(B&D daily. Highchairs, boosters.)* is known for its baked goods and rainbow trout, which are caught fresh each morning from the property's own trout pond.

Packer Lake Lodge *3901 Packer Lake Rd., 10 mi. north of town, (530) 862-1221. 14 cabins; $. Closed Nov-Apr. Children under 2 free. No TVs; some kitchens & wood-burning stoves; some shared baths. Restaurant. Dogs welcome.*

Located at the end of a road in a remote corner of the Sierra Nevada, this rustic resort has eight housekeeping cabins with sun decks overlooking Packer Lake; they are rented by the week and include use of a rowboat. (No motorboats are permitted on the lake.) Six sleeping cabins are available by the night. Cabins here are often booked up several years in advance. The restaurant is open for dinner to non-guests by reservation.

Salmon Lake Lodge *On Gold Lake Rd., 10 mi. north of town, (415) 681-7985 (reservations number is in San Francisco). 14 cabins; $-$$; 1-week min. June-Oct. Closed Nov-Apr. No TVs; some kitchens & wood-burning fireplaces & stoves; some shared baths. Dogs welcome.*

Located in the glaciated high country of Sierra County, this remote resort has been in continuous operation for almost a century. Guests park their cars at the east end of Salmon Lake and are transported by a staff-operated barge across the lake. There they sleep in one of the cabins or tent-cabins and are provided free access to an assortment of boats. Some cabins are fully equipped, but guests in tent-cabins must provide their own bedding, kitchen utensils, and supplies. The experience is like luxurious camping. To ease cooking chores, guests are invited twice each week to a catered barbecue (additional fee) held on an island in the center of the lake.

Sierraville

GETTING THERE

Located 80 miles northeast of Nevada City, where Highway 49 meets Highway 89. Highway 89 continues north to Plumas County and south to Truckee and Lake Tahoe.

WHAT TO DO

Sierra Hot Springs *1 Campbell Hot Springs Rd., off Hwy. 89, (530) 994-3773, fax (530) 994-3479; www.sierrahotsprings.org. Baths open 24-hours daily. Day-use: Adults $10-$15, 5-12 half price, under 5 free.*

Swimsuits are optional in the indoor and outdoor hot springs at this secluded spa, which has been open since the 1850s. An organic vegetarian restaurant serves brunch and dinner on weekends.

Rooms can be rented in the renovated 1909 **Globe Hotel** *(20 rooms; $.)*, as well as in a rustic lodge. Rates are inexpensive and include unlimited use of the springs.

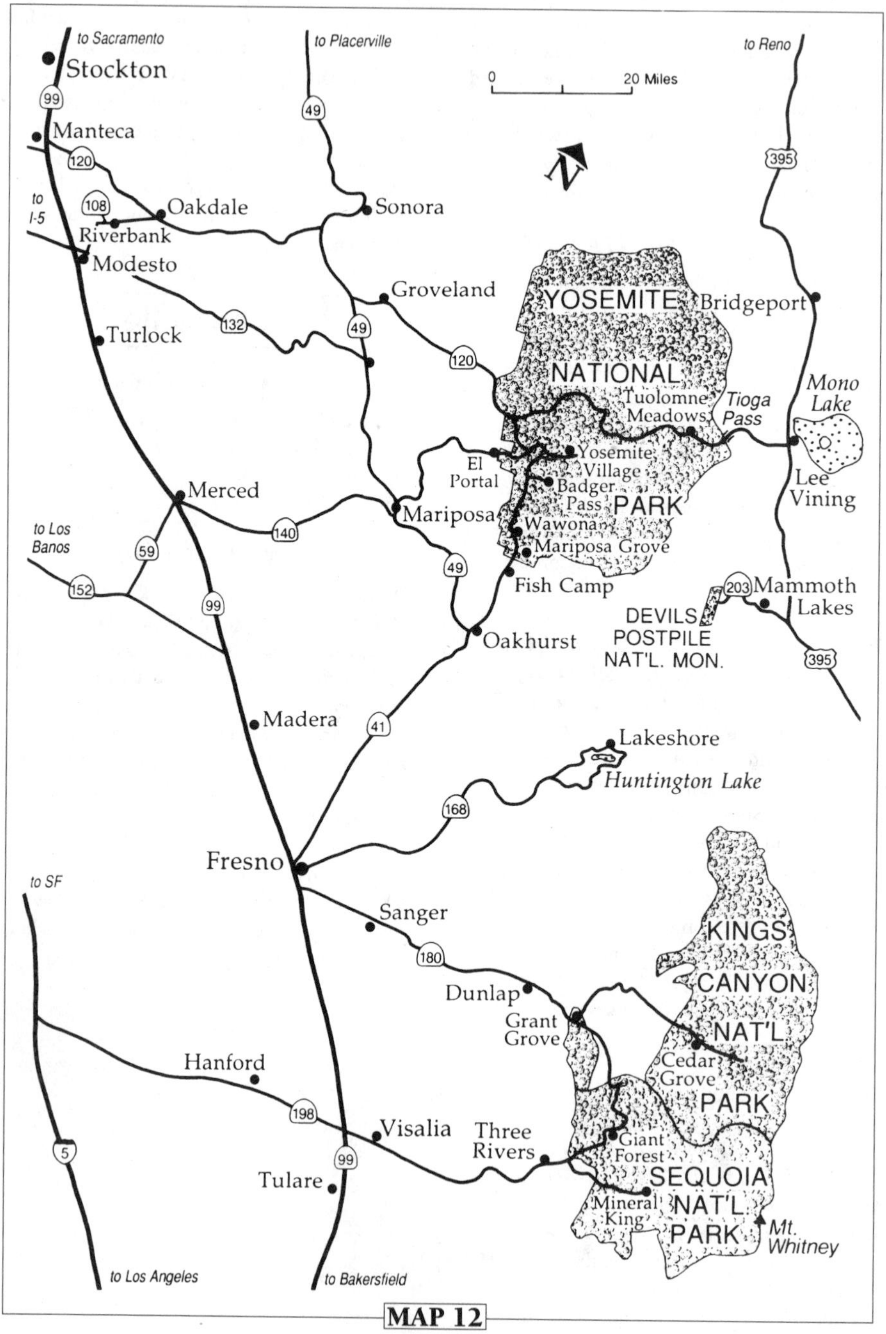
to Sacramento
Stockton
99
to Placerville
49
to Reno
0
20 Miles
Manteca
120
395
N
to
I-5
108
Oakdale
Sonora
Riverbank
Modesto
Groveland
YOSEMITE
Bridgeport
132
49
Turlock
120
NATIONAL
Mono
Lake
Tuolomne
Meadows
Tioga
Pass
El
Portal
Yosemite
Village
Badger
Pass
PARK
Lee
Vining
Merced
Mariposa
to Los
Banos
140
59
Wawona
Mariposa Grove
49
152
99
Fish Camp
203
Mammoth
Lakes
DEVILS
POSTPILE
NAT'L. MON.
Oakhurst
395
Madera
41
Lakeshore
Huntington Lake
168
Fresno
to SF
Sanger
KINGS
CANYON
NAT'L
PARK
180
Dunlap
Grant
Grove
Cedar
Grove
Hanford
198
Visalia
Three
Rivers
Giant
Forest
5
99
Tulare
SEQUOIA
NAT'L
PARK
Mineral
King
Mt.
Whitney
to Los Angeles
to Bakersfield

MAP 12

The High Sierra

Yosemite National Park

A LITTLE BACKGROUND

Yosemite Park is a place of rest. A refuge . . . in which one gains the advantage of both solitude and society . . . none can escape its charms. Its natural beauty cleanses and warms like fire, and you will be willing to stay forever . . .

— John Muir

Yosemite is worth returning to in every season. Doing so permits enjoying the spectacular beauty of the park's dramatic seasonal changes. Most visitors see this grand national park in the summer, when it is at its busiest, with congested roads and accommodations filled to capacity. All this makes it difficult to focus on what was the original draw—the scenic, natural beauty of the High Sierra. To catch a glimpse of the Yosemite described by Muir, it is essential to visit in the off-season: in fall when the colorful foliage change is spectacular; in winter when snow blankets the valley floor; in spring when the falls are at their fullest.

Yosemite's high country was designated a national park in 1890. The valley, which was under state supervision, was added to the

national park in 1906. (It is amazing to realize that the valley comprises just 1 percent of the park's terrain. In fact, Yosemite is as big as the state of Rhode Island.) Among the park's scenic wonders are El Capitan—the largest piece of exposed granite in the world—and Yosemite Falls—the highest waterfall in North America.

Bear in mind that falls and rivers can be dangerous as well as beautiful. Be careful, especially when hiking with children.

A $20 per car admission fee, which is good for 7 days, is collected at all park entrances. Visitors are given a copy of the *Yosemite Guide* activities newsletter and a park map.

VISITOR INFORMATION

National Park Service *Yosemite National Park 95389, (209) 372-0200; www.nps.gov/yose.*

Yosemite Sierra Visitors Bureau *(209) 683-4636; www.yosemite-sierra.org.*

Call to request a free *Visitors Guide* covering areas outside the national park.

GETTING THERE

Located approximately 240 miles east of San Francisco. Take Highway 80 to Highway 580 to Highway 205 to Highway 120. To minimize the need for chains in winter, take low-elevation Highway 140 in from Merced.

ANNUAL EVENTS

Chefs' Holidays *January & February. At The Ahwahnee.*

Guest chefs give cooking presentations and prepare gala banquets.

Vintners' Holidays *November & December. At The Ahwahnee.*

Two days of free wine seminars hosted by esteemed wine-makers culminate in a sumptuous feast in The Ahwahnee Dining Room. Courses are especially designed to complement wines sampled in the seminars.

Bracebridge Dinner *December 22, 24, & 25. At The Ahwahnee. $285/person, 4-12 $212, not appropriate for under 8.*

Since 1927 the fare at this 3-hour mock-medieval feast has been seven courses of elegant Christmas dishes. Pageantry, carols, and jesters entertain diners in between. Attending this memorable dinner is a pleasure not many get to enjoy. Though participants must apply for reservations a full year in advance, applications are so numerous that guests must be chosen by lottery.

STOPS ALONG THE WAY

Attractions are listed in the order encountered driving in from the San Francisco Bay Area.

Manteca Waterslides at Oakwood Lake RV Campground *874 E. Woodward Rd., Manteca, (877) OAKWOOD, (209) 249-2500, fax (209) 239-2060; www.oakwoodlake.com. Daily 10-6 in summer; May & Sept, weekends only 10-5. Over 4' tall $20.99, 42"-48" $13.99, admission without slide use $11.99, under 42" free; parking $4.*

This was North America's first waterslide park, and it is where the world's first fiberglass waterslide was invented in 1976. Now with over 1 mile of fiberglass waterslides, it has the state's tallest speed slide—the 8-story-high V-MAX—as well as three new Thunder Falls thrill slides. Most slides have over 400 feet of enclosed flume and multiple 360-degree turns. Among the other attractions are the River Rapids, maneuvered on an inner tube, and Jet Scream, a two-person inner tube ride. The giant Castaway Bay children's slide and activity pool

provides fun for the little ones, too. Campground facilities include a fishing lake, a playground, and acres of shady barbecue and picnic areas. Campsites are available year-round.

Hershey's Visitors Center *120 S. Sierra Ave., Oakdale, approx. 102 miles from San Francisco, (209) 848-8126, fax (209) 847-2622; www.hersheys.com. Tours M-F 8:30-3. Free. Strollers not permitted.*

A good way to prepare for a visit to this factory, which supplies 13 western states with Hershey's chocolates, is by reading the children's book, or seeing the movie, titled *Charlie and the Chocolate Factory.* Tour participants sign in at the visitors center and then ride a shuttle bus to the factory. Upon entering the factory, the lucious chocolate aromas become intense, and when viewing the multiple 10,000-gallon vats of liquid chocolate being stirred by heavy granite rollers, it's easy to become quite stirred up oneself. And though the sound can't be heard on the tour, it's fun to know that the candy machines make a puckering noise as they deposit chocolate kisses on a moving conveyor belt—thus the name "kiss." Workers in this noisy, warm, and fragrant factory look happy. *Real* happy. Maybe that's because they get to eat as much chocolate as they want for *free.* At the end of the 30-minute tour, each participant receives a sweet treat and the opportunity to purchase official Hershey's souvenirs.

A **Chocolate Festival** is held annually in May. It features chocolate tastings and a Hershey's kiss-eating contest. Yum!

Fast-food heaven seems to be in Oakdale. Numerous cafes and produce stands are also located along Highway 120.

Knight's Ferry Covered Bridge *12 mi. east of Oakdale, (209) 881-3517, fax (209) 881-3203. Visitor center M-F 8-4:30; in summer also Sat & Sun 10-2. Free.*

Built in 1863 and measuring 330 feet long, this bridge is the longest and oldest covered bridge west of the Mississippi. It is closed to cars now, but pedestrian traffic is still permitted. A park on the highway side of the Stanislaus River provides picnicking and fishing spots. On the other side of the river is a rustic Gold Rush-era town with a general store, several restaurants, and another park.

Unguided raft, canoe, and kayak rentals can be arranged through **River Journey** *((800) 292-2938, (209) 847-4671, fax (209) 847-1300; www.riverjourney.com.).*

Groveland.

This rustic mountain town is home to the **Iron Door Saloon** *(18763 Main St., (209) 962-8904.)*, which was built in 1853 and claims to be the oldest saloon in the state. In summer, the **Groveland Motel** *((888) 849-3529, (209) 962-7865, fax (209) 962-0064. ¢-$$$.)* gives pooped parents the option of renting a cabin for themselves and an adjacent carpeted tepee for the kids; mobile home units are also available.

WHAT TO DO

Park Activities

The Ansel Adams Gallery *In Yosemite Village, (209) 372-4413; www.anseladams.com.*

Special edition photographs by this well-known photographer can be purchased here.

Bicycle Rentals *Yosemite Lodge: (209) 372-1208; daily 9-5. Curry Village: (209) 372-8319; daily 8-8; Apr-Oct only. $5.25/hr., $20/day.*

All rental bikes are old-fashioned one-speeds. A map to the park's 8 miles of bike paths is provided, and helmets are available at no charge. Child carriers are not available.

Big Trees Tram Tour *On Hwy. 41, in Wawona, 35 mi. from valley. Tours 9-4; May-Oct only. $4.50-$8.50.*

Approximately 500 giant sequoias are located in the 250-acre Mariposa Grove. Some measure 15 to 25 feet in diameter, and some are over 2,000 years old. Open-air trams take visitors on guided tours of a 6-mile scenic loop. In winter, this is a choice spot for cross-country skiing.

Bus Tours *(209) 372-1240. Valley floor $8.50-$16, grand tour $21.50-$42.*

Float Trip.

Scenic and calm is the area on the Merced River between Pines Campground and Sentinel Bridge. Raft rentals complete with life jackets and paddles are available in June and July at Curry Village.

Glacier Point *Bus tour $5.50-$10.50 one-way, $11-$20.50 round trip.*

From this spot, gazers enjoy a 270-degree view of the high country and a bird's-eye view of the valley 3,214 feet below. Several trails lead down to the valley. Consider arriving in the morning (get a one-way ticket on the Glacier Point Hiker's Bus) and spending the rest of the day hiking back down. The bus tour takes about 4 hours.

Hiking.

Participate in a ranger-guided walk or take any of the many self-guided trails. Maps can be purchased in park stores. The most popular trail is said to be the Mist Trail to Vernal Fall; it features breathtaking vistas and a close-up view of the 317-foot-tall waterfall.

Indian Cultural Museum *In Yosemite Village, next to the **Village Visitor Center.** W-Sun 9-12 & 1-4.*

Visitors learn about the Awaneechee Indians through artifacts, cultural demonstrations, and recorded chants. A reconstructed village located behind the museum has a self-guided trail that points out plants used by the Native American residents for food, clothing, and shelter.

Junior Ranger Program.

This program is available June through August for children ages 8 through 12. Consult the *Yosemite Guide* for details.

Movies.

Scenic movies and slide shows are scheduled some evenings. Check the *Yosemite Guide* for times and locations.

Pioneer Yosemite History Center *On Hwy. 41, in Wawona, 25 mi. from valley. Daily dawn-dusk.*

This village of restored historic pioneer buildings is reached by walking across an authentic covered bridge. Originally located in different areas around the park, the various structures were moved here in the 1950s and '60s. In summer, history comes to life with demonstrations of soap making, yarn spinning, rail-splitting, and other pioneer crafts, and horse-drawn carriage rides are sometimes available.

Rock Climbing Lessons *Curry Village: (209) 372-8344; daily, year-round. Tuolumne Meadows: (209) 372-8435; summer only. $65-$80. Participants must be 14 or older.*

Learn rock climbing at the **Yosemite Mountaineering School**, one of the finest in the world. Beginners are taught safety essentials for dealing with the area's granite rock and can expect to climb as high as 80 feet in the first lesson. Oddly, snow and ice climbing are offered only in the summer.

Valley Stables *(209) 372-8348. Apr-Oct only. Guided 2-hr. horse rides at 8, 10, & 1; $35/person. Half-day mule rides/$45, all-day/$67. Riders must be 7 or older.*

Said to have the largest public riding stock in the world, this concession can arrange for custom pack and fishing trips.

Winter Activities.

See pages 407 to 409.

Yosemite Chapel. *In the Valley.*

Built in 1879, this charming structure is the oldest building in the park.

Activities Outside the Park

The first three destinations are reached via the Tioga Pass. Note that this pass is closed in winter.

Bodie State Historic Park *8 mi. south of Bridgeport, (760) 647-6445. Daily 8-dusk; tour of stamp mill June-Oct, call for times. $2, under 5 $1.*

Located at the end of a 13-mile side road off Highway 395, the last 3 miles of which are unpaved, this 486-acre park is the largest unrestored ghost town in the West. In 1879, when 10,000 people lived here, there were 2 churches, 4 newspapers, and 65 saloons. It was said to be quite rowdy. A little girl who moved here in its heyday wrote in her diary, "Good, by God! We're going to Bodie." This passage has also been interpreted as "Good-bye God! We're going to Bodie." Due to fires in 1892 and 1932, only about 5 percent of the town structures remain. No food service or picnic facilities are available.

Devil's Postpile National Monument *(760) 934-2289. Daily 7:30-5:30.*

This 60-foot-high formation is constructed of polygonal basaltic columns formed long ago by quickly cooling lava. Though the road is closed to vehicles, visitors can take a pleasant 1-mile walk through the monument; another short hike leads to 101-foot-high Rainbow Falls. In summer, a **shuttle bus** *((760) 924-5500. $7, 5-12 $4.)* is available from the Mammoth Mountain area.

Mono Lake *Off Hwy. 395 (call for directions), (760) 647-3000. Nature Center: Daily 9-8; guided nature walks daily in summer at 10 & 1, rest of year Sat & Sun at 1.*

John Muir described this desolate area as, "A country of wonderful contrasts, hot deserts bounded by snow-laden mountains, cinder and ashes scattered on glacier-polished pavement, frost and fire working together in the making of beauty." Mark Twain called it the "Dead Sea of the West." An ancient Ice Age lake, estimated to be at least 1 million years old, Mono Lake features an unusual terrain of pinnacles and spires formed by mineral deposits. It is filled with water that contains more than 2 1/2 times the salt found in ocean water. Perhaps this is what attracts the 50,000-plus vacationing seagulls that flock in during April, stay into August, and then head back to the coast. Situated at over 7,000 feet above sea level, it is one of the largest lakes in the state. Fall is the ideal time for a visit. Campsites are available. For restaurant and lodging information, call (760) 647-6629.

• **Mono Basin Visitor Center** *Off Hwy 395, just outside of Lee Vining, (760) 647-3044. Daily 9-4:30, summer only; interpretive walk at 1.*

Overlooking the lake, this new facility has interpretive displays that provide insight into the area. Nature study outings and hikes are scheduled daily in July and August.

• **Mono Lake Committee Information Center** *On Hwy. 395/Third St., Lee Vining, (760) 647-6595, fax (760) 647-6377. Daily 9-9 in summer; rest of year closes earlier.*

Get oriented here with a brief slide show about the lake. In summer a free hour-long sunset walk is led daily at 6 p.m. Naturalist-led canoe tours are offered on summer weekends, with a small charge for use of equipment.

Yosemite Mountain Sugar Pine Railroad *56001 Hwy. 41, Fish Camp, 4 mi. south of park's southern entrance, 1-hr. drive from valley, (559) 683-7273, (559) 683-8307; www.ymsprr.com. Call for schedule. Train: $11.50, 3-12 $5.75. Jenny rail cars: $7.50, 3-12 $3.75.*

A reconstruction of the Madera Sugar Pine Co. Railroad that made its last run in 1931, this narrow-gauge steam train takes passengers on a 45-minute, 4-mile scenic excursion through the Sierra National Forest. Passengers sit in open-air touring cars upon logs that have been carved out to form long benches and are given live narration on the area's history. A stop-over at the midway point to picnic or hike is optional. Moonlight rides, which include a steak barbecue and campfire program, are scheduled on Saturday nights in summer. Smaller Jenny rail cars, powered by Model A engines, take passengers on shorter 30-minute rides along the same route when the train is not operating. A picnic area and snack shop are available.

WHERE TO STAY

Reservations are essential. Call (559) 252-4848 for information or to make reservations at any park lodging facility. It is especially difficult to obtain accommodations in the summer and on holiday weekends. Rates for two range from $37 to $292. A bargain Midweek Ski Package is available in winter.

Park Lodging: In the Valley

The Ahwahnee *123 rooms; $$$+. Some fireplaces. Pool (seasonal), tennis courts. Afternoon tea; restaurant, room service. Free valet parking.*

Built in 1927 of granite blocks and concrete beams, this sedate luxury hotel is a National Historic Landmark. It is decorated with priceless Native American baskets and oriental rugs, and interesting historic photos and artwork hang on the walls. The grand Great Lounge, with a walk-in fireplace at either end, is delightful to sit in. Some cottages are available.

Campgrounds *(800) 436-7275; www.reservations.nps.gov. ¢. Most Apr-Oct only; several open year-round.*

Curry Village *628 units; ¢-$. No TVs; some shared baths. Pool. Restaurant.*

Accommodations include standard rooms, cabins with and without baths, and inexpensive tent-cabins located along the Merced River that sleep up to six people.

Housekeeping Camp *266 units; ¢.*

Cook in an outdoor pit grill and experience camping beside the Merced River without the bother of setting up a tent. Units sleep up to six people and consist of three concrete walls, a concrete floor, a canvas roof, and a canvas curtain closure. Basic furniture is provided.

Yosemite Lodge *245 rooms; $-$$. No TVs; some shared baths. Pool (seasonal). 3 restaurants.*

Accommodations are comfortable modern hotel rooms.

Park Lodging: Elsewhere

High Sierra Camps *204 beds; $. June-Sept only. Unsuitable for children under 7. No TVs; communal bath house. Dining tent.*

Five camps provide dormitory-style tent accommodations and two meals. Guests provide their own linens. Reservations are assigned by lottery, with applications accepted October 15 through November 30 for the mid-December drawing.

Tuolumne Meadows Lodge *69 units; $. Summer only. No TVs; all wood-burning stoves; communal bath house. Dining tent.*

This all tent-cabin facility is located at the park's eastern entrance.

Wawona Hotel *On Hwy. 41, in Wawona, 30 mi. from valley. 104 rooms; $-$$. Open Apr-Nov & Christmas vacation; weekends only Jan-Easter. No TVs; some shared baths. Unheated pool, 1 tennis court, 9-hole golf course. Restaurant.*

Built in 1879, this Victorian hotel is located 6 miles from the park's southern entrance, near the Mariposa Grove of Big Trees. A National Historic Landmark, it is said to be the oldest resort hotel in the state. Most rooms accommodate only two people; a few in the annex, added in 1918, accommodate three. Facilities include a "swimming tank" built in 1917.

A special **Christmas program** is scheduled each year. Details vary from year to year, but in 1991 it included a stagecoach ride across the covered bridge to the Pioneer History Center, where all the cabins were decorated for the holidays. Santa arrived in a horse-drawn wagon dating from the 1800s, and a special Christmas Eve and New Year's Eve dinner was served. Call for current details.

White Wolf Lodge *At Tioga Pass, 31 mi. from the valley. 28 cabins; ¢. Summer only. No TVs; shared bath house. Dining tent.*

This complex consists of tent-cabins and a few cabins with private baths. Breakfast and dinner are available.

Lodging Unaffiliated with the Park

The Redwoods In Yosemite *In Wawona, 4 mi. inside park's south entrance, (209) 375-6666, fax (209) 375-6400; www.redwoodsinyosemite.com. 130 units; $-$$$; 2-night min., 3-night min. in summer. Children under 4 free. Some TVs & VCRs; all kitchens; most wood-burning fireplaces or stoves. Pets welcome in some units.*

These rustic cabins and modern homes are furnished with linens and kitchenware.

Tenaya Lodge at Yosemite *1122 Hwy. 41, Fish Camp, 2 mi. outside park's south entrance, (800) 635-5807, (209) 683-6555, fax (209) 683-8684; www.tenayalodge.com. 4 stories; 244 rooms; $$-$$$+. Children under 18 free. 1 indoor heated pool & hot tub, 1 outdoor heated pool & hot tub, 2 saunas, 2 steam rooms, fitness room. 2 restaurants, room service.*

Built in 1990, this plush lodging facility is a cross between the park's Yosemite Lodge and The Ahwahnee hotel. A majestic public reception area features 3-story-tall beamed ceilings, and all of the rooms have forest views. Guided nature walks are scheduled most mornings, weather permitting. In winter, ski and snowshoe rentals are available at the hotel, and guests can strike out on a scenic cross-country ski trail through adjacent Yosemite National Forest. In summer, campfire programs, wagon rides, and rentals of mountain bikes are added to the agenda. Camp Tenaya children's program for ages 5 through 12 operates evenings from 6 to 10 on weekends and holidays fall through spring, and nightly in summer *($35)*.

WHERE TO EAT

Park Dining

All of these valley facilities are open daily and equipped with highchairs and boosters.

The Ahwahnee Dining Room *(2059) 372-1489. B,L,&D; $-$$$. Child portions. Reservations essential for D.*

The best time to dine in the rustic splendor of this magnificent dining room is during daylight hours, when the spectacular views of the valley offered by 50-foot-tall, floor-to-trestle-beamed ceiling leaded-glass windows can be fully enjoyed. Dinner is expensive, and men are expected to wear a sport or suit jacket and women to dress accordingly. Guests of the hotel get first choice at reservations, so non-guests should be prepared for either an early or late seating. Children fit in best at breakfast or lunch.

Cafeterias *At Curry Village & Yosemite Lodge. B,L,&D; $.*

Meals here are quick and informal.

Garden Terrace *At Yosemite Lodge. L&D; $-$$. Closed in winter.*

Meals here are buffet-style.

Mountain Room Broiler *At Yosemite Lodge. D; $$-$$$. Child portions.*

The walls in this stunning room are papered with striking black-and-white photo murals of mountain climbers, and floor-to-ceiling windows look out on Yosemite Falls. The menu features broiled fresh fish and aged beef as well as smoked trout, sautéed button mushrooms, and warm cheese bread.

Get rid of the kinks developed on the long ride in at the adjacent **Mountain Room Bar**.

Picnic Pick-Ups.

Box lunches can be reserved at hotel kitchens the evening before they are needed. Supplies can also be picked up at **Degnan's Deli** in Yosemite Village.

Wawona Hotel Dining Room *(209) 375-1425. B,L,&D, SunBr; $-$$. Child portions. Reservations advised for D.*

A visit for the inexpensive Sunday brunch is highly recommended. Served in the hotel's wonderful vintage dining room, where expansive multi-paned windows provide views of the surrounding pines, it consists of simple, satisfying fare. Breakfast or lunch during the rest of the week is also pleasant.

Dining Outside the Park

Erna's Elderberry House *48688 Victoria Ln., Oakhurst, 15 mi. outside park's south entrance, (559) 683-6800, fax (559) 683-0800. L W-Sat, D daily, SunBr; in summer, D also on Tu; $$$.*

Closed 1st 3 weeks of Jan. Highchairs, child portions. Reservations essential.

Hillside dining "in the classic tradition of old Europe" is promised here. The staff prepares a different six-course, fixed-price meal every night. One meal enjoyed here in the elegantly appointed front room began with a flute of elderberry-flavored champagne. It continued with a scallop and sorrel timbale artistically positioned on a nest of pasta, followed by corn and cilantro soup, and then fresh pears poached in Riesling. The main course was alder wood-smoked chicken sausages served with wild rice and a colorful array of vegetables. A simple, elegant salad followed. Dessert, which is served outside on a candle-lighted garden terrace, was a duo of Chocolate Decadence in fresh mint sauce and puff pastry filled with caramelized apples and creamed gourmand. Three wines selected to complement each dinner are offered by the glass.

Elegant lodging is available in the property's castle-like **Chateau du Sureau** *((559) 683-6860, fax (559) 683-0800; www.chateausureau.com. 10 rooms; 100% non-smoking; $$$+, 12% gratuity added to bill; 2-night min. on weekends. Unsuitable for children under 7. TVs & VCRs by request; all wood-burning fireplaces. Unheated pool. Afternoon snack, full breakfast; restaurant, room service.)*, which features an outdoor chess court and serene walking paths. Maids wearing black dresses topped with white ruffled aprons keeps things spiffy. ("Sureau" is the French word for "elderberry.")

Sequoia and Kings Canyon National Parks

A LITTLE BACKGROUND

Though located just south of Yosemite National Park, about a 3-hour drive away, these two scenic national parks are often overlooked. It's a shame because they, too, offer spectacular scenery and are much less crowded.

Sequoia National Park was established in 1890. It was California's first national park and is the country's second-oldest national park. (Yellowstone is the oldest.) Kings Canyon National Park was established in 1940. Combined, they encompass over 860,000 acres.

The main attraction at these parks is the enormous sequoia trees, with their vibrant cinnamon-colored bark. The trees can be viewed in both Sequoia Park's Giant Forest and Kings Canyon's Grant Grove. The largest is the **General Sherman Tree** in Sequoia National Park. It towers 275 feet high, measures 36 1/2 feet in diameter, and is approximately 2,100 years old. This makes it higher than Niagara Falls, as wide as a city street, and the largest living tree on the planet.

Mt. Whitney is also located in Sequoia park and, at 14,494 feet, is the highest point in the United States outside of Alaska. It can't be viewed from the parks without a long hike. From the east side of the Sierra, it is a 1- to 3-day hike to its peak; from the west side it is a 7- to 9-day hike.

Admission to the parks is $10 per vehicle.

VISITOR INFORMATION

Sequoia and Kings Canyon National Parks
47050 Generals Hwy., Three Rivers 93271-9651, (559) 565-3341; www.nps.gov/seki.

GETTING THERE

Located approximately 250 miles southeast of San Francisco. Take Highway 80 to Highway 580 to Highway 99 south, to either Highway 180 east or Highway 198 east.

ANNUAL EVENTS

Caravan to Nation's Christmas Tree *December. (559) 875-4575.*

Since 1926, the 267-foot-tall **General Grant Tree** in Kings Canyon National Park has been the site of a special Christmas service. In honor of its official status as the Nation's Christmas Tree, a wreath is placed at its base each year by members of the National Park Service. A car caravan leaves from the tiny town of Sanger, and seats are also available by reservation on a chartered bus.

WHAT TO DO

Caves.

• **Boyden Cavern** *In Sequoia National Forest, just outside Kings Canyon N.P., (559) 736-2708; www.caverntours.com. Tours daily 10-5, June-Sept only. Adults $6, 6-12 $3. Strollers not permitted.*

This cave is located in spectacular 8,000-foot-deep Kings River Canyon—the deepest canyon in the United States. The guided tours take about 45 minutes.

• **Crystal Cave** *In Sequoia N.P., (559) 565-3759. Schedule varies; mid-May to Sept only. Adults $6, 6-11 $3.*

This 48-degree marble cavern is reached via a steep 1/4-mile trail. The guided tour takes about an hour.

Fishing.

The most popular spots are along Kings River and at the forks of the Kaweah River. A California fishing license is required. Ask about fishing regulations at park visitor centers.

Horse Rentals *In Cedar Grove, Wolverton, Grant Grove, & Mineral King.*

Junior Ranger Program.

Kids can earn a patch while discovering the parks' resources and learning how to protect them. Ages 5 through 8 earn the Jay Award, ages 9 through 12 the Raven Award. To get started, purchase a Junior Ranger booklet in any visitor center and follow the instructions. Program operates year-round.

Trails.

Over 900 miles of hiking trails are in these parks.

Unusual Trees.

Many of these trees are encountered on the drive along the 46-mile **Generals Highway** connecting the two national parks. Some require either a short walk to reach or a drive down a side road. From December through May, this highway is occasionally closed by snow.

• **Auto Log.** Cars can be driven onto this fallen sequoia for a photograph.

• **Senate Group** and **House Group of Sequoias.** These are among the most symmetrically formed and nearly perfect of the sequoias. They are reached via the Congress Trail, an easy 2.1-mile walk that begins at the General Sherman Tree.

• **Tunnel Log.** Cars can drive through this tunnel carved through a tree that fell across the road in 1937.

Visitor Centers *Lodgepole: (559) 565-3782; daily in summer 8-6, F-M in winter 10-4. Grant Grove: (559) 565-4307; daily in summer 8-6, in winter 9:30-4:30. Foothills: (559) 565-3135; daily 8-4:30, in summer to 5. Free.*

See exhibits on the area's wildlife as well as displays on Native Americans and the sequoias. Inquire here about the schedule of nature walks and evening campfire programs.

WHERE TO STAY

Montecito-Sequoia Lodge.

See pages 408 and 412.

Park Lodging *Sequoia N.P.: (888) 252-5757; www.visitsequoia.com. Kings Canyon N.P.: (559) 335-5500; www.sequoia-kingscanyon.com. $$-$$$. Children under 12 free. No TVs; some shared baths. Restaurant. Campgrounds: (800) 365-2267.*

At Sequoia, the new 102-room **Wuksachi Lodge** that opened in 1999 offers deluxe hotel rooms in three price categories. Facilities include a restaurant, and ranger programs are scheduled several nights each week.

Arrangements can also be made to backpack 11 miles into the **Bearpaw High Sierra Camp**, where facilities are tent-cabins with canvas sides and wooden floors. Hot showers, cots, and linens are provided, and dinner and breakfast are included. Reservations are necessary.

Kings Canyon has both deluxe hotel rooms and rustic cabins.

Campsites are available on a first-come, first-served basis. In summer, reservations are accepted, and highly recommended, for Lodgepole and Dorst campgrounds in Sequoia National Park.

For more information, request a park brochure that explains the various options in detail.

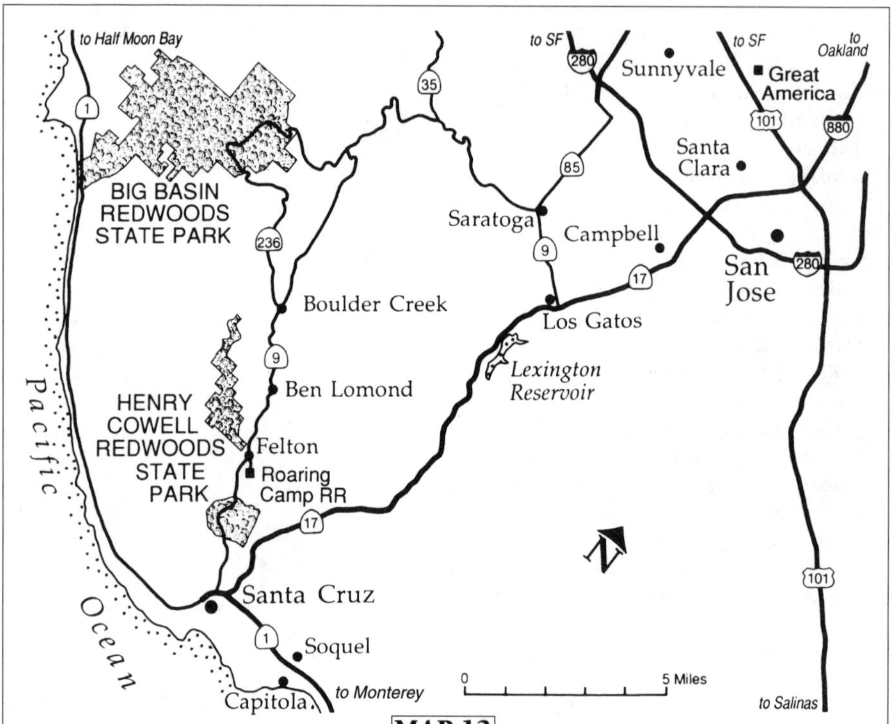
to Half Moon Bay
to SF
to SF
to Oakland
Sunnyvale
Great America
Santa Clara
Saratoga
Campbell
San Jose
BIG BASIN REDWOODS STATE PARK
Boulder Creek
Los Gatos
Lexington Reservoir
Ben Lomond
HENRY COWELL REDWOODS STATE PARK
Felton
Roaring Camp RR
Pacific Ocean
Santa Cruz
Soquel
Capitola
to Monterey
0
5 Miles
to Salinas
1
35
280
101
880
85
236
9
17
N

MAP 13

Los Gatos and Saratoga

A LITTLE BACKGROUND

Tucked in the lush, green Santa Cruz mountains, Los Gatos is known for its many antique shops. It was originally a logging town, and its name is Spanish for "the cats," in reference to the wildcats that once roamed the hills in large numbers. Nearby Saratoga is a smaller, quieter, and even more picturesque town.

VISITOR INFORMATION

Saratoga Chamber of Commerce
20460 Saratoga-Los Gatos Rd., Saratoga, (408) 867-0753, fax (408) 867-5213; www.saratoga chamber.org. Located inside an 1865 cottage built for a local blacksmith, this information resource is worth a stop in.

GETTING THERE

Located approximately 60 miles south of San Francisco. Take Highway 101 to Highway 17 to the Los Gatos exit.

WHAT TO DO

Garrod Farms Stables *22600 Mt. Eden Rd., Saratoga, (408) 867-9527, fax (408) 741-1169. Daily 8:30-4:30; M-F by reservation, Sat & Sun first-come, first-served. Horses $25/hr., riders must be 8 or older; ponies $15/1/2-hr.*

Shetland ponies are available for children under 8 to ride; an adult must walk them with a lead rope. Horse trails roam over 200 acres.

The **Cooper-Garrod Vineyards** *((408) 741-8094, fax (408) 741-1169. Tasting Sat & Sun 11-4:30.)* winery is also located here. It produces estate Chardonnay and Cabernet Sauvignon on 21 acres farmed by the family for over a century. Tasting occurs in the historic Fruit House.

Hakone Japanese Gardens *21000 Big Basin Way, Saratoga, (408) 741-4994. M-F 10-5, Sat & Sun 11-5. By donation; parking $3-$5.*

Now a city park, this garden was originally constructed by a private citizen to typify a mid-17th-century Zen garden. Now it is composed of four separate gardens: a Hill and Pond Garden, a Tea Garden, a Zen Garden, and Kizuna En—a Bamboo Garden. Among its special features are a Japanese-style house built without nails or adhesives, a pond stocked with colorful koi, and an authentic Tea Ceremony room, where a demonstration tea ceremony is held every Thursday afternoon. It also boasts the largest collection of Japanese bamboo in the western world. A tea ceremony is performed on the first Thursday of each month, and tea is served in the garden on summer weekends.

Los Gatos Art Museum *4 Tait St., Los Gatos, (408) 354-2646. W-Sun 12-4. By donation.*

Housed in a Spanish-style building dating

from 1907, this small museum features exhibits on natural science and contemporary fine arts.

The tiny **Forbes Mill History Museum** *(75 Church St., (408) 395-7375. W-Sun 12-4. By donation.)*, located in the remains of a flour mill dating from 1854, focuses on town history.

Montalvo Center for the Arts and Arboretum *15400 Montalvo Rd., Saratoga, (408) 741-3421; www.villamontalvo.org. Arboretum: daily 9-5. Gallery: call for schedule. Free.*

Once the summer home of Senator James Phelan, this majestic 1912 Mediterranean-style estate is now the county center for fine arts. It also serves as a bird sanctuary. Self-guided nature trails wind through the 175-acres of gardens. Performing arts events, some especially for children, are presented June through September in a natural outdoor amphitheater and year-round in an indoor Carriage House.

Parks.

- The 12-acre **Oak Meadow Park** *(Off Blossom Hill Rd., Los Gatos, (408) 354-6809.)* has picnic facilities, baseball diamonds, hiking trails, a 1910 hand-carved, English clockwise **carousel** *($1)*, a well-equipped playground with an authentic fire engine and airplane to climb on, and a steam locomotive pulling the train at the narrow-gauge **Billy Jones Wildcat Railroad** *((408) 395-7433. Daily in summer 10:30-4:30; rest of year Sat & Sun, 11-3. $1, under 3 free.)*.
- The 151-acre **Vasona Lake County Park** *(Off Blossom Hill Rd., Los Gatos, (408) 358-3741, fax (408) 358-3245. Daily 8-dusk. $3/vehicle.)* is dominated by a huge reservoir where visitors can fish and rent rowboats and paddle boats. Visitors can also use the barbecue facilities and playground and see the exhibits on water ecology and conservation at the **Youth Science Institute** *(296 Garden Hill Dr., (408) 356-4945; www.ysi-ca.org. M-F 9-4:30. Free.)*.

Saso Herb Gardens *14625 Fruitvale Ave./Farwell, Saratoga, (408) 867-0307. Sat 9-2:30; closed Oct-Mar. Free.*

Taking advantage of the ideal climate for cultivating herbs, this nursery has one of the largest collections of organically grown culinary, medicinal, and ornamental herbs on the West Coast. Browse in its beautiful natural setting, or plan ahead to attend a workshop or free lecture tour.

Wineries.

- **Mirassou Champagne Cellars** *300 College Ave., Los Gatos, (408) 395-3790, fax (408) 395-5830; www.mirassou.com. Tasting W-Sun 12-5; tours on Sat & Sun at 2.*

  High in the hills above town, this historic site was formerly occupied by the Novitiate Winery. All of the champagnes are field-pressed from night-harvested Monterey County grapes.
- **Savannah Chanel Vineyards** *23600 Congress Springs Rd./Hwy. 9, Saratoga, (408) 741-2930, fax (408) 867-4824. Tasting daily 11-5; tours by appt.*

  Established in 1892, with original plantings dating from 1910 and 1920, this winery's rustic tasting room is located at the end of a steep, woodsy back road. It is surrounded by tall redwoods and 14 acres of vineyards. Picnic tables are available.

WHERE TO STAY

Garden Inn of Los Gatos *46 E. Main St., Los Gatos, (800) 888-8248, (408) 354-6446, fax (408) 354-5911. 28 rooms; $-$$. Children under 10 free. Some kitchens. Heated pool (unavail. Nov-Apr). Continental breakfast.*

These rustic Spanish-style bungalows are in a quiet area just 2 blocks from town. Complimentary use of a nearby health club is available to guests.

The Inn at Saratoga *20645 Fourth St., Saratoga, (800) 543-5020, (408) 867-5020, fax (408) 741-0981; www.innatsaratoga.com. 5 stories; 46 rooms; $$$+. Children under 18 free. Afternoon snack, continental breakfast.*

Combining an old-time Victorian feeling with modern luxurious amenities and a contemporary decor, this hotel is set in a quiet canyon behind busy Highway 9. Its rooms all face a forest of old eucalyptus through which winds gurgling Saratoga Creek. Afternoon wine and appetizers are served inside in the cozy lobby and outdoors on a sylvan patio. Families will appreciate that Wildwood Park, with its ample playground, is just across the creek.

La Hacienda Inn *18840 Saratoga-Los Gatos Rd., Los Gatos, (800) 235-4570, (408) 354-9230, fax (408) 354-7590; www.LaHaciendaInn.com. 20 rooms; $$-$$$. Children under 6 free. Some kitchens & wood-burning & gas fireplaces. Heated pool (seasonally heated), indoor hot tub, fitness center. Continental breakfast; restaurant, room service.*

Tucked away from the main highway at the base of the Santa Cruz Mountains, this pleasant inn was founded in 1901 by a former representative of the China-Japan Trading Company, who designed it to incorporate a Japanese style and landscaping. Now this newer inn, built in 1961, has cozy rooms with 12-foot-tall redwood-beamed ceilings and pine and oak furnishings. The 4-acre site features a lushly landscaped garden with colorful flower beds and an expansive lawn area, and the adjacent **La Hacienda Inn Restaurant** offers fine dining.

Los Gatos Lodge *50 Saratoga Ave., Los Gatos, (800) 231-8676, (408) 354-3300, fax (408) 354-5451; www.losgatoslodge.com. 123 rooms; $$-$$$. Children under 12 free. Some kitchens & fireplaces. Heated pool, hot tub. Restaurant, room service. Dogs welcome.*

Located on attractive, spacious grounds, this contemporary motel provides a putting green and shuffleboard area.

Sanborn Park Hostel *15808 Sanborn Rd., Saratoga, (408) 741-0166. 39 beds; private rooms.*

This rustic arts and crafts-style building dates from 1908. It is constructed of logs and located in a secluded redwood grove in the area's foothills. The naturally fragrant, quiet spot has plenty of hiking trails plus a volleyball court and barbecue facilities. See also page 417.

Just down the road in Sanborn-Skyline County Park are campsites, picnic tables, and the **Youth Science Institute**.

WHERE TO EAT

Andale Mexican Restaurant *6 N. Santa Cruz Ave., (408) 395-4244; also at 21 N. Santa Cruz Ave., (408) 395-8997.*

For description, see page 167.

The Chart House *115 N. Santa Cruz Ave., Los Gatos, (408) 354-1737, fax (408) 395-4553; www.chart-house.com. D daily; $$-$$$. Highchairs, boosters, child portions. Reservations advised.*

Located inside a stately old Victorian mansion, this restaurant features an a la carte menu of prime rib, steaks, and fresh seafood. Salads include housemade dressing, and both hot sourdough and squaw breads are available.

The Good Earth *206 N. Santa Cruz Ave., Los Gatos, (408) 395-6868. B,L,&D daily; $-$$. Highchairs, boosters, booths, child menu. No reservations.*

A good spot for a quick, light meal or snack, this restaurant's menu offers whole grain breads, fish and chicken specialties, and a large selection of vegetarian items. Housemade soups, sandwiches, salads, hot entrees, omelettes, and fruit and yogurt shakes are also available. An extensive children's menu includes pancakes, noodles, a peanut butter & jelly sandwich, and several burgers.

Pedro's Cabo Grill *316 N. Santa Cruz Ave., Los Gatos, (408) 354-7570, fax (408) 395-8578. L&D daily; $$. Highchairs, boosters, booths, child portions. Reservations advised.*

This popular spot features an authentic Mexican decor, including an adobe-style interior courtyard, and serves huge portions of delicious Mexican dishes. Especially tasty menu items include chimichangas (deep-fried flour tortillas filled with spicy shredded beef and topped with guacamole and sour cream) and quesadillas (large flour tortillas filled with Jack cheese and topped with guacamole and sour cream). If there is a wait, a cozy bar and pleasant glassed-in patio invite sipping margaritas and munching tortilla chips and salsa.

San Lorenzo Valley

A LITTLE BACKGROUND

Tucked into a dense redwood forest, this area has simple motels and cabins that are mostly relics left from a long ago heyday. Still, the abundance of tall trees, trails, and swimming holes, as well as reasonable prices, make the area a choice destination for bargain-hunting vacationers.

Traveling is best done in daylight. Though the back roads are lightly traveled, they are also curvy and slow. And, of course, the forest scenery is part of the reason for coming here.

VISITOR INFORMATION

San Lorenzo Valley Chamber of Commerce *P.O. Box 67, Felton 95018, (831) 335-2764; www.slv.net.*

GETTING THERE

Located approximately 70 miles south of San Francisco. Take Highway 280 to Highway 84 to Highway 35 to Highway 9.

WHAT TO DO

Ben Lomond Park *9525 Mill St., Ben Lomond, (831) 454-7956, fax (831) 462-8330. Daily sunrise-sunset. $1.*

This dammed-up deep-water swimming hole has a sandy beach, a playground, and shaded picnic tables with barbecue facilities. In summer, equipment rentals are available, and lifeguards are on duty.

Big Basin Redwoods State Park *21600 Big Basin Way, Boulder Creek, (831) 338-8860, fax (831) 338-8863. Daily 7am-10pm. $6/vehicle.*

California's first and oldest state park, Big Basin has over 80 miles of hiking and equestrian trails through its 20,000 acres of redwood forest. The easy .6-mile self-guiding Redwood Trail leads to interesting redwoods such as the Animal Tree and the Chimney Tree. Other hikes include the 10.3-mile trail leading to 70-foot-high Berry Creek Falls, and the especially popular Skyline to the Sea trail. A Nature Lodge features exhibits, and campfire programs are often scheduled. Campsites and 36 inexpensive tent cabins can be reserved (an optional package includes food and bedding); hike-in campsites are also available.

Felton Covered Bridge Park *Off Graham Hill Rd./Mt. Hermon Rd., Felton, (831) 454-7956, fax (831) 462-8330. Daily sunrise-sunset. Free.*

Built over the San Lorenzo River in 1892, this redwood bridge has been restored to its original condition and can be walked on. A State Historical Landmark, it measures 34 feet high and is the tallest bridge of its kind in the U.S. Facilities include picnic tables, barbecues, and a playground.

Hallcrest Vineyards *379 Felton Empire Rd., Felton, (831) 335-4441. Tasting & tours daily 11-5:30.*

Situated atop a scenic hill, this winery boasts good views of both its half century-old vineyard and of Henry Cowell Redwoods State Park. All wines here are made from organically grown grapes, and their Organic Wine Works division is the only federally licensed organic wine processor in the United States (no sulfites are used, and they are approved for vegans). The Estate White Riesling, for which the winery is noted, and the non-alcoholic premium varietal grape juice, which children can also sample, are of particular interest. A picnic area features an expansive lawn and tables shaded by oak trees; some provisions are available for purchase during summer.

Henry Cowell Redwoods State Park *101 N. Big Tree Park Rd., off Hwy. 9, Felton, (831) 335-4598. Daily sunrise-sunset. $5/vehicle.*

A number of trails lead through this park's redwood groves, including the easy, mile-long Redwood Circle Trail that visits the hollow General Fremont Tree within which it is said the general once camped. Trail guides can be secured at the Nature Center. Campsites are available.

Highlands County Park *8500 Hwy. 9, Ben Lomond, (831) 454-7956. Daily 7am-sunset. $2/vehicle in summer; free rest of year. Pool: M-F 2-4, Sat & Sun 1:15-5:30; summer only. $1, under 3 free.*

The grounds of this old estate have been transformed into a park with pool, playground, two softball diamonds, three tennis courts, a volleyball court, and picnic tables. Nature trails lead to a sandy river beach.

Roaring Camp & Big Trees Narrow-Gauge Railroad *Graham Hill Rd., Felton, (831) 335-4484, fax (831) 335-3509; www.roaringcamp.com. Call for schedule. Adults $14, 3-12 $9.50.*

This 6-mile, hour-long steam train ride winds through virgin redwoods and crosses over a spectacular trestle. About the time passengers start feeling a little restless, the train makes a short stretch stop at Cathedral Grove—an impressive circle of tall, 800-year-old redwood trees said to have a 3,000-year-old root system! Another stop is made at Bear Mountain, where riders may disembark for a picnic or hike and then return on a later train. Remember to bring warm wraps. Though this area enjoys warm to hot weather in the summer, it can get chilly on the train ride.

Another train, the **Big Trees & Pacific Railway** *(Adults $15, 3-12 $11)*, makes two trips each day between Roaring Camp and the Santa Cruz Beach Boardwalk. The round-trip excursion takes 2 1/2 hours.

An outdoor **chuck wagon barbecue** *(Sat & Sun 12-3; May-Oct.)* operates near the depot, and the **Red Caboose Saloon** dispenses short-order items. Be sure to save some tidbits for hungry ducks and geese in the lake.

Many special events are scheduled each year, including the **Civil War Encampment and Battles** in May and a chocolate **Easter egg hunt** for kids during spring vacation.

WHERE TO STAY

Fern River Resort Motel *5250 Hwy. 9, Felton, (831) 335-4412, fax (831) 335-2418. 13 cabins; 100% non-smoking; $. Children under 3 free. Most kitchens; some gas fireplaces.*

These modern cabins are located on the river across from Henry Cowell Redwoods State Park. The 5-acre lot features a redwood-shaded outdoor recreation area with volleyball, tetherball, and Ping-Pong, and guests have use of a private beach on the river.

Jaye's Timberlane Resort *8705 Hwy. 9, Ben Lomond, (831) 336-5479. 10 cabins; $-$$; 2-night min. in summer. All kitchens; some fireplaces. Solar-heated pool (unavail. Oct-Apr).*

These renovated cabins are scattered on spacious grounds shaded by redwoods.

Merrybrook Lodge *13420 Big Basin Way, Boulder Creek, (831) 338-6813. 8 rooms; $; 2-night min. on weekends. Some kitchens & wood-burning fireplaces & stoves. Dogs sometimes welcome (fee).*

Tucked among towering redwoods, some of these units overlook Boulder Creek.

WHERE TO EAT

Scopazzi's Restaurant *13300 Big Basin Way, Boulder Creek, (831) 338-4444. L&D Tu-Sun; $$. Highchairs, boosters, child menu. Reservations advised.*

This spacious, rustic mountain lodge has operated as a restaurant since 1902. Known for Italian meals, its menu offers cannelloni, veal scaloppine, and chicken cacciatora along with fried prawns, pepper steak flambé, and quail en cocotte. Children should be pleased to see the options of a hamburger, a grilled cheese sandwich, pizza, and spaghetti.

Tyrolean Inn & Cottages *9600 Hwy. 9, Ben Lomond, (831) 336-5188, fax (831) 336-2804. L&D W-Sun, SunBr; $$. Highchairs, boosters. Reservations advised.*

Appearing as something right out of Germany's Black Forest, this family-operated restaurant prepares exquisite Austrian-German cuisine. An interesting assortment of imported beers is available, including a refreshing Weiss Bier cloudy with yeast and served in a tall glass over a wedge of lemon. Entrees include sauerbraten and schnitzels, and among the desserts are a housemade fresh apple strudel and Black Forest cake. With 24 hours notice the kitchen will prepare any venison, hare, or duck specialty dish desired. In good weather, lunch is available on a patio sheltered by mature redwoods. Dinner is served in a romantic, cozy dining room heated by two fireplaces.

Vintage **cottages** *(7 units; $; 2-night min. on summer weekends. Some kitchens; 1 gas fireplace.)* sporting warmly patinaed redwood paneling are also available.

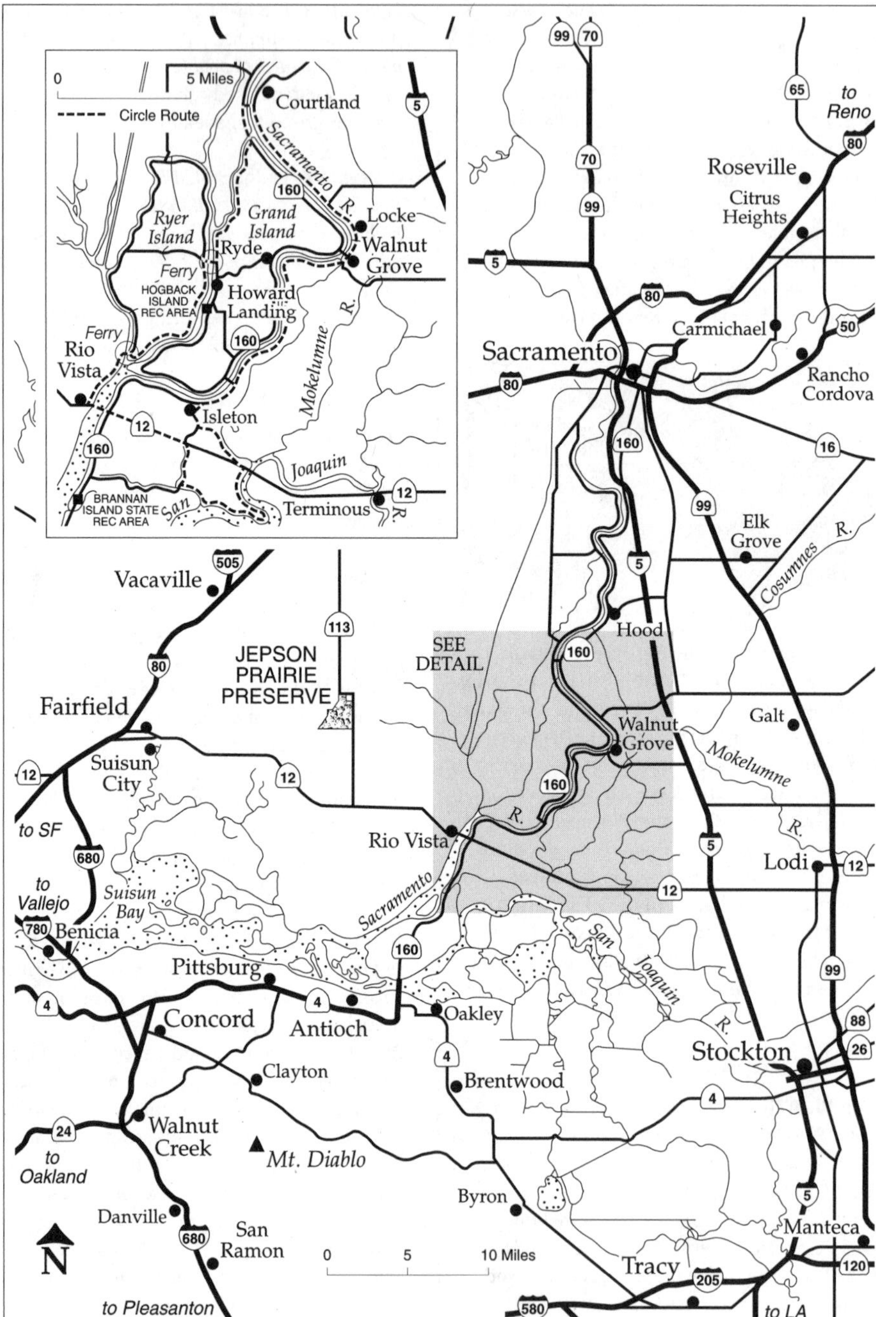
0
5 Miles
Circle Route
Courtland
Sacramento R.
Ryer Island
Grand Island
Locke
Ryde
Walnut Grove
Ferry
HOGBACK ISLAND REC AREA
Howard Landing
Mokelumne R.
Ferry
Rio Vista
Isleton
Joaquin
Terminous
BRANNAN ISLAND STATE REC AREA
San
R.
to Reno
Roseville
Citrus Heights
Carmichael
Sacramento
Rancho Cordova
Elk Grove
Cosumnes R.
Hood
Vacaville
JEPSON PRAIRIE PRESERVE
SEE DETAIL
Fairfield
Suisun City
Walnut Grove
Galt
Mokelumne R.
to SF
Rio Vista
Lodi
to Vallejo
Suisun Bay
Sacramento
Benicia
San Joaquin R.
Pittsburg
Concord
Antioch
Oakley
Stockton
Clayton
Brentwood
Walnut Creek
Mt. Diablo
to Oakland
Byron
Danville
San Ramon
0
5
10 Miles
Manteca
N
Tracy
to Pleasanton
to LA
MAP 14

The Delta

A LITTLE BACKGROUND

Composed of flat land, crisscrossed by more than 700 miles of rivers and sloughs (pronounced "slews"), this area is filled with scenic roads running along raised levees. Bridges abound (there are at least 70), and many raise to accommodate large boats. Popular for a houseboat vacation (see page 414), this area is also pleasant for just a day trip. Pack a good detailed map, as the roads here are maze-like, and try to avoid driving at night, when the levee roads can be dangerous.

Trendy hasn't yet hit this area and probably never will. Food is basic, and wine is sometimes mistreated. However, people in the area enjoy a good time, and many eating establishments book live entertainment in the evening.

VISITOR INFORMATION

California Delta Chambers & Visitor's Bureau *P.O. Box 6, Isleton 95641, (707) 374-5007, fax (707) 374-6134; www.californiadelta.org.*

Hal Schell's Delta Map and Guide *P.O. Box 9140, Stockton 95208, (209) 951-7821.*

This indispensable aid is available in many Delta stores for $2.75. To secure one in advance, send $3.75 to the above address.

GETTING THERE

Located approximately 60 miles east of San Francisco. Take Highway 80 north to Highway 4 east. Continue following Highway 4 as it turns into Highway 160 (River Road) and crosses the gigantic arch that is the John A. Nejedly Bridge. Highway 160 continues north into Sacramento.

ANNUAL EVENTS

Pear Fair *July. In Courtland; (707) 374-5007.*

The Delta is the foremost pear-growing area in the country. This annual celebration of the harvest features a parade, kiddie rides, and, of course, plenty of pear foods. Contests include pear bobbing, pear pie-eating, and pear peeling—in which the longest continuous peel after ten minutes wins. A competition to find the area's largest pear is also part of the fun.

The following towns are listed in the order in which they appear on the circle tour highlighted with broken lines on the map on page 344. It is possible to start the tour at any point. Following it takes drivers through the area's most scenic towns, across several different types of bridges, and on two car ferries.

Isleton

A LITTLE BACKGROUND

Located at the geographic center of the Delta, this picturesque, isolated town is one of the larger in the area. Once a bustling port city with a population of more than 2,000, it is now home to only 840 people.

VISITOR INFORMATION

Isleton Chamber of Commerce *308 Second St., (916) 777-5880, fax (916) 777-4330; www.isletoncoc.org.*

ANNUAL EVENTS

Chinese New Year Festival *March. (916) 777-5880.*

The town celebrates its Asian heritage with the Great March of China, lion dancers, an Asian gift bazaar, ancient cultural rites, Asian foods, and the Invitational Rickshaw Races.

Great Isleton Crawdad Festival *June; Father's Day weekend. (916) 777-5880. Free.*

Benefiting this small town's Children's Fund, this festival features live music and entertainment, activities such as a Crawdad Race and a Crawdad Petting Zoo, and plenty of cooked crawdads for eating.

WHERE TO EAT

Hotel Del Rio *209 2nd St., (916) 777-6033. B,L,&D daily; $-$$. Child portions. Reservations advised.*

The specialty of the house here is prime rib in three sizes: petite, regular, and double. Broasted chicken and deep-fried prawns round out the menu, and big plates of Cajun-style crawdads are sometimes available. All entrees include visits to the salad bar. Live music is scheduled in the bar on Saturday and Sunday nights. Inexpensive **rooms**, furnished attractively with antiques, are available upstairs.

Walnut Grove

A LITTLE BACKGROUND

This town, which grew up on both sides of the river, is linked by the first cantilever bridge built west of the Mississippi. Most of the decaying east side of town, which holds the remnants of a Chinatown, is on the National Register of Historic Places. The west side is a well-maintained residential area.

VISITOR INFORMATION

Walnut Grove Area Chamber of Commerce *14133 Market St., (916) 776-1442.*

WHERE TO EAT

Giusti's *On Walnut Grove Rd., 4 mi. west of town, (916) 776-1808. In summer: L&D Tu-Sun, SunBr; call for off-season schedule; $$. Highchairs, boosters, child menu. No reservations. No cards.*

In a rustic landmark building standing at the junction of the North Fork of the Mokelumne River and Snodgrass Slough, this restaurant has been dishing up family-style Italian dinners since 1896. For lunch, burgers, pastas, and steaks are available. The dining room overlooks the river, and the ceiling is covered with more than 1,250 baseball caps.

Locke

A LITTLE BACKGROUND

Said to be the only town in the country that was built entirely by and for Chinese immigrants, this tiny town dates back to 1915. Its narrow Main Street is lined with picturesque weathered wooden buildings, many of which are still inhabited. Aging Chinese residents are often seen sitting on benches on the wooden walkways, just watching. When leaving here, continue the circle tour as indicated or backtrack to Walnut Grove, cross the river, and continue south to Ryde.

WHAT TO DO

Dai Loy Museum *On Main St., (916) 776-1684. Thur-Sun 11-4:15. Adults $1, children 50¢-75¢.*

Located within what was the town gambling hall from 1916 to 1951, this museum fills visitors in on the town's history as a Chinese outpost. The Central Gaming Hall, with its original furniture and gaming tables, and the low-ceilinged dealers' bedrooms located upstairs can be viewed, and interesting era photographs hang on the walls throughout.

WHERE TO EAT

Al the Wop's Restaurant *On Main St., (916) 776-1800. L&D daily; $. Highchairs, boosters. No reservations. No cards.*

Once a speakeasy, this restaurant's unsavory looks might cause many people to pass it by. But once through the bar, which can be rowdy even at lunchtime, diners enter a windowless back room and can seat themselves at simple Formica picnic tables with benches. In addition to a steak sandwich served with a side of tasty grilled garlic bread, which used to be the only thing on the menu, hamburgers and chicken sandwiches are now available. Jars of peanut butter and jam adorn each table and are meant to be used with the steak. Parents can sometimes strike a deal with a waitress to bring extra bread so their kids can make peanut butter & jelly sandwiches. At dinner, when the place gets more crowded, the steak goes up a bit in price and is served with side dishes of fries, pasta, French bread, and grilled mushrooms. Chicken and pasta plates are also available. When leaving, stop by the bar to find out how dollar bills get stuck to the 2-story-high ceiling. It only costs $1 to find out. Stuck without a buck? A convenient ATM machine is on the premises.

Ryde

WHAT TO DO

Car Ferries. *Free.*

Catch the old-time diesel-powered, cable-guided **Howard's Landing Ferry**, also known as the *J-Mack*, off Grand Island Road. It holds about six cars, and waits are usually short. (Note that it closes down for lunch from 12 to 12:30.) Once on Ryer Island, take Ryer Road south to the **Ryer Island Ferry**, also known as *The Real McCoy*. After crossing, follow the road into Rio Vista.

Hogback Island Recreation Area *On Grand Island Rd. $3/vehicle.*

A grassy picnic area is bounded on one side by Steamboat Slough and on the other by a boat-launching lagoon. This isn't a good swimming area, but there are access spots that are fine for getting feet wet.

The Real McCoy

WHERE TO EAT

Grand Island Mansion *13415 Grand Island Rd., Walnut Grove, (916) 775-1705; www.grandislandmansion.com. SunBr; $$. Boosters, child portions. Reservations required.*

Across the island, this spot is open only on Sunday for an opulent brunch.

Ryde Hotel *14340 Hwy. 160, 3 mi. south of Walnut Grove, (888) 717-RYDE, (916) 776-1318, fax (916) 776-1195; www.rydehotel.com. L Sat, D F & Sat, SunBr; $$. Highchairs, boosters, child portions. Reservations advised.*

Built in 1926 and once owned by actor Lon Chaney, this colorful pink stucco art deco hotel operated a basement speakeasy during Prohibition. It is claimed that Herbert Hoover, who was a Prohibitionist, announced his presidential candidacy in 1928 in this very hotel while standing, ironically, above a large stash of bootleg booze. Now beautifully restored, the hotel once again serves elegant dinners in its dining room. Live music accompanies Saturday night dinner. **Guest rooms** *(4 stories, 32 rooms; $-$$$.)* are also available.

Rio Vista

VISITOR INFORMATION

Rio Vista Chamber of Commerce *75 Main St., (707) 374-2700, fax (707) 374-2424; www.riovista.org.*

WHAT TO DO

Brannan Island State Recreation Area *17645 Hwy. 160, 3 mi. south of town, (916) 777-6671. Open daily, 24-hrs. $12-$16/vehicle.*

Located on a knoll, this 350-acre park offers slough-side picnic and swimming areas. Campsites are available.

Victorian Homes *On Second St.*

Second Street is also known as Millionaires' Row.

WHERE TO EAT

Foster's Big Horn *143 Main St., (707) 374-2511. L&D Tu-Sun; $-$$. Highchairs, boosters, booths, child menu. Reservations accepted.*

Opened in 1931, this restaurant features walls lined with more than 300 mounted big game heads—including a full-grown elephant that is the largest mammal trophy in any collection in the world, the largest mounted moose head in the world, and a rare giraffe head. Gathered by the late hunter William Foster, who shot most of the wild animals himself, it is the world's largest collection of big game trophies. An attractive bar area in front leads to an open dining room with high ceilings and comfortable booths. Sandwiches and hamburgers are on the lunch menu, and steak and seafood on the dinner menu.

The Point Restaurant *120 Marina Dr., in Delta Marina, (707) 374-5400. L&D Tu-Sun, SunBr; $$. Highchairs, boosters, booths, child menu.*

Overlooking the Sacramento River at its widest point, this comfortable, well-maintained restaurant has many roomy booths. The lunch menu features housemade soups and sandwiches. At dinner, entrees include prime rib, scampi, and chicken Dijon. Photos illustrating Humphrey the Whale's well-publicized visit to the area are displayed in the entryway.

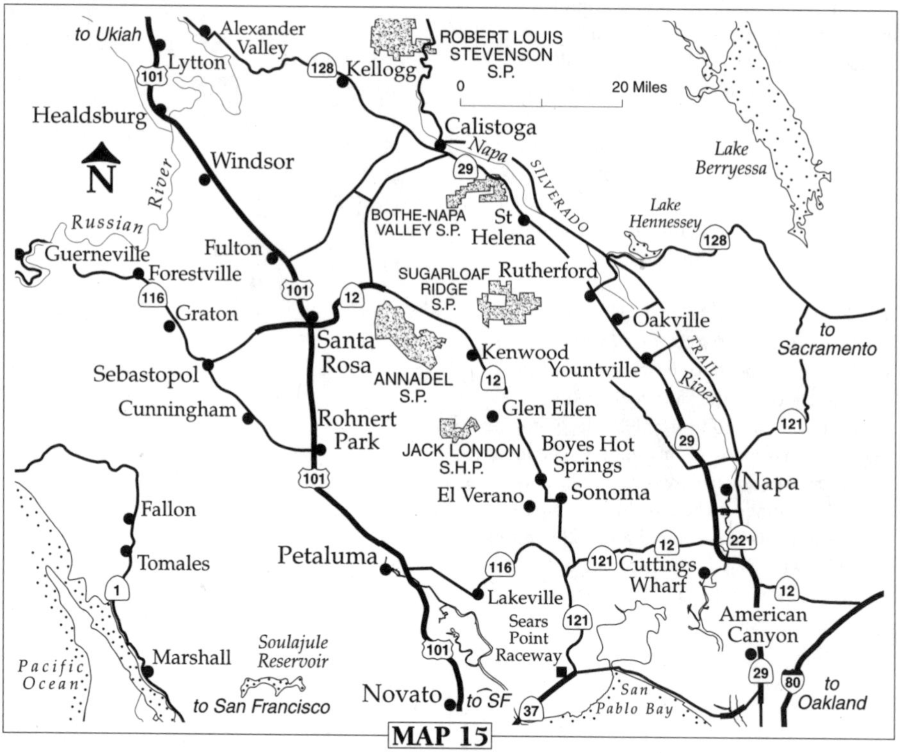
to Ukiah
Alexander Valley
Lytton
101
128
Kellogg
ROBERT LOUIS STEVENSON S.P.
0
20 Miles
Healdsburg
Calistoga
Napa
N
Windsor
29
SILVERADO
Lake Berryessa
River
Russian
BOTHE-NAPA VALLEY S.P.
St Helena
Lake Hennessey
128
Guerneville
Fulton
Forestville
SUGARLOAF RIDGE S.P.
Rutherford
116
101
12
Graton
Oakville
to Sacramento
Santa Rosa
Kenwood
TRAIL
Sebastopol
ANNADEL S.P.
12
Yountville
River
Cunningham
Glen Ellen
Rohnert Park
121
JACK LONDON S.H.P.
Boyes Hot Springs
29
101
El Verano
Sonoma
Napa
Fallon
12
221
Tomales
Petaluma
116
121
Cuttings Wharf
1
Lakeville
12
Sears Point Raceway
121
American Canyon
Soulajule Reservoir
Marshall
101
Pacific Ocean
29
80
to Oakland
to San Francisco
Novato
to SF
37
San Pablo Bay
MAP 15

A LITTLE BACKGROUND

California's first wineries were appendages of the 21 Franciscan missions that were built a day's ride (by horseback) from each other in a chain reaching from San Diego to Sonoma. The wine was produced by the missions for sacramental use. Eventually the church gave up making wine, and the art passed into the realm of private enterprise.

Presently Sonoma County and Napa County are literally erupting with new small family wineries. Wine-making has become a hobby with many city folks who have bought themselves modest vineyard retreats.

The most popular route for wine tasting is in the Napa Valley along Highway 29 between Oakville and Calistoga. Not far behind is scenic Highway 12 in the Sonoma Valley. When visiting these stretches of highway, which are heavily concentrated with wineries, try to remain selective in tasting. Experts suggest not planning to taste at more than four wineries in one day.

Though a visit to the Wine Country is enjoyable at any time of year, fall just might be the most beautiful season. This is when the grapevine leaves turn brilliant hues of gold and red, and "the crush" is in full swing. Workers are seen in the fields, and gondolas, laden with grapes, move slowly down the highway delivering their bounty to the wineries. But because everyone is working to beat the clock, winery staff are less available to give visitors quality time. However, the crowds, like the hot temperatures, have subsided, making it the perfect time of year for sampling some wine, doing a little feasting, and relaxing among this area's beauty.

Young children can be difficult on a winery tour. Out of courtesy to the other tour participants (a noisy child interferes with the guide's presentation), parents might consider having a member of their party stay with the children while the others go on a tour. Most wineries don't require taking a tour before tasting. Or visit a winery with a self-guided tour. It's a nice idea to bring along some plastic wine glasses and a bottle of grape juice so children can "taste," too.

Many wineries have picnic areas. An ideal itinerary is to tour a winery, taste, and then purchase a bottle of wine to drink with a picnic lunch.

A wrinkle in the pleasure of wine tasting is that many wineries now charge for tasting. Sometimes the charge permits tasters to keep their glass as a souvenir, and sometimes the charge is applied to a wine purchase. Tasting fees tend to be imposed by smaller wineries with more expensive vintages, and their purpose seems to be to keep the less serious tasters away.

Some tasting rooms will provide vertical tastings, which portray the aging process of a varietal, and cross tastings, which show the different results that varied treatment of the same grapes can cause. To arrange a special tasting, call ahead.

ANNUAL EVENTS

Carols in the Caves *December. (707) 224-4222. $30.*

In spectacular settings, David Auerbach performs selections using rare and unusual instruments he has collected from around the world: the panpipes of South America, the Celtic harp of Ireland, the steel drums of Trinidad. Instruments and winery sites change each year. Mr. Auerbach also performs in winery caves during the summer and fall; call for current schedule.

WHAT TO DO

California Wine Tours *22455 Broadway, Sonoma, (800) 294-6386, (707) 939-7225, fax (707) 939-7240; www.californiawinetours.com; 5-hr. tour $49/person.*

Customized winery tours to any region of the wine country can be arranged. Riders just sit back and relax in a stretch limo, sipping something cool from the complimentary beverage bar while leaving the driving to a classy tuxedoed professional. Printed itineraries are provided. Round-trip ferry rides from Pier 39 in San Francisco can be included for an additional fee.

Sonoma

VISITOR INFORMATION

Sonoma Valley Visitors Bureau *453 First St. East, (707) 996-1090, fax (707) 996-9212; www.sonomavalley.com.*

GETTING THERE

Located approximately 45 miles north of San Francisco. Take Highway 101 to Highway 37 to Highway 121 to Highway 12.

ANNUAL EVENTS

Valley of the Moon Vintage Festival *September. (707) 996-2109. Free.*

Begun in 1887 as a celebration of the harvest, this old-time event kicks off in the historic Barracks each year with an evening tasting of elite Sonoma Valley wines. Free daytime events include a Blessing of the Grapes, several parades, and a re-enactment of the Bear Flag Revolt. (During the revolt American soldiers seized the town from General Vallejo, taking down the Mexican flag and raising the bear flag—which later became California's state flag.) Messy grape stomping competitions, in which one person stomps and the other holds a bottle under the spicket, are also part of the fun.

WHAT TO DO

Depot Park Museum *270 First St. West, (707) 938-1762. W-Sun 1-4:30. Free.*

Operated by volunteers from the Sonoma Historical Society, this tiny museum is housed in the restored Northwestern Pacific Railroad Depot and features changing historical and railroad exhibits. Adjacent Depot Park has a playground and picnic area. A bicycle path following the old railroad tracks here originates at Sebastiani Winery.

Ramekins *450 W. Spain St., (707) 933-0452, fax (707) 933-0451; www.ramekins.com.*

Newly constructed in a semi-rural setting, this unusual building of solid, 2-foot-thick rammed-earth walls holds a delightful cooking school. The building features subtle, whimsical, food-related decorative touches, such as stair railings resembling asparagus stalks, and is furnished with rustic light pine pieces. Students dice and measure and stir while learning new techniques in a well-equipped teaching kitchen. Short classes are scheduled year-round in all styles of cooking, and eating the results with fellow students is a big part of the fun.

Five spacious, tastefully decorated **guest rooms** *($$-$$$+; 2-night min. on weekends. Continental breakfast.)* are available upstairs. Some have high four-poster beds. Bathrooms are particularly interesting. Some are equipped with an unusual raised stone sink placed so that its bottom is flush with the counter top, and some have contemporary-style open showers. Stainless steel soup ladles double as towel racks.

Sears Point Raceway *At intersection of Hwys. 37 & 121, (800) 870-RACE, (707) 938-8448, fax (707) 938-8430; www.searspoint.com. Closed Dec-Jan. Call for schedule & ticket prices; under 12 free.*

Facilities for car races here include a 2.52-mile course with 12 turns and a 1/4-mile drag strip. Concession stands dispense fast food, and an assortment of grassy hillsides provide perfect picnic perches.

Sonoma Plaza.

This town square, the largest in the state and a National Historic Landmark, was designed by General Vallejo in 1834 for troop maneuvers. Basically an old-fashioned park, it is great for picnics and has a playground and tiny duck pond. City Hall, which is located here, acted as the Tuscany County Courthouse on TV's *Falcon Crest.*

Sonoma State Historic Park *On the plaza, along Spain St., (707) 938-1519. Daily 10-5. Adults $3, 6-12 $2.*

This extensive park preserves structures dating from the early 1800s, when General Mariano Guadalupe Vallejo, founder of Sonoma, was Mexico's administrator of Northern California. The 2-story, whitewashed adobe **Barracks,** which once housed Vallejo's soldiers, now contains historical exhibits. Vallejo drilled his soldiers across the street in what is now the town square.

Next door and across the street from the Barracks is the re-created **Mission San Francisco Solano**. Founded in 1823 and the most northerly and last in the chain of California missions, this historic site has been through a lot. It was burned to the ground twice, was the victim of a Native American uprising, and was seriously damaged in the 1906 earthquake. Then it went through a period of being used as a saloon, a winery, and even a hennery. It now houses a museum and an 1840s parish church with a plain façade and air of rugged dignity. An adobe section of the mission's original quadrangle is located near the church. Currently it exhibits a permanent collection of watercolors depicting each of California's 21 missions. The paintings were done in 1903 by Chris Jorgensen, who traveled from mission to mission via horse and buggy. An impressive old prickly pear cactus forest graces the mission courtyard, and the chapel is said to host a ghost.

General Vallejo's Home *(At W. Third St./W. Spain St., (707) 938-9559. Self-guided tours daily; docent tours on F, Sat, & Sun at 2.),* a classic 2-story Victorian Gothic with its original furnishings, is located at the end of a long, tree-shaded lane 1/2 mile west of the plaza. Shaded picnic tables and another giant prickly pear cactus garden are found here.

Sonoma Traintown Railroad *20264 Broadway, (707) 938-3912; www.traintown.com. F-Sun 10-5; daily in summer. Train: adults $3.75, 55+ & 2-16 & $2.75. Other rides: $1.50.*

A miniature steam train (a diesel engine is used on weekdays) winds through10 acres during the 20-minute ride here. It passes through forests and tunnels and crosses both a 70-foot double truss bridge and a 50-foot steel girder bridge. During a 10-minute stop at a miniature 1800s mining town, where the train takes on water, riders detrain at a petting zoo inhabited by sheep, goats, ducks, and llamas. An antique merry-go-round, full-size Ferris wheel, airplane ride, snack bar, and picnic area are available at the station.

Toscano Hotel *20 E. Spain St., on the plaza, (707) 938-0510. Tours F-Sun 1-4. By donation.*

This beautifully restored mining-era hotel was built in 1858.

Vasquez House *129 E. Spain St., in El Paseo de Sonoma, (707) 938-0510. W-Sun 1:30-4:30.*

Built in 1856, this refurbished wood-frame house features a tearoom where visitors can relax over homemade pastries and a pot of tea.

Vintage Aircraft Co. *23982 Arnold Dr., at airport off Hwy. 121, 2 mi. north of Sears Point Raceway, (707) 938-2444. Rides: Sat & Sun, weekdays by appt. $89-$299. Reservations advised.*

A pilot here claims an aerobatic ride in an authentic 1940 Stearman biplane, once used to train World War II combat pilots, "tops any roller coaster ever built." Calmer scenic rides and glider rides are also available, and old and antique planes can be viewed at the airport.

WINERIES

Bartholomew Park Winery *1000 Vineyard Ln., (707) 935-9511, fax (707) 935-0549; www.bartholomewparkwinery.com. Tasting daily 10-4:30 (vertical tasting of library wines $10, by appt.); tours by request.*

Situated in the heart of peaceful 400-acre Bartholomew Memorial Park, this winery is a newcomer to the area. Though wine grapes were planted on the property in the early 1830s and the land was once owned by Agoston Haraszthy, known as the father of the Calfornia wine industy (and connected with the Vallejo family), the new winery has been in business just since 1994. The winery makes only 100 percent varietal wines and produces just 4,000 cases each year. Because production is so small, the flavorful premium wines are sold only at the winery. Just off the tasting room, a small but interesting museum chronicles the property's history and current grape-growing practices. It also holds a fascinating topographical map and photograpic displays of contemporary area winemakers and of images by Victorian photographer Eadweard Muybridge dating back to the early 1870s. Visitors can picnic in a spacious area with a vineyard view, and a 3-mile hiking trail leads through a fragrant old-growth conifer forest with the promise that on a clear day you can see forever—or at least to San Francisco. Monthly jazz concerts are scheduled, and during harvest visitors are invited to help punch down the grapes.

Buena Vista Winery *18000 Old Winery Rd., (800) 926-1266, (707) 938-1266, fax (707) 939-0916; www.buenavistawinery.com. Tasting daily 10:30-5; tour daily at 2, in summer also at 11.*

Founded in 1857, this is California's oldest winery. Visitors park among the grapevines and take a short, pleasant walk in. After tasting wines in the welcoming old Press House (don't miss the nutty cream sherry, available only at the winery), select a bottle for a picnic outside at one of the tables shaded by stately old eucalyptus trees growing on the banks of a tiny brook. If kids are along, purchase a chilled bottle of Gewurztraminer grape juice for them. A variety of picnic supplies are also available in the winery's shop.

Cline Cellars *24737 Arnold Dr. (Hwy. 121), 2 mi. south of town, (707) 935-4310. Tasting & tours daily 10-6.*

Situated on the original site of Mission San Francisco de Solano, this winery is known for its Rhone-style wines. Grapes for the wines are grown on the family ranch in Oakley. Six thermal pools filled by underground mineral springs dot the property. Once warm, they have been cool since the last big earthquake, and some are now populated with fish and turtles. A picnic area bounded by rose bushes and three of the ponds is located behind the farmhouse tasting room.

Gloria Ferrer Champagne Caves *23555 Hwy. 121, (707) 996-7256, fax (707) 996-0720. Tasting daily 10:30-5:30 (fee $2.75-$5/glass); tours 11-4, on the hour.*

Located back from the highway, atop a hill in a Catalan hacienda-style building, this tasting room provides views across the vineyards. In warm weather, tasters can relax on a patio; in cooler weather, they can gaze at the view from inside, warmed by a large fireplace. The winery is part of Spain's Freixenet family, which has been making wine since the 12th century. The tour visits the man-made caves and provides insight into the making of sparkling wine.

Gundlach-Bundschu Winery *2000 Denmark St. (another entrance is on Thornsberry Rd.), (707) 938-5277, fax (707) 938-9460; www.gunbun.com. Tasting daily 11-4:30; self-guided tour.*

Located in the back country, off a winding road about 3 miles from the plaza, this pioneer winery was established in 1858. Now the great-great grandson of German founder Jacob Gundlach's partner continues the tradition. Jim Bundschu, who has been referred to as the "clown prince of wines," and his merry winemakers produce wines they like to drink themselves—wines with intense varietal character. White wines here are dry and flavorful, reds dark and complex. Unique to the winery, the Kleinberger varietal, which is a kind of Riesling, is produced by vines brought over in 1860 and is sold only at the winery. Picnic tables are perched on a small hill overlooking a pond and the vineyards. When leaving, be sure

"If you can't say 'Gundlach-Bundschu Gewurztraminer,' you shouldn't be driving!"

to take the alternate road out. Each route provides different scenery.

Ravenswood *18701 Gehricke Rd., (800) NO-WIMPY, (707) 938-1960, fax (707) 938-9459. Tasting daily 10-4:30; tours by appt.*

A prime producer of Zinfandel, this winery sells fresh barbecue on summer weekends. A picnic area overlooks the vineyards.

Sebastiani Vineyards *389 Fourth St. East, (800) 888-5532, (707) 938-5532. Tasting daily 10-5; tours daily 10:30-4.*

This winery has been owned continuously by the same family since 1904—longer than any other in the country. It is home to Northern California's first vineyard, planted in 1825 by Franciscan padres and purchased from them by Sebastiani in 1904. The winery is best known for its Symphony and Pinot Noir Blanc, which are available only at the winery. While here, take time to view the world's largest collection of carved oak wine casks, and, across the street, a display featuring an extensive collection of Native American mortars and pestles. A pleasant picnic area is also available.

Viansa Winery *25200 Arnold Dr. (Hwy. 121), 5 mi. south of town, (800) 995-4740, (707) 935-4700, fax (707) 996-4632. Tasting & self-guided tours daily 10-5.*

Built on top of a hill commanding magnificent views of the area, this winery opened in 1990. Owned by Sam Sebastiani and his wife Vicki (and named by merging the first two letters of each of their first names), this beautifully crafted Tuscan-style winery building was inspired by a monastery near Farneta, Italy. Noteworthy wines include the Barbera Blanc, a light blush wine perfect for picnics and sold only at the winery, and the Cabernet Sauvignons. They can be tasted in the state-of-the-art tasting room that features a magnificent "wall of wines" behind the two tasting bars. Wines are available for purchase only at the winery and by mail order.

The **Italian Marketplace** food hall is designed after the mercato in Lucca, Italy, and the extraordinary food offerings *almost* overshadow the wines. Using Vicki's recipes, the kitchen staff prepares wonderful things for picnics: country pâté, torta rustica, hot-sweet mustard, focaccia bread, panini (Italian sandwiches), a triple-chocolate chunk cookie, tiramisu. More goodies include porcini mushroom tomato sauce (made with Viansa Cabernet Sauvignon) and spiced figs (made with Sonoma black mission figs and Viansa Cabernet Sauvignon using Vicki's grandmother's recipe). Some of the items make use of produce from the winery's adjacent vegetable garden. On nice days, picnics can be enjoyed at a bevy of tables located outside on a knoll with a panoramic view of the Sonoma and Napa valleys. On cooler days, tables are available inside. The winery welcomes children and provides them with a complimentary souvenir balloon.

January through March are the prime months to view birds here at the expansive **Viansa wetlands.** That is when the greatest numbers are in transit on their southward trek. Guided tours are given in the summer and fall *(Sat & Sun at 10:30 & 2).*

WHERE TO STAY

El Dorado Hotel *405 First St. West, on the plaza, (800) 289-3031, (707) 996-3030, fax (707) 996-3148; www.hoteleldorado.com. 26 rooms; 100% non-smoking; $$-$$$+. Heated pool. Continental breakfast; restaurant. Small dogs welcome.*

Built in 1843, this historic inn was gutted and remodeled with plenty of Mexican paver tiles and beveled glass. Each of the contemporary rooms contains a goose-down comforter to chase the chill and handmade furnishings, including iron four-poster beds and large mirrors softened by rustic twig frames. A complimentary split of wine greets guests upon arrival.

On the first floor of the hotel, appealing **Piatti** ristorante *((707) 996-2351. L&D daily; $$-$$$. Boosters, child portions. Reservations advised.)* has outside seating at heavy marble tables on a rustic tiled patio dominated by a majestic old fig tree. On cooler days, the large inside dining room is equally inviting. The menu of deliciously innovative Italian cuisine changes regularly and always has several daily specials and a risotto. A variety of unusual pizzas are baked in a wood-burning oven, and most of the pastas are made by hand in-house. Piatti oil—a delicious dipping sauce for bread made with virgin olive oil, balsamic vinegar, salt, pepper, garlic, red pepper flakes, and chopped parsley—is served gratis upon request. Both local and imported Italian wine varietals are available by the glass, and trendy tiramisu is always on the dessert menu.

MacArthur Place *29 E. MacArthur St., (800) 722-1866, (707) 938-2929, fax (707) 933-9833; www.macarthurplace.com. 35 rooms; $$-$$$+; 2-night min. on weekends Apr-Nov. Pool, hot tub, health spa. Continental breakfast; restaurant.*

Featuring a combination of restored Victorian buildings and newly constructed units, this historic estate has been transformed into a luxurious country inn. Rooms are sumptuously decorated with splendid fabrics and furniture, and bathrooms have oversize, open showers. Guests can stroll through 4 acres of manicured gardens, and get a relaxing treatment in the spa. Upon leaving the property, a sign indicates New York is 3,562 miles thataway and Sonoma Plaza is 4 blocks straight ahead. It's a no-brainer which way to go.

Saddles *((707) 933-3191. D daily, SunBr.)* is situated in a beautifully transformed 100-year-old barn said to be fashioned after Thomas Jefferson's barn in Monticello. It has saddles for chairs in the waiting area, and serves good grub, including delicious potato-skin cups filled with salsa, exquisite garlic bread, and really good salads. Entrees include an assortment of prime steaks, plus baby back ribs, roasted chicken, a vegetarian pasta of the day, and fresh fish. At "The Finish Line," as the dessert menu is called, don't miss the signature brownie mousse parfait wrapped in a cowboy kerchief.

Sonoma Hotel *110 W. Spain St., on the plaza, (800) 468-6016, (707) 996-2996, fax (707) 996-7014. 17 rooms; $-$$$+; 2-night min. on weekends in season. Unsuitable for children under 12. No TVs; some shared baths. Continental breakfast; restaurant.*

Dating from the 1870s, when it was the town theater, this hotel's rooms are furnished in carefully selected turn-of-the-century antiques and have private bathrooms with clawfoot tubs. The friendly resident ghost, a Chinese man named Fred who dresses in coolie-style clothing, is said to roam the third floor and has been seen late at night sweeping the sidewalk outside.

Sonoma Mission Inn & Spa *18140 Hwy. 12, Boyes Hot Springs, 3 mi. north of town, (800) 862-4945, (707) 938-9000, fax (707) 938-4250; www.sonomamissioninn.com. 228 rooms; 100% non-smoking; $$$+; 2-night min. on Sat. Children under 14 free. Some wood-burning fireplaces. 2 heated mineral pools, 2 mineral hot tubs, sauna, health spa, fitness center, 2 tennis courts (fee; night lights), 18-hole golf course. 2 restaurants, room service.*

Built in 1927 and surrounded by 10 acres of beautifully landscaped, fragrant grounds, this sedate luxury resort's pink adobe architecture is reminiscent of the town mission. Its immense lobby features beautifully tiled floors and massive ceiling beams and is outfitted with comfortable oversize furniture. The vintage rooms in the original building sport enormous closets and are cooled with both efficient old-fashioned ceiling fans and modern air-conditioning. The most requested room, located in the turret, is completely round and has a view of the pool and gardens. Newer, contemporary-style rooms and luxury suites are also available.

Though children are welcome, this is an adult-oriented resort: Children under 18 are not permitted in the well-equipped, full-service spa, but can use the hotel pool. People have been coming to this spot for the therapeutic 135-degree mineral waters long before the hotel was built, so it is fitting a fabulous spa should take form here. An entire day can be used to good advantage. Start by decompressing with the Bathing Ritual, soaking first in the 92-degree Tepiderium Roman Bath, then moving on to the 102-degree Caldarium hot pool, then cooling under 2-foot-wide Mega showerheads, and finally entering the herbal steam room and then the sauna. That ought to do it! An array of treatments are available, including the fabulous Wine Country Kur. Nicknamed the "scrub, tub, and rub," it consists of an exfoliation rub with local grape seed crush, a soak in a hot grape seed-enhanced bath, and then a massage with rich grape seed oil and lotion. Men might especially enjoy a Rejuvenating Facial designed just for them. An outdoor pool and several private outdoor hot tubs are also part of the spa.

Recently spiffed up, the gorgeous **Mission Grill** *(D daily; $$$.)* operates just off the lobby. The seasonal menu changes regularly but might include a tasty salad with spicy pecans and blue cheese as a starter, and perhaps a horseradish-crusted grouper or a black pepper and corainder-crusted rack of lamb. The spacious, casual dining room of the **Big 3 Diner** *(18140 Hwy. 12 (707) 938-9000. B,L,&D daily, Sat & SunBr; $-$$. Highchairs, boosters, booths, child menu. Reservations advised.)* offers seating at tables and in comfy booths. The restaurant is well-known for its extensive and delicious breakfast menu, which has everything from oatmeal with raisins and brown sugar to eggs Benedict. At lunch and dinner, the menu features eclectic American foods such as sandwiches, soups and salads, a delicious hamburger, and trendy pizzas. During the week before Christmas, **Breakfast with Santa** is scheduled each morning, when Santa visits each table with gifts for children. Make reservations by calling (707) 939-2410. Low-fat spa cuisine options are available in both restaurants.

WHERE TO EAT

The Coffee Garden *415-421 First St. West, on the plaza, (707) 996-6645. B,L,&D daily; $. Highchairs. No reservations.*

Located within the historic 1830s Captain Salvador Vallejo Adobe, this inviting cafe offers salads, sandwiches, and coffees. Order in front, then sit out back in the casual patio garden planted with a large variety of native flora.

The General's Daughter *400 W. Spain St., (707) 938-4004, fax (707) 938-4099. L M-Sat, D nightly, SunBr; $$. Highchairs, boosters, booths. Reservations advised.*

General Vallejo's third daughter, Natalia, built this Victorian in 1864 with her husband, Attilla Haraszthy, whose family grew grapes in the valley. Situated just 3 blocks from the plaza, the house has been beautifully renovated, and its warm-colored walls are adorned with striking farm-themed paintings by Rod Knutson. Diners have a choice of several seating spaces, plus a patio area in good weather. And the food lives up to the surroundings. Starters include crisp buttermilk-and-cornmeal-coated onion rings with lemon-pepper aioli, and a flavorful salad of Sonoma County mixed greens with roasted goat cheese, sun-dried tomatoes, and hazelnuts dressed lightly with a roasted garlic-balsamic vinaigrette. Main courses include light sandwiches—a particularly tasty curry lamb-Feta cheese on cracked wheat is served with a delicious potato salad—and a vegetarian mixed grill, as well as more substantial meat and fish items. Desserts are made on the premises by a full-time pastry chef. Ending a meal with a cigar on the west porch is an intriguing possibility.

Picnic Pick-Ups.

• **Cucina Viansa** *400 First Street East, on the plaza, (707) 935-5656, fax (707) 935-5651.*

This simple self-service deli is operated by Viansa Winery. Sandwiches, such as an eggplant on focaccia, and salads, including spinach-ricotta ravioli with sun-dried tomato sauce and a tube pasta with pesto, are among the items available for take-out or to eat on the premises. Desserts include a tasty and good-for-you housemade fig newton. Boxed lunches are available by advance order. Seating on high stools at a window counter overlooking the Sonoma Mission is particularly appealing. Free wine tasting is available with purchase; otherwise it's $1.

• **Sonoma Cheese Factory** *2 W. Spain St., on the plaza, (800) 535-2855, (707) 996-1931, fax (707) 996-1912. Daily 8:30-5:30.*

This crowded shop stocks hundreds of cheeses (including their famous varieties of Sonoma Jack made from old family recipes) plus cold cuts, salads, and marvelous marinated artichoke hearts. Sandwiches are made to order. A few tables are available inside, and more are outside on a shaded patio. The workings of the cheese factory can be observed through large windows in the back of the shop, and cheese samples are provided for tasting.

• **Sonoma French Bakery** *470 First St. East, on the plaza, (707) 996-2691. M 7am-1:30pm, Tu-F 7-5:30, Sat 7:30-6, Sun 7:30-4.*

This renowned bakery makes both sweet and sourdough French breads without yeast. They are so delicious people are willing to wait in a long line to purchase them. Flutes, rolls, croissants, gâteau Basque bread, French and Danish pastries, and cream puffs are just a few of the other delights available.

Glen Ellen and Kenwood

A LITTLE BACKGROUND

Like the curve of a scimitar blade, the Valley of the Moon stretched before them, dotted with farm houses and varied by pasture-lands, hay-fields, and vineyards. The air shimmered with heat and altogether it was a lazy, basking day. Quail whistled to their young from thicketed hill-side behind the house. Once, there was a warning chorus from the foraging hens and a wild rush for cover, as a hawk, high in the blue, cast its drifting shadow along the ground.

— Jack London, *Burning Daylight,* 1910

Jack London, a man with an eye for landscapes, didn't coin the name "Valley of the Moon." The valley stretching north from Sonoma was referred to as "Valle de la Luna" as early as 1841. But London, who lived on a ranch here when he wasn't on the road, popularized the term—and the place—in his novels.

Now, almost a hundred years later, there are still no high-rise buildings or shopping malls here. Instead visitors are treated to unimpeded views of tree-covered hills and vineyards that appear to stretch forever. It is the perfect antidote to the congestion of civilization and is where food guru M.F.K. Fisher spent her last 20 years, and where actress Sharon Stone is rumored to have a home.

GETTING THERE

Glen Ellen is located on Arnold Drive, 7 miles north of Sonoma via Highway 12. Kenwood is 3 miles farther north on Highway 12.

ANNUAL EVENTS

World Pillow Fighting Championship *July. In Kenwood; (707) 833-2440. $4, under 12 free.*

This very serious all-day competition takes place on a greased pipe positioned over a muddy morass into which losers, and sometimes winners, are buffeted.

WHAT TO DO

Jack London Bookstore *14300 Arnold Dr., Glen Ellen, (707) 996-2888, fax (707) 996-4107. W-M 10:30-5.*

To get in the mood for this trek, read a London classic such as *The Call of the Wild* or *Martin Eden*. Or stop in at this wee shop, which in addition to stocking rare and out-of-print books, especially those by Jack London, also has a good selection of mysteries. The proprietor can provide assistance in selecting a London title.

Jack London State Historic Park *2400 London Ranch Rd., Glen Ellen, (707) 938-5216. Daily 9:30-5, to 7 in summer; museum 10-5. $6/vehicle.*

Jack London, who wrote 191 short stories and 51 books, was once one of the highest paid authors in the country. This 830-acre park contains the ruins of his 26-room Wolf House (reached via a pleasant half-mile trail), his grave, and **The House of Happy Walls**—a museum built in his memory by his widow. Beauty Ranch includes the cottage he actually lived in as well as Pig Palace, a deluxe piggery designed by London. It all was donated to the state by London's nephew.

Guided horse rides, some with a picnic included, are available within the park. For information and reservations contact the **Sonoma Cattle Co.** *((707) 996-8566, fax (707) 938-8366. $45/2 hrs. Riders must be 8 or older.).*

Jack London Village *14301 Arnold Dr. , Glen Ellen.*

This bucolic, rustic, quiet, low-key complex has a creek-side location with an operating waterwheel and a few picnic tables, and it holds several nice gift shops purveying unusual merchandise, several restaurants, and **The Olive Press** *((707) 939-8900, fax (707) 939-8999; www.theolivepress.com; daily 10-5:30.),* where olives are custom-pressed, a process that can be viewed in fall. The product can be tasted and purchased year-round.

Morton's Warm Springs *1651 Warm Springs Rd., Kenwood, (707) 833-5511, fax (707) 833-1077. mid-June to mid-Sept only; call for schedule. Adults $3.50-$5, 2-11 $3-$4.*

Long ago these mineral springs were used by Native Americans to heal their sick. Nowadays they are used for recreational purposes. Two large pools and one toddler wading pool are filled each day with fresh mineral water averaging 86 to 88 degrees. Lifeguards are on duty. Facilities include picnic tables and barbecue pits shaded by large oak and bay trees, a snack bar, a large grassy area for sunbathing, a softball field, horseshoe pits, a basketball court, and two volleyball courts. A teenage rec room is equipped with a jukebox, Ping-Pong tables, and pinball machines, and dressing rooms and lockers are also available.

There are a few rules: no cutoffs in the pools; no glass allowed.

Sugarloaf Ridge State Park *2605 Adobe Canyon Rd., Kenwood, (707) 833-5712. Daily dawn-dusk. $5/vehicle.*

Here, 25 miles of wilderness trails, a horseback-riding concession, and campsites await.

WINERIES

Benziger Family Winery *1883 London Ranch Rd., Glen Ellen, (800) 989-8890, (707) 935-4046; www.benziger.com. Tasting daily 10-4:30; tram tours daily, call for schedule.*

Just up the hill from the little crook in the road that is Glen Ellen, this family-operated winery provides a free 30-minute tram tour through the vineyards and hands-on experience with vines, grapes, and trellising techniques. The tour is followed by tasting a wide selection of wines. A shorter, self-guided walking tour is also available. In addition, there is a gallery displaying original art from which various of their wine labels are designed, some caged peacocks, and extensive picnic facilities.

B.R. Cohn Winery *15140 Sonoma Hwy. 12, Glen Ellen, (707) 938-4064, fax (707) 938-4585. Tasting daily 10-4:30; no tours.*

Originally part of a Spanish land grant and a dairy during the '40s and '50s, this 65-acre estate is now a winery owned by the manager of the Doobie Brothers. All of the old farm buildings have been converted into winery buildings, and Sonoma Valley's largest olive orchard—8 acres of Picolini olive trees planted over 125 years ago—is now farmed for premium extra-virgin olive oil and bottled in tall, long-necked French bottles. The winery's distinctive, intense Cabernets are credited to the area's unique microclimate. Several picnic areas are available, and music and theater performances are sometimes scheduled in an amphitheater.

Château St. Jean Vineyards and Winery *555 Sonoma Hwy. 12, Kenwood, (800) 543-7572, (707) 833-4134, fax (707) 833-4200; www.chateaustjean.com. Tasting M-F 10-4:30, Sat & Sun to 5; self-guided tour.*

This winery specializes in white varietals. The tasting room is inside a 1920s château, and the grassy, shaded picnic area has several fountains and fish ponds.

Kunde Estate Winery *10155 Sonoma Hwy. 12, Kenwood, (707) 833-5501, fax (707) 833-2204; www.kunde.com. Tasting daily 11-5; guided tours F-Sun, self-guided tours daily.*

Tucked between expansive vineyards and the Surgarloaf foothills, this fourth-generation family-owned and -operated winery produces a spicy Zinfandel from gnarled vines growing in a 28-acre vineyard planted over 113 years ago. Tours are given of the half-mile-long aging caves, which are camouflaged by a hill planted with Chardonnay grapes. Children are given grape juice to drink while adults taste wine, and a picnic area is situated by a fountain and pond under a shady grove of oak trees.

Smothers/Remick Ridge Winery *9575 Sonoma Hwy. 12, Kenwood, (800) 795-WINE, (707) 833-1010, fax (707) 833-2313. Tasting daily 10-4:30; no tours.*

Many people stop here just to see if Tommy is around. (Dick is no longer involved with the winery.) Those after the label's cachet might be disappointed to learn that the wines are labeled Remick Ridge. Children get grape juice and pretzels while their parents taste, and a small shaded area is equipped with picnic tables.

WHERE TO STAY

Gaige House Inn *13540 Arnold Dr., Glen Ellen, (800) 935-0237, (707) 935-0237, fax (707) 935-6411; www.gaige.com. 15 rooms; 100% non-smoking; $$$-$$$+; 2-night min. on weekends. Unsuitable for children under 12. Some gas fireplaces, all CD players. Heated pool (unheated Nov-Apr), hot tub. Afternoon cookies & mineral water (always available), evening wine & hors d'oeuvres, full breakfast.*

Because of its 1890 Queen Anne-Italianate exterior, most guests are surprised by the fresh, understated, clean-lined, definitely un-Victorian interior. With Asian touches and gorgeous orchids throughout, the simple but elegant style is refreshing and easy to become accustomed to. A gorgeous pool and hot tub area, with a perfectly manicured half-acre of lawn lined with flowering oleander trees, and a sheltered creekside deck offer perfect afternoon relaxation. Among the most interesting rooms are the Gaige Suite, with a 12-foot ceiling, four-poster lace-canopy bed, and wrap-around balcony; and the Creek Side Suite, with a Jacuzzi for two and a double-headed shower, a private porch overlooking Calabasas Creek, and a stunning tree-filled view from the bed. A gourmet, two-course breakfast is served at private tables in an airy, open room. It might include an appetizer plate of ripe fruits, plus a hot plate of polenta and goat cheese topped with perfectly poached eggs and a mild salsa—all served on beautifully glazed, Japanese-style rectangular plates. Coffee is the best, Peet's, and orange juice is fresh-squeezed.

Kenwood Inn & Spa *10400 Sonoma Hwy. 12, Kenwood, (800) 353-6966, (707) 833-1293, fax (707) 833-1247; www.kenwoodinn.com. 12 rooms; 100% non-smoking; $$$+; 2-night min. on Sat. Unsuitable for children under 21. No TVs; all wood-burning fireplaces. Unheated pool, hot tub, spa treatments. Full breakfast.*

Hugging a hillside covered with olive trees, this sensual, aesthetically pleasing Tuscan-style inn looks very much like an old Italian villa. Guests are greeted at the desk by an inviting arrangement of seasonal fruits. Painted in gray and ochre tones, the various buildings enclose a center courtyard, mixing attractively with the green of the garden and seasonally punctuated by orange globes hanging from persimmon trees and yellow orbs ripening on lemon bushes housed in terra-cotta pots. Fountains and archways are everywhere. Rooms are furnished with a combination of antiques and comfortable newer pieces, and the blissful beds feature both a feather bed and a lofty down comforter.

WHERE TO EAT

The Bistro *13740 Arnold Dr., Glen Ellen, (707) 996-4401, fax (707) 996-0850. L M-Sat, Sun Br, D daily; $$.*

Situated in the crook in the road known as the center of town, this spot is particularly popular with locals. Prime tables overlook the town creek, and outside seating on a tree-sheltered deck is delightful in warm weather. One dinner enjoyed here started with a scrumptious shared butter lettuce salad with goat cheese and dried figs, followed by enormous portions of a house-smoked pork chop with buttermilk mashed potatoes and the Sunday night special Yankee pot roast. Dessert was a tart dried-cherry bread pudding brioche topped with butterscotch ice cream and sauce. More regional dishes and comfort foods round out the menu. Wines are poured in delightfully oversize glasses.

Glen Ellen Inn Restaurant *13670 Arnold Dr., Glen Ellen, (707) 996-6409; www.glenelleninn.com. D Tu-M; $$. Boosters. Reservations advised.*

This modest, charming place is sort of a California-style roadhouse. Diners are seated in one of several small rooms, and in warm weather more tables are tucked into a sunken herb garden outside. Husband Christian Bertrand produces a non-stop parade of delicious fare. Dinner begins with a basket of scones fresh from the oven, often delivered to the table by co-owner and wife Karen, who sometimes waits tables all by herself. Items on the dinner menu have included an exquisitely light puff pastry pocket filled with mushrooms and sausage in a brandy cream sauce, and a late harvest ravioli stuffed with the unexpected taste sensation of a mixture of pumpkin, walnuts, and sun-dried cranberries served on a bed of oven-glazed butternut squash. Save room for one of the killer desserts: perhaps a vertical chocolate mousse contained within a tall chocolate "basket," or maybe housemade vanilla ice cream topped with a marvelous caramel-toasted coconut sauce.

Picnic Pick-Up.

• **Glen Ellen Village Market** *13751 Arnold Dr., Glen Ellen, (707) 996-6728. Daily 7:30am-9pm.*

The perfect place to select a picnic lunch, this full-service deli prepares sandwiches to order and offers a variety of salads and desserts. Fresh local produce, cold drinks, and the usual market staples are also available.

Napa

BACKGROUND INFORMATION

Considered by most tourists to be the center of the Wine Country, this town is more accurately referred to as the "Gateway to the Wine Country." The center of its old town is of interest on its own merits, but the Wine Country's heaviest concentration of wineries is further north. Recently, a group of wineries has also developed south of town.

VISITOR INFORMATION

Napa Valley Conference and Visitors Bureau *1310 Napa Town Center, (707) 226-7459; www.napavalley.com.*

GETTING THERE

Located approximately 50 miles north of San Francisco. Take Highway 101 to Highway 37 to Highway 121 to Highway 12 to Highway 29.

ANNUAL EVENTS

Napa Valley Mustard Festival *February-March. (707) 938-1133, fax (707) 938-0123; www.mustardfestival.org.*

Designed to bring visitors into this area at a beautiful, unhurried time of year, this festival includes a variety of unusual events held around the Napa Valley. Events include tastings as well as art, sporting, and recipe competitions.

Napa Valley Wine Auction *June. Events held throughout the valley; (707) 963-5246; www.napavintners.com.*

Though tickets run $1,250 per couple, this 4-day event usually sells out early. Tickets to individual events, which run from $500 to $800 per couple, are sometimes available at the last minute. Its popularity might be explained by the fact that many wine-makers open their homes and wineries to unique public events in the interest of helping raise money for local health centers. For example, one year the Rutherford Hill Winery hosted a refined candlelight dinner in their hillside caves, while Stag's Leap Wine Cellars hosted a festive Greek dinner and dancing extravaganza on their courtyard. A Friday night Vintner Dinner and Saturday afternoon auction take place at the lush Meadowood Resort.

WHAT TO DO

Di Rosa Preserve *5200 Carneros Hwy. 121/near Duhig Rd., 6 mi. west of town, (707) 226-5991, fax (707) 255-89346; www.dirosapreserve.org. Call for tour times. $10/person; free 1st & 3rd W. Reservations required.*

Wrought iron sheep greet visitors in the parking lot of this expansive 215-acre complex. Tours last 2 1/2 hours. So extensive is the collection of more than 1600 pieces of local contemporary art assembled by owner Rene di Rosa, who never has sold a work of art he acquired, that a tram is used to shuttle guests between the four gallery buildings. One of the largest regional art collections in the country, it is displayed in a 19th-century stone winery building that was converted into a house and now into a gallery, in the tractor barn, in two new architecturally striking structures, and outdoors among the meadows and rolling hills. With its towering oaks, 100-year-old olive orchard, and 35-acre lake, the property is also a bit of a nature preserve. It has its own flock of peacocks and is a stopping point for migratory birds.

Napa Valley Wine Train *1275 McKinstry St., (800) 427-4124, (707) 253-2111; www.winetrain.com. Daily; call for schedule; closed 1st week in Jan. $30-$75. Reservations required.*

This leisurely 3-hour, 36-mile excursion takes passengers through the heart of the Wine Country. Unfortunately, there are no stops to visit wineries. However, the train consists of opulently restored vintage lounge cars and a 1916 Pullman converted into a kitchen complete with a stainless steel galley and a window-wall allowing chefs to be viewed in action. The ticket includes Saturday or Sunday brunch, lunch, or dinner on board, served in richly appointed dining cars outfitted with the refined pleasures of damask linen, bone china, and silver flatware. Almost everything is prepared right on the train using fresh ingredients, and the menu offers several choices in each category. One lunch enjoyed aboard included a tasty baby lettuce salad with Cambozola cheese and a hazelnut-sherry vinaigrette, filet mignon with Cabernet-Roquefort sauce, and a creamy tiramisu served in an oversize cappuccino cup. A deli car that is perfect for families with young children offers an inexpensive a la carte menu. Special events such as private winery tours and murder mystery dinners are also often scheduled.

WINERIES

Artesa *1345 Henry Rd. (call for directions), (707) 224-1668, fax (707) 224-1672; www.artesawinery.com. Tasting (fee $4) & tours M-Thur 10-5, F-Sun 10-3.*

Situated off Highway 121, this spectacular Spanish-owned winery can be difficult to find but is well worth the effort. Its stunning minimalist architecture has it set right into a grassy hill that acts as a sod roof, helping insulate wines stored beneath. Visitors reach the tasting room by walking up a pyramid-like staircase on either side of a cascading man-made waterfall. Stunning panoramic views are enjoyed at the top. In the spirit of the Codorniu family's creation of the first methode champenoise sparkling wine in Spain in 1872, the winery is creating a distinctly California sparkling wine here. After sampling in the spacious tasting room or outside on the inviting deck, a mini-museum of wine-related artifacts awaits leisurely perusal.

Domaine Carneros *1240 Duhig Rd., 6 mi. southwest of town, (707) 257-0101, fax (707) 257-3020; www.domaine.com. Tasting daily 10:30-6 (fee $4-$6); tours M-F at 11, 1, & 3, Sat & Sun hourly 11-3.*

Situated off Highway 121, this imposing classic French château sits atop a hill surrounded by vineyards. The château is inspired by the Château de la Marquetterie, an historic 18th-century residence in Champagne, France owned by the winery's principal founder. After climbing a *lot* of steps, visitors reach the elegant tasting salon and garden terrace. Here information is dispensed about the methode champenoise procedure that produces the champagnes of French founder Taittinger, as well as their local sparking wines made in the same tradition. Flavored mineral water is provided to children while their parents taste.

The Hess Collection Winery *4411 Redwood Rd., (707) 255-1144, fax (707) 253-1682; www.hesscollection.com. Tasting daily 10-4 (fee $2.50); self-guided tours. Gallery admission free.*

Located on the slopes of Mt. Veeder, off a road that winds first through the suburbs and then through scenic woods, this unusual winery is owned by Swiss entrepreneur Donald Hess. Here he grows grapes in rocky soil on steep, terraced hillsides and turns them into premium wines. Built in 1903, the winery was once the original Napa Valley home for the Christian Brothers. Extensively remodeled, it features the original stone walls and a stunning 13,000-square-foot art gallery. The gallery's eclectic collection holds 130 contemporary paintings and sculptures, including works by Robert Motherwell and Frank Stella, as well as an absolutely stunning portrait by Swiss artist Franz Gertsch titled "Johanna II." At various points in the galleries, portholes look into rooms where steel fermentation tanks and bottling machines are located. Visitors can also view a 12-minute narrated slide presentation of the wine-making operations. The winery is known for its Chardonnays and Cabernet Sauvignons, and its Mt. Veeder Estate Merlot is available for purchase only at the winery. Valser mineral water from Switzerland is provided to children accompanying their tasting parents.

RMS Alambic Distillery *1250 Cuttings Wharf Rd., (707) 253-9055, fax (707) 253-0116; www.rmsbrandy.com. Sensory evaluation (fee $2; permits 10% discount on retail merchandise, excluding spirits) & tours daily 10-4:30.*

Situated off Highway 121 amid a peaceful expanse of vineyards, this producer of rare, expensive, traditional French-style Alambic brandy is the first facility of its kind in the U.S. It houses the largest stock of aging Alambic brandies in the country. Since its French owners is Remy Martin Cognac, it makes sense that the distillery resembles those found in the brandy-making regions of France. Though federal law prohibits brandy tasting, visitors are permitted to enjoy a comprehensive "aroma evaluation" after a tour.

Trefethen Winery *1160 Oak Knoll Ave./Hwy. 29, (800) 556-4847, (707) 255-7700, fax (707) 255-0793; www.trefethen.com. Tasting daily 10-4:30; tours by appt.*

Built in 1886, this historic building is a superb example of a wooden gravity-flow winery. Though it can be a bit difficult to find, it is worth the effort just to drive through the majestic gates, then down an impressive private road through expansive vineyards to the tasting room.

WHERE TO STAY

Embassy Suites Napa Valley *1075 California Blvd., (800) EMBASSY, (707) 253-9540, fax (707) 224-7708; www.embassynapa.com. 205 suites; $$-$$$. Children under 12 free. All kitchens. Indoor heated pool, hot tub, sauna. Evening drinks, full breakfast; restaurant (fall only), room service.*

This branch offers suites equipped with a bedroom, a front room with hide-a-bed, a kitchenette, and two TVs. Breakfast is the all-you-can-eat variety with eggs cooked to order, bacon, sausage, pancakes, fried potatoes, toast, fresh fruit, muffins, cereals, and beverages, and it can be enjoyed either in a pleasant indoor atrium or outside by a pond inhabited by ducks and both black and white swans.

The Hennessey House Bed & Breakfast Inn *1727 Main St., (707) 226-3774, fax (707) 226-2975; www.hennesseyhouse.com. 10 rooms; 100% non-smoking; $-$$$; 2-night min. on Sat. 1 TV & VCR; some wood-burning & gas fireplaces. Sauna. Full breakfast.*

Listed in the National Register of Historic Places, this 1889 Eastlake Queen Anne Victorian's exterior is painted stylishly in five different colors. Six rooms are in the main residence, four more in a carriage house. Some have oversize whirlpool tubs or clawfoot tubs, others have featherbeds. Breakfast is served in what is claimed to be Napa County's finest 19th-century hand-painted, stamped-tin ceiling. It is, indeed, magnificent. Complimentary sherry is provided in each room, and a wine and cheese hour is hosted on weekends.

WHERE TO EAT

Alexis Baking Company *1517 Third St., (707) 258-1827. B&L daily, D M-F; $. Highchairs, boosters.*

This combination bakery/cafe is a must-stop for breads and pastries to take home. But most people wind up having a casual meal, too. Breakfast offerings include Dutch babies and hot cinnamon rolls. Lunch is a selection of pastas, sandwiches, soups, and salads, and dinner includes fussy appetizers such as baked goat cheese coated with pistachios and served with sweet potato fries, plus fresh fish and pizza.

Downtown Joe's *902 Main St., (707) 258-2337. B,L,&D daily; $. Highchairs, boosters, child menu.*

Situated within an historic building constructed in 1894, then updated in 1926 with an art deco tile façade, this centrally located brewpub serves up housemade soups, salads, pizzas, steaks, and seafood, plus a burger, ribs, and pulled pig sandwich. Beers include Golden Thistle Bitter Ale (an English-style bitter) and a dark, full-bodied Slipknot Stout; a refreshing housemade root beer is also available. Seating is inside at a comfortable bar and outside on a patio overlooking the west bank of the Napa River. Live music is scheduled Thursday through Saturday evenings.

P.J.'s Cafe *1001 Second St., (707) 224-0607, fax (707) 224-0228. B F-Sun, L&D daily; $. Highchairs, boosters, booths. Reservations advised.*

Located on Alexandria Square in one of Napa's historic buildings, this comfortable spot dishes up big portions of simple foods. The menu offers sandwiches, pastas, pizzas, salads, and soups—all made from scratch and served with fresh-baked oatmeal and cheese breads. Special requests are accommodated.

The Silverado Trail

A LITTLE BACKGROUND

Stretching approximately 30 miles from Napa to Calistoga, this scenic route offers a quieter, less-crowded wine tasting experience.

GETTING THERE

Located 50 miles northeast of San Francisco. Take I-880 north to Highway 29 north to Napa. Turn right on Trancas Street. After about 10 minutes, turn left at the sign onto the Silverado Trail.

WHAT TO DO

Lake Berryessa *In Napa take Hwy. 128 east, (707) 966-2111, fax (707) 966-0409. Open daily.*

This man-made lake is over 25 miles long, 3 miles wide, and has 165 miles of shoreline. Boats and water-skis can be rented, and the swimming and fishing are excellent. Camping and lodging facilities are available.

WINERIES

Mumm Napa Valley Winery *8445 Silverado Trail, Rutherford, (800) MUM-NAPA, (707) 942-3434, fax (707) 942-3470; www.aboutwines.com. Tasting 10-5, in summer 10:30-6 (fee $3.50+); tours daily 11-3, in summer to 4.*

In good weather tasters can sample sparkling wines while sitting under umbrellas on a patio with a magnificent view of the valley's vineyards. A permanent exhibit of Ansel Adams photographs tells "The Story of a Winery," and changing exhibits of fine art photography can be viewed in the winery's art galleries.

Nichelini Winery *2950 Sage Canyon Rd. (Hwy. 128), 11 mi. east of Rutherford, (800) WE-TASTE, (707) 963-0717, fax (707) 963-3262. Tasting & tours Sat & Sun 10-5; in summer to 6; weekdays by appt.*

Established in 1890, this historic, out-of-the-way winery is in a gorgeous location well off the main drag, down a rural side road leading to Lake Berryessa. Pack a picnic to enjoy at tables sheltered by old, old trees. Operated now by four of founder Anton Nichelini's grandchildren, it is the oldest continuously owned family winery in Napa Valley. The winery produces great Zinfandels using vines planted long, long ago by the elder Nichelini.

Pine Ridge Winery *5901 Silverado Trail, Napa, (800) 575-9777, (707) 252-9777, fax (707) 253-1493; www.pineridge.com. Tasting daily 11-5 (fee $3); tours by appt. at 10:15, 1, & 3.*

The tiny tasting room here is a pleasant place to sample the premium Cabernets produced by this winery's Stags Leap District grapes. Tasters can also stroll through a Demonstration Vineyard. A picnic area is situated under a young grove of tall pines, and two board swings await the kiddies.

Rutherford Hill Winery *200 Rutherford Hill Dr., Rutherford, (800) 726-5226, (707) 963-1871, fax (707) 963-4231; www.rutherfordhill.com. Tasting daily 10-4:30 (fee $3; keep tasting glass); tours daily at 11:30, 1:30, & 3:30, also at 12:30 & 2:30 on Sat & Sun.*

Visitors pass through massive 15-foot-tall doors as they enter the tasting room here. The tour includes seeing the most extensive wine-aging cave system in the U.S. A sylvan hillside picnic area, with spacious tables sheltered by old oaks and a pleasant view of the valley, beckons across the street from the tasting room.

WHERE TO STAY

Auberge du Soleil *180 Rutherford Hill Rd., Rutherford, (800) 348-5406, (707) 963-1211, fax (707) 963-8764; www.aubergedusoleil.com. 52 units; $$$+; 2-night min. on weekends. All fireplaces. Pool, hot tub, steam rooms, fitness room, 3 tennis courts. Unsuitable for children under 16. Continental breakfast; restaurant, room service.*

With a name meaning literally "inn of the sun," this upscale Mediterranean-style bungalow village cascades down a peaceful wooded hillside, spreading over the 33-acre property. Each room has a private deck with panoramic views of the valley, a wood-burning fireplace, and an oversize bathtub big enough for two. Beds are made with Frette linens, and breakfast is brought to the room. Paths crisscross the property, passing through a 5-acre **Olive Grove Sculpture Garden** featuring nearly 75 works by 40 California sculptors; all pieces are for sale.

The inn's elegant French **restaurant** *(B,L,&D daily; $$$. Highchairs, child portions. Reservations advised.)* has plush indoor seating as well as more rustic, and more desirable, outside seating on a heated terrace with sweeping views of the valley. Sumptuous, full-flavored entrees might include cumin-scented crab cakes or flame-roasted Spanish-style stuffed peppers as appetizers and a rosemary-grilled-shrimp salad with haricot verts and shaved fennel, or ravioli stuffed with woodland mushrooms and topped with a thyme cream sauce. Desserts are not boring: a Valrhona chocolate soufflé, profiteroles stuffed with cappuccino-chip ice cream, a Meyer lemon-and-white chocolate mousse tart with raspberry sauce.

Meadowood Resort & Hotel *900 Meadowood Ln., St. Helena, (800) 458-8080, (707) 963-3646, fax (707) 963-3532; www.meadowood.com. 85 rooms; $$$+; 2-night min. on weekends. Children under 12 free. Some kitchens & fireplaces. 2 heated pools, hot tub, health spa, fitness room, 7 tennis courts (fee); 9-hole golf course. 2 restaurants, room service.*

This luxury resort allows guests an escape from reality. Cabins with skylights and old-fashioned porches dot the secluded property, providing plenty of privacy, and room service can deliver a breakfast basket to the door. Rooms are equipped with heated bathroom floors, terry robes, and down comforters. Facilities on the 250 acres of lush wooded grounds include a children's playground (one of the two pools is also dedicated to children), two regulation English croquet lawns, and 3 miles of hiking trails. Bike rentals are also available. The health spa offers a massage using a unique Chardonnay lotion developed just for the resort, as well as a grape seed mud massage and grape seed body polish. The resort also operates a **Wine School**. A package includes classes, winery tours, meals, and lodging.

The Restaurant at Meadowood *(D daily, SunBr; $$$.)* complements its refined menu by serving exclusively Napa Valley wines and is said to have the most comprehensive selection in the world. Downstairs, the slightly less formal **Grill** *(B,L,&D daily; $$$.)* serves delicious California bistro fare and features a terrace overlooking the green, green golf course.

For twelve nights in December, the resort hosts **The Twelve Days of Christmas**. Celebrity chefs from around the country prepare sumptuous menus at nearby Merryvale Vineyards. Guests are seated at one very long candelabra-lit table in the winery's magnificent 2-story Cask Room, the stone walls of which are lined with century-old 2,000-gallon wooden wine barrels. Packages that include lodging and dinner are available.

Silverado Resort *1600 Atlas Peak Rd., Napa, 1 mi. northeast of town, (800) 532-0500, (707) 257-0200, fax (707) 257-5400; www.silveradoresort.com. 280 units; $$$-$$$+. Children under 14 free. All kitchens & wood-burning fireplaces. 1 heated pool, 9 unheated pools, hot tub, sauna, health spa, 17 tennis courts (fee; 3 with night lights), 2 18-hole golf courses. 2 restaurants, room service.*

Once part of General Vallejo's Rancho Yajome, this 1,200-acre resort is now the largest tennis complex in Northern California. Its heart is a gracious 1875 mansion, where guests are greeted and registered and within which are the resort's two restaurants. Though all accommodations are in individually-owned condominiums, the location, architectural style, and decor of each vary. Some units are available on the grounds adjacent to the mansion, allowing an easy walk to most of the facilities, while larger condos, some opening right onto the golf course, are farther away and require a 1- or 2-mile drive. Facilities include jogging trails, bicycle rentals, and two golf courses designed by Robert Trent Jones, Jr. The impressive new 16,000-square-foot spa is fashioned after a classic Roman spa and is the largest private spa facility in the Wine Country. **The Vintners**

Court is famous for its Friday night seafood buffet, while the more casual **Bar & Grill** serves smaller meals and offers a soothing view of the golf course.

Silver Rose Inn & Spa *351 Rosedale Rd., Calistoga, (800) 995-9381, (707) 942-9581, fax (707) 942-0841; www.silverrose.com. 20 rooms; 100% non-smoking; $$$-$$$+. No TVs; some fireplaces. 2 hot spring pools, 2 hot tubs, health spa, weight room, tennis courts, putting green. Continental breakfast.*

Sitting amid acres of vineyards and mountains, this peaceful enclave provides quiet, serene views. Architecture is contemporary, with huge stone fireplaces and rustic beams in the public rooms. Themed guest rooms—The Porch Room, Cleopatra's Room, Hello Hollywood, and The Library—are found in the Inn the Vineyard building, where many rooms feature up-close vineyard-side views and in-room whirlpool tubs for two. However, the property's original building, the Inn on the Knoll, has a more impressive public room and pool area and is just a few steps from the property's small spa. A large, wine bottle-shaped pool is located between the two buildings. The spa, which is available only to guests, offers a variety of water treatments and massage. The pools, hot tubs, and spa tubs are all fed by underground hot springs. A restaurant and winery will open soon.

Yountville

VISITOR INFORMATION

Yountville Chamber of Commerce *6516 Yount St., (800) 4-YOUNTVILLE, (707) 944-0904, fax (707) 944-4465.*

WHAT TO DO

Hot Air Balloon Rides.

Tour the Napa Valley via hot air balloon. Trips average 1 hour in the air; altitude and distance depend on which way the wind blows.

- **Adventures Aloft of Napa Valley** *6525 Washington St., in Vintage 1870, (800) 944-4408, (707) 944-4408, fax (707) 944-4406; www.napavalleyaloft.com. Adults $175, 13-18 $150, 6-12 $125. Reservations required.*

This is the Wine Country's oldest balloon company, with the most experienced pilot team available. The adventure includes pre-flight coffee and pastry and a post-flight sit-down breakfast enhanced with a local sparkling wine.

- **Napa Valley Balloons** *6975 Washington St., (800) 253-2224, (707) 944-0228, fax (707) 944-0219; www.napavalleyballoons.com. Adults $165, 5-9 $85.*

This business offers a similar experience, plus an enamel lapel balloon pin and a photo of either the launch or landing.

Vintage 1870 *6525 Washington St., (707) 944-2451, fax (707) 944-2453; www.vintage 1870.com. Daily 10-5:30.*

This lovely old brick building, a former winery, now houses a number of interesting specialty shops and restaurants. **Gillespie's** dispenses ice cream concoctions and delicious housemade candies. Hot air balloons can often be viewed from a children's play area outside.

WINERIES

Domaine Chandon *One California Dr., (707)944-2280; www.dchandon.com. Daily May-Oct; W-Sun Nov-Apr. Tasting 11-6 (fee); tours 11-5:30.*

This attractive French-owned winery specializes in sparkling wines produced by the traditional methode champenoise. It is reached by crossing a wooden bridge spanning a scenic duck pond surrounded by beautifully landscaped grounds. Built with stones gathered on the site, its arched roofs and doorways were inspired by the caves of Champagne, France. For tasting, visitors are seated at tiny tables covered with French Provençale floral cloths in the Vins Le Salon. Sparkling wine can be purchased by the glass, and a variety of sparkling wine cocktails are also available. Complimentary bread and cheese are provided to help keep things steady. Children can order mineral water or orange juice.

The spacious, elegant dining room in the winery **restaurant** *((707) 944-2892, fax (707) 944-1123. L daily May-Oct, W-Sun Nov-Apr; D W-Sun; $$$. Reservations advised.)* is lovely, but in good weather the terrace is the première spot to be seated. Dishes are designed especially to complement the winery's sparkling wines which are available by the glass. The wine list also includes still varietals from neighboring vintners. Men are requested to wear jackets at dinner.

WHERE TO STAY

Bordeaux House *6600 Washington St., (800) 677-6370, (707) 944-2855, same fax. 7 rooms; 100% non-smoking; $-$$. Some wood-burning fireplaces. Continental breakfast.*

This ultra-modern inn features a curved red-brick exterior and lush French- and English-style gardens.

Burgundy House *6711 Washington St., (707) 944-0889. 6 rooms; 100% non-smoking; $-$$; 2-night min. on weekends. Unsuitable for children under 12. No TVs; 1 wood-burning fireplace. Full breakfast.*

Built in 1890 as a brandy distillery, this house was constructed of local field stone and river rock and has walls that are 22 inches thick. The rustic construction of the interior is complemented by lace-covered windows and antique pine and oak furniture. An inspired breakfast is served in either the downstairs lobby or the backyard rose garden, depending on the weather.

Maison Fleurie *6529 Yount St., (800) 788-0369, (707) 944-2056, fax (707) 944-9342; www.foursisters.com. 13 rooms; 100% non-smoking; $$-$$$. Children under 2 free. Some gas fireplaces. Heated pool (unheated Nov-Apr), hot tub. Afternoon snack, full breakfast.*

The rustic, vine-covered main building was constructed in the center of town as a hotel in 1873. It has 2-foot-thick brick walls, lots of terra cotta tile, and romantic multi-paned windows. Rooms, some of which are located in two adjacent buildings, are decorated in French country style. Amenities include oversize pool towels, complimentary use of mountain bikes, evening turndown, and a morning newspaper. Cookies, fruit, and beverages are always available, and wine and hors d'oeuvres are served in the afternoon. Though breakfast is delightful taken in the cozy dining room, upon request it is delivered to the room.

Napa Valley Lodge *2230 Madison St., (800) 368-2468, (707) 944-2468, fax (707) 944-9362; www.woodsidehotels.com. 55 rooms; 100% non-smoking; $$-$$$. Some fireplaces. Heated pool, hot tub, sauna, fitness center. Continental breakfast.*

Located on the outskirts of town, this Spanish-style motel is across the street from a park and playground. Each room has a private patio or balcony.

Napa Valley Railway Inn *6503 Washington St., (707) 944-2000. 9 units; $$-$$$+; 2-night min. on weekends. Children under 7 free. No TVs.*

Railroad enthusiasts are sure to enjoy a night in a brass bed at this unusual lodging facility. Three cabooses and six rail cars—authentic turn-of-the-century specimens sitting on the original town tracks—have been whimsically converted into comfortable suites complete with private bath, sitting area, and skylight. Guests are greeted with a chilled bottle of wine.

Vintage Inn *6541 Washington St., (800) 351-1133, (707) 944-1112, fax (707) 944-1617; www.vintageinn.com. 80 rooms; $$$-$$$+; 2-night min. on Sat, Mar-Nov. Children under 1 free. All wood-burning fireplaces. Heated pool, hot tub, 2 tennis courts. Afternoon snack, continental breakfast. Pets welcome.*

This attractive modern lodging facility is centrally located next to Vintage 1870. In summer, bicycles are available for guests to rent.

WHERE TO EAT

BRIX *7377 St. Helena Hwy. (Hwy. 29), (707) 944-2749, fax (707) 944-8320. L&D daily; $$-$$$. Highchairs, boosters, booths. Reservations taken.*

Comfortable booths and tables, with views of both the expansive kitchen garden and vineyard as well as the action in the open kitchen, welcome diners here. Tasty sesame cracker bread is provided for munching and served in an interesting sculpted metal basket with a grapevine design echoed throughout the restaurant in lighting fixtures and furnishings. The menu of East-West fusion cuisine changes daily and might include a chilled puréed gazpacho soup made with heirloom tomatoes from the kitchen's garden; a salad of baby mixed greens (also from the garden) tossed with a sesame-citrus dressing; a delicious chicken salad with crisp won ton strands and a tropical fruit dressing; stir-fried noodles tossed with chicken, vegetables, and a delicate orange-ginger-soy sauce dressing; and a simply superb, not-too-sweet strawberry-almond shortcake.

The Diner *6476 Washington St., (707) 944-2626. B,L,&D Tu-Sun; $. Closed last 2 weeks in Dec. Highchairs, boosters, booths, child portions. No reservations. No cards.*

This unpretentious, chef-owned cafe offers counter seating as well as tables and booths, and a decor brightened by a Fiesta Ware pitcher collection. Delicious California-ized Mexican specialties enhance the cafe menu, and all items are made with quality ingredients. Breakfast is served until 3 p.m. Choices include German potato pancakes, housemade sausage patties, and old-fashioned oatmeal as well as the house specialty of crispy cornmeal pancakes served with smoky links. At lunch it's hamburgers, sandwiches, and soda fountain treats, among them an unusual buttermilk shake said to taste like liquid cheesecake. Dinners include sophisticated specials and, in season, a delectable dessert cobbler is available made with fresh apricots and blackberries and topped with a scoop of vanilla ice cream.

The French Laundry *6640 Washington St., (707) 944-2380. L F-Sun, D Tu-Sun, in summer D daily; $$$. Closed part of Jan. Reservations essential.*

Indeed once an actual French laundry, this rustic old stone building now holds one of the Wine Country's most popular culinary gems. Owner-chef Thomas Keller offers diners either a five-course or seven-course menu, as well as a five-course vegetarian menu. The kitchen specializes in freshly prepared, innovative, labor-intensive dishes. A first course with a sense of humor is the "tongue and cheek," a mold of tender meats topped with baby leeks and a tad of horseradish cream. Main courses have included a roasted monkfish with minced vegetables flavored with lemon verbena, a long-roasted breast of veal, and a vegetarian Provençale cannelloni. The cheese course might be grilled goat cheese with wilted endive and candied beets or a roasted Anjou pear with blue cheese and walnuts. Great desserts include a tarte tatin made with peaches and topped with sour cream ice cream, and "coffee and doughnuts"—a cappuccino semifreddo and a cinnamon sugar doughnut. Several complimentary surprise sweets end the meal, and the check appears tabulated on a laundry tag. The noteworthy wine list concentrates on Napa Valley vintages that are, amazingly, marked up just a few dollars. Be warned: this tiny 19-table restaurant is so popular and so difficult to get a reservation at that one busy San Francisco executive is said to have hired a temporary worker to spend the day on the phone trying to get him a reservation! Reservations are accepted two months in advance to the day.

Mustards *7399 St. Helena Hwy. (Hwy. 29), (707) 944-2424, fax (707) 944-0828. L&D daily; $$. Boosters. Reservations advised.*

The best place to be seated at this popular bar and grill is on the cool, screened porch. Though tables are set with crisp white napery, the atmosphere is casual and chic and the menu imaginative. Selections include soups, salads, and sandwiches (a great grilled ahi tuna with basil mayonnaise and a good hamburger) as well as entrees such as barbecued baby backribs, mesquite-grilled Sonoma rabbit, and marinated skirt steak. Fresh fish specials are also available. The thin, light onion rings are superb, and housemade ketchup can be ordered with them. Garlic lovers will be pleased with a roasted head to spread on the complimentary baguette. Varietal wines are available by the glass. Rich desserts, among them a good bread pudding, and specialty coffees invite lingering.

The **Cosentino Winery** *(7415 St. Helena Hwy. (Hwy. 29), (707) 944-1220, fax (707) 944-1254; www.cosentinowinery.com. Tasting daily 10-5 (fee $2; applies to purchase & keep tasting glass); self-guided tour.)* is located just next door. Built in 1990, this winery is known for producing the country's first designated Meritage wine. Referred to as The Poet, this wine is composed of a marvelous blend of Cabernet Sauvignon, Cabernet Franc, and Merlot. It is pleasant to reserve a picnic lunch from Mustards to enjoy at the winery's bocce ball court-side tables.

Piatti *6480 Washington St., (707) 944-2070 or (707) 944-9317. L&D daily; $$. Highchairs, boosters, booths, child portions. Reservations advised.*

On a warm day, the patio here is the perfect place to share a long, leisurely lunch. Menu options might include an appetizer mix of olives and smoked almonds; a delicately flavored toasted pearl pasta with scallops, corn, and cherry tomatoes in a lobster broth; housemade potato gnocchi with tomatoes, basil, roasted garlic, and fresh mozzarella; and a refreshing dessert of fresh fruit with a warm chocolate-caramel dipping sauce. Tasty "Piatti oil" is provided for dipping bread, and jazz is included on Sundays from noon to 3 p.m. This is the original location in what has become a chain.

Oakville and Rutherford

ANNUAL EVENTS

Robert Mondavi Summer Festival *July & August. 7801 St. Helena Hwy. (Hwy. 29), Oakville; (800) MONDAVI, (707) 226-1395; www.robertmondavi.com. Tasting (fee $3-$25) & tours daily 9:30-5:30.*

Ah, the pleasure of sitting on the grass, surrounded by vineyards and rolling foothills, while listening to great jazz. The entertainers (who in the past have included Ella Fitzgerald, Al Hirt, and the Preservation Hall Jazz Band—on the *same bill!*) probably enjoy the dusk concerts as much as their audience. After an intermission for wine and cheese tasting, the concerts conclude under the stars. Picnics are encouraged, and catered repasts are available by advance reservation. Ticket-holders may begin selecting seats at 4:30 p.m. The winery's retail shop remains open until 7, when the concerts begin.

This winery also hosts a **Great Chefs at the Robert Mondavi Winery** series each year. Both one-day and weekend-long formats are scheduled. The $750 and up fee includes meals and cooking classes, plus demonstrations by world-famous chefs. A variety of special visitors programs are available, including an Advanced Winegrowing Tour *($30)* and an Appellation Tour of the Napa Valley in a six-passenger plane followed by lunch at the winery *($250)*.

WINERIES

Beaulieu Vineyard *1960 St. Helena Hwy. (Hwy. 29), Rutherford, (800) 264-6918, (707) 967-5230, fax (707) 963-5920; www.bv-wine.com. Tasting & tours daily 10-5.*

Founded in 1900 by Frenchman Georges deLatour, this winery is known for its Cabernet Sauvignons and Chardonnays. A $10 fee is charged for a special tasting of four or five library or reserve wines.

Cakebread Cellars *8300 St. Helena Hwy. (Hwy. 29), Rutherford, (707) 963-5221, fax (707) 963-1067; www.cakebread.com. Tasting daily 10-4; tours daily by appt.*

At this family-owned and -operated winery, Dennis Cakebread says his "handmade wines are made a barrel at a time." The winery is probably best know for its Chardonnays and Sauvignon Blancs, which can be sampled in the cozy tasting room.

La Famiglia Di Robert Mondavi Winery *1595 Oakville Grade, Oakville, (800) VICHON-1, (707) 944-2811, fax (707) 944-9224; www.lafamigliawines.com. Tasting daily 10-4:30; tours Sat & Sun at 11 & 3, also by appt. M-F at 10:30 & 2.*

After driving about a mile up a scenic side road off busy Highway 29, visitors are greeted by an informal tasting room and shaded picnic tables with a magnificent vineyard view. A bocce ball court is also available to customers. A catered picnic and tour that includes a visit to the Robert Mondavi Winery is available May thorough October *($25. Reservations required.).*

Niebaum-Coppola Estate Winery *1991 St. Helena Hwy. (Hwy. 29), Rutherford, (800) RUBICON, (707) 963-9099, fax (707) 963-9084; www.neibaum-coppola.com. Tasting daily 10-5 (fee $5); tours by appt.*

Founded in 1879 by a Finnish sea captain who made his fortune in the Alaskan shipping trade, this is one of the oldest wineries in the Napa Valley. Until recently known as Inglenook Vineyards, it is now owned by legendary film director Francis Ford Coppola, who has owned a home on part of the property since the 1970s and who, when the winery was up for sale, made them an offer they couldn't refuse. Now, after driving down a long lane, through some iron gates, past newly planted vineyards, visitors arrive at an impressive old estate. A gift shop extraordinaire dispenses such essentials as *The Godfather* t-shirts and enormous macaroni. This winery is known for its premium red Rubicon wine, which goes for $50 to $70 a bottle. More affordable everyday wines are also available. In addition to a tasting bar, wines can be ordered by the glass in a small cafe, and a terrace provides space for picnicking. Coppola's Oscars and an authentic Tucker automobile are displayed on the floor above the tasting room, and the **Centennial Museum** documents the winery's history.

Opus One *7900 St. Helena Hwy. (Hwy. 29), Oakville, (800) 292-6787, (707) 944-9442, fax (707) 944-2753; www.opusonewinery.com. Tasting daily 10:30-3:30 (fee $15 for 4-oz.); tours daily at 10:30 & 1:30 by reservation.*

The gated entrance to this exceptional winery is just north of town. A merging of American (Robert Mondavi) and French (Baron Philippe de Rothschild) wine-making skills, this exclusive label boasts a facility that is as impressive as its wine. Though from the highway it looks like a squat pyramid, up close and personal it resembles more a contemporary monastery. Constructed of Texas limestone and landscaped with a softening planting of olive trees, the winery uses gentle gravity-flow production and plants its vines in dense French Bordeaux style. This requires costly hand work and helps explain the $90 tab attached to its young bottles of Cabernet Sauvignon. A highlight of the tour is seeing the immense barrel room, which is somehow reminiscent of the pods lined up waiting to hatch in *The Body Snatchers*, only here it is great wine aging in French oak barrels that is waiting patiently to be born.

Sequoia Grove *8338 St. Helena Hwy. (Hwy. 29), Rutherford, (707) 944-2945, fax (707) 963-9411; www.sequoiagrove.com. Tasting daily 11-5 (fee $3 for 5 wines; keep souvenir glass); no tours.*

Family-owned and -operated, this small winery gets its name from the 100-year-old cluster of tall sequoia redwoods its tasting room sits beneath. Known for its Rutherford-style Cabernet Sauvignons, it claims to be the only winery with underground production facilities. Things are real casual here, with several mellow dogs lounging about while tasters sample the wares.

St. Supery Winery *8440 St. Helena Hwy. (Hwy. 29), Rutherford, (800) 942-0809, (707) 963-4507, fax (707) 963-4526; www.stsupery.com. Tasting daily 9:30-6 (fee $2.50; includes lifetime tasting pass); tours on the hour, M-F 11-3, Sat & Sun 10-4.*

This French-owned winery's **Wine Discovery Center** is an absolutely super place to get an introduction to wine-making. The tour here includes a viewing of the Queen Anne Victorian **Atkinson House**, once occupied by the winery's founder and now furnished with unusual Victorian pieces representative of the era, and an educational visit to a 1-acre demonstration vineyard where, in season, varietal grapes can be tasted. A highlight of the tour is a SmellaVision display that permits a whiff of the various scents used to describe wines (grassy, peppery, etc.). This winery produces award-winning Sauvignon Blancs and bottles a French-produced Viognier as well as several premium kosher wines. Children get a coloring book and crayons to occupy them while parents taste.

WHERE TO EAT

Picnic Pick-Ups.

• **Oakville Grocery Co.** *7856 Hwy. 29, Oakville, (707) 944-8802, fax (707) 944-1844. Daily 10-6.*

Everything needed to put together a fantastic gourmet picnic can be found here. Select from a large variety of mustards, vinegars, jams, fresh fruits, imported beers, and natural juices, as well as cheeses, sandwiches, salads, sausages, and other deli items, plus a large assortment of enticing desserts. If the choices seems overwhelming, call 48 hours in advance to order a pre-packed picnic box and let them pick the contents.

• **Pometta's Deli** *7787 Hwy. 29, on Oakville Grade, Oakville, (707) 944-2365, fax (707) 944-1513. M-Sat 9-5, Sun 10-4.*

Located just off busy Highway 29, this down-home-style deli has been here since 1952. Known for its wine-marinated barbecued chicken, it also offers made-to-order sandwiches, housemade salads and soups, and cold soft drinks. Informal indoor and outdoor seating is available.

St. Helena

VISITOR INFORMATION

St. Helena Highway, Main Street, and Highway 29 are all the same road.

St. Helena Chamber of Commerce *1080 Main St., (800) 799-6456, (707) 963-4456, fax (707) 963-5396; www.sthelena.com.*

GETTING THERE

Located approximately 15 miles north of Yountville via Highway 29.

WHAT TO DO

Bale Grist Mill State Historic Park *3369 Hwy. 29, 3 mi. north of town, (707) 942-4575. Daily 10-5. Adults $2, children $1, under 6 free.*

Reached via a shaded, paved, stream-side path, this grist mill ground grain for farmers from the 1840s through the turn of the century. The damp site and slow-turning millstones were reputedly responsible for the exceptional cornmeal produced here. Now interpretive displays are located inside the gable-roofed granary, and the 36-foot-diameter water wheel has been restored to full operation. Corn and wheat are ground at 1 and 3 p.m. on weekends and are available for purchase. Picnic tables are provided in several shaded areas.

Cameo Theater *1340 Main St., (707) 963-9779.*

This tiny first-run movie theater is equipped with posh velvet seats and Dolby digital sound, making it well worth a visit. Special performances are sometimes scheduled. When offered, *Silverado Squatters,* based on the book by Robert Louis Stevenson and performed live by local resident Donald Davis, is a don't-miss.

Silverado Museum *1490 Library Lane, (707) 963-3757, fax (707) 963-0917. Tu-Sun 12-4. Free.*

This museum contains over 8,500 pieces of Robert Louis Stevenson memorabilia. There are paintings, sculptures, and manuscripts as well as his childhood set of lead toy soldiers. Consider a family read-in of *A Child's Garden of Verses* or *Treasure Island* before or after this visit. This modern stucco library building, situated on the edge of a scenic vineyard, also contains the **Napa Valley Wine Library**.

WINERIES

Beringer Vineyards *2000 Main St., just north of town, (707) 963-4812, fax (707) 963-8129; www.beringer.com. Tours daily 9:30-4, on the half hour; tasting follows.*

Established in 1876, this winery's Visitor Center is located in a beautiful oak-paneled, stained-glass-laden reproduction of a 19th-century German Tudor mansion known as the Rhine House. Its tour is considered to be one of the most historically informative. The winery is noted for its Chardonnays and Cabernet Sauvignons, and its best vintages can be tasted in the Founder's Room for a $2 to $3 per sample tasting fee. Unfortunately, picnicking is not permitted on the beautifully landscaped grounds.

Domaine Charbay Winery & Distillery *4001 Spring Mountain Rd., (800) M-DISTIL, (707) 963-9327, fax (707) 963-3343; www.domainecharbay.com. $10/person, tasting included; by appt.*

Located off a remote scenic road, at almost 2,300 feet, this "still on the hill," as it is fondly nicknamed, is totally family-run and -operated. Co-owner Miles Karakasevic, who hails from Yugoslavia, is a 12th-generation wine maker and master distiller. Spirits are double-distilled by hand in classic Alambic pot stills. The winery is known for exceptional ports, brandies, and liqueurs—among them a grappa and a black walnut liqueur—and California's first pastis.

Freemark Abbey *3022 St. Helena Hwy. N., 2 mi. north of town, (707) 963-9694, fax (707) 963-0554; www.freemarkabbey.com. Tasting daily 10-4:30 (fee $5; applies to wine purchase or keep tasting glass); tour at 2.*

The large, lodge-like tasting room here has oriental carpets covering its hardwood floor. Comfortable furniture arranged around a fireplace invites leisurely sampling, and a picnic area is provided for purchasers of wine. The winery is noted for its Chardonnays and Cabernet Sauvignons.

Next door, **Hurd Beeswax Candles** *(3020 St. Helena Hwy. N., (800) 977-7211, (707) 963-7211, fax (707) 963-4358. Daily 10-5.)* operates in a vintage stone building constructed in 1896. Candles are either rolled or pressed from sheets of pure beeswax. No molds are used. The factory area is open to view, and an active beehive, hidden behind two wooden window covers, can be observed.

Prager Winery and Port Works *1281 Lewelling Ln., (800) 969-PORT, (707) 963-PORT, fax (707) 963-7679; www.pragerport.com. Tasting daily 10-4:30 (fee $5; applies to port purchase); no tours.*

Located down a country lane, the valley's premier port purveyor offers a rustic, informal tasting room for sampling the wares.

Trinchero Family Estates *277 St. Helena Hwy. S., (707) 963-3104; www.sutterhome.com. Tasting daily 10-5; garden tours W-Sun, on the hour 11-4.*

Bob Trinchero, son of Mario who bought the winery in 1947, introduced a fruity, pink-colored Sutter Home (the winery's former name) White Zinfandel in 1971. It took the country by storm. That inexpensive signature version is still available, but the winery now also produces some premium Chardonnays and Cabernets. The tasting room is inside a barn that housed the original winery. The renowned Butchart Gardens in Victoria, B.C. provided the inspiration for the garden surrounding the winery's showcase 1884 Victorian home, now operating as a **bed & breakfast.** Highlights include a rose garden with over 150 varieties and a garden of dwarf Japanese maples.

V. Sattui Winery *1111 White Lane, (800) 799-2337, (707) 963-7774, fax (707) 963-4324; www.vsattui.com. Tasting & self-guided tour daily 9-5; in summer to 6.*

Established in the North Beach area of San Francisco in 1885, this winery was shut down during Prohibition, then re-established in St. Helena in 1976. Family-owned for four generations, the current winemaker is the great-grandson of founder Vittorio Sattui. V. Sattui wines are sold only at the winery. The Johannisberg Rieslings and Cabernet Sauvignons that they are best known for, as well as both the Gamay Rouge that was once voted the best hot tub wine and the nation's oldest port-style Madera, can all be tasted in the stone winery building featuring 3-foot-thick walls and chiseled archways. The goal here is to be user-friendly and to take wine off the pedestal. Picnic supplies are available in a deli well-stocked with housemade salads and pâtés, and with what is claimed to be the largest selection of international cheeses on the West Coast. Plenty of oak-shaded picnic tables are provided on a 2-acre picnic grounds.

WHERE TO STAY

Ambrose Bierce House *1515 Main St., (707) 963-3003; www.ambrosebiercehouse.com. 3 rooms; 100% non-smoking; $-$$; 2-night min. on Sat. Unsuitable for children under 12. No TVs. Continental breakfast.*

Named for the witty author who wrote *The Devil's Dictionary* and who was portrayed by Gregory Peck in the movie *The Old Gringo*, this 1872 house was once Ambrose Bierce's home. One pleasantly decorated room is named after Eadweard Muybridge, who is known as the "father of the motion picture." It holds two interesting artifacts: an 1897 Eastman Kodak No. 2 Hawk-eye camera and a Smith and Wesson No. 2 that is just like the one Muybridge used in 1874 to shoot his wife's lover. Located at the northern end of town, the inn is within convenient walking distance of shopping and dining.

El Bonita Motel *195 Main St., (800) 541-3284, (707) 963-3216, fax (707) 963-8838; www.elbonita.com. 42 rooms; $-$$$; 2-night min. on weekends. Some kitchens. Heated pool, hot tub, sauna. Some pets welcome.*

Featuring an art deco decor, this motel has a shaded, grassy pool area and offers an alternative to classy, cutesy, and expensive Wine Country lodgings.

Harvest Inn *One Main St., (800) 950-8466, (707) 963-WINE, fax (707) 963-4402; www.harvestinn.com. 54 rooms; $$$-$$$+; 2-night min. on weekends. Some fireplaces. 2 heated pools, 2 hot tubs. Continental breakfast. Small pets welcome.*

Situated on a 21-acre working vineyard, this contemporary English Tudor-style inn has beautifully landscaped grounds and rooms furnished with antiques. Bicycles are available to rent.

La Fleur *1475 Inglewood Ave., (707) 963-0233, same fax. 7 rooms; 100% non-smoking; $$; 2-night min. on weekends. Unsuitable for children under 12. No TVs; some wood-burning fireplaces. Full breakfast*

Set back from the main highway, this charming 1882 Queen Anne Victorian B&B is *real quiet.* A large rose garden invites relaxing, and some of the spacious rooms feature claw-foot tubs. Breakfast is served in a cheery solarium with vineyard views, sometimes permitting guests to see hot air balloons floating above the vines.

It's just a short stroll through the flower garden to the tiny **Villa Helena Winery** *(1455 Inglewood Ave., (707) 963-4334, fax (707) 963-4748. Tasting & tours by appt.)* located next door. Call ahead to alert the owner, a former metallurgical engineer from Los Angeles, so that he can be in his office to assist with tasting his Charbono, dessert wines, and unusual Viognier white varietal. He also provides what he calls "the shortest tour in the Napa Valley."

The Wine Country Inn *1152 Lodi Ln., (707) 963-7077. 24 rooms; 100% non-smoking; $-$$$+; 2-night min. on some rooms. Unsuitable for children under 13. No TVs; some fireplaces. Heated pool, hot tub. Evening snack, full breakfast.*

Built in the style of a New England inn, without a lot of fuss and frill, this attractive, quiet lodging is located back from the main highway on top of a small country hill. Rooms are decorated with floral wallpapers and tasteful antiques, and many have views of the surrounding vineyards and hills. An evening wine tasting features different wineries, sometimes with the wine maker in attendance, and the filling breakfast, served on attractive handmade crockery, includes housemade granola and breads.

WHERE TO EAT

Brava Terrace *3010 N. St. Helena Hwy., (707) 963-9300, fax (707) 963-9581. L&D daily; $$. Closed W in winter & 2 weeks in Jan. Highchairs, boosters, child portions. Reservations advised.*

On warm afternoons and evenings, the casual deck seating here, amid trees and a gurgling creek, is highly desirable, but two attractive indoor rooms are also most welcoming. A great hamburger shares the menu along with a cassoulet (made with green lentils imported from Puy, France) and both a pasta and risotto du jour. Desserts include a chocolate chip crème brulee and an old-fashioned apple-raisin pie with vanilla-chocolate chip ice cream. Coffees and dessert wines are also available.

Gillwoods *1313 Main St., (707) 963-1788. B&L daily, D Thur-Sun; $. Highchairs, boosters. Reservations advised for D.*

This comfortable downtown cafe is known for its breakfasts. All kinds of egg dishes and an assortment of three-egg omelettes are on the menu, as is preservative-free Mother Lode bacon and toasted house-baked bread. And then there's corned-beef hash, buttermilk pancakes, French toast, hot cereals, and granola. Beginning at 11 a.m., salads and sandwiches are also available, and for dinner it's large portions of American-style home cooking.

Picnic Pick-Ups.

• **Dean & Deluca** *607 S. St. Helena Hwy., (707) 967-9980, fax (707) 967-9983. M-Sat 10-7, Sun 10-6.*

A branch of the fabled Manhattan store in SoHo, this impressively stocked, airy, European-style market hall is a gustatory delight. It stocks truffled butter and Devon cream as well as hand-cut tortilla chips and fresh flowers. It is a pleasure to shop for a picnic or for dinner to take home, choosing from the fresh breads, the expansive array of deli items, and the organic produce—all of which can be tasted. The store is home to the Wine Country's largest cheese-aging room, and professional quality cookware is also for sale.

• **The Model Bakery** *1357 Main St., (707) 963-8192. Tu-Sat 7-6, Sun 8-4.*

Among the great breads baked in the 1920s-era brick-and-sand ovens here are pain de vin (whole-wheat sourdough made with a starter derived from grape yeasts), sour rye, crusty sourdough, and both sweet baguettes and rounds. Then there are panini, mini pizzas, and croissants stuffed with either ham and cheese or spinach and Feta cheese. Chocolate chocolate chip cookies, oatmeal-raisin cookies, and biscotti make pleasing desserts, and coffee and espresso drinks are also available. Seating is provided for on-the-spot indulgence.

• **Napa Valley Olive Oil Manufacturing Co.** *835 McCorkle Ave., between Charter Oak & Allison, (707) 963-4173, fax (707) 963-4301. Daily 8-5.*

Everything needed for a picnic is available here: cheese, sausage, olives, bread sticks, focaccia, biscotti. This Old World-style Italian deli also offers a variety of pastas, sauces, and dried mushrooms, plus its own cold-pressed olive oil and homemade red wine vinegar—all placed helter-skelter in barrels and on make-shift tables. It's really quite unusual. A picnic area is provided outside.

Pinot Blanc *641 Main St., (707) 963-6191, fax (707) 963-6192. L&D daily; $$$. Booths, child portions. Reservations suggested.*

Among the area's hot new dining spots, this one stands out. Owned by superchef Joachim Splichal, who also owns several acclaimed restaurants in Los Angeles, this impressive venue on the southern edge of town offers indoor seating in a comfortable open room (opt for one of the three-quarter-moon booths) and, in good weather, patio dining. The unusual French-California bistro-style dishes are meant to tantalize: mashed potatoes topped with giant scallops and a truffle vinaigrette; ricotta gnocchi served with long-braised veal cheeks and tiny, tiny baby artichokes; and an absolutely superb chocolate croissant pudding. Assistance in picking wines to complement each is a house specialty.

Terra *1345 Railroad Ave., (707) 963-8931. D W-M; $$$. Closed 1st 2 weeks of Jan. Reservations advised.*

Fronted by planter boxes filled with gorgeous flowers, this magical spot has a stone-walled, cave-like interior and offers a cool respite from the area's often warm weather. Creative menu selections offered by owner-chef Hiro Sone, formerly of Spago in Los Angeles, combine the styles of France, northern Italy, and the Pacific Rim. They are unusual and flavorful and change periodically: radicchio salad tossed with a balsamic vinaigrette and lots of Parmesan; broiled sake-marinated sea bass with shrimp dumplings in shiso broth; grilled salmon with red Thai curry sauce and basmati rice. Desserts are wicked: rich, moist chocolate bread pudding with sun-dried cherries, or maybe chocolate truffle cake with espresso ice cream.

Tra Vigne *1050 Charter Oak Ave., (707) 963-4444, fax (707) 963-4444. L&D daily; $$. Highchairs, boosters, booths, child portions. Reservations advised.*

Situated in a rustic stone building, with a stunning high-ceilinged room furnished with both comfortable tables and booths, this justly popular restaurant specializes in northern Italian cuisine. Outside seating on the stone patio, under mulberry trees that twinkle with tiny lights at night, is quite desirable on warm days and evenings. A round of crusty bread and some olive oil for dipping are provided to enjoy while perusing the menu. Interesting house-made pastas and pizzas share the menu with fresh fish, meats, and poultry, and it seems there is nothing that is not delicious. Antipasti items and daily specials are often intriguing, and desserts include such goodies as fresh fruit gelato and biscotti with sweet wine. Wine varietals are available by the glass and include both local and Italian selections.

Take-out sandwiches and salads are available in the adjoining **Cantinetta** *((707) 963-8888.)*, where informal outdoor seating is also an option. The restaurant's own olive oils—infused variously with garlic, rosemary, mint, chives, or porcini mushroom—can also be purchased here.

Stop in next door at **Merryvale Vineyards** *(1000 Main St., (800) 326-6069, (707) 963-2225, fax (707) 963-1949; www.merryvale.com. Tasting daily 10-5:30 ($3 fee); tours by appt.)*, which has made its home in the former Sunny St. Helena Winery—the first winery built in the Napa Valley after the repeal of Prohibition. Merryvale hosts a **wine component tasting seminar** *(Sat at 10am. $10. Reservations required.)*.

Wine Spectator Greystone Restaurant *2555 Main St., (707) 967-1010; www.ciachef.edu. L&D daily. Free valet parking.*

This magnificent 1889 landmark building was constructed of locally quarried volcanic tufa stone and is the largest stone building west of the Mississippi. Formerly home to The Christian Brothers winery, it now houses **The Culinary Institute of America at Greystone**—the only center in the world dedicated exclusively to continuing education and career development for professionals in the food, wine, and hospitality fields. A visit to the restaurant affords the opportunity to enjoy Mediterranean tapas, mezze, and antipasti as well as more substantial entrees. **Brother Timothy's corkscrew collection**, which consists of over 1,800 corkscrews from around the world, can be viewed adjacent to the well-stocked gift shop. Building tours and cooking demonstrations are available; call for schedule. The Cannard Herb Garden consists of seven terraces and features both an edible flower garden and an herbal tea garden. Across the street, the Organic Garden grows vegetables, fruits, and flowers—many from rare and heirloom seeds.

Calistoga

A LITTLE BACKGROUND

Calistoga sits on top of a hot underground river. Originally called "Indian Hot Springs," the town's current name was devised from a combination of California and Saratoga—a spa area in New York that was the inspiration for an early 25-cottage spa development by town founder Sam Brannan, California's first millionaire. More of the town's history is to be discovered in *The Silverado Squatters* by Robert Louis Stevenson. When Stevenson quipped that "sightseeing is the art of disappointment," he couldn't have meant it to apply to this scenic area.

Calistoga is enjoying a renaissance as a popular weekend and summer retreat. Its many unpretentious spas are geared to helping visitors relax, unwind, and get healthy in pools filled from hot springs. Most offer services such as mud baths, steam baths, and massages, and many make their mineral pools available for day use for a small fee.

While here, don't miss taking a **mud bath**, one of life's great experiences. The mud is prepared using a mixture of volcanic ash (collected from nearby Mount St. Helena), peat moss, and naturally heated mineral water. After a period of nude immersion, the bather takes a mineral bath and a steam bath, and then, swaddled in dry blankets, rests and cools. Ahhh. (A few notes: Pregnant women, people with high

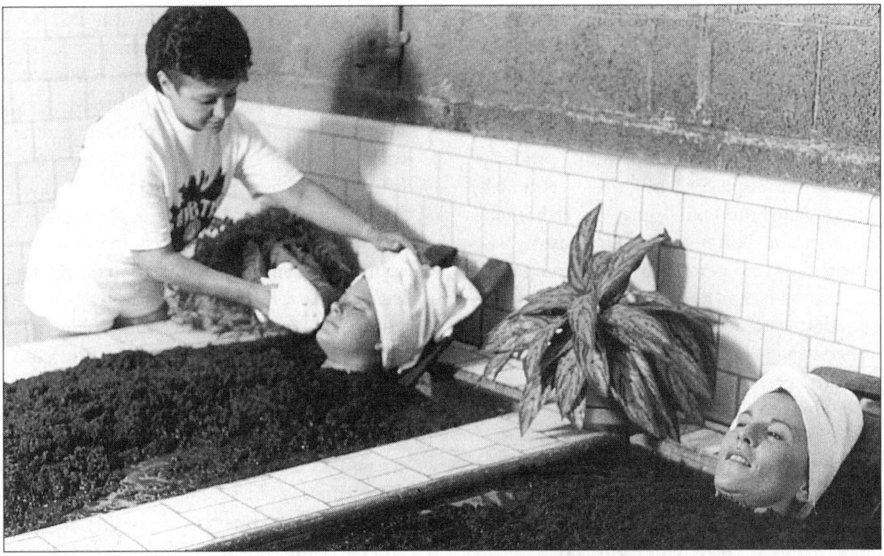

blood pressure or heart conditions, and children under 14 are cautioned against taking mud baths. Technicians are all licensed by the city.)

VISITOR INFORMATION

Calistoga Chamber of Commerce *1458 Lincoln Ave. #9, (707) 942-6333, fax (707) 942-9287; www.calistogafun.com.*

GETTING THERE

Located approximately 10 miles north of St. Helena, and 25 miles north of Napa, via Highway 29.

WHAT TO DO

Bothe-Napa Valley State Park *3801 St. Helena Hwy. N., (707) 942-4575. Daily 8-sunset. $5/vehicle. Pool: Summer only; adults $3, under 18 $1.*

Swimming in the naturally heated pool is a favorite activity at this lovely park, but picnicking and hiking are also popular. Campsites are available.

Getaway Adventures *1117 Lincoln Ave., (800) 499-BIKE, (707) 942-0332, fax 707-763-5458; www.getawayadventures.com. 1 day $89/person.*

Guided bicycle trips visit several small wineries and include a gourmet picnic lunch. Overnight trips, complete with inn stays, are also available. Airport tranfer can be arranged.

Old Faithful Geyser of California *1299 Tubbs Ln., (707) 942-6463, fax (707) 942-6898; www.oldfaithfulgeyser.com. Daily 9-5; in summer to 6. Adults $5, 65+ $4, 6-12 $2.*

Located in the crater of an extinct volcano, this idyllic site is home to one of only three geysers in the world that erupt regularly and merit the name Old Faithful. (The other two are in Yellowstone National Park in Wyoming and on North Island in New Zealand.) This one erupts approximately every 40 minutes and shoots 350-degree water 60 feet into the air. The show lasts from 3 to 4 minutes. Plenty of picnic tables and a snack bar are available.

Petrified Forest *4100 Petrified Forest Rd., 4 mi. west of town, (707) 942-6667; www.petrifiedforest.org. Daily 10-5; in summer to 6. Adults $3, 55+ $2, 4-11 $1.*

A self-guided 1/4-mile path leads through this unusual forest holding the world's largest petrified trees. Open to the public since 1870, it contains petrified redwood trees that are over 3 million years old and as long as 126 feet. Facilities include a small museum and picnic tables.

The Sharpsteen Museum & Sam Brannan Cottage *1311 Washington St., (707) 942-5911; www.sharpsteen-museum.org. Daily 12-4; in summer 10-4. Free.*

Created by Ben Sharpsteen, a Walt Disney Studio animator and Oscar-winning producer (his Oscar is displayed here), this exceptionally well-designed museum displays an elaborate and extensive diorama of Calistoga as it appeared in 1865 when Sam Brannan opened the town's first spa and began its reputation as a restorative resort area. The beautifully furnished cottage exemplifies the style in which wealthy San Franciscans lived when they vacationed here in the late 1800s. A working model of the Napa Valley Railroad is also displayed, and an early kitchen, blacksmith shop, and stagecoach round out the exhibits.

Smith's Mount St. Helena Trout Farm *18401 Ida Clayton Rd., 14 mi. from town (call for directions), (707) 987-3651, fax (707) 987-0105. Sat & Sun 10-6, Feb-Oct; closed Nov-Jan. $1-$5.*

All ages can enjoy fishing on this lake. Poles and bait are free. The charge for fish caught is determined by size, and cleaning and packaging are included.

WINERIES

Château Montelena Winery *1429 Tubbs Ln. (call for directions), (707) 942-5105, fax (707) 942-4221; www.montelena.com. Tasting daily 10-4 (fee $5; applies to purchase of $20+); tours at 11 & 2, reservations required.*

Noted for its Chardonnays and Cabernet Sauvignons, this winery can be difficult to find. Reservations are needed for the unusual island picnic area in Jade Lake where two islets, reached via footbridge, hold miniature picnic pavilions. The lake features a berthed Chinese junk and is populated with ducks, swans, and geese.

Clos Pegase *1060 Dunaweal Ln., (800) 366-8583, (707) 942-4981, fax (707) 942-4993; www.clospegase.com. Tasting daily 10:30-5 (fee $2.50); tours at 11 & 2.*

Because of its stark stucco architecture, this winery opened in 1987 amid much controversy. There were those who liked it and those who didn't. (It is interesting to note that its post-modern design was the winner in a contest sponsored by the San Francisco Museum of Modern Art.) Surrounded by young vineyards, with tall, thin cypress trees lining an outdoor walkway and modern sculpture dotting the landscape, it has a surreal quality. Named after Pegasus, the winged horse of Greek mythology that gave birth to wine and art, the winery appropriately displays a collection of fine art within its caves. Among the treasure-trove are ancient vineyard tools and rare free-blown wine bottles, carafes, and glasses dating from the 3rd century B.C. to the present. An elaborate slide presentation following wine from the birth of the grape, through its celebration in art, and on into the present is scheduled on the third Saturday of each month (except December and January); call to confirm current dates and time. Picnic tables are available.

Schramsberg *1400 Schramsberg Rd., 2 mi. south of town, (800) 877-3623, (707) 942-4558, fax (707) 942-5943; www.schramsberg.com. Tasting (fee $7.50-$15) & tours by appt.*

Established in 1862, this California Historical Landmark was written about extensively by Robert Louis Stevenson in *Silverado Squatters*. He was a guest, as was Ambrose Bierce. Further recognition for its distinctive bottle-fermented sparkling wines made from hand-picked grapes came in 1972 when President Nixon and Premier Chou En-lai poured a bottle of Schramsberg Blanc de Blancs sparkling wine (which, by the way, was the country's first commercial sparkling wine using Chardonnay) for the "Toast to Peace" in Beijing. An informative tour goes through portions of the 2 miles of caves, taking in sections draped with ancient cobwebs and sometimes bumping into the famous "riddler" whose job it is to turn approximately 50,000 bottles each day (the perfect job for a compulsive-neurotic). Tasting occurs in a private room with participants seated appropriately at a glass table supported by an old riddling rack. It is interesting to note that some of the winery buildings were built from redwoods grown on the property, and the house was constructed without nails by a shipbuilder.

Sterling Vineyards

Sterling Vineyards *1111 Dunaweal Ln., (800) 726-6136, (707) 942-3344, fax (707) 942-3445; www.sterlingvienyards.com. Tasting & self-guided tour daily 10:30-4:30. Gondola ride: Adults $6, under 18 $3.*

Accessible via a 4-minute gondola ride, this winery was built to resemble a Greek monastery. It features a stunning and unusual white stucco, cubist style of architecture. Spectacular views of the Napa Valley are provided throughout the self-guided winery tour. For tasting, visitors are seated at tables either in a spacious interior room or on an outdoor terrace, and children are given a complimentary juice drink. A picnic terrace with a magnificent view is also available.

WHERE TO STAY

Brannan Cottage Inn *109 Wapoo Ave., (707) 942-4200. 6 rooms; 100% non-smoking; $-$$$; 2-night min. on weekends. Unsuitable for children under 12. 1 TV. Full breakfast.*

Located a pleasant 2-block walk from town, this Greek Revival Victorian cottage was built by Sam Brannan in 1860. It is listed on the National Register of Historic Places. A large palm tree planted by Brannan, and mentioned by Robert Louis Stevenson in *The Silverado Squatters*, still grows in the garden. Rooms are named after flowers and most open onto a quiet courtyard, where breakfast is served in warm weather.

Calistoga Spa Hot Springs *1006 Washington St., (707) 942-6269; www.calistogaspa.com. 57 units; 100% non-smoking; $-$$; 2-night min. on weekends. Children under 1 free. All kitchens. 3 hot spring pools, hot tub, fitness center.*

This conveniently located, unpretentious, and particularly family-friendly spa offers motel rooms that open onto the pool area. Four outdoor mineral water pools are available: a 100-degree soaking pool, an 83-degree lap pool, a 93-degree children's wading pool, and a 104-degree covered hot tub. Non-guests can also use the pools *(8:30am-9pm. $10/person.).* Mud baths, mineral baths, steam baths, and massage are available.

Cottage Grove Inn *1711 Lincoln Ave., (800) 799-2284, (707) 942-8400, fax (707) 942-2653; www.cottagegrove.com. 16 cabins; 100% non-smoking; $$$-$$$+. All wood-burning fireplaces, VCRs. Afternoon wine, continental breakfast.*

Individual cottages, each decorated in a different theme, nestle here in an historic elm grove. All are equipped with a deep whirlpool soaking tub for two, a stereo system, and a refrigerator.

Dr. Wilkinson's Hot Springs *1507 Lincoln Ave., (707) 942-4102; www.drwilkinson.com. 42 rooms; $-$$; 2-night min. on weekends. Children under 2 free. Some kitchens. 1 indoor heated pool, 2 outdoor heated pools, hot tub, health spa, steam room.*

Operated by the Wilkinson family, this pleasant spa features a 104-degree indoor mineral pool with a view of the nearby foothills, a cooler 92-degree outdoor mineral pool, and a refreshing 82-degree outdoor swimming pool. Pools are not open to non-guests. Mud baths, mineral baths, steam baths, and massage are available, and a separate facial salon offers an assortment of treatments. Lodging is in motel units. The **Hideaway Cottages** and **The Victorian House**, which are unsuitable for children, are also available nearby.

Indian Springs Spa & Resort *1712 Lincoln Ave., (707) 942-4913, fax (707) 942-4919;www.indianspringscalistoga.com. 17 units; $$$-$$$+. Children under 2 free. All kitchens; some gas fireplaces. Heated mineral water pool, health spa, 1 clay tennis court.*

Dating back to 1910 and built on the site of the town's first spa (which was built in 1860 by Sam Brannan), this resort is where Robert Louis Stevenson vacationed in 1880 and is said to have written part of *The Silverado Squatters.* It is the state's oldest continuously operating pool and spa facility. It includes a Mission-style, Olympic-size swimming pool filled with 90- to 102-degree geyser mineral water and is open to non-guests for day use *(Adults $10-$20, children $7-$10.)* and especially enjoyed by children. And this is the only spa in town offering relaxing all ash mud baths. Accommodations are refurbished 1940s housekeeping bungalows. Croquet is also available to guests.

Mountain Home Ranch *3400 Mountain Home Ranch Rd., 6 mi. from town, (707) 942-6616, fax (707) 942-9091. 14 units; $$-$$$. Closed Dec & Jan. Children under 1 free. No TVs; some kitchens & wood-burning fireplaces & stoves. 2 unheated pools (summer only), 1 tennis court. Continental breakfast (Sept-June only); restaurant (Sept-June only). Pets welcome.*

Guests at this informal rural spot can stay in either modern cabins with a private deck or porch, lodge rooms, or rustic cabins (summer only). Summer activities include swimming, hiking, and fishing. Rates are higher in summer and include both breakfast and dinner.

Mount View Hotel *1457 Lincoln Ave., (800) 816-6877, (707) 942-6877, fax (707) 942-6904; www.mountviewhotel.com. 33 rooms; 100% non-smoking; $$-$$$+; 2-night min. on Sat. Unsuitable for children under 16. Some VCRs. Heated pool, hot tub, health spa. Restaurant.*

This beautifully restored grand hotel, built in 1918 and furnished with an eclectic mix of contemporary and antique pieces, is a National Historic Landmark. Nine theme suites are furnished in period pieces, including two in art deco style, and three private cottages have their own decks and hot tubs. An upscale European-style spa offers a variety of treatments; packages are available.

Operated by celebrity chef Jan Birnbaum, **Catahoula Restaurant** *((707) 942-BARK. L&D W-Mon; $$. Closed Jan. Reservations advised.)* offers an imaginative menu of delicious Southern-style American cuisine as well as spectacular desserts. Strong points are items from the kitchen's wood-burning brick oven, braised dishes, and freshly baked sourdough breads. **The Saloon** serves lunch daily and hosts a popular Sunday Blues Brunch. Special events centered around food and wine are scheduled regularly.

The Pink Mansion *1415 Foothill Blvd., (800) 238-PINK, (707) 942-0558, same fax; www.pinkmansion.com. 5 rooms; $-$$$. Some fireplaces. Indoor pool & hot tub. Full breakfast.*

Nestled against a hillside on the outskirts of town, this restored 1875 mansion is painted a pleasant shade of pink. A large front porch equipped with a couch swing invites leisurely contemplation of the surroundings, and the indoor pool and hot tub have a relaxing view of a redwood grove behind the house. Several rooms have clawfoot tubs, and the Angel Room is bedecked with former owner Aunt Alma's angel collection. A lavish breakfast is served in the elegant dining room.

WHERE TO EAT

All Seasons Cafe & Wine Shop *1400 Lincoln Ave., (707) 942-9111, fax (707) 942-9420. L&D Thur-Tu, Sat & SunBr; $$-$$$. Highchairs, boosters. Reservations advised.*

Dress is very casual in this narrow dining room, and children are welcome and accommodated. One dinner enjoyed here began with great housemade bread and a flawless warm spinach salad prepared with pancetta, house-smoked chicken, and Feta cheese. It was followed by a perfectly roasted chicken accompanied by perfectly roasted potatoes, whole cloves of garlic, artichokes, and olives. Dessert was a memorable fresh cherry cobbler with housemade vanilla ice cream arranged artistically on a plate strewn with flower petals.

Calistoga Inn *1250 Lincoln Ave., (707) 942-4101, fax (707) 942-4919. B,L,&D daily; $$-$$$. Highchairs, boosters. Reservations advised.*

With a delightful collection of turkey platters decorating the walls here, it isn't too much of a surprise that the house specialty is big portions of old-fashioned hardwood-grilled meats and vegetables, though 40-clove garlic chicken and fresh fish are also offered. Irresistible down-home desserts include creamy peanut butter pie and housemade brownies "smushed" with vanilla ice cream and topped with hot fudge. In warm weather diners are seated outside on a patio overlooking the Napa Valley River. An informal **brewpub** operating in the cozy old-time bar area offers four house brews—one of them a Pilsner-style lager (the house specialty)—and inexpensive pub food such as housemade potato chips, a variety of salads, a good hamburger, and jerk chicken.

Modest, inexpensive **lodging** *(18 rooms; $. All shared baths.)* in cozy, pleasant rooms equipped with sinks is available upstairs. Several sets of adjoining rooms are suitable for families.

Cinnabar Cafe *1440 Lincoln Ave., (707) 942-6989. B,L,&D daily; $-$$. Highchairs, boosters, booths, child portions. Reservations advised.*

Attractive and unpretentious, this spot serves reasonably priced, honest food. Breakfast is the expected items plus 19 kinds of three-egg omelettes, sautéed boned fresh trout, buttermilk or buckwheat pancakes, and housemade granola. Lunch includes made-from-scratch soups and breads and a large variety of sandwiches and hamburgers. Dinner is a pricier selection of fresh fish and prime rib.

Smokehouse Cafe *1458 Lincoln Ave., in historic Calistoga Depot, (707) 942-6060, fax (707) 942-5431. B,L,&D daily; $-$$.*

Chef extraordinaire Hunter Austin promises no vertical food, aloof waiters, or staggering prices in his restaurant. Instead, diners get delicious down-home American barbecue served in unpretentious surroundings. Hunter smokes his own meats on-site, and the only frozen item he uses is ice cream. Particularly good appetizers include Sacramento Delta crawfish cakes and 101-proof Wild Turkey sausage. Memorable main courses include tasty Arkansas slow pig, fabulous mesquite-smoked beef back ribs, and Texarkana cherrywood-smoked barbecued chicken. Meals are served with lumpy mashed potatoes, a root vegetable and greens sauté, and unlimited cornbread. Call ahead to find out what's cooking in the way of weekend entertainment.

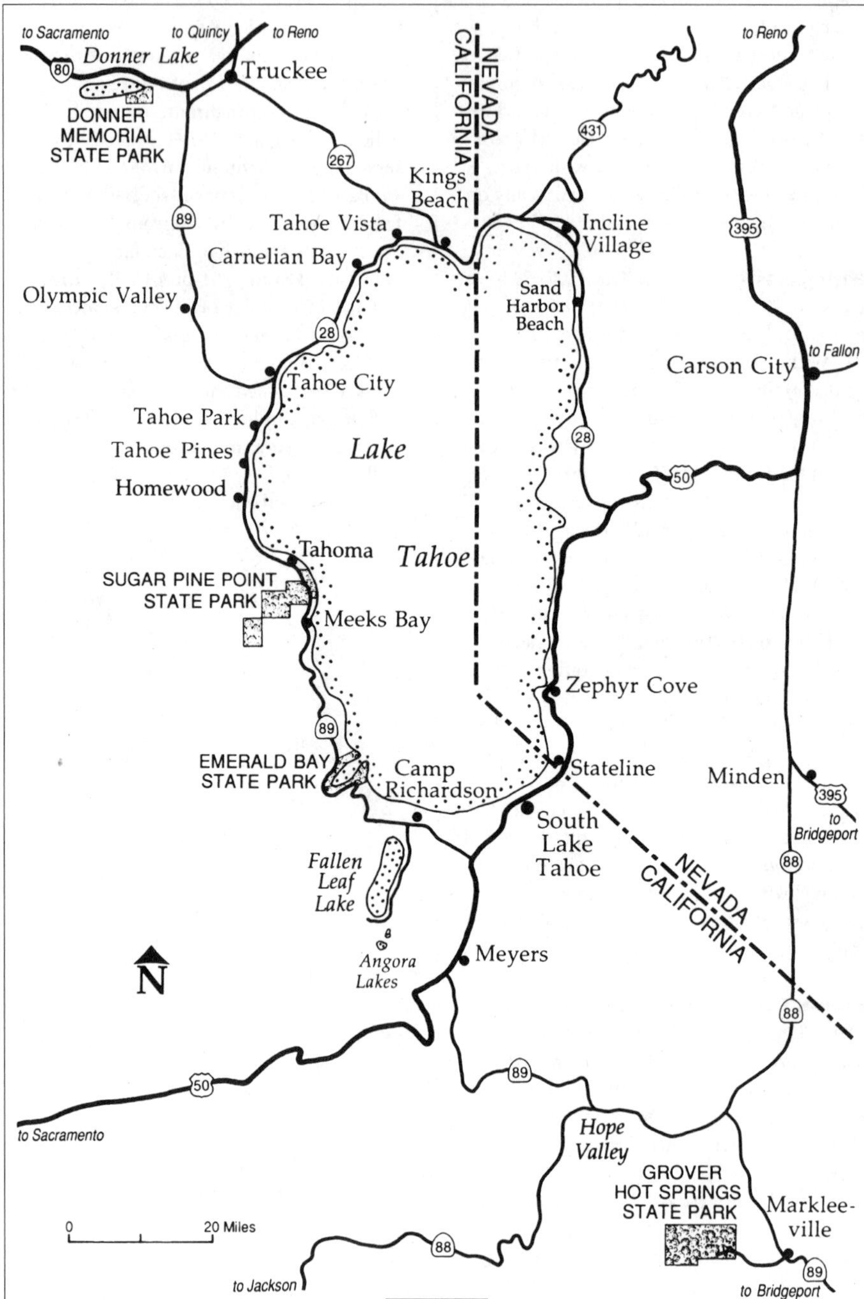

to Sacramento
to Quincy
to Reno
80
Donner Lake
Truckee
DONNER
MEMORIAL
STATE PARK
NEVADA
CALIFORNIA
to Reno
431
267
Kings
Beach
89
Tahoe Vista
Incline
Village
395
Carnelian Bay
Sand
Harbor
Beach
Olympic Valley
28
to Fallon
Carson City
Tahoe City
Tahoe Park
Tahoe Pines
Lake
28
50
Homewood
Tahoma
Tahoe
SUGAR PINE POINT
STATE PARK
Meeks Bay
Zephyr Cove
89
EMERALD BAY
STATE PARK
Camp
Richardson
Stateline
Minden
395
to
Bridgeport
South
Lake
Tahoe
88
Fallen
Leaf
Lake
NEVADA
CALIFORNIA
Angora
Lakes
Meyers
N
88
89
50
to Sacramento
Hope
Valley
GROVER
HOT SPRINGS
STATE PARK
Marklee-
ville
0
20 Miles
88
89
to Jackson
to Bridgeport

MAP 16

South Lake Tahoe

A LITTLE BACKGROUND

. . . At last the Lake burst upon us—a noble sheet of blue water lifted six thousand three hundred feet above the level of the sea, and walled in by a rim of snowclad mountain peaks that towered aloft full three thousand feet higher still!

It was a vast oval. As it lay there with the shadows of the great mountains brilliantly photographed upon its surface, I thought it must surely be the fairest picture the whole earth affords . . .

— Mark Twain

Lake Tahoe lies two-thirds in California and one-third in Nevada. It is the largest (192 square miles surface) and deepest (1,645 feet) Alpine lake in North America and the second largest in the world. At 6,227 feet above sea level, its crystal-clear, deep-blue summer waters provide a striking contrast with the extensive green forests and majestic mountains encircling it.

Once a remote area, Tahoe is now a popular and well-equipped vacation destination offering a wide range of recreational activities along with its spectacular scenery. Swimming, hiking, boating, tennis, golf, bicycling, horseback riding, river rafting, camping, fishing, water-skiing, and backpacking are among the summer outdoor activities to be enjoyed. In winter, the skiing is excellent.

On the Nevada side, gambling is another big attraction. Most lodgings provide transportation to the casinos and have discount casino coupons for their guests. In addition, the casinos offer on-demand pick-up shuttle service from most lodgings.

Children may go into a casino with adults but are not allowed to "loiter" (not even babies in backpacks!) or play the slot machines. Fortunately, childcare is relatively easy to find in this area. Many lodging facilities maintain a list of local sitters, and childcare centers that take drop-ins are listed in the Yellow Pages. Also, the Lake Tahoe Visitors Authority provides a free listing of day care providers.

In addition to having more slot machines than any other casino at Lake Tahoe, Harrah's has an unsupervised Video Game Room and Family Fun Center for children that is open year-round from 9 a.m. to midnight. It is a safe, well-lighted, non-smoking, and alcohol-free environment and is stocked with the latest video and arcade games as well as some old classics. Sure beats sitting on the curb reading comic books like some people did when they were kids. For further information call (800) 648-3773. Harvey's operates a nightly Kid's Camp for ages 6 through 13. Rates are $40 per child for a 6 to 10 p.m. session. For further information call (800) 553-1022.

VISITOR INFORMATION

Lake Tahoe Visitors Authority *1156 Ski Run Blvd.; (800) AT-TAHOE (lodging reservations referral service); (530) 544-5050, fax (530) 544-2386; www.virtualtahoe.com (road and weather conditions).*

GETTING THERE

Located approximately 200 miles north of San Francisco. Take Highway 80 to Highway 50 to the lake.

ANNUAL EVENTS

Lights on the Lake *July 4.*

This spectacular show is the largest display of fireworks west of the Mississippi. Each shell is choreographed and computer synchronized to a soundtrack.

Autumn Colors *October.*

The area around Kirkwood Mountain Resort (see page 401) is home to groves of aspen. Hope Valley, north of Kirkwood on Highway 89, is particularly colorful.

STOPS ALONG THE WAY

I-80 North. See pages 247 through 275.

Folsom *Off Hwy. 50, 25 mi. east of Sacramento.*

This small town provides an easy stop. Restored Gold Rush-era homes and buildings, many now inhabited by antique shops, line historic Sutter Street.

• **Folsom Chamber of Commerce** *200 Wool St., (800) 377-1414, (916) 985-2698, fax (916) 985-4117; www.FolsomChamber.com.*

Information about the town is available at the chamber's office located inside the town's old train depot.

• **Folsom City Zoo** *Natoma/Stafford, (916) 985-7347. Tu-Sun 10-4. Adults $2, 5-12 $1.*

This tiny zoo exhibits native non-releasable North American animals, a few exotics, and the largest captive wolf pack in Northern California.

• **Folsom Dam** *7794 Folsom Dam Rd., (916) 989-7275, fax (916) 989-7208. Tours M-Sat 10-1. Free.*

Built between 1948 and 1956, this impressive dam measures 340 feet high and 1,400 feet long.

• **Folsom History Museum** *823 Sutter St., (916) 985-2707. W-Sun 11-4. Adults $1, under 12 free.*

Exhibits change frequently. Gold-panning demonstrations occur on Sundays.

• **Folsom Lake State Recreation Area** *7806 Folsom-Auburn Rd., (916) 988-0205. Daily 6am-10pm; Oct-Mar 7-7. $6/vehicle.*

Overnight camping is permitted in this 18,000-acre park.

• **Folsom Prison Museum** *(916) 985-2561. Daily 10-4.*

Located just inside the visitor's gate, this small museum documents the history of this massive granite structure. An inmate art show is held annually in the spring and fall

• **Lake Forest Cafe** *13409 Folsom Blvd., (916) 985-6780. B&L W-Sun; $. Highchairs, boosters, child portions.*

Among the breakfast items here are 43 kinds of omelettes, a variety of Jewish specialties, and freshly-baked giant cinnamon rolls. Some breakfast items are also available at lunch.

Poor Red's. See page 316.

Placerville. See page 317.

WHAT TO DO

Amusement Centers.

These family fun spots are open daily in summer and as the weather permits in winter.

• **Magic Carpet Golf** *2455 Lake Tahoe Blvd. (Hwy. 50), (530) 541-3787.*

This is the kind of colorful miniature course that has giant plaster dinosaurs and a new theme at each hole. Choose from either 19- or 28-hole rounds.

• **Tahoe Amusement Park** *2401 Lake Tahoe Blvd. (Hwy. 50), (530) 541-1300.*

Facilities include a variety of kiddie rides, a giant slide, and go-carts.

Angora Lakes Trail *On Spring Creek Rd., off Hwy. 89.*

Take the road to Fallen Leaf Lake, which passes a waterfall, and then turn left at the sign to Angora Lakes. It is an easy 1/2-mile hike from the end of the road to the lakes, where quiet picnic and swimming spots can be found.

Beaches and Biking.

The **Pope-Baldwin Recreation Area** *(On Hwy. 89, between the Y & Emerald Bay, (530) 573-2674. Daily 8-6; closed in winter. $3/vehicle.)* is lined with good beaches. This same stretch of highway has several bike rental facilities and a nice bike trail.

Boat Rentals.

Various kinds of boats are available at **Ski Run Marina** *((530) 544-0200)*, **Tahoe Keys Marina** *((530) 541-2155)*, and **Timber Cove Marina** *((530) 544-2942)*. Water-skiing and wind-surfing lessons and rentals also are available at Ski Run Marina.

Boat Tours.

- **M.S. Dixie II Paddlewheeler** *760 Hwy. 50, Zephyr Cove, Nevada, 4 mi. south of Stateline, (775) 882-0786, (775) 588-3508. Call for schedule. Adults $17, seniors $15, 3-11 $5. Reservations advised.*

Actually used on the Mississippi River as a cotton barge in the 1920s, this three-deck paddle wheel steamer cruises to Emerald Bay. She is the largest boat on the lake and boasts a glass-bottom viewing window. Dinner cruises with live music for dancing and breakfast/ brunch cruises are available at additional charge.

- **Tahoe Queen** *At foot of Ski Run Blvd., (800) 23-TAHOE, (530) 541-3364. Call for schedule. Adults $18, under 12 $8. Reservations required.*

This big paddle wheeler offers 2-hour cruises to Emerald Bay. The boat has a large window in its floor for underwater viewing. Call for information on the sunset dinner-dance cruise and the winter ski shuttle to the North Shore.

- **Woodwind II** *760 Hwy. 50, Zephyr Cove, Nevada, (800) 867-6394, (775) 588-3000. Call for schedule; closed Nov-Apr. Adults $20, seniors $18, 2-12 $10. Reservations advised.*

Only 35 passengers fit on this 55-foot catamaran with two underwater observation windows. A sunset champagne cruise is available at additional charge.

Camp Richardson Corral and Pack Station *On Hwy. 89 N., Camp Richardson, (530) 541-3113. Daily; June-Sept only. Guided rides $20/hr. Riders must be 6 or older. Reservations required.*

M.S. Dixie & Tahoe Queen

Operated by the same family since 1934, this stable has breakfast rides *($28)*, dinner rides *($35)*, and wagon rides *($10, under 3 free)*. Fishing trips, overnight pack trips, and spot pack trips can be arranged, and sleigh rides are available December through March when there is enough snow.

Casino Shows. Big name entertainment is always booked into these showrooms. Call ahead for reservations at the early or late cocktail shows. Seats are assigned. Children 6 and older are usually admitted, but it depends on the show's content.

- **Caesars Circus Maximus** *(800) 648-3353, (775) 588-3515.*
- **Harrah's South Shore Room** *(800) 648-3773.*
- **Harvey's Emerald Theater** *(800) 553-1022, (775) 588-2411. 100% non-smoking.*

Holding just 288 seats, this is said to be the only mini-showroom in the world. There are no bad seats.

- **Horizon's Grande Lake Theatre** *(800) 322-7723, (775) 588-6211.*

Drive Around the Lake.

A leisurely drive around the 72-mile perimeter of Lake Tahoe takes about 3 hours. Allow all day, though, as there are many tempting places to stop for picnicking, swimming, and exploring.

Grover Hot Springs State Park *3415 Hot Springs Rd., 4 mi. east of Markleeville, 35 mi. southeast of town, (530) 694-2248. Daily 9-9 in summer; rest of year M-F 2-9, Sat & Sun 9-9. Adults $4, under 18 $2; parking $5.*

Beautifully situated in a valley meadow ringed by pine-covered slopes, this state park features a 3-foot deep, 104-degree mineral pool filled by six nonsulfurous springs and a 70- to 80-degree fresh-water pool. The pools are well-maintained, and lifeguards are on duty. Because the number of bathers permitted is limited, there is sometimes a wait, and swimsuits are always required. Short hiking trails, picnic facilities, and campsites are also available. In winter this is a popular après-ski destination.

Lake Tahoe Historical Society Museum *3058 Lake Tahoe Blvd., (530) 541-5458; www.tahoenevada.com. Daily 11-4 in summer; rest of year Sat & Sun 12-4. Adults $1, 65+ 75¢, 5-14 50¢.*

The history of Lake Tahoe's south shore is chronicled here.

Lake Tahoe Visitor Center *On Hwy. 89, north of Camp Richardson, (530) 573-2674. Daily 8-5:30. Closed Nov-May. Free.*

Campfire programs and guided nature tours are scheduled regularly, and there are several self-guided trails. Mountain stream life can be viewed from an underwater perspective in the Taylor Creek Stream Profile. Visit in October to see the annual run of the Kokanee salmon and to take part in the annual **Kokanee Salmon Festival.**

Tahoe Trout Farm *1023 Blue Lake Ave., off Hwy. 50, (530) 541-1491. Daily 10-7; June-Aug only. Charge determined by size of fish caught.*

Though there is, of course, no challenge to catching trout here, there are some compelling reasons to give it a try. No license in required, bait and tackle are furnished free, and there is no limit. Anglers are virtually guaranteed to go home with tasty dinner fare. Even young children, who frustrate easily, will probably succeed in catching a fish. (Do bear in mind that some children are appalled at just the *idea* of catching a fish—let alone actually *eating* it.)

Tallac Historic Site *Off Hwy. 89, 3 mi. north of Hwy. 50, (530) 541-5227, fax (530) 573-2693. Museum: Daily 10-4 in summer; grounds open rest of year. Free.*

Three early 20th-century summer estates and 23 cottages are situated on this 74-acre site. Special cultural and historical programs are sometimes scheduled, and picnic tables and barbecues are available.

A **Great Gatsby Festival** is held here each August. Celebrating the area's partying past, this festival brings history to life with era arts and crafts demonstrations, plus some old-fashioned fun and games.

Vikingsholm Castle *On Hwy. 89, Tahoma, (530) 525-7277. Tours daily 10-4; June-Aug only. Adults $2, 6-17 $1. Strollers not permitted on tour.*

Butterflies, waterfalls, and wildflowers are enjoyed on the steep, dry 1-mile trail that descends to this magnificent 39-room, sod-roof Swedish castle home built in 1928. Constructed completely by hand using native materials, it was completed in one summer. It is part of **Emerald Bay State Park** and **Sierra State Park**. Picnic tables are available, and swimming is permitted in an area with a sandy beach.

Winter Activities. See pages 401 to 402.

WHERE TO STAY

Lakefront

Inn By the Lake *3300 Lake Tahoe Blvd. (Hwy. 50), (800) 877-1466, (530) 542-0330, fax (530) 541-6596; www.innbythelake.com. 100 rooms; $-$$$+. Children under 12 free in existing beds. Some kitchens; 1 wood-burning fireplace. Heated pool, hot tub, sauna. Continental breakfast.*

Located in a grove of pine trees across the street from the lake, this attractive contemporary hotel offers comfortable, quiet accommodations.

Royal Valhalla Lodge *4104 Lakeshore Blvd., (800) 999-4104, (530) 544-2233, fax (530) 544-1436. 80 units; $-$$$. Some kitchens. Heated pool (unavail. Nov-Apr), hot tub. Continental breakfast.*

Pick from one-, two-, or three-bedroom units, many of which have lake views. Guests have use of a private beach.

Tahoe Beach & Ski Club *3601 Lake Tahoe Blvd. (Hwy.50), (530) 541-6220, fax (530) 541-6187. 128 rooms; $-$$$+. All kitchens. Heated pool (unavail. Oct-Apr), 2 hot tubs, 2 saunas.*

Located 1 mile from the casinos, this lakeside hotel has 400 feet of private beach plus a **Marie Callenders** restaurant located just next door.

Timber Cove Lodge Marina Resort *3411 Lake Tahoe Blvd. (Hwy. 50), (800) 972-8558, (530) 541-6722, fax (530) 541-7959; www.TimberCoveTahoe.com. 262 rooms; $-$$$; 2-night min. on Sat, July-Sept. Children under 16 free. Heated pool, hot tub. Restaurant, room service.*

This well-situated motel has a private beach, marina, and pier, and many of the rooms have lake views.

Casinos

The major casinos offer large numbers of luxury hotel rooms.

- **Caesars** *(800) 648-3353; www.caesars.com.*
- **Harrah's** *(800) 648-3773; www.harrahs.com.*
- **Harvey's** *(800) 648-3361; www.harveys.com.*
- **Horizon** *(800) 648-3322; www.horizoncasino resort.com.*

Condos and Homes

Accommodation Station *(800) 344-9364, (530) 542-5850, fax (530) 542-4863; www.tahoe lodging.com. 85+ units; $-$$$+; 2-night min. Most VCRs; all kitchens & fireplaces.*

Privately-owned condominiums, cabins, and houses can be rented through this agency. Rate is determined by the number of bedrooms and type of accommodation.

Lake Tahoe Accommodations *((800) 544-3234, (530) 542-1860; www.tahoe accommo dations.com.)* is a similar service.

Lakeland Village *3535 Lake Tahoe Blvd. (Hwy. 50), (800) 822-5969, (530) 544-1685, fax (530) 541-6278; www.Lakeland-Village.com. 207 units; $$-$$$+; 2-night min. on weekends. Children under 18 free. Some VCRs; all kitchens & wood-burning or gas fireplaces. Heated pool, children's wading pool (unavail. Oct-May), 2 hot tubs, sauna, 2 tennis courts (fee).*

Though located beside a bustling highway, this condominium complex manages to retain a secluded, restive feeling. Some units are lakefront; all are within a short walk. Amenities include a private beach, children's playground, horseshoe pit, watercraft rentals, and free shuttle to the casinos. During the Christmas holidays, sleigh rides are available through the resort's 19 wooded acres.

Other

The Christiana Inn *3819 Saddle Rd., (530) 544-7337, fax (530) 544-5342; www.christiana inn.com. 6 rooms; 100% non-smoking; $-$$$; 2-night min. on weekends. Closed for 3 weeks at end of ski season. Children under 12 free. Some wood-burning fireplaces. Continental breakfast; restaurant.*

Built in 1965, this charming Tyrolean-style inn sits high above the lake near the slopes of Heavenly Valley. Each suite is uniquely decorated (several have private saunas), and the inn is furnished with antiques throughout. A decanter of warming brandy awaits guests in each room, and breakfast is delivered to the room in the morning.

The inn's elegant **restaurant** *(D daily. Boosters, booths, child portions. Reservations advised.)* serves American Continental cuisine—rack of lamb, cherries jubilee, baked Alaska—at tables lighted by a fireplace. Known for its extensive wine cellar, it is also open to non-guests.

Embassy Suites Resort Lake Tahoe *4130 Lake Tahoe Blvd. (Hwy. 50), (800) 998-9892, (800) EMBASSY, (530) 544-5400, fax (530) 544-7643; www.embassytahoe.com. 9 stories; 400 rooms; $$-$$$+. Children under 12 free. All VCRs. Indoor heated pool, hot tub, sauna, steam room, fitness center. Evening cocktails, full breakfast; 3 restaurants, room service. Valet parking $2.*

The first new hotel built in the Tahoe Basin since restrictions were imposed, this link in the popular Embassy Suites chain features a nightclub and a 7-story-tall indoor atrium with waterfalls. Winter amenities include on-site ski rental, repair, and storage, plus next-day lift ticket sales and a complimentary shuttle to the Heavenly Valley ski area. And, as an ad for the hotel declares, "... you don't have to gamble to get a free breakfast and free drinks": An all-you-can-eat breakfast and evening cocktails are complimentary to guests. But for those who *do* want to gamble, Harrah's is right next door.

Tahoe Seasons Resort *3901 Saddle Rd., (800) 540-4874, (530) 541-6700, fax (530) 541-7342; www.tahoeseasons.com. 8 stories; 180 units; $$-$$$. Children free. All VCRs; some gas fireplaces. Heated pool, hot tub, 2 tennis courts. Restaurant, room service.*

Each unit here is a spacious suite equipped with a microwave and refrigerator as well as an oversize whirlpool bathtub big enough for two. And since it is located across the street from the Heavenly Valley ski area, skiers who stay here can just walk there in the morning. No chains. No parking hassles. But if someone in the party doesn't want to ski, it's possible to get a room with a view of the slopes so they can stay cozy in front of a fireplace and just watch. The resort also provides on-site ski rentals and both chain installation and removal services.

Motel Row.

Highway 50 into town is littered with more motels than is to be believed. However, this might be changing. South Lake Tahoe's redevelopment plan, which focuses on upgrading rather than expanding, dictates that for every new hotel room built, 1.31 old rooms must be removed.

Farther Away

Sorensen's Resort. See page 401.

Zephyr Cove Resort *760 Hwy. 50, Zephyr Cove, Nevada, 4 mi. north of Stateline, (775) 588-6644, fax (775) 588-9627. 31 units; $-$$$+. Some kitchens & wood-burning fireplaces. Restaurant.*

Located in a lovely forested area by the lake, these rustic cabins and lodge rooms provide a convenient, yet out-of-the-way spot to stay. Facilities include a beach, marina with boat rentals, stable, and arcade. Campsites are also available. Do reserve early; cabins are usually booked-up a year in advance!

WHERE TO EAT

Cantina Bar & Grill *765 Emerald Bay Rd., 1/4 mi. north of the Y, (530) 544-1233, fax (530) 544-0823; www.cantinatahoe.com. L&D daily; $-$$. Highchairs, boosters, booths, child menu. No reservations.*

There is almost always a wait to be seated in this festive and popular spot, but that's no reason to stay away. Waiting time can be passed sitting in the bar with a pitcher of margaritas (tasty niña coladas for kids) and some nachos. The menu has changed a lot over the years, but it just keeps getting better. Delicious choices include carnitas (roast pork), a large variety of giant burritos, and fresh fish.

Casinos.

For some of the best and least expensive food in this area, try the casino restaurants and buffets. Among the best are:

- **Bill's Casino.**

  When the lines at the casino restaurants are just too long, the **McDonald's** here can be a sanity saver. It is the first McDonald's ever built in a casino and has a separate entrance for families. In Bill's, be sure to take a free pull on **Billy Jean**—the world's largest free-pull slot machine.

- **Caesars Cafe Roma** *(800) 648-3353, (775) 588-3515. B,L,&D daily; $. Highchairs, boosters, child portions. No reservations.*

  This coffee shop is open round-the-clock. Caesars also has a **Planet Hollywood**.

• **Harrah's Forest Buffet** *(800) 648-3773, (775) 588-6611. B&L M-Sat, D daily, SunBr; $-$$. Highchairs, boosters, child portions. No reservations.*

Located on the 18th floor, this classy restaurant provides spectacular lake and mountain views, plus outstanding food at a reasonable price.

Harrah's **North Beach Deli** is the place to get a picnic lunch packed to go in a Harrah's fanny pack.

In addition to bargain dining, the casinos also offer fine dining. The elegant **Summit** restaurant *((800) 648-3773. D daily; $$$. Reservations advised.)* on the 16th and 17th floors of Harrah's, offers heady views and refined cuisine. Located in what was originally the Star Suite, where the rich and famous headliners were once put up, it offers a new menu every day. Items are beautifully presented, and service is impeccable. One meal enjoyed here began with crispy-crusted mini baguettes and sweet butter shaped like roses. An appetizer of chilled gulf shrimp was arranged in a red seafood sauce swirled with horseradish hearts, and a salad of baby lettuces was arranged in a scooped-out tomato so that it resembled a bouquet. The entree was a perfect rack of lamb with an anise crust and a side of mashed potatoes sprinkled with truffles, followed by a dessert Frangelico soufflé with a hazelnut-praline crème fraîche.

• **Harvey's Carriage House** *(800) 553-1022, (800) 648-3361, (775) 588-2411. B,L,&D daily; $-$$. Highchairs, boosters, child portions. No reservations.*

Open round-the-clock, this restaurant is known for its delicious fried chicken dinners.

Harvey's also has a **Hard Rock Cafe** and the largest video arcade at the lake.

The Fresh Ketch Lakeside Restaurant *2435 Venice Dr. E., (530) 541-5683. L&D daily; $$. Highchairs, boosters, child portions. Reservations advised.*

Located at the Tahoe Keys Marina, the lake's only protected inland marina, this restaurant offers water views and fresh seafood. In addition to a daily special, the menu also has scampi, calamari steak topped with anchovy butter, cioppino, king crab legs, and live Maine lobster. Plenty of non-fish items are also offered, including steaks and hamburgers, and dessert brings on Key lime and hula pies.

Heidi's Pancake House *3485 Lake Tahoe Blvd. (Hwy.50), (530) 544-8113, fax (530) 544-4118. B&L daily; $. Highchairs, boosters, booths, child menu. No reservations.*

Breakfast is served all day in this cozy, casual restaurant. The menu includes pancakes, French toast, crêpes, Belgian waffles, and omelettes, as well as just about any other breakfast item imaginable, and orange juice is fresh-squeezed. At lunch, a variety of sandwiches, hamburgers, and salads are added to the menu.

Monument Peak Restaurant *Top of Ski Run Blvd., Wildwood/Saddle Dr., (775) 586-7000. L&D daily; call for winter D schedule; $-$$. Closed Oct, Nov, & May. Highchairs, boosters, child portions. Reservations advised. Tram: adults $12.50, 5-12 $9.50.*

A bright red aerial tram lifts diners 2,000 feet above Lake Tahoe to enjoy magnificent views while dining. Call for the current menu and for details on the tram/dinner package.

The moderately strenuous 2-mile Tahoe Vista Trail begins here and offers a panoramic view of the lake. Free 1½-hour guided hikes are scheduled daily; call for details.

North Lake Tahoe

VISITOR INFORMATION

Tahoe North Visitors & Convention Bureau *950 North Lake Blvd., Tahoe City, (800) TAHOE-4-U (reservations service), (530) 583-3494, fax (530) 581-4081; www.tahoefun.org.*

North Lake Tahoe Chamber of Commerce *245 North Lake Blvd., Tahoe City, (530) 581-6900, fax (530) 581-6904.*

Incline Village Crystal Bay Visitors & Convention Bureau *969 Tahoe Blvd., Incline Village, Nevada, (800) GO-TAHOE, (775) 832-1606, fax (775) 832-1605; www.gotahoe.com.*

GETTING THERE

Located approximately 210 miles north of San Francisco. Take Highway 80 to Truckee, then Highway 267 south to the lake.

The Chicago-bound Amtrak train leaves Emeryville daily at 9:35 a.m. and arrives in Truckee at 3:11 p.m. For fare and schedule information and to make reservations, call (800) 872-7245.

ANNUAL EVENTS

Music at Sand Harbor *July. At Sand Harbor State Park in Nevada; (530) 583-7625. Tickets $20-$25.*

Imagine sitting in a natural sand-bowl amphitheater overlooking beautiful Lake Tahoe while enjoying great, live contemporary music. Then add a sprinkling of stars, both celestial and earthly. That's "Tunes in the Dunes"— the nickname given by locals to this event.

Concours d'Elegance *August. In Carnelian Bay; (800) TAHOE-4-U. Adults $16, 62+ $13, 6-16 $8.*

The Tahoe Yacht Club organizes this annual extravaganza of boats.

Lake Tahoe Shakespeare Festival *August. At Sand Harbor State Park in Nevada; (800) 74-SHOWS, (775) 832-1606; www.laketahoeshakespeare.com. Tickets $20-$50.*

"Bard on the Beach," another nickname bestowed by fond locals, is the biggest event of the summer at the lake. Bring a picnic, a blanket, and some low-leg beach chairs.

STOPS ALONG THE WAY

I-80 North. See pages 247 through 276.

Auburn. See page 318.

Grass Valley. See page 319.

Nevada City. See page 321.

WHAT TO DO

Best Beaches.

• **Commons Beach** *In Tahoe City; stairway across from 510 North Lake Blvd.; parking lot behind Tahoe City Fire Station.*

This family beach boasts a large grassy area and a lakefront playground.

• **Sand Harbor State Park** *In Nevada, 4 mi. south of Incline Village. $4/vehicle.*

This is a perfect beach. The sand is clean and fine, lifeguards are usually on duty, and there are plenty of parking spaces and picnic tables.

• **William Kent Beach** *South of Tahoe City. $2/vehicle.*

Parking is difficult, but this small, rocky beach is worth the hassle.

Bike Trails.

One begins in Tahoe City, following the shoreline and the Truckee River. Bike rentals are available in Tahoe City and at other locations along the lake.

Fishing Charters.

Get a fishing license and names of captions at one of the local sporting goods shops. The captain usually supplies bait and tackle.

Gatekeeper's Museum *130 West Lake Blvd., in William B. Layton Park, Tahoe City, (530) 583-1762, fax (530) 583-8992. Daily 11-5, June-Aug; W-Sun in May & Sept; closed Oct-Apr. Free.*

The replica 1910 lodgepole pine log cabin this museum is located within was originally inhabited by a succession of keepers whose job it was to raise and lower the gates of the dam. Displays include Native American artifacts and Lake Tahoe memorabilia. A new annex holds the **Marion Steinbeck Basket Museum**, which displays 800 Native American baskets and other artifacts. The surrounding 3 1/2-acre lakeside park is equipped with picnic tables and barbecue facilities.

Ponderosa Ranch *100 Ponderosa Ranch Rd., Incline Village, Nevada, (775) 831-0691; www.ponderosaranch.com. Daily 9:30-5; May-Oct only. Adults $9.50, 5-11 $5.50; breakfast hayride $2 additional/person, summer only.*

Created especially for filming scenes for the TV series *Bonanza*, this ranch is now open to the public for tours. Visitors get a bumpy ride from the parking lot up the hill to the ranch, and then a guided tour. After the tour, there is time to explore and visit both a petting farm and what is said to be the world's largest collection of antique farm equipment. Fast-grub is available, and the tin cups in which beer and soft drinks are served make great souvenirs. A bargain breakfast hayride begins at 8 a.m. and ends at 9:30 a.m.

Squaw Valley Stables *1525 Squaw Valley Rd., Olympic Valley, (530) 583-RIDE, fax (530) 583-6187. Daily 9-4:30; June-Sept only. Guided rides $20/hr., riders must be 6 or older; ponies $6.*

The proprietor here says, "We have all kinds of horses . . . gentle horses for gentle people, spirited horses for spirited people, and for those who don't like to ride we have horses that don't like to be ridden." Pony rides in a large arena are available for children ages 2 through 6; parents must lead the pony.

Sugar Pine Point State Park *On west shore, Tahoma, 9 mi. south of Tahoe City, (530) 525-7232, in summer (530) 525-7982. Daily 8-dusk. $5/vehicle. Mansion: Tours on the hour 11-4; July & Aug only.*

In this gorgeous, peaceful setting, the 3-story 1902 Queen Anne **Ehrman Mansion** has 16 rooms open for public viewing. The General Phipps Cabin, built in 1872 of hand-split logs, is also on the property. A magnificent beach invites swimming and sunning. Picnic tables, hiking trails, and a 1930s tennis court are also available, and campsites are open year-round. In winter, cross-country skiing and ranger-led snowshoe walks join the agenda.

Truckee River Bridge *At junction of Hwys. 89 & 28 (the Y), Tahoe City.*

The only outlet from the lake, the dam below this bridge has gates that control the flow of water into the river. Spectators gather here to view and feed the giant rainbow trout that congregate beneath the bridge. (They like to eat bread and crackers.) The nickname **"Fanny Bridge"** comes from the sight that develops as people bend over the bridge railing to view the fish.

Truckin' on the Truckee/River Rafting *Begins at the Y in Tahoe City. Daily 9-3:30; June-Oct only. Rates vary. Rafters must be 4 or older.*

What better way to spend a sunny summer Alpine day than floating down the peaceful Truckee River a la Huckleberry Finn? All that's needed is a swimsuit, water-friendly shoes, and some suntan lotion. Packing along a picnic and some cold drinks is also a good idea, and a day-pack keeps hands free for paddling. White-water enthusiasts stay away. This trip is so tame that there are even portable toilets placed strategically along the riverbank. The 4-mile, 3-hour trip ends at **River Ranch** *(On Hwy. 89, (800) 535-9900, (530) 583-4264.)*, where the restaurant prepares an outdoor barbecue lunch on an expansive deck overlooking the river; lodging is also available. Tahoe City concessionaires offer a package that includes raft, life jacket, paddles, and return ride. It is first-come, first-served, so arrive before 11 a.m. to avoid crowds and to get an early-bird discount. (The drought of the early 1990s dried up the river and stopped the fun here for a while. Check with the Visitors Bureau for the current status of the river.)

A 3 1/2-mile off-road bicycle trail runs along the river here from the River Ranch into Tahoe City.

Watson Cabin Museum *560 North Lake Blvd., Tahoe City, (530) 583-1762, fax (530) 583-8992. Daily 12-4; mid-June through Aug only. Free.*

Built in 1908 and 1909, this log cabin is the oldest building in town still on its original site. Furnished as it was in 1909, it illustrates turn-of-the-century life.

Winter Activities. See page 402.

WHERE TO STAY

Condos on the Lake

Rates in condos vary tremendously depending on number of people, length of stay, and time of year. Most units are equipped with kitchens and TVs.

Brockway Springs *101 Chipmunk St., Kings Beach, (530) 546-4201, fax (530) 546-4202; www.brockwaysprings.com. 78 units. All VCRs; most wood-burning fireplaces. Heated pool, children's wading pool, sauna, 2 tennis courts.*

Most units here have stone fireplaces and balconies overlooking the lake. The resort features 1/2 mile of private lakefront.

Chinquapin *3600 North Lake Blvd., Tahoe City, (800) 732-6721, (530) 583-6991, fax (530) 583-0937. 172 units. All TVs, kitchens, & fireplaces. Heated pool (June-Sept only), sauna, 7 tennis courts.*

The one- to four-bedroom units here feature vaulted, beamed ceilings, natural rock fireplaces, and lake views. Some of these units also have private saunas, and all are equipped with washers and dryers. Additional resort amenities include three private beaches, boating facilities, a fishing pier, and a 1-mile paved beachfront path.

Coeur du Lac *136 Juanita Dr., Incline Village, Nevada, (800) 869-8308, (775) 831-3318, fax (775) 831-8668. Heated pool (June-Aug only), indoor hot tub, sauna.*

Located 1 block from the lake, this attractive complex also has a recreation center.

Condos Farther Out

Carnelian Woods *5005 North Lake Blvd., Carnelian Bay, (530) 546-5547, fax (530) 583-8540. 1/4 mi. from lake. 30 rental units. Recreation center with heated pool (June-Sept only), 2 hot tubs, 2 saunas, 3 tennis courts, 1-mile parcourse.*

Further amenities here include sports facilities and bicycle rentals. In winter, a 2-mile cross-country ski course and snow play area are available.

Granlibakken *End of Granlibakken Rd., Tahoe City, (800) 543-3221, (530) 583-4242; www.granlibakken.com. 1 mi. from lake. 160 rooms. Children under 2 free. Some kitchens & fireplaces. Heated pool & children's wading pool (May-Sept only), parcourse, 6 tennis courts, hot tub, sauna. Full breakfast.*

Situated in a 74-acre forested valley, this resort also has a jogging trail. In winter it maintains a ski and snow play area. See also page 403.

Kingswood Village *1001 Commonwealth Dr., off Hwy. 267, Kings Beach, (530) 546-2501 (call collect for reservations). 3/4 mi. from lake. 60 rental units. Heated pool (June-Aug only), hot tub, sauna, 3 tennis courts.*

Amenities here include access to a private lakefront beach club.

Northstar-at-Tahoe *Northstar Dr., off Hwy. 267, Truckee, (800) GO-NORTH, (530) 526-1010, fax (530) 562-2215; www.skinorthstar.com. 6 mi. from lake. 260 units. All VCRs; most kitchens & wood-burning fireplaces. 2 heated pools, 3 hot tubs, 2 saunas, fitness center, parcourse, 10 clay tennis courts, 18-hole golf course. 5 restaurants.*

In addition to the condos here, hotel rooms and homes can be rented. A complimentary shuttle bus makes it unnecessary to use a car within the complex. Facilities include a teen center and, at an additional fee, horseback riding and a supervised summer children's recreation program for ages 2 through 10. Tahoe's largest mountain bike park is here, with 100 miles of trails. An Adventure Park with rope courses, a climbing wall, and orienteering courses is also available. See also page 403.

Squaw Valley Lodge *201 Squaw Peak Rd., Olympic Valley, (800) 922-9970, (530) 583-5500, fax (530) 583-0326; www.squawvalleylodge.com. 10 mi. from lake. 178 rooms. All kitchens, some gas fireplaces. Heated pool (June-Sept only), 3 indoor & 2 outdoor hot tubs, sauna, steam room, health spa, fitness center, 2 tennis courts.*

Claiming to be "just 84 steps from the Squaw Valley tram," this resort is convenient for both skiers and non-skiers. Staying here allows skiers to avoid a congested early morning commute to Squaw's parking lot. When ready to ski, it is possible to just walk, or even ski, to the lifts. For non-skiers, a room facing the slopes allows complete warmth and comfort while watching the rest of the group whiz by. It is interesting to note that the pool here is treated with gentle-on-the-eyes bromine instead of chlorine.

Lakefront Motels

Mourelatos Lakeshore Resort *6834 North Lake Blvd., Tahoe Vista, (800) 2RELAX-U, (530) 546-9500, fax (530) 546-2744. 33 units; $$-$$$+. Children under 1 free. Some kitchens & fireplaces.*

The woodsy housekeeping cottages are gone now, replaced by new rooms and suites. The pine forest opening onto a private beach on the lake remains, and a children's playground is provided in summer.

Villa Vista Resort *6750 North Lake Blvd., Tahoe Vista, (530) 546-1550, fax (530) 546-4100. $-$$; 2-night min. in cottages. Children under 1 free. Some kitchens & fireplaces. Solar-heated pool (June-Aug only).*

Both vintage motel rooms and cottages are available. Facilities include a sandy beach and a deck overlooking the lake.

Other

Hyatt Regency Lake Tahoe Casino *On Lakeshore/Country Club Dr., Incline Village, Nevada, (800) 510-4891, (775) 832-1234, fax (775) 831-7508; www.laketahoehyatt.com. 11 stories; 458 rooms; $-$$$. Children under 18 free. Some fireplaces. Heated pool, indoor hot tub, fitness center, 2 tennis courts. 3 restaurants, room service.*

Guests here have a choice between a room in an 11-story high-rise, in a 3-story annex, or in a lakeside cottage, and Lady Luck can be tested 24 hours a day in the 13,000-square-foot casino. Of special note is the resort's magnificent private beach, complete with beach boys who set up lounge chairs and umbrellas wherever desired. In summer, guests can relax with the water lapping at the shore just beneath their toes. When thirsty, a server can be beckoned by raising a little red flag on the lounge chair, causing one to ponder, "Can it get better than this?" Jet skis and paddle boats can be rented at an adjacent marina. At night, an oceanfront fire pit equipped with comfortable chairs and a hammock invites lingering under the tall pines. During ski season, free shuttle service is provided to nearby ski areas, and both ski rentals and discounted lift tickets can be purchased on the premises. Packages come and go; when making reservations, inquire about current specials.

Camp Hyatt, a program for children ages 3 through 12, operates year-round on weekends and daily during summer and holidays. There is a fee to participate during the day, but the evening program is always free. An inexpensive room service menu for kids is unbelievable: applesauce, corn-on-the-cob, gooey chocolate cake, and hot chocolate with marshmallows!

The resort's imposing **Lone Eagle Grille** features an Old Tahoe-style atmosphere, with massive wood-beamed ceilings, gigantic fireplaces made of local rock, and large windows with lake views. Lunch is soups and salads, some pastas and pizzas, and plenty of tempting desserts. The dinner menu offers updated surf-and-turf and a good Caesar salad.

Resort at Squaw Creek *400 Squaw Creek Rd., Olympic Valley, (800) 327-3353, (530) 583-6300, fax (530) 581-5407; www.squawcreek.com. 9 stories; 403 rooms; $$$+; 2-night min. on weekends. Children under 16 free. Some kitchens & gas fireplaces. 2 heated pools, 1 children's wading pool, 4 hot tubs, sauna, health spa, fitness center, parcourse, 2 tennis courts (fee), 18-hole golf course. 5 restaurants, room service.*

This sleek, black-toned, high-rise hotel is almost invisible tucked up against a mountain. The majestic property is impressively landscaped, with a 250-foot man-made waterfall feeding a rushing stream that cascades over boulders. One of the pools has a twisting 20-foot-long waterslide, and the toddler pool includes a large sandy beach for extra diversion. Two-story windows in the large lobby provide a magnificent valley view. A Mountain

Buddies children's program operates year-round for ages 4 through 13; reservations are required and there is an additional fee. Bicycles can be rented and ridden along a scenic route beside the Truckee River. In winter, ski-in/ski-out access is available to Squaw Valley, and both an ice-skating pavilion and horse-drawn sleigh rides are available.

Motel Row.

Last-minute lodging can usually be found among the numerous motels and cabins lining the lake in Kings Beach and Tahoe Vista. Chances are best, of course, on weekdays and in the off-season.

WHERE TO EAT

Alexander's Bar & Grill *Olympic Valley, (530) 583-2555. L&D daily; in summer D only. Boosters, child menu. Reservations advised for D; not taken for L. Tram: (530) 583-6985; daily 10-4; in summer 10-10; adults $15, 65+ $5-$12, under 13 $5; after 5pm everyone $5; High Camp facilities additional.*

This restaurant is located on the slopes of the Squaw Valley ski area and is reached via a scenic **aerial tram ride**. Call the restaurant for dining details.

A lovely, though difficult, hike to Shirley Lake begins at the tram building. Hikers pass waterfalls and huge boulders while following Squaw Creek about 2 1/2 miles to the lake.

At 8,200-foot elevation, the **High Camp Bath & Tennis Club** is open year-round. Facilities include an Olympic-size outdoor ice-skating rink, six tennis courts, a pool and hot tub, and a stable. Mountain biking, volleyball, and bungee-jumping are also available.

Hacienda del Lago *760 North Lake Blvd., in Boatworks Shopping Center, Tahoe City, (530) 583-0358. D daily; in summer L&D daily; $. Highchairs, boosters, child portions. No reservations.*

It is definitely worth the wait to be seated here in the front room featuring a panoramic lake view, perhaps passing the time sipping fruit margaritas in the bar. (Smoothies are popular with children.) Beware. Anesthetized by these potent, tangy drinks, it is quite easy to over-indulge on the large portions of tasty Mexican food. The menu includes a variety of burritos, chimechangas, and enchiladas. A colossal taco salad consists of a crispy-fried flour tortilla bowl filled to the brim with salad goodies, and make-your-own tacos are available with pork, turkey, or beef stuffing. For those who know when to stop, there are a la carte portions. For those who don't, there is flan topped with whipped cream.

Lakehouse Pizza *120 Grove St., Tahoe City, (530) 583-2222. L&D daily; $. Highchairs, boosters. No reservations.*

This casual spot offers lakefront views and a choice of sitting either inside or outside on a deck. Menu choices include pizza, sandwiches, salads, hamburgers, and exceptionally good housemade potato chips.

Sunnyside Resort *1850 West Lake Blvd., Tahoe City, (800) 822-2-SKI, (530) 583-7200; www.sunnysideresort.com. B M-Sat, L&D daily, SunBr; $$-$$$. Highchairs, boosters, child portions. Reservations advised.*

It is hard to beat a summer meal here, especially when taken outside on the huge deck while watching the sailboats on the lake or listening to live jazz on Sunday afternoons. This restaurant has a history of regularly changing its menu format and phone numbers, so call before visiting. Overnight **lodging** is also available.

Water Wheel *1115 West Lake Blvd., Tahoe City, (530) 583-4404. D daily; $$. Closed M Mar-May & Sept-Nov. Boosters. Reservations advised.*

Diners here are treated to a view of the Truckee River and some of the tastiest Chinese Szechwan cuisine in Northern California. Hailing from Taipei, Taiwan, chef Nelson has a way with a wok and whips up old family recipes to delight his loyal customers. The portion of the menu devoted to spicy Szechwan dishes appears flawless. Highly recommended are the beef Szechwan (beef in a tangy, crunchy sauce of minced wood ear, water chestnuts, and green onions), twice-cooked pork (a colorful arrangement of brilliant chartreuse cabbage, bright orange carrot rounds, and pork in a spicy hot sauce redolent of sesame oil and garlic), and Szechwan spicy pork (shredded pork with minced water chestnuts, mushrooms, garlic, and peppers in a flavorful sauce—served with little pancakes). Drinks mixed by Lily are almost as tasty as the food.

Wolfdale's Cuisine Unique *640 North Lake Blvd., Tahoe City, (530) 583-5700. D W-M; daily in July & Aug; $$-$$$. Child portions. Reservations advised.*

The attractive circa 1880 house this restaurant is located within was floated over on a barge from the Nevada side of the lake at the turn of the century and converted into a restaurant in the 1960s. During the two seatings scheduled each evening, talented owner-chef Douglas Dale combines Italian and Japanese cooking techniques to produce exceptional fresh fish and meat entrees—all artistically arranged and served with house-baked herb bread. The appetizers and house-made desserts are also exceptional. Adding to the aesthetics of this dining experience, everything is served on handmade pottery designed especially to enhance the food.

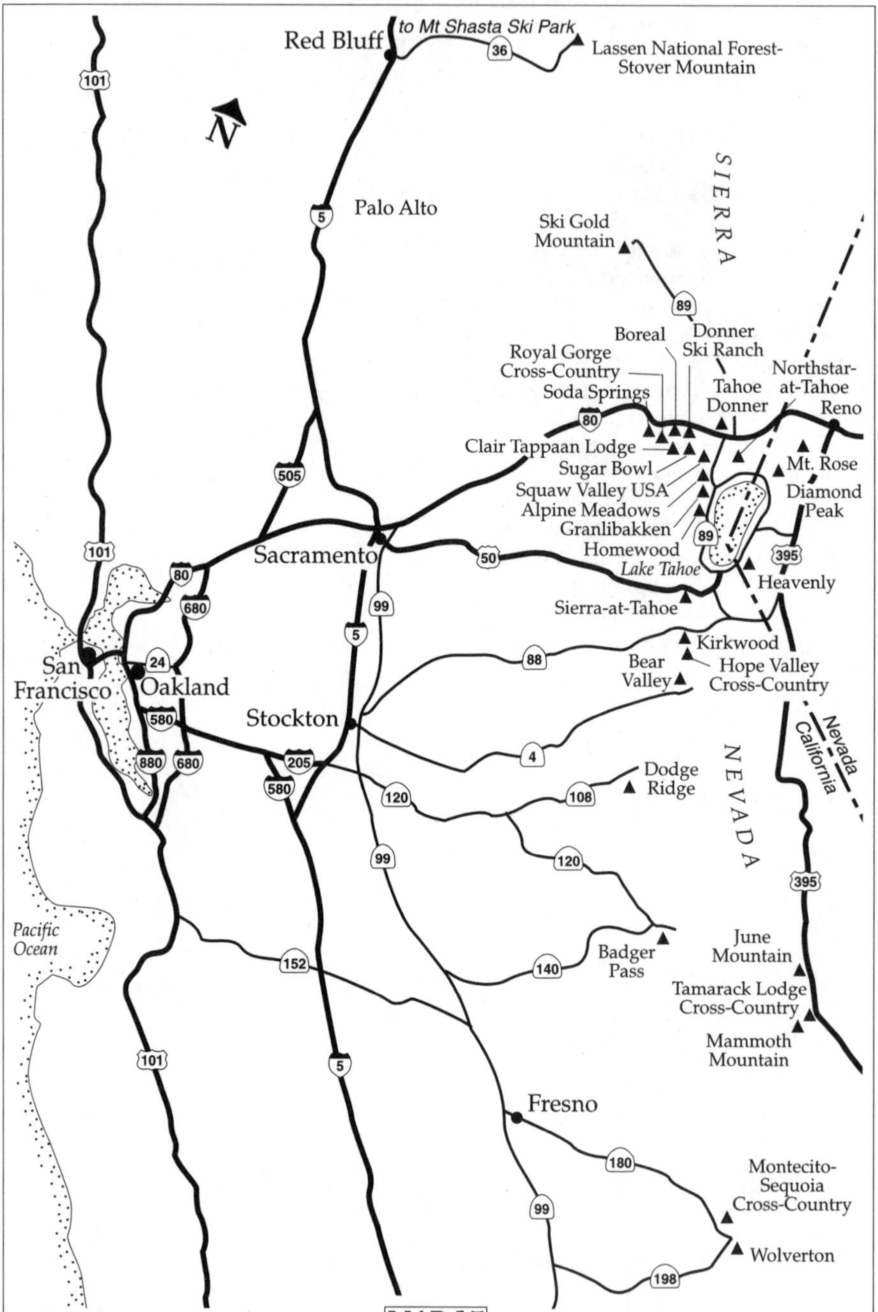
Red Bluff
to Mt Shasta Ski Park
36
Lassen National Forest-
Stover Mountain
101
N
5
Palo Alto
Ski Gold
Mountain
SIERRA
89
Boreal
Donner
Ski Ranch
Royal Gorge
Cross-Country
Northstar-
at-Tahoe
Soda Springs
Tahoe
Donner
Reno
80
Clair Tappaan Lodge
Sugar Bowl
Mt. Rose
Squaw Valley USA
Diamond
Peak
Alpine Meadows
Granlibakken
89
Homewood
395
Lake Tahoe
Heavenly
505
Sacramento
50
101
80
680
99
Sierra-at-Tahoe
5
Kirkwood
San
Francisco
24
Oakland
88
Bear
Valley
Hope Valley
Cross-Country
580
Stockton
Nevada
California
NEVADA
4
880
680
205
Dodge
Ridge
580
120
108
99
120
395
Pacific
Ocean
Badger
Pass
June
Mountain
152
140
Tamarack Lodge
Cross-Country
Mammoth
Mountain
101
5
Fresno
180
Montecito-
Sequoia
Cross-Country
99
Wolverton
198
MAP 17

Downhill Skiing

Downhill ski areas are plentiful in Northern California. The season runs from the first snow, usually in late November, through the spring thaw in April. Several resorts are known for staying open longer.

Lifts usually operate daily from 9 a.m. to 4 p.m. To avoid parking problems and long lines for lift tickets and rentals, arrive early. On-site equipment rentals are usually available and convenient, and lift tickets are often discounted mid-week.

The least crowded times at the resorts are the three weeks after Thanksgiving, the first two weeks in January, and late in the season. The two weeks around Christmas are ridiculous.

Those who know say it is worthwhile to buy ski equipment if someone skis more than 10 days per season. Otherwise, it is financially beneficial to rent. Avoid buying children plastic skis; they break very easily.

Cross-country Skiing

Cross-country skiing becomes more popular each year. One reason for this surging popularity is the advantages it has over downhill skiing: no lift tickets to purchase; equipment is less expensive; is considered safer; can be enjoyed in groups; allows escape from crowds. However,

the sport also has several disadvantages: requires more stamina; is less exhilarating.

Specialized cross-country centers offer equipment rentals, maintained trails with maps, and warming huts. Some centers also offer lodging, guided tours, and the option of downhill facilities.

Children age 4 and older are usually taught in classes with their parents, but some centers have special children's classes. Parents who have the strength can carry younger children in a backpack or pull them along in a "pulk."

It is a good idea for beginners to rent equipment and take a few lessons to learn safety guidelines and basic skiing techniques.

Once the basics are learned, this sport can be practiced just about anywhere there is a foot of snow.

The state **Sno-Park** program makes it easier to park at popular trail heads. Parking areas are kept cleared of snow, and overnight RV camping is permitted at some locations. The permit costs $25 and is good from November 1 through May 30. One-day permits cost $5. For more information call (916) 653-8569.

Snow Play

Toboggans, saucers, inner tubes, and sleds are the equipment for snow play. For safety's sake, take note that sleds are lots of fun to use but extremely dangerous. Truck inner tubes are also dangerous because the rider is high off the ground with nothing to hold on to and no way to steer.

When people do not pay attention to safety rules, snow play can become dangerous. (I once had the wind knocked out of me by an antsy bear of a man who didn't wait for me and my young child to come to a stop before he pushed down the same hill in his saucer. After the collision he said, "Sorry. But you shouldn't have been there." I'm sure worse stories are waiting to be told.)

Some commercial snow play areas allow people to bring their own equipment, but others require that people rent equipment on-site.

Dress for cold, wet weather. Wear wool when possible, and pack a change of clothes. Protect feet with boots. When boots aren't available, an inexpensive improvisation is to wrap feet in newspapers, then in plastic bags, and then put on shoes. Also, cutting a few holes in a large plastic garbage bag allows it to serve as a raincoat. Always wear gloves to protect hands from sharp, packed snow.

The high-speed fun of snowmobiling is an exciting adventure. Many snowmobile concessions provide protective clothing and equipment. Though not inexpensive, especially for a family, it is an exhilarating, memorable experience.

Note: In the following listings, difficulty of terrain at downhill ski resorts is specified in percentages: %B (beginner), %I (intermediate), %A (advanced).

Way Up North

Coffee Creek Ranch. See page 299.

Lassen National Forest—Stover Mountain *(530) 258-3987; 3 mi. southwest of Chester. Open Sat & Sun only. Downhill: 1 surface. 50%B, 50%I. Lifts $12, under 12 $8. Lodging nearby; packages available. Snow play area.*

California's "undiscovered National Park" is an excellent area for families and beginners. The scenery includes hot steam vents and mud pots.

Mt. Shasta Ski Park *104 Siskiyou Ave., Mt. Shasta, (800) SKISHASTA, (530) 926-8610, fax (530) 926-8607, snow phone (530) 926-8686; www.skipark.com; 10 mi. east of Mt. Shasta City. Downhill: 3 triples, 1 surface. 20%B, 55%I, 25%A. Lifts $31, 65+ $17, 1-6 $3. Children's ski school (4-7); lessons (8-12). Snowboard facilities. Cross-country: 17 mi. groomed trails. $10, 65+ $6, 8-12 $6. Lodging nearby, (530) 926-3446, (530) 926-3030.*

Night skiing is available at this low-key, family-oriented ski area.

Ski Gold Mountain *In Johnsville, in Plumas-Eureka State Park, (530) 836-2317;www.skigold mountain.org; 25 mi. east of Quincy & 60 mi. north of Truckee. Downhill only. F-Sun only. 2 poma lifts. 25%B, 50%I, 25%A. Lifts $24, 13-18 $16, 6-12 $12.*

A low-key area that is particularly nice for beginners and families, this old-time ski center is way off the beaten track and is said to be the site of the world's first ski lift. Dog-sled racing, snowshoeing, sleigh rides, sledding, and ice-fishing are all available nearby.

In January and February, the historic **Longboard Ski Revival Races** are held to commemorate the first recorded ski racing in the western hemisphere, held here in 1860. Back then, work for local miners slowed down in winter, and they found themselves with time on their hands. So they devised "long board" skis, measuring up to 12 feet long, and started competing. Today racers wearing period costumes and compete on similar wooden skis with leather bindings, using homemade wax and, as the miners did, just a single wooden pole between their legs for stopping. Other 1800s traditions are part of the fun.

South Lake Tahoe

Heavenly Ski Resort *South Lake Tahoe, (800) 2-HEAVEN, (775) 586-7000, fax (775) 541-2643, snow phone (800) 2-HEAVEN; www.skiheavenly.com. Downhill only. 1 tram, 1 six, 5 quad, 8 triple, 5 double, 7 surface. 20%B, 45%I, 35%A. Lifts $54, 13-18 $44, 6-12 & 65+ $25. Children's ski school (4-12). Snowboard terrain park. Lodging nearby, (800) 2-HEAVEN; adjacent townhouses, (800) 822-5967; packages avail.*

Situated in two states, this is the largest, and one of the most scenic, ski areas in the country. Runs on the California side offer breathtaking views of Lake Tahoe. This resort has been rated as having the best intermediate skiing in California. It also has exhilarating expert slopes, offers both night and helicopter skiing, and has the longest descent—5 1/2 miles—in the west.

Hope Valley Cross-Country Ski Center at Sorensen's Resort *14255 Hwy. 88, Hope Valley, (800) 423-9949, (530) 694-2203, (530) 694-2266; www.sorensonsresort.com; on Hwy. 88, 16 mi. south of Lake Tahoe. Cross-country only; 60 mi. marked trails. By donation. Children's ski school (8-12). Lodging on premises.*

Small and informal, this is a great place for families. Lodging is available in 29 housekeeping cabins. Some are newish log cabins equipped with kitchenettes and wood-burning fireplaces. Others are older and smaller. The resort is open year-round and is 100 percent non-smoking, with a sauna and cafe among its facilities. In the summer it offers a family-oriented fly fishing school, history tours of the Emigrant Trail and Pony Express Trail, and both kayak and mountain bike rentals.

Kirkwood Mountain Resort *1501 Kirkwood Meadows Dr., Kirkwood, (800) 967-7500, (209) 258-6000, fax (209) 258-8899, snow phone (877) KIRKWOOD; www.skikirkwood.com; on Hwy. 88, 30 mi. south of South Lake Tahoe. Downhill: 2 quad, 7 triple, 1 double, 2 surface. 15%B, 50%I, 35%A. Lifts $46, 65+ $24, 13-22 $36, 6-12 $10. Childcare center (2-6); children's ski school (4-12). Snowboard terrain parks and halfpipe. Cross-country: (209) 258-7248; 48 mi. groomed*

Vintage longboard skiing

trails. Trail fee $16, 65+ $12, 7-12 $5. Lodging on premises in condominiums, (800) 967-7500; packages avail.

This very large, uncrowded family resort is reputed to have the deepest snow in North America. It is often snowing here when it is raining at other Tahoe ski areas. A new family fun area with a tubing and sledding hill has been added, and a swim complex is coming. Horse-drawn sleigh rides are available, and the cross-country area offers inexpensive Family Days as well as guided snowshoe adventures and night hikes.

Sierra-at-Tahoe *1111 Sierra-at-Tahoe Rd., Twin Bridges, (530) 659-7453, fax (530) 659-7453, snow phone (530) 659-7475; www.sierratahoe.com; on Hwy. 50, 12 mi. west of South Lake Tahoe. Downhill only. 3 quad, 1 triple, 5 double, 1 surface. 25%B, 50%I, 25%A. Lifts $46, 70+ $5, 13-19 $33, 6-12 $8. Childcare center (2-5); children's ski school (3-12). Snow play area $10/2 hrs., $20/day. Snowboard terrain parks. Lodging nearby (800) AT-TAHOE.*

This ski area is reputed to be particularly popular with college students and families with teenagers. Free shuttles are available from South Lake Tahoe.

SNOW PLAY

Borges' Family Sleigh Rides *On Hwy. 50 next to Caesar's Tahoe casino, Stateline, (530) 541-2953. Daily 10-dusk, weather permitting. Adults $10, 1-10 $5.*

Take a ride around a meadow in an old-fashioned "one-horse open sleigh." Five hand-made sleighs are used, ranging from a cozy two-seater to a 20-passenger model. Sleighs are pulled either by 2,000-pound Blonde Belgian horses or by one rare American-Russian Baskhir Curly.

Hansen's Resort *1360 Ski Run Blvd./Needle Peak Rd., 3 blocks from Heavenly ski area, South Lake Tahoe, (530) 544-3361. Daily 9-5. 1-hr. session $6/person.*

Facilities include a saucer hill and a packed toboggan run with banked turns. All equipment is furnished. Lodging in secluded cabins is available.

Husky Express Dog Sled Tours *In Hope Valley, 25 mi. south of South Lake Tahoe, (775) 782-3047; www.highsierra.com/sst. Adults $60, under 12 $25. Reservations required.*

As the sled swooshes over the scenic trails and through the trees on these enjoyable excursions, the frisky, well-tempered huskies seem to be having as much fun as their passengers. So does the "musher," who never utters the word "mush" but instead hollers "Hike!" or "Let's Go!" Two sleds are available, and each can carry two adults or a combination of kids and adults that doesn't exceed 375 pounds.

Snow Hikes *Sierra District, P.O. Box 266, Tahoma 96142, (530) 525-7232.*

Request a schedule of free ranger-led snowshoe and cross-country hikes in Lake Tahoe area state parks by sending a stamped, self-addressed, legal size envelope to the above address. Hikes are scheduled October through April, depending on the snow level.

North Lake Tahoe

Alpine Meadows *2600 Alpine Meadows Rd., Tahoe City, (800) 441-4423, (530) 583-4232, fax (530) 583-0963, snow phone (530) 581-8374; www.skialpine.com; off Hwy. 89, 6 mi. north of Tahoe City. Downhill only. 2 quad, 2 triple, 7 double, 1 surface. 25%B, 40%I, 35%A. Lifts $50, 70+ free, 13-18 $38, 7-10 $10, 1-6 $6. Children's snow school (4-6); children's ski lessons (7-12). Snowboarding not permitted. Lodging nearby, (800) TAHOE-4-U; packages avail.*

Alpine is usually open through Memorial Day and some years is open into July, giving it the longest ski season at Lake Tahoe. Free 1-hour guided tours that show skiers the main runs and how to avoid crowds are offered daily at 10 a.m. The **Tahoe Adaptive Ski School** *((530) 581-4161)* for people with disabilities operates here, and the **Family Ski Challenge** is scheduled each March.

Granlibakken *Tahoe City, (800) 543-3221, (530) 581-7333, fax (530) 583-7641; www.granlibakken.com. 1 mi. south of Tahoe City. 2 surface. 50%B, 50%I. Lifts $15, 65+ & 1-12 $8; 50% discount to lodging guests. Children's ski school (5+). Snow play area $4/person.*

This small ski area is protected from the wind and caters to beginners and families with small children. It is said to be the oldest ski resort at Tahoe and to have the least expensive lift ticket. See also page 393.

Homewood Mountain Resort *5145 West Lake Blvd., Homewood, (530) 525-2992, fax (530) 525-0417, snow phone (530) 525-2900; www.skihomewood.com; on Hwy. 89, 6 mi. south of Tahoe City. Downhill only. 1 quad, 2 triple, 1 double, 4 surface. 15%B, 50%I, 35%A. Lifts $38, 13-18 $25, 60+ & 11-12 $9. Childcare center (2-6); children's ski school (4-12). Snowboard terrain park. Lodging nearby, (800) 822-5959.*

The slopes here are ideal for intermediates and provide panoramic views of Lake Tahoe. Ferry service from South Lake Tahoe is provided by the *Tahoe Queen.*

Northstar-at-Tahoe *Fax (530) 562-2221, snow phone (530) 562-1330; www.skinorthstar.com; off Hwy. 267, 6 mi. south of Truckee. Downhill: (530) 562-1010. 1 gondola, 4 quad, 2 triple, 2 double, 4 surface. 25%B, 50%I, 25%A. Lifts $49, 60-69 $25, 70+ $5, 13-22 $39, 5-10 $10. Childcare center (2-6); children's ski school (5-12); children's ski lessons (3+). Snow tubing area $13. Snowboard terrain parks. Cross-country: (530) 562-2475; 40 mi. groomed trails. Trail fee $19, 5-12 $10, under 5 free. Lodging in modern condos on premises, (800) GO-NORTH; packages avail.*

This attractive ski area is said to be the least windy at Tahoe. Catering to families, it is good for beginners and excellent for intermediates. Lift ticket sales are limited to assure that the slopes don't get overcrowded, so arrive early. Organized activities are scheduled throughout the week, and free 1-hour introductory tours, in which participants are shown the best runs and given a history of the area, are given daily at 10 a.m. Sleigh rides and snowmobile tours are available, and Polaris Park is open on Friday and Saturday evenings with lighted slopes for tubing, snowshoeing, and other selected snow sports. See also page 393.

Squaw Valley USA *1960 Squaw Valley Rd., Olympic Valley, (800) 545-4350, (530) 583-6985, fax (530) 581-7106, snow phone (530) 583-6955; www.squaw.com; off Hwy. 89, 5 mi. north of Tahoe City. Downhill: 1 tram, 1 funitel, 4 quad, 9 triple, 13 doubles, 4 surface. 25%B, 45%I, 30%A. Lifts $52, 65-75 & 13-15 $26, & 1-12 $5, 76+ free. Childcare (2-3); children's ski school (4-12). Snow play area $8-$11. Snowboarding permitted. Cross-country: 10 mi. groomed trails. Trail fee: $12, 65+ & 1-13 $10. Lodging on premises; packages avail.*

Squaw Valley made its name in 1960 when it was home to the VIII Winter Olympic Games. Today it is a top ski area known internationally for its open slopes and predictably generous snowfall, which usually allows Squaw to stay open into May. Expert skiers consider it to be the best ski resort in the state because it has the steepest, most challenging slopes. Indeed, there are good slopes for every ability level. A special area for children ages 2 through 12 is equipped with two rope tows and a magic carpet. A snowtubing area with a dedicated lift and ice-skating are available at High Camp, and 3 miles of night skiing is available mid-December through mid-March from 4 to 9 p.m. nightly.

SNOW PLAY

Carnelian Woods Condominiums. See page 393.

Snowfest! *(775) 832-7625, fax (775) 832-2232; www.snowfest.org.*

Held for a week each year in March, this is the largest winter carnival in the West. In the past activities have included a fireworks display over the slopes at Squaw Valley followed by the awe-inspiring sight of scores of torch-bearing skiers making a twisting descent down Exhibition Run. Other popular events include The Great Ski Race (a 30-kilometer Nordic ski competition) and the Localman Triathlon (a competition in winter survival skills in which participants must stack firewood, shovel snow, and put on tire chains).

Sugar Pine Point State Park. See page 392.

Tahoe Snowmobile Adventures *Tahoe Vista, (530) 546-6115; off Hwy. 28 at end of National Ave. Snow play & cross-country $3/person; call for snowmobile rates; parking $3.*

This 108-acre park has a snow play area for toboggans and saucers. Snowmobiles can be rented for use on a 1/4-mile oval racing track and 1 3/4 miles of trails. Eight miles of groomed cross-country trails and picnic tables round out the facilities.

Donner Summit

Boreal *(530) 426-3666, snow phone same, fax (530) 426-3173; www.borealski.com; Castle Peak exit off Hwy. I-80, 10 mi. west of Truckee. Downhill only. 2 quad, 3 triple, 4 double. 30%B, 55%I, 15%A. Lifts $31, 5-12 $10. Children's ski school (4-12). Snow play area $10. Snowboard terrain park. Lodging on premises, (530) 426-3668; packages avail.*

Known for being relatively inexpensive and convenient to the Bay Area, this resort has the Sierra's most extensive night skiing facilities. Slopes are especially good for beginners and intermediates, and skiers of all ability levels can ride on the same chairs together. The "Shared Parent" program allows two parents to buy just one ticket if they want to take turns skiing and babysitting their children.

Clair Tappaan Lodge *Norden, (530) 426-3632; www.sierraclub.com/outings/lodges/tappaan.html; on Hwy. 40, 3 mi. east of Norden/Soda Springs exit off Hwy. I-80. Cross-country only. 7 mi. groomed trails. Trail fee: $5 donation.*

This area is said to be the snowiest in the continental U.S. Both the massive timbered lodge, which was built by volunteers in 1934, and the track system are owned and operated by the Sierra Club. A special package *($46+, members $41+, 4-12 $18+)* includes dormitory-style bunk bed lodging, three hearty meals served family-style, and use of the trails. As at hostels, everyone is expected to do a chore, and guests bring their own bedding. Overnight trips to wilderness areas can be arranged. Special programs and workshops are scheduled throughout the year. Children under 4 are free but are not permitted on winter weekends or on holidays.

Donner Ski Ranch *Norden, (530) 426-3635, fax (530) 426-9350, snow phone (530) 321-SNOW; www.donnerskiranch.com; on Hwy. 40, 3 mi. from the Norden/Soda Springs exit off Hwy. I-80. Downhill only. 1 triple, 5 double. 25%B, 50%I, 25%A. Lifts $25, 5-12 $10. Snowboard terrain park. Lodging on premises; packages avail.*

Best for beginners and intermediates, this area offers no frills. Bargain rates are available midweek.

Royal Gorge Cross Country Ski Resort *9411 Hillside Dr., Soda Springs, (800) 500-3871(outside No.Calif.), (530) 426-3871, fax (530) 426-9221, snow phone (530) 426-3871;*

www.royalgorge.com; 1 mi. from Soda Springs/ Norden exit off Hwy. I-80, near Donner Pass. Cross-country only. 190 mi. groomed trails. Trail fee $21.50, 13-16 $8.50. Children's ski school (4-12). Lodging on premises; packages avail.

Modeled after Scandinavian ski resorts, this was the first cross-country ski resort in California. The overnight **Wilderness Lodge** here is not accessible by road. Guests are brought in by snowcat-drawn sleigh (sorry, no reindeer or horses) and leave by skiing the 2 miles back out. Accommodations are rustic. In the old 1920s hunting lodge, everyone shares the same toilet areas. Bathing facilities—showers, a sauna, and an outdoor hot tub—are located in an adjacent building and are reached by a short trek through the snow. Sleeping facilities are tiny roomettes, each with either a double bed or a bunk bed and a cloth-covered doorway, and several three-bed rooms for families. Some private cabins are also available. The food, however, is remarkably civilized. A chef works full-time in the kitchen preparing attractive, tasty, and bountiful French repasts. Oh, yes. The skiing. Guests may cross-country ski whenever they wish, and the capable staff gives lessons each morning and guided tours each afternoon. Guided moonlight ski tours are scheduled after dinner. The per person nightly fee *($129-$169)* includes everything except equipment, which can be rented on the premises. Lower rates are available midweek.

Royal Gorge also operates a more accessible B&B, **Rainbow Lodge** *((530) 426-3871)*, nearby.

The cross-country ski center is open to non-guests and features the largest cross-country track system in the U.S. Facilities include ten warming huts, four trail-side cafes, and four surface lifts. The Rainbow Interconnect Trail allows skiers to enjoy 8 miles of scenic downhill cross-country skiing; shuttle buses return skiers to the trailhead. A special program is available for skiers with disabilities.

Soda Springs Ski Area *Soda Springs, (530) 426-3901, snow phone (530) 426-1010, fax (530) 426-3173; www.skisodasprings.com; at Soda Springs exit off Hwy. I- 80, 4 mi. west of Donner Summit. Downhill only. 1 triple, 1 double, 2 surface. 30%B, 50%I, 20%A. Lifts $20, 8-17 $16. Children's ski school (4-12); children's lessons. Snowtubing area $10-$20. Snowboarding permitted. Lodging nearby.*

Built on the former site of one of the first Sierra ski resorts, this relatively new ski area is among the closest to the Bay Area and is particularly well-designed for beginners. It is owned by the Boreal ski area and shares some facilities with it. All or part of the resort can be rented on weekdays.

Sugar Bowl Ski Resort *Norden, (530) 426-3651, fax (530) 426-3723, snow phone (530) 426-3847; www.sugarbowl.com; on Hwy. 40, 2 mi. east of Soda Springs exit off Hwy. I-80. Downhill only. 1 gondola, 4 quad, 3 double, 2 surface. 17%B, 45%I, 38%A. Lifts $48, 60+ $20, 13-18 $39, 5-12 $10. Childcare (3-6); children's ski school & lessons (6-12). Snow play area, free to lodge guests. Snowboard terrain park. Lodging on premises; packages avail.*

Exuding a 1930s Tyrolean charm, this ski resort is one of the Sierra's oldest and is said to have had the first chairlift in the state. It is further known for having short lift lines, good runs at all ability levels, and a lack of hotdoggers. Skiers park their cars carefully (to avoid tickets), and then ride a gondola or chairlift up to the resort.

Tahoe Donner *11603 Snowpeak, Truckee, fax (530) 587-0685, snow phone (530) 587-9494; www.tahoedonner.com; off Hwy. I-80. Downhill: (530) 587-9444. 1 quad, 1 double, 2 surface. 40%B, 60%I. Lifts $26, 70+ free, 56-69 & 7-12 $12. Children's ski school (3-6); children's ski lessons (7-12). Snow play area $2-$4. Snowboard terrain park. Cross-country: (530) 587-9484. 42 mi. groomed trails. Trail fee $15, 70+ free, 60-69 $13, 7-12 $9. Children's ski school (5-9). Lodging in modern condos & homes on premises, (530) 587-6586 or (530) 587-5411.*

This small resort is especially good for families. The number of lift tickets sold each day is limited, assuring that it never gets too crowded. Snow-biking a la the Beatles in *Help!* was introduced in 1998. The cross-country ski center offers lighted night skiing and schedules special tours: Ski With Santa, Morning Nature Tour, Sauna Tour, Donner Trail Tour.

SNOW PLAY

Western Ski Sport Museum *At Boreal Ridge exit off Hwy. I-80, (530) 426-3313, fax (530) 426-3501. In winter W-Sun 10-4; in summer Sat & Sun 10-4. Free.*

See just how cumbersome that charming old-time ski equipment really was. Skis were used by pioneers to help open this mountain area. This museum chronicles the history of skis in the West from gold camp days to current times. Vintage ski films are shown upon request.

Nevada

Diamond Peak Ski & Cross Country Resort *1210 Ski Way, Incline Village, (800) 00-TAHOE, (775) 832-1177, fax (775) 832-1281, snow phone (775) 831-3211; www.diamondpeak.com; off Hwy. 28. Downhill: 3 quad, 3 double. 18%B, 46%I, 36%A. Lifts $38, 13-17 $31, 60+ & 6-12 $14. Childcare center (2-6) & children's ski school (4-6); children's ski lessons (3-12). Snowboard terrain park. Cross-country: 20 mi. groomed trails. Trail fee: $14, 60-69 $10, 6-12 $8, 70+ & under 6 free. Lodging nearby, (800) GO-TAHOE.*

This well-sheltered, family-oriented resort is especially good on inclement days. It is the area's first and only ski resort to use the European-style easy-loading "Launch Pad" system—similar to a moving walkway—on both quad chairlifts. The cross-country center also has snowshoe facilities, and complimentary shuttle service is available to Incline Village.

Mt. Rose-Ski Tahoe *22222 Mt. Rose Hwy., Reno, (800) SKI-ROSE, (775) 849-0704, fax (775) 849-9080, snow phone (775) 849-0704; www.skirose.com; on Hwy. 431, 11 mi. northeast of Incline Village. Downhill only. 3 triple, 2 quad. 30%B, 35%I, 35%A. Lifts $42, 60+ $21, 13-19 $35, 6-12 $10. Children's ski school (4-10). Snowboard terrain parks.*

At 8,260 feet, this is the highest base elevation at Tahoe.

East

Bear Valley Ski Area *Bear Valley, on Hwy. 4, 45 mi. east of Angels Camp. Downhill: (209) 753-2301, fax (209) 753-6421, snow phone (209) 753-2308; www.bearvalley.com. 2 triple, 7 double, 2 surface. 30%B, 40%I, 30%A. Lifts $37, 13-19 $30, 7-12 $13, 65+ & under 7 free. Childcare center (2-6); children's ski school (4-8). Snowboard terrain park. Cross-country: (209) 753-2834, fax (209) 753-2669; www.bearvalleyxc.com; 40 mi. groomed trails. Trail fee $17, 60+ & 13-17 $11, 9-12 $8, under 9 free. Snow play area $6. Lodging in condos, homes, & lodge 3 mi. from ski area, (209) 753-BEAR; www.bearvalleylodge.com.*

Intermediate or better skiers staying in this secluded resort village can ski the 3-mile Home Run trail back to the resort area at the end of the day. A bus takes skiers to and from the village area lodgings and the slopes. Bear is one of the biggest ski areas in the state and generally has short lift lines. However, that Ski Bare campaign must have caught people's attention: Now there are lines where once there were none. The resort is popular with families and especially good for beginners and intermediates.

The cross-country area has snowshoeing, a kid's sledding hill for ages 4 through 10 *(Must rent sled, $6; child must be accompanied by adult.)*, and an **ice-skating rink** *(Dec-Feb only. $4, skate rental $3.)* on a natural frozen pond. Stays can be arranged at ski-in snowbound cabins.

Inexpensive modern rooms, with bathrooms down the hall, are available at nearby **Base Camp Lodge** *((209) 753-2344).*

Dodge Ridge *Pinecrest, (209) 965-3474, fax (209) 965-4437, snow phone (209) 965-4444; www.dodgeridge.com; 32 mi. east of Sonora off Hwy. 108. Downhill only. 1 quad, 2 triple, 5 double, 4 surface. 20%B, 40%I, 40%A. Lifts $39, 62+ $10, 13-19 $30, 7-12 $15. Children's ski school (4-12). Snowboarding permitted. Lodging nearby, (800) 446-1333.*

This low-key, family-oriented ski area is known for short lift lines.

SNOW PLAY

Bear River Lake Resort *40800 Hwy. 88, on Bear River Reservoir, Pioneer, (209) 295-4868; 42 mi. east of Jackson, 3 mi. off Hwy. 88. F-Sun 7-7. Free; parking $5/vehicle. Lodging on premises.*

Visitors may use their own equipment in this groomed snow play area. Back country cross-country trips can be arranged.

Long Barn Lodge Ice Rink *Long Barn, (800) 310-3533, (209) 586-3533; 23 mi. east of Sonora off Hwy. 108. W-F 6:30-9, Sat 10-9, Sun 10-7. $6.50, skates included.*

Located behind a bar and restaurant built in 1925, this rink is covered but has two sides open to the outdoors.

South

Badger Pass *In Yosemite National Park, off Hwy. 41 on Glacier Point Rd., 23 mi. from the valley; www.badgerpass.com. Downhill: (209) 372-8430, snowphone (209) 372-1000, fax (209) 372-8673. 1 triple, 3 double, 1 surface. 35%B, 50%I, 15%A. Lifts $17-$28, under 13 $10-$16, 65+ free midweek. Childcare center (3-9); children's pre-ski school (4-6). Snowboarders welcome. Cross-country: (209) 372-8444; 21 mi. groomed trails. Trail use free with park admission. Lodging nearby; packages avail.*

Badger Pass opened in 1935, making it California's first, and oldest, organized ski area. A prime spot for beginners and intermediates and especially popular with families, it has a natural bowl with gentle slopes that provide shelter from wind. A free shuttle bus delivers valley guests to the slopes. Ask about the bargain Midweek Ski Package.

The old days

Yosemite's first ski lift
(Skier's stood skis upright in center of "upski," then sat down beside them to be pulled up the hill via funicular cable.)

Cross-country skiing is arranged through **Yosemite Cross-Country School**—the oldest cross-country ski school on the West Coast. Survival courses, snow camping, and overnight tours that include lodging and meals are also available.

June Mountain *June Lake, (888) JUNEMTN, (760) 648-7733, snow phone (760) 934-2224, fax (760) 648-7367; www.junemountain.com; 4 mi. south of Hwy. 395, 58 mi. north of Bishop. Downhill only. 1 tram, 2 quad, 4 double. 35%B, 45%I, 20%A. Lifts $42, 13-19 $32, 65+ & 7-12 $22. Childcare center (newborn-6); children's ski school (3+). Snow play area $10. Snowboarding permitted. Lodging nearby; packages avail.*

This compact, uncrowded area is excellent for beginners and popular with families. Snowboard rentals and lessons are available.

For lodging try **June Lodge** *((760) 648-7713)*. A former hunting lodge, it was once a popular retreat for Clark Gable, Humphrey Bogart, and other era movie stars.

Mammoth Mountain *1 Minaret Rd., Mammoth Lakes, (800) MAMMOTH, (760) 934-0745, fax (760) 934-0603, snow phone (888) SNOWRPT; www.mammoth-mtn.com; 50 mi. north of Bishop. Downhill only. 2 gondolas, 6 quad, 7 triple, 14 double, 1 surface. 30%B, 40%I, 30%A. Lifts $52, 13-19 $39, 65+ & 7-12 $29. Childcare center (infant-12); children's ski school (4-12); children's ski lessons (7-12). Snowboarding permitted. Lodging on premises, (800) 367-6572, (760) 934-2581.*

One of the three largest ski areas in the country, Mammoth is located on a dormant volcano and has the highest elevation of any California ski area. It also is said to have some of the longest lift lines and one of the longest seasons—usually staying open through June and sometimes into July. A 7-hour drive from the Bay Area, it is understandably more popular with Southern Californians.

Montecito-Sequoia Cross Country & Winter Sports Resort *(800) 227-9900, (650) 967-8612, fax (650) 967-0540, snow phone (559) 565-3324; www.mslodge.com; on Hwy. 180 between Kings Canyon & Sequoia National Parks. Cross-country only. 37 mi. groomed trails. Babysitting (2-4); children's lessons (5-11). Lodging on premises; packages avail.*

Skiers here enjoy breathtaking ski tours and snowshoe walks through groves of giant sequoias. Arrangements can be made for videotaping lessons, and parents can rent "pulkas" to pull their children along in. Because of its high altitude location at 7,500 feet, this resort usually retains its snow and stays open for skiing through spring.

Lodge guests have plenty to do besides skiing. In the lodge they feast on "California fresh" cuisine and have access to snacks around the clock. There are board games, Ping-Pong, and plenty of movies for the VCR. Outside activities include snow sculpture, igloo building, and ski football. A session on the naturally frozen **ice-skating rink** *((559) 565-3388. Daily. Adults $8, children $5, includes skates.)* is also a possibility, as is a soak in the outdoor hot tub overlooking the Great Western Divide or a romp on the tubing hill complete with tow. But just resting in front of the massive stone fireplaces is also an option. See also page 412.

Tamarack Lodge Resort and Cross-Country Ski Center *Mammoth Lakes, (800) 237-6879, (760) 934-2442, fax (760) 934-2281; www.tamaracklodge.com; on Twin Lakes, 2.5 mi. from Mammoth Lakes Village. Cross-country only. 30 mi. groomed trails. Trail fee $16, 65+ & 11-17 $11. Children's ski lessons (6-11). Lodging on premises; packages avail.*

Lodging is a choice of either rooms in a rustic 1923 Alpine lodge or housekeeping cabins, some of which have fireplaces or wood-burning stoves.

Wolverton Ski Area *Sequoia National Park; Giant Forest, (559) 565-3435; Grant Grove, (559) 335-2314. Cross-country only. 45 mi. marked trails. Trail use free with park admission. Children's lessons. Lodging nearby.*

The big attraction here is the scenic national park ski trails leading through groves of cinnamon-colored giant sequoias. Free hot drinks are provided, and moonlight and overnight tours are available. Snow play areas are located at Azalea campground and Big Stump picnic areas.

SNOW PLAY

Yosemite National Park.

Ice skate in the shadow of Glacier Point, with a spectacular view of Half Dome, at the scenic outdoor **ice-skating rink** in Curry Village *((209) 372-8341. Call for schedule. Adults $5, under 13 $4.50, skates $2.).*

Free ranger-led **snowshoe walks** are also available at Badger Pass *($3 snowshoe maintenance fee. Unsuitable for children under 10.).* A good place to snowshoe without a guide is in the Mariposa Grove of Giant Sequoias.

Family Camps

Most adults remember the good old days when they were kids and got to go away to summer camp, and most adults think those days are gone for good. Well, they're not. A vacation at a family camp can bring it all back!

Family camps provide a reasonably priced, organized vacation experience. They are sponsored by city recreation departments, university alumni organizations, and private enterprise. The city and private camps are open to anyone, but some university camps require a campus affiliation.

And it isn't necessary to have children to attend. One year at one camp a couple was actually *honeymooning*! Elderly couples whose children have grown occasionally attend alone, and family reunions are sometimes held at a camp. Whole clubs and groups of friends have been known to book in at the same time.

Housing varies from primitive platform tents and cabins without electricity, plumbing, or bedding to comfortable campus dormitory apartments with daily maid service. Locations vary from the mountains to the sea. Predictably, costs also vary with the type of accommodations and facilities. Some camps allow stays of less than a week, but most require a week-long commitment. Children are usually charged at a lower rate according to their age.

Most family camps operate during the summer months only. Fees usually include meal preparation and clean-up, special programs for children, and recreation programs for everyone. Activities can include river or pool swimming, hikes, fishing, volleyball, table tennis, badminton, hayrides, tournaments, campfires, crafts programs, songfests, tennis, and horseback riding.

Each camp has its own special appeal, but all offer an informal atmosphere where guests can really unwind. Often over half the guests return the following year. Repeat guests and their camp friends tend to choose the same week each year.

For detailed rate information, itemization

of facilities, session dates, and route directions, contact the camp reservation offices directly and request a descriptive brochure. Reserve early to avoid disappointment.

City/Group Camps

Berkeley Tuolumne Family Camp *Berkeley Camps Office, Berkeley, (510) 644-6520, fax (510) 883-6519; www.berkeleycamps.com. Located on the south fork of the Tuolumne River near Yosemite National Park. Daily rates. Platform tents without electricity; provide own bedding; community bathrooms; family-style meals. Programs for toddlers-6, 6-12, & teens. Swimming in river; evening programs & breakfast hikes.*

Camp Concord *Concord Department of Leisure Services, Concord, (925) 671-3273, fax (925) 671-3449. Located near Camp Richardson at South Lake Tahoe. Daily rates. Cabins with electricity; provide own bedding; community bathrooms; cafeteria-style meals. Special program for ages 3-6 & 7-16. Horseback riding & river rafting at additional fee.*

Camp Mather *San Francisco Recreation and Park Department, San Francisco, (415) 666-7073, fax (415) 668-3330. Located on the rim of the Tuolumne River gorge near Yosemite National Park. Daily rates. Cabins with electricity; provide own bedding; community bathrooms; cafeteria-style meals. Playground area; program for age 6 and older. Pool, lake swimming, tennis courts (no fee); horseback riding at additional fee.*

Camp Sacramento *Department of Parks and Recreation, Sacramento, (916) 277-6098, fax (916) 454-3956; www.cityofsacramento.org/recreation/campsac. Located in the El Dorado National Forest 17 mi. south of Lake Tahoe. Daily & weekly rates. Cabins with electricity; provide own bedding; community bathrooms; cafeteria-style meals. Programs for all ages.*

Co-op Camp *Berkeley, (800) 708-CAMP, (510) 595-0873; www.coopcamp.com. Located in a pine forest between Huntington & Shaver Lakes 65 mi. east of Fresno. Daily & weekly rates. Cabins with electricity, lodge rooms, or bring own tent; provide own bedding; community bathrooms; family-style meals. Special activities for teens, playground and crafts program for younger children. Discussion groups.*

Feather River Camp *Office of Parks & Recreation, Oakland, (510) 238-3791, fax (510) 238-2224; www.oaklandnet.com/frc.html. Located in the Plumas National Forest north of Lake Tahoe near Quincy. Daily rates. Cabins & platform tents with electricity; provide own bedding; community bathrooms; family-style meals. Play area & activities for ages 2-6; program for age 6 and older. Theme weeks.*

San Jose Family Camp *San Jose Conventions, Arts & Entertainment, San Jose, (408) 277-4666, fax (408) 277-3270. Located in Stanislaus National Forest 30 mi. from Yosemite National Park. Daily rates; tent cabins without electricity (electricity avail. at additional fee); provide own bedding; community bathrooms. Cafeteria-style (B&L) & family-style (D) meals. Play area, program for age 3 and older. Dammed-off river pool.*

Silver Lake Family Resort *Department of Parks and Recreation, Stockton, (209) 937-8371, fax (209) 937-8260; Located 40 mi. south of Lake Tahoe. Daily rates. Platform tents & cabins with electric lights; provide own bedding; community bathrooms; cafeteria-style meals. Program for toddlers & older children. Swimming in lake, horseback riding nearby.*

Private Enterprise Camps

Coffee Creek Ranch. See page 299.

Emandal Farm. See page 229.

Montecito-Sequoia High Sierra Vacation Camp *(800) 227-9900, (650) 967-8612, fax (650) 967-0540; www.mslodge.com. Located in Sequoia National Forest between Kings Canyon & Sequoia National Parks. Weekly rates. Lodge; bedding provided; private baths. Also rustic cabins; community bathrooms. Buffet meals. Parent-child program for babies 6mo.-23mo.; programs for age 2 and older. 2 tennis courts, lake swimming, pool, hot tub, sailing, canoeing,* *boating, archery, fishing, riflery, mountain biking, golf cage; extra fee for water-skiing and horseback riding.* See also page 408.

University Camps

Lair of the Golden Bear *Sponsored by California Alumni Association at University of California, Berkeley, (888) CAL-ALUM, (510) 642-0221, fax (510) 642-6252; www.alumni.berkeley.edu. Located in Stanislaus National Forest near Pinecrest. Weekly rates. Tent cabins with electricity; provide own bedding; community bathrooms; family-style meals. Organized activities for ages 2-adult. Heated pool, 3 tennis courts, swimming and tennis lessons, complete athletic facilities.*

This is actually three separate camps—**Camp Blue, Camp Gold,** and **Camp Oski**—that operate side by side. Each has its own staff and facilities.

Houseboats

Living in a houseboat for a few days is an unusual way to get away from it all. It is possible to dive off the boat for a refreshing swim, fish for dinner while sunbathing, and dock in a sheltered, quiet cove for the night.

Houseboats are equipped with kitchens and flush toilets. Most rental agencies require that renters provide their own bedding, linens, and groceries, but almost everything else is on the floating hotel, including life jackets.

Rates vary quite dramatically depending on the time of year, the size and quality of the boat, and how many people are in the party. Summer rentals are most expensive, and a group of six to ten people gets the best rates. Weekly rates range from $450 to $4,200. Fuel is additional. Some rental facilities have enough boats to offer midweek specials and 3-day weekends; some offer a Thanksgiving special that includes the turkey and pumpkin pie. During the off-season, rates drop by approximately one-third, and some facilities will rent their boats for just a day. Contact rental facilities directly for current stock and rates.

Lake Oroville

- **Bidwell Marina** *(800) 637-1767, (530) 589-3152, fax (530) 589-4873; www.funtime-fulltime.com.*
- **Lake Oroville State Recreation Area** *(800) 444-7275, (530) 538-2200. Apr-Oct; $85/night.*

  Floating campsites have fully equipped kitchens, bathrooms, and sleeping space for up to 15 people.
- **Lime Saddle Marina** *(800) 834-7517, (530) 877-2414, fax (530) 877-6552.*

For more information on this area contact:
Oroville Chamber of Commerce
1789 Montgomery St., (800) 655-GOLD, (530) 538-2542, fax (530) 538-2546; www.orovillecity.com/chamber.

Lake Shasta

• **Bridge Bay Resort** and **Digger Bay Marina** *(800) 752-9669; www.sevencrown.com. Bridge Bay: (530) 275-3021, fax (530) 275-8365. Digger Bay: (530) 275-3072.*

• **Holiday Harbor** *(800) 776-BOAT, (530) 238-2383, fax (530) 238-2102; www.lakeshasta.com.*

• **Packers Bay Marina/Holiday Flotels** *(800) 331-3137, (530) 275-5570, fax (530) 275-5570; www.shastacascade.org/packersbay.*

Trinity Lake

• **Cedar Stock Resort and Marina.** See page 298.

The Delta

• **Herman & Helen's Marina** *(800) 676-4841, (209) 951-4634, fax (209) 951-6505; www.houseboats.com.*

• **Paradise Point Marina** *(800) 752-9669, (209) 952-1000, fax (209) 952-7974; www.sevencrown.com.*

River Trips

The adventure of rafting down a changing and unpredictable river offers a real escape for the harried, city-weary participant. But don't expect it to be relaxing. Participants are expected to help with setting up and breaking camp, and sometimes they are exposed mercilessly to the elements. While usually not dangerous when done with experienced guides, an element of risk is involved. Still, most participants walk away ecstatic and addicted to the experience.

The outfitter provides shelter, food, and equipment for the trip. Participants need only bring sleeping gear and personal items. Costs range from $185 to $590 per person for an overnight run. Some day trips are available. Seasons and rivers vary with each company.

Most outfitters offer special trips for families with young children. The minimum age requirement for children ranges from 4 to 8. For details, contact the tour operators directly.

• **The American River Touring Association** *Groveland, (800) 323-ARTA, (209) 962-7873, fax (209) 962-4819; www.arta.org.*

• **ECHO: The Wilderness Company** *Oakland, (800) 652-ECHO, (510) 652-1600, fax (510) 652-3987; www.echotrips.com.*

• **Mariah Wilderness Expeditions** *Point Richmond, (800) 4-MARIAH, (510) 233-2303; fax (510) 233-0956; www.mariahwe.com.*

This is California's only woman-owned and operated white water raft and wilderness company. Family trips are accompanied by a professional storyteller and include both female and male guides.

• **O.A.R.S.** *Angels Camp, (800) 3-GO-OARS, (209) 736-4677, fax (209) 736-2902; www.oars.com.*

• **Outdoor Adventures** *Wofford Heights (in Southern California), (800) 323-4234, (760) 376-3370, fax (760) 376-8830; www.gorafting.com.*

This company caters to families with campfire games and songs and other activities.

• **Turtle River Rafting Company** *Mt. Shasta, (800) 726-3223, (530) 926-3223, fax (530) 926-3443; www.turtleriver.com.*

Among the special trips are personal growth workshops and family river trips.

• **Whitewater Connection** *Coloma, (800) 336-7238, (916) 622-6446, fax (916) 622-7192; www.whitewaterconnection.com.*

• **Whitewater Voyages** *El Sobrante, (800) 488-RAFT, (510) 222-5994, fax (510) 758-7238; www.whitewatervoyages.com.*

Several discounted Clean-Up Trips are scheduled each year. Participants get the same amenities as on any other trip, but they are expected to pick up any debris they encounter.

For information on more California river outfitters, contact **California Outdoors** on the web at www.caloutdoors.org.

Pack Trips

Packing equipment onto horses or mules allows for a much easier and more comfortable trek into the wilderness than does backpacking.

Campers need simply choose the type of pack trip desired. On a spot pack trip the packers will load the animals with gear, take them to a prearranged campsite, unload the gear, and return to the pack station with the pack animals. They return to repack the gear on the day campers are scheduled to leave. Campers can either hike or ride on horses to the campsite. If riding, campers usually have a choice of keeping the horses at the campsite or of having the packers take them back out. If keeping the horses, campers need to arrange in advance for a corral and feed, and they should be experienced with horses. Children who haven't had at least basic riding instruction should not be included on such a trip.

A more rugged trip (where the campsite is moved each day) or an easier trip (with all expenses and a guide included) can also usually be arranged with the packer.

This is not an inexpensive vacation. Prices will vary according to which of the above options are selected. Often there are special rates for children, who must be at least 5 years old to participate. Trips are usually available only in the summer.

For general information and a list of packers, contact the **Eastern High Sierra Packers Association** *(690 N. Main St., Bishop 93514, (760) 873-8405), fax (760) 873-6999).*

One of the biggest and most organized packers is **Red's Meadow Pack Station** *(Mammoth Lakes, (800) 292-7758, (760) 934-2345, fax (760) 872-4940; http://reds-meadow.com.),* which schedules a large number of pack trips each summer. Horses, saddles, and meals are included. Day rides can be arranged, and special family trips, horse drives, and wagon rides are scheduled.

Camping

Because there are excellent resources available on campgrounds, this book mentions only briefly those that fit into the text. For convenience, they are also included in the index under "campsites."

A Kamping Kabin at a KOA Kampground, listed in each section under "Where to Stay," is a great option for those who don't own a tent yet long for an outdoors camping vacation. Renting for $25 to $50 per night, these rustic cabins provide all the fun and excitement of camping out with all the security and comfort of sleeping in. Each one-room cabin sleeps four and is equipped with a double bed plus kid-pleasing bunk beds. A two-room cabin sleeps six. Campers need bring only sleeping bags and cooking gear. A few locations also have Kamping Kottages, complete with fully-equipped kitchenette and bathroom. Of course, those who own a tent or RV can also camp here. Most of the campgrounds in the KOA chain have swimming pools, and some offer additional recreational facilities. To get a free KOA Directory, visit any KOA Kampground, or send $3 to: KOA Directory, P.O. Box 30558, Billings, MT 59114-0558.

For more complete camping information, consult the following references:

- *CampBook* for California-Nevada. This book and its companion maps list camping facilities and fees. They are available free to California State Automobile Association members.
- *The California State Parks Guide.* This informative brochure includes a map pinpointing all state parks, reserves, recreation areas, historic parks, and campgrounds. It is available free by calling (916) 653-6995.

Reservations are advised at most state park campgrounds. For a small service fee, they can be made by phone as early as 7 months in advance. For general information on state park campgrounds and to make reservations, call (800) 444-7275 *(www.cal-parks.ca.gov).*

Miscellany

American Hiking Society *Washington, D.C., (301) 565-6704, fax (301) 565-6714; www.americanhiking.org.*

This group organizes vacations using teams of volunteers for work trips in remote back country areas. Their annual directory, *Helping Out in the Outdoors*, tells how to get a job as a state park or forest volunteer—hosting a campground, helping improve trails, collecting data on wildlife, or explaining an area's history to visitors. Very few of these jobs reimburse travel and food costs or provide accommodations. Opportunities are available in all 50 states; most are not appropriate for children. For a copy of the directory, send $7 to: American Hiking Society, P.O. Box 20160, Washington, D.C. 20041-2160.

Backroads *Berkeley, (800) GO-ACTIVE, (510) 527-1555, fax (510) 527-1444; www.backroads.com.*

Packaged bicycle trips include the Wine Country, Russian River, and Point Reyes Seashore. Many more trips are scheduled in other states and countries. The emphasis is not on endurance but on getting some exercise. Two or three tour guides accompany bikers, and a support vehicle transports equipment and tired cyclists. Allowing for different ability levels, several routes are available on each trip. Accommodations are in either interesting hotels or comfortable campgrounds, and meals are included. Special family trips are available. Children are welcome on most other trips as well, and they qualify for discounted rates. Walking and cross-country ski trips are also available.

Bed & Breakfast California *Saratoga, (800) 872-4500, (408) 867-9662, fax (408) 867-0907; www.bbintl.com. $-$$$+; 2-night min. on weekends. Children under 2 free. Continental or full breakfast.*

This B&B reservations service books travelers into over 350 private homes, inns, and vacation homes throughout California. Among the more interesting options are a houseboat in Sausalito and a "painted lady" in San Francisco. Though most properties cannot accommodate more than two people in a room, some are appropriate for children. Amenities, of course, vary with the property.

Bike California *Oakland, (800) LUNG-USA.*

Sponsored by the American Lung Association of California, these bicycle trips are fully supported and are led by an experienced staff. Vans carry gear, and mechanics are available for repairs. Camping accommodations and both breakfast and dinner are provided. Though prices are reasonable, if participants raise pledges for the organization, they can go along for even less.

Cal Adventures *Dept. of Recreational Sports, University of California, Berkeley, (510) 642-4000, fax (510) 642-3730; www.strawberry.org/caladv.*

Adventure trips include backpacking, rafting, rock climbing, sailing, sculling, sea kayaking, windsurfing and more. Day classes and a special program for children in grades 3 through 12 are also available.

California Academy of Sciences *San Francisco, (415) 750-7098, fax (415) 750-7346; www.calacademy.org.*

These nature study trips are led by members of the academy staff. On some trips participants camp out and cook their own meals. On other less strenuous trips, motel lodging and restaurant meals are included. Destinations include Mount Lassen National Park and Santa Cruz Island. The Junior Academy offers similar 1-day and weekend trips for children ages 6 through 15.

Coastwalk *Sebastopol, (800) 550-6854, (707) 829-6689, same fax; www.coastwalk.org/coastwalk. Adults $45/day, students $20, under 13 $15.*

Since 1983, Coastwalk has organized summer hikes in California's coastal counties. Hikers can sign up for walks ranging from 4 to 7 days, with camping gear shuttled by vehicle. The goals of this non-profit organization are to nurture an awareness of the coastal environment and to promote development of a continuous California Coastal Trail.

Green Tortoise *San Francisco, (800) 867-8647, (415) 956-7500, fax (415) 956-4900; www.greentortoise.com.*

Travel on this groovy, laid-back, alternative bus line is enjoyed at bargain rates. The clientele tends to be the under-30s crowd, but all ages are welcome. Trips are available to almost anywhere on this continent. There are river rafting trips to Baja and cross-country trips with stops at national parks. Usually the scenic route, which is not necessarily the most direct route, is followed. Overnight accommodations are often arranged in hostels, but sometimes riders must bring their own bedding and sleep onboard on padded platforms. The jack-of-all-trades bus drivers often organize cookouts, and they get out and fix breakdowns themselves. Passengers have also been known to get out and push when necessary. All in all, a trip on this bus line is really a *trip*.

Hostelling International/American Youth Hostels *San Francisco, (415) 863-1444, fax (415) 863-3865; www.norcalhostels.org.*

The idea behind hosteling is to save money, so accommodations are simple. Women bunk in one dormitory-style room, men in another. Some hostels have separate rooms for couples and families. Guests provide their own bedding and linens (sleepsheets can be rented), and bathrooms and kitchens are shared. All guests are expected to do a chore, except in urban hostels. Most hostels are closed during the day, usually from 9:30 to 4:30. Fees are low, ranging from $11 to $20 per person per night, and children under 18 with a parent are half of that. Members receive a discount at most hostels and get a newsletter and handbook describing U.S. hostels. Package tours are available. Call for a free brochure detailing the hostels in Northern California. (Note: In this book, hostels are included in the "Where to Stay" section.)

Junior Ranger Program *At California State Parks, (916) 653-8959.*

Children ages 7 through 12 can participate in a program designed to help them discover the rich natural and cultural heritage in California's state parks. Sessions last about an hour each day for several days, and awards are presented as the kids progress. A child can begin the program at one park and continue at a later date in another location. A similar program operates at the national parks.

Sierra Club *San Francisco, (415) 977-5630, fax (415) 977-5795; www.sierraclub.org/outings.*

Nature appreciation trips, special family trips, and service trips that take participants to remote wilderness areas to maintain trails and clean up trash are all scheduled. All trips are 1 or 2 weeks long and are described in the January/February issue of *Sierra Magazine*, which is sent free to all club members. Shorter day and overnight trips are scheduled through local chapters.

University Extension and Research Programs.

Many state colleges and universities have travel/study programs.

- **San Jose State University** *(408) 924-2625, fax (408) 924-5037.*

  On-location natural history programs are offered through the Extension Division. Special programs that include children 6 through 16 are scheduled in summer.

- **University of California** *(530) 752-0692, fax (530) 752-0681.*

  These research expeditions are not appropriate for children under 16.

Annual Events Index

JANUARY

FEBRUARY

MARCH

APRIL

MAY

JUNE

JULY

AUGUST

SEPTEMBER

OCTOBER

NOVEMBER

DECEMBER

Alphabetical Index

—A—

—B—

—C—

—H—

—N—

—O—

—T—

—X—

—Y—

—Z—